EDUGORILLA
PUBLICATION

HARCO Bank

Clerk Prelims Exam

Latest Edition
Practice Kit

17 Tests
08 Mock Test
09 Sectional Test

Based On Real Exam Pattern

✓ Thoroughly Revised and Updated

✓ Detailed Analysis of all MCQs

<table>
<tr><td>Title</td><td>: HARCO Bank Clerk Prelims Exam</td></tr>
<tr><td>Author Name</td><td>: Mr. Rohit Manglik</td></tr>
<tr><td>Published By</td><td>: EduGorilla Community Pvt. Ltd.</td></tr>
<tr><td>Publishers Address</td><td>: 12/651, First Floor Opp. Arvindo Park, Near Jama Masjid, Indira Nagar, Lucknow, Uttar Pradesh-226016, India</td></tr>
</table>

Copyright EduGorilla

Disclaimer EduGorilla

Compiled and created by EduGorilla Community Pvt. Ltd

Printed By EduGorilla Community Pvt. Ltd.

ROHIT MANGLIK
CEO, EduGorilla

Dear Applicants,

People say *"Success comes to those who work hard."* But I've seen people working hard for their exams day in and day out for marginal success. While others succeed in their examinations by putting in just half the work. So are they God Gifted? No! I believe that it's because they work *smart* and not just *hard*. Similarly, for your exams, you should strategize your preparation so as to increase the likelihood of success. Well with EduGorilla get ready to increase your *chances of selection* in your exam by *16x*.

EduGorilla helps you in not only working *hard* but also working in a *smart and strategic* manner. With EduGorilla's preparation package, you get a chance to make your exam preparation easy, and a fun learning path towards selection. Finding the right path to your preparations can be difficult if you don't know in which direction to head. Don't worry, we have you covered! EduGorilla will be your guide to success in your journey. With our Preparation Package, you can prepare strategically and beat the exam in just one attempt.

EduGorilla's Preparation Package includes-

• **Test Series**   • **Books**

Our preparation package is handcrafted as per the latest changes, expert opinions, and students' discretion. Thus, enabling you to get through each stage of the selection process for your exam.

Our Books are designed by the teachers and experts of the respective exam with a combined 150+ years of experience; to provide you with easy, efficient, and effective learning. Our books are smart, in the sense that not only do they give you the answers to the questions but also provide similar questions for practice.

EduGorilla's competent Test Series gives you real-time experience and confidence through which you can clear your offline or online exam in just one attempt. We currently host 83,000+ mock tests for 1,440+ competitive and academic exams.

Thus, EduGorilla misses no chance to assist you in your preparation and covers all stages of the exam, so that you don't have to look anywhere else.

We provide complete preparation packages for defense, banking, teaching, and other National & State-Level exams. Hence, it doesn't matter which exam you aspire to because you will reach your success.

ALL THE BEST !
Let EduGorilla be your Guide to Success.

Rohit Manglik,
Founder and CEO, EduGorilla

INTRODUCTION

EduGorilla focuses on guiding students to succeed in their examinations. With that in mind, our book, titled "HARCO Bank : Clerk Prelims Exam", has been drafted through the collective efforts of our distinguished experts with 150+ years of combined experience. This book consists of questions that are created following the latest changes in the syllabus and exam pattern. We compiled the book on the basis of questions that are most likely to appear in the HARCO Bank Clerk (Prelims) Exam. Through EduGorilla's "HARCO Bank : Clerk Prelims Exam" your chances of success will increase 16x.

EduGorilla does this through our Complete Preparation Package. This package consists of well-conceptualized and structured content in the form of questions that are tailor-made according to your needs and will help you practice for exams in a smart way by pinpointing all the necessary information. It also provides hints and solutions, along with a smart answer sheet for your self-evaluation. You can assess your shortcomings and work accordingly on areas that may require more of your attention.

EduGorilla promises to help you succeed in your examination and accomplish your dream goals. We believe in our aspirants and see them at the top of the merit list. And the first step towards the top is to start preparing with us. EduGorilla's "HARCO Bank : Clerk Prelims Exam" includes the following attributes.

➤ Well-Researched Content

➤ Top-Notch Quality

➤ Detailed Answers and Analysis

➤ Smart Answer Sheet

➤ Exam Relevant Questions

Therefore, EduGorilla fortifies your preparation and makes it durable enough to help you stand tall and beat the examination.

HARCO Bank Clerk (Prelims) Exam
Scan QR code for Eligibility, Exam Pattern, Syllabus and more.

Book ID: 0179

TABLE OF CONTENTS

Reasoning Ability

Ques (1-3):Direction: Study the information given carefully and answer the question given below.

In a certain code language,

"love france ban fresh" is written as N2G D2P H4J H4G.

"became risk chief put" is written as R2V T3M D3G E3H.

"how given team threat" is written as V2O I3P J2Y V4V.

"taken outfit too used" is written as V1Q Q3V V3P W2F.

Q.1 What does the code J2Y" denote?

A. How
B. Given
C. Team
D. Threat
E. None of these

Q.2 What will be the code for "love is blind"?

A. N2G K1U D4F
B. K2G N1U F4D
C. F2D N4K K1U
D. F1U NIK D4F
E. None of these

Q.3 How will "X4C" be coded as?

A. Varia
B. Vellupura
C. Vadodara
D. Cannot be determined
E. None of these

Ques (4-8):Direction: Study the following arrangement carefully and answer the question:

H % 1 P ! F S ? * X 7 C T 4 $ 9 3 > @ / 6 N Q 5

Q.4 If all the symbols are dropped from the arrangement then what would be the sixth element from the right end?

A. 9
B. T
C. 4
D. C
E. 7

Q.5 If all the numbers are dropped from the above arrangement, which of the following will be the fifth to the right of fourth from the left end?

A. ?
B. S
C. *
D. X
E. C

Q.6 In the given arrangement, how many numbers are there which are immediately followed by a symbol?

A. None
B. One
C. Two
D. Three
E. Four

Q.7 What is the sum of the numbers between the element '*' and '>'?

A. 24
B. 17
C. 19
D. 23
E. 21

Q.8 How many letters are immediately preceded by consonants and immediately followed by a symbol?

A. None
B. One
C. Two
D. Three
E. Four

Q.9 Direction: In the following question assuming the given statements to be true, find which of the conclusion among given three conclusions is /are definitely true and then give your answers accordingly.

Statements:

$$A > B; \quad B > F; \quad C < F; \quad D > C; \quad E > D$$

Conclusions:

I. $A > F$

II. $C > A$

III. $B > D$

A. None is true
B. Only I is true
C. Only I and II is true
D. Only II and III is true
E. Only III is true

Ques (10-14):Direction: Read the information carefully and answer the questions given below.

Eight people A, B, C, D, E, F, G, and H are sitting around a circular table facing towards the table and not in the same order. Each of them likes a different color i.e., Purple, pink, red, green, blue, black, yellow, and orange but not necessarily in the same order.

The one who likes red sits to the immediate left of the one who likes black. D does not like the yellow color. F sits third to the left of A, who likes purple and the person who likes purple sits to the immediate left of G. C sits to the immediate right of E and neither of them likes blue. The one who likes green and B has two people sitting in between them. C, F, and G, neither of them like green color. F and the person who likes blue has one person in between them. D sits second to the right of H. E sits opposite the person who likes yellow and the person who likes yellow sits immediately next to the one who likes orange.

Q.10 Who among the following likes black color?

A. D
B. H
C. C
D. F
E. G

Q.11 Which color does the person who sits third to the right of D likes?

A. Blue
B. Red
C. Pink
D. Orange
E. Purple

Q.12 Four of the following five are alike in a certain way and hence form a group. Which is the one that does not belong to that group?

A. Blue, D
B. Yellow, B
C. Pink, A
D. Black, C

E. Orange, H

Q.13 How many people sit between the one who likes orange and C, when counted from right of C?
A. One
B. Two
C. Three
D. Four
E. More than four

Q.14 Who among the following is an immediate neighbor of the one who likes Red color?
A. D
B. C
C. E
D. F
E. H

Ques (15-16):Direction: Read the following information carefully to answer the question given below:

M, N, O, P, Q, R, S, T and U are members in a family. They are somehow related to one another. They have different blood groups such as A+, A-, B+, B-, AB+, AB-, O+ and O-.

Two members have blood group of the same type. There are more male members than female members.

The parents of S have positive blood groups. One married couple in the family is a positive donor and positive recipient. N has two off-springs and his off-springs are universal donors of both types. R is the maternal uncle of U. N and his maternal grandson, T has a negative blood group. P's son-in-law has an A- blood group. Q is married to a positive universal donor and has a positive blood group. U is the maternal grandson of P and has an A+ blood group. O's daughter is a negative universal recipient.

Q.15 How is R related to O?
A. Brother
B. Sister
C. Brother-in-law
D. Sister-in-law
E. None of these

Q.16 How is P related to S?
A. Maternal Grandfather
B. Maternal Grandmother
C. Paternal Grandfather
D. Paternal Grandmother
E. None of these

Q.17 In the word 'DOORSTEP' if all the vowels are replaced with the letter immediate next to it in the english alphabet series and all the consonants are replaced with the letter immediate before it in the english alphabet series, then how many vowels are there in the new word so formed?
A. Zero
B. One
C. Two
D. More than two
E. None of these

Ques (18-22):Direction: Study the following information carefully and answer the question given below.

Eight chocolate boxes namely Fivestar, Dairy Milk, KitKat, Snicker, Twix, Bournville, Cadbury and Candy are placed one above the other but not necessarily in the same order. Three chocolate boxes are placed between Dairy Milk and Snicker. Two boxes are placed between Twix and Dairy Milk. Twix is placed below Dairy Milk. Four boxes are placed between Twix and Cadbury. The number of boxes above Cadbury is the same as the number of boxes below Candy. Bournville is placed above Kitkat but below Fivestar. Bournville is not placed just above KitKat.

Q.18 Which of the following box is placed immediately below the box of Candy?
A. KitKat
B. Dairy Milk
C. Bournville
D. Snicker
E. None of these

Q.19 Which of the following chocolate box is placed between Bournville and Fivestar?
A. Cadbury
B. Dairy Milk
C. Candy
D. KitKat
E. Twix

Q.20 How many boxes are placed above Cadbury?
A. None
B. One
C. Two
D. Three
E. Four

Q.21 How many boxes are placed between Twix and Snicker?
A. None
B. Two
C. Three
D. Four
E. More than four

Q.22 Which of the following box is placed at the top?
A. Fivestar
B. Cadbury
C. KitKat
D. Twix
E. Snicker

Ques (23-25):

Direction: Read the following information carefully and answer the questions that follow.

A & B means A is 5 km to the south of B.

A % B means A is 5 km to the east of B.

A + B means A is 1 km to the south of B.

A - B means A is 1 km to the east of B.

Q.23 If it is given that: X - Y & A; X + Z + W - V; W % U. What is the direction of X with respect to U?
A. East
B. West
C. North-East
D. South-West
E. South-East

Q.24 If it is given that: C + B % A; D + E - B. What is the distance between C and D?
A. 1 km
B. 2 km
C. 3 km
D. 4 km
E. 5 km

Q.25 If it is given that: C + B % A; C % D. What is the distance between A and D?
A. 1 km
B. 2 km
C. 3 km
D. 4 km
E. 5 km

Ques (26-28):Directions: Study the following information and answer the question following:

Tony Stark has a shelf in which he kept seven electronic items such as, Transformer, Fuse, Switch, Capacitor, Relay, Battery, and Microcontroller but not necessary in the same order. The top of the shelf is numbered as the 7th shelf. Only two items are kept between Relay and Transformer. The Switch is kept just above the Capacitor. Only three items are kept between Capacitor and Battery. More than three boxes are kept below Battery. The transformer is kept above the Battery. Fuse is kept above Relay and below Microcontroller.

Q.26 Which electronic item is kept just above the Switch?

A. Capacitor   **B.** Battery
C. Relay   **D.** Fuse
E. Transformer

Q.27 How many items are kept between Capacitor and Transformer?

A. One   **B.** Two   **C.** Three   **D.** Four
E. Five

Q.28 Find the odd one out?

A. Switch   **B.** Relay
C. Fuse   **D.** Transformer
E. Capacitor

Ques (29-30):Direction: In the following question assuming the given statements to be True, find which of the conclusion among given conclusions is / are definitely true and then give your answers accordingly.

Q.29 Statements: P = Q < R > S = T; A < T < B; C > T < D

Conclusions:

I. C < A

II. D < A

A. None is true
B. Both I and II are true
C. Only II is true
D. Only I is true
E. Either I and II is true

Q.30 Statements: P = Q ≤ R ≤ S; S > A < B; C > D > A

Conclusions:

I. P > A

II. R < C

A. None is true
B. Both I and II are true
C. Only II is true
D. Only I is true
E. Either I and II is true

English Language

Ques (31-35):Direction: Select a segment of sentence that contains grammatical error. If there is no error, mark 'No error' as your answer.

Q.31 The National Commission for Rural (A) Labour argue way back in 1991 (B) that unequal development was (C) the main cause of labour migration. (D)

A. (A)   **B.** (B)   **C.** (C)   **D.** (D)
E. No error

Q.32 He looked after (A) the former (B) and a latter (C) in an effective way (D).

A. (A)   **B.** (B)   **C.** (C)   **D.** (D)
E. No error

Q.33 Everyone's waiting (A) anxious (B) for the concert (C) tickets to go on sale (D).

A. (A)   **B.** (B)   **C.** (C)   **D.** (D)
E. No error

Q.34 Awareness programmes (A) is also being initiated at (B) a community level to (C) prevent such incidents. (D)

A. (A)   **B.** (D)   **C.** (B)   **D.** (C)
E. No error

Q.35 Neither Raj (A) or Rajesh (B) went to (C) school today (D).

A. (A)   **B.** (B)   **C.** (C)   **D.** (D)
E. No error

Ques (36-40):Directions: Read the passage carefully and answer the question that follow:

Although Greece (or Hel′las) is only half as large as the State of New York, it holds a very important place in the history of the world. It is situated in the southern part of Europe, cut off from the rest of the continent by a chain of high mountains which form a great wall on the north. It is surrounded on nearly all sides by the blue waters of the Med-it-er-ra′ne-an Sea, which stretch so far inland that it is said no part of the country is forty miles from the sea or ten miles from the hills. Thus shut in by sea and mountains, it forms a little territory by itself, and it was the home of a **noted** people.

The history of Greece goes back to the time when people did not know how to write and kept no record of what was happening around them. For a long while the stories told by parents to their children were the only information which could be had about the country and its former inhabitants; and these stories, slightly changed by every new teller, grew more and more extraordinary as time passed. At last, they were so changed that no one could tell where the truth ended and fancy began.

The beginning of Greek history is therefore like a fairy tale; and while much of it cannot, of course, be true, it is the only information we have about the early Greeks.

About two thousand years before the birth of Christ, in the days when Isaac wanted to go down into Egypt, Greece was inhabited by a **savage** race of men called the Pe-las′gi-ans. They lived in the forests, or in caves **hollowed** out of the mountainside, and hunted wild beasts with great clubs and stone-tipped arrows and spears. They were so rude and wild that they ate nothing but raw meat, berries, and the roots which they dug up with sharp stones or even with their hands.

For clothing, the Pelasgians used the skins of the beasts they had killed; and to protect themselves against other savages, they gathered together in families or tribes, each having a chief who led in war and in the chase.

There were other far more civilized nations in those days. Among these were the E-gyp′tians, who lived in Africa. They had long known the use of fire, had good tools and were much further advanced than the Pelasgians. They had learned not only to build houses but to erect the most wonderful monuments in the world,--the Pyr´a-mids, of which you have no doubt heard.

In Egypt there were at that time a number of learned men. They were **acquainted** with many of the arts and sciences and recorded all they knew in the particular writing of their own invention. Their neighbors, the Phoe-ni´-cians, whose land also bordered on the Mediterranean Sea, were quite civilized too; and as both of these nations had shipped, they soon began to sail all around that great inland sea.

As they had no compass, the Egyptian and Phoenician sailors did not venture out of sight of land. They first sailed along the shore, and then to the islands which they could see far out on the blue waters.

When they had come to one island, they could see another still farther on; for, as you will see on any map, the Mediterranean Sea, between Greece and Asia, is dotted with islands, which look like stepping-stones going from one coast to the other.

Advancing thus carefully, the Egyptians and Phoenicians finally came to Greece, where they made settlements and began to teach the Pelasgians many useful and important things.

Q.36 Which of the following is an antonym of the word "noted"?

A. Common
B. Important
C. Prominent
D. Acclaimed
E. Renowned

Q.37 Which of the following is an antonym of the word "savage"?

A. Vicious
B. Ferocious
C. Peaceful
D. Barbarian
E. Fierce

Q.38 Why does the author consider Egyptians a civilized people?

A. The Egyptians knew how to read and write
B. The Egyptians knew how to use fire
C. The Egyptians had good tools
D. The Egyptians were more advanced than the Greeks
E. More than one of the above

Q.39 Which of the following is an antonym of the word "hollow"?

A. Shallow
B. Empty
C. Full
D. Deep
E. Solid

Q.40 Which of the following can be inferred from the passage?

A. The author of the passage is most probably a historian
B. The tone of the passage is analytical
C. The source of the passage is most probably a newspaper article
D. The author believes that the Egyptians were wrong to assume that the Greeks were uncivilized
E. None of the above

Ques (41-45):Direction: Which of the option (A), (B), (C) and (D) given below, should replace the phrase printed in bold in the sentence to make it grammatically correct? If the sentence is correct as it is given and no correction is required, mark (E) as the answer.

Q.41 The Bar Council of Delhi's directive to the Big Four accountancy firms not to offer legal services to their clients in India **has been a responsive move that is transparent protectionist in intent.**

A. Is a rhetoric move that is transparent protectionist in intent
B. Is a retrograde move that is transparently protectionist of intent
C. Is a rhetoric move that is transparently puerile in intent
D. Is a retrograde move that is transparently protectionist in intent
E. No correction required

Q.42 The **commander-in-chiefs of both** the armies shook hands with each other and sat down on their respective chairs.

A. Commander-in-chiefs in both
B. Commanders-in-chief of both
C. Commanders-in-chiefs of both
D. Commander-in-chiefs in each army
E. No improvement required

Q.43 There is an argument that it is health that Mr. Modi does not bargain with caste, linguistic and region-oriented interests groups.

A. There is an argument that is healthy
B. There is an argumentative that it is healthy
C. There is an argument that health
D. There is an argument that it is healthy
E. No correction required

Q.44 The Punjab National Bank fraud **demonstrates the extent of** operational and risk management failures in PSBs.

A. Demonstrateing the extent of
B. Demonstrates the extent in
C. Demonstrates the extent with
D. Demonstrates the extention of
E. No correction required

Q.45 The stage is **all set** for the elections to the Mandal and Zilla Parishad territorial constituencies across the State.

A. All sets
B. All setting
C. Set out
D. All setted
E. No replacement required

Ques (46-50):Direction: In the following question, the sentence given with blank to be filled in with an appropriate word. Select the correct alternative out of the five and indicate it by selecting the appropriate option.

Q.46 Balu has _________ coins than Rani.

A. less
B. lower
C. fewer
D. more
E. None of these

Q.47 The girls ____ to go on a picnic.
A. wanting
B. wants
C. want
D. have been wanted
E. None of these

Q.48 Roshni's house is just ________ the road.
A. beside
B. besides
C. between
D. next
E. None of these

Q.49 On hearing the noise, the rabbit jumped _______ the bed.
A. of
B. to
C. off
D. for
E. None of these

Q.50 I wish someday they _____ understand the importance of hard work.
A. can be
B. will be
C. were
D. will
E. None of these

Ques (51-55):Direction: In the following question, two statements and five connectors are given. Only one of the connectors from those given can be used to combine the given two statements into one sentence without changing the meaning. Choose that connector as your answer.

Q.51 I. The floors had been waxed and the furniture got polished by afternoon.
II. The house sparkled but in an empty kind of way.
A. Once
B. As
C. When
D. Wherever
E. If when

Q.52 I. Unlike other business leaders she has not shunned political leaders but engaged with them
II. She believes that society needs political leaders to bring about change and citizens need to engage with them.
A. In lieu of
B. Because
C. As in
D. As of
E. As if

Q.53 I. I live only a few blocks from work
II. I walk to work and enjoy it.
A. Now that
B. Rather than
C. Even though
D. Only if
E. Just as

Q.54 I. Thunderstorms brought the first significant rainfall in weeks to the UK
II. Belfast international airport received 88.2 mm in a matter of hours, more than the region's monthly July average.
A. As
B. If
C. Because
D. So
E. Now

Q.55 I. The man goes to the park every Sunday
II. He loves watching the ducks in the lake.
A. Until
B. Once
C. As
D. Although
E. Until

Ques (56-60):Direction: In the following passage some of the words have been left out. Read the passage carefully and select the correct answer for the given blank out of the given alternatives.

In an attempt to take on fake news, Google News has ___(1)___ new measures. Google has updated its guidelines to prohibit sites that misrepresent or ___(2)___ their country of origin or are ___(3)___ at users in another country under false premises. "Sites included in Google News must not misrepresent, misstate, or conceal information about their ownership or primary purpose, or engage in coordinated activity to ___(4)___ users," states the company guidelines. Google also allows publishers to file a spam report if they believe that another publisher has ___(5)___ Google News inclusion guidelines. "While we may not take manual action in response to every report, spam reports are ___(6)___ based on user impact, and in some cases may lead to complete ___(7)___ of a spam site from Google News results," Google said. This move to keep dishonest sites from ___(8)___ in Google News has been cheered by users worldwide. It comes in the wake of ___(9)___ pressure on the Internet giant take initiative to stop the spread of fake news after allegations of Russian attempts to ___(10)___ the 2016 US presidential election surfaced.

Q.56 Which of the following word fits the blank labelled as (6)?
A. Invaded
B. Prioritized
C. Shielded
D. Fielded
E. Boxed

Q.57 Which of the following word fits the blank labelled as (1)?
A. Adored
B. Adorned
C. Adopted
D. Advised
E. Objected

Q.58 Which of the following word fits the blank labelled as (4)?
A. Engage
B. Mislead
C. Direct
D. Divert
E. Dilute

Q.59 Which of the following word fits the blank labelled as (5)?
A. Shaped
B. Manned
C. Shipped
D. Violated
E. Volatile

Q.60 Which of the following word fits the blank labelled as (10)?
A. Oust
B. Influence
C. Jest
D. Ban
E. Conflict

Numerical Ability

Q.61 If repetition of the digits is allowed, then the number of even natural numbers having three digits is:
A. 250
B. 350
C. 450
D. 550
E. 200

Ques (62-66):Direction: What should come in place of the question mark '?' in the following number series?

Q.62 504, 252, 84, 42, ?, 7
A. 16
B. 15
C. 14
D. 13
E. 17

Q.63 6, 6, 12, 36, 144, ?
A. 620   **B.** 700   **C.** 720   **D.** 520
E. 820

Q.64 7, 8, 14, 45, 176, ?
A. 885   **B.** 775   **C.** 475   **D.** 445
E. 945

Q.65 5, 6, 13, 40, 161, ?
A. 987   **B.** 806   **C.** 876   **D.** 888
E. 654

Q.66 3.5, 4.5, 8.5, 17.5,?, 58.5
A. 32.5   **B.** 33.5   **C.** 31.5   **D.** 34.5
E. 35.5

Q.67 A and B together do a job in 6.75 days and A could do the job in 9 days if he worked alone. How many days would B take to do the job if he worked alone?
A. 27   **B.** 18   **C.** 24   **D.** 21
E. 22

Q.68 Sruti and Shankya started a business by invest in the ratio 3 : 7. If 10% of the total profit goes to repair their house and the share of Sruti is Rs.5400, what is the total profit?
A. 78000   **B.** 65000
C. 20000   **D.** 70000
E. None of these

Q.69 The average of seven numbers is 9. If the average of the first four numbers is 12 and that of last four numbers is 10, Find the fourth number.
A. 30   **B.** 25   **C.** 40   **D.** 50
E. 35

Q.70 The diagonal of rectangle is 15 cm and length is 12 cm. Find the area of the rectangle.
A. 114 cm^2 **B.** 108 cm^2 **C.** 116 cm^2 **D.** 112 cm^2
E. 115 cm^2

Ques (71-75):Direction: Study the given bar graph and answer the following question accordingly.

The bar graph shows the number of students from all three departments.

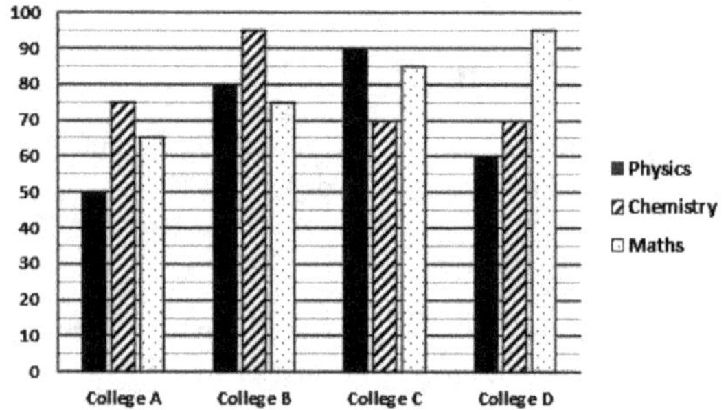

Q.71 The total number of students from college C is approximate what percentage more or less than that of college D?
A. 10%   **B.** 8%   **C.** 9%   **D.** 11%
E. 13%

Q.72 Find the average of all students from the physics department of all four colleges.
A. 70   **B.** 60
C. 50   **D.** 80
E. None of these

Q.73 Find the ratio between the students from physics and math from college A and the students from chemistry and math from college C.
A. 31 : 23   **B.** 23 : 31
C. 13 : 21   **D.** 15 : 25
E. None of these

Q.74 Find the total number of students from the chemistry department from all four colleges.
A. 210   **B.** 410
C. 320   **D.** 310
E. None of these

Q.75 Find the difference between the total number of students from the chemistry department from college B and college C and the total number of students from the physics department from college A and college D.
A. 45   **B.** 55   **C.** 65   **D.** 75
E. 35

Ques (76-77):Direction: What approximate will come in the place of the question mark '?' in the following question?

Q.76 $\dfrac{\left(\left(\frac{2.56}{10.89}\right)+\left(\frac{2.36}{4.58}\right)-\left(\frac{0.99}{4.79}\right)\right)}{[7.05+74.88\%\ of\ 11.88]}$

A. $\frac{1}{55}$ **B.** $\frac{13}{440}$ **C.** $\frac{3}{55}$ **D.** $\frac{4}{55}$
E. $\frac{6}{55}$

Q.77 55% of $99.999 +?^2 = 56\%$ of $850 - 20\%$ of 150
A. 10   **B.** 20   **C.** 45   **D.** 62
E. 36

Q.78 What will come in the place of the question mark '?' in the following question?
$32^{0.16} \times 32^{0.4} \times 32^{0.5} = 128^{?} \div 2$
A. 10   **B.** 1.1   **C.** 9   **D.** 0.9
E. 7

Q.79 What will come in the place of the question mark '?' in the following question?
42% of 250 + 115% of 480 = ?
A. 655   **B.** 657
C. 659   **D.** 653
E. None of the above

Q.80 What should come in the place of the question mark '?' in the following question?

$$57\frac{1}{7}\% \text{ of } 490 + 22.22\% \text{ of } 729 - \sqrt{2500} \times \sqrt{25} \div 5^2 = ?$$

A. 440	**B.** 322
C. 432	**D.** 452

E. None of these

Q.81 Tap A can fill a tank in 12 hours and tap B can emptied it is 15 hours. Tap A starts filling and they opened for 1 hour each alternatively in what time will the tank be full?

A. 102 hours	**B.** 99 hours
C. 100 hours	**D.** 111 hours

E. None of these

Q.82 Mayank threw two dice simultaneously. What is the probability of getting a total of 7?

A. $\frac{1}{6}$	**B.** $\frac{1}{4}$
C. $\frac{2}{3}$	**D.** $\frac{3}{4}$

E. None of these

Q.83 Direction: In the following questions two equations numbered I and II are given. You have to solve both equations and give the answer:

I. $m^3 + 5m^2 = 6m$

II. $n^3 = 5n^2 - 6n$

A. $m = n$ or the relationship cannot be established

B. $m \leq n$

C. $m < n$

D. $m \geq n$

E. $m > n$

Q.84 Direction: In the following question two equations numbered I and II are given. You have to solve both equations and give the answer.

I. $35\,m^2 + 26\,m + 3 = 0$

II. $7n^2 - 12n - 4 = 0$

A. $m > n$

B. $m \geq n$

C. $m < n$

D. $m \leq n$

E. $m = n$ or the relationship cannot be established

Q.85 Direction: In the following question, two equations numbered I and II are given. You have to solve both the equations and give the answer.

I. $x^2 - 2x - 15 = 0$

II. $y^2 - 4y - 12 = 0$

A. $x > y$

B. $x \geq y$

C. $x < y$

D. $x \leq y$

E. $x = y$ or no relation can be established between x and y.

Q.86 A certain sum of money amounts to Rs. 720 in 2 years and Rs. 870 in 4.5 years, with same rate of simple interest. Find the rate of interest.

A. 12%	**B.** 15%	**C.** 10%	**D.** 8%

E. 11%

Q.87 A sum of Rs.1600 was invested at 10% simple interest per annum for 2 years. If the same sum was invested at the same rate of compound interest compounded half-yearly for 1 year, then find the difference between the simple interest and compound interest.

A. Rs. 320	**B.** Rs. 162	**C.** Rs. 160	**D.** Rs. 156

E. Rs. 175

Q.88 Direction: Find the value of '?' in the given question:-
31.25% of 37.5% of 14.28% of (?) = 15% of 500

A. 4480	**B.** 5120	**C.** 5440	**D.** 4860

E. 5020

Q.89 A, B, C subscribe Rs. 60,000 for a business, A subscribes Rs. 16000 more than B and B Rs. 10000 more than C. Out of a total profit of Rs. 80,000, (B + C) receives how much amount?

A. Rs. 45676.56	**B.** Rs. 31355.55
C. Rs. 29376.38	**D.** Rs. 34666.66

E. Rs. 3650.66

Q.90 A bus running at 54 km/h takes 60 seconds to cross a light pole. Find the length of the bus.

A. 900 meters	**B.** 800 meters
C. 950 meters	**D.** 850 meters

E. 810 meters

// Smart Answer Sheet //

Correct   Indicates percentage of students who answered questions correctly.

Skipped   Indicates percentage of students who skipped questions.

Q.	Ans.	Correct / Skipped	Q.	Ans.	Correct / Skipped	Q.	Ans.	Correct / Skipped	Q.	Ans.	Correct / Skipped	Q.	Ans.	Correct / Skipped
1	A	82.58 % / 0.0 %	17	B	82.04 % / 0.0 %	33	B	83.12 % / 0.0 %	49	C	55.1 % / 1.99 %	65	B	55.72 % / 1.27 %
2	A	88.28 % / 0.0 %	18	A	53.56 % / 1.73 %	34	C	77.67 % / 0.0 %	50	D	88.86 % / 0.0 %	66	B	77.66 % / 0.0 %
3	C	80.62 % / 0.0 %	19	A	12.62 % / 4.16 %	35	B	76.47 % / 0.0 %	51	A	59.81 % / 1.23 %	67	A	89.62 % / 0.0 %
4	A	84.68 % / 0.0 %	20	C	43.24 % / 1.13 %	36	A	45.57 % / 1.96 %	52	B	64.25 % / 1.15 %	68	C	62.74 % / 1.35 %
5	D	76.91 % / 0.0 %	21	E	57.26 % / 1.68 %	37	C	45.39 % / 1.5 %	53	A	86.1 % / 0.0 %	69	B	52.01 % / 1.46 %
6	C	89.85 % / 0.0 %	22	E	47.67 % / 1.2 %	38	E	67.31 % / 1.99 %	54	A	65.0 % / 1.68 %	70	B	67.91 % / 1.31 %
7	D	86.58 % / 0.0 %	23	E	45.71 % / 1.07 %	39	E	44.27 % / 1.88 %	55	C	80.51 % / 0.0 %	71	C	60.74 % / 1.82 %
8	B	84.8 % / 0.0 %	24	A	57.94 % / 1.68 %	40	A	57.0 % / 1.69 %	56	B	66.28 % / 1.05 %	72	A	68.15 % / 1.27 %
9	B	88.42 % / 0.0 %	25	A	84.17 % / 0.0 %	41	D	64.57 % / 1.33 %	57	C	54.49 % / 1.02 %	73	B	48.89 % / 1.46 %
10	D	62.21 % / 1.63 %	26	C	68.28 % / 1.19 %	42	B	78.97 % / 0.0 %	58	B	68.61 % / 1.78 %	74	D	77.94 % / 0.0 %
11	C	42.67 % / 1.24 %	27	D	58.72 % / 1.92 %	43	D	13.79 % / 4.54 %	59	D	54.87 % / 1.95 %	75	B	79.92 % / 0.0 %
12	D	53.41 % / 1.41 %	28	B	42.06 % / 1.22 %	44	E	23.44 % / 3.91 %	60	B	55.06 % / 1.19 %	76	B	58.78 % / 1.93 %
13	A	87.25 % / 0.0 %	29	A	53.21 % / 1.15 %	45	E	49.6 % / 1.89 %	61	C	78.85 % / 0.0 %	77	B	44.17 % / 1.88 %
14	D	57.25 % / 1.85 %	30	A	50.74 % / 1.91 %	46	C	59.27 % / 1.22 %	62	C	11.62 % / 3.63 %	78	D	53.03 % / 1.2 %
15	C	24.04 % / 4.65 %	31	B	86.9 % / 0.0 %	47	C	57.8 % / 1.68 %	63	C	78.72 % / 0.0 %	79	B	55.77 % / 1.62 %
16	B	67.37 % / 1.32 %	32	C	77.45 % / 0.0 %	48	A	66.05 % / 1.44 %	64	A	42.71 % / 1.52 %	80	C	61.42 % / 1.98 %

Q.	Ans.	Correct		Q.	Ans.	Correct		Q.	Ans.	Correct		Q.	Ans.	Correct		Q.	Ans.	Correct
		Skipped				Skipped				Skipped				Skipped				Skipped
81	D	28.66 %		83	A	41.03 %		85	E	46.75 %		87	D	67.96 %		89	D	67.18 %
		3.35 %				1.7 %				1.04 %				1.5 %				1.7 %
82	A	40.21 %		84	E	68.03 %		86	C	50.57 %		88	A	67.68 %		90	A	52.65 %
		1.72 %				1.23 %				1.81 %				1.99 %				1.68 %

Performance Analysis

Avg. Score (%)	41.11%
Toppers Score (%)	64.44%
Your Score	

//Hints and Solutions//

Ques (1-3): Logic:

1st element → First letter of the word + 2 (According to the alphabetical positions of the letters).

2nd element → Number of consonants.

3rd element → Last letter of the word + 2 (According to the alphabetical positions of the letters).

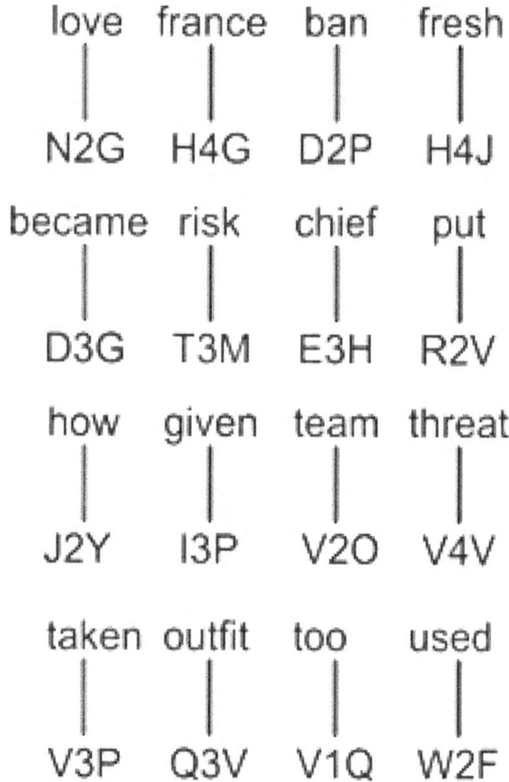

1. So, "J2Y" is the code for "How".

Hence, the correct option is (A).

2. According to the given coding language,

"love" can be coded as "N2G".

"is" can be coded as "K1U".

"blind" can be coded as "D4F".

So, "love is blind" can be coded as "N2G K1U D4F".

Hence, the correct option is (A).

3. According to the given coding language,

"X4C" will be coded as,

1st element is "X". So, the first letter of the word will be X - 2 = V

2nd element is "4". So, the word should consist of 4 consonants.

3rd element is "C". So, the last letter of the word will be C - 2 = A

So, the possible word from the given options is "Vadodara".

Hence, the correct option is (C).

4. Given Series: H % 1 P ! F S ? * X 7 C T 4 $ 9 3 > @ / 6 N Q 5

1) On dropping all the symbols, the arrangement is.

Left Side H 1 P F S X 7 C T 49 3 6 N Q 5 Right Side

2) Element which is sixth from the right end.

Left Side H 1 P F S X 7 C T 4 9 3 6 N Q 5 Right Side

So, 9 is sixth from the right end.

Hence, the correct option is (A).

5. Given Series: H % 1 P ! F S ? * X 7 C T 4 $ 9 3 > @ / 6 N Q 5

1) On dropping all the numbers, the arrangement is.

Left Side H % P ! F S ? * X C T $ > @ / N Q Right Side

Right Side + Left Side = Left Side

5th to the Right + 4th to the Left = 9th from the Left

Left Side H % P ! F S ? * X C T $ > @ / N Q Right Side

So, X is fifth to the right of fourth to the left end.

Hence, the correct option is (D).

6. Given Series: H % 1 P ! F S ? * X 7 C T 4 $ 9 3 > @ / 6 N Q 5

1) Numbers which are immediately followed by a symbol.

H % 1 P ! F S ? * X 7 C T **4 $** 9 3 **>**@ / 6 N Q 5

So, two numbers are there which are immediately followed by a symbol- 4$ and 3>.

Hence, the correct option is (C).

7. Given Series: H % 1 P ! F S ? * X 7 C T 4 $ 9 3 > @ / 6 N Q 5

1) Numbers between '*' and '>'

H % 1 P ! F S ? * X 7 C T 4 $ 9 3> @ / 6 N Q 5

So, the sum of the numbers between '*' and '>' = 7 + 4 + 9 + 3 = 23

Hence, the correct option is (D).

8. Given series: H % 1 P ! F S ? * X 7 C T 4 $ 9 3 > @ / 6 N Q 5

1) Letters which are immediately preceded by consonants and immediately followed by a symbol.

H % 1 P ! **F S ?** * X 7 C T 4 $ 9 3 > @ / 6 N Q 5

Hence, only one letter is there which is immediately preceded by consonants and immediately followed by a symbol i.e., FS?.

Hence, the correct option is (B).

9. Given statements: $A > B; \quad B > F; \quad C < F; \quad D > C; \quad E > D$

On combining: $A > B > F > C < D < E$

Conclusions:

I. $A > F \rightarrow$ True (as $A > B > F \rightarrow A > F$)

II. $C > A \rightarrow$ False (as $A > B > F > C \rightarrow A > C$)

III. $B > D \rightarrow$ False (as $D > C < B \rightarrow$ thus, clear relation between B and D cannot be determined)

Hence, the correct option is (B).

Ques (10-14):Eight people: A, B, C, D, E, F, G, and H

Eight Colors: Purple, pink, red, green, blue, black, yellow, and orange

1) F sits third to the left of A, who likes purple, and the person who likes purple sits to the immediate left of G.

2) F and the person who likes blue has one person in between them.

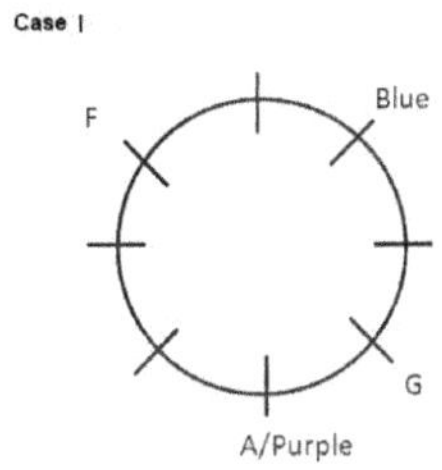
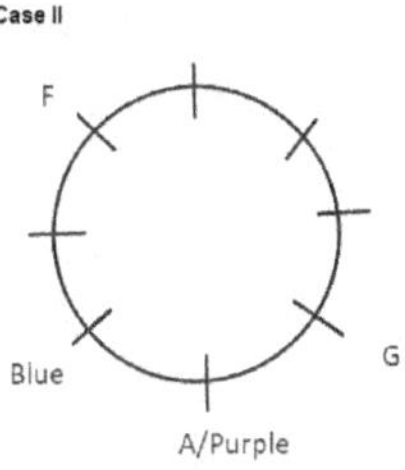

3) C sits to the immediate right of E and neither of them likes blue.

4) E sits opposite the person who likes yellow and the person who likes yellow sits immediately next to the one who likes orange.

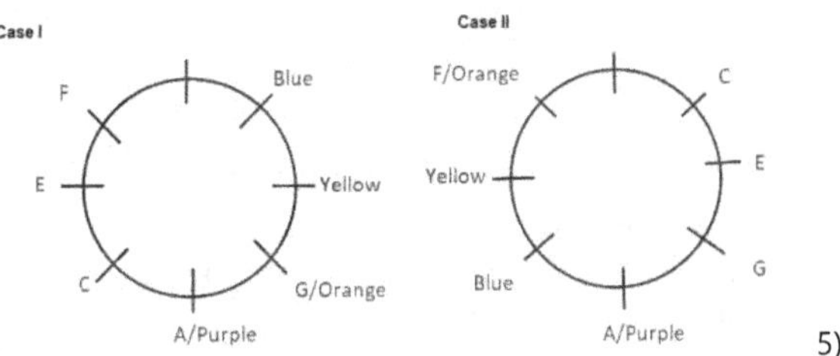

5) The one who likes green and B has two people sitting in between them.

6) C, F and G, neither of them like green color.

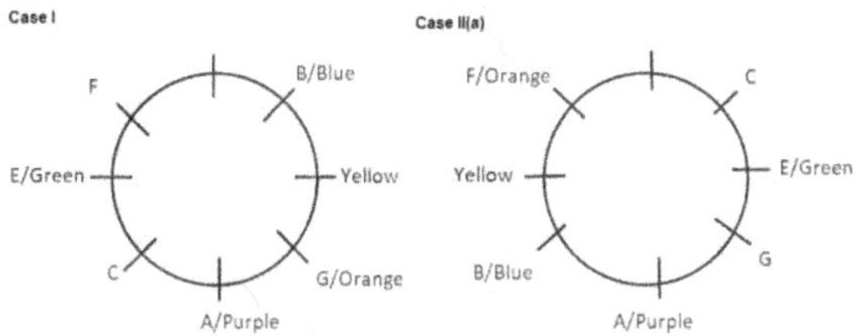

Case II(b)

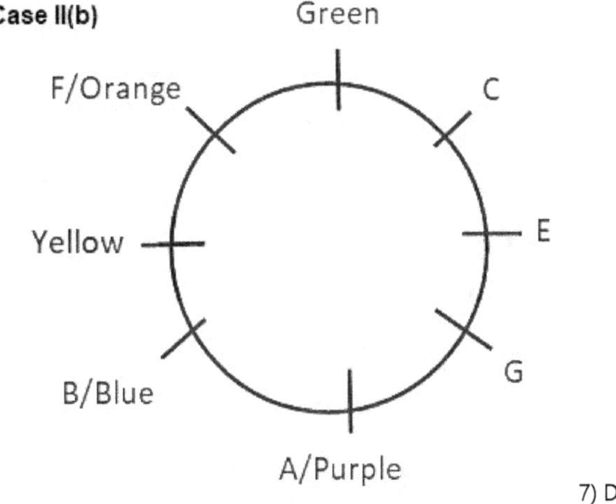

7) D sits second to the right of H.

8) D does not like the yellow color.

This is not possible in cases II(a) and II(b), therefore both the cases get eliminated.

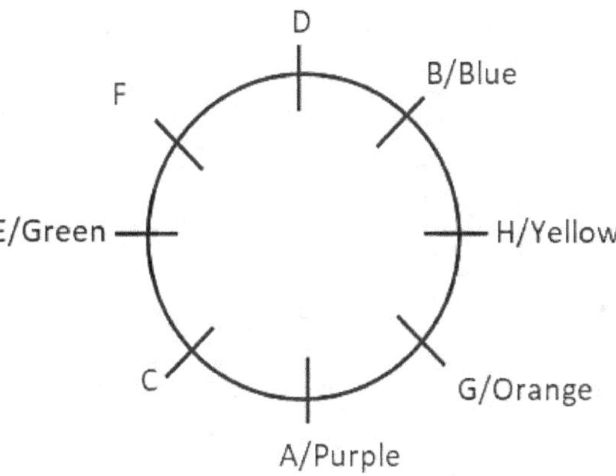

9) The one who likes red sits to the immediate left of the one who likes black.

Thus, the final arrangement is:

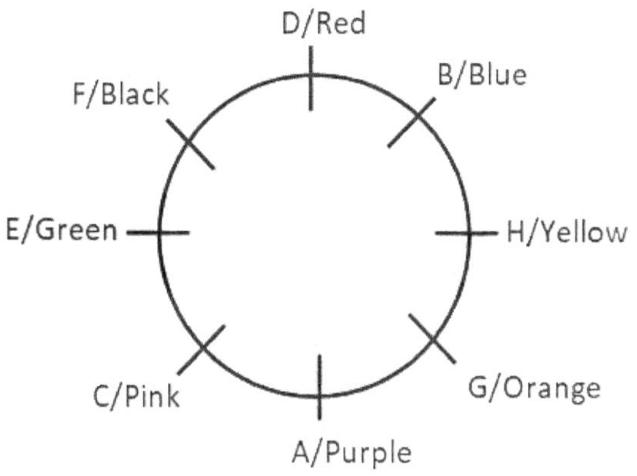

10. Clearly, F likes the black color.

Hence, the correct option is (D).

11. Clearly, the person sitting third to the right of D likes pink color.

Hence, the correct option is (C).

12. Clearly, "Black and C" does not belong to the group as all the other pairs sit adjacent to each other.

Hence, the correct option is (D).

13. Clearly, only one person sits between the one who likes orange and C, when counted from C's right.

Hence, the correct option is (A).

14. Clearly, F is an immediate neighbor of the one who likes red color.

Hence, the correct option is (D).

Symbol in Diagram	Meaning
○	Female
□	Male
═══	Married Couple
───	Siblings
│	Difference of A Generation

Ques (15-16):

Hint: Two members have blood group of the same type.

There are more male members than female members.

One married couple in the family is a positive donor and positive recipient.

Note: The Blood group O+ and O- are universal donors.

The Blood group AB+ and AB- are universal recipients.

Members: M, N, O, P, Q, R, S, T and U.

Blood Groups: A+, A-, B+, B-, AB+, AB-, O+ and O-.

1) N has two off-springs and his off-springs are universal donors of both types.

2) P's son-in-law has an A- blood group.

3) Q is married to a positive universal donor and has a positive blood group.

4) R is the maternal uncle of U.

5) U is the maternal grandson of P and has an A+ blood group.

6) The parents of S have positive blood groups.

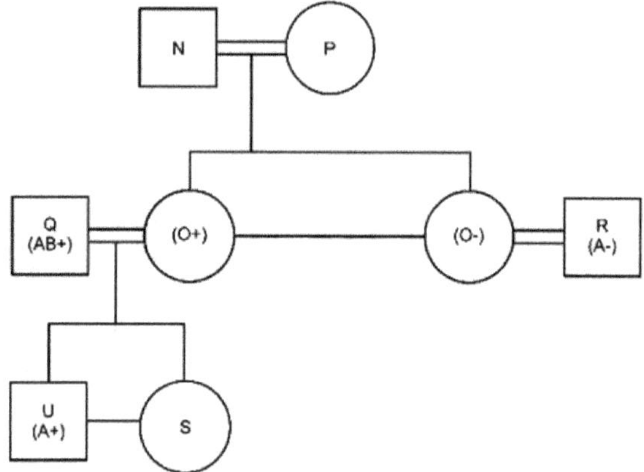

7) O's daughter is a negative universal recipient.

8) N and his maternal grandson, T has a negative blood group. (So the only group left is B-, and as already stated that two members have the same blood group.)

(Thus, P has a B+ blood group and M is a negative universal donor.)

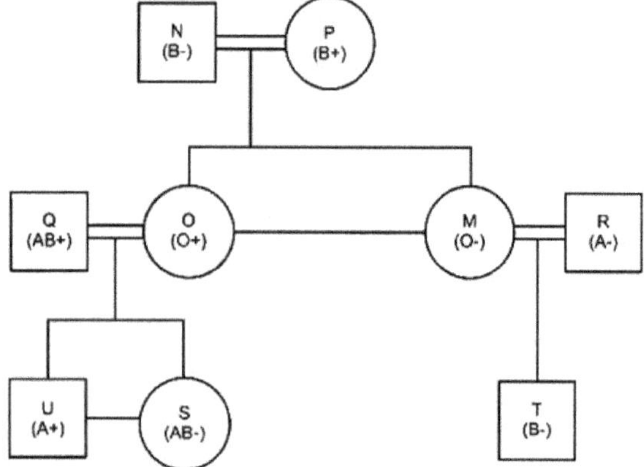

15. Thus, R is the Brother-in-law of O.

Hence, the correct option is (C).

16. Thus, P is the Maternal Grandmother of S.

Hence, the correct option is (B).

17. The given word:

DOORSTEP

Applying the above condition, we have new word:

CPPQRSFO

Then the final arrangement of old and new words are:

D	O	O	R	S	T	E	P
C	P	P	Q	R	S	F	O

Thus 'O' is the only vowel in the new arrangement.

Hence, the correct option is (B).

Ques (18-22):Eight chocolate boxes name: Fivestar, Dairy Milk, KitKat, Snicker, Twix, Bournville, Cadbury and Candy.

1) Three chocolate boxes are placed between Dairy Milk and Snicker.

2) Two boxes are placed between Twix and Dairy Milk.

3) Twix is placed below Dairy Milk.

Case 1	Case 2
Snicker	Dairy Milk
	Twix
Dairy Milk	Snicker
Twix	

4) Four boxes are placed between Twix and Cadbury.5) The number of boxes above Cadbury is the same as the number of boxes below Candy.

Case 1	Case 2
Snicker	Cadbury
Cadbury	Dairy Milk
Dairy Milk	
Candy	Twix
	Snicker
Twix	Candy

6)Bournville is placed above Kitkat but below Fivestar.7)
Bournville is not placed just above KitKat. (This eliminates case 2)

Case 1	Case 2
Snicker	Cadbury
Fivestar	Fivestar
Cadbury	Dairy Milk
Bournville	Bournville

Dairy Milk	Kitkat
Candy	Twix
Kitkat	Snicker
Twix	Candy

Final arrangement:

Case 1
Snicker
Fivestar
Cadbury
Bournville
Dairy Milk
Candy
Kitkat
Twix

18. Therefore, Kitkat is placed just below the Candy.

Hence, the correct option is (A).

19. Therefore, Cadbury is placed between Bournville and Fivestar.

Hence, the correct option is (A).

20. Therefore, 'two' boxes are placed above Cadbury.

Hence, the correct option is (C).

21. Six boxes are placed between Twix and Snicker.

Therefore, more than four boxes are placed between Twix and Snicker.

Hence, the correct option is (E).

22. Therefore, Snicker is placed at the top.

Hence, the correct option is (E).

23. Following the above instructions will lead to the below diagram:

X - Y & A → X is 1 km to the east of Y which is 5 km to the south of A

X + Z + W - V → X is 1 km to the south of Z which is 1 km to the south of V

W % U → W is 5 km to the east of U

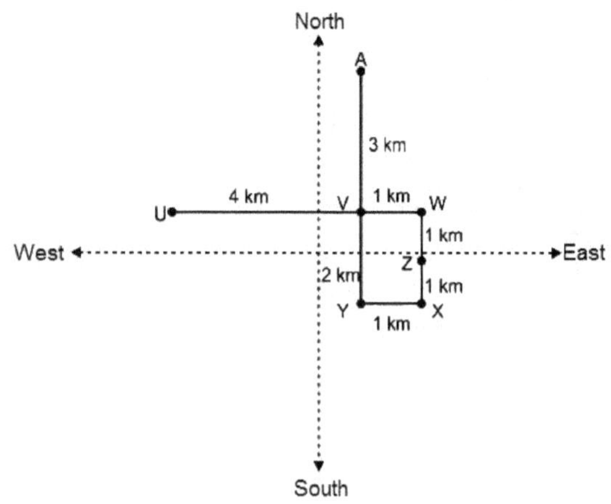

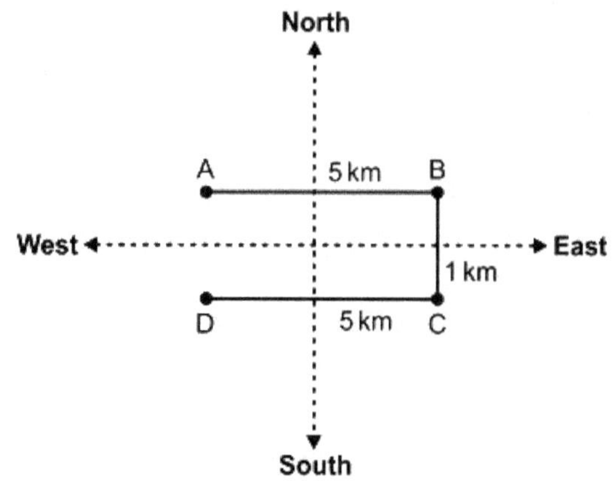

Therefore, X is in the South-East direction with respect to U.

Hence, the correct option is (E).

24. Following the above instructions will lead to the below diagram:

C + B % A= C is 1 km to the south of B which is 5 km to the east of A

D + E - B → D is 1 km to the south of E which is 1 km to the east of B

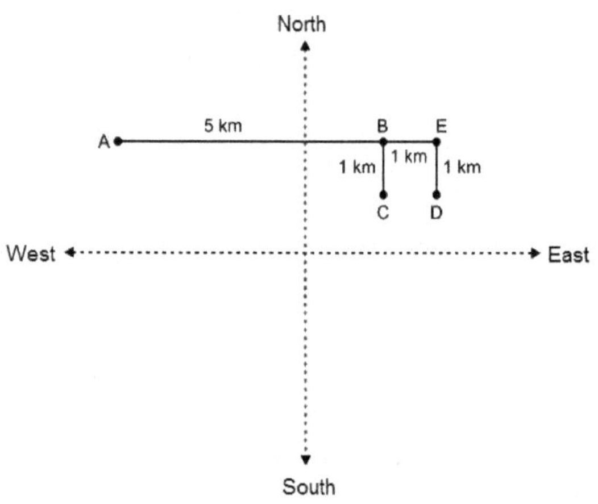

The distance between C and D is 1 km.

Hence, the correct option is (A).

25. Following the above instructions will lead to the below diagram:

C + B % A → C is 1 km to the south of B which is 5 km to the east of A

C % D → C is 5 km to the east of D

The distance between A and D is 1km.

Hence, the correct option is (A).

Ques (26-28):Items: Transformer, Fuse, Switch, Capacitor, Relay, Battery, and Microcontroller.

I. More than three boxes are kept below Battery. (considering 3 cases)

II. Only three items are kept between Capacitor and Battery.

III. The Switch is kept just above the Capacitor.

Case 1:

7	
6	
5	Battery
4	
3	
2	Switch
1	Capacitor

Case 2:

7	
6	Battery
5	
4	
3	Switch
2	Capacitor
1	

Case 3:

7	Battery
6	
5	
4	Switch
3	Capacitor
2	
1	

IV. The transformer is kept above the Battery. (case 3 canceled)

V. Only two items are kept between Relay and Transformer.

Case 1:

7	Transformer
6	
5	Battery
4	Relay
3	
2	Switch
1	Capacitor

Case 1B:

7	
6	Transformer
5	Battery
4	
3	Relay
2	Switch
1	Capacitor

Case 2:

7	Transformer
6	Battery
5	
4	Relay
3	Switch
2	Capacitor
1	

VI. Fuse is kept above Relay and below Microcontroller. (case 1 and case 2 canceled)

Case 1B:

7	Microcontroller
6	Transformer
5	Battery
4	Fuse
3	Relay
2	Switch
1	Capacitor

The above arrangement will be the final arrangement.

26. Relay is kept just above the Switch.

So, Relay is the correct answer.

Hence, the correct option is (C).

27. Four items are kept between Capacitor and Transformer.

Hence, the correct option is (D).

28. All except Relay are kept on even-numbered shelves.

Hence, the correct option is (B).

29. Given statements: P = Q < R > S = T; A < T < B; C > T < D

On combining: P = Q < R > S = T < D, B; C > T > A

Conclusions:

I. C < A → False (as C > T > A)

II. D < A → False (as D > T > A)

Thus, none is true.

Hence, the correct option is (A).

30. Given statements: P = Q ≤ R ≤ S; S > A < B; C > D > A

On combining: P = Q ≤ R ≤ S > A < B; A < D < C

Conclusions:

I. P > A → False (as P = Q ≤ R ≤ S > A → therefore we cannot determine the relation between P and A)

II. R < C → False (as P = Q ≤ R ≤ S > A < B; A < D < C → therefore we cannot determine the relation between R and C)

Thus, none is true.

Hence, the correct option is (A).

31. In part (B), the verb 'argue needs to be replaced with 'argued'.

If past time is given in a sentence then only the simple past tense will be used.

Past time example: Yesterday, two days ago, last Sunday, in 2010, etc.

Here, in the sentence past time i.e. '1991' is given and will require the verbs in simple past.

Thus, the correct sentence is "The National Commission for Rural Labour argued way back in 1991 that unequal development was the main cause of labour migration."

Hence, the correct option is (B).

32. The error lies in part (C) of the sentence.

The correct article will be 'the' instead of 'a'.

"The" is the indefinite article used for specifying nouns.

Here, 'former' is specified and so 'latter' will be specified.

So, the correct sentence will be- "He looked after the former and the latter in an effective way."

Hence, the correct option is (C).

33. The error lies in part (B) of the sentence.

'Anxiously' is the correct adverb to be used instead of 'anxious'.

Adverb- An adverb is a word that modifies (describes) a verb (he sings loudly), an adjective (very tall), another adverb (ended too quickly), or even a whole sentence (Fortunately, I had brought an umbrella). Adverbs often end in -ly, but some (such as fast) look exactly the same as their adjective counterparts.

Example- He ate dinner quickly.

So, the correct sentence is- Everyone's waiting anxiously for the concert tickets to go on sale.

Hence, the correct option is (B).

34. In part (B), the verb 'is' needs to be replaced with 'are'.

The subject of the sentence i.e. 'Awareness programmes' is a plural noun and will require plural verb according to subject-verb agreement.

Subject-verb Agreement- It states that if the subject is singular then the verb should be singular and if the subject is plural then the verb should be plural.

Thus, the correct sentence is "Awareness programmes are also being initiated at a community level to prevent such incidents."

Hence, the correct option is (C).

35. The error lies in part (B) of the sentence.

Correlative conjunctions are pairs such as neither, nor, not, only, either-or, and but also.

Neither, nor: It puts two negative sentences into one simple sentence.

Example- Ali doesn't live in New York. Bob doesn't live in New York.

These conjunctions connect two balanced clauses, phrases, or words.

The two elements that correlative conjunctions connect are usually similar in length and grammatical structure.

Example- Neither Norway nor Switzerland is in the European Union.

Hence, the correct option is (B).

36. 'Noted' means 'important'. From the options, the word that is opposite in meaning to this word is 'common'. All the other words are synonyms of the word 'noted'.

Hence, the correct option is (A).

37. The word savage means fierce, violent, and uncontrolled. Among the options, the word that is opposite in meaning to this word is 'peaceful'.

Hence, the correct option is (C).

38. Refer to the following sentences from the sixth paragraph of the passage: "There were other far more civilized nations in those days. Among these were the E-gyp´tians, who lived in Africa. They had long known the use of fire, had good tools and were much further advanced than the Pelasgians". So, the author considers the Egyptians civilized because they knew how to read and write, they knew how to use fire, they had good tools, etc.

Hence, the correct option is (E).

39. The word 'hollow' means 'being empty from inside'. The word that is opposite in meaning to this word is 'solid', which means having substance inside.

Hence, the correct option is (E).

40. The tone of the passage is narrative. Also, it is unlikely that the source of the passage is a newspaper article. The source is more likely to be a book on history.

The author himself believes that the Greeks were an uncivilized people. So, he is not wrong to assume that the Egyptians believed the same thing.

It is likely that the author is a historian.

Hence, the correct option is (A).

41. Option (D) replaces the bold part most appropriately.

The correct sentence will therefore be:

The Bar Council of Delhi's directive to the Big Four accountancy firms not to offer legal services to their clients in India **is a retrograde move that is transparently protectionist in intent.**

As we can observe that the sentence nowhere implies the context of a perfect tense and therefore the verb 'has been' should be replaced by 'is' here.

Secondly, the word 'rhetoric' which means 'language designed to have a persuasive or impressive effect' doesn't seem to go well with the context of the sentence. This eliminates options (A) and (C) immediately.

'Retrograde' means 'reverting to an earlier and inferior condition' does make sense in the sentence and therefore must replace the given adjective 'responsive' in the bold part.

Usage of the adjective 'transparent' in the bold phrase is also ungrammatical. It should be replaced by the adverb 'transparently'.

Besides, the usage of the preposition 'in' right before the noun 'intent' is absolutely correct.

Hence, the correct option is (D).

42. The plural form of the expression 'commander-in-chief' is 'commanders-in-chief'. It refers the officer holding supreme command of the forces in an area or operation.

Example: Let's hope our commanders in chief have taken that on board as we go off, yet again, into battle.

Correct Sentence:

The **commanders-in-chief of both** the armies shook hands with each other and sat down on their respective chairs.

Hence, the correct option is (B).

43. There is an error in the bold part of the sentence since it is not expressing the correct meaning that it is healthy for the democracy of India that Mr. Modi does not take into account the caste, language and region-oriented issues while deciding on any policy.

Only Option (D) is there that explains the correct meaning of the statement.

The correct statement is:

There is an argument that it is healthy that Mr. Modi does not bargain with caste, linguistic and region-oriented interest groups.

Option (A) can be eliminated since it is not expressing the desired meaning whereas Option (B) is not making any sense. The same can be said regarding Option (C) also. Only Option (D) is there that explains the correct meaning of the statement.

Hence, the correct option is (D)

44. Demonstrates means to show something clearly by giving proof.

Extent of means the length, area, size or importance of something.

So, the original sentence is absolutely correct and hence the bold part needs no replacement.

Hence, the correct option is (E).

45. The bold part is already correct, thus no replacement is required.

As the common meaning of the phrase **all set** is "completely ready" or "wholly prepared," or to put it another way "in the proper state for some purpose, use, or activity."

Hence, the correct option is (E).

46. 'Coin' is a countable noun. Therefore, 'fewer' should be used to fill the blank. 'Less' should be used to compare uncountable items.

Hence, the correct option is (C).

47. Plural 'girls' should take a plural verb. So, (B) is rejected. Options (A) and (D) do not fit grammatically in the blank. Option (C) makes perfect sense, as it is the one only with the plural form of the verb.

Correct sentence: The girls want to go on a picnic.

Hence, the correct option is (C).

48. Roshni's house is just **beside** the road.

"Beside" is a preposition that means "close to" or "next to." "Besides" is also a preposition that means "in addition to" or "apart from." It's can also serve as an adverb that means "furthermore" or "another thing." Example: Come and sit beside me. "Beside" is the most appropriate word for the blank.

Hence, the correct option is (A).

49. On hearing the noise, the rabbit jumped **off** the bed.

"Off" is usually used as an adverb or a preposition. In both cases, it indicates separation or disconnection. 'Jumped off' is the correct usage as per the context.

Hence, the correct option is (C).

50. As the person wishes something to happen in the future, so 'will' fits best in the blank. 'Were' talks of past tense so cannot be the answer. Also helping the verb 'be' in options A and B make them wrong.

Correct sentence: I wish someday they will understand the importance of hard work.

Hence, the correct option is (D).

51. The sentences given suggest that the house sparkled in an empty kind of way after it was waxed and the furniture got polished.

We use once as a conjunction meaning 'as soon as' or 'after'.

The connected statement would be:

"Once" the floors had been waxed and the furniture got polished by afternoon, the house sparkled but in an empty kind of way.

Hence, the correct option is (A).

52. If we read the two sentences, we can observe that they are related by cause and effect relationship. And among the choices available, only 'because' can be used in this context since it means 'the reasons thereof'.

The connected statement would be:

Unlike other business leaders she has not shunned political leaders but engaged with them **"Because"** she believes that society needs political leaders to bring about change and citizens need to engage with them.

Hence, the correct option is (B).

53. If we read the two sentences, we can observe that they are related by cause and effect relationship. And among the choices available, only 'now that' can be used in this context as we use it to give an explanation of a new situation.

The connected statement would be:

"Now that" I live only a few blocks from work, I walk to work and enjoy it.

Hence, the correct option is (A).

54. If we read the two sentences, we can observe the second sentence discusses an event which happens while another is in progress. And among the choices available, only 'as' can be used because we use as to introduce two events happening at the same time

The connected statement would be:

"As" thunderstorms brought the first significant rainfall in weeks to the UK, Belfast international airport received 88.2 mm in a matter of hours, more than the region's monthly July average.

Hence, the correct option is (A).

55. The given sentences suggest that the man goes to a park and the second sentence gives the reason behind his action.

We use as to state the purpose of an object or action.

The connected statement would be:

The man goes to the park every Sunday **"As"** he loves watching the ducks in the lake.

Hence, the correct option is (C).

56. Prioritized means to treat something as being more important than other things.

Example- The organization was formed to prioritize the needs of older people.

- The sentence suggests that the spam reports are divided in a certain way.
- So, the blank must contain a verb that reflects the meaning 'divided'.
- Only 'prioritized' or divided according to priority is the apt solution here.

Hence, the correct option is (B).

57. Adoption is the act of taking something on as your own.

To adore is to love something.

To adorn is to decorate something.

To advise is to guide or counsel.

To object is to speak against a given point.

The sentence suggests that the blank must contain a verb that means 'to implement' or 'to take up'.

The only verb that reflects this meaning is 'adopted'.

Therefore, the correct answer is option (C).

Hence, the correct option is (C).

58. Mislead (a verb) means to make somebody have the wrong idea or opinion about somebody/something.

Example- He then again said he really wanted to remain friends and he hadn't meant to mislead me.

- The passage talks about website malpractices, so the sentence must also be related to the context.
- The blank must contain a verb that means 'misdirect' or 'falsely guide' the users.
- The only option that reflects this meaning is 'mislead'.

Hence, the correct option is (B).

59. Violated means to break a rule, an agreement, etc; to not respect something; to spoil or damage something.

Example- She was attacked and violated by an unknown intruder.

- The sentence suggests that the blank must contain a verb that means 'did not agree with' or 'refused'.
- The only option that reflects this meaning is 'violated', which means abused.

Hence, the correct option is (D).

60. Influence means the power to affect, change or control somebody/something.

Example- She claims that her personal problems played no influence upon her decision to resign.

- The sentence suggests that the blank must contain a verb that means 'to tamper with' or to try to be associated with.
- The only option that reflects this meaning is 'influence'.

Hence, the correct option is (B).

61. In a three digit number, 1st place can be filled in 5 different ways with (0, 2, 4, 6, 8).

10th place can be filled in 10 different ways.

100th place can be filled in 9 different ways.

So, the total number of ways = 5 × 10 × 9 = 450

Hence, the correct option is (C).

62. The pattern is as follows:

Logic: Alternate division by 2 and 3

$504 \div 2 = 252$

$252 \div 3 = 84$

$84 \div 2 = 42$

$42 \div 3 = 14$

$14 \div 2 = 7$

∴ The value of ? is 14.

Hence, the correct option is (C).

63. The pattern is as follows:

$6 \times 1 = 6$

$6 \times 2 = 12$

$12 \times 3 = 36$

$36 \times 4 = 144$

$144 \times 5 = 720$

∴ The value of ? is 720.

Hence, the correct option is (C).

64. The pattern is as follows:

$7 \times 1 + 1 = 8$

$8 \times 2 - 2 = 14$

$14 \times 3 + 3 = 45$

$45 \times 4 - 4 = 176$

$176 \times 5 + 5 = 885$

∴ The value of ? is 885.

Hence, the correct option is (A).

65. The pattern is as follows:

$5 \times 1 + 1 = 6$

$6 \times 2 + 1 = 13$

$13 \times 3 + 1 = 40$

$40 \times 4 + 1 = 161$

$161 \times 5 + 1 = 806$

∴ The value of '?' is 806.

Hence, the correct option is (B).

66. The pattern is as follows:

$4.5 - 1 = 3.5 \quad (\because 1 = 1^2)$

$8.5 - 4 = 4.5 \quad (\because 4 = 2^2)$

$17.5 - 9 = 8.5 \quad (\because 9 = 3^2)$

$33.5 - 16 = 17.5 \quad (\because 16 = 4^2)$

$58.5 - 25 = 33.5 \quad (\because 25 = 5^2)$

∴ The value of ? is 33.5.

Hence, the correct option is (B).

67. Let the total work be 'a'.

Work done by A in 1 day = $\dfrac{a}{9}$

Work done by A and B in 1 day = $\dfrac{a}{6.75}$

Let the work done by B in 1 day be b.

Work done by B in 1 day = $\dfrac{a}{6.75} - \dfrac{a}{9}$

$\Rightarrow$ Work done by B in 1 day = $\dfrac{4a}{27} - \dfrac{3a}{27} = \dfrac{a}{27}$

∴ Total days taken by B to complete the work = $\dfrac{a}{\left(\frac{a}{27}\right)} = 27$

Hence, the correct option is (A).

68. Given:

The investment ratio of Sruti and Shankya = 3 : 7

Share of Sruti = Rs. 1800

Let, the total profit = Rs. 100x

Profit percent after repairing of house = 100x - (100x × 10%) = 90x

Share of Sruti = 90x × $\left(\dfrac{3}{10}\right)$ = 27x

According to the question,

$\Rightarrow$ 27x = 5400

$\Rightarrow$ x = 200

∴ Total profit = 100x = 100 × 200 = 20000

Hence, the correct option is (C).

69. Given:

Average of seven numbers = 9

Average of first four numbers = 12

Average of last four numbers = 10

We know that,

Average = $\dfrac{Sum\ of\ observations}{Total\ number\ of\ observations}$

Let the numbers be a_1, a_2, a_3, a_4, a_5, a_6 and a_7 respectively.

$\Rightarrow \dfrac{(a_1+a_2+a_3+a_4+a_5+a_6+a_7)}{7} = 9$

$\Rightarrow a_1+a_2+a_3+a_4+a_5+a_6+a_7 = 63$ ----(i)

$\Rightarrow \dfrac{(a_1+a_2+a_3+a_4)}{4} = 12$

$\Rightarrow a_1+a_2+a_3+a_4 = 48$ ----(ii)

$\Rightarrow \dfrac{(a_4+a_5+a_6+a_7)}{4} = 10$

$\Rightarrow a_4+a_5+a_6+a_7 = 40$ ----(iii)

$\Rightarrow$ on adding equation (ii) and (iii) we get,

$\Rightarrow a_1+a_2+a_3+a_4+a_4+a_5+a_6+a_7 = 48 + 40$

$\Rightarrow a_1+a_2+a_3+a_4+a_4+a_5+a_6+a_7 = 88$

$\Rightarrow (a_1+a_2+a_3+a_4+a_5+a_6+a_7)+a_4 = 88$

$\Rightarrow 63 + a_4 = 88$

$\Rightarrow a_4 = 25$

So, the fourth term is 25.

Hence, the correct option is (B).

70. Let the breadth of rectangle is x.

So, $15^2 = 12^2+x^2$

$225 = 144+x^2$

$x^2 = 225 - 144 = 81$

$x = 9$ cm

Therefore, area of the rectangle=12×9 = 108 cm^2

Hence, the correct option is (B).

71. Number of students from physics department from college $C = 90$

Number of students from chemistry department from college $C = 70$

Number of students from math department from college $C = 85$

Number of students from physics department from college $D = 60$

Number of students from chemistry department from college $D = 70$

Number of students from math department from college $D = 95$

Total number of students from college $C = (90 + 70 + 85) = 245$

Total number of students from college $D = (60 + 70 + 95) = 225$

Now, the total number of students from college C is more than that of college D.

Difference between them $= (245 - 225) = 20$

So, Required percentage $= \left(\dfrac{20}{225} \times 100\right)\% = \left(\dfrac{80}{9}\right)$

$= 8.88\% \approx 9\%$

∴ The students from college C are 9% more than that of college D.

Hence, the correct option is (C).

72. Number of students from physics department from college $A = 50$

Number of students from physics department from college $B = 80$

Number of students from physics department from college $C = 90$

Number of students from physics department from college $D = 60$

As we know,

$$\text{Average} = \frac{\text{Total sum of all numbers}}{\text{Total number of the item in the set}}$$

Average of all students from the physics department of all four colleges $= \frac{50+80+90+60}{4} = \frac{280}{4}$

$= 70$

∴ The average of all students from the physics department of all four colleges is 70.

Hence, the correct option is (A).

73. Students from the physics department from college A = 50

Students from the math department from college A = 65

Students from chemistry department from college C = 70

Students from the math department from college C = 85

Total number of students from physics and math department from college A = (50 + 65) = 115

Total number of students from chemistry and math department from college C = (70 + 85) = 155

Now, the ratio between them = 115 : 155

= 23 : 31

∴ The ratio between the students from physics and math from college A and the students from chemistry and math from college C is 23 : 31.

Hence, the correct option is (B).

74. Number of students from chemistry department from college $A = 75$

Number of students from chemistry department from college B $= 95$

Number of students from chemistry department from college C $= 70$

Number of students from chemistry department from college D $= 70$

Total number of students $= (75 + 95 + 70 + 70)$

$= 310$

∴ The total number of students from the chemistry department from all four colleges is 310.

Hence, the correct option is (D).

75. Number of students from chemistry department from college B = 95

Number of students from chemistry department from college C = 70

Number of students from physics department from college A = 50

Number of students from physics department from college D = 60

Total students from the chemistry department from both college B and college C = (95 + 70) = 165

Total students from the physics department from both colleges A and college D = (50 + 60) = 110

So, the difference between the students from two departments = (165 - 110) = 55

∴ The difference between the total number of students from the chemistry department from college B and college C and the total number of students from the physics department from college A and college D is 55.

Hence, the correct option is (B).

76. Given:

$$\frac{\left(\left(\frac{2.56}{10.89}\right)+\left(\frac{2.36}{4.58}\right)-\left(\frac{0.99}{4.79}\right)\right)}{[7.05+74.88\% \text{ of } 11.88]}$$

Taking approximate value, we get

$$\frac{\left(\left(\frac{3}{11}\right)+\left(\frac{2}{5}\right)-\left(\frac{1}{5}\right)\right)}{[7+75\% \text{ of } 12]}$$

$$\Rightarrow \frac{\frac{(15+22-11)}{55}}{(7+9)}$$

$$\Rightarrow \left(\frac{26}{55}\right) \div 16$$

$$\Rightarrow \frac{26}{(55\times16)}$$

$$\Rightarrow \frac{13}{440}$$

Hence, the correct option is (B).

77. Given:

$$55\% \text{ of } 99.999 +?^2 = 56\% \text{ of } 850 - 20\% \text{ of } 150$$

Taking approximate value, we get

$$55\% \text{ of } 100 +?^2 = 56\% \text{ of } 850 - 20\% \text{ of } 150$$

$$\Rightarrow (55 \div 100 \times 100) + ?^2 = (56 \div 100 \times 850) - (20 \div 100 \times 150)$$

$$\Rightarrow 55 + ?^2 = 476 - 30$$

$$\Rightarrow 55 + ?^2 = 446$$

$$\Rightarrow ?^2 = 446 - 55$$

$$\Rightarrow ?^2 = 391$$

$$\therefore ? \approx 20$$

Hence, the correct option is (B).

78. Follow BODMAS rule to solve this question, as per the order given below:

B	Brackets in order (), {}, []	ब्रेकट (), {}, [] क्रम
O	Of	का
D	Division (÷)	विभाजन (÷)
M	Multiplication (×)	गुणा (×)
A	Addition (+)	जोड़ (+)
s	Subtraction (-)	घटाव (-)

$32^{0.16} \times 32^{0.4} \times 32^{0.5} = 128^? \div 2$

$$\Rightarrow 2^{5 \times 0.16} \times 2^{5 \times 0.4} \times 2^{5 \times 0.5} = 2^{7 \times ?} \div 2$$

$$\Rightarrow 0.8 + 2 + 2.5 = 7 \times ? - 1$$

$$\Rightarrow 5.3 = 7 \times ? - 1$$

$$\Rightarrow 7 \times ? = 6.3$$

$$\Rightarrow ? = 0.9$$

Hence, the correct option is (D).

79. Given:

42% of 250 + 115% of 480 = ?

Follow the BODMAS rule according to the table given below:

B	Brackets in order (), {}, []	ब्रेकट (), {}, [] क्रम
O	Of	का
D	Division (÷)	विभाजन (÷)
M	Multiplication (×)	गुणा (×)
A	Addition (+)	जोड़ (+)
s	Subtraction (-)	घटाव (-)

42% of 250 + 115% of 480 = ?

$$\Rightarrow \left(\frac{42}{100}\right) \times 250 + \left(\frac{115}{100}\right) \times 480 = ?$$

$$\Rightarrow 105 + 552 = ?$$

$$\Rightarrow 657 = ?$$

$\therefore$ The value of ? is 657

Hence, the correct option is (B).

80. $57\frac{1}{7}\%$ of 490 + 22.22% of 729 - $\sqrt{2500} \times \sqrt{25} \div 5^2 = ?$

Follow the BODMAS rule according to the table given below:

B	Brackets in order (), {}, []	ब्रेकट (), {}, [] क्रम
O	Of	का
D	Division (÷)	विभाजन (÷)
M	Multiplication (×)	गुणा (×)
A	Addition (+)	जोड़ (+)
s	Subtraction (-)	घटाव (-)

$57\frac{1}{7}\%$ of 490 + 22.22% of 729 - $\sqrt{2500} \times \sqrt{25} \div 5^2 = ?$

$$\Rightarrow \left(\frac{4}{7}\right) \times 490 + \left(\frac{2}{9}\right) \times 729 - 50 \times 5 \div 25 = ?$$

$$\Rightarrow 4 \times 70 + 2 \times 81 - 10 = ?$$

$$\Rightarrow 280 + 162 - 10 = ?$$

$$\Rightarrow 442 - 10 = ?$$

$$\Rightarrow ? = 432$$

$\therefore$ The value of '?' Is 432.

Hence, the correct option is (C).

81. Let tank capacity is = 60 ltr

LCM of 12 and 15-

So tap A can fill it in 12 hours

$\therefore$ Tap A can fill per hours = $\dfrac{60}{12}$ = 5 ltr

Tap B can emptied it in 15 hours-

$\therefore$ Tap B can empty per hours = $\dfrac{60}{15}$ = 4 ltr

Tank filled after 2 hour = 5 - 4 = 1 ltr

(If taps open alternatively)

In last hour tap A filled tank 5 ltr

So rest part of tank need to be filled is = 60 - 5 = 55 ltr

In 2 hours tank filled = 1 ltr

So 55 ltr to be filled in = 55 $\times$ 2 = 110

So total time = 110 + 1 = 111 hours

Hence, the correct option is (D).

82. On throwing two dice, n(S) = 6 × 6 = 36

Number of events of getting a total of 7, n(E) = 6, i.e., (1,6), (2,5) , (3,4), (4,3) , (5,2), (6,1)

$\therefore$ Probability of getting a total of 7 = $\dfrac{n(E)}{n(S)}$ = $\left(\dfrac{6}{36}\right)$ = $\left(\dfrac{1}{6}\right)$

Hence, the correct option is (A).

83. I. $m^3 + 5m^2 = 6m$

$$\Rightarrow m(m^2 + 5m - 6) = 0$$

$$\Rightarrow m^2 + 6m - m - 6 = 0$$

$$\Rightarrow m(m + 6) - (m + 6) = 0$$

$\Rightarrow (m+6)(m-1) = 0$

$\Rightarrow m = -6, 1$ and 0

II. $n^3 = 5n^2 - 6n$

$\Rightarrow n(n^2 - 5n + 6) = 0$

$\Rightarrow n^2 - 3n - 2n + 6 = 0$

$\Rightarrow n(n-3) - 2(n-3) = 0$

$\Rightarrow (n-3)(n-2) = 0$

$\Rightarrow n = 3, 2$ and 0

When $m = -6, m < n$ for $n = 3, m < n$ for $n = 2$ and $m < n$ for $n = 0$

When $m = 1, m < n$ for $n = 3, m < n$ for $n = 2$ and $m > n$ for $n = 0$

When $m = 0, m < n$ for $n = 3, m < n$ for $n = 2$ and $m = n$ for $n = 0$

$\therefore$ The relationship cannot be established

Hence, the correct option is (A).

84. I. $35m^2 + 26m + 3 = 0$

$\Rightarrow 35m^2 + 21m + 5m + 3 = 0$

$\Rightarrow 7m(5m + 3) + 1(5m + 3) = 0$

$\Rightarrow (5m + 3)(7m + 1) = 0$

$\Rightarrow m = \dfrac{-3}{5}$ or $m = \dfrac{-1}{7}$

II. $7n^2 - 12n - 4 = 0$

$\Rightarrow 7n^2 - 14n + 2n - 4 = 0$

$\Rightarrow 7n(n-2) + 2(n-2) = 0$

$\Rightarrow (n-2)(7n + 2) = 0$

$\Rightarrow n = 2$ or $n = \dfrac{-2}{7}$

When $m = \dfrac{-3}{5}, m < n$ for $n = 2$ and $m < n$ for $n = \dfrac{-2}{7}$

And when $m = \dfrac{-1}{7}, m < n$ for $n = 2$ and $m > n$ for $n = \dfrac{-2}{7}$

$\therefore$ The relationship cannot be established.

Hence, the correct option is (E).

85. Given,

I. $x^2 - 2x - 15 = 0$

$\Rightarrow x^2 - 5x + 3x - 15 = 0$

$\Rightarrow x(x-5) + 3(x-5) = 0$

$\Rightarrow (x-5)(x+3) = 0$

Then, $x = (5)$ or $x = (-3)$

II. $y^2 - 4y - 12 = 0$

$\Rightarrow y^2 - 6y + 2y - 12 = 0$

$\Rightarrow y(y-6) + 2(y-6) = 0$

$\Rightarrow (y+2)(y-6) = 0$

Then, $y = (6)$ or $y = (-2)$

So, when $x = (5), x < y$ for $y = (6)$ and $x > y$ for $y = (-2)$

And when $x = (-3), x < y$ for $y = (6)$ and $x < y$ for $y = (-2)$

$\therefore$ So, the relationship cannot be determined.

Hence, the correct option is (E).

86. Given:

Amount in 2 years $=$ Rs. 720

Amount in 4.5 years = Rs. 870

Formula used:

Simple interest(SI) $= \dfrac{[\,\text{Principal }(P) \times \text{Rate} \times \text{Time}\,]}{100}$ And Amount $=$ Principal $+ SI$

Let the sum(principal) be P and the rate of interest be R

So, $720 =$ Principal $+ SI$

$\Rightarrow 720 = P + \dfrac{(P \times R \times 2)}{100}$ ... (i)

And $870 = P + SI$

$\Rightarrow 870 = P + \dfrac{(P \times R \times 4.5)}{100}$ ... (ii)

Equation (ii) - (i)

$\dfrac{(2.5 \times P \times R)}{100} = 150$

$\Rightarrow P \times R = 6000$ ... (iii)

Now, from eq.(i),

$720 = P + \dfrac{(6000 \times 2)}{100}$

$\Rightarrow P = 720 - 120 =$ Rs. 600

From eq. (iii)

$600 \times R = 6000$

$\Rightarrow R = 10\%$

$\therefore$ The rate of interest is 10%.

Hence, the correct option is (C).

87. Given:

Principle $=$ Rs. 1600

Time $= 2$ years $(S.I)$

Rate of Interest $= 10\%$

Formula Used:

Simple interest $= \dfrac{(P \times R \times T)}{100}$

Compound interest, C.I. $= P\left(1 + \dfrac{r}{100}\right)^t - P$

If interest compounded half-yearly, then

Rate $= \dfrac{r}{2}$ Time $= 2t$

Single equivalent increase of two successive increase of $x\%$ and $y\% = x + y + \dfrac{xy}{100}$

S.I. $= \dfrac{(1600 \times 10 \times 2)}{100}$ $\Rightarrow$ S.I. $=$ Rs. 320

Now Compound interest is compounded half-yearly.

Rate $= 10\%$

If interest compounded half-yearly, then

Rate $= \dfrac{10}{2} = 5\%$

$\therefore$ Single equivalent rate of first two years $= 5 + 5 + \dfrac{(5 \times 5)}{100}$

$= 10 + 0.25 = 10.25\%$

Compound Interest $= 1600 \times \dfrac{10.25}{100} \times 1$

$\Rightarrow$ Compound Interest = Rs. 164

Difference between the compound interest and simple interest = Rs. $(320 - 164) =$ Rs. 156

$\therefore$ Difference between the compound interest and simple interest is Rs. 156

Hence, the correct option is (E).

88. Given:

31.25% of 37.5% of 14.28% of $(?) = 15\%$ of 500

Now,

$31.25\% = (25 + 6.25)\% = \dfrac{1}{4} + \dfrac{1}{16} = \dfrac{5}{16}$

$37.5\% = \dfrac{3}{8}$

$14.27\% = \dfrac{1}{7}$

Putting these values,

$\left(\dfrac{5}{16}\right) \times \left(\dfrac{3}{8}\right) \times \left(\dfrac{1}{7}\right)$ of $(?) = 75$

$(?) = 5 \times 16 \times 8 \times 7 = 4480$

Hence, the correct option is (A).

89. Let C be the amount subscribed by C

Then amount subscribed by B = C + 10000

And amount subscribed by A = C + 10000 + 16000 = C = 26000

Now the total amount 3 × C + 36000 = 60000

$\Rightarrow$ 3 × C = 24000

$\Rightarrow$ C = 8000

$\therefore$ B = 8000 + 10000 = 18000

And A = 18000 + 16000 = 34000

Now the ratio is 34000 : 18000 : 8000

$\Rightarrow$ 34 : 18 : 8

$\Rightarrow$ 17 : 9 : 4

Now, to find amount received by (B + C) out of a profit of 80000

(B + C) = (9 + 4) = 13

(B + C)'s profit = 80000 × $\left(\dfrac{13}{30}\right)$

$\Rightarrow$ 34666.66

$\therefore$ (B + C) receives Rs. 34666.66

Hence, the correct option is (D).

90. Given:

Speed of bus = 54 km/h

Time = 60 seconds

Concept used:

When a train crosses a light pole, it covers the distance equal to its length

To convert km/hr into m/sec, multiply the number by $\dfrac{5}{18}$

We know that,

Distance = Speed × Time

Calculation:

The length of the bus = [54 × $\dfrac{5}{18}$ × 60] = 900 meters

$\therefore$ The length of the bus is 900 meters.

Hence, the correct option is (A).

Reasoning Ability

Q.1 Direction: Relationship between different elements is shown in the statements below. These Statements are followed by 2 Conclusions. Mark your answer on the basis of given statements and conclusions.

Statements: $A < B \leq C > D; C > E \geq F; E > B$

Conclusions:

(i) $A < F$

(ii) $D < B$

A. Only conclusion (i) follows

B. Only conclusion (ii) follows

C. Either conclusion (i) or conclusion (ii) follows

D. Both conclusions follow

E. None Follows

Q.2 Direction: In these Question, Relationship between different elements is shown in the statements. These Statements are followed by 2 Conclusions. Marks Answer as Option Given.

Statements: $X = Y \geq Z > V; V < P > Q; Q = T$

Conclusions:

(I) $X > V$

(II) $T \leq Z$

A. Only (I) Follows

B. Only (II) Follows

C. Only (I) & (II) Follows

D. Neither (I) nor (II) follows

E. Either (I) or (II) follows

Q.3 Direction: In the following question assuming the given statements to be true, Find which conclusion among the given conclusions is/are definitely true and then give your answers accordingly.

Statements:

$J < K \geq L = Y > X; L < V \geq D > I; D = R \geq P$

Conclusions:

I. $P < K$

II. $X \leq D$

III. $R > K$

A. Only II is true

B. II and III are true

C. Only III is true

D. Only I is true

E. None is true

Ques (4-5):Directions: These questions are based on the following information.

P's mother is the sister of R who is Q's daughter. R's brother-in-law has only one son whose grandparents are Q and S, and they have only two daughters. A's husband B is Q's son-in-law.

Q.4 Who is R's sister?

A. P

B. Q

C. S

D. A

E. Cannot be determined

Q.5 Who is B's mother-in-law?

A. P

B. Q

C. S

D. B

E. Cannot be determined

Q.6 Direction: Study the following information carefully and answer the question given below.

Each consonant of the word 'TERMINATION' is changed to the previous letter in the English alphabetical series and each vowel is changed to the next letter in the English alphabetical series. If the new alphabets thus formed are arranged in alphabetical order (from left to right), which of the following will be the sixth letter from the right end?

A. M   **B.** S

C. P   **D.** L

E. None of these

Ques (7-11):Direction: Answer the question based on the information given below.

9 movies (A, B, C, D, E, F, G, H and I) are released on 4th, 17th and 25th during June, July and August. Neither H nor E is released in June and 3 movies are released between H and E. F is released immediately after E but not on 17th of any month. 2 movies are released between F and G. 3 movies are released between G and D. C and B are released in the same month. C is not the first movie to be released. I is released neither before A nor immediately before H.

Q.7 Movie I is released on _____.

A. 17th July   **B.** 4th August

C. 4th July   **D.** 25th June

E. None of the above

Q.8 Movie A is released immediately before movie __.

A. E   **B.** H

C. G   **D.** B

E. None of these

Q.9 How many movies are released between E and B?

A. 2   **B.** 4

C. 3   **D.** 6

E. None of these

Q.10 ___ is released on 17th August.

A. Movie I   **B.** Movie E

C. Movie A   **D.** Movie D

E. None of these

Q.11 Number of movies released before G is equal to the number of movies released after _____.

A. H
B. D
C. A
D. F
E. None of these

Ques (12-14):Direction: Study the following information carefully and answer the given questions.

In a certain code language

'da mi ge he' means 'David is going school'

'da ta ri' means 'David stays there'

'he mi ri' means 'school is there'

'ra ta li he' means 'Roshni stays in school'

Q.12 How will 'Roshni is going there' be written in that code language?

A. ra mi ge ri
B. li mi ge ri
C. Either (A) or (B)
D. da mi ge ri
E. None of the above

Q.13 How will 'David is Roshni' be written in that language?

A. da mi ra
B. da mi li
C. da mi ri
D. Either (A) or (B)
E. Either (A) or (C)

Q.14 What is the meaning of 'li' in that language?

A. Roshni
B. David
C. in
D. stays
E. Either (A) or (C)

Ques (15-19):Direction: Study the following series carefully and answer the question given below.

Q.15 A @ D 1 5 % K & 6 I 9 # V 8 E 3 ¥ 7 M L 2 U € F S © 9 1 X Z

How many such letters are there in the series each of which is immediately preceded by a symbol and followed by cube number?

A. One
B. Two
C. Three
D. Four
E. None

Q.16 A @ D 1 5 % K & 6 I 9 # V 8 E 3 ¥ 7 M L 2 U € F S © 9 1 X Z

If all the numbers in the above arrangement are deleted then which among the following element is ninth form the right end?

A. ¥
B. U
C. M
D. V
E. #

Q.17 A @ D 1 5 % K & 6 I 9 # V 8 E 3 ¥ 7 M L 2 U € F S © 9 1 X Z

If '@' is related to 'X', '5' is related to '©' in a certain way then 'K' is related to which of the following in the same way?

A. €
B. F
C. ¥
D. S
E. 8

Q.18 A @ D 1 5 % K & 6 I 9 # V 8 E 3 ¥ 7 M L 2 U € F S © 9 1 X Z

Which among the following element is second to the left of the tenth element from the left end?

A. 2
B. €
C. I
D. #
E. &

Q.19 A @ D 1 5 % K & 6 I 9 # V 8 E 3 ¥ 7 M L 2 U € F S © 9 1 X Z

Four of the five given in the options are same in a certain way. Choose the option which is different from others.

A. M7L
B. %5K
C. V#8
D. U2€
E. I96

Ques (20-24):Direction: Study the following information and answer the given questions.

Eight friends K, L, M, N, O, P, Q and R are sitting in a circle, not necessarily in the same order. Four of them are facing outside and four of them are facing the centre. O faces outside and both the immediate neighbours of O face the centre. R sits second to the right of O. L sits third to the left of O. N faces the centre. Both the immediate neighbours of N face outside. K sits second to the left of Q. L sits third to the right of R. P is an immediate neighbour N. M is an immediate neighbour of Q. P is not an immediate neighbour of L.

Q.20 How many friends are sitting between L and O (counting clockwise from L)?

A. Two
B. One
C. Three
D. Four
E. Five

Q.21 Who amongst the following sits exactly between R and N taking clockwise from R?

A. M
B. O
C. Q
D. P
E. L

Q.22 Which is the one that does not belong to the group?

A. R
B. P
C. L
D. Q
E. O

Q.23 Who amongst the following sits third to the right of K?

A. Q
B. O
C. M
D. K
E. P

Q.24 Who amongst the following sits to the immediate right of M?

A. K
B. L
C. N
D. O
E. P

Ques (25-27):Direction: Read the following information carefully and answer the question given below.

There are MN axis in such a way that M is in north and N is in south direction. There is IJ axis in such a way that I is in west direction and J is in east direction. MN axis and IJ axis intersect at a point O in such a way that MO is 15m, ON is 17m, OI is 12m, OJ is 24 m. A starts from point M and walks 20m in south direction and then he turns his left and walks 32m. B starts from point M and walks 20m in east direction. C starts from point J and walks 5m in north direction and then he turns his left and walk 4m and again he turns his left and walks 22m.

Q.25 Point N is in which direction with respect to B's current position?

[Bank of Maharashtra Clerk, 2017], [IBPS Clerk, 2017], [Indian Bank Clerk, 2017]

A. North – East
B. South – East
C. South – West
D. North – West
E. South

Q.26 Point M is in which direction with respect to C's current position?

[Bank of Maharashtra Clerk, 2017], [IBPS Clerk, 2017], [Indian Bank Clerk, 2017]

A. South – East
B. South
C. South – West
D. North – West
E. North

Q.27 What is the distance between B's current position and A's current position?

[Bank of Maharashtra Clerk, 2017], [IBPS Clerk, 2017], [Indian Bank Clerk, 2017]

A. $\left(4\sqrt{29}\right)$ km
B. $\left(2\sqrt{29}\right)$ km
C. $\left(8\sqrt{23}\right)$ km
D. $\left(4\sqrt{23}\right)$ km
E. None of these

Ques (28-30):Directions: Read the instructions carefully and answer the question below.

Seven friends, Archi, Lalit, Kanika, Raju, Pankaj, Taruna, and Shiva took a test. They all scored different marks in that test. Archi scored 45 marks more than the least scorer. Taruna scored 10 marks fewer than the topper. At least four person scored more than Pankaj. Both Archi and Lalit scored more than Kanika. The difference between the score of the second lowest scorer and Pankaj is of 5 marks. Two persons scored more than Raju and less than Taruna. At least three persons scored more than Lalit. The difference between the score of Taruna and Kanika is of 45 marks and the sum of their scores is 115. Raju scored more than at least two persons.

Q.28 If Pranay also take the test and score 78 marks then which of the following would be true about Pranay?
A. Second highest scorer
B. Second lowest scorer
C. Third highest scorer
D. Fourth highest scorer
E. Highest scorer

Q.29 How many people scored less than Archi?
A. One
B. Four
C. Three
D. Two
E. Five

Q.30 Who is the second lowest scorer?
A. Raju
B. Pankaj
C. Kanika
D. Taruna
E. Archi

English Language

Ques (31-33):Direction: Which of the following phrases (A), (B), (C), (D) given below in the statement should replace the phrase printed in bold in the sentence to make it grammatically correct? If the sentence is correct as it is given and 'No Correction is required', mark (E) as the answer.

Q.31 My superior liked the first candidate **more better** than the second one whom I liked.
A. Better
B. More good
C. As good as
D. Almost similar
E. No correction is required

Q.32 It is **an urgent that the** banks work exclusively for the betterment of the common people due to the duress caused by demonetization.
A. The urgent that the
B. A urgent that the
C. Urgent that the
D. An urgents that the
E. No improvement

Q.33 The opposition party is likely to win the elections **by the sweeping majority.**
A. with the sweeping majority
B. by a sweeping majority
C. with sweeping a majority
D. in a sweeping majority
E. No correction required

Ques (34-35):Direction: In the following question, a sentence is given with certain words in bold. Choose the pair/s of such words which need to be interchanged so as to make the sentence grammatically correct and meaningful.

Q.34 A significant number of hearths have been (A) **unearthed** around the 76,000-year mark and there is (B) **controlled** archaeological evidence of (C) **diminishing** fire the further back you go, so the (D) **assumption** is that once we became modern, we worked out how to cook.
A. B-C
B. A-B, C-D
C. C-D
D. A-C, B-D
E. A-B

Q.35 Mori's hypothesis states that as a robot is made more humanlike in its (A) **appearance** and motion, the (B) **repulsion** response from a human being to the robot will become increasingly positive and (C) **empathic** until a point is reached beyond which the (D) **response** quickly becomes that of strong (E) emotional.
A. A-D, B-E
B. C-D
C. B-E
D. B-D, C-E
E. B-D

Ques (36-38):

Direction: Which of the following phrases (A), (B), (C), (D) given below in the statement should replace the phrase printed in bold in the sentence to make it grammatically correct? If the sentence is correct as it is given and 'No Correction is required', mark (E) as the answer.

Q.36 The whole class **looks forward** to the class teacher because of her commendable personality.
A. Looks towards
B. Looks upon
C. Looks up to
D. Looks beyond
E. No correction

Q.37 The teacher has been conducting a test in an hour.

A. Has conducted
B. Will conduct
C. Would conduct
D. Having being conducted
E. No correction

Q.38 Raj can borrow my bike as far as he wants.
A. As much as   B. As long as
C. As unless   D. As fur as
E. No correction

Ques (39-43):Directions: Find out which part has an error and mark it as your answer. If there is no error, mark 'No error' as your answer.

Q.39 None of these (A) two officers (B) has been looking after (C) his department well. (D)
A. (A)   B. (B)   C. (C)   D. (D)
E. No error

Q.40 The strict boss (A) did not give her ascent (B) to the employee's (C) whimsical request. (D)
A. (A)   B. (B)   C. (C)   D. (D)
E. No error

Q.41 The Party Chief (A) and the Chief Minister (B) expressed his views (C) on demonetization in India. (D)
A. The Party Chief
B. and the Chief Minister
C. expressed his views
D. on demonetization in India.
E. No error

Q.42 Unlike Indian laws, US laws provides (A) for a contingency fee of lawyering (B) where the costs of litigation (C) are borne by lawyers. (D)
A. Unlike Indian laws, US laws provides
B. for a contingency fee of lawyering
C. where the costs of litigation
D. are borne by lawyers
E. No error

Q.43 India's Swachh Bharat Mission is (A) receiving globe praise (B) for attempting (C) to close the sanitation gap. (D)
A. India's Swachh Bharat Mission is
B. receiving globe praise
C. for attempting
D. to close the sanitation gap.
E. No error

Ques (44-48):Direction: The given question has one blank indicating that something has been omitted. Choose the word from the given options that could fit in the blank correctly.

Q.44 Exportable technology can ___ around the world.
A. Ceremony   B. Function
C. Ritual   D. Formal
E. Traditional

Q.45 The UN refused to ___ in the civil war, apart from some troop convoys for humanitarian aid.

A. Egalitarian   B. Diverse
C. Intervene   D. Dissolve
E. Frosted

Q.46 The great image of Lochana Buddha at Nara, for example, would ________138 ft.
A. Measure   B. Millimetre
C. Width   D. Height
E. Weight

Q.47 Louis was a man of strong frame, who loved the chase, and did not ___ from the hardships of war.
A. Disgust   B. Shrink   C. Contract   D. Expand
E. Illustrate

Q.48 His ___ and energy met everywhere with conspicuous success.
A. Thrive   B. Advance   C. Deposit   D. Zeal
E. Hoard

Ques (49-53):Directions: Read the passage carefully and select the best answer to each question out of the given five alternatives.

In a bid to ensure timely support to depositors of stressed banks, the government may bring amendment to DICGC Act in the monsoon session with the objective to provide account holders easy and time-bound access to funds to the extent of the deposit insurance cover. Last year, the government raised insurance cover on deposit five-folds to Rs 5 lakh with a view to provide support to depositors of **ailing** lenders like Punjab and Maharashtra Co-operative (PMC) Bank. Following the collapse of PMC Bank, Yes Bank and Lakshmi Vilas Bank NSE 4.79 % too came under stress leading to restructuring by the regulator and the government.

The amendment to the Deposit Insurance and Credit Guarantee Corporation (DICGC) Act, 1961 is the budget announcement made by the Finance Minister and the Bill is almost ready, sources said. It is expected that the Bill will be tabled in the upcoming monsoon session after being vetted by the Union Cabinet, sources added. Once the Bill becomes the law, it will provide immediate relief to thousands of depositors who had their money parked in stressed lenders such as PMC Bank and other small cooperative banks.

As per the current provisions, the deposit insurance of up to Rs 5 lakh comes into play when the licence of a bank is cancelled and liquidation process starts. DICGC, a wholly-owned subsidiary of the Reserve Bank of India, provides insurance cover on bank deposits. Finance Minister Nirmala Sitharaman in the Budget speech in February said the government had approved an increase in the Deposit Insurance cover from Rs 1 lakh to Rs 5 lakh for bank customers last year. It could not be presented in the Budget session due to **curtailment** of the last session following the spread of the second wave of COVID-19 pandemic.

It is to be noted that the enhanced deposit insurance cover of Rs 5 lakh is effective from February 4, 2020. The increase was done after a gap of 27 years as it was static since 1993. The cover is provided by the Deposit Insurance and Credit Guarantee Corporation (DICGC), a wholly-owned subsidiary of the RBI. With increased insurance cover, the banks are paying a higher premium of 12 paise against 10 paise per Rs 100 deposited without any additional burden on account holders. The deposit insurance scheme covers all banks operating in India, including private sector, cooperative, and even branches of foreign banks. There are some exemptions such as deposits of foreign governments, deposits of central and state governments, and inter-bank deposits.

It can be recalled that way back in 2009, the Raghuram Rajan committee on financial sector reforms had recommended strengthening the capacity of the DICGC, a more explicit system of prompt, corrective action, and making deposit insurance premia more risk-based.

Q.49 What is the main reason to make an amendment in the law?

A. to give the opportunity of easy access to the banking
B. to provide the useful services in any situation
C. to provide account holders easy and time-bound access
D. for the welfare of the customer experience
E. to put limits on the different frauds

Q.50 What changes will come after the bill has passed?

A. It will help the govt to gain the profits.
B. it will ease the banking conetivity.
C. The banks gain profit after it.
D. it will provide immediate relief to thousands of depositors.
E. It is important for the future of the banking system.

Q.51 Who can be benefitted from the deposit insurance scheme?

A. Only nationalized banks
B. All private banks with other foreign banks
C. mains branches of the banks
D. Rural banks
E. All private sector, cooperative and even branches of foreign banks.

Q.52 What can we infer from the passage?

A. The amendment is a good step to ease the burden of the depositors.
B. It can be harmful for the economy.
C. It will be a big gamble for the govt.
D. The insurance policy is just a mean of attraction for people.
E. This is a historic step in banking system.

Q.53 Consider the following statements and answer the question.

A. the government raised insurance cover on deposit five-folds to Rs. 5 lakh.

B. The amendment is brought by the suggestion of RBI.

C. The amendment is made to ease the burden of the depositors.

A. A is correct but B is wrong.
B. A and B are correct but C is wrong.
C. B and C are correct but A is wrong.
D. A and C are correct but B is wrong.
E. All are correct.

Ques (54-55):Direction: In the question below, a part of the sentence is bold. Below are given alternatives to the bold part which may improve the sentence. Choose the correct alternative. In case no improvement is needed, choose 'No improvement'.

Q.54 Things didn't **pan out** the way we expected it to.

A. Pan to
B. Pan up
C. Pan for
D. Pan in
E. No improvement

Q.55 With the help of a dictionary, **you may** learn new words easily.

A. You might
B. You can
C. You need
D. You ought
E. No improvement

Ques (56-60):Direction: Given sentences are not in their exact position. Rearrange them to make a coherent paragraph and then answer the questions given below.

A. We do need to guard against unfair trade practices, such as goods made in China being routed through some countries with which India has an FTA, flouting all rules of origin and local value-addition norms.

B. This is integral to the ongoing process of eliminating from Indian business assorted means of enrichment that have little do with efficient creation of value.

C. India can hope to end its present exclusion from global value chains — across various industry segments — through membership of RCEP.

D. At the same time, the government needs to appreciate that global trade and exposure to import competition constitute a sure method of raising the Indian industry's competitiveness.

E. In parallel, there's the need to put in place clear-cut safeguards measures to prevent dumping of goods, especially from China.

Q.56 Which of the following should be the FOURTH sentence after the rearrangement?

A. A   **B.** B   **C.** C   **D.** D
E. E

Q.57 Which of the following should be the SECOND sentence after the rearrangement?

A. A   **B.** B   **C.** C   **D.** D
E. E

Q.58 Which of the following should be the THIRD sentence after the rearrangement?

A. A   **B.** B   **C.** C   **D.** D
E. E

Q.59 Which of the following should be the FIRST sentence after the rearrangement?

A. A   **B.** B   **C.** C   **D.** D
E. E

Q.60 Which of the following should be the FIFTH sentence after the rearrangement?

A. A   **B.** B   **C.** C   **D.** D
E. E

Numerical Ability

Q.61 Two dice are tossed. The probability that the total score is a prime number is?

A. $\frac{1}{6}$ **B.** $\frac{5}{12}$ **C.** $\frac{1}{2}$ **D.** $\frac{7}{9}$
E. $\frac{8}{9}$

Q.62 Length of the rectangular field is three times the width. If area of the field is 192m², then find the cost of fencing it at Rs. 2/m.

A. 160   **B.** 135   **C.** 128   **D.** 320
E. 115

Q.63 Three pipes A, B, and C can fill a tank from empty to full in 30 minutes, 20 minutes, and 10 minutes respectively. When the tank is empty, all three pipes are opened. A, B, and C discharge chemical solutions P, Q, and R respectively. What is the proportion of the solution R in the liquid in the tank after 3 minutes?

A. $\frac{5}{11}$ **B.** $\frac{6}{11}$ **C.** $\frac{7}{11}$ **D.** $\frac{8}{11}$
E. $\frac{9}{11}$

Q.64 Direction: In the following question two equations numbered I and II are given. You have to solve both equations and give the answer:

I. $25p^2 - 30p + 8 = 0$

II. $q^2 - 2q + 1 = 0$

A. $p > q$
B. $p \geq q$
C. $p < q$
D. $p \leq q$
E. $p = q$ or the relationship cannot be established

Q.65 In the given question, two equations numbered I and II are given. You have to solve both the equations and mark the appropriate answer

I. $7p^2 - 168p = 0$

II. $11q^2 - 891 = 0$

A. $p < q$
B. $p \leq q$
C. $p > q$
D. $p \geq q$
E. $p = q$ or the relationship cannot be determined

Q.66 A boat running upstream takes 8 hours 48 minutes to cover a certain distance, while it takes 4 hours to cover the same distance running downstream. What is the ratio between the speed of the boat and speed of the water current respectively?

A. 2 : 1   **B.** 3 : 2
C. 8 : 3   **D.** 9 : 5
E. None of these

Q.67 A certain sum of money lent at simple interest becomes $\frac{6}{5}$ of itself in 6 years. Find the rate of interest.

A. $\left(\frac{10}{3}\right)$ %   **B.** $\left(\frac{13}{12}\right)$ %
C. 12.5%   **D.** 13.5%
E. None of these

Q.68 A man invested a sum of money at compound interest. It amounted to Rs. 4840 in 2 years and to Rs. 5324 in 3 years. Find the sum.

A. 2000   **B.** 6000   **C.** 4000   **D.** 10164
E. 10000

Q.69 The time taken by A and B to complete a piece of work is 12 days and 8 days respectively. They start working together and B leaves the work after 4 days of starting. How many days will A take to complete the rest of the work?

A. 1 day   **B.** 2 days   **C.** 2.5 days   **D.** 3 days
E. 5 days

Ques (70-74):Direction: Study the following Bar graph and answer the questions based on it.

A Computer made by two companies LENVO and COMPAQ. The Bar value is given in thousands.

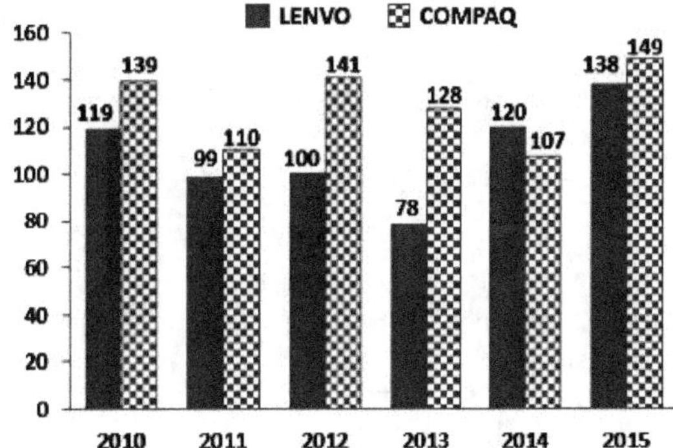

Q.70 The production of Company COMPAQ in 2013 was approximately what percent of the production of Company LENVO in the same year?

A. 136.6%   **B.** 90.8%
C. 120.8%   **D.** 164.10%
E. None of these

Q.71 In which of the following years, the difference between the productions of Companies LENVO and COMPAQ was the maximum among the given years?

A. 2013   **B.** 2015
C. 2014   **D.** 2011
E. None of these

Q.72 What is the average number of Computers manufactured by Company LENVO over the given period?

A. 119000   **B.** 109000
C. 115000   **D.** 99000
E. None of these

Q.73 What is the difference between the numbers of Computers manufactured by Company COMPAQ in 2011 and 2012?
A. 31000
B. 41000
C. 21000
D. 76000
E. None of these

Q.74 What is the difference between the two companies in the given question?
A. 150,000
B. 135,000
C. 120,000
D. 189,000
E. None of these

Q.75 What will come in place of question mark (?) in the following question?
13.33 + 33.31 + 331.13 = ?
A. 377.77
B. 354.77
C. 355.67
D. 301.67
E. None of these

Q.76 What will come in the place of the question mark '?' in the following question?
14.28% of 490 – 71.43% of 63 = ?
A. 25
B. 49
C. 64
D. 81
E. None of the above

Q.77 What will come in the place of the question mark '?' in the following question?
450 ÷ 15 × 12 – 120 ÷ 4 × 12 + 1 = ?
A. -1
B. 0
C. 1
D. 2
E. -2

Q.78 What will come in the place of the question mark '?' in the following question?

$$\sqrt{\left[1331^{\left(\frac{1}{3}\right)} + 1728^{\left(\frac{1}{3}\right)} + 2\right]} = ?$$

A. 5
B. 6
C. 7
D. 8
E. 9

Q.79 As Jio entered into market, other telecom sectors have to struggle alot in order to remain in the market. The effect is also seen on the share price of the companies. A survey is being conducted for share price fluctuation of Airtel. It has been observed that share price of Airtel rose by 10% from July to August. Then, it has been dropped 20% from August to September and again rose by 50% from September to October. What was the percentage increase for the whole quarter in 2017?
A. 31%
B. 24%
C. 26%
D. 32%
E. 23%

Ques (80-82):Direction: What should come in place of the question mark '?' in the following number series?

Q.80 0, 6, 24, 60, 120, ?
A. 210
B. 150
C. 186
D. 225
E. 250

Q.81 4, 8, 10, 30, 33, 132, 136, 680, ?

A. 682
B. 684
C. 685
D. 690
E. 687

Q.82 6, 7, 18, 63, 268, ?
A. 1315
B. 1365
C. 1644
D. 1572
E. 1700

Q.83 A dishonest shopkeeper sells his grocery at celling price and earns a profit equal to 20% of his selling price. If he uses false weight to make this gain, find the weight lose per kilogram that lead to the profit if he sold 25 Kg of goods at Rs. 20 per kilogram.
A. 100 g
B. 150 g
C. 200 g
D. 250 g
E. 300 g

Q.84 If $C(20, n + 2) = C(20, n - 2)$ then what is n equal to?
A. 8
B. 10
C. 12
D. 16
E. 20

Q.85 Direction: In the given question, two equations numbered I and II are given. Solve both the equations and mark the appropriate answer.

I. $2x^2 + 18x + 40 = 0$

II. $2y^2 + 15y + 27 = 0$

A. x > y
B. x < y
C. x ≥ y
D. x ≤ y
E. x = y or the relationship between x and y cannot be established

Q.86 In Aditya hospital, the average salary of 9 nurses is Rs. 3600 while the average salary of 11 ward boys is Rs. 4400 and the average salary of all doctors is Rs. 22000. If average salary of entire staff is Rs. 7632, then find the number of doctors working in Aditya hospital.
A. 25
B. 7
C. 15
D. 5
E. 10

Q.87 What should come in place of the question mark '?' in the following number series?
98, 79, 62, 47, ?, 23
A. 34
B. 32
C. 38
D. 42
E. 36

Q.88 What should come in place of the question mark '?' in the following number series?
1, 5, 11, ?, 29, 41
A. 13
B. 21
C. 25
D. 16
E. 19

Q.89 What will come in the place of the question mark '? in the following question?
$(562.5 \times 6)^4 \div (135 \div 9)^2 \times (37.5 \times 6)^5 = (3.75 \times 4)^{(5-?)}$
A. 5
B. -5
C. 15
D. -15
E. 20

Q.90 In a partnership, P invested Rs. 2000 more than Q. Q invested for two years while P withdrew his share and profit after a year. The profit that this investment offers is 10% for a year. The difference between profits earned by Q and P is Rs. 200. How much money did they invest in total?

A. Rs. 8000

B. Rs. 10000

C. Rs. 12000

D. Rs. 16000

E. Rs. 13300

// Smart Answer Sheet //

Correct   Indicates percentage of students who answered questions correctly.

Skipped   Indicates percentage of students who skipped questions.

Q.	Ans.	Correct / Skipped	Q.	Ans.	Correct / Skipped	Q.	Ans.	Correct / Skipped	Q.	Ans.	Correct / Skipped	Q.	Ans.	Correct / Skipped
1	E	83.64 % / 0.0 %	17	B	45.41 % / 1.03 %	33	B	44.07 % / 1.97 %	49	C	40.72 % / 1.73 %	65	E	55.39 % / 1.88 %
2	A	89.17 % / 0.0 %	18	E	64.23 % / 1.19 %	34	A	61.01 % / 1.85 %	50	D	60.22 % / 1.97 %	66	C	43.09 % / 1.94 %
3	E	82.31 % / 0.0 %	19	E	43.69 % / 1.44 %	35	C	69.92 % / 1.53 %	51	E	55.97 % / 1.92 %	67	A	21.49 % / 4.48 %
4	D	14.85 % / 4.64 %	20	A	42.43 % / 1.06 %	36	C	40.76 % / 1.74 %	52	A	54.41 % / 1.95 %	68	C	12.08 % / 4.5 %
5	E	48.03 % / 1.96 %	21	D	66.4 % / 1.11 %	37	B	48.15 % / 1.75 %	53	D	40.34 % / 1.75 %	69	B	58.64 % / 1.15 %
6	A	89.77 % / 0.0 %	22	D	54.86 % / 1.08 %	38	B	46.07 % / 1.22 %	54	E	65.01 % / 1.79 %	70	D	31.98 % / 3.05 %
7	B	64.32 % / 1.39 %	23	C	67.9 % / 1.23 %	39	A	53.26 % / 1.77 %	55	B	48.49 % / 1.1 %	71	A	54.52 % / 1.64 %
8	C	59.4 % / 1.1 %	24	B	66.94 % / 1.53 %	40	B	69.76 % / 1.44 %	56	D	56.64 % / 1.35 %	72	B	48.58 % / 1.21 %
9	D	69.3 % / 1.52 %	25	C	64.05 % / 1.44 %	41	C	46.01 % / 1.48 %	57	E	68.48 % / 1.97 %	73	A	88.33 % / 0.0 %
10	B	48.04 % / 1.85 %	26	D	52.16 % / 1.98 %	42	A	51.48 % / 1.87 %	58	A	46.56 % / 1.18 %	74	C	11.93 % / 4.51 %
11	A	62.43 % / 1.75 %	27	A	64.52 % / 1.31 %	43	B	53.77 % / 1.54 %	59	C	55.06 % / 1.66 %	75	A	81.58 % / 0.0 %
12	C	55.93 % / 1.07 %	28	C	45.39 % / 1.57 %	44	B	44.92 % / 1.41 %	60	B	60.08 % / 1.26 %	76	A	59.88 % / 1.7 %
13	D	19.67 % / 3.65 %	29	B	51.9 % / 1.36 %	45	C	59.68 % / 1.87 %	61	B	46.48 % / 1.72 %	77	C	53.56 % / 1.26 %
14	E	67.57 % / 1.99 %	30	C	67.37 % / 1.05 %	46	A	58.71 % / 1.6 %	62	C	62.58 % / 1.79 %	78	A	60.32 % / 1.03 %
15	B	69.83 % / 1.29 %	31	A	66.84 % / 1.13 %	47	B	52.82 % / 1.56 %	63	B	58.72 % / 1.54 %	79	D	44.03 % / 1.32 %
16	C	57.1 % / 1.44 %	32	C	57.48 % / 1.05 %	48	D	42.32 % / 1.86 %	64	C	60.45 % / 1.6 %	80	A	82.4 % / 0.0 %

Q.	Ans.	Correct		Q.	Ans.	Correct		Q.	Ans.	Correct		Q.	Ans.	Correct		Q.	Ans.	Correct
		Skipped				Skipped				Skipped				Skipped				Skipped
81	C	77.42 %		83	C	53.26 %		85	E	69.66 %		87	A	41.61 %		89	D	46.52 %
		0.0 %				1.06 %				1.4 %				1.75 %				1.12 %
82	B	66.15 %		84	C	44.99 %		86	D	49.14 %		88	E	43.58 %		90	B	62.18 %
		1.31 %				1.06 %				1.82 %				1.99 %				1.06 %

Performance Analysis	
Avg. Score (%)	65.56%
Toppers Score (%)	72.22%
Your Score	

//Hints and Solutions//

1. Given Statement: A < B ≤ C > D; C > E ≥ F; E > B

(i) A < F: False (A < B ≤ C > E ≥ F; There is no clear relation between A and F, hence can not conclude anything).

(ii) D < B: False (B ≤ C > D; There is no clear relation between B and D, hence can not conclude anything).

So, the correct answer is None follows.

Hence, the correct option is (E).

2. Given statements: X = Y ≥ Z > V; V < P > Q; Q = T

On combining: X = Y ≥ Z > V < P > Q = T

Conclusions:

(I) X > V - True (as per X = Y ≥ Z > V → X > V)

(II) T ≤ Z - False (X = Y ≥ Z > V < P > Q = T → thus clear relation between T and Z cannot be determined)

So, The correct answer is Only (I) Follows.

Hence, the correct option is (A).

3. Given statements:

J < K ≥ L = Y > X; L < V ≥ D > I; D = R ≥ P

Combining the given statements,

J < K ≥ L < V ≥ D > I and

J < K ≥ L < V ≥ D = R ≥ P

I. P < K → false (as K ≥ L < V ≥ D = R ≥ P = > clear relation between P and K cannot be determined)

II. X ≤ D → false (as X < Y = L < V ≥ D = > clear relation between X and D cannot be determined)

III. R > K → false (as K ≥ L < V ≥ D = R = > clear relation between R and K cannot be determined)

So, none of the given conclusions is true.

Hence, the correct option is (E).

Ques (4-5): From the given information,

Symbol in Diagram	Meaning
○	Female
□	Male
═══	Married Couple
───	Siblings
│	Difference of A Generation

1) P's mother is R's sister.

2) R is Q's daughter.

3) R's brother-in-law has only one son whose grandparents are Q and S who have only two daughters.

4) A's husband is B.

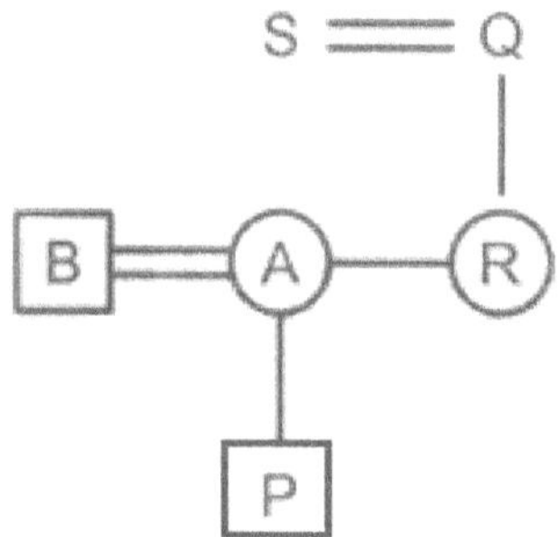

4. So, R's sister is A.

Hence, the correct option is (D).

5. As the gender of Q and S is not specified here, we cannot determine B's mother-in-law.

Hence, the correct option is (E).

6. The given word:

T E R M I N A T I O N

Applying the above condition, we have new word:

S F Q L J M B S J P M

Now, arranging in alphabetical order (from left to right)

B F J J L M M P Q S S

So, M is sixth from the right.

Hence, the correct option is (A).

Ques (7-11): 1. Neither H nor E is released in June and 3 movies are released between them.

2. F is released immediately after E but not on 17th of any month.

3. 2 movies are released between F and G, so the possible cases are:

	Case I			Case II		
Month	4th	17th	25th	4th	17th	25th
June						G
July	H		G		E	F
August		E	F			H

4. 3 movies are released between G and D.

5. C and B are released in the same month.

	Case I			Case II		
Month	4th	17th	25th	4th	17th	25th
June	B/C	D	C/B	B/C	C/B	G
July	H		G		E	F
August		E	F	D		H

6. C is not the first movie to be released.

7. I is released neither before A nor immediately before H, so case II is rejected. The final table is given below:

	Case I		
Month	4th	17th	25th
June	B	D	C
July	H	A	G
August	I	E	F

7. So, Movie I is released on 4th August.

Hence, the correct option is (B).

8. So, Movie A is released immediately before movie G.

Hence, the correct option is (C).

9. So, 6 movies are released between E and B.

Hence, the correct option is (D).

10. So, Movie E is released on 17th August.

Hence, the correct option is (B).

11. So, the Number of movies released before G is equal to the number of movies released after H.

Hence, the correct option is (A).

Ques (12-14):

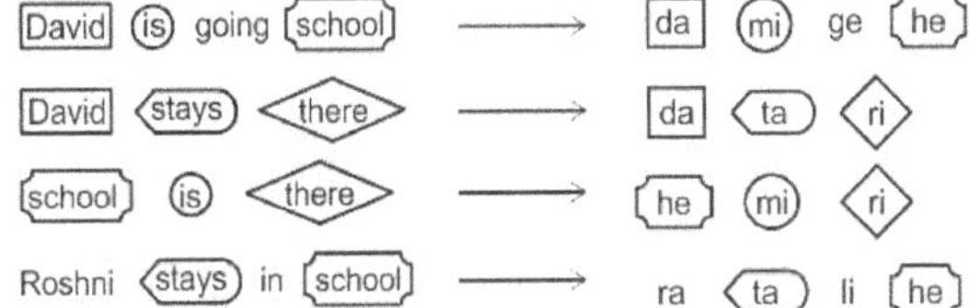

Therefore, in the given code language,

'da' means 'David'

'mi' means 'is'

'he' means 'school'

'ge' means 'going'

'ta' means 'stays'

'ri' means 'there'

12. Either 'ra' or 'li' means 'Roshni' or 'in'

Therefore, either 'ra mi ge ri' or 'li mi ge ri' means 'Roshni is going there'.

Therefore, 'Either (A) or (B)' is the correct answer.

Hence, the correct option is (C).

13. Either 'da mi ra' or 'da mi li' means 'David is Roshni'.

Therefore, 'Either (A) or (B)' is the correct answer.

Hence, the correct option is (D).

14. Therefore, 'li' means either 'Roshni' or 'in' in that language.

So, 'either (A) or (C)' is the correct answer.

Hence, the correct option is (E).

15. **Given Series:** Left side A @ D 1 5 % K & 6 I 9 # V 8 E 3 ¥ 7 M L 2 U € F S © 9 1 X Z Right side

1) Letters are there in the series each of which is immediately preceded by a symbol and followed by cube number.

A @ **D** 1 5 % K & 6 I 9 # **V** 8 E 3 ¥ 7 M L 2 U € F S © 9 1 X Z

So, 'two' letters are there in the series each of which is immediately preceded by a symbol and followed by cube number.

Hence, the correct option is (B).

16. **Given Series:** Left side A @ D 1 5 % K & 6 I 9 # V 8 E 3 ¥ 7 M L 2 U € F S © 9 1 X Z Right side

1) If all the numbers in the above arrangement are deleted, an element which is ninth from the right end is:

A @ D % K & I # V E ¥ **M** L U € F S © X Z

So, if all the numbers in the above arrangement are deleted then 'M' is ninth from the right end.

Hence, the correct option is (C).

17. Given series-

Left side A @ D 1 5 % K & 6 I 9 # V 8 E 3 ¥ 7 M L 2 U € F S © 9 1 X Z Right side

'@' is related to 'X', '5' is related to '©' in a certain way.

The logic is-

1) '@' is second from the left side, 'X' is second from the right side.

2) '5' is fifth from the left side, '©' is fifth from the right side.

Similarly, 'K' is seventh from the left side, 'F' is seventh from the right side.

So, 'K' is related to 'F'.

Hence, the correct option is (B).

18. Given Series: Left side A @ D 1 5 % K & 6 I 9 # V 8 E 3 ¥ 7 M L 2 U € F S © 9 1 X Z Right side

1) Second to the left of the tenth element from the left end

Firstly, the tenth element from the left end

A @ D 1 5 % K & 6 **I** 9 # V 8 E 3 ¥ 7 M L 2 U € F S © 9 1 X Z

Now, second to the left of 'I'

A @ D 1 5 % K **&** 6 I 9 # V 8 E 3 ¥ 7 M L 2 U € F S © 9 1 X Z

So, '&' is second to the left of the tenth element from the left end.

Hence, the correct option is (E).

19. The given series is-

A @ D 1 5 % K & 6 I 9 # V 8 E 3 ¥ 7 M L 2 U € F S © 9 1 X Z

From option (A)- M7L

In the series, M lies between 7 (left) and L (right).

From option (B)- %5K

In the series, % lies between 5 (left) and K (right).

From option (C)- V#8

In the series, V lies between # (left) and 8 (right).

From option (D)- U2€

In the series, U lies between 2 (left) and € (right).

From option (E)- I96

In the series, I lies between 9 (right) and 6 (left).

The logic followed in the first four options is- The first element lies between the second element (left) and the third element (right).

The same logic is not followed in fifth option.

Therefore, I96 is different from others.

Hence, the correct option is (E).

Ques (20-24):1. O faces outside and both the immediate neighbors of O face the center.

2. R sits second to the right of O.

3. L sits third to the left of O.

4. L sits third to the right of R.

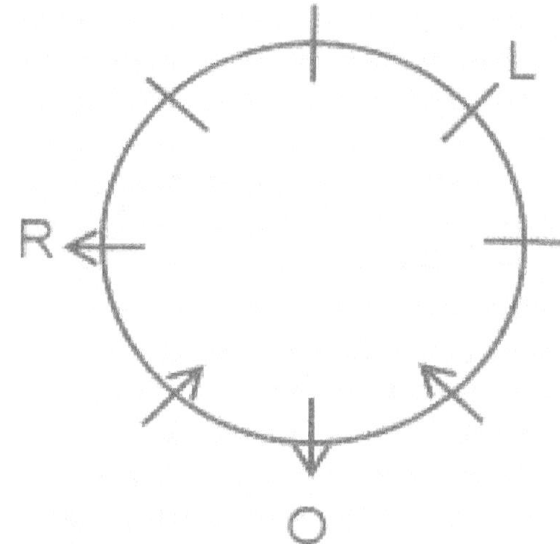

5. N faces the centre.

6. Both the immediate neighbours of N face outside.

7. P is an immediate neighbour N.

8. P is not an immediate neighbour of L.

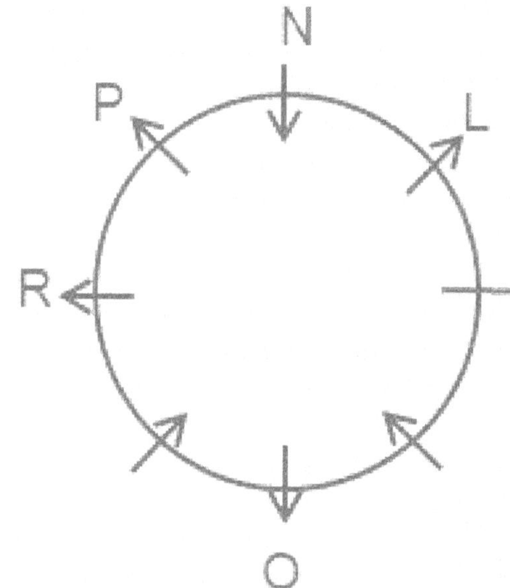

9. K sits second to the left of Q.

10. M is an immediate neighbour of Q.

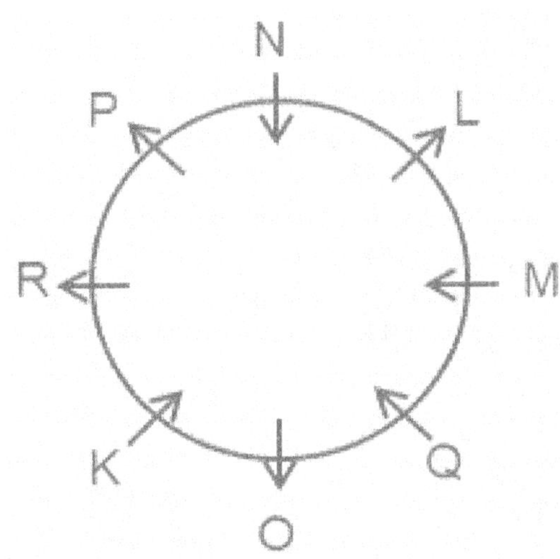

20. Thus, two friends are sitting between L and O (counting clockwise from L).

Hence, the correct option is (A).

21. Thus, P sits exactly between R and N taking clockwise from R.

Hence, the correct option is (D).

22. R, P, L, and O are facing outside whereas Q is facing the center.

Thus, Q does not belong to the group.

Hence, the correct option is (D).

23. Thus, M sits third to the right of K.

Hence, the correct option is (C).

24. Thus, L sits to the immediate right of M.

Hence, the correct option is (B).

Ques (25-27):1. MN axis in such a way that M is in north and N is in south direction. There is IJ axis in such a way that I is in west direction and J is in east direction. MN axis and IJ axis intersect at a point O in such a way that MO is 15m, ON is 17m, OI is 12m, OJ is 24 m.

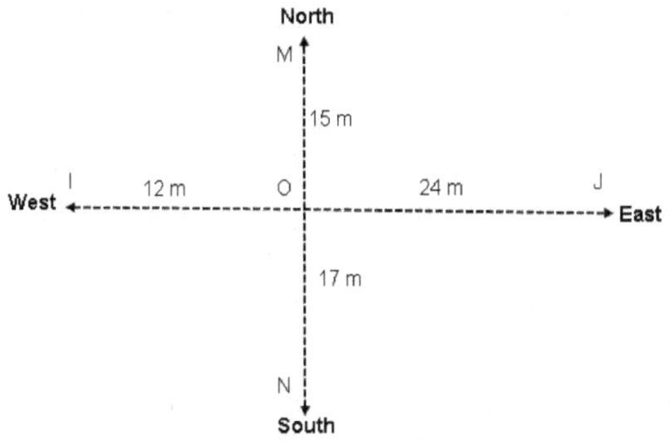

2. A starts from point M and walks 20m in south direction and then he turns his left and walks 32m.

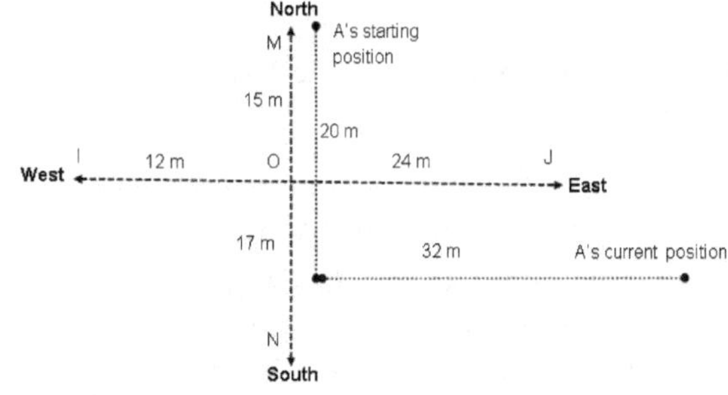

3. B starts from point M and walks 20m in east direction.

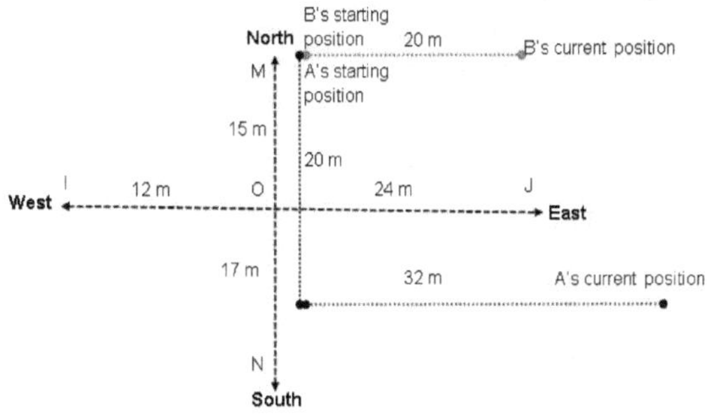

4. C starts from point J and walks 5m in north direction and then he turns his left and walk 4m and again he turns his left and walks 22m.

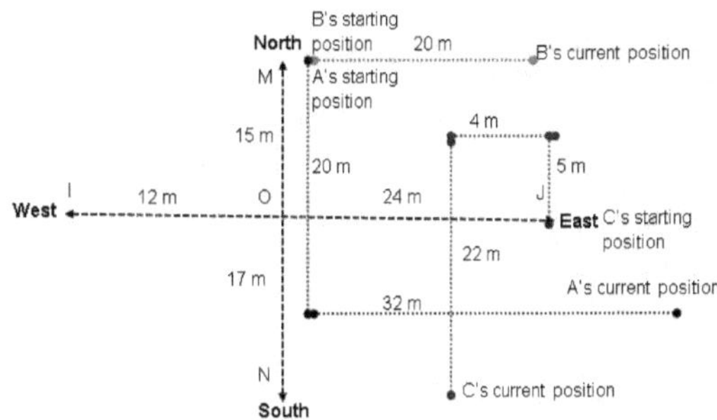

25. Point N is in south – west direction with respect to B's current position.

Hence, the correct option is (C).

26. Point M is in North – west direction with respect to C's current position.

Hence, the correct option is (D).

27. Distance between B's current position and A's current position

$$= \left(\sqrt{(20)^2 + (32-24)^2} = \sqrt{(20)^2 + (8)^2} \right)$$

$$= \left(\sqrt{400 + 64} \right)$$

$$= \left(\sqrt{464} \right) km = \left(4\sqrt{29} \right) km$$

Thus, Distance between B's current position and A's current position is $\left(4\sqrt{29} \right) km$.

Hence, the correct option is (A),

Ques (28-30):1) Two persons scored more than Raju and less than Taruna.

2) Taruna scored 10 marks fewer than the topper.

3) Raju scored more than at least two persons.

(As Taruna scored 10 marks fewer than the topper, implies, Taruna is not the topper. Also, there are at least two persons who scored less than Raju. Implies, there is only one possibility now i.e., Taruna is the second-highest scorer and Raju is the 5th highest scorer.)

Person	Score
	X + 10
Taruna	X
Raju	

4) At least four-persons scored more than Pankaj.

(Now, it is clear that Pankaj is either the lowest or the second-lowest scorer.)

5) The difference between the score of the second-lowest scorer and Pankaj is 5 marks.

(Implies, Pankaj is not the least scorer.)

Person	Score
	X + 10
Taruna	X
Raju	
	Y + 5
Pankaj	Y

6) At least three persons scored more than Lalit.

7) Both Archi and Lalit scored more than Kanika.

(It clearly means that Lalit is not amongst the top three scorers. Also, now there are only two positions left in the bottom four and it is given that Kanika scored fewer marks than Lalit. Thus, it is only possible if Lalit is the fourth-highest scorer and Kanika is the second-lowest scorer.)

Person	Score
	X + 10
Taruna	X
Lalit	
Raju	
Kanika	Y + 5
Pankaj	Y

8) The difference between the score of Taruna and Kanika is 45 marks and the sum of their scores is 115.

(X + Y + 5 = 115

And, X – Y – 5 = 45

Implies, X = The score of Taruna is 80

And, Y + 5 = The score of Kanika is 35.

Also, the score of Pankaj is 30 and the score of the top scorer is 90 (X + 10).)

9) Archi scored 45 marks more than the least scorer.

(Pankaj is the least scorer and he scored 30 marks, implies, Archi scored 75 marks. It further implies Archi is not the top scorer which means Shiva must be the top scorer as he is the only option left now.)

Person	Score
Shiva	90
Taruna	80
Archi	75
Lalit	
Raju	
Kanika	35
Pankaj	30

28. Clearly, Pranay would be the third-highest scorer.

Hence, the correct option is (C).

29. Clearly, four people scored less than Archi.

Hence, the correct option is (B).

30. Clearly, Kanika is the second lowest scorer.

Hence, the correct option is (C).

31. Both 'more' and 'better' are used to indicate comparison. 'Better' is the comparative form of the adjective 'good'. However, in this sentence we are using it as an adverb. It is describing the verb 'like'. So, using 'more' and 'better' together is grammatically wrong.

The sentence can be rephrased in two ways:

My superior liked the first candidate more than the second one whom I liked.

My superior liked the first candidate better than the second one whom I liked.

Among the given options, 'better' has been given and thus it is the right answer.

Hence, the correct option is (A).

32. 'An' is in itself a type of adjective 'Urgent' is an adjective and do not need an article before it here.

Thus, the correct replacement would be **Urgent that the**.

Hence, the correct option is (C).

33. The word 'likely' means probable or might happen. So the usage of the definite article 'the' is not appropriate. We should use the indefinite article 'a' here and so **'by a sweeping majority'** is the correction required.

Hence, the correct option is (B).

34. The phrase 'controlled archeological evidence' does not make any sense. The word 'controlled' means 'the restriction of an activity, tendency, or phenomenon'. Thus, 'archeological evidence' cannot be 'controlled'. Therefore, the word 'controlled' needs to be changed. Out of all the emboldened words, the only word that would fit the sentence grammatically and make the sentence meaningful as well is 'diminishing'. Thus, 'controlled' and 'diminishing' should be interchanged with each other.

Correct sentence: **A significant number of hearths have been unearthed around the 76,000-year mark and there is diminishing archaeological evidence of controlled fire the further back you go, so the assumption is that once we became modern, we worked out how to cook.**

Hence, the correct option is (A).

35. The phrase 'repulsion response' is grammatically incorrect. Therefore, the word 'repulsion' needs to be changed. Out of all the emboldened words, the word 'emotional' would make the sentence more meaningful and grammatically correct as well.

Correct sentence: **Mori's hypothesis states that as a robot is made more humanlike in its appearance and motion, the emotional response from a human being to the robot will become increasingly positive and empathic, until a point is reached beyond which the response quickly becomes that of strong repulsion.**

Hence, the correct option is (C).

36. "Looks up to" means to admire or respect someone.

"Looks forward to" means to anticipate or wait for something.

"Looks towards" means to look in a particular direction.

"Looks upon" means to consider or think of someone or something in a stated way. For example, "We look upon him as a son".

Lastly, "looks beyond" means to look further from what is being seen. As per the meaning of the sentence, "looks up to" is the appropriate phrase.

The correct sentence is- "The whole class looks up to the class teacher because of her commendable personality."

Hence, the correct option is (C).

37. The situation described in the sentence talks about an event which will take place in an hour at the latest. In this case, simple future tense is used.

Therefore, "will conduct" perfectly suits the meaning of the sentence. All the other options are contextually incorrect.

The correct sentence is- "The teacher will conduct a test in an hour."

Hence, the correct option is (B).

38. "As far as" is used to show the degree or distance, or to show regarding what.

"As much as" is used to show two things which are equal in degree.

"As long as" is used to show for how long.

In the given sentence, "as long as" is the appropriate phrase as per the meaning.

All other options are grammatically incorrect.

The correct sentence is- "Raj can borrow my bike as long as he wants."

Hence, the correct option is (B).

39. 'Neither' should be there in place of 'none'.

A pronoun is a word that is used instead of a noun or noun phrase. Pronouns refer to either a noun that has already been mentioned or to a noun that does not need to be named specifically.

'None of the' is used for more than two persons or objects, 'neither of the' is used for two objects.

- E.g. None of the three flowers is red.
- Neither of the two teachers is competent.

The correct sentence should be: Neither of these two officers has been looking after his department well.

Hence, the correct option is (A).

40. 'assent' should be there in place of 'ascent'.

Singular nouns are followed by singular verbs and plural nouns are followed by plural verbs.

"Ascent" means 'a climb or walk to the summit of a mountain or hill' which does not make any sense in the given context.

The correct word in place of 'ascent' would be 'assent' which means 'the expression of approval or agreement'.

- For E.g. The ascent of Fuji presents no difficulties.
- Prince Bagration bowed his head in sign of assent.

The correct sentence is: The strict boss did not give her assent to the employee's whimsical request.

Hence, the correct option is (B).

41. 'their' should be there in place of 'his'.

A pronoun is a word that is used instead of a noun or noun phrase. Pronouns refer to either a noun that has already been mentioned or to a noun that does not need to be named specifically.

When two singular nouns are joined by 'and' refer to two different persons the pronoun used for them should be 'plural'.

- E.g.: Ashwin and Hardik are brothers. They play cricket.

The correct sentence should be: The Party Chief and the Chief Minister expressed their views on demonetization in India.

Hence, the correct option is (C).

42. 'provide' should be there in place of 'provides'

Singular nouns are followed by singular verbs and plural nouns are followed by plural verbs.

A singular noun names one person. place. thing. or idea. while a plural noun names more than one person. place. thing, or idea.

The usage of the verb singular 'provides' is erroneous and needs to be replaced with the plural form of the verb 'provide' to make the sentence grammatically and contextually correct.

According to the subject-verb agreement, if the subject is singular then it is followed by a singular verb and if the subject is plural it is followed by a plural verb. Here the subject is 'US laws' which is plural and hence is followed by a plural verb.

- E.g. The dog chases the cat.
- The dogs chase the cat.

The correct sentence is: Unlike Indian laws, US laws provide for a contingency fee of lawyering, where the costs of litigation are borne by lawyers

Hence, the correct option is (A).

43. 'global' should be there in place of 'globe'

The usage of the noun 'globe' is erroneous and needs to be replaced with the adjective 'global' to make the sentence grammatically and contextually correct. This is because we need an adjective to modify the noun 'praise'. 'Globe' is a noun.

- E.g. This sacrifice was the least he could do for his friend.
- It was as if he'd tossed out a sacrificial lamb to a flock of vultures.

The correct sentence is: India's Swachh Bharat Mission is receiving global praise for attempting to close the sanitation gap.

Hence, the correct option is (B).

44. Function - an activity that is natural to or the purpose of a person or thing.

The sentence should be read as : Exportable technology can function around the world.

Hence, the correct option is (B).

45. Intervene - take part in something so as to prevent or alter a result or course of events.

The sentence should be read as : The UN refused to intervene in the civil war, apart from some troop convoys for humanitarian aid.

Hence, the correct option is (C).

46. Measure - ascertain the size, amount, or degree of (something) by using an instrument or device marked in standard units.

The sentence should be read as: The great image of Lochana Buddha at Nara, for example, would measure 138 ft.

The given blank is followed by a certain numeric measurement and hence, measure is the correct word for the given blank.

Hence, the correct option is (A).

47. Shrink - be averse to or unwilling to do (something difficult or unappealing).

The sentence should be read as : Louis was a man of strong frame, who loved the chase, and did not shrink from the hardships of war.

Hence, the correct option is (B).

48. Zeal - great energy or enthusiasm in pursuit of a cause or an objective.

The sentence should be read as: His zeal and energy met everywhere with conspicuous success.

Hence, the correct option is (D).

49. According to the first sentence of the first passage, the government may bring the amendment to DICGC Act in the monsoon session with **the objective to provide account holders easy and time-bound access to funds to the extent of the deposit insurance cover**.

Hence, the correct option is (C).

50. According to the last sentence of the second passage- it will provide immediate relief to thousands of depositors who had their money parked in stressed lenders such as PMC Bank and other small cooperative banks.

Hence, the correct option is (D).

51. According to the fourth sentence of the fourth passage, The deposit insurance scheme covers all banks operating in India, including private sector, cooperative and even branches of foreign banks.

Hence, the correct option is (E).

52. According to the line of the passage, Once the Bill becomes the law, it will provide immediate relief to thousands of depositors who had their money parked in stressed lenders such as PMC Bank and other small cooperative banks.

All the other options are irrelevant to the passage.

Hence, the correct option is (A).

53. According to the line of the passage, the government raised insurance cover on deposit five-folds to Rs 5 lakh with a view to provide support to depositors of ailing lenders like Punjab and Maharashtra Co-operative (PMC) Bank.

According to another line of the passage, the government may bring the amendment to DICGC Act in the monsoon session with the objective to provide account holders easy and time-bound access to funds to the extent of the deposit insurance cover.

Hence, the correct option is (D).

54. The underlined part of the sentence is grammatically correct and doesn't have to be improved.

The phrasal verb "pan out" means "happen in a particular way."

None of the other alternatives can make the sentence meaningful.

Hence, the correct option is (E).

55. The modal 'can' is used to express 'ability or opportunity', to make general statements about what is possible.

Here the ability to learn new words with the help of a dictionary is conveyed, and thus 'can' fits perfectly.

Hence, the correct option is (B).

Ques (56-60): The first sentence should seem like an introduction to the topic. After reading all the sentences, statement C seems to be the most appropriate choice. It speaks about India's hope to end its present exclusion from global value chains.

Further, statement E picks up where fragment C has left off and they make sense together. The sentence starts with 'in parallel' which indicates other measures that are to be taken to make India's hopes come true. Thus, fragment C and fragment E make a pair.

Now, if we read the sentences carefully, we find that statement E mentions 'dumping of goods' from China and statement A carries on with the mention of 'unfair trade practices' and how goods made in China are routed. They make a meaningful sentence together. Thus, fragment E and fragment A also make a mandatory pair. So far, the correct sequence of statements is: CEA

The fourth sentence should add meaning to the idea being formed. A complete ban on Chinese goods would be impractical and the government should also consider imports to be an essential part of India's trade competitiveness.

Thus, the correct sequence of statements is CEADB.

56. D should be the FOURTH sentence after the rearrangement.

Hence, the correct option is (D).

57. E should be the SECOND sentence after the rearrangement.

Hence, the correct option is (E).

58. A should be the THIRD sentence after the rearrangement.

Hence, the correct option is (A).

59. C should be the FIRST sentence after the rearrangement.

Hence, the correct option is (C).

60. B should be the FIFTH sentence after the rearrangement.

Hence, the correct option is (B).

61. Number of ways of outcomes when two dice are thrown = n(S) = 36 and the possible cases of event when the sum of numbers on two dice is a prime number are

(1, 1), (1, 2), (1, 4), (1, 6), (2, 1), (2, 3), (2, 5), (3, 2), (3, 4), (4, 1), (4, 3), (5, 2), (5, 6), (6, 1), (6, 5).

Number of events = 15

Probability = $\dfrac{15}{36}$ = $\dfrac{5}{12}$

Hence, the correct option is (B).

62. Let the width of the rectangular field be x.

Then the length be 3x.

Area of the field = x × 3x = 192

$\Rightarrow 3x^2 = 192$

$\Rightarrow x^2 = 64$

$\Rightarrow x = 8$

So, width = 8m, and

Length = 3× 8 = 24 m

Also, Perimeter = 2 × (24 + 8) = 64m

As the cost of fencing is Rs.2/m,

$\therefore$ Total cost = 2 × 64 = Rs.128

Hence, the correct option is (C).

63. Given,

Time taken by pipe A to fill the tank with chemical P = 30 minutes

Time taken by pipe B to fill the tank with chemical Q = 20 minutes

Time taken by pipe C to fill the tank with chemical R = 10 minutes

Part filled by A, B and C in 3 minutes $= 3 \times \left(\dfrac{1}{30} + \dfrac{1}{20} + \dfrac{1}{10}\right)$

$= 3 \times \dfrac{11}{60}$

$= \dfrac{11}{20}$

Part filled by C in 3 minutes $= \dfrac{3}{10}$

$\therefore$ Required ratio $= \dfrac{3}{10} \times \dfrac{20}{11}$

$= \dfrac{6}{11}$

Hence, the correct option is (B).

64. I. $25p^2 - 30p + 8 = 0$

$\Rightarrow 25p^2 - 20p - 10p + 8 = 0$

$\Rightarrow 5p(5p - 4) - 2(5p - 4) = 0$

$\Rightarrow (5p - 4)(5p - 2) = 0$

$\Rightarrow p = \dfrac{4}{5}$ or $p = \dfrac{2}{5}$

II. $q^2 - 2q + 1 = 0$

$\Rightarrow q^2 - q - q + 1 = 0$

$\Rightarrow q(q - 1) - 1(q - 1) = 0$

$\Rightarrow (q - 1)(q - 1) = 0$

$\Rightarrow q = 1$

When $p = \dfrac{4}{5}, p < q$ for $q = 1$

And when $p = \dfrac{2}{5}, p < q$ for $q = 1$

$\therefore p < q$

Hence, the correct option is (C).

65. I. $7p^2 - 168p = 0$

$\Rightarrow 7p(p - 24) = 0$

Then, $p = 0$ or $p = 24$

II. $11q^2 - 891 = 0$

$\Rightarrow 11(q^2 - 81) = 0$

$\Rightarrow (q^2 - 9^2) = 0$

Use: $(p^2 - q^2) = (p - q)(p + q)$

$\Rightarrow (q - 9)(q + 9) = 0$

Then, $q = 9$ or $q = -9$

So, when $p = 0, p < q$ for $q = 9$ and $p > q$ for $q = (-9)$

And when $p = 24, p > q$ for $q = 9$ and $p > q$ for $q = (-9)$

$\therefore$ The relationship cannot be determined.

Hence, the correct option is (E).

66. Given,

Time is taken by boat running upstream to cover certain distance = 8 hours 48 minutes

Time is taken by boat running downstream to cover certain distance = 4 hours

Let the boat's rate upstream be x km/h and that downstream be y km/h.

Then, distance covered upstream in 8 hrs 48 min = Distance covered downstream in 4 hrs.

We know,

$$Speed = \frac{Distance}{Time}$$

$$Distance = Speed \times Time$$

According to question,

$$x \times 8\frac{4}{5} = y \times 4$$

$$\Rightarrow \frac{44}{5}x = 4y$$

$$\Rightarrow y = \frac{11}{5}x$$

Therefore,

Required ratio $= \dfrac{y+x}{2} : \dfrac{y-x}{2}$

$= \left(\dfrac{16x}{5} \times \dfrac{1}{2}\right) : \left(\dfrac{6x}{5} \times \dfrac{1}{2}\right)$

$= \dfrac{8}{5} : \dfrac{3}{5}$

$= 8 : 3$

Hence, the correct option is (C).

67. Given:

The principal becomes $\dfrac{6}{5}$ of itself in 6 years.

We know that,

S.I. (Simple interest) $= \dfrac{(P \times R \times T)}{100}$

P $\rightarrow$ Principal,

R $\rightarrow$ Rate of interest per annum,

T $\rightarrow$ Time (in years)

Amount = Principal + S.I.

Let the sum of money lent (Principal) be Rs. x.

S.I. (Simple interest) $= \dfrac{(P \times R \times T)}{100}$

$\Rightarrow$ S.I. = x × R × $\dfrac{6}{100}$

$\Rightarrow \dfrac{6xR}{100}$

Amount = Principal + S.I.

$\Rightarrow \dfrac{6}{5}$ of x = x + $\left(\dfrac{6xR}{100}\right)$

$\Rightarrow \left(\dfrac{6}{5}\right)$x – x = $\dfrac{6xR}{100}$

$\Rightarrow \dfrac{x}{5} = \dfrac{6xR}{100}$

$\Rightarrow$ R = $\dfrac{100}{(5 \times 6)}$% p.a.

$\Rightarrow$ R = $\left(\dfrac{10}{3}\right)$%

$\therefore$ The rate of interest earned is $\left(\dfrac{10}{3}\right)$% p.a.

Hence, the correct option is (A).

68. Given:

Amount (A_1) = Rs. 4840, Time (n_1) = 2 years

Amount (A_2) = Rs. 5324, Time (n_2) = 3 years

We know that

$$A = P\left(1 + \frac{R}{100}\right)^n$$

where A = amount

p = principal

R = rate

n = time

Calculations:

Case I

$$4840 = P\left(1 + \frac{R}{100}\right)^2 \quad ----(i)$$

$$5324 = P\left(1 + \frac{R}{100}\right)^3 \quad ----(ii)$$

By equation (ii) ÷ (i)

$$\frac{5324}{4840} = \left(1 + \frac{R}{100}\right)$$

$$\Rightarrow \frac{R}{100} = \left(\frac{5324}{4840}\right) - 1$$

$$\Rightarrow \frac{R}{100} = \frac{484}{4840}$$

⇒ R = 10%

From equation (i),

$$4840 = P\left(1 + \frac{10}{100}\right)^2$$

$$\Rightarrow 4840 = P \times \left(\frac{121}{100}\right)$$

⇒ P = 4000

∴ The correct answer is 4000.

Hence, the correct option is (C).

69. Given:

A's time = 12 days

B's time = 8 days

B leaves after 4 days

Let total work be 24 (L.C.M of 12 and 8)

A's efficiency = $\frac{24}{12}$ = 2 units/day

B's efficiency = $\frac{24}{8}$ = 3 units/day

4 days work = (3 + 2) × 4 = 20 units

Remaining work = 4 units

Required time = $\frac{4}{2}$ = 2 days

∴ The answer is 2 days

Hence, the correct option is (B).

70. Given:

The production of the Computer by company COMPAQ in the year 2013 = 128000

The production of the Computer by company LENVO in the year 2013 = 78000

Formula used:

Required percentage =

$$\frac{\text{The production of company COMPAQ in the year 2013}}{\text{The production of company LENVO in the year 2013}} \times 100$$

Percentage = $\frac{128000}{78000} \times 100$

Required percentage = 164.10%

Hence, the correct option is (D).

71. Given:

The production of company LENVO in 2010 to 2015 = 119000, 99000, 100000, 78000, 120000, 138000

The production of company COMPAQ in 2010 to 2015 = 139000, 110000, 141000, 128000, 107000, 149000

In years 2010 = 139000 – 119000 = 20000

In year 20011 = 110000 – 99000 = 11000

In year 2012 = 141000 – 100000 = 41000

In year 2013 = 128000 – 78000 = 50000

In year 2014 = 120000 – 107000 = 13000

In year 2015 = 149000 – 138000 = 11000

From the above we can see that in 2013 production is maximum.

Hence, the correct option is (A).

72. Given:

The production of company LENVO in 2010 to 2015 = 119000, 99000, 100000, 78000, 120000, 138000

Formula used:

$$\text{Average} = \frac{\text{Total Computer production by the company LENVO}}{6}$$

Average = $\frac{(119000+99000+100000+78000+120000+138000)}{6}$

Average = $\frac{654000}{6}$

∴ Average = 109000

Hence, the correct option is (B).

73. Given:

The production of company COMPAQ in the year 2011 = 110000

The production of company COMPAQ in the year 2012 = 141000

Formula used:

Difference = the production of company COMPAQ in the year 2012 – The production of company COMPAQ in the year 2011

Difference = 141000 – 110000 = 31000

Hence, the correct option is (A).

74. Given:

The production of company LENVO in 2010 to 2015 = 119000, 99000, 100000, 78000, 120000, 138000

The production of company COMPAQ in 2010 to 2015 = 139000, 110000, 141000, 128000, 107000, 149000

Formula used:

Difference = the production of company COMPAQ from 2010 to 2015 – the production of company LENVO from 2010 to 2015

The production of company LENVO from 2010 to 2015 = 654000

The production of company COMPAQ in 2010 to 2015 = 774000

Difference = 774000 – 654000 = 120,000

Hence, the correct option is (C).

75. Follow the BODMAS rule according to the table given below:

B	Brackets in order (), {}, [ ]	ब्रेकट (), {}, [ ] क्रम
O	Of	का
D	Division (÷)	विभाजन (÷)
M	Multiplication (×)	गुणा (×)
A	Addition (+)	जोड़ (+)
s	Subtraction (-)	घटाव (-)

Given expression,

13.33 + 33.31 + 331.13 = ?

46.64 + 331.13 = ?

? = 377.77

Hence, the correct option is (A).

76. Given:

14.28% of 490 – 71.43% of 63 = ?

To solve this type of question, we can take use of conversion of percentage into fraction.

Also, follow the BODMAS rule according to the table given below:

Also, follow the BODMAS rule according to the table given below:

B	Brackets in order (), {}, [ ]	ब्रेकट (), {}, [ ] क्रम
O	Of	का
D	Division (÷)	विभाजन (÷)
M	Multiplication (×)	गुणा (×)
A	Addition (+)	जोड़ (+)
s	Subtraction (-)	घटाव (-)

Converting given percentages into fraction,

$$\Rightarrow 14.28\% = \frac{1}{7}$$

$$\Rightarrow 71.43\% = \frac{5}{7}$$

According to the given equation,

$$\Rightarrow \frac{1}{7} \text{ of } 490 - \frac{1}{7} \text{ of } 63 = ?$$

$$\Rightarrow \frac{1}{7} \times 490 - \frac{5}{7} \times 63 = ?$$

$\Rightarrow 70 – 45 = ?$

$\Rightarrow 25 = ?$

∴ The value of ? is 25.

Hence, the correct option is (A).

77. Follow BODMAS rule to solve this question, as per the order given below,

B	Brackets in order (), {}, [ ]	ब्रेकट (), {}, [ ] क्रम
O	Of	का
D	Division (÷)	विभाजन (÷)
M	Multiplication (×)	गुणा (×)
A	Addition (+)	जोड़ (+)
s	Subtraction (-)	घटाव (-)

450 ÷ 15 × 12 – 120 ÷ 4 × 12 + 1 = ?

$$\frac{450}{15} \times 12 - \frac{120}{4} \times 12 + 1 = ?$$

30 × 12 – 30 × 12 + 1 = ?

? = 1

∴ The value of '?' is 1.

Hence, the correct option is (C).

78. Follow BODMAS rule to solve this question, as per the order given below,

B	Brackets in order (), {}, [ ]	ब्रेकट (), {}, [ ] क्रम
O	Of	का
D	Division (÷)	विभाजन (÷)
M	Multiplication (×)	गुणा (×)
A	Addition (+)	जोड़ (+)
s	Subtraction (-)	घटाव (-)

$$\sqrt{\left[1331^{\left(\frac{1}{3}\right)} + 1728^{\left(\frac{1}{3}\right)} + 2\right]} = ?$$

$$\sqrt{(11 + 12 + 2)}$$

$$= \sqrt{25} = 5$$

Hence, the correct option is (A).

79. First we calculate multiplier for various percentage changes

⇒ Multiplier for 10% increase = 1 + 0.10 = 1.1

⇒ Multiplier for 20% decrease = 1.1 – 0.20 × 1.1 = 1.1 – 0.22 = 0.88

⇒ Multiplier for 50% increase = 0.88 + 0.50 × 0.88 = 0.88 + 0.44

⇒ Overall Percentage change = 1.32

∴ Answer is 32%.

Hence, the correct option is (D).

80. Given:

0, 6, 24, 60, 120, ?

$1^3 – 1 = 1 – 1 = 0$

$2^3 - 2 = 8 - 2 = 6$

$3^3 - 3 = 27 - 3 = 24$

$4^3 - 4 = 64 - 4 = 60$

$5^3 - 5 = 125 - 5 = 120$

$\Rightarrow 6^3 - 6 = ?$

$\Rightarrow 216 - 6$

$\Rightarrow 210$

∴ The value will come at the place of ? is 210.

Hence, the correct option is (A).

81. The pattern is as follows:

8 + 2 = 10

10 × 3 = 30

30 + 3 = 33

33 × 4 = 132

132 + 4 = 136

136 × 5 = 680

680 + 5 = 685

∴ The value of ? is 685.

Hence, the correct option is (C).

82. The pattern is as follows:

$6 \times 1 + 1^2 = 7$

$7 \times 2 + 2^2 = 18$

$18 \times 3 + 3^2 = 63$

$63 \times 4 + 4^2 = 268$

$268 \times 5 + 5^2 = 1365$

∴ The value of ? is 1365.

Hence, the correct option is (B).

83. Given:

Selling price = Cost price

The gain obtained by selling at cost price = 20% of cost price

Bought 25 Kg of goods at Rs. 20/ Kg.

By selling 25 Kg shopkeeper gains 20%.

Total cost price = 25 × 20 = Rs. 500

The profit obtained on selling 25 Kg = 20% of 500

$$= 500 \times \frac{20}{100} = \text{Rs. } 100$$

That means profit in weight corresponding to profit in money = Profit/cost price

$\Rightarrow$ Profit in weight $= \frac{100}{20}$ = 5 Kg

That is, out of 25 Kg weight, the shopkeeper actually uses only 20 Kg.

The loss per kilogram $= \frac{5}{25}$

$\Rightarrow$ Loss of weight per kilogram $= \frac{1}{5}$ kg = 200g

∴ The weight shopkeeper reduces to get a 20% gain on selling 25kg is 200g per kilogram weight.

Hence, the correct option is (C).

84. The notation $C(n, r)$ is the number of combinations/groups of n different things taking r at a time and is given by:

$$C(n, r) = \frac{n!}{r!(n-r)!}$$

If $C(n, x) = C(n, y)$, then $x + y = n$

Calculation:

Given $C(20, n + 2) = C(20, n - 2)$

As we know that, if $C(n, x) = C(n, y)$, then $x + y = n$.

$\Rightarrow (n + 2) + (n - 2) = 20$

$\Rightarrow 2n = 20$

$\Rightarrow n = 10$

Hence, the correct option is (C).

85.

I. $2x^2 + 18x + 40 = 0$

$\Rightarrow 2x^2 + 10x + 8x + 40 = 0$

$\Rightarrow 2x(x + 5) + 8(x + 5) = 0$

$\Rightarrow (x + 5)(2x + 8) = 0$

$\Rightarrow x = -5, -4$

II. $2y^2 + 15y + 27 = 0$

$\Rightarrow 2y^2 + 6y + 9y + 27 = 0$

$\Rightarrow 2y(y + 3) + 9(y + 3) = 0$

$\Rightarrow (y + 3)(2y + 9) = 0$

$\Rightarrow y = -3, -\frac{9}{2}$

Comparison between x any via tabulation:

Value of x	Value of y	Relation
-5	-3	x < y
-5	$-\frac{9}{2}$	x < y
-4	-3	x < y
-4	$-\frac{9}{2}$	x > y

∴ The relation between x and y can't be established.

Hence, the correct option is (E).

86. Given,

The average salary of 9 nurses is Rs. 3600 while the average salary of 11 ward boys is Rs. 4400:

The average salary of all the doctors is Rs 22000.

$$\text{Average} = \frac{\text{(Total salary of all employees)}}{\text{Number of employees}}$$

Total salary of 9 nurses = 3600 × 9 = Rs. 32400

Total salary of 11 ward boys = 4400 × 11 = Rs. 48400

Let the total number of all doctors in hospital be 'd'.

Total salary of 'd' number of doctors = d × 22000 = Rs. 22000d

The average salary of entire staff is Rs. 7632

Total salary of entire staff = (9 + 11 + d) × 7632 = (20 + d) × 7632

Total salary of entire staff = Total salary of 9 nurses + Total salary of 11 ward boys + Total salary of 'd' number of doctors

⇒ (20 + d) × 7632 = 32400 + 48400 + 22000d

⇒ 152640 + 7632d = 80800 + 22000d

⇒ 22000d - 7632d = 152640 - 80800

⇒ 14368d = 71840

$$\Rightarrow d = \left(\frac{71840}{14368}\right) = 5$$

∴ There are 5 doctors available in Aditya hospital.

Hence, the correct option is (D).

87. The series follows the following pattern:

(10 × 9) + 8 = 98

(9 × 8) + 7 = 79

(8 × 7) + 6 = 62

(7 × 6) + 5 = 47

(6 × 5) + 4 = 34

(5 × 4) + 3 = 23

Hence, the correct option is (A).

88. The series follows the following pattern:

$1 - 0 = 1^2$

$5 - 1 = 2^2$

$11 - 2 = 3^2$

$19 - 3 = 4^2$

$29 - 4 = 5^2$

$41 - 5 = 6^2$

Hence, the correct option is (E).

89. Follow the BODMAS rule according to the table given below:

B	Brackets in order (), {}, []	ब्रेकट (), {}, [] क्रम
O	Of	का
D	Division (÷)	विभाजन (÷)
M	Multiplication (×)	गुणा (×)
A	Addition (+)	जोड़ (+)
s	Subtraction (-)	घटाव (-)

$(562.5 \times 6)^4 \div (135 \div 9)^2 \times (37.5 \times 6)^5 = (3.75 \times 4)^{(5-?)}$

$\Rightarrow (3375)^4 \div (15)^2 \times (225)^5 = (15)^{(5-?)}$

$\Rightarrow (15)^{12} \div (15)^2 \times (15)^{10} = (15)^{(5-?)}$

$\Rightarrow (15)^{20} = (15)^{(5-?)}$

$\Rightarrow 5-? = 20$

$\Rightarrow ? = -15$

Hence, the correct option is (D).

90. Suppose P invested an amount of Rs. T.

So, Q invested an amount of Rs. (T – 2000).

Q invested for two years while P withdrew his share and profit after a year.

The profit that this investment offers is 10% for a year.

Case i) Profit earned by Q in two years - Profit earned by P in one year = Rs. 200

$\Rightarrow (T - 2000) \times \dfrac{10}{100} \times 2 - T \times \dfrac{10}{100}) = 200$

$\Rightarrow 0.2T - 400 - 0.1T = 200$

$\Rightarrow T = \dfrac{600}{0.1} = 6000$

Total money invested = T + T – 2000 = 10000

Case ii) Profit earned by P in one year - Profit earned by Q in two years = Rs. 200

$\Rightarrow T \times \dfrac{10}{100} - T - 2000 \times \dfrac{10}{100} \times 2 = 200$

$\Rightarrow - 0.2T + 400 + 0.1T = 200$

$\Rightarrow T = \left(\dfrac{200}{0.1}\right) = 2000$

In this case, money invested by Q will become 0.

Total money invested = T + T – 2000 = 2000

Although this case is theoretically possible but no option matches the answer produced by it.

∴ Total money invested is Rs. 10000.

Hence, the correct option is (B).

Reasoning Ability

Ques (1-5):Direction: Study the following information carefully and answer the questions following it.

Eight persons B, H, M, J, O, T, D, and K are seated in a row. All of them are facing north. J is sitting to the immediate left of M. D is third to the right of B and one of them is sitting at an extreme end of the row. One person sits between B and O and that person is not K. There are 2 persons sitting between B and T. J is not an immediate neighbour of B.

Q.1 Who is sitting to the immediate left of D?
A. K   **B.** M   **C.** O   **D.** B
E. J

Q.2 How many persons are sitting between K and B?
A. Four   **B.** Five   **C.** Two   **D.** Three
E. None

Q.3 Who among the following sits third to the right of M?
A. O   **B.** D   **C.** K   **D.** T
E. B

Q.4 Which pair among the following does not belong to the group?
A. BD   **B.** KM   **C.** OM   **D.** MH
E. JH

Q.5 If all the persons are asked to sit in alphabetical order from left to right, then who will sit second to the right of K?
A. K   **B.** O   **C.** M   **D.** B
E. J

Ques (6-8):Direction: Study the following information carefully and answer the given questions.

In a certain code language,

'se ma to' means 'India is beautiful''si fe ma' means 'Rohan is smart''ra fe si to' means 'Smart Rohan visits India''si kn ma' means 'Village is smart'

Q.6 What will be the code of Village?
A. ma   **B.** si
C. kn   **D.** to
E. Either ma or si

Q.7 What could be the code of 'Rohan is going Village'?
A. kn sa si fe   **B.** si ma se fe
C. kn ra se fe   **D.** kn ma fe kr
E. kn ma to ra

Q.8 Code 'kn ma se lk to' is for which of the following sentence in given language?
A. Smart India is beautiful
B. Village in India is beautiful
C. India is smart village
D. Village in India is smart
E. Rohan is very smart

Ques (9-13):Direction: Following questions are based on five words given below.

FGT   SDB   TUC   OER   AVY

(The new words formed after performing the mentioned operations may or may not necessarily be meaningful English words)

Q.9 If the letters of given words are arranged in alphabetical order (from left to right) within the words then how many words will have consonant as the first letter?
A. One   **B.** Two   **C.** Three   **D.** Four
E. None

Q.10 If first letter of each word replaced by the 3rd succeeding letter in the English alphabetical series, then how many words thus formed will have no vowel?
A. All   **B.** Three   **C.** Four   **D.** Two
E. One

Q.11 If all the alphabets are assigned numbers starting from A till Z (i.e., A = 1, B = 2 and so on), then which word has the maximum sum value?
A. FGT   **B.** OER   **C.** SDB   **D.** TUC
E. AVY

Q.12 If the middle letter of each word is replaced by immediate preceding letter as per alphabetical series, how many words will have no vowel after rearrangement?
A. One   **B.** Two   **C.** Three   **D.** Four
E. Five

Q.13 If the given words are arranged in the order as they would appear in a dictionary from left to right, which of the following will be third from left?
A. SDB   **B.** TUC   **C.** FGT   **D.** OER
E. AVY

Ques (14-18):Direction: Read the following information carefully and answer the questions which follow.

A, B, C, D, E, and F live on different floors in the same building having six floors numbered one to six (the ground floor is numbered 1, the floor above it, number 2 and so on and the topmost floor is numbered 6).

B lives on an even-numbered floor. Only two people live between the floors on which B and F live. D lives on a floor immediately above the floor on which C lives. D does not live on an odd-numbered floor. A does not live on a floor that is immediately above or immediately below the floor on which E lives. A does not live on the lowermost floor i.e., floor no. 1.

Q.14 Who amongst the following live on the floors exactly between the floors on which B and F live?
A. C, D
B. A, C
C. D, E
D. A, E
E. Cannot be determined

Q.15 Who amongst the following lives on floor number 5?
A. A
B. B
C. E
D. F
E. Cannot be determined

Q.16 On which of the following floors does E live?
A. 3rd
B. 5th
C. 1st
D. 4th
E. Cannot be determined

Q.17 How many people live on the floors above the floor on which A lives?
A. One
B. Two
C. Three
D. None
E. Cannot be determined

Q.18 On which of the following floors does C live?
A. 3rd
B. 5th
C. 1st
D. 4th
E. Cannot be determined

Ques (19-21):Direction: In the question below are given three statements followed by three conclusions numbered I, II, and III. You have to take the given statements to be true even if they seem to be at variance with commonly known facts. Read all the conclusions and then decide which of the given conclusions logically follows from the given statements disregarding commonly known facts.

Q.19 Statements:
Some rich are poor.
Only a few kings are honest.
No honest is rich.
Conclusions:
I. All kings can be honest.
II. Some honest is not rich.
III. All poor is king.
A. Only conclusion I follow
B. Only conclusion II follow
C. Conclusion I and III follow
D. All conclusion follows
E. None conclusion follows

Q.20 Statements:
No Facebook is WhatsApp.
No WhatsApp is App.
No App is Insta.
Conclusions:
I. Some Facebook is Insta.
II. Some App is WhatsApp.
III. Some Insta are WhatsApp.
A. Conclusion II and III follow
B. Only conclusion II follow
C. Conclusion I and III follow
D. Conclusion I and II follow
E. None follow

Q.21 Statements:
Only a few roads are royal.
Few roads are good.
Few royals are kings.
Conclusions:
I. All good can be roads.
II. All kings can be royal.
III. Some good is roads.
A. Only conclusion I follow
B. Only conclusion II follow
C. Conclusion I and III follow
D. All conclusion follows
E. None conclusion follows

Q.22 In a row where all are facing north, Priya is 15th from the left end and Garima is 19th from the right end. They interchange their positions, and Ram who sits 24th from the left end sits at the 5th place to the left of Priya's new position. How many persons were there in the row?
A. 36   **B.** 42   **C.** 47   **D.** 56
E. 57

Q.23 During a prize distribution ceremony, Vikram was ninth from the left while Janhvi was eighth from the right in the front row. If Hariom was thirteenth from the left and was exactly in the middle of Vikram and Janhvi in the same row then what was the total number of people in the front row?
A. 18   **B.** 19   **C.** 21   **D.** 24
E. 25

Q.24 In a north-facing row of NCC Cadets, Trisha is 9th from the left end and Tina is 12th from the right end. There are 5 cadets between Trisha and Tanya which is equal to the number of cadets between Tanya and Tina. Find how many cadets are there in the row?
A. 34   **B.** 32
C. 31   **D.** 33
E. Can't be determined

Ques (25-27):Direction: Study the information given below carefully and answer the question that follow.

Prajakta and Prasann start from a point simultaneously. Prajakta moves 17 km towards west, and Prasann moves towards south and covers 17 km. Prajakta takes a 270° clockwise turn and travel to another 17 km. Prasann takes a 90° turn towards east and moves 23 km. Then Prasann goes 40 km in the same line in exactly the opposite direction.

Q.25 How much distance does Prasann travelled?
A. 75 km
B. 80 km
C. 65 km
D. 60 km
E. None of these.

Q.26 The final position of Prajakta is in which direction with respect to Prasann's initial position?
A. South East
B. South
C. South West
D. Cannot be determined
E. None of these

Q.27 What is the difference between the distance travelled by Prajakta and Prasann?
A. 50 km
B. 35 km
C. 48 km
D. 40 km
E. 46 km

Q.28 If in the word 'SEPTUAGENARIAN' first three and then next three letters are written in reverse order and the rest of the letters are written as they appear in English alphabet, the positions of how many letters get changed in the new arrangement?
A. Nil
B. 2
C. 10
D. 12
E. None of these

Ques (29-30):Direction: Study the following information carefully to answer the given questions:

If 'P # Q' means 'P is the son of Q'

If 'P % Q' means 'P is the father of Q'

If 'P * Q' means 'P is the sister of Q'

If 'P $ Q' means 'Q is the husband of P'

Q.29 Which of the following represent 'X is the brother of Y'?
A. X * Y % K
B. Y # K % X
C. Y * K % X
D. Y * X % K
E. None of these

Q.30 In 'Y * X # F % L', how is Y related to L?
A. Cousin
B. Brother
C. Sister
D. Can't be determined
E. None of these

English Language

Ques (31-35):Direction: Read the passage carefully and answer the questions that follow. Some words are highlighted for your attention.

Overpopulation is a serious threat to our own existence. The whole world needs to address this issue and not just a few countries. The world's population is increasing mainly due to medical advancements and increases in agricultural productivity. Countries like Brazil, China and India add more to their woes by neglecting substantial increases in their populations.

India is now home to 1.2 billion. Furthermore, India's population is expected to grow to 1.8 billion before stabilizing around the middle of this century, if sufficient measures are taken. Today India is stretched to its limit due to overpopulation. 57 billionaires control 70 per cent of India's wealth. This economic inequality leads to poverty, lack of free medical assistance, lack of social security and bad living conditions. The issues are even more critical due to the advancements in Artificial Intelligence and Automation. Automation threatens 69 per cent job losses with millions of job losses already occurring in the IT and production sectors. E-commerce has failed to pick up so far due to job cuts and prices that are not as competitive as in the local marketplace.

Excessive population leads to working institutions dysfunctionality and makes all plans to improve a country's infrastructure, medical assistance facilities and social welfare initiatives ineffective. This includes the Indian Government which has struggled to enact reforms over the past 69 years since independence.

The consequences of population growth are a problem that the whole world will soon face sooner or later. Drinking water, sewage treatment, inadequate rainfall, rapid depletion of natural resources, extinction of many plant and animal species due to deforestation and loss of ecosystems, increased level of life-threatening air and water pollution, high infant and child mortality rate and hunger due to extreme poverty are some of the results of over-population.

Many people are already aware of the social and environmental problems due to overpopulation, but only a few are aware of its adverse effects on health. Most Indian cities are badly polluted and have little fresh air. This leads to countless airborne diseases and skin infections.

It's not just India's struggle, Brazil and China are also coping with the ramifications of overpopulation. It's time for all global forums to provide effective solutions in order to resolve this problem. Overpopulation can only be solved by spreading awareness of and implementing measures like birth control and access to birth control devices. Let us help the world prepare for a better tomorrow.

Q.31 Which of these is not the reason for increase in population?
A. Improvement in medical facilities
B. Increasing agricultural productivity
C. Improving economies
D. None of the above
E. Both (B) and (C)

Q.32 Due to which factors do people face poverty and poor living conditions?
A. Economic inequality
B. Poor medical facilities
C. Overpopulation
D. Both (A) and (C)

E. All of the above

Q.33 Which sectors have faced job losses?
A. Production   **B.** IT
C. Agricultural   **D.** Both (A) and (B)
E. All of the above

Q.34 What are the consequences of overpopulation?
A. Rapid depletion of resources
B. Increasing levels of pollution
C. Extreme poverty
D. Both (A) and (B)
E. All of the above

Q.35 Which of these is not a method to control overpopulation?
A. Creating awareness among people
B. Ensuring economic equality
C. Easy access to birth control devices
D. Both (A) and (B)
E. None of the above

Ques (36-40):Direction: A sentence/a part of the sentence is underlined. Four alternatives are given to the underlined part which will improve the meaning of the sentence. Choose the correct alternative. In case no improvement is needed, click the option corresponding to "No improvement".

Q.36 The most exciting event in the Sydney Olympics <u>for most British viewers were the rowing finals.</u>
A. For most British viewers was the rowing finals
B. For the most British viewers were the rowing finals
C. For the more British viewers were the rowing finals
D. For most British viewers was the rowing final
E. No improvement

Q.37 <u>She performed so enthusiastically as</u> the judges overlooked her inexperience.
A. She performed as enthusiastic that
B. She performed so enthusiastically that
C. She perform so enthusiastically as
D. She performed so enthusiastic as
E. No improvement

Q.38 The more sophisticated the product, <u>more substantial the potential profit.</u>
A. The more substantial the potential profit
B. A more substantial the potential profit
C. The most substantial the potential profit
D. Most substantial the potential profit
E. No improvement

Q.39 The doctor <u>advised him taking</u> a course of antibiotics.
A. Advised him to take
B. Advice him to take
C. Advised him to taking
D. Advised to take
E. No improvement

Q.40 <u>Only if the sun would come</u> out so we could get on with the filming.
A. If only the sun would came
B. Only if the sun will come
C. If only the sun would come
D. Only if the sun would comes
E. No improvement

Q.41 Direction: Fill in the blanks with the appropriate word.
He _____ very little when there are strangers present.
A. had always spoken
B. was always speaking
C. is always speaking
D. always speaks
E. have been speaks

Ques (42-44):Direction: Below, a statement is divided into parts. One or more of these parts may contain an error. Out of the given options, choose the one that gives an 'errorless combination'. If there are no errors, choose option (E), viz, No error.

Q.42 The smaller businesses are (A) / aggressively leveraged technology (B) / like cloud and mobile internet (C) / to bring down their cost of operations.(D)
A. ABD   **B.** BCD   **C.** ACD   **D.** ABC
E. No error

Q.43 With leaders of the Gujjar agitation (A) / for reservations calling of their stir, (B) / the Rajasthan government has averted (C) / what could have been a prolonged crisis. (D)
A. ABD   **B.** ABC   **C.** BCD   **D.** ACD
E. No error

Q.44 Industry organisations will (A) / make a fresh appeal to the (B) / state to intervene and undertaken (C) / necessary steps to provide relief.(D)
A. ABD   **B.** ABC   **C.** BCD   **D.** ACD
E. No error

Ques (45-46):Direction: The following sentences are broken into four parts and two parts may contain an error in them. Find out the combination which contains error. If the sentence is free from error, mark 'No Error'.

Q.45 Hurdles like electric boxes and (A) / hawkers on the sidewalks leaving (B) / very little space for pedestrians (C) / to actually walk in.(D)
A. B and D   **B.** A and C   **C.** A and B   **D.** C and D
E. No Error

Q.46 The man this found, (A) / was soon assaulted by (B) / three armed men for the streets (C) / near his house in Arizona.(D)
A. B and C   **B.** A and D
C. A and C   **D.** C and D
E. No Error

Ques (47-51):Direction: The following passage has five missing words; 1, 2, 3, 4, 5, and 6. Choose the most appropriate option to fill in the respective blanks.

Dennis Arp was feeling optimistic last summer, which is unusual for a beekeeper these days. Thanks to a record wet spring, his hundreds of hives, ______(1) across the central Arizona desert, produced a bounty of honey. Arp would have plenty to sell in stores, but more importantly, the______ (2) harvest would strengthen his bees for their biggest task of the coming year. Like most commercial beekeepers in the US, at least half of Arp's revenue now comes from pollinating almonds. Selling honey is far _____(3) than renting out his colonies to mega-farms in California's fertile Central Valley, home to 80% of the world's almond supply. But as winter approached, with Arp just months away from taking his hives to California, his bees started getting sick. By October, 150 of Arp's hives had been ______(4) by mites, 12% of his inventory in just a few months. Commercial beekeepers who send their hives to the almond farms are seeing their bees die in record numbers, and nothing they do seems to stop the decline. Beekeepers ______(5) the high mortality rate to pesticide exposure, diseases from parasites and habitat loss. However, environmentalists and organic beekeepers ____(6) that the real culprit is something more systemic: America's reliance on industrial agriculture methods, especially those used by the almond industry, which demands large-scale mechanization of one of nature's most delicate natural processes.

Q.47 Which of the following words fits the blank labelled as (1)?

A. Stumbled   **B.** Littered
C. Scattered   **D.** Entrenched
E. Squandered

Q.48 Which of the following words fits the blank labelled as (2)?

A. Inflated   **B.** Piddling   **C.** Flush   **D.** Squat
E. Bumper

Q.49 Which of the following words fits the blank labelled as (3)?

A. Less lucrative   **B.** More expected
C. Little dicey   **D.** More lucrative
E. Less dicey

Q.50 Which of the following words fits the blank labelled as (4)?

A. Manipulated   **B.** Cautioned against
C. Wreaked   **D.** Wiped out
E. Looked after

Q.51 Which of the following words fits the blank labelled as (5)?

A. Heartened   **B.** Coupled
C. Directed   **D.** Attributed
E. Counselled

Ques (52-56):Directions: In the following questions, some part of the sentence is underlined. Which of the options given below the sentence should replace the part underlined to make the sentence grammatically correct? If the sentence is correct as it is given then choose option E 'No Correction required' as the answer.

Q.52 After a great deal of effort she finally <u>managed to success</u> in her venture.

A. managing to succeed
B. managed to succeed
C. managing success
D. manage to success
E. No correction required

Q.53 As she bought <u>quite a number</u> of books she got a heavy discount.

A. quite numbers
B. heavy numbers
C. some numbers
D. many numbers
E. No correction required

Q.54 I woke up early in the morning and <u>had a steamer</u> cup of coffee.

A. has a steamer
B. has a steaming
C. had a steaming
D. had a steam
E. No correction required

Q.55 Tired <u>of being harassed</u> by the goons, I finally called the police and complained.

A. in being harassed
B. of being harass
C. in be harassed
D. of be harassed
E. No correction required

Q.56 One of the <u>base laws of nature</u> is that adaptability is the price of survival.

A. basis laws of
B. basic law of
C. base law of
D. basic laws of
E. no correction required

Ques (57-58):Direction: In the given sentence, a blank is given indicating that a word is missing. Among the four given options, a combination of words fit the blank thereby making it grammatically and contextually correct. Choose that option as your response.

Q.57 Harry held on to his ____________ beliefs for so long that ultimately he saw nothing else but what he thought was true, which was completely wrong.

A. infallible
B. fallible
C. erroneous
D. fallacious

A. AD   **B.** CD
C. DB   **D.** AC
E. None of these

Q.58 After being such a/an ______________ reader for so long, Althea didn't know what to do with all her books once they were banned from the country.

A. voracious

B. vivacious

C.insatiable

D.insufferable

A. AC   **B.** CD

C. DB   **D.** BA

E. None of these

Ques (59-60):Direction: The following question consists of one blank only. You are given six choices and you have to choose any two of them, either of which will make the sentence meaningful.

Q.59 The devoted fans paid homage and _________ to the late singer by placing flowers on his memorial and by holding candles.

A. Tariffs

B. Retrospection

C. Adoration

D. Affection

E. Disloyalty

F. Inconsistency

A. A and C   **B.** B and D   **C.** C and D   **D.** C and E

E. C and F

Q.60 To prove your theory, you need to design an experiment that will provide _________ and pragmatic evidence.

A. Empirical

B. Genuine

C. Hypothetical

D. Conjectural

E. Lamentable

F. Perfunctory

A. A and B   **B.** B and C   **C.** C and D   **D.** E and F

E. A and F

Numerical Ability

Q.61 A and B started a business investing amounts of ₹ 6000 and ₹ 8000 respectively. If both incurred loss at the end of a year and B's share in loss is ₹ 2000, then what is the total loss incurred?

A. ₹ 3500   **B.** ₹ 3000   **C.** ₹ 2500   **D.** ₹ 2000

E. ₹ 1500

Q.62 Length of rectangular field is 3 times its breadth, if area of the field is 432 m². Find the cost of fencing it at Rs. 2 per metre.

A. 200   **B.** 192   **C.** 165   **D.** 250

E. 175

Ques (63-67):Directions: The line chart given below represent the salary and expenditure (in Rs.) of Rakesh for the given period.

Q.63 In the year 2015, Rakesh invested 50% of his saving in the stock market, where he earned a profit of 300%. What was the profit?

A. 500   **B.** 3000   **C.** 1500   **D.** 780

E. 2000

Q.64 According to a non-government company if a person save at least 27% of his salary in a year that year can be called as "a year of investment". How many years are "a year of investment" during the given period?

A. 5   **B.** 3   **C.** 1   **D.** 7

E. 2

Q.65 Find in which year the percentage increase in the salary of Rakesh was maximum.

A. 2012   **B.** 2013   **C.** 2014   **D.** 2015

E. 2016

Q.66 Find by what percent the salary of Rakesh was increased in 2016 over 2012.

A. 35%   **B.** 230%   **C.** 450%   **D.** 350%

E. 92%

Q.67 Find the compound annual growth rate (CAGR) of the salary of Rakesh during 2011-16. (Given: $9^{\frac{1}{5}} = 1.55$)

A. 55%   **B.** 23%   **C.** 45%   **D.** 88%

E. 92%

Q.68 In how many ways can the letters of word AVERAGE be rearranged so that all the vowels are together and all the consonants are together, but no two same letters are together?

A. 12   **B.** 24   **C.** 36   **D.** 48

E. 60

Q.69 Mike and Mindy can make paintings in 6 days, Mindy and Josh can make those paintings in 10 days. If Mike, Mindy & Josh together can finish the work in 4 days, then Mike & Josh together will do it in how many days?

A. $\frac{2}{15}$ days   **B.** $\frac{7}{30}$ days   **C.** $\frac{8}{17}$ days   **D.** 10 days

E. $\frac{30}{7}$ days

Q.70

A motorboat, whose speed is 15 km/hr in still water goes 30 km downstream and comes back in a total of 4 hours 30 minutes. The speed of the stream (in km/hr) is:

A. 4   **B.** 5   **C.** 6   **D.** 10
E. 12

Q.71 What will come in the place of the question mark '?' in the following question?

$$9.89\% \text{ of } 199.88 + 2.22\% \text{ of } 56499.70 - 4.78\% \text{ of } 7300.2 = ?^2 + 1$$

A. 18   **B.** 20   **C.** 21   **D.** 28
E. 35

Q.72 What will come in the place of the question mark '?' in the following question?

$$(76 \div 0.25 \div 0.3) \times 1.2 \times 1.2 \times 3.6 = ?$$

A. 5253   **B.** 5203   **C.** 5313   **D.** 5103
E. 525

Q.73 What value should come in place of "?" in the following equation:

$$32.98\% \text{ of } 4399.89 - (17.03 \times 22.94) = (?)^2 - (5.03^2 \times 3.97) + 5.01$$

A. 34   **B.** 1156
C. 36   **D.** 32
E. None of these

Q.74 What value should come in place of "?" in the following equation:

$$\left\{(784.03)^{\frac{1}{2}} \times 3.97\right\} + (29.07 \times 12.96) = (?)^2 - (7.92 \times 5.01)$$

A. 529   **B.** 8
C. 24   **D.** 23
E. None of these

Q.75 What value will come in the place of the question mark '?' in the following question:

$$\sqrt{6241} - 34.898 + 2 \times ?^3 - 9.899 = 216 + 504$$

A. 6   **B.** 2401   **C.** 343   **D.** 49
E. 7

Ques (76-80):Direction: What should come in place of the question mark '?' in the following number series?

Q.76 60.5, 72, 84.5, 98, 112.5, ?
A. 125   **B.** 122   **C.** 126   **D.** 128
E. 132

Q.77 10, 18, 8, 20, 6, ?
A. 20   **B.** 22   **C.** 2   **D.** 12
E. 30

Q.78 4, 4, 6, 12, ?, 90
A. 30   **B.** 20   **C.** 40   **D.** 50
E. 70

Q.79 500, 505, 515, 526, 539,?
A. 592   **B.** 544   **C.** 556   **D.** 567
E. 542

Q.80 100, 325, 521, 690, 834, 955, ?

A. 1055   **B.** 1000   **C.** 2000   **D.** 3500
E. 1200

Q.81 Manoj earns a profit of 30% by selling books. What would be the approximate percent change in the profit, if he had paid 20% less and sold at 20% more?
A. 165%   **B.** 251%
C. 195%   **D.** 217%
E. None of these

Q.82 The average temperature in the first three days of a week is 45 degrees and average for the second, third and fourth day is 46 degrees. The temperature on the first day is $93\frac{3}{4}\%$ of the temperature on the fourth day. Find the average temperature on the first and fourth day of the week.
A. 31.0 degrees   **B.** 42.5 degrees
C. 46.5 degrees   **D.** 48.5 degrees
E. 47.5 degrees

Ques (83-85): In the following question, two equations numbered I and II are given. Solve both the equations and give an answer.

Q.83 I. $2x^2 - 17x + 36 = 0$
II. $3y^2 - 4y - 32 = 0$
A. x > y
B. x < y
C. x ≥ y
D. x ≤ y
E. x = y or no relationship could be established.

Q.84 (I). $3x + 5y = 18$
(II). $7x + 8y = 42$
A. if $x < y$
B. If $x \geq y$
C. If $x \leq y$
D. If $x > y$
E. If $x = y$ or no relationship can be established

Q.85 I. $15x^2 - 19x + 6 = 0$
II. $45y^2 - 47y + 12 = 0$
A. x < y
B. x ≤ y
C. x > y
D. x ≥ y
E. x = y or no relationship can be obtained

Q.86 A sum of money was invested for 2 years at the rate of 10% compounded annually. After that, the received amount is invested for another 3 years at rate of 15% simple interest. Finally, the amount becomes Rs. 1, 75, 450. _____ is the initial sum of money that was invested?

[SBI Clerk, 2019]

A. 110000   **B.** 100000   **C.** 140000   **D.** 160000
E. 130000

Q.87 Ram gave 50% of his total saving Rs. 1682 to his wife and distributed the reaming amount between his two sons

Rahul and Ravi. The age of Rahul and Ravi at that time was 18 years and 16 years respectively. He divides the money in such a way that each son when they attain the age of 21 years, would receive the same amount at 5% interest compounded annually. What was the amount given to Ravi?

A. Rs. 541 **B.** Rs. 841 **C.** Rs. 441 **D.** Rs. 400
E. Rs. 141

Q.88 Two integers are selected from the 1st 10 natural numbers. If the sum is even find the probability that both numbers are odd.

A. $\dfrac{1}{2}$ **B.** $\dfrac{3}{5}$

C. $\dfrac{2}{5}$ **D.** $\dfrac{1}{5}$

E. None of these

Q.89 Two pipes A and B can fill a cistern in $37\dfrac{1}{2}$ minutes and 45 minutes respectively. Both pipes are opened. The cistern will be filled in just half an hour, if the B is turned off after:

A. 5 minutes **B.** 9 minutes

C. 10 minutes **D.** 15 minutes

E. 12 minutes

Q.90 Ram's salary 60% more than Shayam's salary. Ram got a raise of 25% on his salary while Shayam got raise of 40% on his salary. Now by what percent is Shayam's salary less than Ram's salary?

A. 35% **B.** 25%

C. 30% **D.** 40%

E. None of these

// Smart Answer Sheet //

Correct — Indicates percentage of students who answered questions correctly.

Skipped — Indicates percentage of students who skipped questions.

Q.	Ans.	Correct / Skipped	Q.	Ans.	Correct / Skipped	Q.	Ans.	Correct / Skipped	Q.	Ans.	Correct / Skipped	Q.	Ans.	Correct / Skipped
1	C	61.19 % / 1.62 %	17	D	28.68 % / 3.45 %	33	D	80.35 % / 0.0 %	49	A	68.57 % / 1.96 %	65	E	56.43 % / 1.34 %
2	D	57.45 % / 1.86 %	18	A	13.97 % / 3.51 %	34	E	55.67 % / 1.96 %	50	D	59.77 % / 1.78 %	66	D	64.04 % / 1.21 %
3	A	66.55 % / 1.53 %	19	B	78.14 % / 0.0 %	35	B	69.21 % / 1.92 %	51	D	46.79 % / 1.28 %	67	A	44.25 % / 1.43 %
4	D	50.07 % / 1.35 %	20	E	87.67 % / 0.0 %	36	A	43.28 % / 1.93 %	52	B	47.37 % / 1.61 %	68	B	80.1 % / 0.0 %
5	B	45.86 % / 1.16 %	21	D	67.77 % / 1.36 %	37	B	81.45 % / 0.0 %	53	E	53.02 % / 1.78 %	69	E	49.2 % / 1.62 %
6	C	87.02 % / 0.0 %	22	C	47.9 % / 1.42 %	38	A	55.79 % / 1.38 %	54	C	44.53 % / 1.45 %	70	B	51.79 % / 1.4 %
7	D	43.26 % / 1.13 %	23	D	62.4 % / 1.81 %	39	A	88.51 % / 0.0 %	55	E	52.67 % / 1.51 %	71	D	67.58 % / 1.95 %
8	B	65.53 % / 1.4 %	24	B	67.92 % / 1.32 %	40	C	56.74 % / 1.59 %	56	D	55.14 % / 1.43 %	72	A	19.21 % / 3.75 %
9	C	85.85 % / 0.0 %	25	B	52.21 % / 1.93 %	41	D	84.52 % / 0.0 %	57	B	59.4 % / 1.22 %	73	A	14.88 % / 4.53 %
10	D	62.67 % / 1.51 %	26	C	53.47 % / 1.45 %	42	C	51.32 % / 1.81 %	58	A	49.87 % / 1.1 %	74	D	43.27 % / 1.85 %
11	E	56.64 % / 1.27 %	27	E	55.76 % / 1.45 %	43	D	67.88 % / 1.23 %	59	C	60.6 % / 1.18 %	75	E	82.11 % / 0.0 %
12	C	51.67 % / 1.53 %	28	D	60.88 % / 1.43 %	44	A	53.18 % / 1.89 %	60	A	51.67 % / 1.47 %	76	D	78.42 % / 0.0 %
13	D	41.55 % / 1.37 %	29	D	43.98 % / 1.16 %	45	A	67.11 % / 1.99 %	61	A	60.19 % / 1.2 %	77	B	59.64 % / 1.83 %
14	A	19.62 % / 3.28 %	30	C	65.59 % / 1.24 %	46	C	42.39 % / 1.18 %	62	B	51.33 % / 1.91 %	78	A	59.24 % / 1.54 %
15	D	28.84 % / 4.16 %	31	C	62.4 % / 1.52 %	47	C	43.1 % / 1.86 %	63	C	54.79 % / 1.06 %	79	C	10.92 % / 3.42 %
16	C	29.34 % / 5.0 %	32	D	63.55 % / 1.39 %	48	E	67.23 % / 1.24 %	64	A	54.24 % / 1.27 %	80	A	44.77 % / 1.07 %

Q.	Ans.	Correct / Skipped
81	D	57.52 %
		1.66 %
82	C	14.08 %
		4.98 %

Q.	Ans.	Correct / Skipped
83	C	65.83 %
		1.89 %
84	D	51.17 %
		1.47 %

Q.	Ans.	Correct / Skipped
85	D	47.87 %
		1.21 %
86	B	89.57 %
		0.0 %

Q.	Ans.	Correct / Skipped
87	D	41.74 %
		1.47 %
88	A	58.11 %
		1.93 %

Q.	Ans.	Correct / Skipped
89	B	64.75 %
		1.89 %
90	C	51.83 %
		1.54 %

Performance Analysis

Avg. Score (%)	28.89%
Toppers Score (%)	57.78%
Your Score	

//Hints and Solutions//

Ques (1-5): Persons: B, H, M, J, O, T, D, and K

1) D is third to the right of B and one of them is sitting at an extreme end of the row.

Case 1:

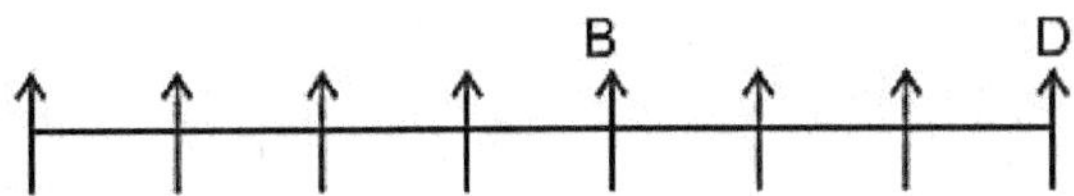

Case 2:

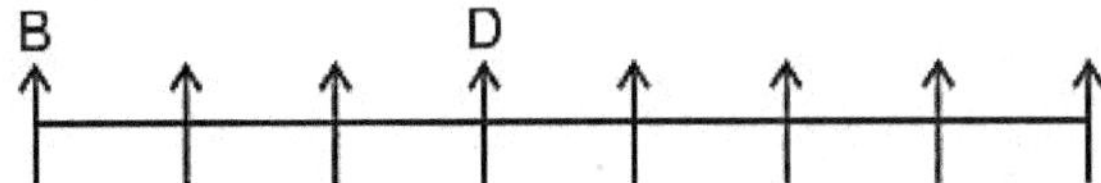

2) There are 2 persons sitting between B and T.

T cannot be placed in case 2. So, Case 2 gets eliminated.

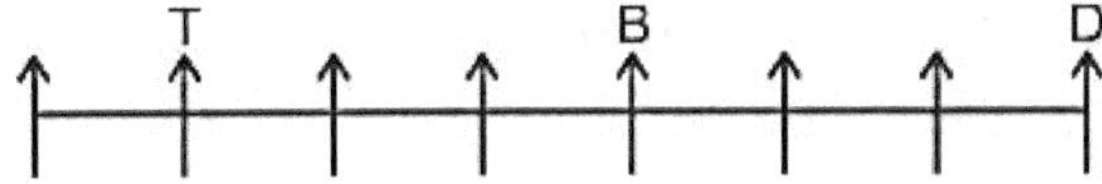

3) J is sitting immediate left of M.

4) J is not an immediate neighbour of B.

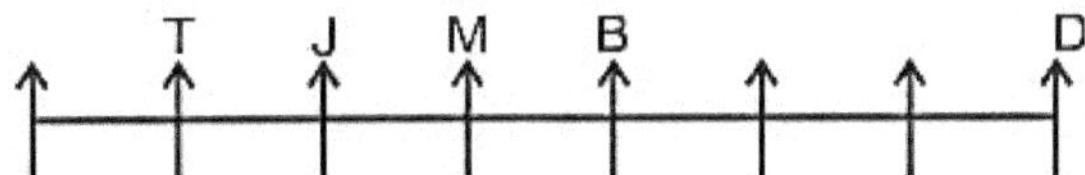

5) One person sits between B and O and that person is not K.

Hence, O is sitting to the immediate left of D and K sits at the extreme left end.

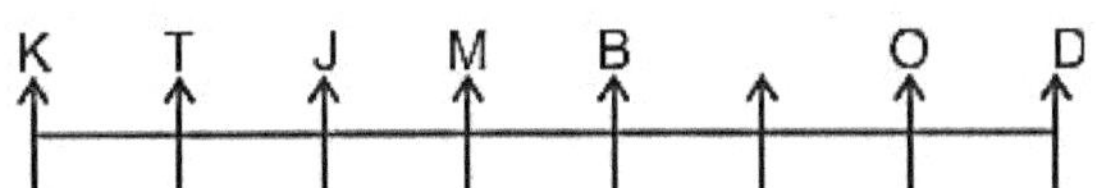

So, H sits at the only place left in the arrangement i.e. between B and O.

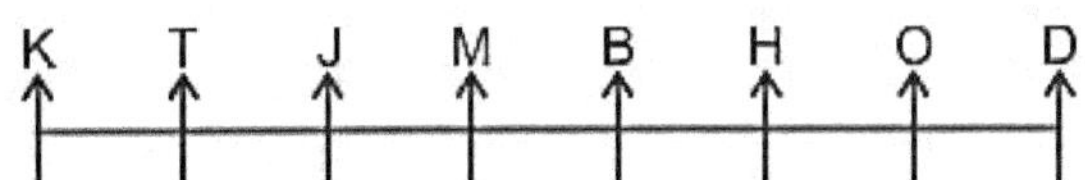

1. So, O is sitting immediate left of D.

Hence, the correct option is (C).

2. So, there are three persons sitting between K and B.

Hence, the correct option is (D).

3. So, O sits third to the right of M.

Hence, the correct option is (A).

4. MH is different from others as there is only one person sitting between M and H whereas in other options two persons are sitting between the persons in pair.

Hence, the correct option is (D).

5. So, if all the persons are asked to sit in alphabetical order from left to right, then O will sit second to the right of K.

Hence, the correct option is (B).

Ques (6-8):

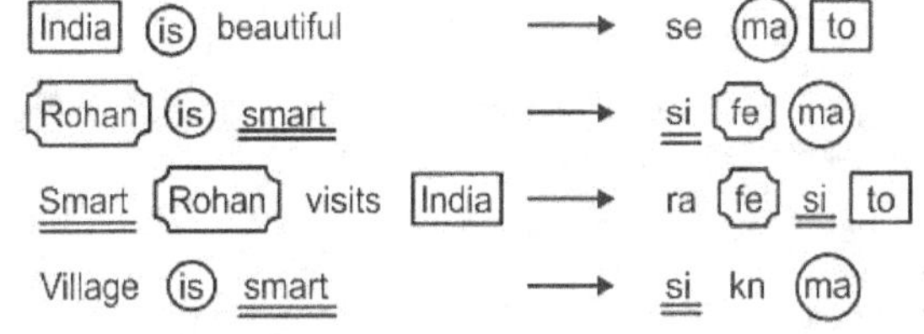

6. So, the code for village is kn.

Hence, the correct option is (C).

7. Code for 'Rohan' is 'fe'

Code for 'is' is 'ma'

Code for 'village' is 'kn'

Possible code for 'going' is 'kr'

So, code for 'Rohan is going village' is 'kn ma fe kr'.

Hence, the correct option is (D).

8. 'kn' stands for 'Village'

'ma' stands for 'is'

'se' stands for 'beautiful'

'to' stands for 'India'

'lk' can possibly stands for 'in'

So, 'kn ma se lk to' means 'Village in India is beautiful'.

Hence, the correct option is (B).

9. Given words: FGT   SDB   TUC   OER   AVY

Arranging letters of words in alphabetical order:

FGT   BDS   CTU   EOR   AVY

Clearly, three words are FGT, BDS and CTU which have consonants as the first letter after rearrangement.

Hence, the correct option is (C).

10. Given words: FGT   SDB   TUC   OER   AVY

Replacing first letters of all words to 3rd succeeding letter:

IGT   VDB   WUC   RER   DVY

Clearly, two words VDB, DVY have no vowel after rearrangement.

Hence, the correct option is (D).

11. Given words: FGT   SDB   TUC   OER   AVY

1) Sum of FGT → 6 + 7 + 20 = 33

2) Sum of SDB → 19 + 4 + 2 = 25

3) Sum of TUC → 20 + 21 + 3 = 44

4) Sum of OER → 15 + 5 + 18 = 38

5) Sum of AVY → 1 + 22 + 25 = 48

So, AVY has maximum sum value.

Hence, the correct option is (E).

12. Given words: FGT   SDB   TUC   OER   AVY

Replacing the middle letter of each word to immediate preceding letter as per alphabetical series:

FFT   SCB   TTC   ODR   AUY

Clearly, three words FFT, SCB and TTC have no vowel after rearrangement.

Hence, the correct option is (C).

13. Given words: FGT   SDB   TUC   OER   AVY

Arranging words as they would appear in a dictionary from left to right:

Left side AVY FGT OER SDB TUC Right side

So, OER is the third from the left side after rearrangement.

Hence, the correct option is (D).

Ques (14-18):People: A, B, C, D, E, and F
Floors: 1 – 6

1. B lives on an even-numbered floor

⇒ This gives us 3 possibilities:

Person	Floor		Person	Floor		Person	Floor
B	6			6			6
	5			5			5
	4		B	4			4
	3			3			3
	2			2		B	2
	1			1			1

2. Only two people live between the floors on which B and F live

Person	Floor		Person	Floor		Person	Floor
B	6			6			6
	5			5		F	5
	4		B	4			4
F	3			3			3
	2			2		B	2
	1		F	1			1

3. D does not live on an odd-numbered floor.

⇒ D lives on an even-numbered floor.
D lives on a floor immediately above the floor on which C lives

Person	Floor		Person	Floor		Person	Floor
B	6		D	6			6
	5		C	5		F	5

	4		B	4		D	4
F	3			3		C	3
D	2			2		B	2
C	1		F	1			1

4. A does not live on a floor that is immediately above or immediately below the floor on which E lives. A does not live on the lowermost floor i.e., floor no. 1.

⇒ In all other possibilities but 3rd A and E will be neighbors. Thus, only possibility 3rd is feasible.
∵ A doesn't live on the 1st floor so he lives on the 6th floor.

Person	Floor
A	6
F	5
D	4
C	3
B	2
E	1

14. Clearly, C and D live on floors between B and F.

Hence, the correct option is (A).

15. Clearly, F lives on floor number 5.

Hence, the correct option is (D).

16. Clearly, E lives on the 1st floor.

Hence, the correct option is (C).

17. ∵ A lives on the topmost floor so no one lives on the floor above him.

Hence, the correct option is (D).

18. Clearly, C lives on the 3rd floor.

Hence, the correct option is (A).

19. The least possible diagram for the given statements is as follows,

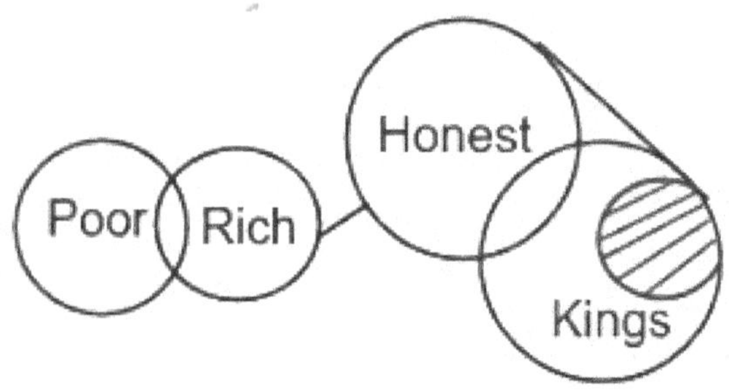

Conclusions:

I. All kings can be honest. → Fales (Only a few kings are honest → some kings are honest and some kings are not honest).

II. Some honest is not rich. → True (No honest is rich → some honest is not rich).

III. All poor is king. → Fales (it is definitely false).

So, only conclusion II follow.

Hence, the correct option is (B).

20. The least possible diagram for the given statements is as follows,

Conclusions:

I. Some Facebook is Insta. → False (it is possible but not definite).

II. Some App is WhatsApp. → False (it is definitely false).

III. Some Insta are WhatsApp. → False (it is possible but not definite).

So, none follow.

Hence, the correct option is (E).

21. The least possible diagram for the given statements is as follows,

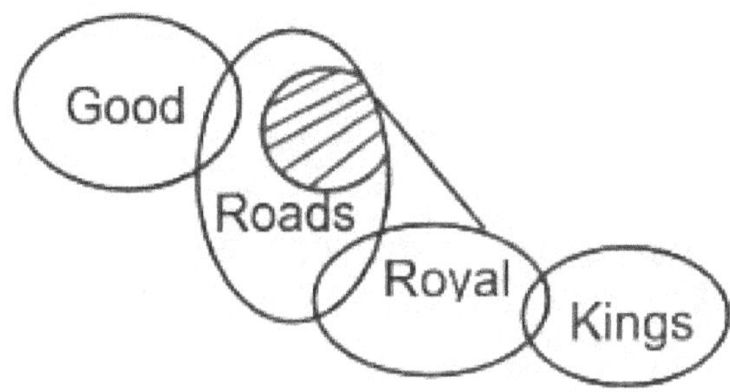

Conclusions:

I. All good can be roads. → True (Possibility is given so it is true).

II. All kings can be royal. → True (Possibility is given so it is true).

III. Some good is roads. → True (it is definitely true).

So, all conclusion are follows.

Hence, the correct option is (D).

22. Using the given information we can create the following figure:

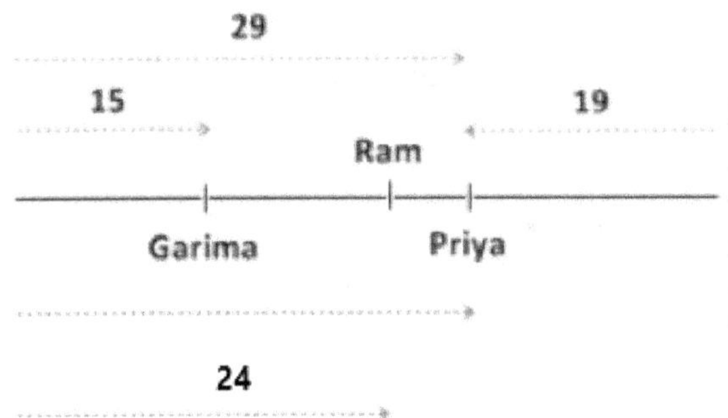

Ram's position from the left end = 24

Priya's position from Ram's position = 5

Priya's position from the left end = Ram's position from the left end + Priya's position from Ram's position

= 24 + 5 = 29

Total number of persons in the queue = [Position of Priya from right + Position of Priya from left] - 1

= (29 + 19 - 1) = 47

Hence, the correct option is (C).

23. Here, we know that Vikram was ninth from the left while Hariom was thirteenth from the left. So, we can say that there were 3 persons between Vikram and Hariom.

And, we also know that Hariom was exactly in the middle of Vikram and Janhvi so the number of persons between Hariom and Janhvi will also be 3.

At this point, using the given information we can create the following figure:

8 Persons	3 Persons	3 Persons	7 Persons
Vikram	Hariom	Janhvi	

Now, total number of people in the queue = (8 + Vikram + 3 + Hariom + 3 + Janhvi + 7)

= (8 + 1 + 3 + 1 + 3 + 1 + 7) = 24

Thus, the total number of people in the queue was 24.

Hence, the correct option is (D).

24. By the given information,

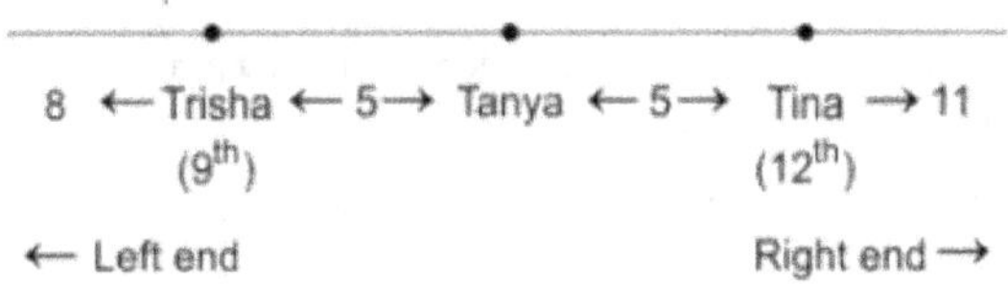

Adding all the persons in the above image, we get

8 + 1(Trisha) + 5 + 1(Tanya) + 5 + 1(Tina) + 11 = 32

Thus there are 32 cadets in the row.

Hence, the correct option is (B).

Ques (25-27):

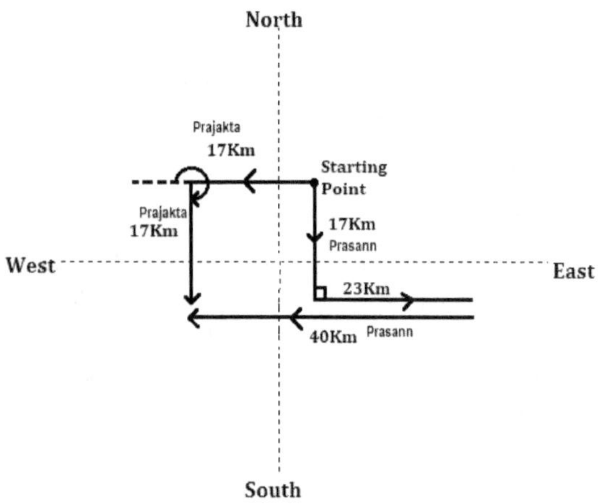

25. Prasann travelled = 17 km + 23 km + 40 km

= 80 km

So,Prasann travelled 80 km.

Hence, the correct option is (B).

26. So, Prajakta is in South West direction with respect to Prasann's initial position.

Hence, the correct option is (C).

27. Distance travelled by Prasann = 17 km + 23 km + 40 km = 80 km

Distance travelled by Prajakta = 17 km + 17 km = 34 km

So, the difference between the distance covered by Prajakta and Prasann is 80 km – 34 km = 46 km.

Hence, the correct option is (E).

28. The given word:

SEPTUAGENARIAN

Applying the above condition, we have a new word:

PESAUTAAEGINNR

Now final arrangements of the old and new words are:

S	E	P	T	U	A	G	E	N	A	R	I	A	N
P	E	S	A	U	T	A	A	E	G	I	N	N	R

So clearly, except E and U the positions of all other 12 letters get changed in the new arrangement.
Hence, the correct option is (D).

Ques (29-30): Let us first decode the given symbols and then draw a family tree.

P is				
Symbol	#	%	*	$
Meaning	Son	Father	Sister	Wife
Of Q				

29. Let us first decode the given symbols and then draw a family tree.

P is				
Symbol	#	%	*	$
Meaning	Son	Father	Sister	Wife
Of Q				

Using option (A):

'X * Y % K' means X is the sister of Y, Y is the father of K.

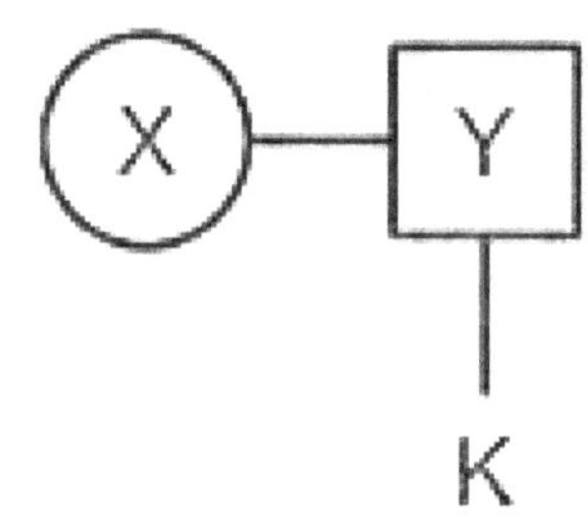

But, here X is the sister of Y.

So, this statement does not follow.

Using option (B):

'Y # K % X' means Y is the son of K, K is the father of X.

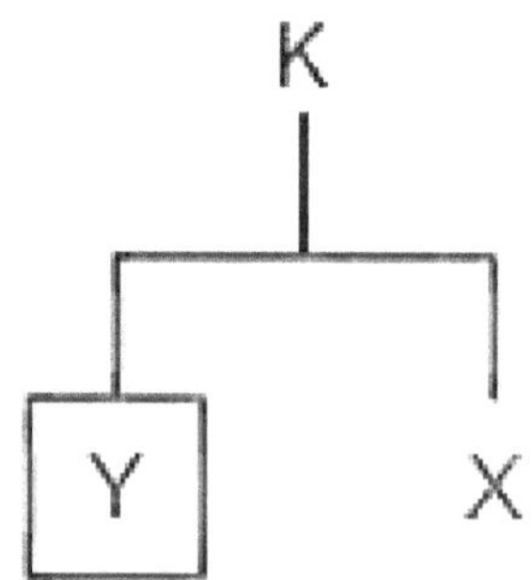

But, here the gender of X is not defined.

So, this statement does not follow.

Using option (C):

'Y * K % X' means Y is the sister of K, K is the father of X.

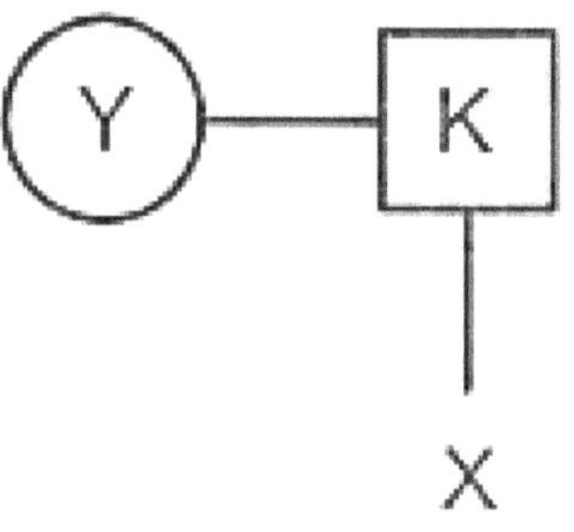

But, here the gender of X is not defined.

So, this statement does not follow.

Using option (D):

'Y * X % K' means Y is the sister of X, X is the father of K.

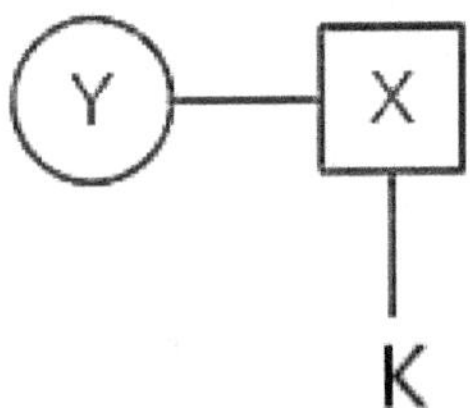

Clearly in this statement X is the brother of Y.

Thus, the correct statement is 'Y * X % K'

Hence, the correct option is (D).

30. 'Y * X # F % L' means Y is the sister of X, X is the son of F, F is the father of L.

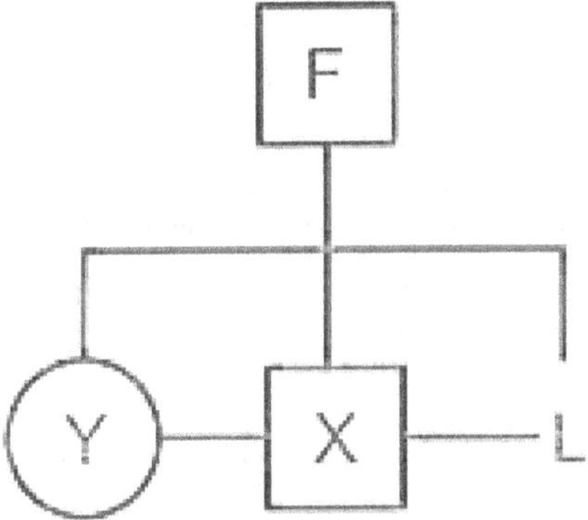

Thus, Y is the sister of L.

Hence, the correct option is (C).

31. It is mentioned that the world's population is increasing mainly due to medical advancements and increases in agricultural productivity. There is no mention of improving the economy as the cause of increasing population.

Hence, the correct option is (C).

32. It is mentioned that economic inequality leads to poverty, lack of free medical assistance, lack of social security, and bad living conditions. High infant and child mortality rates and hunger due to extreme poverty are some of the results of over-population. So, both options (A) and (C) are correct.

Hence, the correct option is (D).

33. It is mentioned that automation threatens 69 percent job losses with millions of job losses already occurring in the IT and production sectors. So,only option (A) and (B) are correct.

Hence, the correct option is (D).

34. It is mentioned that The consequences of population growth are a problem that the whole world will soon face sooner or later. Drinking water, sewage treatment, inadequate rainfall, rapid depletion of natural resources, extinction of many plant and animal species due to deforestation and loss of ecosystems, increased level of life-threatening air and water pollution, high infant and child mortality rate and hunger due to extreme poverty are some of the results of over-population.

Hence, the correct option is (E).

35. It is mentioned that overpopulation can only be solved by spreading awareness of and implementing measures like birth control and access to birth control devices. Economic equality may not solve the problem of overpopulation.

Hence, the correct option is (B).

36. According to the rule of subject-verb agreement, whenever we use the singular subject we have to use the singular verb with it.

In the given sentence, the subject of the sentence is 'Event'. 'The' is the definite article 'most' is a superlative degree and 'exciting' is a present participle which is used to describe 'event'. 'in the Sydney Olympics' is the prepositional phrase hence because of it there will be no effect on the verb. Also 'For most British viewers' is a prepositional phrase and 'the rowing finals' is the object of the sentence.

Correct sentence: The most exciting event in the Sydney Olympics for most British viewers was the rowing finals.

Hence, the correct option is (A).

37. According to grammar, We can use adverbs with 'so, as, too, enough' and when we use so...that co-relative pair of conjunction in this 'that' is used as a conjunction and So...as in this pair 'as' is used as a pronoun.

Hence, in the given sentence, we don't want a pronoun we need a conjunction to join the main clause with the subordinate clause.

There are two clauses because there two verbs which are 'performed' and 'overlooked' the latter one is used for the subject 'judges'.

Correct sentence: She performed so enthusiastically that the judges overlooked her inexperience.

Hence, the correct option is (B).

38. According to grammar, to describe how a change in one thing causes a change in another, we can use two comparative forms with the definite article 'the'.

Correct sentence: The more sophisticated the product, The more substantial the potential profit.

Hence, the correct option is (A).

39. According to grammar, The verbs advise, allow forbid and permit are followed by a gerund when they have no object but when they have the object we have to use an infinitive.

The concept behind it is→ the verbs given are transitive verbs hence after these verbs we have to write an object the object can only be a noun/pronoun/gerund. Whenever we don't have an object after these verbs then, write a gerund to make an object, and whenever an object is written write an infinitive, and the verb, which is written with the preposition 'to' i.e. 'to + v1', is written for the object of the main verb.

Correct sentence: The doctor advised him to take a course of antibiotics.

Hence, the correct option is (A).

40. According to grammar, "wish/if only + would + V1 "usually expresses a desire for someone to change their deliberate behavior in the present or future.

Only if⇒ used for condition whereas If only⇒ used for the wish/imaginary statement.

In the given sentence, 'if only' should be used because in the other part sentence we can say that the sentence is the imaginary one.

Correct sentence: If only the sun would come out so we could get on with the filming.

Hence, the correct option is (C).

41. The complete sentence is: He **always speaks** very little when there are strangers present.

The given sentence is in the simple present tense. We use the simple present tense when an action is happening right now or when it happens regularly or unceasingly.

In the simple present tense, most regular verbs use the root form, except in the third-person singular (which ends in -s).

Hence, the correct option is (D).

42. The given sentence has one error, which lies in part B.

The part B uses the verb 'are leveraged', which is incorrect. Since it is used with the verb 'are', it should be in its progressive form 'leveraging'.

So, the errorless combination is ACD.

Hence, the correct option is (C).

43. The given sentence has one error, which lies in part B.

The part B uses the preposition 'of' (expressing the relation between two things). This is incorrect here, given the context.

The correct adverb/preposition here should be 'off'' (meaning removing or separating), which makes the phrase 'calling off' or canceling.

So, the errorless combination is ACD.

Hence, the correct option is (D).

44. The given sentence has one error, which lies in part C.

The part C uses the past participle form of the verb 'undertaken', which is incorrect here. Since the previous verb is 'to intervene', it must also be in the form 'undertake'.

So, the errorless combination is ABD.

Hence, the correct option is (A).

45. The error lies in parts B and D.

Part B uses the progressive verb form 'leaving', which is incorrect. As the sentence suggests that it is the main verb, it should be either 'leave' or 'left'.

Part D uses the preposition 'in', which is incorrect. The correct preposition should be- to walk 'on' the sidewalks.

Hence, the correct option is (A).

46. The error lies in parts A and C.

Part A uses the determiner 'this' (meaning a thing just referred), which is incorrect. It could be the adverb 'thus' (meaning so, to this point).

Part C uses the preposition 'for', which is incorrect. The correct preposition could be 'on' the streets.

Hence, the correct option is (C).

47. 'Scattered' means 'covering a wide area' and is the appropriate choice.

The meanings of the given words:-

Stumbled - Trip or momentarily lose one's balance; almost fall.

Littered - Make (a place or area) untidy with rubbish or a large number of objects left lying about.

Entrenched - (Adj.) (of an attitude, habit, or belief) firmly established and difficult or unlikely to change; ingrained.

Squandered - (Verb) waste (something, especially money or time) in a reckless and foolish manner.

Hence, the correct option is (C).

48. 'Bumper' means 'exceptionally large, fine, or successful' and is the appropriate choice.

Inflated - distended through being filled with air or gas.

Piddling - pathetically trivial; trifling.

Flush - (of a person's skin, face, etc.) become red and hot, typically as the result of illness or strong emotion.

Squat - Crouch or sit with one's knees bent and one's heels close to or touching one's buttocks or the back of one's thighs.

Hence, the correct option is (E).

49. It is mentioned that 'California's fertile Central Valley, home to 80% of the world's almond supply'. This implies that honey production provides fewer returns than what is obtained by almond pollination. Thus, 'less lucrative' is the appropriate phrase.

The meanings of the other given words:-

More expected - To anticipate or look forward to the coming or occurrence of we expect them any minute now expected a telephone call.

Little dicey - Starting a business can be quite a dicey proposition.

More lucrative - It is something that can lead to a lot of profit or wealth or that has led to a great deal of profit or wealth.

Less dicey - Something that is dicey is slightly dangerous or uncertain.

Hence, the correct option is (A).

50. To wipe out something such as a place or a group of people or animals means to destroy them completely.

The meanings of the given words:-

Manipulated - handle or control (a tool, mechanism, information, etc.) in a skilful manner.

Cautioned against - to warn somebody about the possible dangers or problems of something.

Wreaked - cause (a large amount of damage or harm).

Looked after - to take care of someone or something and make certain that they have everything they need.

Hence, the correct option is (D).

51. 'Attributed' means 'to say or think that something is the result of a particular thing' and is the appropriate choice.

The meanings of the given words:-

Heartened - make more cheerful or confident.

Coupled - linked or connected in a pair or pairs.

Directed - control the operations of manage or govern.

Counselled - give professional help and advice to (someone) to resolve personal or psychological problems.

Hence, the correct option is (D).

52. The underlined part must be replaced with 'managed to succeed' to make it a grammatically correct sentence.

Because here the sentence is talking about achieving the goal, therefore a verb should be used here. Since 'success' is an uncountable noun it should be replaced by succeed which means 'to attain a goal'.

Thus, the correct sentence is:

After a great deal of effort, she finally managed to succeed in her venture.

Hence, the correct option is (B).

53. No correction is required.

So, the given sentence is grammatically correct- As she bought quite a number of books she got a heavy discount.

Hence, the correct option is (E).

54. Use of 'steamer' which means 'a ship that has an engine powered by' is erroneous in the context and must be replaced with the adjective 'steaming' which means 'very hot' to make it a grammatically correct sentence.

Hence, the correct option is (C).

55. No correction is required.

So, the given sentence is grammatically correct- Tired of being harassed by the goons, I finally called the police and complained.

Hence, the correct option is (E).

56. The underlined part must be replaced with 'basic laws of' to make it a grammatically correct sentence.

Base: A position or thing that is a base for something is one from which that thing can be developed or achieved.

Basic: You use basic to describe things, activities, and principles that are very important or necessary, and on which others depend.

Hence, the correct option is (D).

57. The correct answer is option (B), -CD.

To be **infallible** means to be incapable of being able to make a mistake.

To be **fallible** means to be capable of being able to make mistakes or being wrong.

To be **erroneous** means to be wrong or incorrect.

To be **fallacious** means to be based on a mistaken belief.

Thus, the correct answer is option (B), -CD- fallacious and erroneous.

Hence, the correct option is (B).

58. The correct answer is option (A) -AC.

To be **voracious** means to want or devour great quantities of something.

To be **vivacious** means to be full of life, lively and enthusiastic.

To be **insatiable** means to be impossible to satisfy.

To be **insufferable** means to be impossible to tolerate, to be impossible to bear.

Thus, the correct answer is option (A), -AC - voracious and insatiable.

Hence, the correct option is (A).

59. The correct answer is option (C).

The blank is preceded by the conjunction 'and' and the word is 'homage'. This means that a word which has a meaning similar to 'homage' must be used.

'Homage' means 'special honour or respect shown publicly'.

Both 'adoration' and 'affection' are the synonyms of the word 'homage'.

Let us look at the meanings of the other words.

Tariff- A tax levied on a good imported into a country

Retrospection- the act of looking back on or reviewing past events or situations, especially those in one's own life.

Disloyalty and Inconsistency are antonyms of the word 'homage'.

Hence, the correct option is (C).

60. The blank is succeeded by the conjunction 'and' and the word is 'pragmatic'. This means that a word which has a meaning similar to 'pragmatic' must be used.

'Pragmatic' means something that is practical. Both 'empirical' and 'genuine' are the synonyms of the word 'pragmatic'.

Let us look at the meanings of the other words.

'Hypothetical' means something based on a supposition. 'Conjectural' is the synonym of 'hypothesis'.

Lamentable – very bad; deplorable.

Perfunctory - carried out without real interest, feeling, or effort.

Hence, the correct option is (A).

61. Given:

Investment of A = ₹ 6000

Investment of B = ₹ 8000

Profit share of B = ₹ 2000

We know that,

Loss = Investment × Time period

Let loss share of A = x

$$\frac{(Investment\ of\ A)}{(Investment\ of\ B)} = \frac{(Loss\ of\ A)}{(Loss\ of\ B)}$$

$$\frac{6000}{8000} = \frac{x}{2000}$$

$$\Rightarrow x = \frac{(6000 \times 2000)}{8000}$$

$$\Rightarrow x = 1500$$

Total loss = 2000 + 1500 = 3500

∴ Total loss incurred is ₹ 3500.

Hence, the correct option is (A).

62. Given:

Area of the field is 432 m².

Let breadth of the field be x.

Then length will be 3x.

Area = Length × Breadth

$$\Rightarrow 3x \times x = 432$$

$$\Rightarrow 3x^2 = 432$$

$$\Rightarrow x^2 = 144$$

$$\Rightarrow x = 12$$

Length = 3x = 3 × 12 = 36 m and Breadth = x = 12 m.

Length of fencing = Perimeter of the field.

Perimeter = 2(Length + Breadth) = 2(36 + 12) = 96 m.

Rate of fencing is Rs. 2 per m.

Total Cost of fencing = 96 × 2 = Rs. 192.

∴ The cost of fencing is Rs. 192.

Hence, the correct option is (B).

63. Salary in 2015 = Rs. 3000

Expenditure in 2015 = Rs. 2000

Saving = 3000 – 2000 = Rs. 1000

Investment in stock market = $\dfrac{1000}{2}$ = Rs. 500

Profit = 300% of 500 = Rs. 1500

Hence, the correct option is (E).

64. Saving rate = $\dfrac{(Salary - Expenditure)}{Salary} \times 100$

Saving rate for 2011 = $\dfrac{(1000 - 500)}{1000} \times 100 = 50\%$

Saving rate for 2012 = $\dfrac{(2000 - 1500)}{2000} \times 100 = 25\%$

Saving rate for 2013 = $\dfrac{(2500 - 1500)}{2500} \times 100 = 40\%$

Saving rate for 2014 = $\dfrac{(4000 - 2500)}{4000} \times 100 = 37.5\%$

Saving rate for 2015 = $\dfrac{(3000 - 2000)}{3000} \times 100 = 33.33\%$

Saving rate for 2016 = $\dfrac{(9000 - 4500)}{9000} \times 100 = 50\%$

∴ 5 years are a year of investment.

Hence, the correct option is (A).

65. Percentage increase in 2012 = $\dfrac{(2000 - 1000)}{1000} \times 100 = 100\%$

Percentage increase in 2013 = $\dfrac{(2500 - 2000)}{2000} \times 100 = 25\%$

Percentage increase in 2014 = $\dfrac{(4000 - 2500)}{2500} \times 100 = 60\%$

Percentage increase in 2015 = $\dfrac{(3000 - 4000)}{4000} \times 100 = -25\%$

Percentage increase in 2016 = $\dfrac{(9000 - 3000)}{3000} \times 100 = 200\%$

∴ In 2016 the percentage increase in the salary of Mohan was maximum.

Hence, the correct option is (E).

66. Salary in 2012 = Rs. 2000

Salary in 2016 = Rs. 9000

∴ Required increase = $\dfrac{(9000 - 2000)}{2000} \times 100 = 350\%$

Hence, the correct option is (D).

67. Salary in 2011 = Rs. 1000

Salary in 2016 = Rs. 9000

Time period = 5 years

CAGR for period 2011-16 = $\left(\dfrac{Ending\ Salary}{Beginning\ Salary} \right)^{\frac{1}{n}} - 1$

$$\Rightarrow \left[\left(\frac{9000}{1000}\right)^{\frac{1}{5}} - 1\right] \times 100 = 55\%$$

Hence, the correct option is (A).

68. Vowels in word AVERAGE = A, A, E and E

Consonants in word AVERAGE = V, R and G

If all vowels are together and all consonants are together, then either all vowels come and then all consonants come, or vice versa.

All vowels can come together such that no two same letters are together in these ways; AEAE or EAEA.

Three different consonants can come together in 3!, i.e., 6 ways.

∴ Total number of ways = 2 × 2 × 6 = 24

Hence, the correct option is (B).

69. Given:

Mike and Mindy's 1 day work = $\dfrac{1}{6}$

Mindy and Josh's 1 day work = $\dfrac{1}{10}$

Mike, Mindy and Josh's 1 day work = $\dfrac{1}{4}$

So, Mike and Josh's 1 day work = 2 × (Mike, Mindy and Josh's 1 day work) - (Mike and Mindy's 1 day work) - (Mindy and Josh's 1 day work)

$$\Rightarrow 2 \times \left(\frac{1}{4}\right) - \left(\frac{1}{6}\right) - \left(\frac{1}{10}\right)$$

$$\Rightarrow \frac{15-5-3}{30} = \frac{7}{30}$$

∴ Time taken by Mike and Josh to complete the painting

$$= \frac{1}{\left(\frac{7}{30}\right)} = \frac{30}{7} \text{ days.}$$

Hence, the correct option is (E).

70. Given,

Speed of motorboat in still water = 15 km/hr

Distance covered by motorboat in downstream = 30 km

Let the speed of the stream be x km/hr.

Then, Speed in downstream = (15 + x) km/hr.

Speed in upstream = (15 - x) km/hr.

Therefore,

$$\frac{30}{(15+x)} + \frac{30}{(15-x)} = 4\frac{1}{2}$$

$$\Rightarrow \frac{30\times(15-x)+30\times(15+x)}{(15+x)\times(15-x)} = \frac{9}{2}$$

$$\Rightarrow \frac{900}{225-x^2} = \frac{9}{2}$$

$$\Rightarrow 2025 - 9x^2 = 1800$$

$$\Rightarrow -9x^2 = 1800 - 2025$$

$$\Rightarrow -9x^2 = -225$$

$$\Rightarrow 9x^2 = 225$$

$$\Rightarrow x^2 = 25$$

$$\Rightarrow x = 5 \text{ km/hr}$$

Hence, the correct option is (B).

71. Follow the BODMAS rule according to the table given below:

B	Brackets in order (), {}, []	ब्रेकट (), {}, [] क्रम
O	Of	का
D	Division (÷)	विभाजन (÷)
M	Multiplication (×)	गुणा (×)
A	Addition (+)	जोड़ (+)
s	Subtraction (-)	घटाव (-)

In approximation we do not require to find the exact value of the expression but an approximate value through near rounding of.

$$9.89\% \text{ of } 199.88 + 2.22\% \text{ of } 56499.70 - 4.78\% \text{ of } 7300.2 =?^2 + 1$$

$$\Rightarrow 10\% \text{ of } 200 + 2\% \text{ of } 56500 - 5\% \text{ of } 7300 = ?^2 + 1$$

$$\Rightarrow 20 + 1130 - 365 =?^2 + 1$$

$$\Rightarrow 1150 - 365 =?^2 + 1$$

$$\Rightarrow 785 - 1 =?^2$$

$$\Rightarrow 784 =?^2$$

$$\Rightarrow \sqrt{784} =?^2$$

$$\Rightarrow 28 =?$$

∴ The value of $?$ is 28.

Hence, the correct option is (D).

72. Follow the BODMAS rule according to the table given below:

B	Brackets in order ( ), { }, [ ]	ब्रेकट ( ), { }, [ ] क्रम
O	Of	का
D	Division (÷)	विभाजन (÷)
M	Multiplication (×)	गुणा (×)
A	Addition (+)	जोड़ (+)
S	Subtraction (-)	घटाव (-)

In approximation we do not require to find the exact value of the expression but an approximate value through near rounding of.

$$(76 \div 0.25 \div 0.3) \times 1.2 \times 1.2 \times 3.6 =?$$

$$\Rightarrow \left[76 \times \left(\frac{1}{0.25}\right) \times \left(\frac{10}{3}\right)\right] \times 1.2 \times 1.2 \times 3.6 =?$$

$$\Rightarrow \left[76 \times 4 \times \left(\frac{10}{3}\right)\right] \times 1.2 \times 1.2 \times 3.6 =?$$

$\Rightarrow \dfrac{[76\times4\times12\times12\times36\times10]}{[3\times10\times10\times10]}=?$

$\Rightarrow \dfrac{[76\times4\times4\times12\times36]}{[10\times10]}=?$

$\Rightarrow \dfrac{525312}{100}=?$

$\Rightarrow? \approx 5253$

$\therefore$ In the place of ' $?$ ' the value is 5253.

Hence, the correct option is (A).

73. Follow the BODMAS rule according to the table given below:

B	Brackets in order ( ), { }, [ ]	ब्रेकट ( ), { }, [ ] क्रम
O	Of	का
D	Division (÷)	विभाजन (÷)
M	Multiplication (×)	गुणा (×)
A	Addition (+)	जोड़ (+)
S	Subtraction (-)	घटाव (-)

In approximation we do not require to find the exact value of the expression but an approximate value through near rounding of.

$33\% \text{ of } 4400 - (17 \times 23) = (?)^2 - (5^2 \times 4) + 5$

$\Rightarrow 33\% \text{ of } 4400 - (17 \times 23) = (?)^2 - (25 \times 4) + 5$

$\Rightarrow 33\% \text{ of } 4400 - 391 = (?)^2 - 100 + 5$

$\Rightarrow 1452 - 391 = (?)^2 - 95$

$\Rightarrow 1452 + 95 - 391 = (?)^2$

$\Rightarrow 1547 - 391 = (?)^2$

$\Rightarrow (?)^2 = 1156$

$\therefore? = 34$

Hence, the correct option is (A).

74. Follow the BODMAS rule according to the table given below:

B	Brackets in order ( ), { }, [ ]	ब्रेकट ( ), { }, [ ] क्रम
O	Of	का
D	Division (÷)	विभाजन (÷)
M	Multiplication (×)	गुणा (×)
A	Addition (+)	जोड़ (+)
S	Subtraction (-)	घटाव (-)

In approximation we do not require to find the exact value of the expression but an approximate value through near rounding of.

$\left\{(784)^{\frac{1}{2}} \times 4\right\} + (29 \times 13) = (?)^2 - (8 \times 5)$

$\Rightarrow \{28 \times 4\} + (29 \times 13) = (?)^2 - (8 \times 5)$

$\Rightarrow \{28 \times 4\} + 377 = (?)^2 - 40$

$\Rightarrow 112 + 377 = (?)^2 - 40$

$\Rightarrow 489 = (?)^2 - 40$

$\Rightarrow (?)^2 = 489 + 40$

$\Rightarrow (?)^2 = 529$

$\therefore? = 23$

Hence, the correct option is (D).

75. Follow the BODMAS rule according to the table given below:

B	Brackets in order ( ), { }, [ ]	ब्रेकट ( ), { }, [ ] क्रम
O	Of	का
D	Division (÷)	विभाजन (÷)
M	Multiplication (×)	गुणा (×)
A	Addition (+)	जोड़ (+)
S	Subtraction (-)	घटाव (-)

In approximation we do not require to find the exact value of the expression but an approximate value through near rounding of.

$\sqrt{6241} - 34.898 + 2 \times ?^3 - 9.899 = 216 + 504$

$\Rightarrow 79 - 35 + 2 \times ?^3 - 10 = 216 + 504$

$\Rightarrow 79 - 45 + 2 \times ?^3 = 216 + 504$

$\Rightarrow 34 + 2 \times ?^3 = 720$

$\Rightarrow 2 \times ?^3 = 720 - 34 = 686$

$\Rightarrow ?^3 = \dfrac{686}{2} = 343$

$\Rightarrow? = 7$

Hence, the correct option is (E).

76. The pattern is as follows:

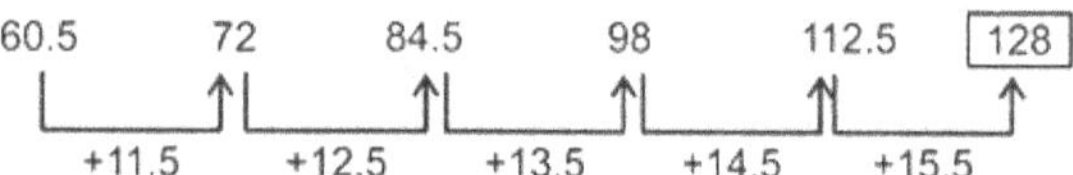

$\therefore$ The value of ? is 128.

Hence, the correct option is (D).

77. The pattern is as follows:

10 + 8 = 18

18 - 10 = 8

8 + 12 = 20

20 - 14 = 6

6 + 16 = 22

$\therefore$ The value of ? is 22.

Hence, the correct option is (B).

78. The pattern is as follows:

4 × 1 = 4

4 × 1.5 = 6

6 × 2 = 12

12 × 2.5 = 30

30 × 3 = 90

∴ The value of ? is 30.

Hence, the correct option is (A).

79. The pattern is as follows:

Next term in the series is obtain by adding the sum of digits to that number.

500 + 5 = 505   (∵ 5 + 0 + 0 = 5)

505 + 10 = 515   (∵ 5 + 0 + 5 = 10)

515 + 11 = 526   (∵ 5 + 1 + 5 = 11)

526 + 13 = 539   (∵ 5 + 2 + 6 = 13)

539 + 17 = 556   (∵ 5 + 3 + 9 = 17)

∴ The value of ? is 556.

Hence, the correct option is (C).

80. The pattern is as follows:

$100 + 15^2 = 325$

$325 + 14^2 = 521$

$521 + 13^2 = 690$

$690 + 12^2 = 834$

$834 + 11^2 = 955$

$955 + 10^2 = 1055$

∴ The value of ? is 1055.

Hence, the correct option is (A).

81. Given,

Original profit = 30%

Let the original Cost Price = Rs. 100

∴ Selling Price = Rs. 130

Now, New Cost Price = Rs. 80

And New Selling Price = 120% of 130 = Rs. 156

∴ New Profit % = $\dfrac{76}{80}$ × 100 = 95%

∴ % change in profit percent = $\dfrac{(95 - 30)}{30}$ × 100

= $\dfrac{65}{30}$ × 100 = 216.66% (approx.)

Hence, the correct option is (D).

82. Average = $\dfrac{sum\ of\ elements}{number\ of\ elements}$

Given,

Let the temperature on the first, second, third and fourth day be a, b, c and d degrees respectively.

The average temperature in the first three days of a week is 45 degrees

$\Rightarrow \dfrac{(a + b + c)}{3} = 45$

⇒ (a + b + c) = 135

⇒ (b + c) = 135 - a

The average for the second, third and fourth day is 46 degrees,

$\Rightarrow \dfrac{(b + c + d)}{3} = 46$

⇒ (b + c + d) = 138

⇒ (135 - a + d) = 138

⇒ d - a = 3

Given,

The temperature on the first day is 93 $\dfrac{3}{4}$% of the temperature on the fourth day.

$\Rightarrow a = \left(\dfrac{375}{4}\right) \times \left(\dfrac{1}{100}\right) \times d$

$\Rightarrow a = \dfrac{15d}{16}$

$\Rightarrow d - \dfrac{15d}{16} = 3$

$\Rightarrow \dfrac{d}{16} = 3$

⇒ d = 48

Temperature on the fourth day is 48 degree

Temperature on the first day = a = $\dfrac{15d}{16} = \dfrac{(15 \times 48)}{16} = 45$ degree

The average temperature on the first and fourth day of the week

=

= $\dfrac{(45 + 48)}{2}$

= $\dfrac{93}{2}$ = 46.5

The average temperature on the first and fourth day of the week is 46.5 degrees.

Hence, the correct option is (C).

83. Given

I. $2x^2 - 17x + 36 = 0$

$\Rightarrow 2x^2 - 8x - 9x + 36 = 0$

$\Rightarrow 2x(x - 4) - 9(x - 4) = 0$

$\Rightarrow (x - 4)(2x - 9) = 0$

$\therefore$ x = 4 or $\dfrac{9}{2}$

II. $3y^2$ - 4y - 32 = 0

$\Rightarrow 3y^2$ - 12y + 8y - 32 = 0

$\Rightarrow$ 3y(y - 4) + 8(y - 4) = 0

$\Rightarrow$ (y - 4) (3y + 8) = 0

$\therefore$ y = 4 or $\dfrac{-8}{3}$

$\Rightarrow$ So, when x = 4, for y = 4 or $\dfrac{-8}{3}$

$\Rightarrow$ And when x = $\dfrac{9}{2}$, for y = 4 or $\dfrac{-8}{3}$

$\therefore$ We can observe that x $\geq$ y

Hence, the correct option is (C).

84. (I) $3x + 5y = 18$

(II) $7x + 8y = 42$

Multiple (I) $\times$ 7 and (II) $\times$ 3

$21x + 35y = 126$

$21x + 24y = 126$

On solving above equations, we get,

$y = 0$

$x = 6$

So, $x > y$

Hence, the correct option is (D).

85. Here,

$\Rightarrow$ P(x) = $15x^2$ - 19x + 6 = 0

$\Rightarrow$ P(y) = $45y^2$ - 47y + 12 = 0

Factorization of P(x) and P(y);

$\Rightarrow$ P(x) = $15x^2$ - 10x - 9x + 6 = 0

$\Rightarrow$ 5x(3x - 2) - 3(3x - 2) = 0

$\Rightarrow$ (3x - 2) (5x - 3) = 0

$\Rightarrow$ x = $\dfrac{2}{3}$ or x = $\dfrac{3}{5}$

$\Rightarrow$ P(y) = $45y^2$ - 27y - 20y + 12 = 0

$\Rightarrow$ 9y(5y - 3) - 4(5y - 3) = 0

$\Rightarrow$ (5y - 3)(9y - 4) = 0

$\Rightarrow$ y = $\dfrac{3}{5}$ or y = $\dfrac{4}{9}$

Here, either value of x and y matches or x is greater than y

Hence, the correct option is (D).

86. Let the initial sum of money be Rs 'x'

Amount after gaining Compound interest = $x\left(\dfrac{1+10}{100}\right)^2$ = Rs 1.21x

Amount after gaining Simple interest = 1.21x

$+ \dfrac{(1.21x \times 3 \times 15)}{100}$ = Rs 1.7545x

Given,

1.7545x = 175450

$\Rightarrow$ x = 1, 00,000

Hence, the correct option is (B).

87. Share of wife $= 50\%$ of 1682 Rs.

$= $ Rs. 841

Rahul $=$ Rs. x

Ravi $=$ Rs. $(841 - x)$

According to question:

$$x\left(1 + \dfrac{5}{100}\right)^3 = (841 - x)\left(1 + \dfrac{5}{100}\right)^5$$

$$\Rightarrow x = 441$$

Ravi share $= 841 - 441 = $ Rs. 400

Hence, the correct option is (D).

88. Let A be the event that both numbers are odd

Let B be the event that the sum is even

$$P\left(\dfrac{A}{B}\right) = \dfrac{P(A \cap B)}{P(B)}$$

Odd + odd = even

Odd + even = odd

Even + even = even

$P(A \cap B) = \dfrac{^5C_2}{^{10}C_2} = \dfrac{2}{9}$

$P(B) = \dfrac{(^5C_2 + {}^5C_2)}{^{10}C_2} = \dfrac{4}{9}$

$\therefore P\left(\dfrac{A}{B}\right) = \dfrac{1}{2}$

Hence, the correct option is (A).

89. Given,

Time taken by pipe A to fill the cistern = $37\dfrac{1}{2}$ minutes

Time taken by pipe B to fill the cistern = 45 minutes

Let B be turned off after x minutes.

Then, Part filled by $(A + B)$ in x minutes + Part filled by A in $(30 - x)$ minutes = 1

Therefore,

$$x\left(\frac{2}{75} + \frac{1}{45}\right) + (30 - x) \times \frac{2}{75} = 1$$

$$\Rightarrow \frac{11x}{225} + \frac{60 - 2x}{75} = 1$$

$$\Rightarrow 11x + 180 - 6x = 225$$

$$\Rightarrow x = 9$$

Hence, the correct option is (B).

90. Given:

Ram's salary 60% more than Shayam's salary.

Ram got a raise of 25% on his salary.

Shayam got raise of 40% on his salary.

$$\therefore 60\% = \frac{3}{5}$$

Let Shayam's salary = $500x$

Than Ram's = 800x

Ram's salary after 25% raise $= (800x) \times \left(1 + \frac{25}{100}\right),$

$$= \frac{125}{100} \times 800x = 1000x$$

Shayam's salary after 40% raise $= (500x) \times \left(1 + \frac{40}{100}\right)$

$$= \left(\frac{140}{100}\right) \times 500x = 700x$$

Ram's salary – Shayam's salary $= = 1000x - 700x = 300x$

Percent of Shayam's salary less than Ram's salary $=$
$$\frac{\text{(Ram's salary - Shayam's salary)}}{\text{Ram's salary}} \times 100$$

Percent of Shayam's salary less than Ram's salary $=$
$$\frac{300x}{1000x} \times 100 = 30\%$$

$\therefore$ Shayam's salary 30% less than the Ram's salary.

Hence, the correct option is (C).

Reasoning Ability

Ques (1-3):Directions: In this question, the relationship between different elements is shown in the statements. These statements are followed by two conclusions.

Q.1 Statement: $C \geq M > F < A = B > S$

Conclusions:

I. $C > B$

II. $F < S$

A. Only conclusion I follow

B. Only conclusion II follows

C. Either conclusion I or II follows

D. Neither conclusion I nor II follows

E. Both conclusions I and II follow

Q.2 Statements: $H = M \leq W; C \geq W < S$

Conclusions:

I. $C = M$

II. $C > M$

A. Only conclusion I is true

B. Only conclusion II is true

C. Either conclusion I or II is true

D. Neither conclusion I nor II is true

E. Both conclusions I and II are true

Q.3 Statement: $H < Y, Y \geq R, R > W$

Conclusions:

I. $W < Y$

II. $R \leq Y$

A. Only conclusion I is true

B. Only conclusion II is true

C. Either conclusion I or II is true

D. Neither conclusion I nor II is true

E. Both conclusion I and II are true

Ques (4-6):Directions: Study the following information carefully and answer the questions given below.

In a certain code language:

'New year special sweet' is written as 'sa re ga ma'.

'Sweet potatoes are tasty' is written as 'pa da ne sa'.

'Favorite sweet is Gulabjamoon' is written as 'sa daa nee saa'.

'Gulabjamoon all are tasty' is written as 'ree nee ne pa'.

Q.4 What is the code for 'Sweet' in the given code language?

A. re

B. ga

C. sa

D. nee

E. None of these

Q.5 What is the code for 'tasty' in the given code language?

A. re

B. ne or pa

C. sa

D. ga

E. None of these

Q.6 What is the code for 'Gulabjamoon' in the given code language?

A. ree

B. sa

C. da

D. nee

E. None of these

Ques (7-8):Direction: These questions are based on the following information:

There are eight family members - Ali, Brinda, Chetna, Dhruv, Esha, Fauzia, Garima and Harish in the family of three generations where the third generation is unmarried. There are three married couples in the family. Either both or none of the parents is alive. Fauzia is the sister-in-law of Chetna who is the husband of Esha. Harish is the grandchild of Ali who has only two children. Esha and Chetna have only one daughter, Garima who is unmarried. Dhruv is the only brother of Chetna and one of the sons of Ali who is the wife of Brinda. There is an equal number of males and females in the family.

Q.7 Who is the brother-in-law of Esha in the family?

A. Ali

B. Harish

C. Dhruv

D. Brinda

E. Cannot be determined

Q.8 How is Brinda related to Chetna?

A. Father

B. Mother

C. Sister

D. Sister - in - law

E. None of these

Ques (9-13):Direction: There are exactly ten stores and no other store on a straight in Bistupur Market. On the northern side of the street, from West to East, are stores 1, 3, 5, 7 and 9; on the southern side of the street, also from West to East, are stores 2, 4, 6, 8 and 10 The stores on the northern side are located directly across the street from those on the southern side, facing each other in pairs, as follows: 1 and 2; 3 and 4; 5 and 6; 7 and 8; 9 and 10. Each store is decorated with lights in exactly one of the following colours: green, red, and yellow. The stores have been decorated with lights according to the following conditions:

1. No store is decorated with lights of the same colour as those of any store adjacent to it.

2. No store is decorated with lights of the same colour as those of the store directly across the street from it.

3. Yellow lights decorate exactly one store on each side of the street.

4. Red lights decorate store 4.

5. Yellow lights decorate store 5.

Q.9 How many store/s are decorated by red colored light?

A. 1
B. 2
C. 3
D. 4
E. Cannot be determined

Q.10 Suppose that yellow lights decorate exactly two stores on the south side of the street and exactly one store on the north side. If all other conditions remain the same, then which one of the following statements must be true?
A. Green lights decorate store 1
B. Red lights decorate store 7
C. Red lights decorate store 10
D. Yellow lights decorate store 2
E. Yellow light decorate store 8

Q.11 Which one of the following statements must be true?
A. Red lights decorate store 1
B. Green lights decorate store 10
C. Red lights decorate store 8
D. Yellow lights decorate store 10
E. Yellow lights decorate store 8

Q.12 If green lights decorate store 7, then each of the following statements could be false Except:
A. Green lights decorate store 2
B. Green lights decorate store 10
C. Red lights decorate store 8
D. Yellow lights decorate store 2
E. Red lights decorate store 9

Q.13 Which one of the following could be an accurate list of the colors of the lights that decorate stores 2, 4, 6, 8 and 10, respectively?
A. Green, red, green, red, green
B. Green, red, green, yellow, red
C. Green, red, yellow, red, green
D. Yellow, green, red, green, red
E. Yellow, red, green, red, yellow

Q.14 If all the letters of the word 'INTROSPECTION' are arranged in a way that all the vowels are arranged in the beginning in alphabetical order and then all the consonants are arranged in the alphabetical order, then the position of how many letters remains unchanged?
A. Zero
B. One
C. Two
D. More than two
E. None of these

Ques (15-19):Direction: What should come in the place of question mark '?' in the following number series?

Q.15 11, 18, 37, 74, 135, ?
A. 231
B. 161
C. 131
D. 226
E. 278

Q.16 8, 27, 125, ?, 1331, 2197
A. 49
B. 343
C. 64
D. 512
E. 729

Q.17 5, 7, 10, ?, 22, 33, 46
A. 12
B. 16
C. 15
D. 18
E. 20

Q.18 5, 19, 41, 71, ?
A. 5
B. 19
C. 41
D. 109
E. 115

Q.19 – 86, – 85, – 93, – 66, – 130, ?
A. 1
B. -5
C. 0
D. 2
E. -2

Ques (20-24):Direction: Study the following information and answer the given questions.

Eight people Prashant, Rekha, Pyare, Manali, Parimal, Vasudha, Sulekha, and Sukumar are sitting around a circular table. Some of them are facing the centre and some of them are facing away from the centre.

Immediate neighbours of Sulekha face the same direction. Pyare is not an immediate neighbour of Prashant. Parimal is to the immediate right of Sulekha and Prashant.

Rekha is facing towards the centre and is sitting opposite Sulekha. Pyare and Vasudha are facing away from the centre the same as Sulekha. Immediate neighbours of Sukumar are facing opposite direction to each other. Manali is to the immediate left of Sukumar and Sulekha.

Q.20 Who is sitting opposite Pyare?
A. Parimal
B. Manali
C. Vasudha
D. Rekha
E. Sulekha

Q.21 What is the position of Prashant with respect to Manali?
A. Third to the right
B. Second to the left
C. Second to the right
D. Third to the left
E. Fourth to the right

Q.22 How many persons are sitting between Rekha and Parimal when counted from the right of Rekha?
A. Three
B. Four
C. One
D. Two
E. Five

Q.23 Who is sitting third to the right of Sulekha?
A. Vasudha
B. Sukumar
C. Prashant
D. Pyare
E. Rekha

Q.24 Sukumar is related to Manali in a certain way. Similarly, Pyare is related to Vasudha. In the same way, Sulekha is related to which of the following?
A. Sukumar
B. Vasudha
C. Rekha
D. Prashant
E. Parimal

Ques (25-27):Direction: Study the following information and answer the question.

Shrivin goes to his Cafe from his house with his wife by bike. He rides the bike from Bus stop. He rides 5 km towards North and reaches point Q then he turns to his left and rides 12 km and reaches a gift store. Here he purchases some gifts for his wife.

Q.25 How far is gift store from Bus stop and in which direction?

A. 13 km, North-West   **B.** 14 km, North-East
C. 11 km, South-West   **D.** 12 km, South-East
E. None of these

Q.26 From the gift store, Shrivin turns to his left and rides 9 km and reaches point R. He then takes a right turn and rides 12 km and reaches dance class and drops his wife. What is the distance between the gift store and the dance class?

A. 10 km   **B.** 13 km
C. 15 km   **D.** 17 km
E. None of these

Q.27 From the dance class he rides 6 km towards North then turns right and rides 4 km and reaches point S. Point S is in which direction of the Bus stop?

A. North-West   **B.** South-West
C. South-East   **D.** North-East
E. None of these

Ques (28-30):Directions: Read the following information carefully and answer the given questions.

Six Students M, N, O, X, Y, and Z participated in an essay writing competition. Each of the scores different marks.

Y scores the third highest marks. M scores more marks than only one person. O scores more marks than Y and M. O does not score the highest number of marks. Z scores fewer marks than O but More marks than M. N does not score the lowest number of marks.

Q.28 Who scores the third-lowest marks?
A. O   **B.** N   **C.** Z   **D.** M
E. X

Q.29 How many students score less marks than O?
A. Three   **B.** Five   **C.** Two   **D.** Four
E. Six

Q.30 If Z scores 28 marks and X scores 15 marks, then what is the possible number of marks did M score?
A. Five   **B.** Twelve
C. Twenty-nine   **D.** Ten
E. Twenty

English Language

Ques (31-35):Direction: Which of the following phrases (A), (B), (C), (D) given below in the statement should replace the phrase printed in bold in the sentence to make it grammatically correct? If the sentence is correct as it is given and 'No Correction is required', mark (E) as the answer.

Q.31 Has your child becomes anxious or nervous about any activity, it is a good idea to inform the team-leader.
A. Should your child   **B.** Were your child
C. Had your child   **D.** When your child
E. No correction

Q.32 When he is rich, he lives in a small hause.
A. Unless he is rich   **B.** Until he is rich
C. Finally he is rich   **D.** Although he is rich
E. No correction

Q.33 If he were in Australia he **would be getting** up now.
A. were been getting   **B.** had been getting
C. has being getting   **D.** has been getting
E. No correction

Q.34 The sound of the stream resembling that of a child's chatter **pleasing to the ears.**
A. Pleasing for the ears
B. Was pleasing to the ears
C. Was pleasing for the ears
D. Pleasure for the ears
E. No correction required

Q.35 The 'Solitary Reaper' is **one of the good** poems composed by William Wordsworth.
A. One of the better
B. A better
C. One of the best
D. One of the well
E. No correction required

Ques (36-40):Direction: Below is some sentences out of which the sentence numbered 4 has been correctly placed. The rest of the sentences A,B,C,D,E,F need to be arranged correctly in order to form a logical order.

A. A derivative is a contract between two or more parties whose value is based on an agreed-upon underlying financial asset (like a security) or set of assets (like an index).

B. Generally belonging to the realm of advanced investing, derivatives are secondary securities whose value is solely based (derived) on the value of the primary security that they are linked to.

C. A futures contract, for example, is a derivative because its value is affected by the performance of the underlying asset.

4. In and of itself a derivative is worthless.

D. Futures contracts, forward contracts, options, swaps, and warrants are commonly used derivatives.

E. Common underlying asset instruments include bonds, commodities, currencies, interest rates, market indexes, and stocks.

F. Similarly, a stock option is a derivative because its value is "derived" from that of the underlying stock.

Q.36 Which of the following is the FIRST statement?
A. F   **B.** D   **C.** C   **D.** A
E. B

Q.37 Which of the following is the SECOND statement?
A. D   **B.** E   **C.** B   **D.** F
E. A

Q.38 Which of the following is the THIRD statement?
A. F   **B.** E   **C.** C   **D.** A
E. B

Q.39 Which of the following is the FIFTH statement?

A. D   **B.** E   **C.** A   **D.** F
E. C

Q.40 Which of the following is the SEVENTH statement?

[LIC AAO (Generalist), 2021]

A. F   **B.** E   **C.** C   **D.** A
E. B

Ques (41-45):Direction: Given below is a passage with five blanks (A-E). A phrase written in brackets is given against each blank. Choose the right word from the options which can replace the phrase most appropriately.

___________ **[A] (Distressed or irritated)** by a large number of Central Americans who have been entering the country from Mexico, President Trump doubled down on his threat to close the Southern U.S. border. This is not the first time Trump has _________ **[B] (conveying some message)** that warning. And so far he has not followed through. _________ **[C] (bring to a stop)** cross-border traffic with one of the nation's biggest trading partners could do serious damage to the U.S. economy, including industries located far from Mexico. Retailers in San Diego got a small taste of what a border closing would look like last November when members of a migrant _________ **[D] (procession of travelers with their vehicles and cargo)** rushed the international boundary and U.S. officials closed one border crossing in response. which lasted only a few hours. But the fallout was severe, costing local merchants an estimated $5.3 million in lost sales. One importer warned that the U.S. would run out of _______ **[E] (pear-shaped fruit)** in three weeks and fresh tomatoes, peppers, melons, and eggplant for the whole country would soon be in short supply.

Q.41 Which of the following fits the blank labeled [A]?

A. Cluster   **B.** Calmed
C. Fearfulness   **D.** Crowded
E. Frustrated

Q.42 Which of the following fits the blank labeled [D]?

A. Profession   **B.** Caravan
C. Parade   **D.** March
E. None of these

Q.43 Which of the following fits the blank labeled [E]?

A. Mangoes   **B.** Apples
C. Melons   **D.** Avocados
E. Grapes

Q.44 Which of the following fits the blank labeled [B]?

A. Sounded   **B.** Gleamed
C. Blistered   **D.** Abundant
E. None of these

Q.45 Which of the following fits the blank labeled [C]?

A. Reciprocating   **B.** Invigilating
C. Emerging   **D.** Halting
E. None of these

Ques (46-50):Direction: Read the sentence to find out whether there is any error in it. The error, if any, will be in one part of the sentence. The number of that part is the answer. If there is no error, the answer is (E). Ignore errors of punctuation, if any.

Q.46 The chairman had not taken (A)/ any decision until (B)/ he had studied (C)/ the case thoroughly. (D)/ No error(E)

A. (A)   **B.** (B)   **C.** (C)   **D.** (D)
E. (E)

Q.47 If I would have realised (A)/ what a bad driver you were, (B)/ I would not have (C)/ come with you. (D)/ No error (E)

A. (A)   **B.** (B)   **C.** (C)   **D.** (D)
E. (E)

Q.48 None of the seven (A) contenders who have been given (B) the chance to join the (C) league plays confidently. (D) No error (E)

A. (A)   **B.** (B)   **C.** (C)   **D.** (D)
E. (E)

Q.49 Within two years, (A)/ the sisters had (B)/ losted their parents in (C) a tragic accident. (D)/ No error (E)

A. (A)   **B.** (B)   **C.** (C)   **D.** (D)
E. (E)

Q.50 I would rather (A) / pay for my (B)/ education than financial (C) / aid. (D) / No error (E)

A. (A)   **B.** (B)   **C.** (C)   **D.** (D)
E. (E)

Ques (51-54):Direction: A sentence with one blank is given, indicating that something has been omitted. Choose the word that fits the blank appropriately.

Q.51 Tom applied for a promotion twice this year, but he was ______ both times.

A. Turned down   **B.** Been turning down
C. Has turned down   **D.** Turned up
E. Turning up

Q.52 India's social fabric has been damaged to an ______ where repair seems impossible.

A. Portent   **B.** Extent
C. Extant   **D.** Extension
E. Expansion

Q.53 With the 2019 general election announced, an inescapable question arises about the ______ of the country: Is it any worse today than it was under the previous governments?

A. States   **B.** Stated   **C.** State   **D.** Stating
E. Start

Q.54 We ______ to thank intrepid journalists, who have painstakingly documented Facebook's wrongdoings.

A. Had many   **B.** Had much
C. Have much   **D.** Have many
E. Have had many

Ques (55-59):Direction: Read the passage and answer the following question.

Marie Curie was one of the most accomplished scientists in history. Together with her husband, Pierre, she discovered radium, an element widely used for treating cancer and studied uranium and other radioactive substances. Pierre and Marie's amicable collaboration later helped to unlock the secrets of the atom. Marie was born in 1867 in Warsaw, Poland, where her father was a professor of physics. She was a Polish and French physicist, chemist and feminist. She did research on radioactivity. She was also the first woman to win a Nobel Prize. She received a Nobel Prize in physics for her research on uncontrolled radiation, which was discovered by Henri Becquerel.

At an early age, she displayed a brilliant mind and a blithe personality. Her great exuberance for learning prompted her to continue with her studies after high school. She became disgruntled, however, when she learned that the university in Warsaw was closed to women. Determined to receive a higher education, she defiantly left Poland and in 1891 entered the Sorbonne, a French university, where she earned her master's degree and a doctorate in physics. Marie was fortunate to have studied at the Sorbonne with some of the greatest scientists of her day, one of whom was Pierre Curie. Marie and Pierre were married in 1895 and spent many productive years working together in the physics laboratory.

Curie discovered radium. It is one of the most radioactive and dangerous metals. She shared this discovery with Pierre Curie and Gustave Bemont. The three found radium in 1898. They discovered it when using a uranium ore. It gave off a lot of radiation. They decided that it was coming from more than uranium. The group found radium in the uranium. Radium is now used for many different things. For example, doctors used to use it to kill cancer cells. Radium was found in paint and watches. Many workers who made radium-containing products developed bone cancer. A short time after they discovered radium, Pierre was killed by a horse-drawn wagon in 1906. Marie was stunned by this horrible misfortune and endured heartbreaking anguish.

Curie's feeling of desolation finally began to fade when she was asked to succeed her husband as a physics professor at the Sorbonne. She was the first woman to be given a professorship at the world-famous university. In 1911 she received the Nobel Prize in chemistry for isolating radium. Although Marie Curie eventually suffered a fatal illness from her long exposure to radium, she never became disillusioned about her work. Regardless of the consequences, she had dedicated herself to science and to revealing the mysteries of the physical world.

Q.55 When did Marie Curie win the Nobel prize for isolating radium?

A. 1911   **B.** 1891   **C.** 1867   **D.** 1906
E. 1895

Q.56 Whom did she discover radium with?

1. Pierre Curie

2. Henri Becquerel

3. Gustav Bemont

A. Only 1   **B.** Only 2
C. Only 3   **D.** All except 2

E. All except 3

Q.57 How did Marie Curie die?

A. She was killed by a horse-drawn wagon
B. Long exposure to radium killed her
C. Long exposure to uranium killed her
D. Old age killed her
E. None of these

Q.58 Which of the following statements is TRUE?

A. Marie Curie received a Nobel Prize in biology.
B. Marie and Pierre got married in 1891.
C. Marie Curie shared the radium discovery with Pierre Curie and Gustave Bemont.
D. Uranium was found from radium by Marie Curie.
E. Marie Curie was a Polish and English physicist

Q.59 What does 'amicable' mean?

A. Characterized by friendliness
B. Showing or feeling opposition or dislike
C. Behaving or done in a determined and forceful way.
D. Relating to ordinary citizens and their concerns
E. Not connected with religious or spiritual matters.

Q.60 Direction: Find out the most effective word from the given options to fill the blanks of the following question.

1. As India prepares to celebrate its Diwali festival, stockbrokers see growing signs of an economic _______.

2. The doctors are worried as he is not showing any signs of _______.

A. replete   **B.** slumps   **C.** recovery   **D.** acquired
E. satisfied

Numerical Ability

Q.61 A, B and C start business with an investment of Rs. 4000, Rs. 8000 and Rs. 12000. The total profit they got after 1 year is Rs. 12,000. Find the profit got B and C together.

A. Rs. 5,000   **B.** Rs. 10,000
C. Rs. 15,000   **D.** Rs. 16,000
E. Rs. 20,000

Ques (62-66):Direction: What should come in place of the question mark '?' in the following number series?

Q.62 5, 4, 0, -18, -114, -714, ?

A. -1000   **B.** -5034   **C.** 2000   **D.** 1100
E. 2300

Q.63 1, 10, 90, 720, 5040, 30240, ?

A. 161200   **B.** 151200   **C.** 171200   **D.** 141200
E. 131200

Q.64 8, 8, 12, ?, 60, 180, 630

A. 24   **B.** 75   **C.** 33   **D.** 36
E. 22

Q.65 3, 6, 11, 18, 27, 38, ?

A. 45   **B.** 46   **C.** 48   **D.** 51
E. 49

Q.66 384, 576, 1440, ?, 22680
A. 5045   **B.** 5540   **C.** 5040   **D.** 5044
E. 5400

Q.67 A boat takes 90 minutes less to travel 36 miles downstream than to travel the same distance upstream. If the speed of the boat in still water is 10 mph, the speed of the stream is:
A. 2 mph   **B.** 2.5 mph
C. 3 mph   **D.** 4 mph
E. None of these

Ques (68-70):Direction: In the given question, two equations numbered I and II are given. Solve both the equations and mark the appropriate answer.

Q.68 I. $x^2 + 36x + 243 = 0$
II. $2y^2 - 32y + 120 = 0$
A. if x > y
B. if x ≥ y
C. if x < y
D. if x ≤ y
E. if x = y or the relationship cannot be established

Q.69 I. $x^2 + 64x + 960 = 0$
II. $y^2 + 32y + 240 = 0$
A. if x > y
B. if x ≥ y
C. if x < y
D. if x ≤ y
E. if x = y or the relationship cannot be established

Q.70 I. $x^2 - 269x + 534 = 0$
II. $6y^2 - 24y + 18 = 0$
A. if x > y
B. if x ≥ y
C. if x < y
D. if x ≤ y
E. if x = y or the relationship cannot be established

Q.71 A question paper has two parts, A and B, each containing 10 questions. If a student has to choose 8 from part A and 5 from part B, in how many ways can he choose the questions?
A. 11340   **B.** 113450   **C.** 40   **D.** 320
E. 12570

Ques (72-76):Direction: Study the following table chart carefully and answer the question given beside.

The table given below shows the percentage of appeared and qualified candidates in a competitive examination from different institutes.

Institutes	Appeared Candidates = 24000	Qualified Candidates =4000
	Percentage of appeared candidates	Percentage of qualified candidates
A	25%	18%
B	10%	12%
C	15%	18%
D	12%	16%
E	18%	20%
F	20%	16%

Q.72 What is the ratio of the qualified candidates from institutes D, E and F together to the appeared candidates from institutes A, B and C together?
A. 11 : 17   **B.** 12 : 67   **C.** 19 : 75   **D.** 17 : 74
E. 13 : 75

Q.73 What percentage of the candidates from institute C has been declared qualified out of the total candidates appeared from this institute?
A. 30%   **B.** 25%   **C.** 40%   **D.** 20%
E. 35%

Q.74 What is the percentage of students who qualified from the institute C and D together with respect to those who appeared from the institute C and D together?
A. 24.98%   **B.** 30.98%   **C.** 20.98%   **D.** 31.98%
E. 25.98%

Q.75 Which institute has the highest percentage of candidates qualified with respect to those who appeared?
A. A   **B.** D   **C.** C   **D.** E
E. B

Q.76 What is the ratio of qualified candidates from institute B to the appeared candidates from institute F?
A. 1 : 10   **B.** 2 : 11   **C.** 3 : 14   **D.** 4 : 17
E. 5 : 19

Q.77 What would be simple interest on the principal amount of Rs. 10000 with 10% p.a. interest rate annually for 5 years?
A. Rs. 18,750   **B.** Rs. 9,000
C. Rs. 15,000   **D.** Rs. 5,000
E. Rs. 1,00,000

Q.78 A sum of Rs. 1,250 amounts to Rs. 1,550 in 4 years. What is the simple interest rate?
A. 8%   **B.** 1%   **C.** 4%   **D.** 6%
E. 5%

Q.79 Mannu can do a piece of work in 9 days while, Naina can do a piece of work in 5 days, The wage of full work is Rs. 420, If they both work together to complete the work then the earnings of mannu is:
A. 300   **B.** 150   **C.** 450   **D.** 250
E. 400

Q.80 A Bag contains 7 red, 8 white and 9 black balls. Four balls are drawn out at random. Find the probability that none of the balls drawn is white.
A. $\frac{130}{759}$ **B.** $\frac{237}{771}$
C. $\frac{110}{759}$ **D.** $\frac{37}{759}$
E. None of these

Q.81 Abhilasha scores an average of 57 marks in each subject of a half-yearly exam of his school. It is known that there are a total of three subjects, and the maximum marks in each subject is 80. What would have been her average marks had she scored 12 marks more in any one of the subjects?

A. 62   **B.** 55   **C.** 65   **D.** 61
E. 69

Q.82 A tank is filled by three pipes with uniform flow. The first two pipes operating simultaneously fill the tank at the same time during which the tank is filled by the third pipe alone. The second pipe fills the tank 5 hours faster than the first pipe and 4 hours slower than the third pipe. The time required by the first pipe is:

A. 6 hours   **B.** 10 hours   **C.** 15 hours   **D.** 30 hours
E. 5 hours

Q.83 What should come in place of the question mark (?) in the following question?

$\frac{1}{4}$th of $\frac{1}{2}$ of $\frac{3}{4}$th of 52000 =?

A. 4875   **B.** 4857
C. 4785   **D.** 4865
E. None of these

Q.84 What should come in place of the question mark (?) in the following question?

$\sqrt[3]{12167} \times \sqrt[3]{5832} =?$

A. 416   **B.** 394
C. 414   **D.** 396
E. None of these

Q.85 What should come in place of the question mark (?) in the following question?

$\frac{3}{7}$ of $\frac{4}{5}$ of $\frac{5}{8}$ of $490 =?$

A. 115   **B.** 105
C. 108   **D.** 116
E. None of these

Q.86 What should come in place of the question mark (?) in the following question?

7855 − 4236 + 388 = ? + 3974

A. 133   **B.** 73
C. 33   **D.** 43
E. None of these

Q.87 What should come in place of the question mark (?) in the following question?

(8.2% of 365) − (1.75% of 108) = ?

A. 16.02   **B.** 28.04
C. 42.34   **D.** 53.76
E. None of these

Q.88 A rectangular area of land is divided into 3 plots of dimensions 50 m × 20 m each, 4 plots of 40 m × 30 m each and 4 plots of 30 m × 25 m each. Which of the following is the possible dimensions of the rectangular land?

A. 140 m × 80 m   **B.** 160 m × 70 m
C. 180 m × 60 m   **D.** 200 m × 50 m
E. 220 m × 40 m

Q.89 Ramesh scored 556 marks in an exam and Rajesh got 69% marks in the same exam which is 4 marks less than Ramesh. If the minimum passing marks in the exam is 34%, then how much more marks did Ramesh score than the minimum passing marks?

A. 284   **B.** 296   **C.** 290   **D.** 280
E. 260

Q.90 Heath has two fake notes of Rs. 100. A customer came to him to buy 3 kg of sugar. Heath buys sugar at Rs. 50 per kg and sells at Rs. 60 per kg. The customer gave him a note of Rs. 500 and he returned him the balance money including both fake notes of Rs. 100. How much profit did Heath earn in this transaction?

A. 120%   **B.** 133.33%   **C.** 153.33%   **D.** 180%
E. 166.67%

// Smart Answer Sheet //

Correct Indicates percentage of students who answered questions correctly.

Skipped Indicates percentage of students who skipped questions.

Q.	Ans.	Correct / Skipped	Q.	Ans.	Correct / Skipped	Q.	Ans.	Correct / Skipped	Q.	Ans.	Correct / Skipped	Q.	Ans.	Correct / Skipped
1	D	45.66 % / 1.23 %	17	C	82.7 % / 0.0 %	33	E	57.06 % / 1.32 %	49	C	44.23 % / 1.77 %	65	D	48.01 % / 1.03 %
2	C	56.88 % / 1.31 %	18	D	51.63 % / 1.68 %	34	B	61.74 % / 1.78 %	50	C	68.61 % / 1.05 %	66	C	55.31 % / 1.12 %
3	E	55.88 % / 1.65 %	19	B	87.33 % / 0.0 %	35	C	44.78 % / 1.05 %	51	A	42.24 % / 1.19 %	67	A	69.37 % / 1.29 %
4	C	40.45 % / 1.96 %	20	A	68.64 % / 1.78 %	36	D	59.44 % / 1.08 %	52	B	57.46 % / 1.67 %	68	C	56.68 % / 1.44 %
5	B	85.87 % / 0.0 %	21	D	65.16 % / 1.33 %	37	B	57.96 % / 1.98 %	53	C	46.29 % / 1.37 %	69	C	53.53 % / 1.78 %
6	D	61.72 % / 1.89 %	22	D	43.85 % / 1.17 %	38	E	43.95 % / 1.17 %	54	C	51.31 % / 1.78 %	70	E	20.37 % / 4.94 %
7	C	52.77 % / 1.17 %	23	A	62.69 % / 1.35 %	39	A	51.61 % / 1.99 %	55	A	41.82 % / 1.15 %	71	A	83.71 % / 0.0 %
8	A	40.56 % / 1.43 %	24	B	69.41 % / 1.57 %	40	A	56.76 % / 1.38 %	56	D	51.72 % / 1.97 %	72	E	68.67 % / 1.09 %
9	E	23.73 % / 4.55 %	25	A	51.6 % / 1.61 %	41	E	46.77 % / 1.41 %	57	B	54.47 % / 1.36 %	73	D	51.64 % / 1.21 %
10	D	22.52 % / 3.48 %	26	C	69.6 % / 1.76 %	42	B	62.69 % / 1.4 %	58	C	58.27 % / 1.57 %	74	C	40.34 % / 1.08 %
11	A	40.5 % / 1.86 %	27	A	53.62 % / 1.19 %	43	D	66.95 % / 1.1 %	59	A	60.94 % / 1.67 %	75	B	60.74 % / 1.74 %
12	E	53.33 % / 1.73 %	28	C	56.26 % / 1.49 %	44	A	66.92 % / 1.78 %	60	C	56.06 % / 1.71 %	76	A	83.34 % / 0.0 %
13	B	13.52 % / 4.18 %	29	D	59.39 % / 1.26 %	45	D	51.58 % / 1.71 %	61	B	69.96 % / 1.31 %	77	D	50.11 % / 1.38 %
14	B	85.27 % / 0.0 %	30	E	58.17 % / 1.41 %	46	A	45.23 % / 1.06 %	62	B	11.48 % / 4.42 %	78	D	77.95 % / 0.0 %
15	D	84.5 % / 0.0 %	31	D	54.45 % / 1.95 %	47	A	40.02 % / 1.66 %	63	B	51.65 % / 1.02 %	79	B	67.14 % / 1.45 %
16	B	83.97 % / 0.0 %	32	D	55.75 % / 1.5 %	48	E	45.64 % / 1.34 %	64	A	69.23 % / 1.38 %	80	A	86.34 % / 0.0 %

Q.	Ans.	Correct		Q.	Ans.	Correct		Q.	Ans.	Correct		Q.	Ans.	Correct		Q.	Ans.	Correct
		Skipped				Skipped				Skipped				Skipped				Skipped
81	D	54.67 %		83	A	53.44 %		85	B	43.19 %		87	B	10.95 %		89	A	47.95 %
		1.6 %				1.42 %				1.06 %				3.21 %				1.46 %
82	C	40.07 %		84	C	41.64 %		86	C	88.53 %		88	C	46.83 %		90	C	40.98 %
		1.25 %				1.16 %				0.0 %				1.61 %				1.78 %

Performance Analysis

Avg. Score (%)	61.11%
Toppers Score (%)	74.44%
Your Score	

//Hints and Solutions//

1. Statement: C ≥ M > F < A = B > S

Conclusions:

I. C > B ⇒ It's not true as C > F and B > F so no direct relationship between C and B can be established.

II. F < S ⇒ It's not true as A > S and A > F so no direct relationship between S and F can be established.

So, neither conclusion I nor II follows.

Hence, the correct option is (D).

2. Given statements are: H = M ≤ W; C ≥ W < S

On rearranging: H = M ≤ W ≤ C; W < S

Conclusions:

I. C = M (False as C ≥ M)

II. C > M (False as C ≥ M)

But both the conclusions form a complementary pair; so either I or II follows.

Hence, the correct option is (C).

3. Given statements are: H < Y, Y ≥ R, R > W

On combining: H < Y ≥ R > W

Conclusions:

I. W < Y (True)

II. R ≤ Y (True)

So, both the conclusion follows.

Hence, the correct option is (E).

Ques (4-6): The codes are as follows:

4. 'Sweet' will be coded as sa.

Hence, the correct option is (C).

5. Therefore, 'tasty' will be coded as ne or pa.

Hence, the correct option is (B).

6. Therefore, 'Gulabjamoon' will be coded as nee.

Hence, the correct option is (D).

Ques (7-8): From the given information,

Symbol in Diagram	Meaning
○	Female
□	Male
══	Married Couple
──	Siblings
│	Difference of A Generation

1) Eight members - Ali, Brinda, Chetna, Dhruv, Esha, Fauzia, Garima and Harish. Three generations in the family.

2) Either both or none of the parents is alive.

3) Fauzia is the sister-in-law of Chetna who is the husband of Esha.

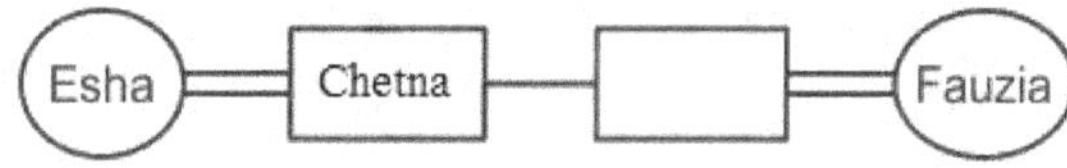

4) Esha and Chetna have only one daughter, Garima who is unmarried implies Garima belongs to the third generation.

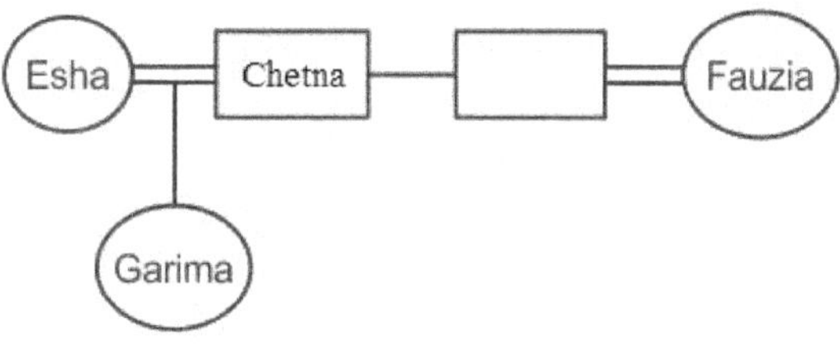

5) Dhruv is the only brother of Chetna and one of the sons of Ali who is the wife of Brinda.

6) Harish is the grandchild of Ali who has only two children.

7) There is an equal number of males and females in the family implies that Harish is a male.

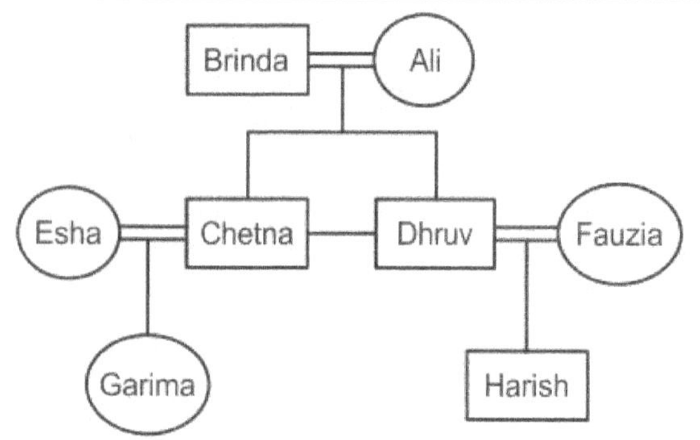

7. Therefore, Dhruv is the brother-in-law of Esha in the family.

Hence, the correct option is (C).

8. Therefore, Brinda is the father of Chetna.

Hence, the correct option is (A).

Ques (9-13): According to the given information in the question, we conclude:

1. No two adjacent and opposite stores have same light.
2. Yellow lights decorate exactly one store on each side of the street.
3. Red lights decorate store 4.
4. Yellow lights decorate store 5.

So, store 6 and store 3 are decorated with green as per given conditions. And so, store 1 must be decorated with Red.

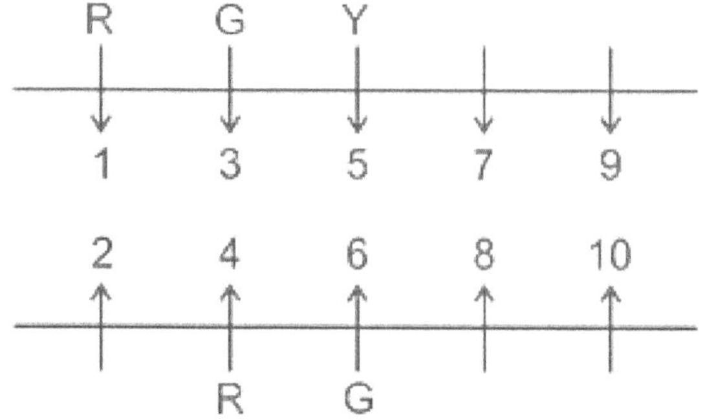

Now, there must be exactly one store in South row that's decorates with yellow lights. Yellow light can decorate either of store 2, 4 or 6.

Case 1:

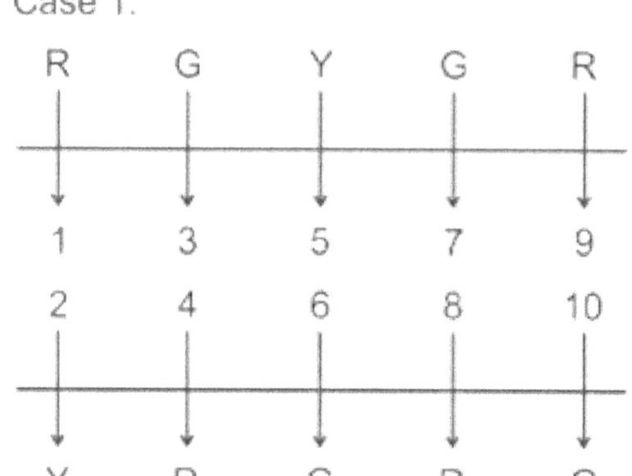

In case 1, 4 store are decorated with red lights.

Case 2:

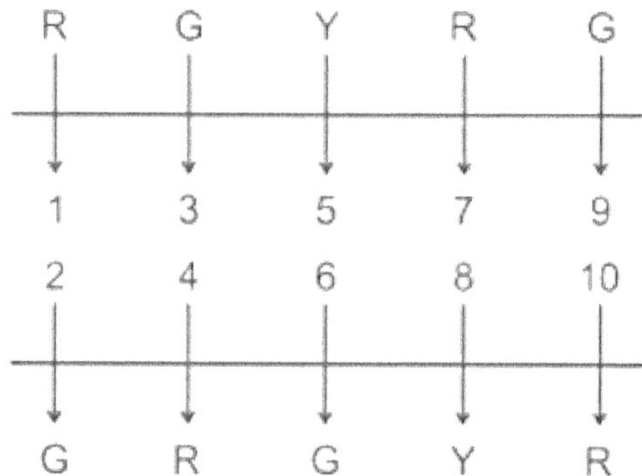

In case 2, 4 store are decorated with red lights.

Case 3:

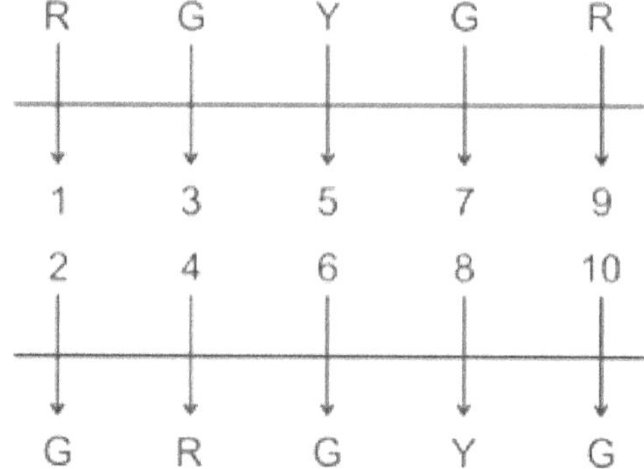

In case 3, 3 store are decorated with red lights.

Case 4:

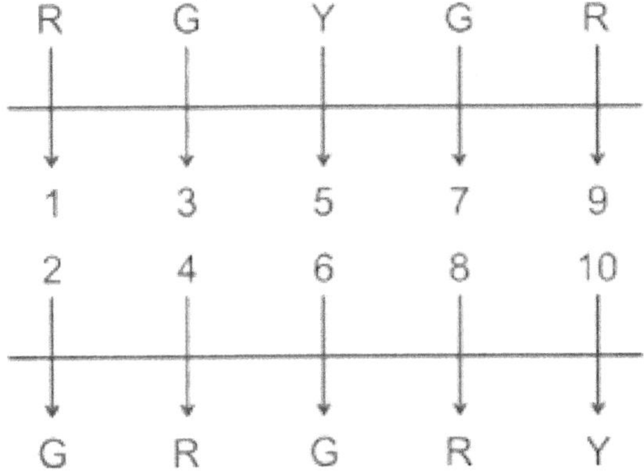

In case 4, again 4 store are decorated with red lights.

9. Clearly, the number of store decorated with red lights is different in different cases.

Hence, the correct option is (E).

10. From the above cases, lets evaluate the given options:

(A). Green lights decorate store 1 $\Rightarrow$ False

(B). Red lights decorate store 7 $\Rightarrow$ False

(C). Red lights decorate store 10 $\Rightarrow$ This is possible but not definite

(D). Yellow lights decorate store 2 $\Rightarrow$ True

(E). Yellow light decorate store 8 $\Rightarrow$ This is possible but not definite

Hence, the correct option is (D).

11. From the above cases, lets evaluate the given options:

(A). Red lights decorate store 1 $\Rightarrow$ This is possible definitely.

(B). Green lights decorate store 10 $\Rightarrow$ This is possible but not definite

(C). Red lights decorate store 8 $\Rightarrow$ This is possible but not definite

(D). Yellow lights decorate store 10 $\Rightarrow$ This is possible but not definite

(E). Yellow lights decorate store 8 $\Rightarrow$ This is possible but not definite

Hence, the correct option is (A).

12. From the above cases, lets evaluate the given options:

(A). Green lights decorate store 2 $\Rightarrow$ This is possible but not definite

(B). Green lights decorate store 10 $\Rightarrow$ This is possible but not definite

(C). Red lights decorate store 8 $\Rightarrow$ This is possible but not definite

(D). Yellow lights decorate store 2 $\Rightarrow$ This is possible but not definite

(E). Red lights decorate store 9 $\Rightarrow$ This is possible definitely.

Hence, the correct option is (E).

13. So, green, red, green, yellow, red list is correct.

Hence, the correct option is (B).

14. The given word:

INTROSPECTION

Applying the above condition, we have a new word:

EIIOOCNNPRSTT

The final arrangements of the old and new words are:

I	N	T	R	O	S	P	E	C	T	I	O	N
E	I	I	O	O	C	N	N	P	R	S	T	T

Thus the position of only one letter i.e, "O" remains unchanged. Hence, the correct option is (B).

15. The series follows following pattern:

$10 + 1^3 = 11$

$10 + 2^3 = 18$

$10 + 3^3 = 37$

$10 + 4^3 = 74$

$10 + 5^3 = 135$

$10 + 6^3 = 226$

$\therefore$ The value of ? is 226.

Hence, the correct option is (D).

16. The given series is the cube of prime numbers:

$2^3 = 8$

$3^3 = 27$

$5^3 = 125$

$7^3 = 343$

$11^3 = 1331$

$13^3 = 2197$

$\therefore$ The value of ? is 343.

Hence, the correct option is (B).

17. The given series is the addition of prime numbers:

$5 + 2 = 7$

$7 + 3 = 10$

$10 + 5 = 15$

$15 + 7 = 22$

22 + 11 = 33

33 + 13 = 46

∴ The value of ? is 15.

Hence, the correct option is (C).

18. The series follows following pattern:

1 × 3 + 2 = 5

3 × 5 + 4 = 19

5 × 7 + 6 = 41

7 × 9 + 8 = 71

9 × 11 + 10 = 109

∴ The value of ? is 109.

Hence, the correct option is (D).

19. The logic of the series can be explained as:

$-86 + 1^3 = -85$

$-85 - 2^3 = -93$

$-93 + 3^3 = -66$

$-66 - 4^3 = -130$

By observing the pattern, we can write

$\Rightarrow -130 + 5^3 = ?$

$\Rightarrow ? = -5$

∴ The value of ? is − 5.

Hence, the correct option is (B).

Ques (20-24):Persons: Prashant, Rekha, Pyare, Manali, Parimal, Vasudha, Sulekha, and Sukumar

1) Parimal is to the immediate right of Sulekha and Prashant.

2) Manali is to the immediate left of Sukumar and Sulekha.

3) Pyare and Vasudha are facing away from the centre the same as Sulekha.

Therefore Sulekha, Vasudha, and Pyare are facing away from the centre.

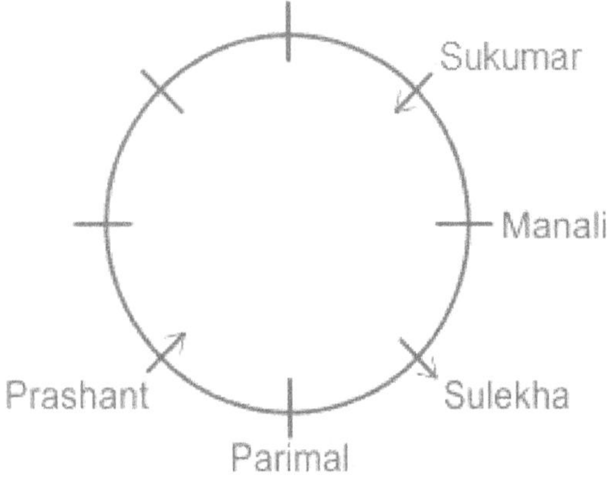

4) Rekha is facing towards centre and is sitting opposite Sulekha.

5) Pyare is not an immediate neighbour of Prashant.

Thus, the position of the only person left Vasudha is also determined.

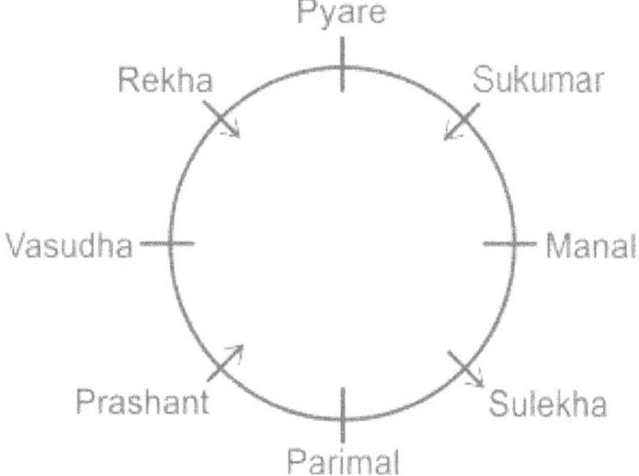

6) Immediate neighbours of Sukumar are facing opposite direction to each other.

7) Immediate neighbours of Sulekha face the same direction.

Point 3) determines the direction of Vasudha and Pyare.

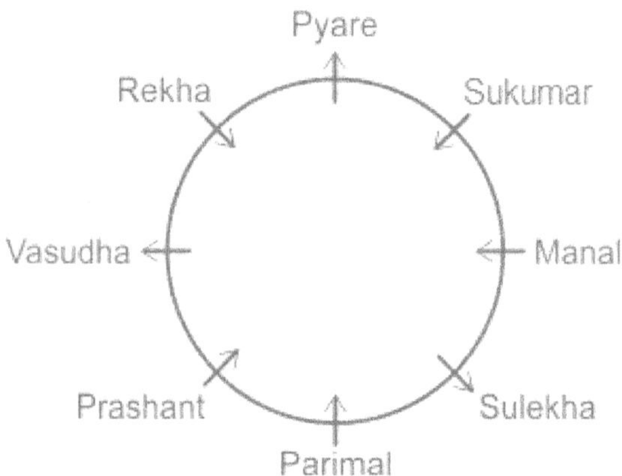

20. Thus, Parimal is sitting opposite Pyare.

Hence, the correct option is (A).

21. Thus, Prashant is third to the left of Manali.

Hence, the correct option is (D).

22. Thus, two persons are sitting between Rekha and Parimal when counted from the right of Rekha.

Hence, the correct option is (D).

23. Thus, Vasudha is sitting third to the right Sulekha.

Hence, the correct option is (A).

24. Here, both the members of the pair are facing the same direction.

Thus, Sulekha is related to Vasudha.

Hence, the correct option is (B).

25. Shrivin rides the bike from Bus stop. Now given information can be analyzed as follows:

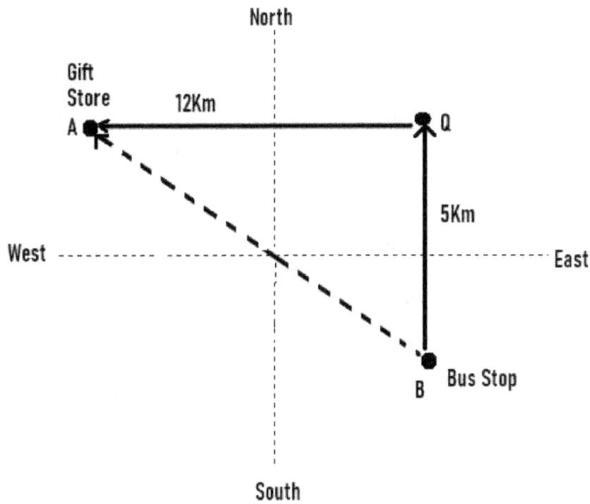

To find the distance of gift store from Bus stop,

Let the gift store be point A.

$$AB = \sqrt{BQ^2 + AQ^2}$$

$$AB = \sqrt{5^2 + 12^2}$$

$$AB = \sqrt{169}$$

$$AB = 13 \text{ km}$$

So, the gift store is 13 km North-West direction of Bus stop.

Hence, the correct option is (A).

26. The given information can be analyzed as follows:

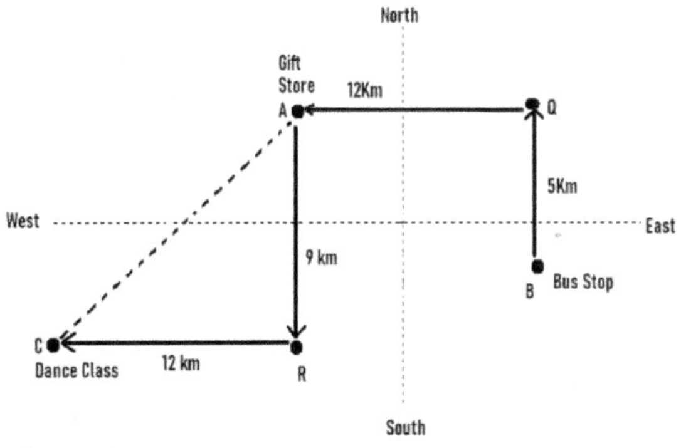

To find the distance between gift store and dance class,

Let, the dance class be point C.

$$AC = \sqrt{AR^2 + CR^2}$$

$$AC = \sqrt{12^2 + 9^2}$$

$$AC = \sqrt{225}$$

$$AC = 15 \text{ km}$$

So, the distance between the gift store and the dance class is 15 km.

Hence, the correct option is (C).

27. Given information can be analyzed as follows:

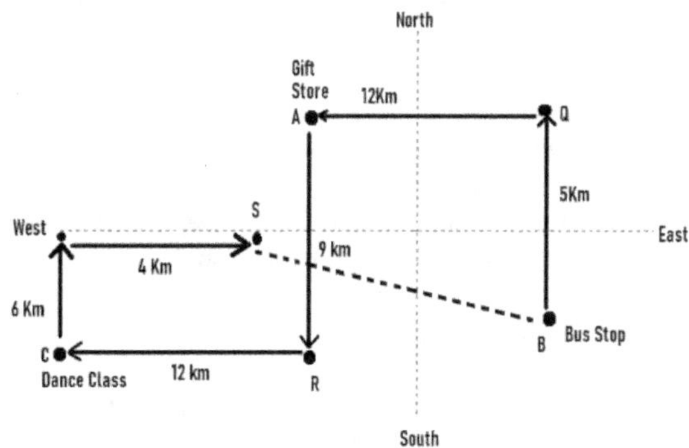

So, Point S is in the North-West direction of Bus stop.

Hence, the correct option is (A).

Ques (28-30):Persons: M, N, O, X, Y, and Z

1) Y scores the third highest marks.

___ > ___ > Y > ___ > ___ > ___

2) M scores more marks than only one person.

___ > ___ > Y > ___ > M > ___

3) O scores more marks than Y and M. O does not score the highest number of marks. (So, O will score second highest marks)

___ > O > Y > ___ > M > ___

4) Z scores less marks than O but More marks than M. (So, Z will score fourth highest marks)

___ > O > Y > Z > M > ___

5) N does not score the lowest number of marks. (So, N will score the highest marks)

N > O > Y > Z > M > ___

Thus, the final arrangement will be:

N > O > Y > Z > M > X

So, Z scores the third lowest marks.

28. So, Z scores the third lowest marks.

Hence, the correct option is (C).

29. So, only four students score less marks than O.

Hence, the correct option is (D).

30. So, the possible number of marks scored by M is Twenty.

Hence, the correct option is (E).

31. Options (A), (B) and (C) can easily be eliminated as they do not convey the intended meaning of the sentence. The only option we are left with is option (D) and so the correct answer.

Hence, the correct option is (D).

32. The sentence contains an irony (He is rich; he lives in a small house). The most appropriate word connecting both the sentences would be 'although' because 'although' indicates a contrast.

Hence, the correct option is (D).

33. The sentence talks of a hypothetical. The future continuous tense is appropriate here. However, the use of 'were" in the sentence means we need to modify 'will' to its 'past tense form' i.e., 'would'. So the correct phrase would be 'would be getting'. Therefore, no correction is needed.

Hence, the correct option is (E).

34. The phrase is missing a verb. 'Was' must be included in the phrase to make it meaningful and grammatically correct. The use of the preposition 'to' would be correct in the sentence.

Hence, the correct option is (B).

35. The sentence is comparing poems by William Wordsworth and thus 'one of the best' poems conveys a superlative degree of comparison between the poems and hence is the right answer.

Hence, the correct option is (C).

36. A defines derivatives and is clearly the introductory sentence. AE is a pair with the common theme of 'underlying asset.' B4 is also a pair with B mentioning that the value of a derivative is linked to its underlying asset and sentence 4 stating that by itself (without the underlying asset) a derivative is useless. E follows sentence 4 by giving some examples of derivatives. CF is a pair. C gives an example of a derivative while F with 'similarly' gives another example of a derivative.

The correct order is AEB4DCF.

The ordered paragraph is: A derivative is a contract between two or more parties whose value is based on an agreed-upon underlying financial asset (like a security) or set of assets (like an index). Common underlying asset instruments include bonds, commodities, currencies, interest rates, market indexes, and stocks. Generally belonging to the realm of advanced investing, derivatives are secondary securities whose value is solely based (derived) on the value of the primary security that they are linked to. In and of itself a derivative is worthless. Futures contracts, forward contracts, options, swaps, and warrants are commonly used derivatives. A futures contract, for example, is a derivative because its value is affected by the performance of the underlying asset. Similarly, a stock option is a derivative because its value is "derived" from that of the underlying stock.

Hence, the correct option is (D).

37. A defines derivatives and is clearly the introductory sentence. AE is a pair with the common theme of 'underlying asset.' B4 is also a pair with B mentioning that the value of a derivative is linked to its underlying asset and sentence 4 stating that by itself (without the underlying asset) a derivative is useless. E follows

sentence 4 by giving some examples of derivatives. CF is a pair. C gives an example of a derivative while F with 'similarly' gives another example of a derivative.

The correct order is AEB4DCF.

The ordered paragraph is: A derivative is a contract between two or more parties whose value is based on an agreed-upon underlying financial asset (like a security) or set of assets (like an index). Common underlying asset instruments include bonds, commodities, currencies, interest rates, market indexes, and stocks. Generally belonging to the realm of advanced investing, derivatives are secondary securities whose value is solely based (derived) on the value of the primary security that they are linked to. In and of itself a derivative is worthless. Futures contracts, forward contracts, options, swaps, and warrants are commonly used derivatives. A futures contract, for example, is a derivative because its value is affected by the performance of the underlying asset. Similarly, a stock option is a derivative because its value is "derived" from that of the underlying stock.

Hence, the correct option is (B).

38. A defines derivatives and is clearly the introductory sentence. AE is a pair with the common theme of 'underlying asset.' B4 is also a pair with B mentioning that the value of a derivative is linked to its underlying asset and sentence 4 stating that by itself (without the underlying asset) a derivative is useless. E follows sentence 4 by giving some examples of derivatives. CF is a pair. C gives an example of a derivative while F with 'similarly' gives another example of a derivative.

The correct order is AEB4DCF.

The ordered paragraph is: A derivative is a contract between two or more parties whose value is based on an agreed-upon underlying financial asset (like a security) or set of assets (like an index). Common underlying asset instruments include bonds, commodities, currencies, interest rates, market indexes, and stocks. Generally belonging to the realm of advanced investing, derivatives are secondary securities whose value is solely based (derived) on the value of the primary security that they are linked to. In and of itself a derivative is worthless. Futures contracts, forward contracts, options, swaps, and warrants are commonly used derivatives. A futures contract, for example, is a derivative because its value is affected by the performance of the underlying asset. Similarly, a stock option is a derivative because its value is "derived" from that of the underlying stock.

Hence, the correct option is (E).

39. A defines derivatives and is clearly the introductory sentence. AE is a pair with the common theme of 'underlying asset.' B4 is also a pair with B mentioning that the value of a derivative is linked to its underlying asset and sentence 4 stating that by itself (without the underlying asset) a derivative is useless. E follows sentence 4 by giving some examples of derivatives. CF is a pair. C gives an example of a derivative while F with 'similarly' gives another example of a derivative.

The correct order is AEB4DCF.

The ordered paragraph is: A derivative is a contract between two or more parties whose value is based on an agreed-upon underlying financial asset (like a security) or set of assets (like an

index). Common underlying asset instruments include bonds, commodities, currencies, interest rates, market indexes, and stocks. Generally belonging to the realm of advanced investing, derivatives are secondary securities whose value is solely based (derived) on the value of the primary security that they are linked to. In and of itself a derivative is worthless. Futures contracts, forward contracts, options, swaps, and warrants are commonly used derivatives. A futures contract, for example, is a derivative because its value is affected by the performance of the underlying asset. Similarly, a stock option is a derivative because its value is "derived" from that of the underlying stock.

Hence, the correct option is (A).

40. A defines derivatives and is clearly the introductory sentence. AE is a pair with the common theme of 'underlying asset.' B4 is also a pair with B mentioning that the value of a derivative is linked to its underlying asset and sentence 4 stating that by itself (without the underlying asset) a derivative is useless. E follows sentence 4 by giving some examples of derivatives. CF is a pair. C gives an example of a derivative while F with 'similarly' gives another example of a derivative.

The correct order is AEB4DCF.

The ordered paragraph is: A derivative is a contract between two or more parties whose value is based on an agreed-upon underlying financial asset (like a security) or set of assets (like an index). Common underlying asset instruments include bonds, commodities, currencies, interest rates, market indexes, and stocks. Generally belonging to the realm of advanced investing, derivatives are secondary securities whose value is solely based (derived) on the value of the primary security that they are linked to. In and of itself a derivative is worthless. Futures contracts, forward contracts, options, swaps, and warrants are commonly used derivatives. A futures contract, for example, is a derivative because its value is affected by the performance of the underlying asset. Similarly, a stock option is a derivative because its value is "derived" from that of the underlying stock.

Hence, the correct option is (A).

41. Here, one can easily find the answer from the given words if the context and the relative word in brackets are understood.

Let's know the meaning of the words given in options.

- Cluster means a group of similar things or people.
- Calmed means absolute quietness or to be at peace.
- Fearfulness refers to having fear or filled with terror.
- Crowded refer to full of people or things; completely packed.
- Frustrated refers to feeling or expressing distress and annoyance.
- Among the given words, it is clear that frustrated will be the most suitable word for the blank.

Hence, the correct option is (E).

42. Here one can easily find the answer from the given words if the context and the relative word in brackets are understood.

- Let's know the meaning of some of the other words given in options.
- Profession refers to the occupation or job done by someone
- Caravan refers to a group of people, traveling across the borders along with vehicles and cargo.
- Parade refers to a public procession especially one celebrating a special day or event.
- March refers to walk in a military manner with a regular measured tread.
- Among the given words, it is clear that caravan would be the most suitable word for the blank as it completes the sentence appropriately making it meaningful and grammatically correct.

Hence, the correct option is (B).

43. Here one can easily find the answer from the given words if the context and the relative word in brackets are understood. If one looks at the options, all are names of fruits mentioned but the answer should be something related to the shape of a pear.

Avocados refer to a pear-shaped fruit with rough leathery skin.

Mangoes, apples, grapes and melons are clearly not pear-shaped so they can be eliminated.

So the correct answer will be avocados.

Hence, the correct option is (D).

44. Here, one can easily find the answer from the given words if the context and the relative word in brackets are understood.

Let's know the meaning of the words given in options.

- Sounded refers to convey a message of information.
- Gleamed refers to shine brightly.
- Blistered refers to swelling or having blisters on the skin.
- Abundant refers to existing or available in large quantities.
- Among the given words, it is clear that sounded will be the most suitable word for the blank as it completes the sentence appropriately making it meaningful and grammatically correct.

Hence, the correct option is (A).

45. Here, one can easily find the answer from the given words if the context and the relative word in brackets are understood.

Let's know the meaning of the words given in options.

- Halting refers to an abrupt or sudden stop.
- Reciprocating refers to respond or a to-fro motion.
- Invigilating refers to overseeing a test or exam.
- Emerging refers to starting to exist or growing and developing,
- Among the given words, it is clear that halting will be the most suitable word for the blank as it completes

the sentence appropriately making it meaningful and grammatically correct.

Hence, the correct option is (D).

46. In this sentence, there are two action verbs. The action verb tells us what the subject of our clause or sentence is doing- physically or mentally.

E.g. - Marie **walked** to school. (Walked tells us what Marie was doing.)

E.g. - Louis **thought** about the math problem. (Thought tells us what Louis was doing (mentally).)

First action verb – "he had studied" is the past perfect tense. Second action verb – "The chairman had not taken"

Since the first action word is in past perfect tense, the second action word should also be in simple past tense to maintain it's past perfect sense meaning i.e. to indicate something that has occurred in the simple past contrary to past perfect, which shows the past of the past (he had studied).

The correct sentence is:

The chairman **did not** take any decision until he had studied the case thoroughly.

Hence, the correct option is (A).

47. In this sentence, it is important to understand the properties of conditionals (if-clause statements). Now, the correct construction says that if 'would + have + 3rd form of the verb is used in the main clause, which in this case is 'would not have come'. Then, the if clause should contain had + 3rd form of verb, which is not the case in this sentence. So, 'would have realised' shall be replaced by 'had realised'.

The correct sentence is :-

If I **had** realized what a bad driver you were, I would not have come with you.

Hence, the correct option is (A).

48. No improvement is required here.

This is because both plays and play in the (D) part are correct.

None of the seven contenders who have been given the chance to join the league here, **who** is a relative pronoun for 7 contenders and after that the verb **plays** reflect the subject **none** which can take both singular and plural in any case. The single rule for none: In pure form, None takes only singular e.g., None likes him.

Hence, the correct option is (E).

49. The error lies in the third part of the sentence.

In the given sentence, the usage of tenses is inappropriate. Here, verbs are discussed here, i.e. lost. Remember that, 'lost' remains same in all the tenses. Thus, replace 'losted' with 'lost'.

Correct Sentence- Within two years, the sister had lost their parents in a tragic accident.

Hence, the correct option is (C).

50. On analysing the sentence, we find that it is based on the parallel structure problem. Parallel structure means using the same pattern of words to show that two or more words or ideas are of equal importance.

When analyse part (A) and (B) of the sentence we find that a noun (education) and a verb (pay), but in part (C) and (D) of the sentence, there is only a noun (financial aid). We can't find any verb out there.

The correct sentence is:-

I would rather pay for my education than **receive/get** financial aid.

Hence, the correct option is (C).

51. Tom applied for a promotion twice this year, but he was _turned down_ both times.

Since the structure of the sentence is past tense, 'turned down' is the appropriate verb. **Turn something/somebody down** is a phrasal verb that means 'to refuse an offer or request'. For example: He turned down the job because it involved too much travelling.

The rest of the options are canceled as they make the sentence meaningless and are not in agreement with the tense of the sentence.

Hence, the correct option is (A).

52. The sentence suggests that the blank should contain a noun as it is used with the article 'an'.

Given the context, the word should mean 'level'.

The only option that gives the intended meaning is 'extent'.

Hence, the correct option is (B).

53. The sentence suggests that the blank should contain a noun as it is used with the article 'the'.

The word is referred to by the pronoun 'it', indicating that it must be in its singular form.

The only option that gives the intended meaning is 'state'.

Hence, the correct option is (C).

54. Options (A), (D) and (E) can be straightaway discarded because 'many' is used for 'countable nouns'. 'Many' denotes 'large number', whereas **'much' denotes 'large quantity' of an 'uncountable noun'.**

Since journalists are to be thanked for their efforts and support, 'much' must be used.

The sentence is in Present tense. Thus, 'had' is incorrect.

'Have much' must be used to fill the blank.

Hence, the correct option is (C).

55. The passage is about Marie Curie and her contribution to the field of science which won her the Nobel Prize.

According to the passage, "In 1911 she received the Nobel Prize in chemistry for isolating radium."

Hence, the correct option is (A).

56. The passage is about Marie Curie and her contribution to the field of science which won her the Nobel Prize.

According to the passage, "Curie discovered radium. She shared this discovery with Pierre Curie and Gustave Bemont."

Hence, the correct option is (D).

57. The passage is about Marie Curie and her contribution to the field of science which won her the Nobel Prize.

According to the passage, "Curie eventually suffered a fatal illness from her long exposure to radium."

Hence, the correct option is (B).

58. The passage is about Marie Curie and her contribution to the field of science which won her the Nobel Prize.

According to the passage, "Curie discovered radium. She shared this discovery with Pierre Curie and Gustave Bemont."

Hence, the correct option is (C).

59. In the passage, 'amicable' is used to refer to the friendly relationship shared between Pierre and Curie.

An example of the same is: "I hope that they will be able to reach amicable agreement."

Hence, the correct option is (A).

60. The meaning of the word 'recovery' is 'the process of getting better or improvement'.

The word 'economic' is an adjective. So, a noun should be used after it. Clearly, options (A),(B), (D), and (E) should be eliminated.

'recovery' is the only word that fits well here.

Complete sentences:

1. As India prepares to celebrate its Diwali festival, stockbrokers see growing signs of an economic *recovery*.

2. The doctors are worried as he is not showing any signs of *recovery*.

Hence, the correct option is (C).

61. Given:

Investment of A, B and C are Rs.4000, Rs. 8000 and Rs. 12000 respectively

Total profit they got after 1 year = Rs. 12,000

Concept used:

Profit is directly proportional to product of amount invested and time period of investment.

Profit ratio of A : B : C = Rs. 4000 : Rs. 8000 : Rs. 12,000

$\Rightarrow$ 1 : 2 : 3

Total profit = (1 + 2 + 3) units

$\Rightarrow$ 6 units

Profit of B and C together = (2 + 3) units

$\Rightarrow$ 5 units

According to the question,

6 units = Rs. 12,000

$\Rightarrow$ 5 units = Rs. $\left(\dfrac{12,000}{6}\right) \times 5$

$\Rightarrow$ Rs. 10,000

$\therefore$ The profit of B and C together is Rs. 10,000

Hence, the correct option is (B).

62. The pattern is as follows:

$5 \times 2 - 6 = 4$

$4 \times 3 - 12 = 0$

$0 \times 4 - 18 = -18$

$-18 \times 5 - 24 = -114$

$-114 \times 6 - 30 = -714$

$-714 \times 7 - 36 = -5034$

$\therefore$ The value of ? is -5034.

Hence, the correct option is (B).

63. The pattern is as follows:

$10 = 1 \times 10$

$90 = 10 \times 9$

$720 = 90 \times 8$

$5040 = 720 \times 7$

$30240 = 5040 \times 6$

$? = 30240 \times 5$

$? = 151200$

$\therefore$ The value of ? is 151200.

Hence, the correct option is (B).

64. The pattern is as follows:

$8 \times 1 = 8$

$8 \times 1.5 = 12$

$12 \times 2 = 24$

$24 \times 2.5 = 60$

$60 \times 3 = 180$

$180 \times 3.5 = 630$

$\therefore$ The value of ? is 24.

Hence, the correct option is (A).

65. The pattern is as follows:

$1^2 + 2 = 3$

$2^2 + 2 = 6$

$3^2 + 2 = 11$

$4^2 + 2 = 18$

$5^2 + 2 = 27$

$6^2 + 2 = 38$

$? = 7^2 + 2$

$? = 51$

$\therefore$ The value of ? is 51.

Hence, the correct option is (D).

66. The pattern is as follows:

$384 \times \dfrac{3}{2} = 576$

$576 \times \dfrac{5}{2} = 1440$

$1440 \times \dfrac{7}{2} = 5040$

$5040 \times \dfrac{9}{2} = 22680$

$\therefore$ The value of ? is 5040.

Hence, the correct option is (C).

67. Given,

Speed of boat in still water $= 10mph$

Distance covered by boat in downstream and upstream $= 36$ miles

Let the speed of the stream be x mph.

Then,

Speed in downstream $= (10 + x)mph$

Speed in upstream $= (10 - x)mph$

Therefore,

$\dfrac{36}{10-x} - \dfrac{36}{10+x} = \dfrac{90}{60}$

$\Rightarrow \dfrac{36\times(10+x)-36\times(10-x)}{(10-x)\times(10+x)} = \dfrac{90}{60}$

$\Rightarrow \dfrac{72x}{(100-x^2)} = \dfrac{90}{60}$

$\Rightarrow 72x \times 60 = 90(100 - x^2)$

$\Rightarrow x^2 + 48x - 100 = 0$

$\Rightarrow (x + 50)(x - 2) = 0$

$\Rightarrow x = 2mph$

Hence, the correct option is (A).

68. First Equation:

$x^2 + 36x + 243 = 0$

$\Rightarrow x^2 + 27x + 9x + 243 = 0$

$\Rightarrow x(x + 27) + 9(x + 27) = 0$

$\Rightarrow (x + 27)(x + 9) = 0$

$\Rightarrow x = -27$ or $x = -9$

Second Equation:

$2y^2 - 32y + 120 = 0$

$\Rightarrow 2y^2 - 12y - 20y + 120 = 0$

$\Rightarrow 2y(y - 6) - 20(y - 6) = 0$

$\Rightarrow (y - 6)(2y - 20) = 0$

$\Rightarrow y = 6$ or $y = 10$

$\therefore x < y$

Hence, the correct option is (C).

69. First Equation:

$x^2 + 64x + 960 = 0$

$\Rightarrow x^2 + 40x + 24x + 960 = 0$

$\Rightarrow x(x + 40) + 24(x + 40) = 0$

$\Rightarrow (x + 40)(x + 24) = 0$

$\Rightarrow x = -40$ or $x = -24$

Second Equation:

$y^2 + 32y + 240 = 0$

$\Rightarrow y^2 + 20y + 12y + 240 = 0$

$\Rightarrow y(y + 20) + 12(y + 20) = 0$

$\Rightarrow (y + 20)(y + 12) = 0$

$\Rightarrow y = -20$ or $y = -12$

$\therefore x < y$

Hence, the correct option is (C).

70. First Equation:

$x^2 - 269x + 534 = 0$

$\Rightarrow x^2 - 2x - 267x + 534 = 0$

$\Rightarrow x(x - 2) - 267(x - 2) = 0$

$\Rightarrow (x - 2)(x - 267) = 0$

$\Rightarrow x = 2$ or $x = 267$

Second Equation:

$6y^2 - 24y + 18 = 0$

$\Rightarrow 6y^2 - 18y - 6y + 18 = 0$

$\Rightarrow 6y(y - 3) - 6(y - 3) = 0$

$\Rightarrow (y - 3)(6y - 6) = 0$

$\Rightarrow y = 3 \text{ or } y = 1$

$\therefore$ we can observe that no clear relationship cannot be determined between x and y.

Hence, the correct option is (E).

71. There are 10 questions in part A out of which 8 question can be chosen $= {}^{10}C_8$

Similarly, 5 questions can be chosen from 10 questions of Part $B = {}^{10}C_5$

So, total number of ways $= {}^{10}C_8 \times {}^{10}C_5$

$= \dfrac{10!}{8!(10-8)!} \times \dfrac{10!}{5!(10-5)!}$

$= \dfrac{10!}{2! \times 8!} \times \dfrac{10!}{5! \times 5}$

$= \left(10 \times \dfrac{9}{2}\right) \times \left(\dfrac{10 \times 9 \times 8 \times 7 \times 6}{5 \times 4 \times 3 \times 2 \times 1}\right)$

$= 11340$

Hence, the correct option is (A).

72. Given,

Qualified candidates $= 4000$

Qualified candidates from D, E and F $= \dfrac{(16+20+16)}{100} \times 4000$

$= \dfrac{52}{100} \times 4000$

$= 52 \times 40$

Appeared candidates from A, B and C $= \dfrac{(25+10+15)}{100} \times 24000$

$= \dfrac{50}{100} \times 24000$

$= 50 \times 240$

Required ratio $= \dfrac{52 \times 40}{50 \times 240}$

$= 13 : 75$

Hence, the correct option is (E).

73. Given,

Qualified candidates = 4000

Qualified candidates from institute C = 18% × 4000

$= \dfrac{18}{100} \times 4000$

$= 18 \times 40$

Appeared candidates from institute C = 15% × 24000

$= \dfrac{15}{100} \times 24000$

$= 15 \times 240$

Required % $= \dfrac{18 \times 40 \times 100}{15 \times 240}$

$= 20\%$

Hence, the correct option is (D).

74. Given,

Qualified candidates = 4000

Appeared Candidates =24000

Percentage of Qualified candidates from C =18%

Percentage of Qualified candidates from D = 16%

Percentage of appeared candidates from C =15%

Percentage of appeared candidates from D = 12%

Qualified candidates from C and D together = (18 + 16) % × 4000

$= \dfrac{(18+16)}{100} \times 4000$

$= 34 \times 40$

Appeared candidates from C and D together = (15 + 12) % × 24000

$= \dfrac{(15+12)}{100} \times 24000$

$= 27 \times 240$

Required $\%$ $= \dfrac{34 \times 40 \times 100}{27 \times 240}$

$= 20.98\%$

Hence, the correct option is (C).

75. Given,

Percentage of candidates qualified with respect to those appeared:

$A = \dfrac{18 \times 4}{24 \times 25}$

$B = \dfrac{12 \times 4}{10 \times 24}$

$C = \dfrac{18 \times 4}{15 \times 24}$

$D = \dfrac{16 \times 4}{12 \times 24}$

$E = \dfrac{20 \times 4}{18 \times 24}$

$F = \dfrac{16 \times 4}{20 \times 24}$

In these values $\dfrac{4}{24}$ can be discarded because it is common in comparison.

So,

$$A = \frac{18}{25}$$

$$B = \frac{12}{10}$$

$$C = \frac{18}{15}$$

$$D = \frac{16}{12}$$

$$E = \frac{20}{18}$$

$$F = \frac{16}{20}$$

Here, A and F are less than 1, so they are removed without solving.

B = 1.2

C = 1.2

D = 1.33

E = 1.1

D has the highest percentage of qualified candidates with respect to those who appeared.

Hence, the correct option is (B).

76. Given,

Qualified candidates = 4000

Appeared Candidates = 24000

Percentage of Qualified candidates from B = 12%

Qualified candidates from institute B = 12% × 4000

Percentage of appeared candidates from F = 20%

Appeared candidates from institute from institute F = 20% × 24000

$$\text{Required ratio} = \frac{12\% \times 4000}{20\% \times 24000}$$

$$= \frac{\frac{12}{100} \times 4000}{\frac{20}{100} \times 24000}$$

$$= 1 : 10$$

Hence, the correct option is (A).

77. Given,

Principal amount $= Rs.\ 10{,}000$

Interest rates $= 10\%$ p.a.

Time $= 5$ years

As we know,

$$\text{Simple interest} = \frac{(P \times R \times T)}{100}$$

Where, $P =$ Principal Amount

$R =$ Interest rate

$T =$ Time for which interest is applied on amount

$$\text{Simple interest} = \frac{10000 \times 10 \times 5}{100} = Rs.\ 5000$$

∴ Simple interest is Rs. 5000.

Hence, the correct option is (D).

78. Given,

P = Rs. 1250, A = Rs. 1550, T = 4 years

$$\text{Simple interest} = \frac{(P \times R \times T)}{100}$$

Let, rate of interest be r%.

Interest earned = Rs (1550 – 1250) = Rs. 300

According to the question,

$$\frac{(1250 \times 4 \times r)}{100} = 300$$

⇒ 5000r = 30000

⇒ r = 6

∴ Rate of interest = 6%

Hence, the correct option is (D).

79. Given,

Mannu can do a piece of work in 9 days while.

Naina can do a piece of work in 5 days.

Total wage = Rs. 420

The wages will be distributed according to the ratio of the efficiency.

Mannu's one day work = 5units / day

Naina's one day work = 9 units / day

Wages will be in ratio - 5 : 9

According to the question,

5x + 9x = 420

9x = 420

x = 30

Earnings of Mannu = 5x = 5 × 30 = Rs. 150

Hence, the correct option is (B).

80. Total number of balls = 7 + 8 + 9 = 24

Let S be the sample space.

n(S) = Number of ways of drawing 4 balls from 24 = $^{24}C_4$ = $\frac{(24 \times 23 \times 22 \times 21)}{(4 \times 3 \times 2 \times 1)}$ = 10626

Let E be the event that none of the drawn balls are white.

∴ n(E) = $^{16}C_4$ = $\frac{(16 \times 15 \times 14 \times 13)}{(4 \times 3 \times 2 \times 1)}$ = 1820

∴ P(E) = $\frac{n(E)}{n(S)} = \frac{1820}{10626} = \frac{910}{5313} = \frac{130}{759}$

Hence, the correct option is (A).

81. Given:

Total number of subjects = 3

Maximum marks in each subject = 80

Average marks scored by Abhilasha in all the three subjects together = 57

We know that:

Average marks scored in each subject =
$$\frac{\text{Total marks scored in all the subjects}}{\text{Total number of subjects}}$$

Total marks scored by her in all the subjects together = 57 × 3 = 171

If she scores 12 marks more in any subject, her new total marks = 171 + 12 = 183

So, her new average marks in all the subjects together = $\frac{183}{3}$ = 61

∴ The new average of total marks scored by Abhilasha in all the three subjects together is 61

Hence, the correct option is (D).

82. Given,

Time taken by first two pipes = Time taken by third pipe alone

Let the first pipe alone takes x hours to fill the tank.

Then, time taken by second pipe = $(x - 5)$ hours

Time taken by third pipe = $(x - 9)$ hours

According to question,

Time taken by first two pipes = Time taken by third pipe alone

$$\frac{1}{x} + \frac{1}{x-5} = \frac{1}{x-9}$$

$$\Rightarrow \frac{x-5+x}{x(x-5)} = \frac{1}{x-9}$$

$$\Rightarrow (2x - 5)(x - 9) = x(x - 5)$$

$$\Rightarrow x^2 - 18x + 45 = 0$$

$$\Rightarrow (x - 15)(x - 3) = 0$$

We will not take x as 3 because this will give the negative value of an hour which is not possible.

Therefore,

$$x - 15 = 0$$

$$\Rightarrow x = 15$$

∴ The time required by the first pipe is 15 hours.

Hence, the correct option is (C).

83. Follow the BODMAS rule according to the table given below:

B	Brackets in order ( ), { }, [ ]	ब्रेकट ( ), { }, [ ] क्रम
O	Of	का
D	Division (÷)	विभाजन (÷)
M	Multiplication (×)	गुणा (×)
A	Addition (+)	जोड़ (+)
S	Subtraction (-)	घटाव (-)

Given:

$\frac{1}{4}$th of $\frac{1}{2}$ of $\frac{3}{4}$th of 52000 =?

$$\Rightarrow \left(\frac{1}{4}\right) \times \left(\frac{1}{2}\right) \times \left(\frac{3}{4}\right) \times 52000 =?$$

$$\Rightarrow \frac{(52000 \times 3)}{32} =?$$

$$\Rightarrow 1625 \times 3 =?$$

$$\Rightarrow 4875 =?$$

∴ The required value of ? is 4875.

Hence, the correct option is (A).

84. Follow the BODMAS rule according to the table given below:

B	Brackets in order ( ), { }, [ ]	ब्रेकट ( ), { }, [ ] क्रम
O	Of	का
D	Division (÷)	विभाजन (÷)
M	Multiplication (×)	गुणा (×)
A	Addition (+)	जोड़ (+)
S	Subtraction (-)	घटाव (-)

Given: $\sqrt[3]{12167} \times \sqrt[3]{5832} =?$

$$\sqrt[3]{12167} = 23$$

Also $\sqrt[3]{5832} = 18$

So, $\sqrt[3]{12167} \times \sqrt[3]{5832} = 23 \times 18$

$$= 414$$

Hence, the correct option is (C).

85. Follow the BODMAS rule according to the table given below:

B	Brackets in order ( ), { }, [ ]	ब्रेकट ( ), { }, [ ] क्रम
O	Of	का
D	Division (÷)	विभाजन (÷)
M	Multiplication (×)	गुणा (×)
A	Addition (+)	जोड़ (+)
S	Subtraction (-)	घटाव (-)

Given:

$\frac{3}{7}$ of $\frac{4}{5}$ of $\frac{5}{8}$ of $490 =?$

$$\Rightarrow \left[\frac{(3\times4\times5)}{(7\times5\times8)}\right] \times 490 =?$$

$$\Rightarrow \left(\frac{60}{280}\right) \times 490 =?$$

$$\Rightarrow \left(\frac{3}{14}\right) \times 490 =?$$

$\Rightarrow 3 \times 35 = ?$

$\Rightarrow ? = 105$

Hence, the correct option is (B).

86. Follow the BODMAS rule according to the table given below:

B	Brackets in order ( ), { }, [ ]	ब्रैकट ( ), { }, [ ] क्रम
O	Of	का
D	Division (÷)	विभाजन (÷)
M	Multiplication (×)	गुणा (×)
A	Addition (+)	जोड़ (+)
S	Subtraction (-)	घटाव (-)

Given:

7855 – 4236 + 388 = ? + 3974

⇒? = 7855 - 4236 + 388 - 3974

⇒? = (7855 + 388) - (4236 + 3974)

⇒ ?= 8243 - 8210 = 33

Hence, the correct option is (C).

87. Follow the BODMAS rule according to the table given below:

B	Brackets in order ( ), { }, [ ]	ब्रैकट ( ), { }, [ ] क्रम
O	Of	का
D	Division (÷)	विभाजन (÷)
M	Multiplication (×)	गुणा (×)
A	Addition (+)	जोड़ (+)
S	Subtraction (-)	घटाव (-)

Given:

(8.2% of 365) – (1.75% of 108) = ?

$$\Rightarrow \left[\left(\frac{8.2}{100}\right) \times 365\right] - \left[\left(\frac{1.75}{100}\right) \times 108\right)\right] = ?$$

$$\Rightarrow \frac{[(8.2 \times 365) - (1.75 \times 108)]}{100} = ?$$

$$\Rightarrow \frac{(2993 - 189)}{100} = ?$$

$$\Rightarrow ? = \frac{2804}{100} = 28.04$$

Hence, the correct option is (B).

88. Area of the rectangular land = area of all the plots

⇒ (3 × 50 m × 20 m) + (4 × 40 m × 30 m) + (4 × 30 m × 25 m)

⇒ 3000 + 4800 + 3000

⇒ 10800 m²

Area of the land with the given options,

⇒ 140 m × 80 m = 11200 m²

⇒ 160 m × 70 m = 11200 m²

⇒ 180 m × 60 m = 10800 m²

⇒ 200 m × 50 m = 10000 m²

⇒ 220 m × 40 m = 8800 m²

∴ The possible dimensions of the rectangular land is 180 m × 60 m.

Hence, the correct option is (C).

89. Let the maximum marks be x.

Given: Ramesh scored = 556 marks

Rajesh scored = 69% marks

Also given that, 69% of x = 556 – 4

Thus, 69% of x = 552

$$\left(\frac{69}{100}\right) \times x = 552$$

∴ x = 800

Therefore, the maximum mark is 800.

Passing marks = 34% of 800

$$= \left(\frac{34}{100}\right) \times 800$$

= 272 marks

Thus, Ramesh scored (556 – 272) = 284 marks more than the minimum passing marks.

Hence, the correct option is (A).

90. Heath buys sugar at Rs. 50 per kg and sells at Rs. 60 per kg.

The customer bought 3 kg of sugar.

Cost price of rice = 3 × Rs. 50 = Rs. 150

Selling price of rice = 3 × Rs. 60 = Rs. 180

The customer gave him a note of Rs. 500 and he returned him the balance money including both fake notes of Rs. 100.

So, Heath earned a profit of Rs. 30 from the actual difference between selling and cost price. Also, he earned Rs. 200 more by returning fake notes.

⇒ On cost price of Rs. 150, profit earned is Rs. 230.

We know, profit percentage = $100 \times \dfrac{Profit}{Cost\ price}$ = 100

$\times \dfrac{230}{150}$ = 153.33%

Hence, the correct option is (C).

Reasoning Ability

Ques (1-3):Direction: Read the information given and answer given question.

In a certain code language,

"google goal nexas device" is written as "H9# O6\$ H4@ E9#"

"android ecosystem open plateform" is written as "P4+ Q18© B12& F18©"

"facebook uses cortana assistant" is written as "V4\$ D12? G16% B18*"

"microsoft focus windows environment" is written as "N18* X10\$ G6\$ F28*"

(note: All the code are 3 element code with 1 letter, 1 symbol and 1 number)

Q.1 What is the possible code for 'assistant' in the code language?
A. B18?　　**B.** D12?　　**C.** B18*　　**D.** G16%
E. B11?

Q.2 In the given code language what does '©' stand for ?
A. D　　**B.** M　　**C.** K　　**D.** A
E. N

Q.3 What is the possible code for "amazon has prime concept" ?
A.　A9# H2\$ P6# C10*
B.　B7# I3\$ Q6# D10*
C.　B9+ I2\$ Q6# D10*
D.　B9? H2\$ Q6# C10*
E.　B9* I2# Q6\$ D10?

Ques (4-8):Direction: Read the following information carefully and answer the given questions:

Six persons P, Q, R, S, T and U are sitting in a row. R sits one of the extreme ends of the row. S sits third from the right end. Only one person sits between P and U, where U is to the right of P. Neither P nor U is a neighbour of R. T does not sit at an extreme ends. Number of persons to the left of Q is same the number of persons to the right of R.

Q.4 How many person(s) does not change their positions when they arranged in English alphabetical order from the left side?
A. One　　**B.** Two　　**C.** None　　**D.** Three
E. Four

Q.5 Who among the following sit at an extreme end?
A. S　　**B.** T　　**C.** P　　**D.** U
E. Q

Q.6 How many persons sit between T and U?

A. None　　**B.** One　　**C.** Two　　**D.** Three
E. Four

Q.7 Who is an immediate neighbour of Q?
A. P　　**B.** S　　**C.** R　　**D.** U
E. T

Q.8 Who sits second from the left end?
A. R　　**B.** T　　**C.** P　　**D.** S
E. U

Ques (9-13):Direction: Study the following information carefully to answer the given questions.

Certain number of persons lives in a building with less than twelve floors. Some floors are vacant. The ground floor is numbered 1, the floor above ground floor is numbered 2 and so on.

B lives on the bottommost floor. Number of floors above E is same as number of floors below A. F lives on a floor which is an even numbered below A's floor. There is a gap of two floors between G and E. D lives on even numbered floor. There are five floors between A and C. There is a gap of two floors between A and B. G lives on a floor which is immediately above C.

Q.9 How many vacant floors are there in the building?
A. One　　**B.** Four　　**C.** Three　　**D.** Five
E. Two

Q.10 D lives on which floor?
A. 2nd floor　　　　　　**B.** 4th floor
C. 8th floor　　　　　　**D.** 10th floor
E. None of the above

Q.11 How many persons live between D and B?
A. One　　**B.** Five　　**C.** Three　　**D.** Two
E. Zero

Q.12 How many floors are there in the building?
A. Nine　　**B.** Ten　　**C.** Eleven　　**D.** Thirteen
E. Twelve

Q.13 Who lives on floor number 8?
A. G　　**B.** C　　**C.** D　　**D.** E
E. Vacant

Q.14 If it is possible to form only one meaningful word using the first, third, fifth and eighth letters of the word 'APPECIATION', then which of the following will be the second letter of the word? If no such word can be formed, mark 'Y' as the answer and if any such word can be formed, mark 'Z' as the answer.
A. M　　**B.** X　　**C.** A　　**D.** Y
E. Z

Ques (15-16):Direction: A series is given with one term missing. Select the correct alternative from the given ones that will complete the series.

Q.15 Y, V, Q, J, ?

A. B **B.** Y
C. A **D.** X
E. None of these

Q.16 ?, HI, OP, WX

A. AB **B.** BC
C. DE **D.** EF
E. None of these

Ques (17-19):Direction: Following questions are based on five words given below.

(The new words formed after performing the mentioned operations may or may not necessarily be meaningful English words)

EDC, TGF, VBJ, QAL, KJU

Q.17 If the given words are arranged in the order as they would appear in a dictionary from left to right, how many alphabets are there in English alphabetical series between first and last letter of the word which will be fourth from right?

A. One **B.** Seven **C.** Eight **D.** Four
E. Nine

Q.18 If the first and last alphabet of each word is changed to the previous alphabet and the middle alphabet is changed to its next alphabet in the English alphabetical series, how many words having only consonants will be formed?

A. One **B.** Three **C.** Four **D.** Two
E. Five

Q.19 If in each word, we interchange both alphabets present at odd positions, how many words ending with vowels will be formed?

A. Four **B.** Three
C. One **D.** Two
E. None of these

Ques (20-22):Directions: In the question below are given two statements followed by two conclusions numbered I and II. You must take the given statements to be true even if they seem to be at variance with commonly known facts. Read all the conclusions and then decide which of the given conclusions logically follow (s) from the given statements disregarding commonly known facts.

Q.20 Statements:

All papers are pens.

All papers are pencils.

Conclusions:

I. Some pens are pencils.
II. All pencils are pens.

A. Only I follows
B. Only II follows
C. Both I and II follow
D. Neither I nor II follows
E. Either I or II follows

Q.21 Statements:

All RBI is Bank.

No SEBI is Bank.

Conclusions:

I. No RBI is SEBI.
II. Some RBI is SEBI.

A. Either I or II follows
B. Neither I nor II follows
C. Both I and II follow
D. Only I follows
E. Only II follows

Q.22 Statements:

Only a few mobiles are smartphones.

Some smartphones are iPhones.

Conclusions:

I. Some iPhones are mobile.
II. Some mobiles are not iPhones.

A. Only I follows
B. Only II follows
C. Either I or II follows
D. Neither I nor II follows
E. Both I and II follow

Q.23 In a queue of students facing north, Ayesha and Anisha are standing at 10th and 8th position from the left and right end respectively. If another student Ariva who is 12th from the left end is exactly in between Ayesha and Anisha then find the position of Ayesha from right end?

A. 10th **B.** 12th
C. 15th **D.** 8th
E. Can't be determined

Q.24 In a class of 35 students, Ziya is placed 7th from the bottom where as Sofia is placed 9th from the top. Shahruk is placed in between the two. What is Ziya's position from Shahruk?

A. 10 **B.** 15 **C.** 19 **D.** 21
E. 25

Q.25 There are 25 students in a class and all of them are sitting in a row to do yoga. Meena is 11th from the top and Sneha is 6th from the bottom. Two students are sitting between Ananya and Reena. What is the position of Reena from the top?

A. 12th **B.** 13th
C. 16th **D.** 14th
E. Can't be determined

Ques (26-28):Directions: Study the following information to answer the given Questions:

In the following questions, the symbols #, %, &, @ are used with the following meaning illustrated.

P @ Q → Point P is in east of point Q.

P * Q → Point P is in west of Point Q.

P # Q → Point P is in south of Point Q.

P & Q → Point P is in north of Point Q.

P @20 → means point P is 20 km in the east of point Q.

Two persons V and U started from point A and point G respectively and finally meet at point W. Point G is exactly in the east of point A.

V follows: A *16 B #10 C @8 D #14 E *23 F &16 W

U follows: G #4 H @9 I &6 J @5 K #9 L @10 W

Q.26 In which direction is point F with respect to the point I?
[Union Bank of India Clerk, 2020], [IBPS Clerk, 2020], [Bank of Maharashtra Clerk, 2020]

A. North   **B.** South-West
C. North-East   **D.** North-West
E. None of the above

Q.27 What is the shortest distance between point B and point W?
[Union Bank of India Clerk, 2020], [IBPS Clerk, 2020], [Bank of Maharashtra Clerk, 2020]

A. 16 km   **B.** 20 km   **C.** 17 km   **D.** 18 km
E. 21 km

Q.28 What is the distance between point A and G?
[Union Bank of India Clerk, 2020], [IBPS Clerk, 2020], [Bank of Maharashtra Clerk, 2020]

A. 55 km   **B.** 54 km
C. 60 km   **D.** 44 km
E. None of the above

Ques (29-30):Direction: Study the information given below carefully and answer the questions that follow.

There are 7 members in the family. There are 2 married couples. R is son of H. S is mother of A. H is son of S. Y and H are married couples. A is aunt of I who is the daughter of Y. I is sister-in-law of J.

Q.29 What is relationship between A and R?
A. Aunt– Nephew   **B.** Father – Son
C. Mother – daughter   **D.** Aunt – Niece
E. Brother – Sister

Q.30 How is Y related to J?
A. Daughter – in – law   **B.** Uncle
C. Daughter   **D.** Mother– in – law
E. Son

English Language

Ques (31-35):Direction: In the following question, a paragraph is given with three blanks, followed by six words. You have to choose the most suitable combination of words from the five options forming a grammatically correct and contextually meaningful paragraph. If none of the combinations appropriately fill the blank, mark option E, 'None of these' as the answer.

Q.31 The compact city is commonly identified as a high-density and mixed-use development pattern. This pattern is considered to be effective in ______ urban sprawl by intensifying activity density in urban areas, ______ trips in personal vehicles, and providing diverse services through mixed land use, and by ______ old urban areas and preserving rural areas by promoting infill development.

i. Restructuring
ii. Reducing
iii. Relaxing
iv. Revitalizing
v. Restraining
vi. Revamping

A. ii, v, vi   **B.** v, ii, vi
C. i, iii, v   **D.** ii, iv, vi
E. None of these

Q.32 An enterprise is classified as proprietary if an individual is its sole ______ and as a partnership if there are two or more owners on a partnership basis with our ______ formal registration. It ______ all corporate entities, registered co-operatives, trusts, and other legal entities which do not conform with the conditions.

i. Without
ii. Lacking
iii. Excludes
iv. Includes
v. Discusses
vi. Owner

A. vi, i, iii   **B.** v, iv, iii
C. iv, ii, vi   **D.** ii, iv, v
E. None of these

Q.33 Life on earth depends on energy from the ______. About 30 percent of the sunlight that beams toward Earth is deflected by the outer atmosphere and scattered back into ______. The rest reaches the planet's surface and is reflected upward again as a type of slow-moving ______ called infrared radiation.

i. power
ii. Milky way
iii. Energy
iv. Space
v. Sun
vi. Sunlight

A. vi, i, iii   **B.** v, iv, iii
C. iv, ii, vi   **D.** ii, iv, v
E. None of these

Q.34 JNNURM requires certain reforms to be undertaken by states/ cities in Community Participation, with the ______ of institutionalizing citizen participation as well as ______ the concept of the Area Sabha in urban areas. The larger objective is to ______ citizens in municipal functions, e.g. setting priorities, budgeting provisions, etc.

i. Introduction
ii. Introducing

iii. Ornery

iv. Objective

v. Involvement

vi. Involve

A. vi, i, iii　　　　**B.** v, iv, iii

C. iv, ii, vi　　　　**D.** ii, iv, v

E. None of these

Q.35 While the greenhouse effect is an essential environmental ______ for life on Earth, there really can be too much of a good thing. The problems begin when human activities ______ and accelerate the natural process by creating more greenhouse gases in the atmosphere than are necessary to warm the planet to an ____ temperature.

i. Straighten

ii. Prerequisite

iii. Energy

iv. Distort

v. Ideal

vi. Idle

A. vi, i, iii　　　　**B.** v, iv, iii

C. iv, ii, vi　　　　**D.** ii, iv, v

E. None of these

Ques (36-40):Directions: Seven sentences are given, in which one sentence is jumbled; also one sentence is going to be filled with the appropriate word. Firstly, arrange the jumbled sentence to form a meaningful sentence and then finally arrange the sentences to form a meaningful paragraph. Out of the seven sentences, there is one sentence that does not fit into the theme of the passage thus formed. Read the sentences carefully and answer the questions that follow.

P: Second, act as a platform for attracting private excess global debt capital and Third, bring to the market innovative financial solutions that reduce risk and improve return profiles.

Q: garnering adequate capital(A)/sector seems a mammoth task(B)/With the pandemic,(C)/for the infrastructure(D)/

R: To give India's infrastructure sector a further boost, a National Infrastructure Bank can be the third key element along with the already existing ______ project pipeline and favorable public policy.

S: This bank can be formed with a vision of achieving three key objectives First, provide long-term and flexible funding for Infrastructure projects that match the project tenure requirements.

T: Infrastructure investment in digital technology increased access to mobile broadband, fiber-optic cable connections, and power-supply expansion combined with the expansion of low-cost smartphones has enabled millions of Indians to connect to the internet for the first time.

U: This is the appropriate time for the country to set up a National Infrastructure Bank.

V: The solution lies in setting up a robust financial institution, which can be at the forefront of India's infrastructure growth story.

Q.36 What will come at the LAST place?
[Punjab National Bank Clerk, 2021], [Union Bank of India Clerk, 2021], [UCO Bank Clerk, 2021]

A. Q　　　**B.** R　　　**C.** S　　　**D.** V

E. U

Q.37 What will come at SECOND place?
[Punjab National Bank Clerk, 2021], [Union Bank of India Clerk, 2021], [UCO Bank Clerk, 2021]

A. P　　　**B.** U　　　**C.** V　　　**D.** S

E. R

Q.38 What will come at the FOURTH place?
[Punjab National Bank Clerk, 2021], [Union Bank of India Clerk, 2021], [UCO Bank Clerk, 2021]

A. Q　　　**B.** P　　　**C.** R　　　**D.** U

E. S

Q.39 Arrange the jumbled sentence into a meaningful sentence.

garnering adequate capital(A)/sector seems a mammoth task(B)/With the pandemic,(C)/ / for the infrastructure(D) /
[Punjab National Bank Clerk, 2021], [Union Bank of India Clerk, 2021], [UCO Bank Clerk, 2021]

A. CADB　　　**B.** BDAC　　　**C.** DBAC　　　**D.** ADCB

E. ABCD

Q.40 Find the appropriate word to fill the blank.

To give India's infrastructure sector a further boost, a National Infrastructure Bank can be the third key element along with the already existing ______ project pipeline and favorable public policy.
[Punjab National Bank Clerk, 2021], [Union Bank of India Clerk, 2021], [UCO Bank Clerk, 2021]

A. Weak　　　　　**B.** Fragile

C. Determined　　　**D.** Languid

E. Robust

Ques (41-45):Direction: Read the sentence to find out whether there is an error in it or not. The error, if any, will be in one part of the sentence. The number of that part is the answer. If there is no error, the answer is (E). Ignore errors of punctuation, if any.

Q.41 The aforementioned position / (1) was to be close for the / (2) candidates possessing a / (3) score of 160 or lower. / (4)
[SBI Clerk, 2019]

A. (1)　　　**B.** (2)　　　**C.** (3)　　　**D.** (4)

E. No Error

Q.42 The cold mist have (1) / engulfed the entire town (2) / as if reclaimed in (3) / its own parallel dimension. (4)/
[SBI Clerk, 2019]

A. (1)　　　**B.** (2)　　　**C.** (3)　　　**D.** (4)

E. No Error

Q.43 Try hard as he might, (1) / Alvira knew her brother (2) / could never hoped to (3) / regain his health. (4) /
[SBI Clerk, 2019]

A. (1)   **B.** (2)   **C.** (3)   **D.** (4)
E. No Error

Q.44 Little does the King / (1) know that an evil plan / (2) was already being hatched in his / (3) palace at that moment. / (4)

[SBI Clerk, 2019]

A. (1)   **B.** (2)   **C.** (3)   **D.** (4)
E. No error

Q.45 He was aware (1)/ that the oath he (2)/ had taken was soon to (3)/ be proven to disastrous.(4) /

[SBI Clerk, 2019]

A. (1)   **B.** (2)   **C.** (3)   **D.** (4)
E. No Error

Ques (46-50):Direction: Which of the option (A), (B), (C) and (D) given below, should replace the phrase printed in bold in the sentence to make it grammatically correct? If the sentence is correct as it is given and no correction is required, mark (E) as the answer.

Q.46 A federal government climate-change report released last year shows the Pacific Northwest is already **seeing damage from rising temperatures**.
A. Seen damages for rising temperatures
B. Seeing damaging rising temperatures
C. Seen damaging from rising temperatures
D. Seeing damages for rising temperatures
E. No correction required

Q.47 The article explores the problem and the **consequences damage arises** out of dumping about 5 to 13 million tonnes of plastic into the ocean each year.
A. Consequences damaging arising
B. Consequential damaging arising
C. Consequences for damages arising
D. Consequential damage arising
E. No correction required

Q.48 A comedian analyzes the mundane from a variety of angles and **find the thread among two points.**
A. Found the threading between two points
B. Finds the thread between two points
C. Finding the thread among two points
D. Is finding the thread between more than two points
E. No correction required

Q.49 Getting to hire as the assistant to a pastry chef seemed like a dream come true.
A. Get to hire
B. Getting to be hired
C. Getting hired
D. Having got hired
E. No correction required

Q.50 Students from around the world **have increasing started opting to** online education.
A. Has increasingly started opt to
B. Have increasing starting opted to

C. Have increasingly started opting for
D. Have increasingly starting opting for
E. No correction required

Ques (51-55):Direction: Read the passage given below and then answer the questions given below the passage. Some words may be highlighted for your attention.

The big fuss about consensus management is an issue that boils down to a lot of noise about not much. The consensus advocates are great **admirers** of the Japanese management style. Consensus is what Japan is famous for. Well, I know the Japanese fairly well: They still remember Douglas MacArthur with respect, and they still bow down to their Emperor. In my dealings with them, I found that they talk a lot about consensus, but there's always one guy behind the scenes who ends up making the tough decisions. It doesn't make sense to me to think that Mr. Toyoda or Mr. Morita of Sony sits around in committee meetings and says, "We've got to get everybody in this organization, from the janitor up, to agree with this move". The Japanese believe in their workers' involvement early on in the decision-making process and in feedback from employees. And they probably listen better than we do. But you can bet that **when the chips are down**, the yen stops at the top guy's desk. So, we're wasting time trying to **emulate something I don't think really exists.**

Business structures are microcosms of other structures. There were no corporations in the fifteenth century. But there were families. There were city governments, provinces, and armies. There was the Church. All of them had, for lack of a better word, a pecking order.

Why? Because that's the only way you can steer clear of **anarchy**. Otherwise, you'll have somebody come in one morning and tell you: "Yesterday I got tired of painting red convertibles, so today I switched to all baby-blues on my own". You'll never get anything done right that way.

What's to admire about consensus management anyway? By its very nature, it's slow. It can never be daring. There can never be real accountability - or flexibility. About the only plus that I've been able to figure out is that consensus management means consistency of direction and objectives. And so much consistency can become faceless, and that's a problem too. In any event, I don't think it can work in this country. The fun of business for entrepreneurs, big or small, lies in the free enterprise system, not in the greatest agreement by the greatest number.

Q.51 What is the tone of the given passage?
A. Optimistic   **B.** Sarcastic
C. Sensitive   **D.** Empathetic
E. None of the above

Q.52 Which of the following is true as per the given passage?
A. The author suggests that the Japanese practice consensus management in letter and spirit
B. Consensus management is a very daring practice
C. According to the author, consensus management cannot work in India
D. Japan is famous for its army

E. None of the above

Q.53 What is the central idea behind the passage?

A. The Japanese do not practice consensus management completely and only pretend to do so

B. Consensus management stands a high chance in a free enterprise system

C. Consensus management exists more in theory than in practice

D. Japan is a superpower because it follows consensus management

E. None of the above

Q.54 Based on the passage, which of the following can be concluded?

A. Corporations have been with us since the 15th century

B. The author himself is of Japanese origin

C. The Japanese have done away with the concept of kings and emperors

D. Japanese companies encourage feedback from their employees

E. None of the above

Q.55 What did the author mean by 'They still remember Douglas MacArthur with respect, and they still bow down to their Emperor'?

A. The notion that the Japanese companies work on consensus management cannot be more accurate because they respect each and every citizen as much as they respect the emperor

B. Both the Emperor and Douglas MacArthur hold the same position and were at an equal level when it came to power and authority over the general public

C. The respect the Japanese have for their Emperor is much more than what they have for Douglas MacArthur

D. Since the Japanese hero-worship their leaders, which conveys their respect for authority, the concept of consensus management is fundamentally incompatible with them

E. All of the above

Ques (56-60):Direction: In the following passage some of the words have been left out. Read the passage carefully and select the correct answer for the given blank out of the given alternatives.

One of Britain's __(1)__ centres for research and training in plant and microbial science has launched a new scholarship for post-graduate students. The scholarship will be awarded to students from developing countries in honour of a botanist who was __(2)__ the first women from India to obtain a PhD in botany. The John Innes Centre in Norfolk has chosen to __(3)__ Dr. Janaki Ammal for her work at the John Innes Horticultural Institution. The Janaki Ammal Scholarship Scheme will award a scholarship to post-graduate research applicants from 88 eligible countries who __(4)__ to study plant and microbial sciences at the John Innes Centre.

"We take great __(5)__ in our international alumni and we are delighted to name this new scheme in her honour," said Professor Dale Sanders, director of the John Innes Centre. The scheme has been set up to reduce the financial __(6)__ of UK

tuition fees on international students from less developed and lower-income countries, including India.

"At the John Innes Centre, we strive for a level playing field on which all students compete on scientific merit, __(7)__ of nationality, economic status or gender. For this reason, we've __(8)__ this mechanism to support students from low-income countries with their tuition fees," added Sanders. The award applies to graduate students from least developed, low income or lower-middle-income countries as __(9)__ by the Development Assistance Committee of the Organisation for Economic Cooperation and Development (OECD).

Janaki Ammal's research led to the publication of the 'Chromosome Atlas of Cultivated Plants'. She ultimately returned to India to continue a __(10)__ career in science before she passed away in 1984.

Q.56 Which of the following word fits the blank labelled as (1)?

A. Distilled   **B.** Talented
C. Leading   **D.** Fame
E. Registered

Q.57 Which of the following word fits the blank labelled as (2)?

A. Thrive   **B.** Around   **C.** Amid   **D.** About
E. Among

Q.58 Which of the following word fits the blank labelled as (3)?

A. honour   **B.** pride   **C.** abstain   **D.** remove
E. construct

Q.59 Which of the following word fits the blank labelled as (4)?

A. eradicate   **B.** willing   **C.** acquire   **D.** aspire
E. honour

Q.60 Which of the following word fits the blank labelled as (5)?

A. complement   **B.** pride
C. respect   **D.** reserve
E. refill

Numerical Ability

Ques (61-63):Direction: In the given question, two equations numbered I and II are given. Solve both the equations and mark the appropriate answer.

Q.61 I. $x^2 - 11x + 24 = 0$
II. $y^2 - 13y + 40 = 0$

[IDBI Bank Assistant Manager, 2021]

A. x > y
B. x < y
C. x ≥ y
D. x ≤ y
E. x = y or relation between x and y can not be established.

Q.62 I. $x^2 - 16x + 63 = 0$
II. $y^2 - 13y + 42 = 0$

[IDBI Bank Assistant Manager, 2021]

A. x < y
B. x > y

C. $x \leq y$

D. $x \geq y$

E. x = y or the relation between x and y can't be established.

Q.63 I. $3x^2 - 14x + 15 = 0$

II. $15y^2 - 34y + 15 = 0$

[IDBI Bank Assistant Manager, 2021]

A. $x \leq y$

B. $x > y$

C. $x \geq y$

D. No relation in x and y or x = y

E. $x < y$

Ques (64-68):Direction: Study the following pie chart carefully and answer the question given beside.

There are six types of employees working in an organization. The pie chart given below shows the different types of employees working in the organization in the year 2017.

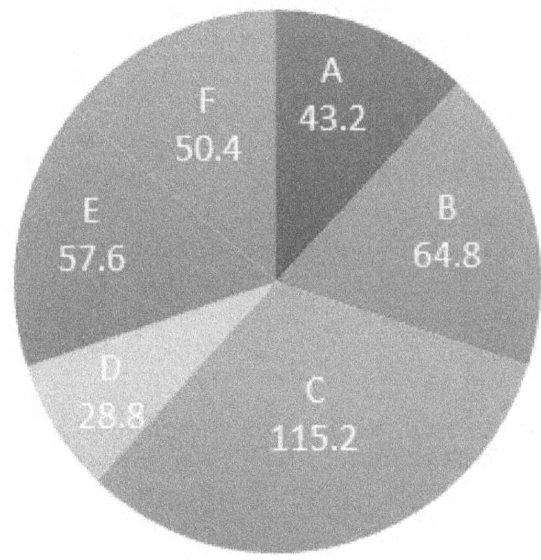

Q.64 In the year 2017, total number of 500 employees was working in the organization. In the year 2018, 50 more joined the organization out of which 20 was F type employees then in the year 2018, total number of F type employees was what percentage of the total number of employees? (rounded off two decimal)

A. 18.33%   **B.** 18.67%   **C.** 17.33%   **D.** 16.37%

E. 15.37%

Q.65 In the year 2017, the difference between B type employees and D type employees was 40, then find the total number of F type employees working in the organization?

A. 58   **B.** 42   **C.** 56   **D.** 55

E. 60

Q.66 In the year 2017, the number of D type employees was what percent less than the number of A type employees?

A. 34.28%   **B.** 33.33%   **C.** 32.67%   **D.** 32.98%

E. 31.98%

Q.67 In the year 2018, the ratio of the number of B type employees to the number of E type employees was 11: 9 then what is the total percentage increase in the number of B type employee and E type employees together?

A. 15%   **B.** 17.65%

C. 18.24%   **D.** 19%

E. Can't be determined

Q.68 In the year 2017, the difference between C type employees and F type employees was 126 then in that year what was the difference between F type employees and D type employees?

A. 25   **B.** 35

C. 42   **D.** 49

E. None of these

Q.69 There are 12 points in a plane out of which 5 are collinear. The number of triangles formed by the points as vertices are:

A. 185   **B.** 210   **C.** 220   **D.** 175

E. 200

Q.70 A lends Rs. 700 to B and a certain amount to C at the same time at 3% annual simple interest. Ifafter 2 years, A receives Rs. 252 as interest from both. Then what amount did A give to C?

[IBPS SO Marketing Officer, 2019], [IBPS SO HR Officer, 2019], [IBPS SO IT Officer, 2019]

A. Rs. 3200   **B.** Rs. 4000   **C.** Rs. 3500   **D.** Rs. 2400

E. Rs. 3000

Q.71 A person invested Rs. 46875 at some rate of compound interest for 3 years. At the end of 3 years, he receives Rs. 12174 as interest. Find the rate of compound interest.

[IBPS Agriculture field Officer (AFO), 2019], [IBPS SO HR Officer, 2019], [IBPS SO Marketing Officer, 2019]

A. 10%   **B.** 8%   **C.** 12%   **D.** 6%

E. 9%

Q.72 From a class of 50 students, some students were selected randomly for the republic day parade but the condition was that the number should be either multiple of 2 or multiple of 5. The average weight of all the students who were not selected was 56 kg and the average weight of all the students who were selected was 58 kg. What was the average weight (in kg) of the class?

A. 57.8   **B.** 57.2

C. 56.9   **D.** 57.6

E. None of these

Q.73 The total area of square and rectangle is 955 m², and diagonal of square is $25\sqrt{2}$ m. find sum of parameter of square and rectangle if length of rectangle is 22 m.

A. 124 m   **B.** 160 m   **C.** 174 m   **D.** 156 m

E. 170 m

Q.74 A cistern has two taps attached to it. Tap B can empty the cistern in 45 minutes. But Tap A can fill the cistern in just 30 minutes. Rohit started both taps unknowingly but realized his mistake after 30 minutes. He immediately closed Tap B. Now after this, in how much time will the cistern be filled?

A. 30 minutes   **B.** 45 minutes
C. 15 minutes   **D.** 20 minutes
E. 10 minutes

Ques (75-79):Direction: Find the missing number in place of the question mark (?) in the given series.

Q.75 120, 145, ?, 197, 224, 257
A. 170   **B.** 168
C. 165   **D.** 171
E. None of these

Q.76 47, 58, 71, 79, 95, ?
A. 108   **B.** 107
C. 105   **D.** 109
E. None of these

Q.77 8, 39, 79, 394, 789, ?
A. 2149   **B.** 3542
C. 2862   **D.** 3944
E. None of these

Q.78 15, 17, 26, 47, 86, ?
A. 132   **B.** 149   **C.** 169   **D.** 172
E. 152

Q.79 3, 9, 24, 57, ?, 267, 552
A. 121   **B.** 118
C. 114   **D.** 126
E. None of these

Q.80 464 articles marked 50% above cost price. These articles sold at some discount such that after selling 348 articles total cost price is recovered. What is discount

[Bank of Maharashtra Clerk, 2017], [IBPS Clerk, 2017], [Indian Bank Clerk, 2017]

A. $33\frac{1}{3}\%$ **B.** $16\frac{2}{3}\%$
C. $6\frac{2}{3}\%$ **D.** $11\frac{1}{9}\%$
E. None of these

Q.81 Around a round table, 13 persons are sitting on 13 chairs. Harry is one among them. A person is chosen randomly from them (other than Harry). What is the probability that there will be exactly 2 persons between Harry and the chosen person?
A. $\frac{1}{3}$ **B.** $\frac{1}{6}$ **C.** $\frac{1}{5}$ **D.** $\frac{2}{13}$
E. $\frac{1}{8}$

Ques (82-86):Direction: Simplify the given expression.

Q.82 $\dfrac{18\times\frac{8}{15}+10\% \text{ of } 624}{?} = 4$

A. 16   **B.** 18   **C.** 22   **D.** 24
E. 26

Q.83 $\sqrt{1024} \times 40 + 20^2 + 0.5\% \text{ of } 9600 + 469 = ?^3$

[IBPS Clerk, 2021]

A. 23   **B.** 13   **C.** 17   **D.** 19
E. 21

Q.84 $4\frac{3}{5}\%$ of $6500 + 3\frac{2}{7}\%$ of $3500 = ?$
A. 424   **B.** 414   **C.** 418   **D.** 404
E. 401

Q.85 $(4.5 \times 4.5 \times 4.5 \times 4.5) \div 225 \div 25 + 3^3 = ?$
A. 27.729   **B.** 277.29   **C.** 27.0729   **D.** 2772.90
E. 2.7729

Q.86 $3\frac{1}{2} \times \dfrac{7\frac{2}{5}}{9\frac{3}{5}} \times 8^2 \times 60 = 2^4 \times ?$
A. 624   **B.** 2364   **C.** 647.5   **D.** 1864
E. 1946

Q.87 A, B and C three friends started the business in which A invested for 4 months, B initially didn't invest and started as a working partner, while C invested for 6 months. They decided to donate 9% of total profit and to give 21% of total profit to B as salary. Find the ratio of their profit shares if A and C invested in the ratio of 3 : 2 and B also invested an amount which is 80% of total amount invested by A and C together for a single month.
A. $4:5:6$ **B.** $7:8:9$
C. $30:31:30$ **D.** Can't be determined
E. None of these

Q.88 The ratio of the speed of train Before accident and after accident is 3 : 2. After an accident train travels 400 km in 5 hours. Find the original speed of train before the accident.
A. 40 km/hr   **B.** 80 km/hr
C. 120 km/hr   **D.** 160 km/hr
E. 200 km/hr

Q.89 Kuldeep decides to improve his running by running around a circular playground on daily basis. On the first day of the month, he completed one round of the playground at a speed of 10 km/hr in 6 minutes. And on the last day of the month, he completed one round of the playground in 4 minutes. How much in (m/s) Kuldeep improved upon his speed in one month?
A. 25 m/s   **B.** $\frac{25}{18}$ m/s   **C.** $\frac{18}{25}$ m/s   **D.** 5 m/s
E. 8 m/s

Q.90 Speed of boat A is 50% more than speed of boat B in still water, if both boats start in a lake at same time from point P downstream at the same time and reach point Q, which is 72 km away from point P at the same time. Boat A lost 120 minutes during the journey because the engine did not work properly. Find time taken by boat A to cover a given distance upstream with 50% of its speed?
A. 8 hr   **B.** 10 hr   **C.** 6 hr   **D.** 12 hr
E. 14 hr

// Smart Answer Sheet //

Correct   Indicates percentage of students who answered questions correctly.

Skipped   Indicates percentage of students who skipped questions.

Q.	Ans.	Correct / Skipped
1	C	18.92 % / 4.96 %
2	B	30.59 % / 4.5 %
3	C	29.17 % / 3.0 %
4	A	32.38 % / 3.0 %
5	E	47.56 % / 1.66 %
6	C	30.01 % / 4.55 %
7	D	41.02 % / 1.16 %
8	B	77.44 % / 0.0 %
9	B	43.32 % / 1.6 %
10	E	52.97 % / 1.6 %
11	D	58.02 % / 1.67 %
12	C	59.64 % / 1.72 %
13	D	58.87 % / 1.45 %
14	E	42.67 % / 1.98 %
15	B	55.98 % / 1.16 %
16	B	89.4 % / 0.0 %
17	E	47.88 % / 1.15 %
18	D	65.89 % / 1.13 %
19	C	57.4 % / 1.51 %
20	A	58.11 % / 1.28 %
21	D	53.28 % / 1.47 %
22	D	57.55 % / 1.39 %
23	B	63.92 % / 1.14 %
24	A	51.51 % / 1.01 %
25	E	65.6 % / 1.4 %
26	D	28.3 % / 4.16 %
27	C	65.76 % / 1.62 %
28	A	67.07 % / 1.76 %
29	A	57.17 % / 1.24 %
30	D	61.91 % / 1.7 %
31	B	45.22 % / 1.83 %
32	A	50.15 % / 1.49 %
33	B	42.61 % / 1.71 %
34	C	43.71 % / 1.66 %
35	D	68.99 % / 2.0 %
36	B	29.27 % / 4.61 %
37	C	65.67 % / 1.39 %
38	E	61.97 % / 1.71 %
39	A	58.99 % / 1.43 %
40	E	41.07 % / 1.68 %
41	B	57.13 % / 1.57 %
42	A	57.99 % / 1.53 %
43	C	50.72 % / 1.69 %
44	A	50.46 % / 1.27 %
45	D	52.14 % / 1.38 %
46	E	53.06 % / 1.42 %
47	D	62.82 % / 1.38 %
48	B	49.06 % / 1.63 %
49	C	42.04 % / 1.97 %
50	C	66.31 % / 1.83 %
51	B	60.32 % / 1.52 %
52	E	66.4 % / 1.43 %
53	C	65.15 % / 1.42 %
54	D	56.18 % / 1.85 %
55	D	54.18 % / 1.21 %
56	C	40.41 % / 1.68 %
57	E	87.6 % / 0.0 %
58	A	56.65 % / 1.21 %
59	D	56.25 % / 1.54 %
60	B	69.19 % / 1.76 %
61	E	65.25 % / 1.64 %
62	D	63.05 % / 1.65 %
63	C	56.01 % / 1.21 %
64	D	12.69 % / 3.64 %
65	C	68.54 % / 1.79 %
66	B	45.67 % / 1.61 %
67	E	47.55 % / 1.3 %
68	C	69.78 % / 1.86 %
69	B	53.83 % / 1.59 %
70	C	66.12 % / 1.28 %
71	B	47.53 % / 1.06 %
72	B	47.88 % / 1.16 %
73	C	43.15 % / 1.62 %
74	D	60.16 % / 1.03 %
75	B	78.5 % / 0.0 %
76	D	82.89 % / 0.0 %
77	D	68.87 % / 1.09 %
78	B	43.21 % / 1.7 %
79	D	81.13 % / 0.0 %
80	D	63.85 % / 1.51 %

Q.	Ans.	Correct		Q.	Ans.	Correct		Q.	Ans.	Correct		Q.	Ans.	Correct		Q.	Ans.	Correct
		Skipped				Skipped				Skipped				Skipped				Skipped
81	B	59.09 %		83	B	44.79 %		85	C	41.09 %		87	C	25.55 %		89	B	56.25 %
		1.38 %				1.1 %				1.05 %				3.18 %				1.11 %
82	B	80.58 %		84	B	66.7 %		86	C	63.19 %		88	C	56.68 %		90	A	44.56 %
		0.0 %				1.44 %				1.36 %				1.85 %				1.02 %

Performance Analysis

Avg. Score (%)	38.89%
Toppers Score (%)	67.78%
Your Score	

//Hints and Solutions//

Ques (1-3):Logic:

Here as we can see that code contain 3 element 1 letter, 1 number and 1 symbol.

1) **1st element:** First element is letter which is an immediate next letter of first letter of word as per English alphabet.

2) **2nd Element:** 2nd element is number which is product of number of vowel and number of consonant in the word.

3) **3rd Element:** Third element is symbol which represent last letter of word.

(Which symbol is used for which letter is shown below)

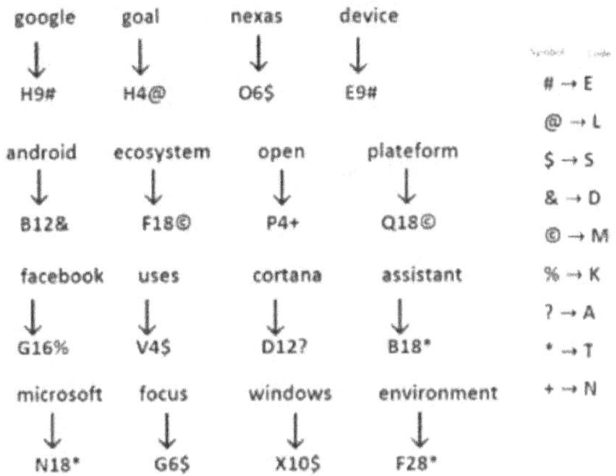

1. So, 'assistant' will be coded as "B18*"

Hence, the correct option is (C).

2. So, '©' stand for 'M' in this code language.

Hence, the correct option is (B).

3. As per logic given above

"Amazon" will be coded as "B9+"

"has" will be coded as "I2$"

"prime" will be coded as "Q6#"

"concept" will be coded as "D10*"

So, "amazon has prime concept" will be coded as "B9+ I2$ Q6# D10*"

Hence, the correct option is (C).

Ques (4-8): Six persons: P, Q, R, S, T and U

1.R sits one of the extreme ends of the row.

2.S sits third from the right end.

Following are the possibilities we get,

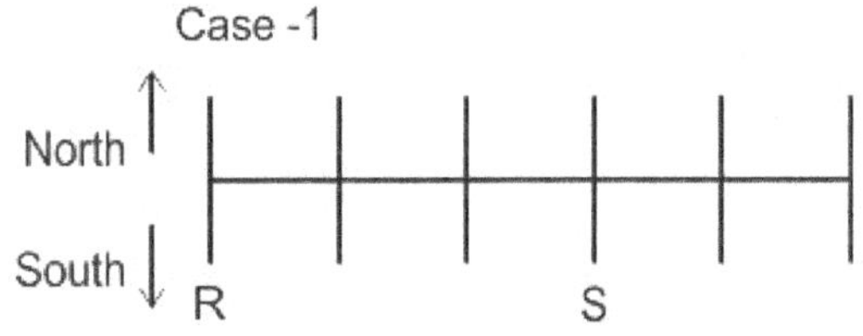

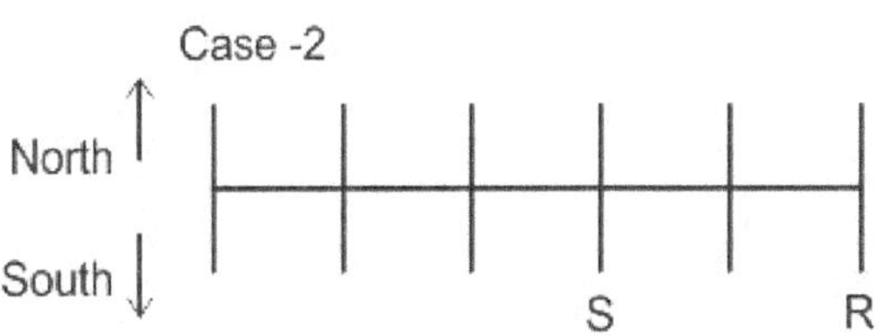

3. Only one person sits between P and U.

4. Neither P nor U is a neighbor of R, where U is to the right of P.

5. Number of persons to the left of Q is same the number of persons to the right of R.

6. T does not sit at an extreme end.

Here, this statement is violated in case II. so it is eliminated and the final arrangement is:

541nal arrangement is:

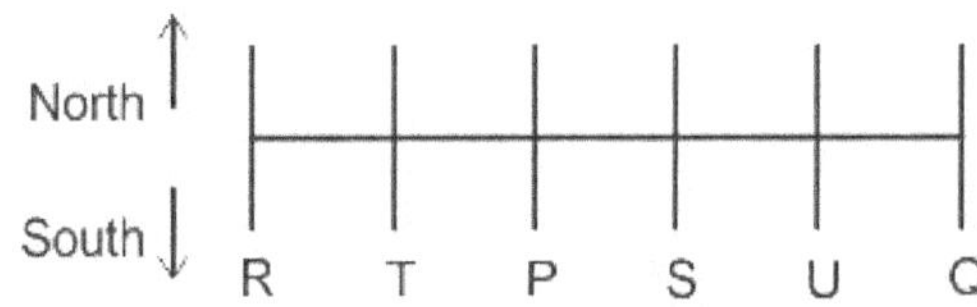

4. So, one person does not change its position.

Hence, the correct option is (A).

5. So, Q sits at an extreme end.

Hence, the correct option is (E).

6. So, two persons sit between T and U.

Hence, the correct option is (C).

7. So, U is an immediate neighbour of Q.

Hence, the correct option is (D).

8. So, T sits second from the left.

Hence, the correct option is (B).

Ques (9-13):1) B lives on bottom most floor.

2) There is a gap of two floors between A and B.

3) F lives on a floor which is an even numbered below A's floor.

Floor	Person
4	A
3	

2	F
1	B

4) There are five floors between A and C.

5) G lives on a floor which is immediately above C.

Floor	Person
11	G
10	C
9	
8	
7	
6	
5	
4	A
3	
2	F
1	B

6) Number of floors above E is same as number of floors below A.(From this statement we can conclude that E must live on floor numbered 8, as there building contains less than 12 floors)

7) D lives on even numbered floor.

Floor	Person
11	G
10	C
9	Vacant
8	E
7	Vacant
6	D
5	Vacant
4	A
3	Vacant
2	F
1	B

9. So, there are four vacant floors in the building.

Hence, the correct option is (B).

10. Here, D lives on 6th floor.

So, "None of the above" is the correct answer.

Hence, the correct option is (E).

11. So, two persons live between D and B.

Hence, the correct option is (D).

12. So, there are "Eleven" floors in the building.

Hence, the correct option is (C).

13. So, "E" live on floor number 8.

Hence, the correct option is (D).

14. The given word:

APPECIATION

The first, the third, the fifth, and the eighth letters of the given word above, we have:

A, P, C, and T

Here, from the above letter, we can make a meaningful word 'PACT'.

Hence, the correct option is (E).

15. The pattern followed here is,

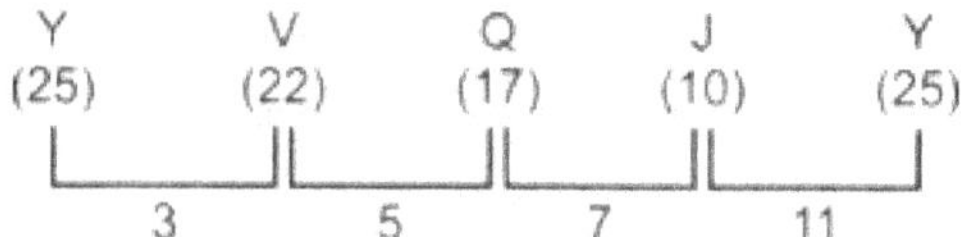

Therefore, Y is the correct answer.

Hence, the correct option is (B).

16. If we observe given series we will find that,

Term given in series have 2 consecutive letter of English alphabet.

(HI, OP, WX)

Now if look carefully we will find that,

$\Rightarrow$ W – P = 7

$\Rightarrow$ O – I = 6

$\Rightarrow$ H – ? = 5

$\Rightarrow$? = 8 - 5

$\Rightarrow$? = C

Therefore "BC" will be missing term.

Hence, the correct option is (B).

17. Given words are: EDC, TGF, VBJ, QAL, KJU

On arranging words in the order as they appear in a dictionary from left to right, we get:

Left side to Right side - EDC KJU QAL TGF VBJ

The fourth word from the right is KJU and first and last letters are K and U respectively.

There are nine letters in English alphabetical order between K and U i.e. L, M, N, O, P, Q, R, S, T

Thus, nine is the correct answer.

Hence, the correct option is (E).

18. Given words are: EDC, TGF, VBJ, QAL, KJU

On changing the first and last alphabet of each word to the previous alphabet and the middle alphabet to its next alphabet in the English alphabetical series:

DEB, SHE, UCI, PBK, JKT

Clearly, two words PBK and JKT having only consonants will be formed.

In English alphabetical series there are 5 vowels i.e. A, E, I, O, U else all are consonants.

Thus, two words will be formed.

Hence, the correct option is (D).

19. Given words are: EDC, TGF, VBJ, QAL, KJU

Odd positions: 1st and 3rd positions

On interchanging both alphabets of each word present at odd positions

CDE, FGT, JBV, LAQ, UJK

Clearly, only one word, CDE ending with vowel will be formed.

In English alphabetical series there are 5 vowels i.e. A, E, I, O, U else all are consonants.

Thus, only one word will be formed.

Hence, the correct option is (C).

20.

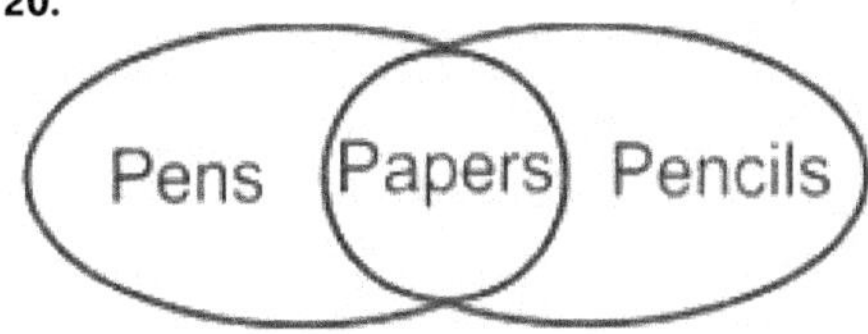

Conclusions:

I. Some pens are pencils à True (The papers which are pens are pencils as all papers are pencils)

II. All pencils are pens à False (It is possible but not definite)

Thus, only conclusion I follows.

Hence, the correct option is (A).

21. The least possible diagram for the given statements is as follows

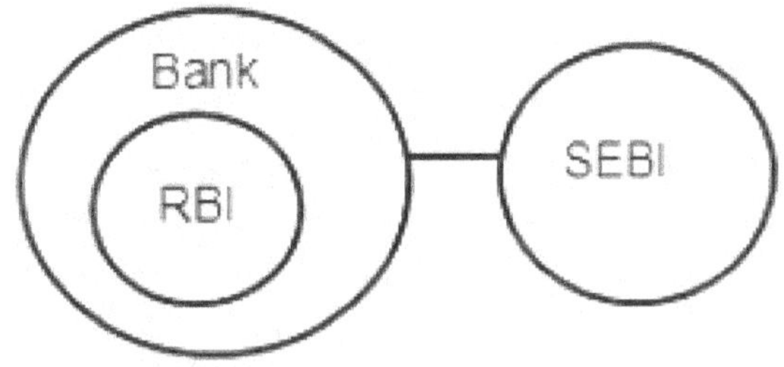

Conclusions:

I. No RBI is SEBI. → True (It is definitely true as RBI is under Bank)

II. Some RBI is SEBI. → False (It is definitely false)

Thus, only I follows.

Hence, the correct option is (D).

22. The least possible diagram for the given statements is as follows

Conclusions:

I. Some iPhones are mobile. → False (it is possible but not definite)

II. Some mobiles are not iPhones. → False (it is possible but not definite)

Thus, Neither I nor II follows.

Hence, the correct option is (D).

23. Given,

In a queue of students facing north, Ayesha and Anisha are standing at 10th and 8th position from the left and right end respectively.

From the given image it is clear that Ayesha is 12th from the right end.

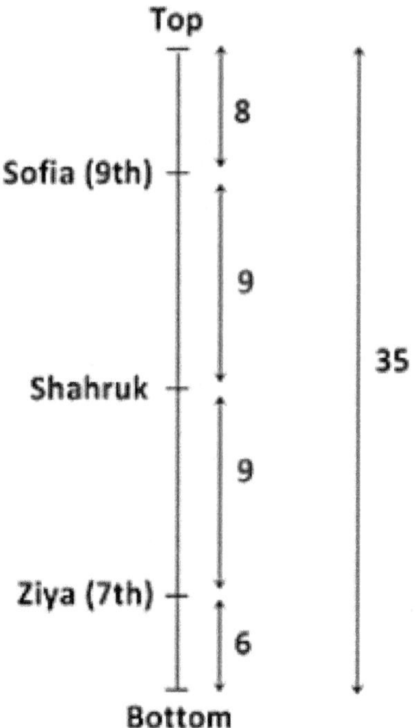

Position of Ayesha from right end = 7 + 1(Anisha) + 1 + 1(Ariva) +1 + 1 = 12

Hence, the correct option is (B).

24. As seen in the figure, Shahruk is between Sofia and Ziya.

It's given that Ziya is 7th from the bottom and Sofia is 9th from the top.

Therefore, number of persons between Sofia and Ziya = 35 - (9 + 7) = 19

Sharuk's position between Sofia and Ziya = $\dfrac{19+1}{2}$ =10

Thus, Shahruk is at the middle i.e., at 10th position from both. Ziya, therefore, is at the 10th position from Shahruk.

Hence, the correct option is (A).

25. Given,

There are 25 students in a class and all of them are sitting in a row to do yoga. Meena is 11th from the top and Sneha is 6th from the bottom. Two students are sitting between Ananya and Reena.

From the above information, we cannot be sure about the position of Reena, as we don't have enough information about the position of Ananya and Reena.

Hence, the correct option is (E).

Ques (26-28): Given code: A *16 B #10 C @8 D #14 E *23 F &16 W and G #4 H @9 I &6 J @5 K #9 L @10 W

By decoding given information:

@	*	#	&
Means			
East	West	South	North

Point A is 16km in the west of point B, which is 10km in the south of point C, which is 8km in the west of point D, which is 14km in the south of point E, which is 23km in the west of point F, which is 16km in the north of point W.

Point G is the 4km in the south of point H, which is 9km in the east of point I, which is 6km in the north of point J, which is 5km in the east of point K, which is 9km in the south of point L, which is 10km in the east of point W.

According to the given information, we get the following figure,

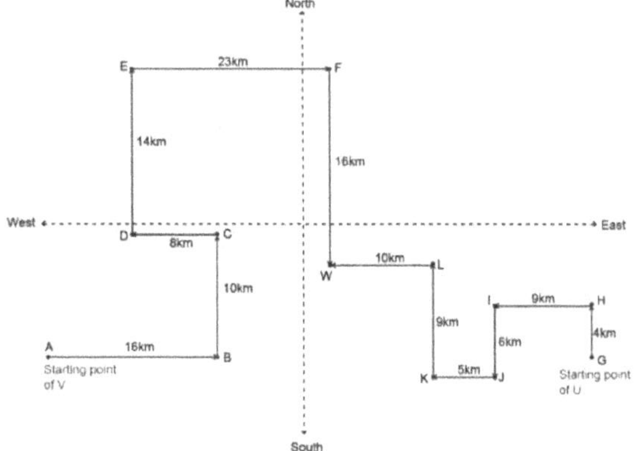

26. So, point F is in the north-west of the point I.

So, 'North-West' is the correct answer.

Hence, the correct option is (D).

27. By using Pythagoras theorem,

Shortest distance between B and W = $\sqrt{(15^2 + 8^2)}$ = $\sqrt{(225 + 64)} = \sqrt{289} = 17$

So, 17km is the correct answer.

Hence, the correct option is (C).

28. The distance between point A and point G = 16 + 15 + 10 + 5 + 9 = 55

So, 55 km is the correct answer.

Hence, the correct option is (A).

Ques (29-30): Number of people: 7

There are two married couples.

Preparing the family tree using the following symbols:

Symbol in Diagram	Meaning
◯	Female
☐	Male
═══	Married Couple
───	Siblings
│	Difference of A Generation

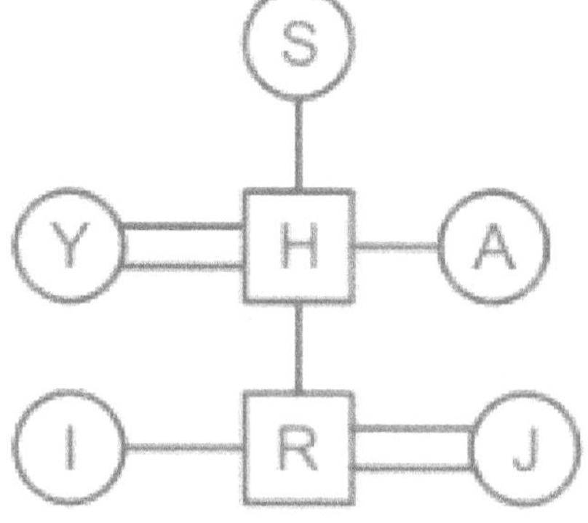

29. Thus, the relationship between A and R is Aunt – Nephew.

Hence, the correct option is (A).

30. Thus, Y is mother – in – law of J.

Hence, the correct option is (D).

31. The first sentence in the given passage talks about the identifying features of a 'compact city'.

The second sentence talks about the advantages associated with such a city. Since 'urban sprawl' (Sprawl: spread out over a large area in an untidy or irregular way) is considered a negative aspect of urbanization, 'compact cities' would more likely try to decrease its spread.

Thus, alternatives (ii) and (v) can be used in the first blank. But alternative (ii) is a more suitable word for the second blank as a decrease in vehicular transport will support sustainable development.

As per the passage, the compact city has numerous advantages. Thus, older urban areas can be 'revamped' which means to give them a new and improved form, structure, or appearance.

Hence, the correct option is (B).

32. The given passage defines the associated words with the word 'enterprise'. If 'partnership' is because of two or more 'owners' then by association 'propriety' should also depend on the number of owners. Thus, alternative (vi) is appropriate for the first blank.

This makes options A and C viable. To maintain continuity, the second blank should have 'without' in it to show opposition to 'with'. The basis of classification of an enterprise has already been provided and it can be inferred that those entities which do not conform with the requisites will not fall under this category.

Thus, alternative (iii) is correct for the third blank.

Hence, the correct option is (A).

33. The given passage is about Sunlight as a source of energy and its propagation on Earth. The sentence after the first blank mentions the amount of sunlight entering the Earth's atmosphere.

Thus the first blank should have 'sun' in it as it is the source of said light. For the second blank, possible options are (ii) and (iv) but since there is no definite article before the second blank, 'space' is the appropriate choice. The third blank should have 'energy' in it as 'radiation' is defined as the emission of energy.

Hence, the correct option is (B).

34. The last blank should have a verb in its base form (as a 'to-infinitive' structure takes the base form of the verb) which denotes the participation of the citizens. 'Involvement' is a noun while 'involve' is a verb which makes alternative (vi) appropriate for the last blank. The concept of 'Area Sabha' needs to be introduced to the citizens in the urban areas.

Thus, the present participle form (used in the case of verbs of perception such as look, hear, listen, feel, and introduce) of the verb 'introducing' should be used in the second blank.

This makes option C viable for the given blanks. 'Objective' means a goal and fits correctly in the first blank making option C the correct answer.

Hence, the correct option is (C).

35. The meaning of the given alternatives is listed below:

Straighten – make or become straight.

Prerequisite – a thing that is required as a prior condition for something else to happen or exist.

Energy – the strength and vitality required for sustained physical or mental activity.

Distort – give a misleading or false account or impression of.

Ideal – most suitable

Idle – lazy

'Distort' is correct for the second blank while 'ideal' is correct for the third blank.

Off the other alternatives, in the given context 'prerequisite' is ideal for the first blank.

Hence, the correct option is (D).

36. After arranging the paragraph meaningfully, the correct sequence is: QVUSPR

Thus, the paragraph is:

With the pandemic, garnering adequate capital for the infrastructure sector seems a mammoth task. The solution lies in setting up a robust financial institution, which can be at the forefront of India's infrastructure growth story. This is the appropriate time for the country to set up a National Infrastructure Bank. This bank can be formed with a vision of achieving three key objectives First, provide long-term and flexible funding for Infrastructure projects that match the project tenure requirements. Second, act as a platform for attracting private excess global debt capital, and Third, bring to the market innovative financial solutions that reduce risk and improve return profiles. To give India's infrastructure sector a further boost, a National Infrastructure Bank can be the third key element along with the already existing robust project pipeline and favorable public policy.

Hence, the correct option is (B).

37. After arranging the paragraph meaningfully, the correct sequence is: QVUSPR

Thus, the paragraph is:

With the pandemic, garnering adequate capital for the infrastructure sector seems a mammoth task. The solution lies in setting up a robust financial institution, which can be at the forefront of India's infrastructure growth story. This is the appropriate time for the country to set up a National Infrastructure Bank. This bank can be formed with a vision of achieving three key objectives First, provide long-term and flexible funding for Infrastructure projects that match the project tenure requirements. Second, act as a platform for attracting private excess global debt capital, and Third, bring to the market innovative financial solutions that reduce risk and improve return profiles. To give India's infrastructure sector a further boost, a National Infrastructure Bank can be the third key element along with the already existing robust project pipeline and favorable public policy.

Hence, the correct option is (C).

38. After arranging the paragraph meaningfully, the correct sequence is: QVUSPR

Thus, the paragraph is:

With the pandemic, garnering adequate capital for the infrastructure sector seems a mammoth task. The solution lies in setting up a robust financial institution, which can be at the forefront of India's infrastructure growth story. This is the appropriate time for the country to set up a National Infrastructure Bank. This bank can be formed with a vision of achieving three key objectives First, provide long-term and flexible funding for Infrastructure projects that match the project tenure requirements. Second, act as a platform for attracting private excess global debt capital, and Third, bring to the market innovative financial solutions that reduce risk and improve return profiles. To give India's infrastructure sector a further boost, a National Infrastructure Bank can be the third key element along with the already existing robust project pipeline and favorable public policy.

Hence, the correct option is (E).

39. 'With the pandemic,' is a prepositional phrase and generally, it behaves like an adjective or adverb modifying noun or verb. Here, it is behaving like an adverb modifying the verb 'garnering' so part C will come in the first place.

Since the prepositional phrase is working as an adverb modifying the verb 'garnering', part A will come in the second place.

Part D will come in third place as 'for' when used as the preposition means 'having the purpose of' and is expressing the relation between capital and infrastructure.

Line up the last part.

Thus, the correct sentence is: 'With the pandemic, garnering adequate capital sector seems a mammoth task'.

Hence, the correct option is (A).

40. Let's explore the meaning of the given options:

- Weak: lacking the power to perform physically demanding tasks; lacking physical strength and energy.
- Fragile: easily broken or damaged.
- Determined: having made a firm decision and being resolved not to change it.
- Languid: displaying or having a disinclination for physical exertion or effort; slow and relaxed.
- Robust: strongly formed or constructed.

According to the context of the passage, the correct option is (E).

Thus, the correct sentence is: 'To give India's infrastructure sector a further boost, a National Infrastructure Bank can be the third key element along with the already existing robust project pipeline and favorable public policy.

Hence, the correct option is (E).

41. The error lies in part (2).

The sentence uses the form' to be close', which is incorrect.

Since the sentence uses the form 'to be' before 'close', the correct form here must be the verb form 'closed' meaning 'not open'.

The corrected sentence is: The aforementioned position was to be closed for the candidates possessing a score of 160 or lower.

Hence, the correct option is (B).

42. The error lies in part (1).

The sentence uses the form 'have engulfed', which is incorrect here.

The correct form here should be either 'has' or 'had', since the 'mist' is singular and so the corresponding auxiliary verb form must also be singular.

The corrected sentence will be: The cold mist has engulfed the entire town as if reclaimed in its own parallel dimension.

Hence, the correct option is (A).

43. The error lies in part (3).

The sentence uses the form 'could never hoped', which is incorrect.

The correct form here should be the simple present tense form of the verb, viz, 'hope', as the modal verb 'could' already expresses the tense and ability of the verb.

The corrected sentence will be: Try hard as he might, Alvira knew her brother could never hope to regain his health.

Hence, the correct option is (C).

44. The error lies in part (1).

The sentence uses the form 'little does' one know, which is incorrect here.

As the sentence uses the past tense verb 'was', the correct form here should be 'little did' the King know.

'Little did/does one know' is a way of expressing the ignorance of a person about something.

The corrected sentence is: Little did the King know that an evil plan was already being hatched in his palace at that moment.

Hence, the correct option is (A).

45. The error lies in part (4).

The sentence uses the preposition 'to' after the verb form 'to be proven', which, given the context of the sentence is unnecessary. It should be 'to be proven disastrous' and not 'to be proven to disastrous'.

Note here that both past participle forms 'proved' and 'proven' are correct.

The corrected sentence will be: He was aware that the oath he had taken was soon to be proven disastrous.

Hence, the correct option is (D).

46. The original sentence "A federal government climate-change report released last year shows the Pacific Northwest is already **seeing damage from rising temperatures**." is grammatically correct in the given form and therefore the bold part needs no replacement.

Hence, the correct option is (E).

47. The given part is grammatically as well as contextually incorrect as two nouns 'consequences' and 'damage' are coming together and making no sense. Instead of 'consequences' the adjective 'consequential' would make sense in the given context of the sentence.

Clearly, among the given choices option (D) replaces the bold part most appropriately.

The sentence after replacement becomes:

The article explores the problem and the **consequential damage arising** out of dumping about 5 to 13 million tonnes of plastic into the ocean each year.

Hence, the correct option is (D).

48. Reason: The verb 'find' is not in agreement with the subject 'A comedian' which is singular in number. Besides, 'for two points' usage of 'among' is erroneous. Instead of 'among' 'between' must be used to make the sentence grammatically correct.

Clearly, among the given choices option (B) replaces the bold part most appropriately.

The sentence after replacement becomes:

A comedian analyzes the mundane from a variety of angles and **finds the thread between two points.**

Hence, the correct option is (B).

49. The sentence is starting with a gerund and implying as the narrator is feeling happy to have got the job of the assistant to a pastry chef. Therefore, instead of 'to hire', the past participle 'hired' must be used to make the sentence meaningful.

Clearly, among the given choices option (C) replaces the bold part most appropriately.

The sentence after replacement becomes:

Getting hired as the assistant to a pastry chef seemed like a dream come true.

Hence, the correct option is (C).

50. As we can observe that the sentence is made in Present Perfect Tense (Have + V3), usage of 'increasing' is ungrammatical in the sentence. Instead of it, the adverb 'increasingly' should be used here.

Besides, the verb 'opt' always takes preposition 'for' after it. Therefore, 'to' must be replaced by 'for' to make it a grammatically correct sentence.

Clearly, among the given choices option (C) replaces the bold part most appropriately.

The sentence after replacement becomes:

Students from around the world **have increasingly started opting for** online education.

Hence, the correct option is (C).

51. Reading the passage we find that:

The given passage highlights the author's personal views on 'Consensus Management' while taking Japan as one of the key examples. He very confidently speaks out against the concept and is very sly while making his remarks. He exposes the hypocrisy of the Japanese and seems to be mocking them. To find the tone of the given passage we need to look at the given words and it's meanings.

Let's look at the meaning of the marked option.

Sarcastic: Marked by or given to using irony in order to mock or convey contempt.

Let's look at the meaning of the other options.

Optimistic: Hopeful and confident about the future; positive.

Sensitive: Having or displaying a quick and delicate appreciation of others' feelings

Empathetic: Showing an ability to understand and share the feelings of another.

The author speaks in a negative way and does not seem to be empathetic or sensitive towards the Japanese or the concept of Consensus Management.

Hence, the correct option is (B).

52. Reading the passage we find that:

'To do something in letter and spirit' means 'to follow the rules surrounding it and their intentions completely' and nowhere in the entire passage does the author ask the Japanese to practise consensus management. Thus, Option (A) is incorrect.

The last paragraph states: 'What's to admire about consensus management anyway? By its very nature, it's slow. It can never be daring.' Thus, Option (B) is also incorrect.

Nowhere in the passage does the author talk about 'India' or about 'Japan's army'. Which shows that Option (C) and (D) are incorrect.

Thus, it is clear that the first four options are factually incorrect as they completely disregard what's been said in the passage.

Hence, the correct option is (E).

53. Reading the passage we find that:

The author tries to convey that consensus management is impractical, especially in a free enterprise system. Even the Japanese pretend to follow it but they actually don't. No one can actually follow it in order to become a superpower.

"The Japanese believe in their workers' involvement early on in the decision-making process and in feedback from employees. And they probably listen better than we do. But you can bet that when the chips are down, the yen stops at the top guy's desk. So, we're wasting time trying to emulate something I don't think really exists."

A general agreement regarding something sounds great, but it is impossible to practise it as it would result in anarchy or a state of disorder.

So, it can be concluded that consensus management exists more in theory than practice. The phrase 'in theory' is used to say that something seems to be true or possible as an idea but may not actually be true or possible.

Other options are rejected because Option (A) is an integral message of the passage but cannot be stated as the central idea of the passage. Option (B) and (D) are factually incorrect.

Hence, the correct option is (C).

54. Reading the passage we find that:

The first three options are incorrect for the following reasons.

Option (A) is incorrect because the passage says: 'There were no corporations in the fifteenth century.'

Option (B) is incorrect because the author's origin has not been revealed.

Option (C) is incorrect because the passage says: 'They still remember Douglas MacArthur with respect, and they still bow down to their Emperor.'

Thus only Option (D) can be correctly concluded from the passage as it says:

'The Japanese believe in their workers' involvement early on in the decision-making process and in feedback from employees. And they probably listen better than we do'.

Hence, the correct option is (D).

55. Reading the passage we find that:

The marked option clearly explains the given line from the passage and thus is the correct answer.

It points out to the reverence that the Japanese have for people in power and this conveys their respect for authority.

Through the passage, the author is trying to convey that consensus management is only a theory and not a reality. Even Japan, which is considered to be the great pioneer of consensus management, only appears to be following it and not actually follows it.

Option (A), (B), and (C) are factually incorrect and cannot be considered as correct answers.

Hence, the correct option is (D).

56. The sentence suggests that the blank must contain a word that is an adjective since it comes before the noun, 'centers'. The only option that can make a meaningful sentence is 'leading'.

Hence, the correct option is (C).

57. The sentence suggests that the blank must contain a preposition. The only option that can make a meaningful sentence is 'among'.

Among: being a member or members of (a larger set)

Hence, the correct option is (E).

58. The blank must contain a word that means 'to felicitate' or 'to honour'.

Honour: Regard with great respect

Hence, the correct option is (A).

59. The sentence suggests that the blank should contain a word that means 'wish to'. The only word that gives this meaning is 'aspire'.

Aspire: .direct one's hopes or ambitions towards achieving something.

Hence, the correct option is (D).

60. The sentence suggests that the blank must contain a word that reflects the achievements of the scholarship. The only word that makes a meaningful sentence is 'pride'.

Pride: a feeling or deep pleasure or satisfaction derived from one's own achievements, the achievements of those with whom one is closely associated, or from qualities or possessions that are widely admired

Hence, the correct option is (B).

61. Given,

I. $x^2 - 11x + 24 = 0$

II. $y^2 - 13y + 40 = 0$

From I,

I. $x^2 - 11x + 24 = 0$

$\Rightarrow x^2 - 8x - 3x + 24 = 0$

$\Rightarrow x(x - 8) - 3(x - 8) = 0$

$\Rightarrow (x - 8)(x - 3) = 0$

$\Rightarrow (x - 8) = 0$ or $(x - 3) = 0$

$\Rightarrow x = 8$ or 3

From II,

$y^2 - 13y + 40 = 0$

$\Rightarrow y^2 - 8y - 5y + 40 = 0$

$\Rightarrow y(y - 8) - 5(y - 8) = 0$

$\Rightarrow (y - 8)(y - 5) = 0$

$\Rightarrow (y - 8) = 0$ or $(y - 5) = 0$

$\Rightarrow y = 8$ or 5

Comparison between x and y (via Tabulation):

Value of x	Value of y	Relation
8	8	x = y
8	5	x > y
3	8	x < y
3	5	x < y

∴ x = y or relation between x and y can not be established.

Hence, the correct option is (E).

62. Given,

I. $x^2 - 16x + 63 = 0$

II. $y^2 - 13y + 42 = 0$

I. $x^2 - 16x + 63 = 0$

$\Rightarrow x^2 - 7x - 9x + 63 = 0$

$\Rightarrow x(x - 7) - 9(x - 7) = 0$

$\Rightarrow (x - 7)(x - 9) = 0$

$\Rightarrow x = 7, 9$

II. $y^2 - 13y + 42 = 0$

$\Rightarrow y^2 - 6y - 7y + 42 = 0$

$\Rightarrow y(y - 6) - 7(y - 6) = 0$

$\Rightarrow (y - 6)(y - 7) = 0$

$\Rightarrow y = 6, 7$

Comparison between x and y (via Tabulation):

Value of x	Relation	Value of y
7	>	6
7	=	7
9	>	6
9	>	7

When we compared the values of 'x' and 'y' in the table above, we found that there are two relations between x and y i.e., > and =. So, the relation between x and y is "x ≥ y".

Hence, the correct option is (D).

63. From I,

$3x^2 - 14x + 15 = 0$

$\Rightarrow 3x^2 - 9x - 5x + 15 = 0$

$\Rightarrow 3x(x - 3) - 5(x - 3) = 0$

$\Rightarrow (3x - 5)(x - 3) = 0$

$\Rightarrow 3x - 5 = 0$ or $x - 3 = 0$

$\Rightarrow x = \dfrac{5}{3}$ or $x = 3$

From II,

$15y^2 - 34y + 15 = 0$

$\Rightarrow 15y^2 - 25y - 9y + 15 = 0$

$\Rightarrow 5y(3y - 5) - 3(3y - 5) = 0$

$\Rightarrow (5y - 3)(3y - 5) = 0$

$\Rightarrow 5y - 3 = 0$ or $3y - 5 = 0$

$\Rightarrow y = \dfrac{3}{5}$ or $y = \dfrac{5}{3}$

Comparison between x and y (via Tabulation):

x	y	Relation
$\dfrac{5}{3}$	$\dfrac{3}{5}$	x > y
$\dfrac{5}{3}$	$\dfrac{5}{3}$	x = y
3	$\dfrac{3}{5}$	x > y
3	$\dfrac{5}{3}$	x > y

From the table, we can conclude that the values of variable x are always greater than or equal to y.

∴ We can say that x ≥ y

Hence, the correct option is (C).

64. First covert the given pie chart in the term of percentage:

Types	Percentage
A	$\dfrac{(100 \times 43.2)}{360} = 12\%$
B	$\dfrac{(100 \times 64.8)}{360} = 18\%$
C	$\dfrac{(100 \times 115.2)}{360} = 32\%$
D	$\dfrac{(100 \times 28.8)}{360} = 8\%$
E	$\dfrac{(100 \times 57.6)}{360} = 16\%$
F	$\dfrac{(100 \times 50.4)}{360} = 14\%$

Total number of employees in the year 2017 = 500

The total number of F types employees in the year 2017 = 14% of 500

= 70

Total number of employees in the year 2018 = 500 + 50

= 550

Total number of F type employees in the year 2018 = 70 + 20

= 90

The required percentage $= \dfrac{90 \times 100}{550}$

= 16.37%

Hence, the correct option is (D).

65. First convert the given pie chart in the term of percentage:

Types	Percentage
A	$\dfrac{(100 \times 43.2)}{360} = 12\%$
B	$\dfrac{(100 \times 64.8)}{360} = 18\%$
C	$\dfrac{(100 \times 115.2)}{360} = 32\%$
D	$\dfrac{(100 \times 28.8)}{360} = 8\%$
E	$\dfrac{(100 \times 57.6)}{360} = 16\%$
F	$\dfrac{(100 \times 50.4)}{360} = 14\%$

In the year 2017, let the total number of employees $= 100x$
According to the question,
the difference between B type employees and D type employees
$= 18\%$ of $100x - 8\%$ of $100x$

$\Rightarrow 10\%$ of $100x = 40$
$\Rightarrow 10x = 40$
$\Rightarrow x = 4$
Therefore, the number of employees in the year 2017 = 100 × 4
= 400
The number of F type employees = 14% of 400
$= \dfrac{14 \times 400}{100}$
= 56
Hence, the correct option is (C).

66. First convert the given pie chart in the term of percentage:

Types	Percentage
A	$\dfrac{(100 \times 43.2)}{360} = 12\%$
B	$\dfrac{(100 \times 64.8)}{360} = 18\%$
C	$\dfrac{(100 \times 115.2)}{360} = 32\%$
D	$\dfrac{(100 \times 28.8)}{360} = 8\%$
E	$\dfrac{(100 \times 57.6)}{360} = 16\%$
F	$\dfrac{(100 \times 50.4)}{360} = 14\%$

Let the total number of employees $= 100x$
D type employees $= 8\%$ of $100x = 8x$
A type employees $= 12\%$ of $100x = 12x$

The required percentage $= \dfrac{(12x - 8x) \times 100}{12x}$

$= \dfrac{100}{3}$
= 33.33%
Hence, the correct option is (B).

67. First convert the given pie chart in the term of percentage:

Types	Percentage
A	$\dfrac{(100 \times 43.2)}{360} = 12\%$
B	$\dfrac{(100 \times 64.8)}{360} = 18\%$
C	$\dfrac{(100 \times 115.2)}{360} = 32\%$
D	$\dfrac{(100 \times 28.8)}{360} = 8\%$
E	$\dfrac{(100 \times 57.6)}{360} = 16\%$
F	$\dfrac{(100 \times 50.4)}{360} = 14\%$

Let the total number of employees $= 100x$
B type employees $= 18\%$ of $100x = 18x$
E type employee $= 16\%$ of $100x = 16x$
The ratio $= 18x : 16x$

$= 9 : 8$
In the year 2018, the ratio becomes 11 : 9.
Except ratio, we don't have any information about the number of employees in 2018 therefore answer can't be determined.
Hence, the correct option is (E).

68. First convert the given pie chart in the term of percentage:

Types	Percentage
A	$\dfrac{(100 \times 43.2)}{360} = 12\%$
B	$\dfrac{(100 \times 64.8)}{360} = 18\%$
C	$\dfrac{(100 \times 115.2)}{360} = 32\%$
D	$\dfrac{(100 \times 28.8)}{360} = 8\%$
E	$\dfrac{(100 \times 57.6)}{360} = 16\%$
F	$\dfrac{(100 \times 50.4)}{360} = 14\%$

Let the total number of employees $= 100x$
C type employees $= 32\%$ of $100x$
$= 32x$
F type employees $= 14$
$= 14x$
According to the question,
$32x - 14x = 18x = 126$
$\Rightarrow x = 7$
The required difference $= 14\%$ of $100x - 8\%$ of $100x = 6x$
$= 6 \times 7$
= 42
Hence, the correct option is (C).

69. As given,

There are 12 points in a plane out of which 5 are collinear.

For formation of a triangle we need 3 points if they are not collinear.

So,

Total number of triangles that can be formed with 12 points (if none of them are collinear) $= {}^{12}C_3$

With collinear points, we cannot make any triangle as they are in straight line.

Here 5 points are collinear. Therefore we need to subtract ${}^{5}C_3$ triangles from the above count.

As we know,

$${}^{n}C_k = \dfrac{n!}{k!(n-k)!}$$

Hence, required number of triangles $= {}^{12}C_3 - {}^{5}C_3$

$= \dfrac{12!}{3!(12-3)!} - \dfrac{5!}{3!(5-3)!}$

$= 220 - 10 = 210$

Hence, the correct option is (B).

70. Given,

The total interest for 2 years $=$ Rs. 252

The total interest for 1 year $=$ Rs. $\dfrac{252}{2} =$ Rs. 126

Rate of interest $= 3\%$

The interest that A receives from B for 1 year $=$
$700 \times \dfrac{3}{100} =$ Rs. 21

The interest that A receives from C for 1 year $= 126 - 21 =$ Rs. 105

Let Rs. P be the amount that A gave to C.

As we know,

Simple Interest $(SI) = \dfrac{P \times R \times T}{100}$

where $R =$ Rate of interest and $T =$ Number of years.

$SI = \dfrac{P \times R \times T}{100}$

$\Rightarrow 105 = \dfrac{P \times 3 \times 1}{100}$

$\Rightarrow \dfrac{105 \times 100}{3} = P$

$\Rightarrow P =$ Rs. 3500

$\therefore$ The amount that A gave to C is Rs. 3500.

Hence, the correct option is (C).

71. Given,

Principal $=$ Rs. 46875

Time $= n = 3$ years

The interest received at the end of 3 years $=$ Rs. 12174.

As we know,

$CI = P\left(1 + \dfrac{r}{100}\right)^n - P$

Where, $CI =$ Compound Interest, $P =$ Principal, $r =$ rate of interest, $n =$ number of years.

$CI = P\left(1 + \dfrac{r}{100}\right)^n - P$

$\Rightarrow 12174 = 46875\left(1 + \dfrac{r}{100}\right)^3 - 46875$

$\Rightarrow 12174 + 46875 = 46875\left(1 + \dfrac{r}{100}\right)^3$

$\Rightarrow 59049 = 46875\left(1 + \dfrac{r}{100}\right)^3$

$\Rightarrow \dfrac{19683}{15625} = \left(1 + \dfrac{r}{100}\right)^3$

$\Rightarrow \dfrac{27}{25} = 1 + \dfrac{r}{100}$

$\Rightarrow \dfrac{27}{25} - 1 = \dfrac{r}{100}$

$\Rightarrow \dfrac{2}{25} = \dfrac{r}{100}$

$\Rightarrow \dfrac{2 \times 100}{25} = r$

$\Rightarrow r = 8\%$

Hence, the correct option is (B).

72. Given:

The total number of students is 50 and the number of selected students should be either multiple of 2 or 5.

The average weight of students who were not selected = 56 kg

The average weight of students who were selected = 58 kg

Total students whose number was multiple of 2 = 25

Total students whose number was multiple of 5 = 10

Total students whose number was multiple of 5 and 2 both i.e., of 10 = 5

Total students whose number was either multiple of 2 or multiple of 5 = (25 + 10 − 5)

= 30

It means, 30 students were selected and 20 students were not selected.

According to question,

The sum of the weight of all the students = (56 × 20 + 58 × 30) kg

= 2860 kg

The average weight of all the students = $\dfrac{2860}{50}$

= 57.2 kg

Hence, the correct option is (B).

73. Given:

The total area of square and rectangle is 955 m²

The diagonal of the square is $25\sqrt{2}$ m.

The length of the rectangle is 22 m.

Diagonal of square $= \sqrt{2} \times$ side

Area of rectangle = length × breadth

Area of square = side²

The total area of square and rectangle = Area of rectangle + Area of square

Perimeter of square = 4 × side

Perimeter of rectangle = 2 × (Length + Breadth)

Total Perimeter of square and rectangle = Area of Rectangle + Perimeter of square

Diagonal of square = $\sqrt{2}$ × side

$\Rightarrow 25\sqrt{2} = \sqrt{2}$ × side

$\Rightarrow$ Side = 25 m

Total area of square and rectangle = Area of rectangle + Area of square

$\Rightarrow$ 955 = 22 × breadth + 25 × 25

$\Rightarrow$ Breadth = 15 m

Total Perimeter of square and rectangle = Area of Perimeter + Perimeter of square

$\Rightarrow$ 4 × 25 + 2 × (22 + 15)

$\Rightarrow$ 4 × 25 + 2 × (37)

$\Rightarrow$ 100 + 74

$\Rightarrow$ 174 m

∴ The Sum of the Perimeter of square and rectangle is 174 m.

Hence, the correct option is (C).

74. Given:

Tap B can empty the cistern in 45 minutes.

Tap A can fill the cistern in just 30 minutes.

In 1 minute, cistern filled by Tap A $= \dfrac{1}{30}$

In 1 minute, cistern emptied by Tap B $= \dfrac{1}{45}$

In 1 minute with Taps A and B, cistern filled $= \dfrac{1}{30} - \dfrac{1}{45} = \dfrac{1}{90}$

In 30 minutes, $30 \times \dfrac{1}{90} = \dfrac{1}{3}$ amount of cistern is filled

Remaining cistern $= 1 - \dfrac{1}{3} = \dfrac{2}{3}$

This is filled by Tap A only

In 1 minute, amount of cistern is filled $= \dfrac{1}{30}$

In ? minutes, amount of cistern is filled $= \dfrac{2}{3}$

∴ ? In minutes, the amount of the tank emptied $= \dfrac{\frac{2}{3}}{\frac{1}{30}} = 20$ minutes

Thus, time to fill after Tap B is closed is 20 minutes.

Hence, the correct option is (D).

75. Given series:

120, 145, ?, 197, 224, 257

The pattern is:

$11^2 - 1 = 120$

$12^2 + 1 = 145$

$13^2 - 1 = 168$

$14^2 + 1 = 197$

$15^2 - 1 = 224$

$16^2 + 1 = 257$

So, the missing number is 168.

Hence, the correct option is (B).

76. Given series:

47, 58, 71, 79, 95, ?

The pattern is:

47 + (4 + 7) = 58

58 + (5 + 8) = 71

71 + (7 + 1) = 79

79 + (7 + 9) = 95

95 + (9 + 5) = 109

So, the missing number is 109.

Hence, the correct option is (D).

77. Given series:

8, 39, 79, 394, 789, ?

The pattern is:

8 × 5 − 1 = 39

39 × 2 + 1 = 79

79 × 5 − 1 = 394

394 × 2 + 1 = 789

789 × 5 − 1 = 3944

So, the missing number is 3944.

Hence, the correct option is (D).

78. Given series:

15, 17, 26, 47, 86, ?

The pattern is:

$$15 + (1^3 + 1) = 17$$

$$15 + (2^3 + 3) = 26$$

$$15 + (3^3 + 5) = 47$$

$$15 + (4^3 + 7) = 86$$

$$15 + (5^3 + 9) = 149$$

So, the missing number is 149.

Hence, the correct option is (B).

79. Given series:

3, 9, 24, 57, ?, 267, 552

The pattern is:

3 × 2 + 3 = 9

9 × 2 + 6 = 24

24 × 2 + 9 = 57

57 × 2 + 12 = 126

126 × 2 + 15 = 267

267 × 2 + 18 = 552

So, the missing number is 126.

Hence, the correct option is (D).

80. Let cost price of each article = b Rs

Total cost price $= 464\,b$ Rs

Let, selling price of each article $= a$

Now, $348a = 464b$

Profit% $= 33\frac{1}{3}\%$

Selling price $= \frac{4}{3}b$

Mark price $= \frac{3}{2}b$

Discount $\% = \dfrac{\frac{3}{2}b - \frac{4}{3}b}{\frac{3}{2}b} \times 100\% = 11\frac{1}{9}\%$

Hence, the correct option is (D).

81. Given,

To have exactly 2 persons between Harry and chosen person, the chosen person must be either 3rd to left of Harry or 3rd to right of harry

A person is chosen randomly from them (other than Harry)

∴ The person can be chosen from 12 possible persons

Required probability $= \dfrac{2}{12}$

$= \dfrac{1}{6}$

Hence, the correct option is (B).

82. Given,

$$\dfrac{18 \times \frac{8}{15} + 10\% \text{ of } 624}{?} = 4$$

Follow the BODMAS rule-

$$\Rightarrow 6 \times \frac{8}{5} + 624 \times \frac{10}{100} = 4 \times ?$$

$$\Rightarrow 6 \times \frac{8}{5} + 62.4 = 4 \times ?$$

$$\Rightarrow 6 \times 1.6 + 62.4 = 4 \times ?$$

$$\Rightarrow 9.6 + 62.4 = 4 \times ?$$

$$\Rightarrow 72 = 4 \times ?$$

$$\Rightarrow ? = \frac{72}{4}$$

$$\Rightarrow ? = 18$$

Hence, the correct option is (B).

83. Given,

$$\sqrt{1024} \times 40 + 20^2 + 0.5\% \text{ of } 9600 + 469 = ?^3$$

Follow the BODMAS rule-

$$\Rightarrow 32 \times 40 + 400 + 9600 \times \frac{0.5}{100} + 469 = ?^3$$

$$\Rightarrow 32 \times 40 + 400 + 48 + 469 = ?^3$$

$$\Rightarrow 1280 + 400 + 48 + 469 = ?^3$$

$$\Rightarrow 1280 + 448 + 469 = ?^3$$

$$\Rightarrow 2197 = ?^3$$

$$\Rightarrow ? = \sqrt[3]{2197}$$

$$\Rightarrow ? = 13$$

Hence, the correct option is (B).

84. Given,

$$4\frac{3}{5}\% \text{ of } 6500 + 3\frac{2}{7}\% \text{ of } 3500 = ?$$

Follow the BODMAS rule-

$$\Rightarrow \frac{23}{5}\% \text{ of } 6500 + \frac{23}{7}\% \text{ of } 3500 = ?$$

$$\Rightarrow \left(\frac{23}{500}\right) \times 6500 + \left(\frac{23}{700}\right) \times 3500 = ?$$

$$\Rightarrow 23 \times 13 + 23 \times 5 = ?$$

$$\Rightarrow ? = 23 \times (13 + 5)$$

$$\Rightarrow ? = 23 \times 18$$

$$\Rightarrow ? = 414$$

Hence, the correct option is (B).

85. Given,

$$(4.5 \times 4.5 \times 4.5 \times 4.5) \div 225 \div 25 + 3^3 = ?$$

Follow the BODMAS rule-

$\Rightarrow \left(\dfrac{4.5 \times 4.5 \times 4.5 \times 4.5}{15 \times 15 \times 25}\right) + 27 =?$

$\Rightarrow (0.3 \times 0.3 \times 0.9 \times 0.9) + 27 =?$

$\Rightarrow 0.0729 + 27 =?$

$\Rightarrow ? = 27.0729$

Hence, the correct option is (C).

86. Given,

$$3\dfrac{1}{2} \times \dfrac{7\frac{2}{5}}{9\frac{3}{5}} \times 8^2 \times 60 = 2^4 \times ?$$

Follow the BODMAS rule-

$$\Rightarrow \dfrac{7}{2} \times \dfrac{\frac{37}{5}}{\frac{48}{5}} \times 8^2 \times 60 = 2^4 \times ?$$

$$\Rightarrow \dfrac{7}{2} \times \dfrac{37}{5} \times \dfrac{5}{48} \times 64 \times 60 = 16 \times ?$$

$$\Rightarrow \dfrac{7 \times 37 \times 64 \times 60}{48 \times 2} = 16 \times ?$$

$\Rightarrow ? \times 16 = 7 \times 37 \times 8 \times 5$

$\Rightarrow ? \times 16 = 10360$

$\Rightarrow ? = \dfrac{10360}{16}$

$\Rightarrow ? = 647.5$

Hence, the correct option is (C).

87. Given:

Ratio of invested money by A and $C = 3 : 2$

A invested money for 4 months and C invested money for 6 months.

Formula:

Profit $=$ invested money $\times$ time period

Calculation:

Let A invested $3x$ and C invested $2x$.

Then B invested $= (3x + 2x) \times 80\%$

$\Rightarrow 5x \times \dfrac{80}{100} = 4x$

Let total profit be 100%.

According to question,

9% is given as donation and B gets 21% as salary of total profits.

Then remaining part of profit $= 70\%$

Now ratio of their shares $= 3x \times 4 : 4x \times 1 : 2x \times 6$

$= 3 : 1 : 3$

$\Rightarrow$ A gets $= \dfrac{3}{7}$ of $70\% = 30\%$

$\Rightarrow$ B gets $= \dfrac{1}{7}$ of $70\% + 21\% = 31\%$

$\Rightarrow$ C gets $= \dfrac{3}{7}$ of $70\% = 30\%$

$\therefore$ Ratio of profit shares of A, B and $C = 30 : 31 : 30$

Hence, the correct option is (C).

88. Follow the BODMAS rule:

Given:

The ratio of the speed of train Before accident and after accident $= 3 : 2$

Distance travelled after an accident = 400 km

Time taken = 5 hours

Formula used:

Speed $= \dfrac{distance}{time}$

Calculations:

Let 3x and 2x be the speed of the train before and after an accident respectively.

Speed of train after an accident $= \dfrac{400}{5} = 80$ km/hr

$\Rightarrow$ 2x = 80 km/hr

$\Rightarrow$ x = 40 km/hr

Then, speed of the train before an accident = 3x = 40 × 3 = 120 km/hr

$\therefore$ Original speed of the train before the accident is 120 km/hr.

Hence, the correct option is (C).

89. Given:

Kuldeep completes one round in 6 minutes at the speed of 10 km/h and completes one round in 4 minutes.

Calculation:

Speed of Kuldeep on first day of the month

$= \dfrac{Distance\ Covered}{Time\ Taken}$

Let speed on the first day be S_1 and time be T_1

Speed on the last day be S_2 and time be T_2.

$\Rightarrow S_1 = \dfrac{D}{T_1}$

$\Rightarrow D = S_1 \times T_1$

$\Rightarrow D = 10 \times \left(\dfrac{6}{60}\right)$

$\Rightarrow D = \dfrac{60}{60}$

$\Rightarrow D = 1$ km

Now, Speed of Kuldeep on last day of the month

$$= \frac{Distance\ Covered}{Time\ Taken}$$

$$\Rightarrow S_2 = \frac{D}{T_2}$$

$$\Rightarrow S_2 = \frac{1}{\left(\frac{4}{60}\right)}$$

$$\Rightarrow S_2 = \frac{60}{4}$$

$$\Rightarrow S_2 = 15\ km/h$$

Now, the improvement in Kuldeep's speed = $(S_2 - S_1)$

$= 15 - 10$

$= 5\ km/h$

So, Increase in Kuldeep's speed in m/s = $(S_2 - S_1) \times \left(\frac{5}{18}\right)$

$= 5 \times \left(\frac{5}{18}\right)$

$= \frac{25}{18}\ m/s$

$\therefore$ Kuldeep increased his speed by $\frac{25}{18}$ m/s in one month.

Hence, the correct option is (B).

90. We know that there is no speed of current in lake as lake water is stagnant.

Let's speed of boat B in still water $= x\ km/hr$

Therefore,

Speed of boat A in still water $= 1.5x\ km/hr$

According to question,

$$\left(\frac{Distance}{Speed}\right) Boat\ B - \left(\frac{Distance}{Speed}\right) Boat\ A = Time\ gap$$
between both boats

$$\Rightarrow \frac{72}{x} - \frac{72}{1.5x} = \frac{120}{60}$$

$$\Rightarrow \frac{72}{x} - \frac{48}{x} = 2$$

$$\Rightarrow x = \frac{24}{2}$$

$$\Rightarrow x = 12\ km/hr$$

Speed of boat $A = 1.5 \times 12$

$= 18\ km/hr$

The upstream speed of boat A $= 18 \times \frac{1}{2}$

So, the time taken by boat A to cover the distance in upstream

$$= \frac{72}{18 \times \frac{1}{2}}$$

$= 8$ hr

Hence, the correct option is (A).

Reasoning Ability

Ques (1-5):Direction: Read the information carefully and answer the questions given below.

Eight people, A, B, C, D, E, F, G, and H are sitting around a circular table. Four of these eight people are facing towards the center (inward direction) while four of them are facing away from the center (outward direction). No three consecutive people are facing the same direction.

D is sitting second to the right of G. C is sitting second to the right of B. Both H and E are facing the same direction. F is sitting second to the right of D and they are facing different directions. B is not an immediate neighbour of E. G is facing the inward direction. H is sitting third to the right of E. F is an immediate neighbour of H. Only one person is sitting between G and E.

Q.1 Who is sitting third to the right of A?
A. F   **B.** C   **C.** G   **D.** H
E. D

Q.2 Who is sitting third to the left of C?
A. G   **B.** A   **C.** E   **D.** F
E. D

Q.3 What is the position of H with respect to the position of D?
A. Second to the left   **B.** Immediate right
C. Immediate left   **D.** Third to the left
E. Third to the right

Q.4 Four of the following five are alike in some way and thus form a group. Which of the following does not belong to the group?
A. A   **B.** G   **C.** F   **D.** D
E. C

Q.5 Who are the immediate neighbours of B?
A. D, H   **B.** D, A   **C.** C, G   **D.** G, D
E. A, F

Ques (6-8):Direction: Study the following information carefully and answer the given questions:

In a certain code language,

'people visit many auditorium' is written as 'bh oa pu ki',

'many places like visit' is written as 'pu mh jk oa',

'people like discover places' is written as 'bh jk eg mh'

'auditorium visit discover things' is written as 'ki oa eg qw'.

Q.6 What is the code for word 'discover' in this language?

[IBPS RRB Scale I, 2020]

A. mh   **B.** eg
C. qw   **D.** oa

E. either mh or eg

Q.7 Which of the following word is coded as 'ki' in the given coding language?

[IBPS RRB Scale I, 2020]

A. many   **B.** visit
C. auditorium   **D.** people
E. things

Q.8 What is the code for the word 'visit' in the given language?

[IBPS RRB Scale I, 2020]

A. mh   **B.** oa
C. jk   **D.** bh
E. either 'mh' or 'jk'

Ques (9-10):Direction: Study the following information carefully to answer the given questions:

In a family of 6 people of three-generation, Rupali is the mother of Akshi. Moose is the father of Nikhil, who is the father of Sejal. Rupali is the daughter-in-law of Prena. The number of persons in each generation is the same. Sejal has a sister. No single person has a child. Akshi does not have a brother.

Q.9 How is Sejal related to Akshi?
A. Brother   **B.** Father - in - law
C. Mother   **D.** Sister - in - law
E. Sister

Q.10 Find the odd one out.
A. Akshi   **B.** Nikhil   **C.** Prena   **D.** Rupali
E. Sejal

Ques (11-15):Direction: Answer the question based on the information given below.

Nine students A, B, C, D, E, F, G, H and K are born on 1st of different months among January, February, April, May, June, August, September, October and December in the same year. Students, who were born in months with only 30 days, have different ranks among 1st, 2nd and 3rd.

B was born immediately after the 3rd rank holder. K was born two months after B, who was not born in May. One student was born before D. Two students were born between K and G. A was born immediately before F. E was born after C, who was born after H. A is not 1st rank holder. E doesn't have any rank.

Q.11 How many students are elder than E?
A. Six   **B.** Four
C. Five   **D.** Eight
E. None of the above

Q.12 Who was born immediately after 2nd rank holder?
A. E   **B.** H
C. B   **D.** F
E. None of the above

Q.13 Find the odd one out.

[LIC AAO (Generalist), 2021]

A. H   **B.** F   **C.** D   **D.** B
E. K

Q.14 Who is four months elder than C?
A. G   **B.** F
C. H   **D.** A
E. None of the above

Q.15 Which among the following statements is/are true?
A.   F was born after G
B.   C was born in August
C.   F was born two months after D
D.   H is not the eldest
E.   None of the above statements is true

Ques (16-18):Directions: In the next five questions, the relationship between different characters is given in the statements followed by two conclusions. You have to determine which of the conclusion is true based on the statement.

Q.16 Statements: Y ≤ K < M > B = I, A ≥ M > O ≥ K
Conclusions:
1. A ≥ Y
2. B < O
A.   Only conclusion 1 is necessarily true
B.   Only conclusion 2 is necessarily true
C.   Either conclusion 1 or 2 is necessarily true
D.   Neither conclusion 1 or 2 is necessarily true
E.   Both conclusions are necessarily true

Q.17 Statements: R > P = Q ≤ H ≤ N, H > U < P
Conclusions:
1. U < N
2. N ≥ P
A.   Only conclusion 1 is necessarily true
B.   Only conclusion 2 is necessarily true
C.   Either conclusion 1 or 2 is necessarily true
D.   Neither conclusion 1 or 2 is necessarily true
E.   Both conclusions are necessarily true

Q.18 Statements: D > S ≥ C < U < A, Y = X ≤ B < U
Conclusions:
1. X ≤ C
2. Y > C
A.   Only conclusion 1 is necessarily true
B.   Only conclusion 2 is necessarily true
C.   Either conclusion 1 or 2 is necessarily true
D.   Neither conclusion 1 or 2 is necessarily true
E.   Both conclusions are necessarily true

Ques (19-21):Direction: Read the following information carefully and answer the question which follows.

Point P is 10 km towards the East of point Q. Point R is 16 km North of point Q. Point S is exactly midway between point R and point Q. Point T is 16 km to the South of point S. Point U is 8 km towards the East of point S. Point V is exactly midway between point Q and point P.

Q.19 If a person walks 8 km towards the South from point U, takes a right turn and walks for another 3 km, which of the following points would he reach?
A. Q   **B.** V   **C.** R   **D.** T
E. U

Q.20 If a person walks 8 km towards south from point V, take a right turn and walk 5 km. What is the nearest point to the person?
A. S   **B.** T   **C.** R   **D.** V
E. Q

Q.21 If a person walks 4 km towards the east from point S, take a left turn and walk 8 km. What is the nearest point and how far from the nearest point?
A. R, 4 km   **B.** T, 3 km   **C.** R, 8 km   **D.** S, 3 km
E. S, 5 km

Q.22 If all the vowels of the word 'FRAGMENT' are changed to the letter immediately succeeding them in the english alphabet series and all the consonants are changed to the letter immediately preceding them in the english alphabet series, then how many letters of the new word are similar to the letters of the old word?
A.   Two   **B.**   Three
C.   Four   **D.**   More than four
E.   None of these

Q.23 Suresh is heavier than Anil but not as heavy as Raju. 'Anil' is heavier than Jayesh. 'Krishna' is heavier than Suresh but lighter than 'Raju'. Who is the lightest among them?
A. Krishna   **B.** Suresh   **C.** Jayesh   **D.** Raju
E. Anil

Q.24 Sahil and Gaurav are standing in a row of persons. Sahil is 12th from the left side and Gaurav is 18th from the right side of the row. If they interchanged their positions Sahil becomes 25th from left. What is the total number of persons standing in the row?
A. 42   **B.** 52   **C.** 45   **D.** 46
E. 56

Q.25 In a School, there are 147 people, the ratio of girls : boys is 1:6. Soumya is a girl who stands 15th from the top of that row and 7 girls are in front of her. How many boys are behind her?
A. 100   **B.** 119   **C.** 110   **D.** 120
E. 125

Ques (26-27):Direction: The question is based on the following arrangement. Study the arrangement carefully to answer the question.

I 4 N 5 6 C 7 5 O 6 8 G 3 N 8 I 4 T O 8 M 5 O 3 D 3 4 6 E

Q.26 How many such numbers are there in the above series, each of which is immediately followed by a consonant as well as preceded by a vowel?
A. 5   **B.** 3   **C.** 8   **D.** 4

E. 7

Q.27 After dropping all the consonants, which element will be third to the left of the third vowel from the right end?

A. I   **B.** N   **C.** O   **D.** 3
E. 8

Ques (28-30):Directions: Study the following information carefully to answer the given questions:

Z © H M $ 9 H I 2 E & @ S U V 5 ¥ 3 R O © I T 4 3 % 4 $ L 2 N €

Q.28 If all the numbers are dropped in the above arrangement, then which will be the fifteenth element from the right end?

A. U   **B.** E
C. @   **D.** S
E. None of these

Q.29 How many such numbers are there in the above arrangement each of which is immediately followed by a vowel but not immediately preceded by consonant?

A. One   **B.** Two
C. Three   **D.** More than three
E. None

Q.30 Which of the following is the seventh to the left of the tenth element from the left end of the above arrangement?

A. E   **B.** ¥   **C.** 9   **D.** $
E. H

English Language

Ques (31-35):Direction: Rearrange the following sentences into a meaningful paragraph by choosing the correct sequence of the given sentences, the default order is P, Q, R, S and T, which may or may not be correct.

P. Artificial intelligence and machine learning are core drivers of how Google will pursue its 20-year-old mission

Q. The search engine focused strongly on mobile use and appeared to be growing more like Facebook, encouraging users to linger and explore topics, interests or stories

R. Google unveiled changes Monday aimed at making the leading search engine more visual and intuitive to the point it can answer questions before being asked

S. He described the latest changes as shifting from answers to journeys, providing ways to target queries without knowing what words to use and enhancing image-based searches

T. To organize the world's information and make it accessible to anyone, search vice president Ben Gomes said at an event in San Francisco

Google Images was redesigned to weave in "Lens" technology that enables queries based on what is pointed out in pictures.

Q.31 Which of the following sentences should be the FIRST sentence of the paragraph?

A. P   **B.** R   **C.** S   **D.** Q

E. T

Q.32 Which of the following sentences should be the SECOND sentence of the paragraph?

A. Q   **B.** R   **C.** S   **D.** T
E. P

Q.33 Which of the following sentences should be the THIRD sentence of the paragraph?

A. P   **B.** S   **C.** R   **D.** Q
E. T

Q.34 Which of the following sentences should be the FOURTH sentence of the paragraph?

A. S   **B.** Q   **C.** R   **D.** T
E. P

Q.35 Which of the following sentences should be the FIFTH sentence of the paragraph?

A. P   **B.** Q   **C.** S   **D.** R
E. T

Ques (36-40):Direction: Find out the most effective word from the given options to fill the blanks of the following questions.

Q.36 1. She has played a _______ role in the film.
2. The RBI has done a _______ job in preventing a crisis in the NBFC sector.

A. revival   **B.** commendable
C. notability   **D.** desired
E. attractive

Q.37 1. Tata Iron and Steel Company (TISCO) was _______ by Dorabji Tata on 26 August 1907.
2. In 1990, TISCO began to expand, and _______ its subsidiary, Tata Inc., in New York.

A. impress   **B.** improving
C. established   **D.** clarified
E. appointed

Q.38 1. The pandemic has made more than half of industry _______ negative growth.
2. She came inside the room to _______ her child.

A. extending   **B.** impressed
C. realizes   **D.** embrace
E. approached

Q.39 1. They have _______ the software before launching the new phones in the market.
2. The credit analysis company CARE has _______ ratings on various debt instruments of the bank.

A. increasing   **B.** upgraded
C. improve   **D.** encouraged
E. revises

Q.40 1. The government announces steps to_______ goods and services under Foreign Trade policy.
2. The employees have found a worthy leader to _______ their interest.

A. enroll   **B.** announce

C. celebrate   **D.** promote

E. expect

Ques (41-45):Direction: In the passage given below there are 5 blanks, each followed by a word given in bold. Each blank has four alternative words given in options (A), (B), (C) and (D). You have to tell which word will best suit the respective blank. Mark (E) as your answer if the word given in bold after the blank is your answer i.e No change required.

Introduce a prosecution guided investigation, as is the ___(A) [tradition]across the world. Prosecutors cannot stay ___(B) [abreast]from investigations and only give judgments on the proposed charge sheet. It is often too late to make any changes at all. The prosecution's guidance is necessary in collecting, ___(C) [absolution], sifting, sequencing the evidence and seeking warrant and other legal advice. Separating the prosecution from the police has not helped. The prosecution is unaccountable, and hardly makes any impression on the judiciary. When a case fails, it is routine to criticise the police for every ___(D)[rejoice]and forget the case.

Reviving the nearly___(E)[abysmal]women helpline, women help desk in all police stations, and regular monitoring of all the calls/complaints received and the police's response must be made a criterion for performance evaluation.

Q.41 Which of the following fits in the blank labelled (A)?

A. Liturgy   **B.** Ritual

C. Norm   **D.** Rite

E. No improvement

Q.42 Which of the following fits in the blank labelled (B)?

A. Aloof   **B.** Stray

C. Erratic   **D.** Steady

E. No improvement

Q.43 Which of the following fits in the blank labelled (C)?

A. Conforming   **B.** Collating

C. Persisting   **D.** Acclimating

E. No improvement

Q.44 Which of the following fits in the blank labelled (D)?

A. Alteration   **B.** Lapse

C. Progresssion   **D.** Accustom

E. No improvement

Q.45 Which of the following fits in the blank labelled (E)?

A. Defunct   **B.** Dreary

C. Dismal   **D.** Somber

E. No improvement

Ques (46-50):Directions: In each question, a part of the sentence is made bold. Below are given alternatives to the bold part at (A), (B), (C) and (D) which may improve the sentence. Choose the correct alternative. In case no replacement is needed, mark (E) as your answer.

Q.46 Mr. Tharoor's **urban manners charm friends** and enemies alike.

A. urban manners charming friends

B. urbane manners charming friends

C. urban mannerisms charm friends

D. urbane manners charm friends

E. No correction required

Q.47 Religious **bigots look away on** anyone who does not conform to their beliefs.

A. bigots look away on

B. bigots look down on

C. bigots look behind on

D. bigots look in front of

E. No correction required

Q.48 Having leisure till outdoor activities such as taking a stroll down the park has become a rarity in this fast paced life.

A. Having leisures till outdoor

B. Having laziness for outdoor

C. Having leisure in outdoor

D. Having leisure for outdoor

E. No correction required

Q.49 India lent a helpful handshake to Nepal by giving them 2.1 billion Nepalese rupees for the reconstruction of houses flattened in the 2015 earthquake.

A. India lent a helping handshake

B. India lent a helpful hand

C. India lent a helping hand

D. India lending a helping hand

E. No correction required

Q.50 One is advised **to check the voracity of news** articles before forwarding them on whatsapp and other social media.

A. to check the voracity of news

B. checking the veracity of news

C. to check the veracity of news

D. to check the voracity of new

E. No correction required

Ques (51-55):Direction: In the following sentence, some parts have been printed in bold. One of the bold parts is incorrectly spelled. Pick up that part and choose its number. If there is no error in the bold parts, choose option (E)- No error as the answer.

Q.51 The **association** between the Jews and evil was therefore not a creation of the Nazis, but **dated** back to the Christian Middle Ages, a period when the Jews were first confined in **ghetos** and excluded from **respectable** society.

A. Association   **B.** Dated

C. Ghetos   **D.** Respectable

E. No error

Q.52 The term 'fascism' **derives** from the Italian word fasces, meaning a bundle of rods with an axe-blade **protruding** that signified the **authority** of the **magistrates** in Imperial Rome.

A. Derives   **B.** Protruding

C. Authority   **D.** Magistrates

E. No error

Q.53 In his **classification** of the government into normal and **perverted** forms, Aristotle placed democracy among perverted forms since it **signifies** the rule of the **medeocre** seeking their selfish interests.

A. Classification   **B.** Perverted
C. Signified   **D.** Medeocre
E. No error

Q.54 Tens of **thousands** more workers, **independent** contractors usually working in their homes, also **anotate** data through **crowdsourcing** services like Amazon Mechanical Turk.

A. Thousands   **B.** Independent
C. Anotate   **D.** Crowdsourcing
E. No error

Q.55 Ancient Hindu **shrines** rise over roadside markets at the **southwestern** end of the city — giant towers of **stacked** stone that date to the first **millenium**.

A. Shrines   **B.** Southwestern
C. Stacked   **D.** Millenium
E. No error

Ques (56-60):Direction: Read the passage carefully and select the best answer to each question out of the given five alternatives.

The move by the government to demonetize Rs. 500 and Rs. 1000 notes by replacing them with new Rs. 500 and Rs. 2000 notes have taken the country by surprise. The move by the government is to tackle the menace of black money, corruption, terror funding, and fake currency. From a market perspective, we think that this is a very welcome move by the government and which has taken the black money hoarders by surprise. The total value of old Rs. 500 and Rs. 1000 notes in the circulation is to the tune of Rs. 14.2 trillion, which is about 85% of the total value of the currency in circulation. This means that the total cash has to now pass through the **formal** banking channels to get legitimacy. The World Bank in July 2010 estimated the size of the shadow economy for India at 20.7% of the Gross Domestic Product (GDP) in 1999 and rising to 23.2% in 2007. Assuming that this figure has not risen since then (quite unlikely though) and that the cash component of the shadow economy is also proportional (it could be higher), the estimated unaccounted value of the currency could be to the tune of Rs. 3.3 trillion. Now, post the announcement of demonetization by the government this money would have to either account for by paying the relevant tax and penalties or would get extinguished. There are higher chances of a larger proportion of this unaccounted currency getting extinguished as the tax rate and subsequent legal issues could be prohibitively high for such money.

This move by the government is likely to have long-term benefits for the economy. The extinguishing of the major proportion of unaccounted currency would reduce the liabilities of the government and. would add to its finances. This can have very strong implications as the government would get money to spend without borrowing from the market. This would mean that while interest rates can be low, the government spending on large infrastructure (we assume that the government would use a large proportion for infra spending) projects would kick start the apex cycle and push economic growth higher in the medium term. The move is also

likely to have a habit-changing impact on the Indian populous and there could be an increased belief in keeping cash in the banks rather than stashed at home and use formal banking channels for their spending needs. With a large part of the cash moving through the banking channels, the banking sector is likely to be flush with funds in the near term and this would help them reduce the cost of funds for such period. Also with more money being kept in the banking channel, some of these low-cost deposits may be sticky and improve the medium to long term Current Account and Savings Account (CASA) ratio of the banks. Another element of the demonetization would be a reduction in cash transactions in real estate which has been acting like a **cash cow** for the corrupt.

Q.56 What percentage of the total value of the currency in circulation is made up of the old Rs.500 and Rs.1000 notes?

A. 80%   **B.** 85%   **C.** 90%   **D.** 95%
E. 100%

Q.57 Choose the correct synonym of the word 'formal' as highlighted in the paragraph in context to the whole from the given options.

A. Official   **B.** Ceremonial
C. Informal   **D.** Traditional
E. Orthodox

Q.58 Why are there higher chances of the larger proportion of the unaccounted currency getting extinguished?

A. Black money hoarders would be ashamed to expose their entire holdings and will probably burn or destroy the money they had hoarded.

B. Since the notes that has been demonetized are mostly with black money hoarders, and they no longer have any market value they hoarders have no other option but to destroy them either by burning or by tearing.

C. The unaccounted currency when accounted for through legal channels would attract higher tax rates and even legal actions thereby forcing the hoarders to extinguish them so as to avoid the taxes and legal wrangling.

D. The unaccounted money is in form of large notes that has been demonetized making it illegal for use. Hence they need to be extinguished.

E. A large proportion of the unaccounted currency will be extinguished so to avoid persecution by the legal authorities.

Q.59 What is the full form of CASA?

A. Current Act and Savings Act
B. Current action and Savings Action
C. Current Affirmation and Savings Affirmation
D. Current Account and Savings Account
E. Current Act and Savings Account

Q.60 Choose the correct meaning of the idiom 'cash cow' as underlined in the paragraph in context to the whole from the given options.

A. The cow that gives cash.
B. Cash that buys cows.
C. People with low income from land.
D. An approximate estimate of the cost of land.
E. A product or service that is a regular source of income for

someone.

Numerical Ability

Q.61 If the cost price of 18 pens is equal to the selling price of 12 pens, what is the gain percent?

A. 12.5%   **B.** 22.5%   **C.** 50%   **D.** 36%
E. 60%

Q.62 What will be compound interest (in Rs.) on a sum of Rs.6000 for 2 years at the rate of 10 % per annum?

A. 1260   **B.** 1200   **C.** 1380   **D.** 1140
E. 1139

Q.63 The interest on Rs.1,250 for 15 years at the rate of 1.6 % simple interest per annum will be:

A. Rs.350   **B.** Rs.375   **C.** Rs.360   **D.** Rs.300
E. Rs.400

Ques (64-68):Direction: What should come in place of the question mark '?' in the following number series?

Q.64 9, 17, 33, 65, ?

A. 113   **B.** 131   **C.** 129   **D.** 118
E. 119

Q.65 40, 41, 84, 255, 1024, ?

A. 5125   **B.** 5075   **C.** 5175   **D.** 5025
E. 5235

Q.66 11, 19, 28, 92, ?, 333

A. 117   **B.** 214   **C.** 191   **D.** 217
E. 137

Q.67 70, 140, 420, 1680, ?

A. 8600   **B.** 8500   **C.** 8400   **D.** 9400
E. 9500

Q.68 14, 22, 28, 32, 34, ?

A. 34   **B.** 36   **C.** 38   **D.** 35
E. 37

Q.69 In a box there are 2 dark chocolates, 3 milk chocolates and 4 ice-creams. Find the possible number of ways 3 items can be taken if one milk chocolate is a must.

A. 54   **B.** 64   **C.** 78   **D.** 51
E. 44

Q.70 Two pipes A and B can fill a tank in 15 min and 20 min respectively. Both the pipes are opened together but after 4 min, pipe A is turned off. What is the total time required to fill the tank?

A. 10 min 20 sec   **B.** 11 min 45 sec
C. 12 min 30 sec   **D.** 14 min 40 sec
E. 12 min 40 sec

Ques (71-75):

Direction: The following line graph gives the percentage of the number of candidates who qualified an examination out of the total number of candidates who appeared for the examination over a period of seven years from 1994 to 2000.

Percentage of Candidates Qualified to Appeared in an Examination Over the Years.

Q.71 The difference between the percentage of candidates qualified to appeared was maximum in which of the following pairs of years?

A. 1994 and 1995   **B.** 1995 and 1996
C. 1998 and 1999   **D.** 1999 and 2000
E. 1997 and 1998

Q.72 In which pair of years was the number of candidates qualified, the same?

A. 1994 and 1995   **B.** 1995 and 1997
C. 1998 and 1999   **D.** 1995 and 2000
E. Data inadequate

Q.73 If the number of candidates qualified in 1998 was 21200, what was the number of candidates who appeared in 1998?

A. 32000   **B.** 28500   **C.** 26500   **D.** 25000
E. 27000

Q.74 If the total number of candidates who appeared in 1996 and 1997 together was 47400, then the total number of candidates qualified in these two years together was?

A. 34700   **B.** 32100
C. 31500   **D.** 32500
E. Data inadequate

Q.75 The total number of candidates qualified in 1999 and 2000 together was 33500 and the number of candidates appeared in 1999 was 26500. What was the number of candidates in 2000?

A. 24500   **B.** 22000   **C.** 20500   **D.** 19000
E. 21500

Ques (76-80):Direction: What will come in the place of the question mark (?) in the following question?

Q.76 $\sqrt{144} \div 4 \times 6 - \sqrt{196} \div \sqrt{49} + 5 =?$

[SBI Clerk, 2020]

A. 19   **B.** 20   **C.** 21   **D.** 22
E. 23

Q.77 680 × 24 ÷ 12 ÷ 17 + 12 of 6 = ?

A. 142   **B.** 152
C. 132   **D.** 165
E. None of the above

Q.78 263 – 345 + 180 × 3% of 20 – 1 = ?
A. 30 **B.** 24 **C.** 25 **D.** 26
E. 29

Q.79 250 × 24 ÷ 12 ÷ 125 + 2 of 3 = ?
A. 7 **B.** 8 **C.** 9 **D.** 10
E. 11

Q.80 $\frac{3}{4} + \frac{7}{8} + \frac{11}{12} + \frac{13}{16} = \frac{?+1}{48}$
A. 160 **B.** 140 **C.** 150 **D.** 130
E. 120

Q.81 A train crosses two platforms of length 500 m and 800 m in 80 seconds and 120 seconds respectively, then find the length of the train.
A. 150 m **B.** 180 m **C.** 100 m **D.** 250 m
E. 300 m

Ques (82-84):Direction: In the given question, two equations numbered I and II are given. You have to solve both the equations and mark the appropriate answer.

Q.82 I. $10x^2 – 29x + 10 = 0$
II. $4y^2 – 11y + 6 = 0$
A. x > y
B. x < y
C. x ≥ y
D. x ≤ y
E. x = y or relationship between x and y cannot be established

Q.83 I. $x^2 + 91 = 20x$
II. $10y^2 - 29y + 21 = 0$
A. if x < y
B. if x > y
C. if x ≤ y
D. if x ≥ y
E. if x = y or no relation can be established

Q.84 I. $3x^2 + 25x – 18 = 0$
II. $2y^2 + 15y + 27 = 0$
A. if x > y
B. if x ≥ y
C. if x < y
D. if x ≤ y
E. if x = y or no relation can be established between x and y

Q.85 The ratio between the length and the breadth of a rectangular plot is 6: 5. If the perimeter of the plot is 484 metres, what is its area?
A. 14520 sq.metres **B.** 12500 sq. metres
C. 12000 sq. metres **D.** 13800 sq. metres
E. None of these

Q.86 A boatman goes $2\ km$ against the current of the stream in 1 hour and goes $1\ km$ along the current in 10 minutes. How long will it take to go $5\ km$ in stationary water?
A. 40 minutes **B.** 1 hr
C. 1 hr and 15 min **D.** 1 hr and 30 min
E. 1 hr and 45 min

Q.87 The average weight of 3 children is 20 kg. The weight of Chinu is three times the weight of Bhavya and the weight of Arshi is twice that of Bhavya, Find the weight of Chinu.
A. 20 kg **B.** 30 kg **C.** 10 kg **D.** 15 kg
E. 25 kg

Q.88 In a business, A invested Rs. 50000 for 8 months and B invested for 6 months. The ratio of profit of B to the total profit is 9 : 17. Find the money invested by B.
A. Rs. 35750 **B.** Rs. 75000
C. Rs. 25000 **D.** Rs. 77500
E. Rs. 52850

Q.89 A box contains 4 red and 3 green pens. 3 pens are drawn at random. Find the probability that 2 pens are of red colour and 1 pen is of green colour are drawn from the box.
A. $\frac{2}{18}$ **B.** $\frac{2}{19}$ **C.** $\frac{18}{35}$ **D.** $\frac{1}{7}$
E. $\frac{1}{9}$

Q.90 Two cars are initially 64 km apart and speed of cars is 48 km/h and 'x' km/h . Distance between them will be 4 km after travelling for 't₁' min when travelling towards each other and distance between them will be 84 km after 't₂' min when travelling away from each other. If 't₁ – t₂' is 30, then find the speed of second car.
A. 28 km/h **B.** 24 km/h **C.** 36 km/h **D.** 32 km/h
E. 30 km/h

// Smart Answer Sheet //

Correct Indicates percentage of students who answered questions correctly.

Skipped Indicates percentage of students who skipped questions.

Q.	Ans.	Correct / Skipped
1	C	57.3 % / 1.54 %
2	D	49.57 % / 1.26 %
3	B	67.58 % / 1.03 %
4	C	80.39 % / 0.0 %
5	D	50.09 % / 1.66 %
6	B	52.67 % / 1.68 %
7	C	59.26 % / 1.99 %
8	B	78.46 % / 0.0 %
9	E	76.59 % / 0.0 %
10	B	85.45 % / 0.0 %
11	D	68.56 % / 1.54 %
12	D	56.38 % / 1.7 %
13	C	41.43 % / 1.6 %
14	B	51.34 % / 1.27 %
15	E	10.58 % / 3.45 %
16	D	51.56 % / 1.75 %

Q.	Ans.	Correct / Skipped
17	E	52.49 % / 1.5 %
18	C	44.79 % / 1.14 %
19	B	44.46 % / 1.19 %
20	B	45.12 % / 1.57 %
21	A	64.2 % / 1.47 %
22	C	85.4 % / 0.0 %
23	C	57.84 % / 1.8 %
24	A	62.76 % / 1.2 %
25	B	47.73 % / 1.39 %
26	D	63.95 % / 1.2 %
27	E	63.07 % / 1.09 %
28	C	58.75 % / 1.4 %
29	A	52.42 % / 1.49 %
30	E	49.08 % / 1.62 %
31	B	48.1 % / 1.84 %
32	E	69.83 % / 1.07 %

Q.	Ans.	Correct / Skipped
33	E	46.81 % / 1.12 %
34	B	49.06 % / 1.2 %
35	C	51.86 % / 1.5 %
36	B	40.98 % / 1.75 %
37	C	62.83 % / 1.97 %
38	D	53.85 % / 1.28 %
39	B	57.44 % / 1.18 %
40	D	48.81 % / 1.52 %
41	C	49.47 % / 1.69 %
42	A	61.45 % / 1.98 %
43	B	47.24 % / 1.04 %
44	B	42.72 % / 1.71 %
45	A	58.66 % / 1.17 %
46	D	55.11 % / 1.48 %
47	B	43.09 % / 1.87 %
48	D	66.71 % / 1.62 %

Q.	Ans.	Correct / Skipped
49	C	46.68 % / 1.49 %
50	C	52.91 % / 1.38 %
51	C	41.27 % / 1.82 %
52	E	47.72 % / 1.4 %
53	D	48.31 % / 1.19 %
54	C	42.44 % / 1.46 %
55	D	56.09 % / 1.17 %
56	B	54.56 % / 1.48 %
57	A	61.97 % / 1.93 %
58	C	69.33 % / 1.73 %
59	D	43.78 % / 1.1 %
60	E	65.04 % / 1.17 %
61	C	47.18 % / 1.18 %
62	A	63.34 % / 1.2 %
63	D	60.27 % / 1.5 %
64	C	87.75 % / 0.0 %

Q.	Ans.	Correct / Skipped
65	A	63.22 % / 1.43 %
66	A	44.68 % / 1.86 %
67	C	83.49 % / 0.0 %
68	A	79.67 % / 0.0 %
69	B	49.02 % / 1.53 %
70	D	61.75 % / 1.69 %
71	E	88.8 % / 0.0 %
72	E	88.24 % / 0.0 %
73	C	85.87 % / 0.0 %
74	E	65.31 % / 1.39 %
75	C	46.66 % / 1.63 %
76	C	84.94 % / 0.0 %
77	B	86.16 % / 0.0 %
78	C	44.37 % / 1.5 %
79	D	87.38 % / 0.0 %
80	A	87.05 % / 0.0 %

Q.	Ans.	Correct	
		Skipped	
81	C	47.09 %	
		1.05 %	
82	E	63.17 %	
		1.49 %	

Q.	Ans.	Correct	
		Skipped	
83	B	41.03 %	
		1.78 %	
84	E	45.15 %	
		1.3 %	

Q.	Ans.	Correct	
		Skipped	
85	A	24.35 %	
		3.58 %	
86	C	45.71 %	
		1.47 %	

Q.	Ans.	Correct	
		Skipped	
87	B	45.43 %	
		1.18 %	
88	B	49.45 %	
		1.23 %	

Q.	Ans.	Correct	
		Skipped	
89	C	65.63 %	
		1.91 %	
90	D	57.3 %	
		1.27 %	

Performance Analysis

Avg. Score (%)	57.78%
Toppers Score (%)	68.89%
Your Score	

//Hints and Solutions//

Ques (1-5): Eight person: A, B, C, D, E, F, G and H

1) H is sitting third to the right of E.

2) Both H and E are facing the same direction.

(As it is a circular arrangement, we can randomly pick a seat for E and then we can place H according to the direction that E is facing.)

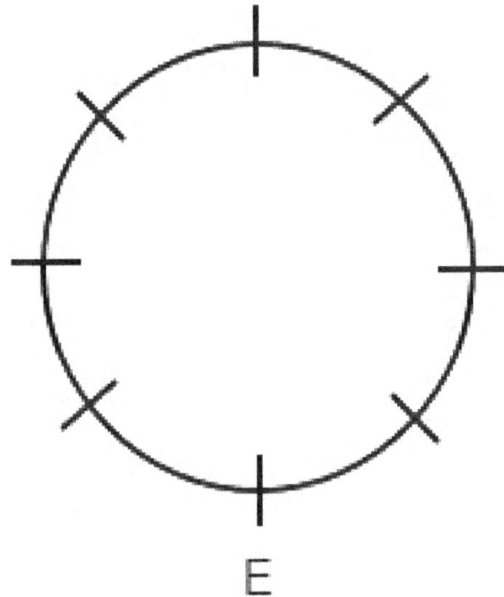

3) G is facing the inward direction.

4) Only one person is sitting between G and E.

5) D is sitting second to the right of G.

(It is only possible if we place E second to the left of G then only we can place D second to the right of G.)

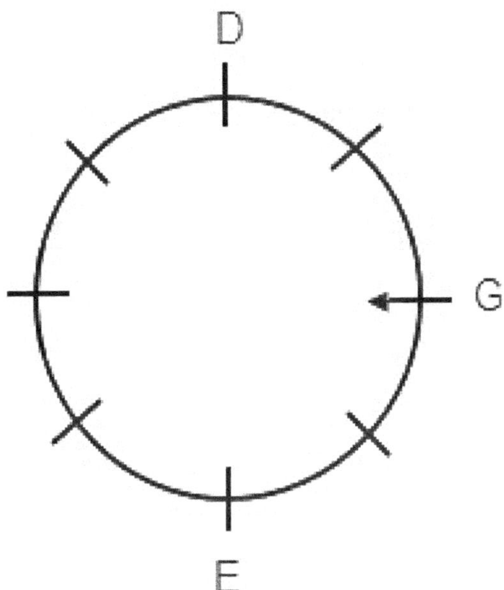

6) If we place H between D and G then that would mean that E is facing inward direction but, in that case, F would not be an immediate neighbour of H. Therefore, both E and H are facing outward direction.

7) H is sitting third to the right of E and immediate neighbour of F. (It further implies that F is sitting to the immediate left of H as it is the only possibility.)

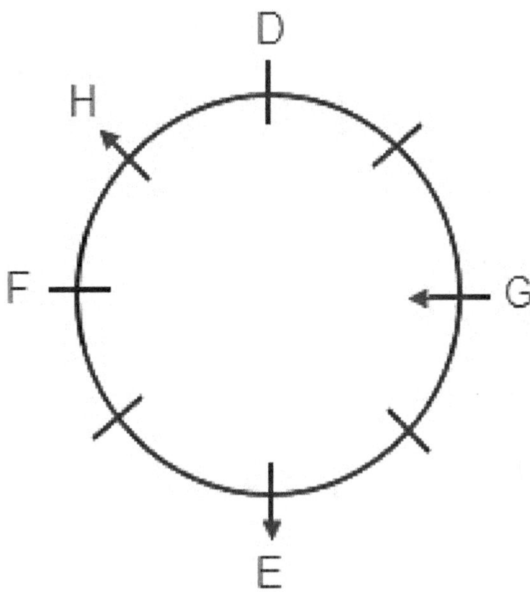

8) F is sitting second to the right of D and they are facing different directions.

(It is only possible if D is facing inward direction and F is facing outward direction. Also, as no three consecutive people are facing the same direction implies that the person sitting to the immediate left of F is facing inward direction.)

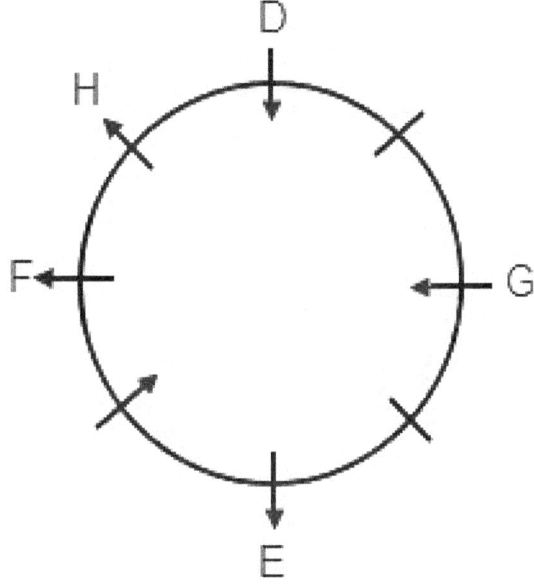

9) B is not an immediate neighbour of E.

(Implies, B is sitting between D and G. It is the only possibility.)

10) C is sitting second to the right of B.

(It is only possible if B is facing outward direction. Also, now that we have identified four people who are facing outward, we can say that the other four are facing inward direction. Therefore, C is facing the inward direction. Also, now only A is left to be placed implies that A is sitting to the immediate left of F.)

Thus, the final arrangement is:

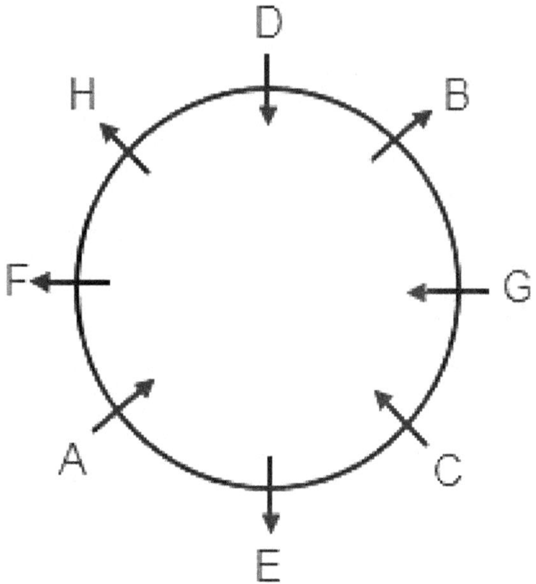

1. Clearly, G is sitting third to the right of A.

Hence, the correct option is (C).

2. Clearly, F is sitting third to the left of C.

Hence, the correct option is (D).

3. Clearly, H is sitting to the immediate right of D.

Hence, the correct option is (B).

4. Except F, all are facing inward direction.

Therefore, F does not belong to the group.

Hence, the correct option is (C).

5. Clearly, G and D, are the immediate neighbours of B.

Hence, the correct option is (D).

Ques (6-8): In a certain coding language:

The words and their code are marked with a specific outline/underlined.

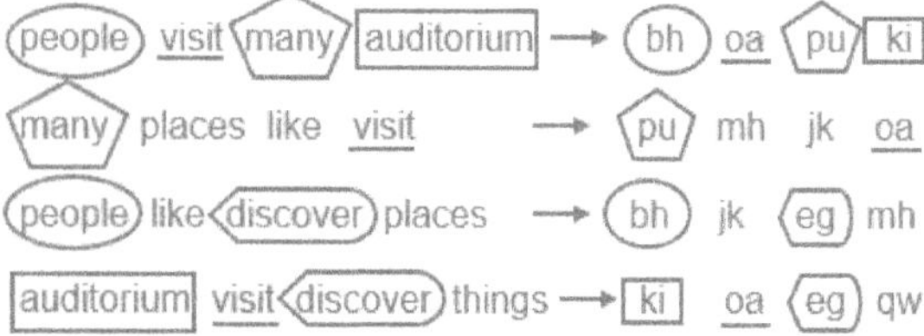

6. 'discover' has the same outline as 'eg'.

Hence, the correct option is (B).

7. 'auditorium' has the same outline as 'ki'.

Hence, the correct option is (C).

8. 'visit' is coded as 'oa'.

Hence, the correct option is (B).

Ques (9-10): Below table represents symbols used to draw a family tree,

Symbol in Diagram	Meaning
○	Female
□	Male
═══	Married Couple
───	Siblings
│	Difference of A Generation

1) Rupali is mother of Akshi.

2) Moose is father of Nikhil, who is father of Sejal.

3) Rupali is daughter - in - law of Prena.

4) Number of persons in each generation is the same. So, there must be 2 persons in each generation.

5) Sejal has a sister.

6) Akshi does not have a brother. So, Sejal must be the sister of Akshi.

We can draw the following Family Tree from the information given above:

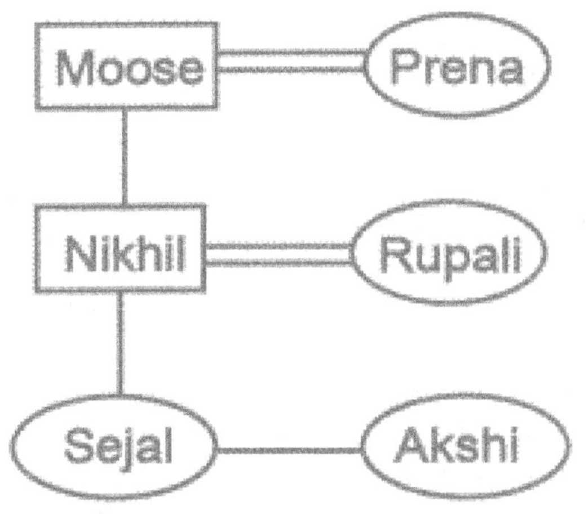

9. Thus, Sejal is sister of Akshi.

Hence, the correct option is (E).

10. All are female except Nikhil.

Hence, the correct option is (B).

Ques (11-15): 1. One student was born before D.
2. B was born immediately after the 3rd rank holder.
3. K was born two months after B, who was not born in May.
4. Two students were between K and G.
So, B was born in either August or October. K was born in either October or December. G was born in either June or August.
Case I: B was born in August:

Month	Student	Rank
January		
February	D	
April		
May		
June	G	3rd
August	B	
September		
October	K	
December		

Case II: B was born in October:

Month	Student	Rank
January		
February	D	
April		
May		
June		
August	G	
September		3rd
October	B	
December		

5. K was born two months after B, this is not possible in case II, so case II is rejected.
6. A was born immediate before F.
7. E was born after C, who was born after H.
8. A is not 1st rank holder. E doesn't have any rank.
So, E was born in December. C was born in September and H is

born in January. C is 1st rank holder and A is 2nd rank holder. The final table is given below:

Month	Student	Rank
January	H	
February	D	
April	A	2nd
May	F	
June	G	3rd
August	B	
September	C	1st
October	K	
December	E	

11. So, Eight students are elder than E

Hence, the correct option is (D).

12. So, F was born immediately after 2nd rank holder.

Hence, the correct option is (D).

13. So, H, F, B, and K were born in January, May, August, and October month respectively which has 31 days but D was born in February.

Hence, the correct option is (C).

14. So, F was born immediately after 2nd rank holder.

Hence, the correct option is (D).

15. So, None of the above statements is true.

Hence, the correct option is (E).

16. Y ≤ K < M > B = I, A ≥ M > O ≥ K

From these statements, we can conclude that Y ≤ K < O < M ≤ A and M > B = I

Conclusion 1 is incorrect as A > Y but they can never be equal.

Conclusion 2 is incorrect as there is no relationship between O and B.

They can be equal, or O can be greater or less than B.

Hence, the correct option is (D).

17. R > P = Q ≤ H ≤ N, H > U < P

From these statements, we can conclude that U < P = Q ≤ H ≤ N and P < R

We can see that both the conclusions follow from the conclusion we have drawn using both statements.

Hence, the correct option is (E).

18. D > S ≥ C < U < A, Y = X ≤ B < U

From these statements, we can conclude that X = Y ≤ B < S < D and A > U > C ≤ S

None of the conclusions definitely follow. But together, they make an exhaustive set i.e. they cover all the possibilities that can be between X(=Y) and C.

Hence, the correct option is (C).

19. The given set of directions is as follows:

1) Point P is 10 km towards the East of point Q.

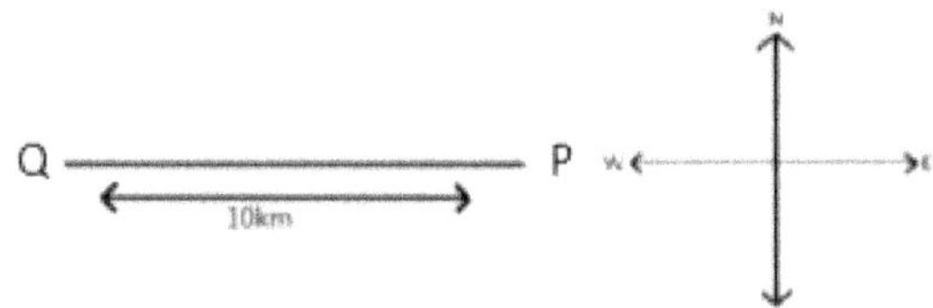

2) Point R is 16 km North of point Q.

3) Point S is exactly midway between point Q and point R.

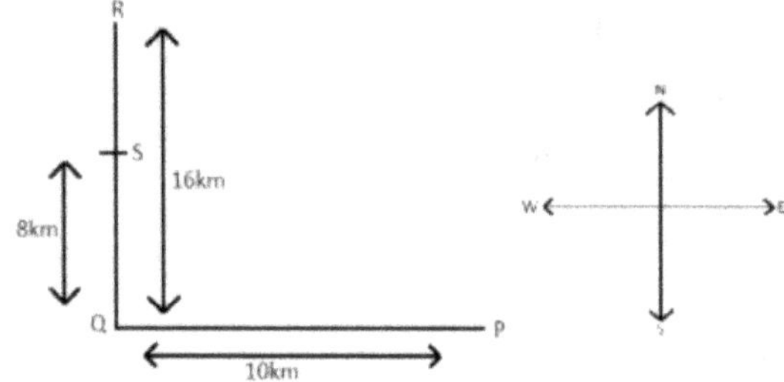

4) Point T is 16 km to the South of point S.

5) Point U is 8 km towards the East of point S.

6) Point V is exactly midway between point Q and point P.

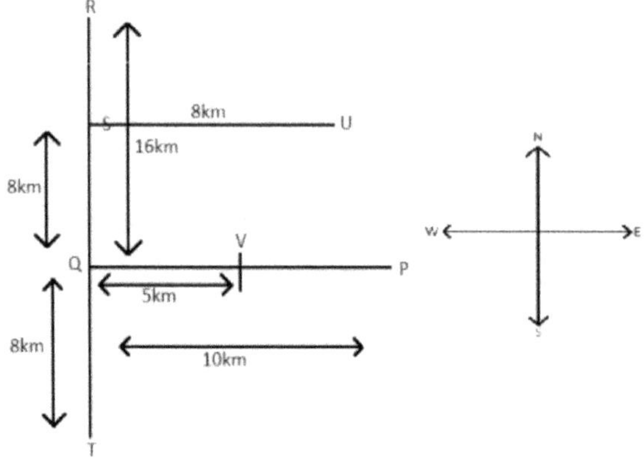

So, the answer is point V.

Hence, the correct option is (B).

20. The given set of directions is as follows:

1) Point P is 10 km towards the East of point Q.

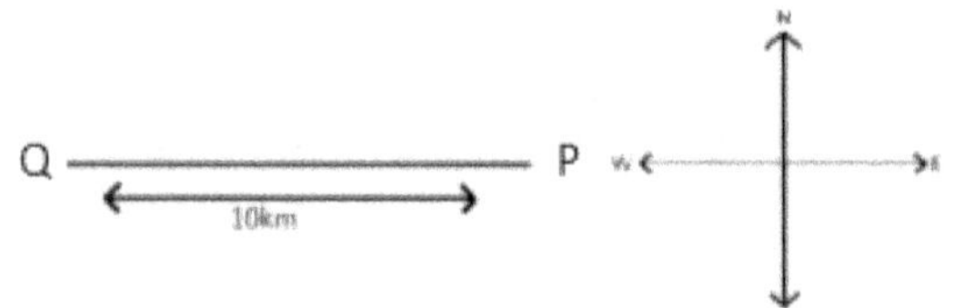

2) Point R is 16 km North of point Q.

3) Point S is exactly midway between point Q and point R.

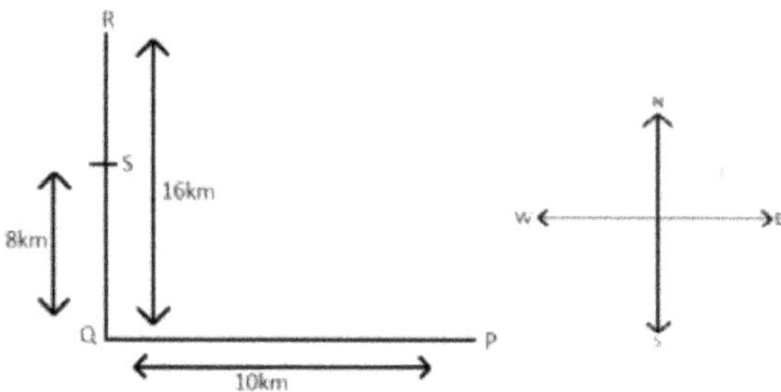

4) Point T is 16 km to the South of point S.

5) Point U is 8 km towards the East of point S.

6) Point V is exactly midway between point Q and point P.

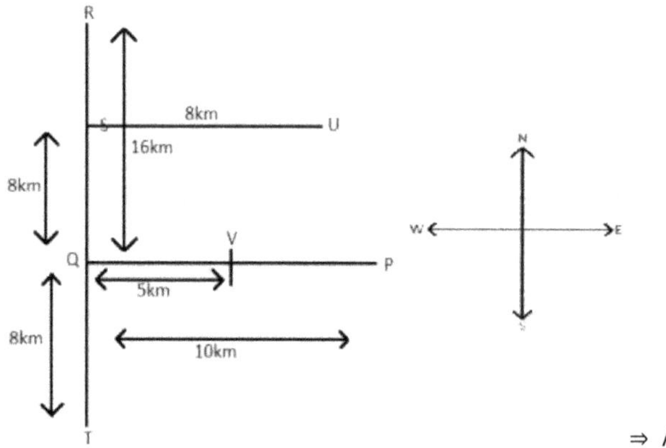

⇒ A person Walk 8 km towards South from v point.

⇒ Take a right turn and walk 5 km.

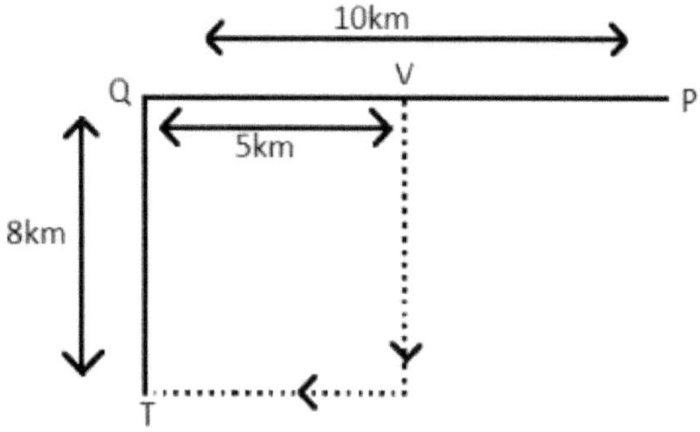

The nearest position is T.

So, the correct answer is T.

Hence, the correct option is (B).

21. ⇒ A person walks 4 km towards east from point S

⇒ take a left turn and walk 8 km.

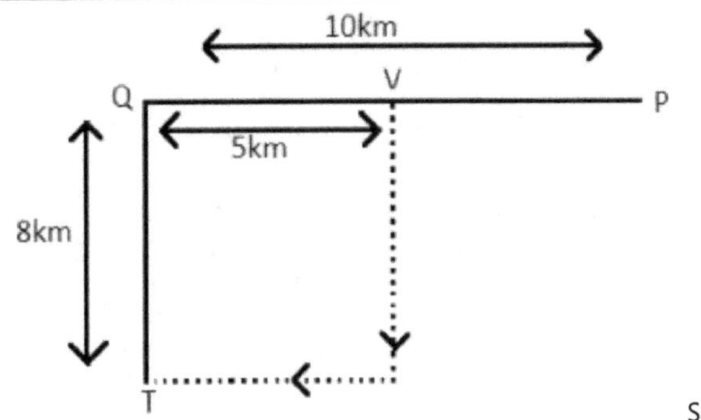

the correct answer is R, 4 km

Hence, the correct option is (A).

22. The given word:

FRAGMENT

Applying the above condition, we have a new word:

EQBFLFMS

Now, the new arrangement of old and new words are:

F	R	A	G	M	E	N	T
E	Q	B	F	L	F	M	S

Apparently, four letters viz. E, F, F and M of the new word are similar to the letters of the old word.
Hence, the correct option is (C).

23. Given,

Suresh is heavier than Anil but not as heavy as Raju. 'Anil' is heavier than Jayesh. 'Krishna' is heavier than Suresh but lighter than 'Raju'.

The sequence is as follows,

$Raju > Krishna > Suresh > Anil > Jayesh$

Thus the lightest one is 'Jayesh'.

Hence, the correct option is (C).

24. Given,

Sahil and Gaurav are standing in a row of persons. Sahil is 12th from the left side and Gaurav is 18th from the right side of the row.

Position of Sahil from Left = 25 (after interchanging)

Total person = Position from Left + Position from right - 1

Position of Sahil from Right = 18 (position of Sahil from right end is same as Gaurav after interchanging) -1

Total person $= 25 + 18 - 1 = 42$

Thus, there are 42 persons in the row.

Hence, the correct option is (A).

25. Given,

In a School, there are 147 people, the ratio of girls: boys is 1:6. Soumya is a girl who stands 15th from the top of that row and 7 girls are in front of her.

Total number of students $= 147$

Girls : Boys $= 1 : 6$

Let the number of girls be x and the number of boys be $6x$.

Then,

$x + 6x = 147$

$\operatorname{\Rightarrow~}7x = 147$

$\operatorname{\Rightarrow~}x = 21$

Then the number of girls $= 21$

The number of boys $= 6 \times 21 = 126$

Now Soumya is in 15th position from the top and 7 girls are in front of her.

Now boys are in front of him $= 7$ as total 14 students are in front of him.

So, the number of boys, behind him $= 126 - 7 = 119$

Hence, the correct option is (B).

26. We know, consonants are letters other than vowels (A, E, I, O, U).

I 4 N 5 6 C 7 5 O 6 8 G 3 N 8 I 4 T O 8 M 5 O 3 D 3 4 6 E

Here we get four numbers which are immediately followed by a consonant and immediately preceded by a vowel.

Hence, the correct option is (D).

27. Given series: I 4 N 5 6 C 7 5 O 6 8 G 3 N 8 I 4 T O 8 M 5 O 3 D 3 4 6 E

New series: I 4 5 6 7 5 O 6 8 3 8 I 4 O 8 5 O 3 3 4 6 E

Here we have 3rd vowel is O and the third element to the left of it is 8.

Hence, the correct option is (E).

28. Given series:

Left Side Z © H M $ 9 H I 2 E & @ S U V 5 ¥ 3 R O © I T 4 3 % 4 $ L 2 N € Right Side

1) If all the numbers are dropped:

Z © H M $ H I E & @ S U V ¥ R O © I T % $ L N €

2) 15th element from the right end is @

Then, the element that is fifteenth from the right end is '@'.

Hence, the correct option is (C).

29. Given series:

Left Side Z © H M $ 9 H I 2 E & @ S U V 5 ¥ 3 R O © I T 4 3 % 4 $ L 2 N € Right Side

1) Numbers that are immediately followed by a vowel but not immediately preceded by consonant:

The pattern should be Consonant Number Vowel

Z © H M $ 9 H I 2 E & @ S U V 5 ¥ 3 R O © I T 4 3 % 4 $ L 2 N €

So, there is only one number which is immediately followed by a vowel but not immediately preceded by consonant: I 2 E.

Hence, the correct option is (A).

30. Given series:

Left Side Z © H M $ 9 H I 2 E & @ S U V 5 ¥ 3 R O © I T 4 3 % 4 $ L 2 N € Right Side

Tips And Tricks: Left - Left = Left

10th from the left - 7th from the left = 3rd from the left

Clearly, 3rd from the left end element is **H.**

Hence, the correct option is (E).

31. There is no doubt that this passage is **related to technology,** and the particular organisation in question is '**Google.**' This is introduced to us in **sentence R.**

The next sentence must be **P** where it says that '**the 20-year old mission**' is referring to the mission of making the search engine more intuitive. This tells us how they are going to achieve it.

The third sentence is **T as this sentence starts with 'to.'**

The fourth sentence is Q. Since the paragraph has already introduced us to 'Google' now it is referring to it as **'the search engine.'** This sentence tells us what they want to achieve and what their focus areas will be. Finally, the fifth sentence will be S.

Thus, the correct chronological order for the passage is RPTQS.

The ordered paragraph is: Google unveiled changes Monday aimed at making the leading search engine more visual and intuitive to the point it can answer questions before being asked artificial intelligence and machine learning are core drivers of how Google will pursue its 20-year-old mission to organize the world's information and make it accessible to anyone, search vice president Ben Gomes said at an event in San Francisco. The search engine focused strongly on mobile use and appeared to be growing more like Facebook, encouraging users to linger and explore topics, interests or stories. He described the latest changes as shifting from answers to journeys, providing ways to target queries without knowing what words to use and enhancing image-based searches. **Google Images was redesigned to weave in "Lens" technology that enables queries based on what is pointed out in pictures.**

Hence, the correct option is (B).

32. There is no doubt that this passage is **related to technology,** and the particular organisation in question is 'Google.' This is introduced to us in sentence R.

The next sentence must be **P** where it says that 'the **20-year old mission**' is referring to the mission of making the search engine more intuitive. This tells us how they are going to achieve it.

The third sentence is **T as this sentence starts with 'to.'**

The fourth sentence is Q. Since the paragraph has already introduced us to 'Google' now it is referring to it as **'the search**

engine.' This sentence tells us what they want to achieve and what their focus areas will be. Finally, the fifth sentence will be S.

Thus, the correct chronological order for the passage is RPTQS.

The ordered paragraph is: Google unveiled changes Monday aimed at making the leading search engine more visual and intuitive to the point it can answer questions before being asked artificial intelligence and machine learning are core drivers of how Google will pursue its 20-year-old mission to organize the world's information and make it accessible to anyone, search vice president Ben Gomes said at an event in San Francisco. The search engine focused strongly on mobile use and appeared to be growing more like Facebook, encouraging users to linger and explore topics, interests or stories. He described the latest changes as shifting from answers to journeys, providing ways to target queries without knowing what words to use and enhancing image-based searches. **Google Images was redesigned to weave in "Lens" technology that enables queries based on what is pointed out in pictures.**

Hence, the correct option is (E).

33. There is no doubt that this passage is **related to technology,** and the particular organisation in question is 'Google.' This is introduced to us in sentence R.

The next sentence must be **P** where it says that '**the 20-year old mission**' is referring to the mission of making the search engine more intuitive. This tells us how they are going to achieve it.

The third sentence is **T as this sentence starts with 'to.'**

The fourth sentence is Q. Since the paragraph has already introduced us to 'Google' now it is referring to it as **'the search engine.'** This sentence tells us what they want to achieve and what their focus areas will be. Finally, the fifth sentence will be S.

Thus, the correct chronological order for the passage is RPTQS.

The ordered paragraph is: Google unveiled changes Monday aimed at making the leading search engine more visual and intuitive to the point it can answer questions before being asked artificial intelligence and machine learning are core drivers of how Google will pursue its 20-year-old mission to organize the world's information and make it accessible to anyone, search vice president Ben Gomes said at an event in San Francisco. The search engine focused strongly on mobile use and appeared to be growing more like Facebook, encouraging users to linger and explore topics, interests or stories. He described the latest changes as shifting from answers to journeys, providing ways to target queries without knowing what words to use and enhancing image-based searches. **Google Images was redesigned to weave in "Lens" technology that enables queries based on what is pointed out in pictures.**

Hence, the correct option is (E).

34. There is no doubt that this passage is **related to technology,** and the particular organisation in question is 'Google.' This is introduced to us in sentence R.

The next sentence must be **P** where it says that '**the 20-year old mission**' is referring to the mission of making the search engine more intuitive. This tells us how they are going to achieve it.

The third sentence is **T as this sentence starts with 'to.'**

The fourth sentence is Q. Since the paragraph has already introduced us to 'Google' now it is referring to it as '**the search engine.'** This sentence tells us what they want to achieve and what their focus areas will be. Finally, the fifth sentence will be S.

Thus, the correct chronological order for the passage is RPTQS.

The ordered paragraph is: Google unveiled changes Monday aimed at making the leading search engine more visual and intuitive to the point it can answer questions before being asked artificial intelligence and machine learning are core drivers of how Google will pursue its 20-year-old mission to organize the world's information and make it accessible to anyone, search vice president Ben Gomes said at an event in San Francisco. The search engine focused strongly on mobile use and appeared to be growing more like Facebook, encouraging users to linger and explore topics, interests or stories. He described the latest changes as shifting from answers to journeys, providing ways to target queries without knowing what words to use and enhancing image-based searches. **Google Images was redesigned to weave in "Lens" technology that enables queries based on what is pointed out in pictures.**

Hence, the correct option is (B).

35. There is no doubt that this passage is **related to technology,** and the particular organisation in question is 'Google.' This is introduced to us in sentence R.

The next sentence must be **P** where it says that '**the 20-year old mission**' is referring to the mission of making the search engine more intuitive. This tells us how they are going to achieve it.

The third sentence is **T as this sentence starts with 'to.'**

The fourth sentence is Q. Since the paragraph has already introduced us to 'Google' now it is referring to it as '**the search engine.'** This sentence tells us what they want to achieve and what their focus areas will be. Finally, the fifth sentence will be S.

Thus, the correct chronological order for the passage is RPTQS.

The ordered paragraph is: Google unveiled changes Monday aimed at making the leading search engine more visual and intuitive to the point it can answer questions before being asked artificial intelligence and machine learning are core drivers of how Google will pursue its 20-year-old mission to organize the world's information and make it accessible to anyone, search vice president Ben Gomes said at an event in San Francisco. The search engine focused strongly on mobile use and appeared to be growing more like Facebook, encouraging users to linger and explore topics, interests or stories. He described the latest changes as shifting from answers to journeys, providing ways to target queries without knowing what words to use and enhancing image-based searches. **Google Images was redesigned to weave in "Lens" technology that enables queries based on what is pointed out in pictures.**

Hence, the correct option is (C).

36. We should find out an adjective to qualify the nouns 'role' and 'job'. So, we should eliminate options A, C, and D.

The article 'a' is used before the blank. So we cannot choose 'attractive' which is an adjective. Therefore, 'commendable' is the only word that fits here.

The meaning of the word 'commendable' is 'praiseworthy or admirable'.

Complete sentences:

She has played a commendable role in the film.

The RBI has done a commendable job in preventing a crisis in NBFC sector.

Hence, the correct option is (B).

37. Past tense is used in both sentences. Therefore, options (A) and (B) should be eliminated.

A company cannot be 'clarified' or 'appointed'. Thus, options (D) and (E) should be eliminated. So, 'established' is the only word that fits here appropriately.

The meaning of the word 'established' is 'set up or brought into being or laid the foundation of something'.

Complete sentences:

Tata Iron and Steel Company (TISCO) was established by Dorabji Tata on 26 August 1907.

In 1990, TISCO began to expand and established its subsidiary, Tata Inc., in New York.

Hence, the correct option is (C).

38. In the second sentence the preposition 'to' is used. Therefore, verb1 should be used after the preposition. Clearly, options (A), (B), (C), and (E) should be eliminated.

So, 'embrace' is the only word that fits well in both blanks.

The word 'embrace' means 'to hold in one's arms or to accept something'.

Complete sentences:

The pandemic has made more than half of the industry embrace negative growth.

She came inside the room to embrace her child.

Hence, the correct option is (D).

39. Both these sentences are written in the present perfect tense. Therefore, the verb3 form should be chosen here. Hence, options (A), (B), and (E) should be eliminated.

Option (E) should also be eliminated as software cannot be encouraged.

So, 'upgraded' is the only word that fits well.

The word 'upgraded' means 'improved or made better or brought up to date'.

Complete sentences:

They have upgraded the software before launching the new phones in the market.

The credit analysis company CARE has upgraded ratings on various debt instruments of the bank.

Hence, the correct option is (B).

40. In the first sentence, the word 'steps' is used and we usually say that steps are taken to further the progress of something. Therefore, the word 'promote' is the only word that fits properly.

The meaning of the word 'promote' is 'to advance the progress of something or to give publicity to something'.

Complete sentences:

The government announces steps to promote goods and services under Foreign Trade policy.

The employees have found a worthy leader to promote their interest.

Hence, the correct option is (D).

41. The sentence conveys the rule followed around the world. So, the required word must mean the same as standard or rule.

Liturgy means a form according to which public religious worship, especially Christian worship, is conducted. There is no mention of form.

Ritual means a religious or other solemn ceremony or act. There is no indication of any religious act.

Norm means something that is usual, typical, or standard. This is correct as it fulfils the requirement.

Rite means relating to or done as a religious or solemn rite. It is inappropriate with respect to the context.

Tradition means the transmission of customs or beliefs from generation to generation or the fact of being passed on in this way. It is unsuitable for the passage.

Hence, the correct option is (C).

42. The sentence wants to convey that it is not possible for the prosecutors to stay away from the investigation. So, the required word must mean the same as uninvolved.

Aloof means conspicuously uninvolved. This is correct as it fulfils the requirement.

Stray means move away aimlessly from a group or from the right course or place. Prosecutors do not move away in groups.

Erratic means not even or regular in pattern or movement; unpredictable. Prosecutors cannot be irregular.

Steady means firmly fixed, supported, or balanced. Prosecutors are not firmly fixed.

Abreast means alongside or level with something. This is inappropriate with respect to the context.

Hence, the correct option is (A).

43. The required word must mean combining..

Conforming means to comply with rules, standards, or laws. The sentence talks about the events in which the prosecution's guidance is necessary. So, this word is inappropriate.

Collating means to collect and combine (texts, information, or data). This is correct as it fulfils the requirement.

Persisting means continue in an opinion or course of action in spite of difficulty or opposition. The prosecution cannot persist.

Acclimating means adjusting. There is no need for adjusting by the prosecution.

Absolution means formal release from guilt, obligation, or punishment. This word is unsuitable.

Hence, the correct option is (B).

44. The sentence conveys how the police are criticized for every failure in the case. So, the required word must mean the same as failure.

Alteration means the process of changing. The police cannot change the case.

Lapse means a brief or temporary failure of concentration, memory, or judgement. This is correct as it fulfils the requirement.

Progression means the process of developing or moving gradually towards a more advanced state. This is the opposite of our requirement.

Accustom means customary; usual. This is inappropriate with respect to the context.

Rejoice means feel or show great joy or delight. There is no joy in the case.

Hence, the correct option is (B).

45. The presence of the word reviving indicates that the required word must mean the same as not functioning.

Defunct means no longer existing or functioning. This is correct as it fulfils the requirement.

Dreary means depressingly dull and bleak or repetitive. This is inappropriate with respect to the context.

Dismal means causing a mood of gloom or depression. The helpline cannot be gloomy.

Sombre means having or conveying a feeling of deep seriousness and sadness. The helpline cannot convey deep sadness.

Abysmal means extremely bad; appalling. The helpline cannot be bad.

Hence, the correct option is (A).

46. The original sentence is erroneous.

Reason: The word 'urban' means 'relating to or characteristic of a town or city' and is unsuitable in this sentence. The correct word to be used here is 'urbane' which means 'courteous and refined in manner'. Hence 'urbane' should be used in place of 'urban' to make the sentence grammatically correct.

Among the given choices, only option D replaces the given bold part most appropriately.

The sentence after replacement becomes:

Mr. Tharoor's urbane manners charm friends and enemies alike.

Hence, the correct option is (D).

47. The original sentence is erroneous.

Reason: Usage of the phrasal verb 'look away' which means 'avert one's gaze' is inappropriate in this sentence.

'Look down on' which means 'to consider someone or something lesser or inferior in some way' would be suitable in this context.

E.g.: She looks down on anyone who hasn't had a university education.

Hence 'look down on' should be used in place of 'look away on' to make the sentence grammatically and contextually correct.

Among the given choices, only option B replaces the given bold part most appropriately.

The sentence after replacement becomes:

Religious bigots look down upon anyone who does not conform to their beliefs

Hence, the correct option is (B).

48. The original sentence is erroneous.

Reason: The word 'leisure' must be followed the preposition 'for' instead of 'till' in this context. The expression "leisure for" means 'free time for'.

Hence 'for' should be used in place of 'till' to make the sentence grammatically and contextually correct.

Among the given choices, only option D replaces the given bold part most appropriately.

The sentence after replacement becomes:

Having leisure for outdoor activities such as taking a stroll down the park has become a rarity in this fast paced life.

Hence, the correct option is (D).

49. The original sentence is erroneous.

Reason: The correct idiomatic expression is 'a helping hand' and not 'a helpful handshake'.

Lend a helping hand (Idiom):

Meaning: To help or assist.

E.g.: Peter is always willing to lend a helping hand around the house.

Hence 'a helping hand' should be used in place of 'a helpful handshake' to make the sentence grammatically correct.

Among the given choices, only option C replaces the given bold part most appropriately.

The sentence after replacement becomes:

India lent a helping hand to Nepal by giving them 2.1 billion Nepalese rupees for the reconstruction of houses flattened in the 2015 earthquake.

Hence, the correct option is (C).

50. The original sentence is erroneous.

Reason: The word 'voracity' means 'the quality of craving or consuming large quantities of food' and is unsuitable in this sentence. The correct word to be used here is 'veracity' which means 'truthfulness or accuracy'. Hence 'veracity' should be used in place of 'voracity' to make the sentence grammatically correct.

Among the given choices, only option C replaces the given bold part most appropriately.

The sentence after replacement becomes:

One is advised to check the veracity of news articles before forwarding them on whatsapp and other social media.

Hence, the correct option is (C).

51. The error lies in part 3 of the sentence as the word "**Ghettos**: the Jewish quarters in a city; a part of a city, especially a slum area, occupied by a minority group or groups" is incorrectly spelled here.

Example sentence: Whole communities of blacks crowded together into **ghettos** in New York City, Chicago and Detroit, where once the poor white immigrants had lived.

The meanings of some of the other words are:

Association: a connection or cooperative link between people or organizations

Hence, the correct option is (C).

52. There are no errors in the above sentence; all words in bold are spelled correctly here.

The meanings of some of the words are:

Protruding: sticking out; projecting.

Magistrates: civil officers who administer the law, especially one who conducts a court that deals with minor offenses and holds preliminary hearings for more serious ones.

Hence, the correct option is (E).

53. The error lies in part 4 of the sentence as the word "**Mediocres**: average; common" is incorrectly spelled here.

Example sentence: Parents don't want their children going to **mediocre** schools.

The meanings of some of the other words are:

Perverted: (of a thing) having been corrupted or distorted from its original course, meaning, or state

Hence, the correct option is (D).

54. The error lies in part 3 of the sentence as the word "Annotate: add notes to (a text or diagram) giving explanation or comment" is incorrectly spelled here.

Example sentence: Historians annotate, check and interpret the diary selections.

The meanings of some of the other words are:

Crowdsourcing: the practice of obtaining information or input into a task or project by enlisting the services of a large number of people, either paid or unpaid, typically via the Internet

Hence, the correct option is (C).

55. The error lies in part 4 of the sentence as the word "**Millennium**: a period of a thousand years, especially when calculated from the traditional date of the birth of Christ" is incorrectly spelled here.

Example sentence: With the advent of the **millennium,** youngsters continue to be carefully evaluated through entrance exams and personal interviews.

The meanings of some of the other words are:

Shrines: places regarded as holy because of its associations with a divinity or a sacred person or relic, marked by a building or other construction

Stacked: put or arranged in a stack or stacks

Hence, the correct option is (D).

56. The paragraph clearly states the following –

"The total value of old Rs. 500 and Rs. 1000 notes in the circulation is to the tune of Rs. 14.2 trillion, which is about 85% of the total value of the currency in circulation."

Therefore from the passage, we can infer that 85% is the correct answer.

Hence, the correct option is (B).

57. The word 'formal' can have two different meanings:

- done in accordance with convention or etiquette; suitable for or constituting an official or important occasion.
- officially sanctioned or recognized.

In the case of the given paragraph, the second meaning is more appropriate.

'Official' means having the approval or authorization of an authority or public body.

So, the correct synonym of the word 'formal' is "official".

Hence, the correct option is (A).

58. The correct answer is: The unaccounted currency when accounted for through legal channels would attract higher tax rates and even legal actions thereby forcing the hoarders to extinguish them so as to avoid the taxes and legal wrangling.

- According to the paragraph the demonetization has been brought forth to combat the black money in circulation within the Indian economy.
- By the various measures, it can be inferred that a certain amount of this money can be legalized through various channels.
- Beyond that certain amount, people who are hoarding the black money would find it difficult to convert the black money as they would be in the spotlight having to account for the money.

- This would attract the notice of the taxation authorities in India and other legal offices.
- Rather than attracting this attention, most black money hoarders would be more comfortable with destroying this unaccounted money
- Thus option (C) is the best-fit answer for the given question.

Hence, the correct option is (C).

59. The correct answer is: Current Account and Savings Account.

The paragraph clearly states the following –

"Also with more money being kept in the banking channel, some of these low-cost deposits may be sticky and improve the medium to long term Current Account and Savings Account (CASA) ratio of the banks."

Hence, the correct option is (D).

60. The correct answer is: 'A product or service that is a regular source of income for someone.'

- The idiom 'cash cow' refers to any products or services that yield a profit or income on a regular basis.
- The 'real estate' sector which often allows black money hoarders to transform their black money to white has been considered to be a cash cow as it yields profits regularly.

Hence, the correct option is (E).

61. Given,

$$CP \text{ of 18 pen} = SP \text{ of 12 pen}$$

Formula used:

$$\text{Gain } \% = \frac{(\text{Gain} \times 100)}{CP}$$

$$\text{Gain} = SP - CP$$

Let SP of 1 pen be $Re\,1$.

So, SP of 18 pens $= Rs.18$

$$CP \text{ of 18 pen} = SP \text{ of 12 pens} = Rs.\,12$$

$$\text{Gain} = 18 - 12 = Rs.\,6$$

$$\text{Gain } \% = \left(\frac{6}{12}\right) \times 100) = 50\%$$

$\therefore$ The Gain $\%$ is 50%.

Hence, the correct option is (C).

62. Given,

The sum $= Rs.\,6000$

Time $= 2$ years

Rate of interest $= 10\%$

$$A = P\left(1 + \frac{r}{100}\right)^t$$

$$= 6000 \times \left(1 + \frac{10}{100}\right)^2$$

$$= 6000 \times \left(\frac{11}{10}\right) \times \left(\frac{11}{10}\right)$$

$$= 6000 \times \left(\frac{121}{100}\right)$$

$$= 7260$$

Now, $CI = 7260 - 6000$

$$\therefore CI = 1260$$

Hence, the correct option is (A).

63. Given:

P = Rs. 1250, t = 15 years, and r = 1.6 %

As we know,

$$SI = \frac{P \times r \times t}{100}$$

$$= \frac{1250 \times 1.6 \times 15}{100}$$

$$\therefore SI = Rs.\ 300$$

Hence, the correct option is (D).

64. The pattern is as follows:

9 × 2 - 1 = 17

17 × 2 - 1 = 33

33 × 2 - 1 = 65

65 × 2 - 1 = 129

∴ The value of ? is 129.

Hence, the correct option is (C).

65. The pattern is as follows:

40 × 1 + 1 = 41

41 × 2 + 2 = 84

84 × 3 + 3 = 255

255 × 4 + 4 = 1024

1024 × 5 + 5 = 5125

∴ The value of ? is 5125.

Hence, the correct option is (A).

66. Logic: Alternate Cube and Square of consecutive numbers.

The series follows the following pattern:

11 + 8 = 19   (∵ 2³ = 8)

19 + 9 = 28   (∵ 3² = 9)

28 + 64 = 92   (∵ 4³ = 64)

92 + 25 = 117   (∵ 5² = 25)

117 + 216 = 333   (∵ 6³ = 216)

∴ The value of ? is 117.

Hence, the correct option is (A).

67. The pattern is as follows:

70 × 2 = 140

140 × 3 = 420

420 × 4 = 1680

1680 × 5 = 8400

∴ The value of ? is 8400.

Hence, the correct option is (C).

68. The pattern is as follows:

14 + 8 = 22

22 + 6 = 28

28 + 4 = 32

32 + 2 = 34

34 + 0 = 34

∴ The value of '?' is 34.

Hence, the correct option is (A).

69. Given that: 1 milk chocolate is must.

So possible selection can be:

(1 milk chocolate and 2 from dark chocolate or ice cream) or (2 milk chocolates and 1 from dark chocolate or ice cream) or (3 milk chocolates)

Possible combinations $= ({}^3C_1 \times {}^6C_2) + ({}^3C_2 \times {}^6C_1) + ({}^3C_3)$

We know that,

$${}^nC_r = \frac{n!}{(n-r)!\, r!}$$

Possible combination $= \left(3 \times \frac{30}{2}\right) + \left(\frac{6}{2} \times 6\right) + 1$

Possible combination $= 45 + 18 + 1$

∴ Possible combination is 64.

Hence, the correct option is (B).

70. Given,

Time taken by pipe A to fill the tank = 15 min

Part filled by A in 1 minutes $= \dfrac{1}{15}$

Time taken by pipe B to fill the tank = 20 min

Part filled by B in 1 minutes $= \dfrac{1}{20}$

Pipe A is off after 4 min.

Part filled by A and B in 4 min $= 4\left(\dfrac{1}{15} + \dfrac{1}{20}\right)$

$= \dfrac{7}{15}$

Remaining part $= 1 - \dfrac{7}{15}$

$= \dfrac{8}{15}$

Time taken to fill the remaining part $= \dfrac{\text{Remaining part}}{\text{Part filled by B in 1 min}}$

$= \dfrac{\left(\frac{8}{15}\right)}{\left(\frac{1}{20}\right)}$

$= \dfrac{32}{3}$

$= 10\dfrac{2}{3}$ min

$= 10\dfrac{2}{3} \times 60$ min

= 10 min 40 sec

Total time required to fill the tank = 4 min + 10 min 40 sec

= 14 min 40 sec

∴ Total time required to fill the tank is 14 min 40 sec.

Hence, the correct option is (D).

71. The difference between the percentage of candidates qualified to appear in different year pairs are:

For 1994 and 1995 = 50% - 30% = 20%

For 1995 and 1996 = 60% - 50% = 10%

For 1998 and 1999 = 80% - 80% = 0

For 1999 and 2000 = 80% - 60% = 20%

For 1997 and 1998 = 80% - 50% = 30%

Thus, the maximum difference is between the years 1997 and 1998.

Hence, the correct option is (E).

72. The given graph gives the data for the percentage of candidates qualified to appear and unless the absolute values of number of candidates qualified or candidates appeared is known we cannot compare the absolute values for any two years.

So, the data is inadequate to solve this question.

Hence, the correct option is (E).

73. Given,

The number of candidates qualified in 1998 = 21200

Let the number of candidates appeared in 1998 be x.

According to question,

80% of x = 21200

$\Rightarrow x = \dfrac{21200 \times 100}{80}$

$\Rightarrow x = 26500$

Hence, the correct option is (C).

74. The total number of candidates qualified in 1996 and 1997 together, cannot be determined until we know at least, the number of candidates appeared in any one of the two years 1996 or 1997 or the percentage of candidates qualified to appear in 1996 and 1997 together.

So, the data is inadequate.

Hence, the correct option is (E).

75. Given,

The total number of candidates qualified in 1999 and 2000 together = 33500

The number of candidates appeared in 1999 = 26500

According to question,

The number of candidates qualified in 1999 = (80% of 26500) = 21200

Therefore the number of candidates qualified in the year 2000 = (33500 - 21200) = 12300

Let the number of candidates appeared in the year 2000 be x.

Then,

60% of $x = 12300$

$\Rightarrow x = \left(\dfrac{12300 \times 100}{60}\right)$

$\Rightarrow x = 20500$

Hence, the correct option is (C).

76. Follow the BODMAS rule according to the table given below:

B	Brackets in order ( ), { }, [ ]	ब्रेकट ( ), {}, [ ] क्रम
O	Of	का
D	Division (÷)	विभाजन (÷)
M	Multiplication (×)	गुणा (×)
A	Addition (+)	जोड़ (+)
S	Subtraction (-)	घटाव (-)

Given,

$\sqrt{144} \div 4 \times 6 - \sqrt{196} \div \sqrt{49} + 5 = ?$

$\Rightarrow 12 \div 4 \times 6 - 14 \div 7 + 5 = ?$

$\Rightarrow 3 \times 6 - 2 + 5 = ?$

$\Rightarrow 18 - 2 + 5 = ?$

$\Rightarrow ? = 21$

∴ The value of $?$ is 21.

Hence, the correct option is (C).

77. Follow the BODMAS rule according to the table given below:

B	Brackets in order ( ), { }, [ ]	ब्रेकट ( ), {}, [ ] क्रम
O	Of	का
D	Division (÷)	विभाजन (÷)
M	Multiplication (×)	गुणा (×)
A	Addition (+)	जोड़ (+)
s	Subtraction (-)	घटाव (-)

Given,

$$680 \times 24 \div 12 \div 17 + 12 \text{ of } 6 = ?$$

$$\Rightarrow 680 \times 2 \div 17 + 12 \times 6 = ?$$

$$\Rightarrow 680 \times \frac{2}{17} + 12 \times 6 = ?$$

$$\Rightarrow 80 + 72 = ?$$

$$\Rightarrow ? = 152$$

$\therefore$ The value of $?$ is 152.

Hence, the correct option is (B).

78. Follow the BODMAS rule according to the table given below:

B	Brackets in order ( ), { }, [ ]	ब्रेकट ( ), {}, [ ] क्रम
O	Of	का
D	Division (÷)	विभाजन (÷)
M	Multiplication (×)	गुणा (×)
A	Addition (+)	जोड़ (+)
s	Subtraction (-)	घटाव (-)

Given,

$$263 - 345 + 180 \times 3\% \text{ of } 20 - 1 = ?$$

$$\Rightarrow 263 - 345 + 180 \times \left(\frac{3}{100} \times 20\right) - 1 = ?$$

$$\Rightarrow 263 - 345 + 180 \times \frac{60}{100} - 1 = ?$$

$$\Rightarrow 263 - 345 + 18 \times 6 - 1 = ?$$

$$\Rightarrow 263 - 345 + 108 - 1 = ?$$

$$\Rightarrow 263 - 238 = ?$$

$$\Rightarrow ? = 25$$

$\therefore$ The value of $?$ is 25.

Hence, the correct option is (C).

79. Follow the BODMAS rule according to the table given below:

B	Brackets in order ( ), { }, [ ]	ब्रेकट ( ), {}, [ ] क्रम
O	Of	का
D	Division (÷)	विभाजन (÷)
M	Multiplication (×)	गुणा (×)
A	Addition (+)	जोड़ (+)
s	Subtraction (-)	घटाव (-)

Given,

$$250 \times 24 \div 12 \div 125 + 2 \text{ of } 3 = ?$$

$$\Rightarrow 250 \times 2 \div 125 + 2 \times 3 = ?$$

$$\Rightarrow 250 \times \frac{2}{125} + 2 \times 3 = ?$$

$$\Rightarrow 2 \times 2 + 2 \times 3 = ?$$

$$\Rightarrow 4 + 6 = ?$$

$$\Rightarrow ? = 10$$

$\therefore$ The value of $?$ is 10.

Hence, the correct option is (D).

80. Follow the BODMAS rule according to the table given below:

B	Brackets in order ( ), { }, [ ]	ब्रेकट ( ), {}, [ ] क्रम
O	Of	का
D	Division (÷)	विभाजन (÷)
M	Multiplication (×)	गुणा (×)
A	Addition (+)	जोड़ (+)
s	Subtraction (-)	घटाव (-)

Given,

$$\frac{3}{4} + \frac{7}{8} + \frac{11}{12} + \frac{13}{16} = \frac{?+1}{48}$$

$$\Rightarrow \frac{36+42+44+39}{48} = \frac{?+1}{48}$$

$$\Rightarrow \frac{161}{48} = \frac{(?+1)}{48}$$

$$\Rightarrow 161 = ? + 1$$

$$\Rightarrow ? = 160$$

$\therefore$ The value of $?$ is 160.

Hence, the correct option is (A).

81. Given,

A train crosses a $500m$ platform in 80 seconds.

A train crosses a $800m$ platform in 120 seconds.

As we know,

$$S_{\text{Train}} = \frac{(L_{\text{Train}} + L_{\text{Platform}})}{T}$$

Where, T = Time taken, L_{Train} = Length of the train, L_{Platform} = Length of Platform, S_{Train} = Speed of train.

Let the length of the train be L.

According to the question,

Speed of the train is same in both cases i.e., while crossing two platforms.

$$\frac{(L+500)}{80} = \frac{(L+800)}{120}$$

$$\Rightarrow \frac{(L+500)}{(L+800)} = \frac{80}{120}$$

$\Rightarrow \dfrac{(L+500)}{(L+800)} = \dfrac{2}{3}$

$\Rightarrow 3(L + 500) = 2(L + 800)$

$\Rightarrow 3L + 1500 = 2L + 1600$

$\Rightarrow L = 100m$

$\therefore$ The length of the train is $100m$.

Hence, the correct option is (C).

82. Given

I. $10x^2 - 29x + 10 = 0$

$\Rightarrow x^2 - \dfrac{29x}{10} + 1 = 0$

$\Rightarrow x^2 - \dfrac{5x}{2} - \dfrac{2x}{5} + 1 = 0$

$\Rightarrow \left(\dfrac{x-2}{5}\right)\left(\dfrac{x-5}{2}\right) = 0$

So, $x = \dfrac{2}{5}, x = \dfrac{5}{2}$

II. $4y^2 - 11y + 6 = 0$

$\Rightarrow 4y^2 - 8y - 3y + 6 = 0$

$\Rightarrow (4y - 3)(y - 2) = 0$

So, $y = \dfrac{3}{4}, y = 2.$

Value of x	Value of y	Relation
$\dfrac{2}{5}$	$\dfrac{3}{4}$	x < y
$\dfrac{2}{5}$	2	x < y
$\dfrac{5}{2}$	$\dfrac{3}{4}$	x > y
$\dfrac{5}{2}$	2	x > y

So, x = y or relationship between x and y cannot be established

Hence, the correct option is (E).

83. Given

$x^2 + 91 = 20x$

$(x - 7)(x - 13)$

Solving we get, x = 7, 13

$10y^2 - 29y + 21 = 0$

$(5x - 7)(2x - 3)$

Solving we get, $y = \dfrac{7}{5}, \dfrac{3}{2}$

So x is greater than y

Hence, the correct option is (B).

84. Given

$3x^2 + 25x - 18 = 0$

$3x^2 + 27x - 2x - 18 = 0$

$(3x - 2)(x + 9) = 0$

Solving we get, x = -9, $\dfrac{2}{3}$

$2y^2 + 15y + 27 = 0$

$2y^2 + 6y + 9y + 27 = 0$

$(y + 3)(2y + 9) = 0$

Solving we get, $y = \dfrac{-9}{2}, -3$

So, y can be less than x or greater than x

Hence, the correct option is (E).

85. Let the length of the rectangular plot be 6x

And the breadth of the rectangular plot be 5x

According to the given information:

The perimeter of the rectangular plot is 484

As we know, the perimeter of a rectangle = 2(l + b)

2(6x + 5x) = 484

$\Rightarrow$ 2(11x) = 484

$\Rightarrow$ 22x = 484

$\Rightarrow$ x = 22

$\Rightarrow$ The length of the rectangular plot is 6 × 22 = 132 m

And the breadth of the rectangular plot is 5 × 22 = 110 m

Thus, the area of the rectangular plot is L × B

$\Rightarrow$ 132 × 110 = 14520 sq.metres

So, the area of the rectangular plot is 14,520 sq. metres.

Hence, the correct option is (A).

86. Given,

Time is taken by a boatman in downstream $= 1hr$

Time is taken by a boatman in upstream $= 10min$

Distance covered by a boatman in downstream $= 2km$

Distance covered by a boatman in upstream $= 1km$

Total distance covered by boatman = Downstream - Upstream

$= 2km - 1km = 1km$

Rate in downstream $= \left(\dfrac{1}{10} \times 60\right) km/hr$

$= 6km/hr$

Rate in upstream $= 2km/hr$

Speed in still water $= \dfrac{1}{2}(6 + 2) km/hr$

$= 4km/hr$

$\therefore$ Required Time $= 1\frac{1}{4} hrs = 1hr\,15min$

Hence, the correct option is (C).

87. Given:

The average weight of 3 children is 20 kg

We know that,

$$\text{Average} = \frac{Sum\ of\ observations}{Total\ number\ of\ observations}$$

Calculations:

Let the weight of Bhavya be x kg

Then the weight of Arshi is 2x kg, and

Weight of Chinu is 3x kg.

$\Rightarrow$ Average weight $= \dfrac{(x+2x+3x)}{3} = 20$

$\Rightarrow \dfrac{6x}{3} = 20$

$\Rightarrow x = 10$

$\therefore$ Weight of Chinu = 3 × 10 = 30 kg

Hence, the correct option is (B).

88. We know that,

Profit = Investment × Time

Let the amount invested by B be Rs. x.

Amount invested by A for 8 months = Rs. 50000

$\Rightarrow$ Profit of A = Rs. 50000 × 8 = Rs. 400000

Time for which B invested = 6 months

$\Rightarrow$ Profit of B = Rs. x × 6 = Rs. 6x

Total profit = Rs. (400000 + 6x)

Ratio of profit of B to the total profit = 9 : 17

$\Rightarrow \dfrac{6x}{(400000+6x)} = \dfrac{9}{17}$

$\Rightarrow$ 6x × 17 = (400000 + 6x) × 9

$\Rightarrow$ 102x = 3600000 + 54x

$\Rightarrow x = \dfrac{3600000}{48}$

$\Rightarrow$ x = Rs. 75000

$\therefore$ The money invested by B is Rs. 75000.

Hence, the correct option is (B).

89. Given:

Total number of pens = 7

$$P(E)\!:\ \frac{Number\ of\ favorable\ outcomes}{Total\ number\ of\ outcomes}$$

Calculation:

n(s) = total number of ways of drawing 3 pens from a total number of 7 pens,

$\Rightarrow {}^{7}C_{3} = \dfrac{(7\times6\times5\times4!)}{(3!\times4!)} = 70$

If nA_1 = The event of drawing 2 red pens from 4 red pens.

$\Rightarrow {}^{4}C_{2} = \dfrac{(4\times3\times2!)}{2!\times2!} = 6$

nA_2 = The event of drawing green pens from 3 pens.

$\Rightarrow {}^{3}C_{1} = \dfrac{(3\times2!)}{1!\times2!} = 3$

Let A is the event of drawing 2 red pens and 1 green pen.

$$\therefore n(A) = \frac{[n(A_1)\times n(A_2)]}{n(s)}$$

$\Rightarrow \dfrac{(6\times3)}{35}$

$\Rightarrow \dfrac{18}{35}$

Hence, the correct option is (C).

90. Given:

Distance between two cars = 64 km apart

Speed of one car = 48 km/h

$t_1 - t_2 = 30$

Formula Used:

Distance = Speed × Time

Let speed of second car = 'x'

Relative speed of cars = (48 + x)

Now,

$$64 - 4 = (48 + x) \times \frac{t_1}{60}$$

$$\Rightarrow (48 + x)t_1 = 3600 \,...\,(1)$$

$$84 - 64 = (48 + x) \times \frac{t_2}{60}$$

$$\Rightarrow (48 + x)t_2 = 1200 \,...\,(2)$$

From (1) and (2):

$$\frac{t_1}{t_2} = \frac{3}{1}$$

Let $t_1 = 3a$ and $t_2 = a$

$t_1 - t_2 = 30$

$\Rightarrow 3a - a = 30$

$\Rightarrow a = 15$

From equation (1):

(48 + x) × 3 × 15 = 3600

$\Rightarrow$ 48 + x = 80

$\Rightarrow x = 32$

$\therefore$ Speed of second car = x = 32 km/h

Hence, the correct option is (D).

Reasoning Ability

Ques (1-3):Directions: In each of the questions given below statements are followed by some conclusions. You have to take the given statements to be True even if they seem to be at variance from commonly known facts. Read all the conclusions and then decide which of the given conclusions logically follows from the given statements disregarding commonly known facts.

Q.1 Statements:

Only a few market are global.

Some global are ground.

Some Ground is not business.

Conclusions:

I. Some market are ground.

II. No ground is market.

III. No Global is business.

A. Either I or II follows

B. Only II and III follow

C. Only I follows

D. None follows

E. Only II follows

Q.2 Statements:

All water is brown.

Some brown is orange.

No orange is green.

Conclusions:

I. Only a few water is orange.

II. Some green being brown is a possibility.

III. Some Water is not Green.

A. Either I or II follows

B. Only II and III follow

C. Only III follows

D. None follows

E. Only II follows

Q.3 Statements:

All maths are orbit.

Only a few orbit is biology.

Some biology are arts.

Conclusions:

I. Some arts are not orbit.

II. All biology are maths.

III. All orbit are biology is a possibility.

A. Only I follows   B. I and II follow

C. I and III follow   D. Only III follows

E. None follows

Q.4 If the letter of the words 'FANTASTIC' are arranged in alphabetic order from left to right then what would be the third letter of the meaningful English word formed using third, fifth, sixth and eighth letter of the word formed after arranging? (If no word is formed mark 'L' as your answer and if more than one word are formed mark 'M' as your answer)

A. R   B. N   C. S   D. L

E. M

Ques (5-9):Directions: Study the following information carefully and answer the questions given below.

Eight friends G, H, J, K, L, M, N and O live on a separate floor of a building but not necessarily in the same order. The ground floor is numbered 1, first floor is numbered 2 and so on until the topmost floor is numbered 8.

G lives on the floor numbered 5. There are two floors between G and N. L lives on an odd-numbered floor but immediately above O. J lives on one of the floors below M but not on the ground floor. There are three people between L and K. As many people live above N as below L.

Q.5 How many people live between M and O?

[SBI Clerk, 2018]

A. One   B. Three   C. Four   D. Five

E. Two

Q.6 Who occupies topmost and ground floor respectively?

[SBI Clerk, 2018]

A. L, H   B. O, K   C. K, N   D. N, H

E. M, H

Q.7 Four among the given five are similar in a certain way, who among is not belong to that group?

[SBI Clerk, 2018]

A. M, O   B. L, O   C. O, J   D. J, N

E. K, H

Q.8 Who among the following lives on the 3 numbered floor?

[SBI Clerk, 2018]

A. L   B. K   C. J   D. M

E. N

Q.9 Who lives immediately below H?

[SBI Clerk, 2018]

A. L

B. O

C. M

D. N

E. No one, As H live on the ground floor.

Ques (10-12):Direction: There are certain defense exercises that are presented by some code. Answer the given questions which are based on the following information.

Exercise Name	Step I	Step II	Code Name
SAMPRITI	IAMPRITS	PR20#	NP10
INDRA	ANDRI	AI14@	CK7
DHANUSH	HHANUSD	HD8@	FB4
EKUVERIN	NKUVERIE	VE9@	TG18
MALABAR	RALABAM	RM1#	PK2
ABHYAS	SBHYAA	HY1@	FW2
SAMUNDRA	AAMUNDRS	UN18#	WL9

Note: In every step operation is performed on the output of the previous step.

Q.10 What will be the code name for exercise 'SURYA KIRAN'?

A. AS21 NK9

B. CQ21 LI9

C. CQ42 LI18

D. YU42 PM18

E. YU21 PM9

Q.11 What is output in step II for excise 'VAJRA PRAHAR'?

A. AV1# AH18@

B. AV1@ AH1#

C. AV1@ AH18@

D. AV1@ AH1@

E. AV18@ AH18@

Q.12 What will be the code name for 'SAUNDRA'?

A. WL9

B. CQ2

C. WL18

D. CQ18

E. UN18

Ques (13-15):Direction: Study the following information carefully and answer the questions given below:

If,

A * B (67km) means A is 56 km north of B.

A % B (45km) means A is 34 km south of B.

A # B (58km) means A is 47 km east of B.

A Ω B (39km) means A is 28 km west of B.

If, P % Q (51km); Q # R (41km); R * S (31km); S # T (41km); T % U (51 km); U Ω V (91km); V * W (91km); W # X (111km); X % Y (111km)

Q.13 What is the shortest distance between R and P?

A. 40 km

B. 50 km

C. 30 km

D. 25 km

E. 35 km

Q.14 What is the direction of U with respect to R?

A. Northwest

B. Northeast

C. Southeast

D. Southwest

E. North

Q.15 What is the direction of W with respect to T?

A. South

B. Northeast

C. Southwest

D. Southeast

E. Northwest

Ques (16-20):Directions: Read the following information carefully and answer the question given below:

Four boys A, B, C, D and their friends - J, K, L, M, not necessarily in the same order, went to Agra in a car. One of them is driving the car. The car has eight seats which are facing north, in such a way that there are two rows of three seats each and the front row has two seats, including the driver's seat. The car has six seats immediately next to six windows. The driver's seat is at the extreme right side in the front row of the car. The seating arrangement follows the pattern as given below.

A, L and their friends do not sit in the front row, which consists of two seats. K and C sit in the 2nd row and the 3rd row respectively. L and M are the only two persons who do not sit next to a window. B sits in the same column as J and one place ahead of him. A is the friend of J and sits in the same row in which C sits, but not on the same side of the window in which the driver sits. No pair of friends sits in the same row or the same column. L is a friend of C.

Q.16 Who among the following is sitting just beside the right window of the last row?

A. B **B.** C **C.** D **D.** K

E. L

Q.17 Who among these eight persons is driving the car?

A. J **B.** A **C.** B **D.** C

E. D

Q.18 Who is sitting to the immediate right of L?

A. J **B.** K **C.** B **D.** C

E. D

Q.19 Which of the following is definitely true regarding their position?

A. D and J are in same row

B. Both J and L are sitting beside window

C. Both K and C are sitting in the same row

D. All are true

E. None is true

Q.20 Who among the following is sitting in the second row?

A. A **B.** M **C.** L **D.** C

E. D

Ques (21-22):Direction: These questions are based on the following information.

There are seven family members – P, Q, R, S, T, U, and V. R is the maternal grandmother of V. Q is the husband of R. S is the brother-in-law of Q. P is the nephew of S. T is the mother of V. U is the son-in-law of Q. There are four males in the family.

Q.21 How is V related to P?

A. Daughter

B. Nephew

C. Niece

D. Son

E. Cannot be determined

Q.22 How is P related to Q?

A. Daughter

B. Son

C. Nephew

D. Son-in-law

E. None of these

Q.23 Direction: Read the following information carefully and answer the question that follow:

There are six chains P, Q, R, S, T and U, each has different length. S length is more than T and less than Q. P length is more than R and less than Q. U length is more than Q. R length is more than S.

How many chains are longer than U?

A. One   **B.** Two   **C.** Three   **D.** Four
E. None

Q.24 Direction: Read the following information carefully and answer the given question.

In an auction, the jewelry made of different metals P, Q, R, S, and T are there. They are tested and ranked against expensiveness. Q and S are equally expensive. T was the least expensive brand among them. S was less expensive than R but more expensive than P.

Which of the following is true?

A. R was the most expensive among them
B. P was more expensive than Q
C. S was in the middle
D. P was the most expensive among them
E. None of these

Q.25 Direction: Study the following information and answer the question based on it.

(A) 'Srikanth' is younger than Neelima.

(B) Pratima is taller than Srikant.

(C) Subhash is taller than Neelima but shorter than Hembrum.

(D) 'Nilima' is taller than Pratima.

If all of them are made to stand in a row in the order of their height, then who among them will be exactly in the middle of the row?

A. Shrikant   **B.** Nilima
C. Pratima   **D.** Hembram
E. Subhash

Ques (26-30):Direction: A series is given with one term missing. Select the correct alternative from the given ones that will complete the series.

Q.26 O, M, R, K, U, I, ?

A. X   **B.** Y
C. V   **D.** W
E. None of these

Q.27 BMO, EOQ, HQS, ?

A. KSU   **B.** LMN   **C.** SOV   **D.** SOW
E. SPW

Q.28 FNC, HQG, JTK, ?

A. LWO   **B.** LMO   **C.** LXO   **D.** KMT
E. KTM

Q.29 ACD, BEC, CGB, ?

A. DIA   **B.** DJA   **C.** EIA   **D.** DIC
E. DCA

Q.30 TAP, VZT, XYX, ZXB, BWF,?

A. EHW   **B.** EVH   **C.** DVJ   **D.** DJV
E. DBJ

English Language

Ques (31-35):Direction: Given below is a paragraph containing three blanks. It is followed by six words. From the given options, choose the most suitable combination of words that would fit in the blanks to form a meaningful and grammatically correct paragraph. If none of the combinations fill the blanks appropriately, mark option E, 'None of these', as the answer.

Q.31 According to Atlas Obscura, Lake Nyos has formed in a volcanic crater __________ 400 years ago. A lake of this kind is generally formed by the volcanic activities that take place deep __________ the surface of the earth, and __________ have high levels of carbon dioxide in them. Usually, this gas is released over time as the lake water evaporates.

i) Around
ii) Below
iii) Beneath
iv) About
v) Therefore
vi) Thus

A. i, ii, iii   **B.** ii, iii, iv
C. i, iii, v   **D.** ii, iv, vi
E. None of these

Q.32 As __________ for having been ignored by an English Rolls Royce salesman in a London showroom, the king bought all the cars the showroom had on offer. He bought the cars on the __________ that the salesman would __________ him to India. Once there, the Maharaja ordered the cars to be used for garbage collection.

i) Revengeii) Condition
iii) Accompanyiv) Avengev) Warrantyvi) Statement

A. i, ii, iii   **B.** ii, iii, iv
C. i, iii, v   **D.** ii, iv, vi
E. None of these

Q.33 __________ to the reporters, Air Vice Marshal RGK Kapoor said that the IAF fighters had been tasked with intercepting Pakistani aircraft and were successful in __________ them. He also said that __________ the Pakistan Air Force jets dropped bombs, they were not able to cause any damage.

i) Althoughii) Despiteiii) Thwartingiv) Defeatingv) Speakingvi) Announcing

A. i, ii, iii   **B.** ii, iii, iv
C. i, iii, v   **D.** ii, iv, vi
E. None of these

Q.34 When you think of a railway __________ in India, the first thing that comes to your mind is crowded __________. But the newly launched premier waiting for __________ at the Madurai Railway Station might just change your opinion.

i) Podiumii) Stationiii) Areaiv) Platformsv) Stagevi) Lounge

A. i, ii, iii   **B.** ii, iii, iv
C. i, iii, v   **D.** ii, iv, vi
E. None of these

Q.35 The candidate's decision to contest from Wayanad, Kerala, is __________ one of the most sensational developments of this election. His move, political pundits contend, is a __________ for the Left Front. The candidate's decision also __________ the idea of opposition parties pooling their votes to vanquish the party currently in power.

i) Literally

ii) Arguably

iii) Setback

iv) Undermines

v) Milestones

vi) Weakens

A. i, ii, iii   **B.** ii, iii, iv

C. i, iii, v   **D.** ii, iv, vi

E. None of these

Ques (36-40):Direction: Which of the option (A), (B), (C) and (D) given below, should replace the phrase printed in bold in the sentence to make it grammatically correct? If the sentence is correct as it is given and no correction is required, mark (E) as the answer.

Q.36 While all rights are available to citizens, persons including foreign citizens **are entitle to the rights** to equality and the right to life, among others.

A. Is entitled to the right

B. Are entitled for the right

C. Are entitled to a rights

D. Are entitled to the right

E. No correction required

Q.37 With the election **round a corner** and data revealing that the unemployment rate has hit a 45-year high, there is a spike in concern for the economic security of the people.

A. In the corner

B. Over the corner

C. Around the corner

D. For in corner

E. No correction required

Q.38 The prospects for Britain's orderly withdrawal from the European Union on March 29 **have receded further**, even as MPs rallied to stop a no-deal scenario.

A. Had recede further

B. Have recedes further

C. Has receded further

D. Have receded for further

E. No correction required

Q.39 Cash transfers to the poor do not **ensue accessibility**, affordability or even sustained economic security given falling real wages.

A. Ensure accessibility

B. Ensure excesses

C. Ensures accessibility

D. Assure formality

E. No correction required

Q.40 Afghanistan has **historically be an difficult place** for external invaders, thanks to its complex tribal equations and its rugged mountainous terrain.

A. Historic has a difficult place

B. Historically been a difficult place

C. Historically being a difficult place

D. Historically been a difficult places

E. No correction required

Ques (41-45):Direction: The following sentences form a paragraph. The first and last sentence is given. The rest of the sentences are numbered as A, B, C, D and E. These five parts are not given in their proper order. Read the sentences and choose the alternative that arranges them in the correct order.

1. Scientific attitude is the ability to think and analyze our surroundings with empirically tested methods and theories.

A. Also, it includes discerning hidden values and thoroughly appraising proposed conclusions.

B. Critical thinking attempts to investigate assumptions and evidence.

C. Both are ways to objectively clear our biases.

D. It serves us by enabling us to think smarter in situations.

E. A similar concept is critical thinking, which in brief means thinking smart.

7. These concepts are driven by science that enables us to gain a better vision of our environment.

Q.41 Which of the following should be the SIXTH after rearrangement?

A. A   **B.** B   **C.** C   **D.** D

E. E

Q.42 Which of the following should be the THIRD after rearrangement?

A. A   **B.** B   **C.** C   **D.** D

E. E

Q.43 Which of the following should be the FOURTH after rearrangement?

A. A   **B.** B   **C.** C   **D.** D

E. E

Q.44 Which of the following should be the FIFTH after rearrangement?

A. A   **B.** B   **C.** C   **D.** D

E. E

Q.45 Which of the following should be the SECOND after rearrangement?

A. A   **B.** B   **C.** C   **D.** D

E. E

Ques (46-50):Direction: Read the sentence to find out whether there is an error in it. The error, if any, will be in one part of the sentence. If there is no error, the answer is option (E). Ignore errors of punctuation, if any.

Q.46 Shooting as well as horse riding (1) are taught (2) to cadets at the National Defence (3) Academy every morning. (4)

[SBI PO, 2019]

A. (1)   **B.** (2)   **C.** (3)   **D.** (4)

E. No error

Q.47 The President, along with several international guests, (1) are to be present (2) during the swearing-in ceremony (3) of the new government. (4)

[SBI PO, 2019]

A. (1)   **B.** (2)   **C.** (3)   **D.** (4)
E. No error

Q.48 India has a long way (1) to go to reach environmental (2) quality similar to that enjoyed (3) in developed economies. (4)

[SBI PO, 2019]

A. (1)   **B.** (2)   **C.** (3)   **D.** (4)
E. No error

Q.49 Stories are all about going further reality (1) and it is no wonder that they (2) let you understand big concepts with only (3) a little bit of reading practice. (4)

[SBI PO, 2019]

A. (1)   **B.** (2)   **C.** (3)   **D.** (4)
E. No error

Q.50 Who wouldn't love to chat (1)/ about who character is their favorite, (2) or predict what will happen in a (3) suspense story they are reading? (4)

[SBI PO, 2019]

A. (1)   **B.** (2)   **C.** (3)   **D.** (4)
E. No error

Ques (51-55):Direction: Fill in the blanks with appropriate words.

Prior to 1991, India's economy and financial system were heavily regulated and ___(1)___ by the public sector. A complicated regulatory regime required firms to obtain licenses for most economic activities, and many industries were ___(2)___ for the public sector, including much of the financial system. Bank nationalizations in 1969 and 1980 increased the public sector share of deposits 5 to over 80 per cent, and further branch licensing was rigidly controlled. Primarily focused on financing government ___(3)___ and serving government priority sectors such as agriculture, India's public banks lacked proper lending ___(4)___ and exhibited a high number of non-performing loans. Following a balance of payments crisis in 1991, however, a number of structural ___(5)___ were implemented that greatly deregulated many economic ___(6)___, and in November 1991, a broad financial reform agenda was established in India by the Committee on the Financial System (CFS). The CFS was appointed by the Government of India to examine the ___(7)___ financial system and make recommendations for improving its efficiency so as to more effectively meet the credit needs of ___(8)___. One of the committee's recommendations to meet this goal was to introduce greater competition into the banking system by ___(9)___ more foreign banks to enter India. It was argued that the entry of additional foreign banks would improve the competitive efficiency of the Indian banking system and induce an ___(10)___ of banking technology.

Q.51 What should come in the place of blank (1)?

A. Neglected   **B.** Dominated
C. Mismatched   **D.** Mismanaged

E. Followed

Q.52 What should come in the place of blank (2)?
A. Open   **B.** Unlocked
C. Unrolled   **D.** Reserved
E. Free

Q.53 What should come in the place of blank (3)?
A. Deficits   **B.** Surplus
C. Profit   **D.** Forward
E. Impassive

Q.54 What should come in the place of blank (4)?
A. Incentives   **B.** Deterrent
C. Disincentive   **D.** Warning
E. Prohibition

Q.55 What should come in the place of blank (5)?
A. Preserve   **B.** Maintain
C. Occupied   **D.** Attain
E. Reforms

Ques (56-60):Direction: Read the passage and answer the questions that follow:

Mosquitoes can transmit pathogens that cause many human **diseases**, such as malaria, yellow fever, dengue fever, chikungunya, and Zika fever. Many of these diseases can be physically devastating and even fatal. For example, according to the World Health Organization (WHO), there are over 200 million new cases of malaria per year worldwide, resulting in over 400,000 deaths, most of them children under the age of 5. Zika fever is caused by a virus transmitted to humans primarily by the bite of Aedes aegypti mosquitoes. Symptoms in infected human adults are typically mild, but if the virus infects a pregnant woman it can be transmitted to the developing fetus and affect brain development, causing a condition called microcephaly. To reduce the number of Aedes aegypti mosquitoes that may carry the Zika virus, researchers at a biotechnology company called Oxitec have produced genetically modified (GM) Aedes aegypti mosquitoes that when released into the wild, mate with wild mosquitoes and any offspring produced die before becoming adults.

The fluorescence gene is used to________ GM mosquitoes. The lethality gene, which is more **accurately** called tetracycline transcriptional activator variant (or tTAV), encodes a protein that blocks **transcription** of several other genes that are essential to mosquito development. GM mosquito larvae that produce the tTAV protein die before reaching maturity. However, the tTAV protein cannot prevent the transcription of other genes when it is bound to the antibiotic tetracycline. Therefore, tetracycline acts as a repressor of the lethality gene, or, in other words, its antidote. In the lab, the GM mosquito larvae are reared in water containing tetracycline and develop normally into adult mosquitoes. When adult GM mosquitoes are released into the wild and breed with wild, non-GM mosquitoes, their offspring inherit the lethality gene. Without tetracycline in the environment to protect them, the offspring die.

In one study, Oxitec scientists released GM mosquitoes into a neighborhood in Brazil. **Sustained** release over the course of a year led to a reduction of the local Aedes aegypti population by 80% to 95% according to different measures (Carvalho et al., 2015). The scientists chose densely populated neighborhoods for their study because mosquito-borne diseases can spread most easily in areas where lots of humans and mosquitoes are present. They hypothesized that if they could reduce both the population size of the Aedes aegypti mosquitoes and the mosquito population density, they would reduce the probability that a person becomes infected with a pathogen spread by these mosquitoes. (An activity that shows how scientists measure mosquito density, based on data from Oxitec scientists, is available on the BioInteractive website as "Tracking Genetically Modified Mosquitoes.")

Q.56 What is the tone of the passage?

[SBI Clerk, 2020], [IBPS PO, 2019]

A. Informative
B. Humorous
C. Sarcastic
D. Apologetic
E. Biased

Q.57 Which of the following is not correct according to the passage?

[SBI Clerk, 2020]

A. Malarial fever is caused by a virus transmitted to humans primarily by the bite of Aedes aegypti mosquitoes.
B. The fluorescence gene is used to identify GM mosquitoes.
C. The lethality gene, which is more accurately called tetracycline transcriptional activator variant (or tTAV), encodes a protein that blocks transcription of several other genes that are essential to mosquito development.
D. Oxitec scientists released GM mosquitoes into a neighborhood in Brazil.
E. None of the these

Q.58 Choose the synonym for the word 'transcription' given in the passage?

[SBI Clerk, 2020]

A. Introduction
B. Copy
C. Variation
D. Induction
E. None of these

Q.59 Which of these is antonym to the the word 'sustained' given in the passage?

[SBI Clerk, 2020]

A. Nourished
B. Sporadic
C. Back
D. Relieved
E. None of these

Q.60 Which of these words can be filled in the blank given in the passage?
The fluorescence gene is used to_______GM mosquitoes.

[SBI Clerk, 2020]

A. mollify
B. quatify
C. identify
D. rectify
E. No word required

Numerical Ability

Ques (61-65):Direction: Simplify the given expression.

Q.61 $(4698 - 3625 - 857) = ?^3 - 42 - \sqrt{7225}$
A. 49
B. 14
C. 7
D. 343
E. 326

Q.62 $\left(\frac{?}{37}\right) = \left(\frac{15}{?}\right) \times \left(\frac{1}{2145}\right) \times \left(\frac{1}{9.25}\right) \times 676 \times 143$
A. 36
B. 26
C. 69
D. 55
E. 52

Q.63 $\sqrt{441} \times (985.35 - 969.35) = ?^{\frac{1}{2}} + 305$
A. 324
B. 900
C. 1225
D. 961
E. 1600

Q.64 $\left[\frac{3}{2} + \frac{1}{2}\left\{\frac{3}{4} - \frac{1}{2}\left(\frac{7}{8} - \frac{3}{4}\right)\right\}\right] = ?$
A. $\frac{59}{15}$
B. $\frac{59}{32}$
C. $\frac{59}{37}$
D. $\frac{58}{11}$
E. None of these

Q.65 $\left(4 + 3\sqrt{2}\right)^2 - \left(3 + 2\sqrt{2}\right)^2 = ?$
A. $24 + 12\sqrt{2}$
B. $24 + 10\sqrt{2}$
C. $23 + 12\sqrt{2}$
D. $23 + 10\sqrt{2}$
E. None of these

Q.66 A invests Rs. 500 and B invests Rs. M into a partnership for a year. After 8 months, A added Rs. 200 to his investment, and B removes Rs. 100 from his investment. If the difference between the profit shares of B and A after a year is Rs. 720 and the total profit of Rs. 3440, then find the ratio between the initial investment of A and B.
A. 4 : 9
B. 4 : 7
C. 9 : 4
D. 5 : 9
E. 5 : 7

Q.67 The difference between CI and SI on an amount at 10% per annum for 3 years is Rs. 1395. If same principal of Rs. __is lends on SI for 4 years at 20% per annum then the Simple Interest is Rs. __ (CI calculated annually).
A. 45000, 36000
B. 45850, 38000
C. 47000, 40000
D. 45000, 38000
E. 47000, 35000

Q.68 A lends an amount of Rs. 35000 to Raj for 4 years at 10% on simple interest of Rs. ___. Raj gives $\frac{6}{7}$th of this amount to Sam on simple interest for 4 years at the same rate and remaining amount kept as it is. The profit or loss Raj had in 4 years is Rs. ___ .
A. Rs. 14000, Rs. 1350
B. Rs. 15000, Rs. 3500
C. Rs. 12000, Rs. 1500
D. Rs. 14000, Rs. 2000
E. Rs. 16000, Rs. 4000

Ques (69-73):Direction: Study the following pie chart carefully and answer the question given beside.

The following pie chart gives the information about the percentage distribution of the JIO users in five different states out of 6 crores users in these states.

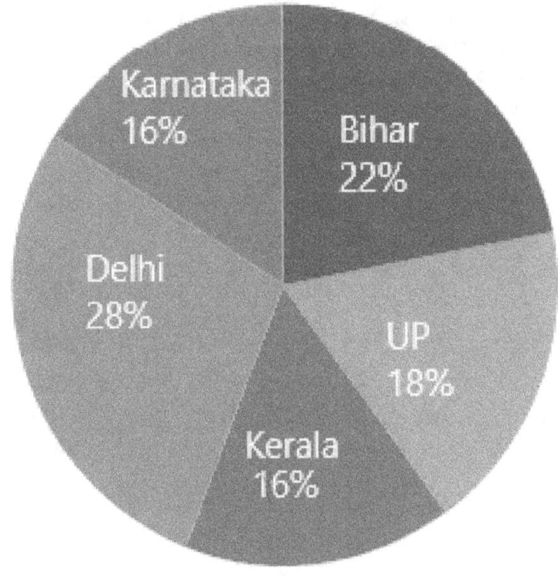

Q.69 If the total number of Airtel users in Bihar is 2500000 less than the total number of JIO users in that state then what is the total number of Airtel users in Bihar?

A. 10700000   **B.** 13200000
C. 11200000   **D.** 11500000
E. 11700000

Q.70 If the total number of Idea users in Delhi is 15% of the sum of the total number of Idea users in these five states then the total number of JIO users in Delhi is what percent more than the total number of Idea users in Delhi? (It is given that the sum of the total number of Idea users in these five states is 2.5 crores)

A. 358%   **B.** 368%   **C.** 348%   **D.** 338%
E. 340%

Q.71 What is the difference between the sum of the JIO users in Delhi and Kerala together and the sum of the JIO users in UP and Bihar together?

A. 2400000   **B.** 2800000   **C.** 1800000   **D.** 2200000
E. 3300000

Q.72 The number of JIO users in Karnataka is approximately what percent less than the number of JIO users in Bihar?

A. 28.28%   **B.** 28.47%   **C.** 27.27%   **D.** 28.48%
E. 26.97%

Q.73 The respective ratio of the total number of JIO users in Bihar and the total number of Airtel users in Kerala is 11: 5 then the total number of Airtel users in Kerala is what percent less than the total number of JIO users in Delhi?

A. 54.28%   **B.** 72.68%   **C.** 58.28%   **D.** 64.29%
E. 68.59%

Q.74 After an accident, a train moving $\frac{3}{4}$ of it's original speed. A train reached its destination 15 minutes late. Find the usual time to reach the destination.

A. 15 min.   **B.** 30 min.   **C.** 45 min.   **D.** 60 min.
E. 75 min.

Q.75 Karan calculates the average of his marks in five subjects. By mistake, he writes a number of two subjects as the reverse of original marks thereby increasing the average by 27 marks. If the incorrect numbers are in the ratio 13:10, what is the sum of the original numbers? (The marks awarded are from 01, 02 ... to 99)

A. 35   **B.** 31
C. 43   **D.** 26
E. None of these

Q.76 By walking $\frac{5}{3}$ of the usual speed a student reaches school 20 minutes earlier. Find his usual time.

A. 60 minutes   **B.** 50 minutes
C. 40 minutes   **D.** 30 minutes
E. 20 minutes

Ques (77-79):Direction: In the given question, two equations numbered I and II are given. Solve both the equations and mark the appropriate answer.

Q.77 I. $3x^2 + 19x + 20 = 0$
II. $6y^2 + 19y + 15 = 0$

[SBI PO, 2021]

A. x > y
B. x < y
C. x ≥ y
D. x ≤ y
E. x = y or the relationship between x and y cannot be established

Q.78 I. $x^2 = 256$
II. $y^2 + 18y + 17 = 0$

[SBI PO, 2021]

A. x > y
B. x < y
C. x ≥ y
D. x ≤ y
E. x = y or the relationship between x and y cannot be established

Q.79 I. $x^2 - 15x + 56 = 0$
II. $y^2 + 17y + 72 = 0$

[SBI PO, 2021]

A. x > y
B. x < y
C. x ≥ y
D. x ≤ y
E. x = y or the relationship between x and y cannot be established

Q.80 Time taken by a boat to cover half of a distance upstream is equal to time taken by boat to cover total distance downstream. If the boat covers a distance $240\ km$ downstream with three different speeds in three different parts in the ratio of $12:13:15$ respectively. Boat cover first parts with usual speed, second part with $\frac{3}{4}th$ of its usual speed and third part with half of its usual speed, if boat takes total 19.5 hours to cover total distance. Find the usual speed of the boat?

A. $12\ km/hr$
B. $10\ km/hr$
C. $8\ hr$
D. $13\ km/hr$
E. $14\ km/hr$

Ques (81-85):Direction: Find the missing number in place of the question mark (?) in the given series.

Q.81 2, 8, 28, 102, 432, ?
A. 1860
B. 1296
C. 2190
D. 2490
E. None of these

Q.82 6, 16, 44, 126, 370, ?
A. 1100
B. 1050
C. 1400
D. 1260
E. None of these

Q.83 51, 77, 175, 250, 279, ?
A. 313
B. 413
C. 512
D. 616
E. None of these

Q.84 2, 2, 5, 15.5, ?, 267.125
A. 58.25
B. 65.25
C. 56.25
D. 62.25
E. None of these

Q.85 219, 223, 232, 248, ?
A. 296
B. 284
C. 257
D. 273
E. 267

Q.86 There are 30 people in a group. If all shake hands with one another, how many handshakes are possible?
A. 870
B. 435
C. 500
D. 625
E. 258

Q.87 The perimeter of a rectangle is 44 cm and the area is 120 cm². Find the length of the rectangle. (length > breath)
A. 10
B. 15
C. 17
D. 12
E. 20

Q.88 Pipe P can fill a tank 8 hours and Pipe Q can fill it in 10 hours. If they are opened an alternate hour and if pipe P is opened first, then in how many hours the tank should be full?
A. 8.8 hours
B. 6.3 hours
C. 7.5 hours
D. 3.6 hours
E. None of these

Q.89 Cards numbered from 107 to 1006 are put in a bag. A card is drawn from it at random. Find the probability that the number on the card is not divisible both by 11 and 37?
A. 0.998
B. 0.105
C. 0.107
D. 0.103
E. None of these

Q.90 The cost price of a set of 2 pants + 4 shirts or 1 pant + 6 shirts is Rs. 5,600. A shopkeeper decided to sell them separately. He sells 10 shirts for Rs. 6,000. Find the amount of profit or loss per shirt.
A. Profit Rs. 1000
B. Loss Rs. 1000
C. Profit Rs. 100
D. Loss Rs. 100
E. Loss Rs. 130

// Smart Answer Sheet //

Correct — Indicates percentage of students who answered questions correctly.

Skipped — Indicates percentage of students who skipped questions.

Q.	Ans.	Correct / Skipped
1	A	63.1 % / 1.22 %
2	E	69.38 % / 1.59 %
3	E	56.9 % / 1.02 %
4	D	13.07 % / 4.08 %
5	A	53.35 % / 1.67 %
6	E	40.0 % / 1.81 %
7	B	51.82 % / 1.61 %
8	B	41.04 % / 1.26 %
9	E	44.33 % / 1.77 %
10	C	76.06 % / 0.0 %
11	D	78.15 % / 0.0 %
12	B	76.53 % / 0.0 %
13	B	41.72 % / 1.43 %
14	A	67.38 % / 1.48 %
15	D	52.93 % / 1.88 %
16	B	58.1 % / 1.79 %

Q.	Ans.	Correct / Skipped
17	C	52.93 % / 1.79 %
18	A	56.2 % / 1.03 %
19	E	50.98 % / 1.28 %
20	C	48.2 % / 1.59 %
21	C	69.06 % / 1.11 %
22	B	45.54 % / 1.02 %
23	E	54.96 % / 1.47 %
24	A	56.39 % / 1.81 %
25	B	59.5 % / 1.63 %
26	A	55.97 % / 1.47 %
27	A	43.4 % / 1.3 %
28	A	62.41 % / 1.74 %
29	A	49.74 % / 1.74 %
30	C	58.86 % / 1.27 %
31	C	12.45 % / 4.02 %
32	A	19.7 % / 4.5 %

Q.	Ans.	Correct / Skipped
33	E	40.53 % / 1.1 %
34	D	29.71 % / 4.17 %
35	B	61.04 % / 1.81 %
36	D	40.45 % / 1.28 %
37	C	61.43 % / 1.29 %
38	E	66.11 % / 1.79 %
39	A	54.17 % / 1.51 %
40	B	59.99 % / 1.29 %
41	C	89.94 % / 0.0 %
42	E	89.02 % / 0.0 %
43	B	60.44 % / 1.39 %
44	A	53.92 % / 1.73 %
45	D	79.21 % / 0.0 %
46	B	57.79 % / 1.08 %
47	B	69.12 % / 1.8 %
48	E	84.08 % / 0.0 %

Q.	Ans.	Correct / Skipped
49	A	46.05 % / 1.35 %
50	B	66.19 % / 1.24 %
51	B	49.63 % / 1.48 %
52	D	49.96 % / 1.7 %
53	A	58.46 % / 1.65 %
54	A	47.96 % / 1.33 %
55	E	67.82 % / 1.51 %
56	A	13.29 % / 4.87 %
57	A	24.58 % / 4.87 %
58	B	20.51 % / 4.85 %
59	B	18.94 % / 4.25 %
60	C	27.75 % / 4.08 %
61	C	81.23 % / 0.0 %
62	E	46.89 % / 1.67 %
63	D	61.22 % / 1.3 %
64	B	21.17 % / 4.38 %

Q.	Ans.	Correct / Skipped
65	E	66.51 % / 1.46 %
66	D	48.52 % / 1.31 %
67	A	67.14 % / 1.94 %
68	D	49.68 % / 1.13 %
69	A	61.16 % / 1.87 %
70	C	76.14 % / 0.0 %
71	A	44.06 % / 1.13 %
72	C	46.04 % / 1.36 %
73	D	46.73 % / 1.89 %
74	C	58.83 % / 1.5 %
75	D	16.81 % / 3.83 %
76	B	63.26 % / 1.16 %
77	E	41.25 % / 1.6 %
78	E	56.76 % / 1.86 %
79	A	41.56 % / 1.39 %
80	A	15.68 % / 4.68 %

Q.	Ans.	Correct		Q.	Ans.	Correct		Q.	Ans.	Correct		Q.	Ans.	Correct		Q.	Ans.	Correct
		Skipped				Skipped				Skipped				Skipped				Skipped
81	C	60.85 %		83	B	57.87 %		85	D	29.31 %		87	D	59.7 %		89	A	48.82 %
		1.76 %				1.9 %				4.95 %				1.94 %				1.63 %
82	A	55.71 %		84	A	46.9 %		86	B	62.53 %		88	A	17.89 %		90	D	63.58 %
		1.44 %				1.43 %				1.16 %				4.08 %				1.58 %

Performance Analysis

Avg. Score (%)	58.89%
Toppers Score (%)	62.22%
Your Score	

//Hints and Solutions//

1. The least Possible Venn diagram is shown below:

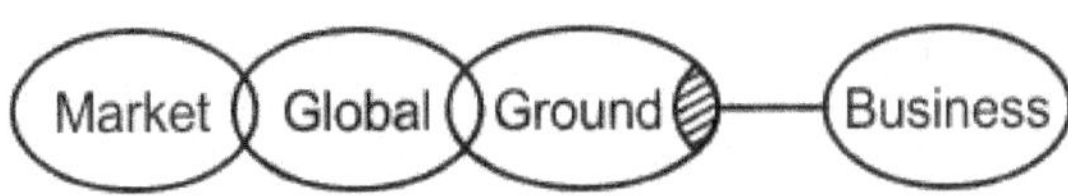

Conclusions:

I. Some market are ground → False (No relation is given)

II. No ground is market → False (No relation is given)

III. No Global is business → False (No relation is given)

Here, Conclusion I and II is a complementary pair so either or is followed.

So, the correct answer is either I or II follows.

Hence, the correct option is (A).

2. The least Possible Venn diagram is shown below:

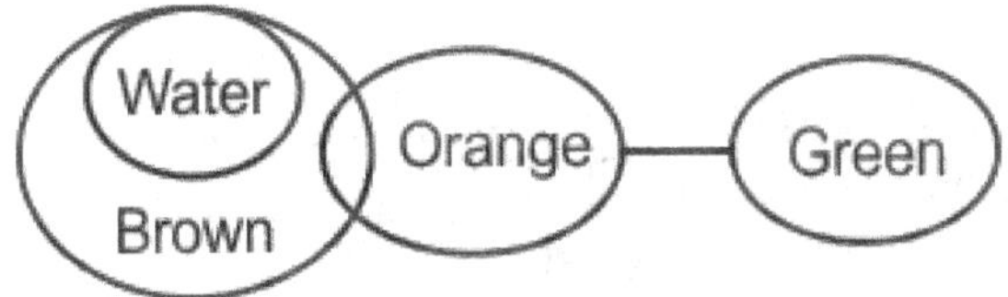

Conclusions:

I. Only a few water is orange → False (No relation is given hence false)

II. Some green being brown is a possibility → True (The possibility is true).

III. Some Water is not Green → False (No relation is given so false)

So, the correct answer is only II follows.

Hence, the correct option is (E).

3. The least Possible Venn diagram is shown below:

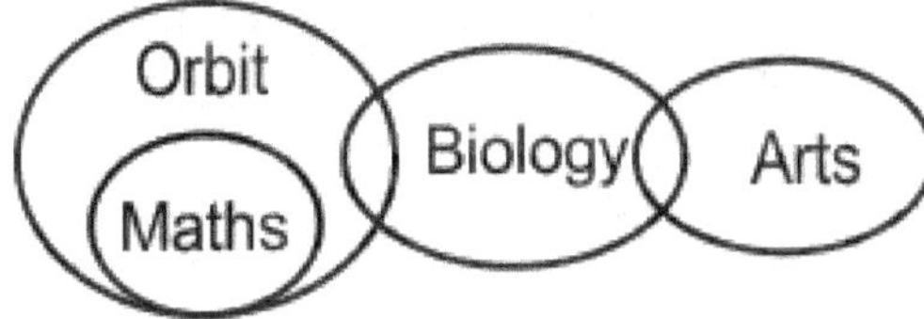

Conclusions:

I. Some arts are not orbit → False (No definite relation is given)

II. All biology are maths → False.

III. All orbit are biology is a possibility → False (as only few biology is orbit given)

So, the correct answer is none follows is the answer.

Hence, the correct option is (E).

4. The given word:

FANTASTIC

After arranging the letters of the word in alphabetic order from left to right, we get:

AACFINSTT

Now, the third, fifth, sixth, and eighth letters of the word 'AACFINSTT' are C, I, N and T.

No meaningful English word can be formed using C, I, N and T.

Hence, the correct option is (D).

Ques (5-9):Friends: G, H, J, K, L, M, N and O

1) G lives on the floor numbered 5.

2) There are two people between G and N.

Floor Number	Case – 1	Case – 2
8		N
7		
6		
5	G	G
4		
3		
2	N	
1		

3) L lives on an odd-numbered floor but immediately above O.

4) As many people live above N as below L.

Thus, Case - 2 gets eliminated.

Floor Number	Case – 1
8	
7	L
6	O
5	G
4	
3	
2	N
1	

5) There are three people between L and K.

Floor Number	Case – 1
8	
7	L
6	O
5	G
4	
3	K
2	N
1	

6) J lives on one of the floors below M but not on the ground floor.

Floor Number	Case – 1
8	M
7	L
6	O

5	G
4	J
3	K
2	N
1	

Therefore, the final arrangement will be:

Floor Number	Case – 1
8	M
7	L
6	O
5	G
4	J
3	K
2	N
1	H

5. Therefore, one person lives between M and O.

Hence, the correct option is (A).

6. Therefore, M and H occupy top and ground floor respectively.

Hence, the correct option is (E).

7. (A) M, O ⇒ Only one floor between M and O.

(B) L, O ⇒ No floor between L and O.

(C) O, J ⇒ Only one floor between O and J.

(D) J, N ⇒ Only one floor between J and N.

(E) K, H ⇒ Only one floor between K and H.

Hence, the correct option is (B).

8. Therefore, K lives on the third floor.

Hence, the correct option is (B).

9. As H live on the ground floor, therefore no one lives below H.

Hence, the correct option is (D).

Ques (10-12): For Step I: First and last alphabets are interchanged.

For Step II:

For Letters: If the number of letters in the word is even then two middle letters are taken.

If the number of letters in the word is odd then first and last letters are taken.

For Number: If the number of letters in the word are even then the number is place value of letter which is 2nd from the last.

If the number of letters in the word is odd then the number is place value of letter which is 2nd from the start.

For Symbol: If the number of vowel in the word is even symbol used is @.

If the number of the vowel in the word is odd symbol used is #.

For Code Name:

For Letter: If the letter in step II is consonant:letter = letter – 2

If the letter in step II is vowel: Letter = letter + 2

For Number: If the number in step II is even then Number = Number ÷ 2

If the number in step II is odd then Number = Number × 2

10.

Exercise Name	Step I	Step II	Code Name
SURYA	AURYS	AS21@	CQ42
KIRAN	NIRAK	NK9@	LI18

So, code name for 'SURYA KIRAN' is 'CQ42 LI18'

Hence, the correct option is (C).

11.

Exercise Name	Step I	Step II
VAJRA	AAJRV	AV1@
PRAHAR	RRAHAP	AH1@

So, the output of second step 'VAJRA PRAHAR' is 'AV1@ AH1@'

Hence, the correct option is (D).

12.

Exercise Name	Step I	Step II	Code Name
SAUNDRA	AAUNDRS	AS1#	CQ2

So, the code name for 'SAMUNDRA' is 'CQ2'.

Hence, the correct option is (B).

Ques (13-15): Decoding the statement:

	A is to the			
Symbol	*	%	#	Ω
Direction	North	South	East	West
	Of B			

The distance between two points is 11 km less than the number given within brackets.

P % Q (51km); Q # R (41km); R * S (31km); S # T (41km); T % U (51 km); U Ω V (91km); V * W (91km); W # X (111km); X % Y (111km) means:

P is 40 km South of Q, Q is 30 km East of R, R is 20 km North of S, S is 30 km East of T, T is 40 km South of U, U is 80 km West of V, V is 80 km North of W, W is 100 km East of X, X is 100 km South of Y.

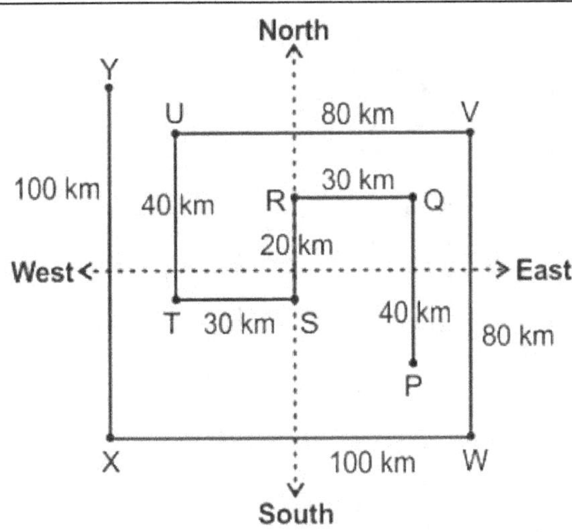

13. Shortest Distance between R and P:

Applying Pythagoras Theorem:

$\rightarrow RP^2 = RQ^2 + QP^2$

$\rightarrow RP^2 = 900 + 1600 = 2500$

$\rightarrow RP = 50$ km

Thus, the distance between R and P is 50 km.

Hence, the correct option is (B).

14. Thus, U is in the Northwest direction with respect to R.

Hence, the correct option is (A).

15. Thus, W is in the Southeast direction with respect to T.

Hence, the correct option is (D).

Ques (16-20): Given:

Four boys A, B, C, D and their friends - J, K, L, M, not necessarily in the same order, go to Agra in a car.

Front row: 2 seats including the driver.

Second row: 3 seats.

Third row: 3 seats.

The driver's seat is at the extreme right side in the front row of the car. The car has six seats immediately next to six windows.

1) K and C sit in the 2nd row and the 3rd row respectively.

2) A is the friend of J and sits in the same row in which C sits, but not on the same of the window in which the driver sits.

3) A, L and their friends do not sit in the front row, which consists of two seats.

4) L and M are the only two persons who do not sit next to a window.

5) L is a friend of C.

6) No pair of friends sit in the same row or the same column.

(Combining all, A sits in 3rd row and L sits in the middle of the 2nd row and M sits in the middle of the 3rd row)

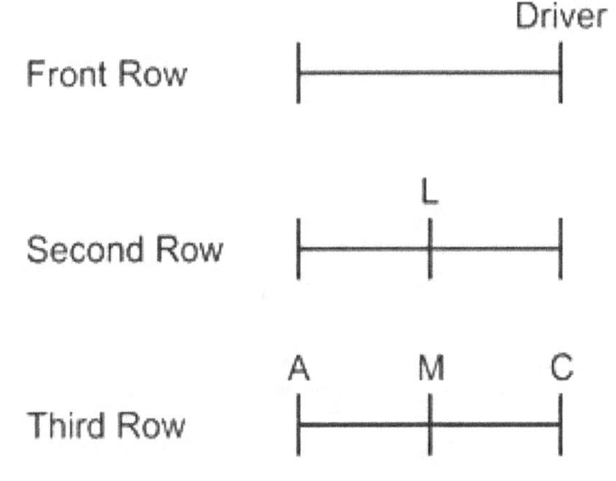

7) A is a friend of J.

8) Neither A nor L nor their friends sit in the front row, which consists of two seats.

9) No pair of friends sits in the same row or the same column.

(So, J sits in the 2nd row and behind the seat of driver)

10) K sits in the 2nd row.

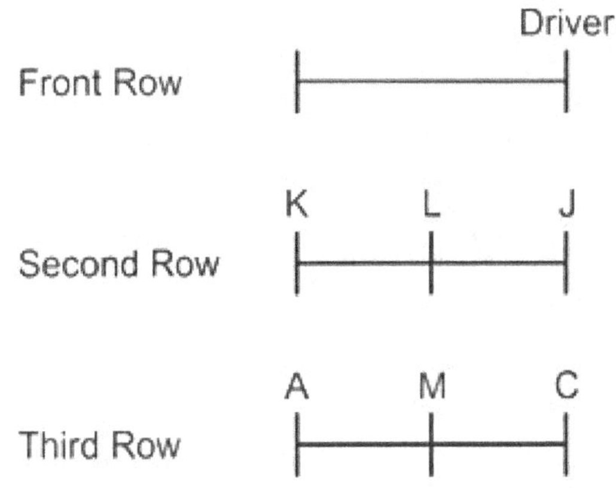

11) B sits in the same column as J and one place ahead of him.

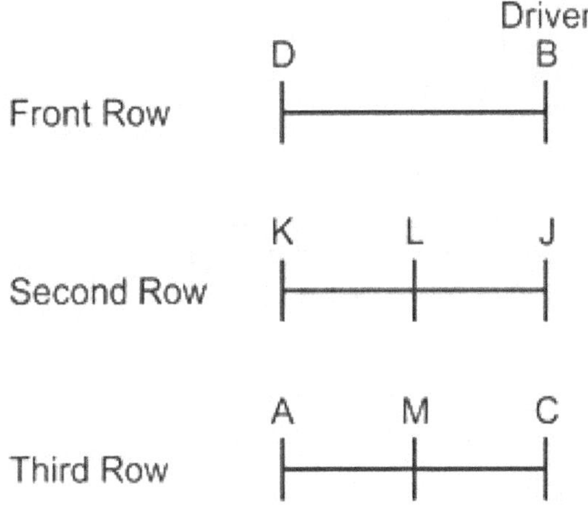

16. Clearly, C is sitting just beside the right window of the last row.

Hence, the correct option is (B).

17. Clearly, B is driving the car.

Hence, the correct option is (C).

18. Clearly, J is sitting to the immediate right of L.

Hence, the correct option is (A).

19. Clearly, none is true.

Hence, the correct option is (E).

20. Clearly, L is sitting in the second row.

Hence, the correct option is (C).

Ques (21-22): From the given information,

(i) T is the mother of V. R is the grandmother of V.

(ii) Q is the husband of R. S is the brother-in-law of Q.

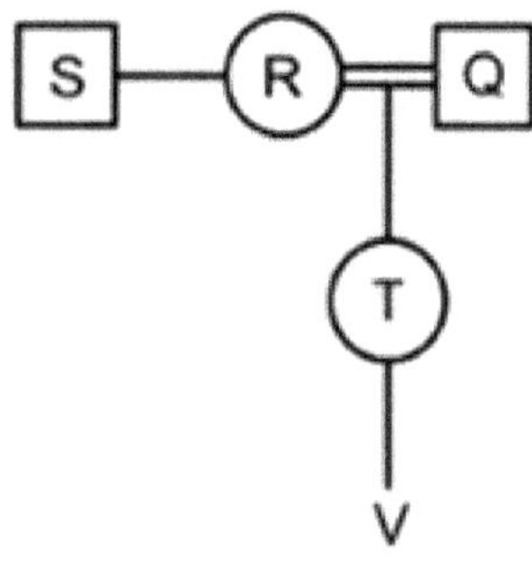

(iii) U is the son-in-law of Q. P is the nephew of S.

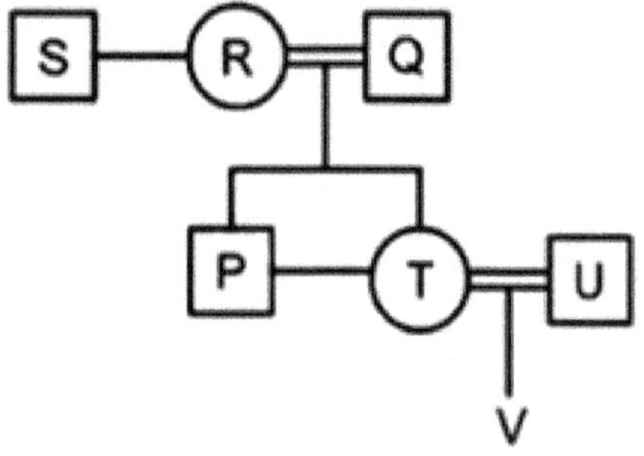

(iv) There are 4 males in the family. It means V is female.

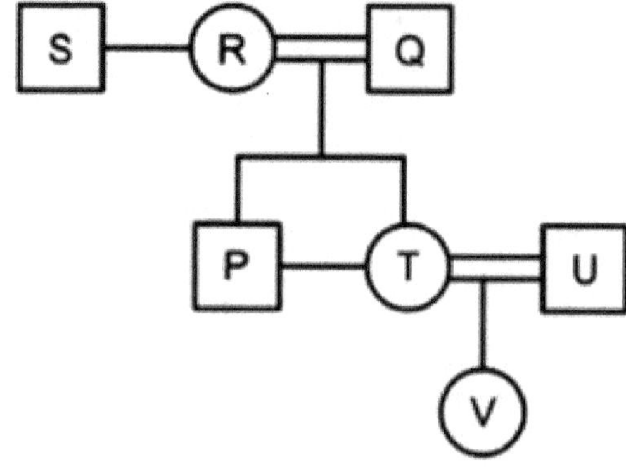

21. So, V is the niece of P.

Hence, the correct option is (C).

22. So, P is the son of Q.

Hence, the correct option is (B).

23. 1) S length is more than T and less than Q.

Q > S > T

2) P length is more than R but less than Q.

Q > P > R

3) U length is more than Q.

U > Q

4) R length is more than S.

R > S

After combining:

U > Q > P > R > S > T

Thus, no chain is longer than U.

Hence, the correct option is (E).

24. 1) Q and S are equally expensive.

Q = S

2) T is the least expensive jewelry.

_ > _ > _ > _ > T

3) S was less expensive than R but more expensive than P.

R > S > P

4) The expensiveness of the R is more than that of Q.

R > Q = S > P > T

Options (A): R was the most expensive among them → True

Option (B): P was more expensive than Q → False

Option (C): S was in the middle. → False (Either Q or S can be at the middle)

Option (D): P was the most expensive among them → False

Thus, R was the most expensive among them is true.

Hence, the correct option is (A).

25. According to the given information, their sequence in the order of height in the queue is as follows-

Shrikant < Neelima = Neelima $>$ Shrikant ...(i)

Pratima $>$ Shrikant ...(ii)

Hembram > Subhash > Neelima...(iii)

Neelima > Pratima ...(iv)

Here ' $>$ ' means 'longer than' and '<' means 'shorter than'.

On arranging their order from equations (i), (ii), (iii) and (iv),

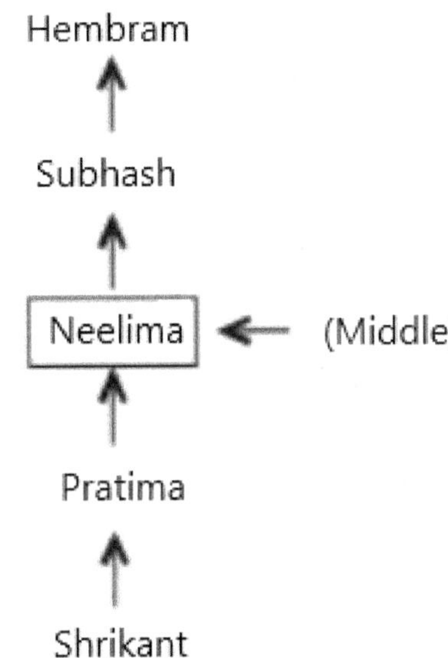

Thus, Neelima will be right in the middle of the row.

Hence, the correct option is (B).

Ques (26-30):

Alpha bets	A	B	C	D	E	F	G	H	I	J	K	L	M
Positional value	1	2	3	4	5	6	7	8	9	10	11	12	13
Positional value	26	25	24	23	22	21	20	19	18	17	16	15	14
Alpha bets	Z	Y	X	W	V	U	T	S	R	Q	P	O	N

26. The pattern followed is:

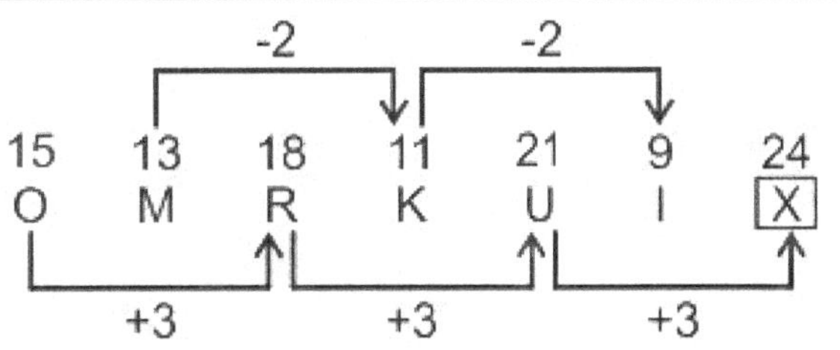

So, the correct answer is "X".

Hence, the correct option is (A).

27. The pattern followed is:

2 13 15
B M O
+3 +2 +2
E O Q
5 15 17
+3 +2 +2
H Q S
8 17 19
+3 +2 +2
K S U
11 19 21

So, the correct answer is "KSU".

Hence, the correct option is (A).

28. The pattern followed is:

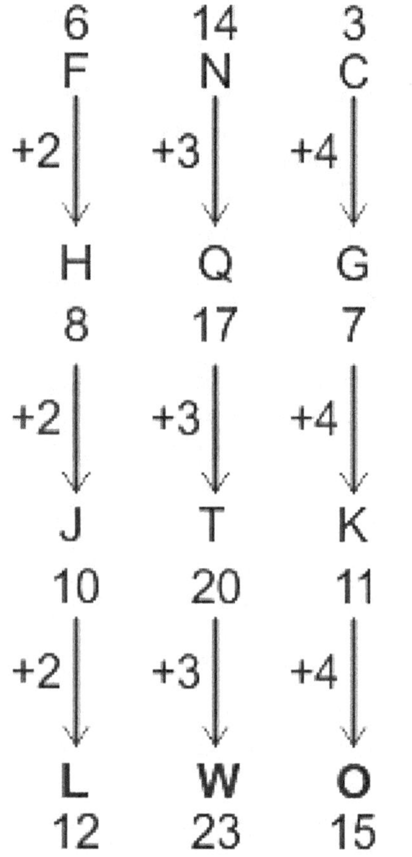

So, the correct answer is "LWO".

Hence, the correct option is (A).

29. The Logic here is as follows:

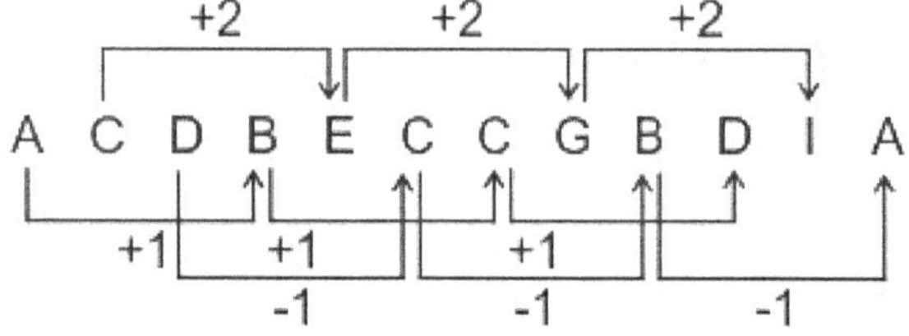

So, the correct answer "DIA"

Hence, the correct option is (A).

30. The logic follows here is:

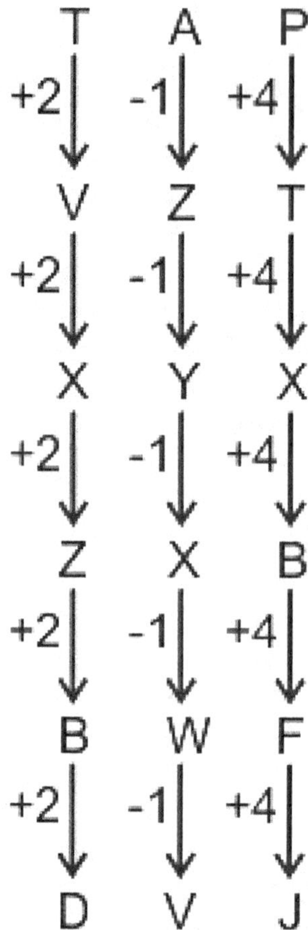

So, "DVJ" is the correct answer.

Hence, the correct option is (C).

31. The first blank is placed just before a vague time period is mentioned. When we have to indicate an approximate time, "around" as well as "about" is used. But since none of the options has (iv) as the first word, "about" can be eliminated.

It is already mentioned that the lake was formed above the volcanic crater. So, all the volcanic activities will take place below or beneath the lake. Thus, alternatives ii & iii fit in the second blank.

The high level of carbon dioxide is due to volcanic activities. In other words, volcanic activities are the cause behind the high level of carbon dioxide. To state conclusions, both 'thus' and 'therefore' can be used.

Complete paragraph: According to Atlas Obscura, Lake Nyos was formed in a volcanic crater around 400 years ago. A lake of this kind is generally formed by the volcanic activities that take place deep beneath the surface of the earth, and therefore have high levels of carbon dioxide in them. Usually, this gas is released over time as the lake water evaporates.

Hence, the correct option is (C).

32. It is understood from the sentence that the salesman ignored the king, and thus, the king took revenge. 'Avenge' is a verb and 'revenge' is a noun. Since the first blank precedes the article 'a', the blank should contain the noun(revenge).

The second blank will also contain a noun as it is preceded by 'the'. Of the remaining alternatives, ii, v & vi, are nouns. "Condition" refers to a situation that must exist before something else is possible or permitted. The word fits appropriately in the second blank to indicate that the king brought all the cars on certain terms.

The third blank will contain a verb, as it is preceded by a modal (would). Of the two verbs in options, the only one that could be performed by the salesman with reference to India is 'accompany'.

Complete paragraph: As revenge for having been ignored by an English Rolls Royce salesman in a London showroom, the king bought all the cars the showroom had on offer. He bought the cars on the condition that the salesman would accompany him to India. Once there, the Maharaja ordered the cars to be used for garbage collection.

Hence, the correct option is (A).

33. Only "speaking" can fit in the first blank as the blank is succeeded by the preposition "to". None of the other verbs can be followed by "to". Since none of the options has the alternative (v) as the first word, none of these is the correct option.

Complete paragraph: Speaking to the reporters, Air Vice Marshal RGK Kapoor said that the IAF fighters had been tasked with intercepting Pakistani aircraft and were successful in defeating them. He also said that despite the Pakistan Air Force jets dropped bombs, they were not able to cause any damage.

Hence, the correct option is (E).

34. Alternatives ii, iv & vi would fit in the first blank as these are the only words that can be associated with 'railway'.

The second blank needs to be a noun that can be crowded and also related to the railways. Keeping these two conditions, options ii, iv & vi are suitable for this blank.

For the last blank either 'area' or the 'lounge' could be used, as these two could be used for 'waiting'. This means that the last option in the correct combination should be either iii or vi.

Both options A & D have these. Option D also has ii & iv in the consecutive sequence.

Complete paragraph: When you think of a railway station in India, the first thing that comes to your mind is crowded platforms. But the newly launched premier waiting for lounge at the Madurai Railway Station might just change your opinion.

Hence, the correct option is (D).

35. The first blank comes after an auxiliary verb, so we would think that the next word should be the main verb. But there is no object for the said verb after the blank. The blank is followed by 'one of the...', which means the word in the blank will not be a verb, but a word to put emphasis on. Both 'literally' and 'arguably' are suitable for this blank.

The presence 'a' before the second blank means that this blank will contain a noun. Of the given options, 'setback' and

'milestones' are nouns. however, the plural noun "milestones" cannot be placed after the article "a". The mentioned developments, thus, could be a setback for the Left Front.

We know that for the second blank, it should be (iii). Only options (B) & (C) have option iii as the second choice. For the first blank, it is either (i) or (ii), and B carries (ii) and C carries (i).

Option (C) carries alternative (v) [milestones] as its choice for the last blank. This is wrong because the last blank will have a verb. Option (B) has a verb (undermines) as the third choice. So, the correct answer is (B).

Complete paragraph: The candidate's decision to contest from Wayanad, Kerala, is arguably one of the most sensational developments of this election. His move, political pundits contend, is a setback for the Left Front. The candidate's decision also undermines the idea of opposition parties pooling their votes to vanquish the party currently in power.

Hence, the correct option is (B).

36. Option (D) is correct grammatically and contextually. Because the statement talks about multiple people and thus '**are**' is correct. And because of this, we can say that option (A) will be wrong because the verb '**is**' is given in it which is wrong.

One is entitled 'to' something and not 'for'. This eliminates option (B).

Option (C) is incorrect as 'a rights' is incorrect grammatically.

Hence, the correct option is (D).

37. The correct phrase is **around/round the corner**. It means something that about to happen, nearby, close by, not far away.

Example- "The commander was claiming that peace was just around the corner".

Hence, the correct option is (C).

38. Recede means to go or move away; retreat; go to or toward a more distant point; withdraw.

Further means in addition; moreover.

So in this sentence, this word group is giving the correct meaning, in its original form and does not need to be changed.

Hence, the correct option is (E).

39. The phrase '**ensure accessibility**' is correct and fits in well meaningfully and grammatically.

Ensue means result/proceed and does not fit in. This does not make sense in the statement.

Ensures means make certain that (something) will occur or be the case.

Accessibility means the quality of being able to be reached or entered.

Thus, Ensures accessibility is best suited here because it shows that only cash transfers are not enough for economic security.

Hence, the correct option is (A).

40. We need the adverb form of 'history'.

Thus, **'historically'** is correct while **'historic'** is incorrect. This eliminates option (A).

Being is incorrect as it is used to refer to an individual/person. Been is correct here. This eliminates option (C).

Due to article 'a', the correct form is 'place' in singular. This elminate option (D).

So, the correct sentence is "Afghanistan has Historically been a difficult place for external invaders, thanks to its complex tribal equations and its rugged mountainous terrain."

Hence, the correct option is (B).

41. We first realise the topic of the given jumbled-up passage to be- scientific attitude and critical thinking.

As the 1st sentence is given, sentence D is the 2nd sentence because it elaborates on the relevance of the topic.

Sentence E is the 3rd sentence because it delivers a deeper meaning by linking the topic to similar concepts.

Sentence B is the 4th sentence because it begins with 'critical thinking and provides more information on it.

Sentence A is the 5th sentence as it is the continuation because it begins with 'also'.

Finally, with the help of the last sentence given, we know sentence C to be the 6th sentence.

So, the correct order of sentences is 1DEBAC7.

Hence, the correct option is (C).

42. We first realise the topic of the given jumbled-up passage to be- scientific attitude and critical thinking.

As the 1st sentence is given, sentence D is the 2nd sentence because it elaborates on the relevance of the topic.

Sentence E is the 3rd sentence because it delivers a deeper meaning by linking the topic to similar concepts.

Sentence B is the 4th sentence because it begins with 'critical thinking' and provides more information on it.

Sentence A is the 5th sentence as it is the continuation because it begins with 'also'.

Finally, with the help of the last sentence given, we know sentence C to be the 6th sentence.

So, the correct order of sentences is 1DEBAC7.

Hence, the correct option is (E).

43. We first realise the topic of the given jumbled-up passage to be- scientific attitude and critical thinking.

As the 1st sentence is given, sentence D is the 2nd sentence because it elaborates on the relevance of the topic.

Sentence E is the 3rd sentence because it delivers a deeper meaning by linking the topic to similar concepts.

Sentence B is the 4th sentence because it begins with 'critical thinking' and provides more information on it.

Sentence A is the 5th sentence as it is the continuation because it begins with 'also'.

Finally, with the help of the last sentence given, we know sentence C to be the 6th sentence.

So, the correct order of sentences is 1DEBAC7.

Hence, the correct option is (B).

44. We first realise the topic of the given jumbled-up passage to be- scientific attitude and critical thinking.

As the 1st sentence is given, sentence D is the 2nd sentence because it elaborates on the relevance of the topic.

Sentence E is the 3rd sentence because it delivers a deeper meaning by linking the topic to similar concepts.

Sentence B is the 4th sentence because it begins with 'critical thinking' and provides more information on it.

Sentence A is the 5th sentence as it is the continuation because it begins with 'also'.

Finally, with the help of the last sentence given, we know sentence C to be the 6th sentence.

So, the correct order of sentences is 1DEBAC7.

Hence, the correct option is (A).

45. We first realise the topic of the given jumbled-up passage to be- scientific attitude and critical thinking.

As the 1st sentence is given, sentence D is the 2nd sentence because it elaborates on the relevance of the topic.

Sentence E is the 3rd sentence because it delivers a deeper meaning by linking the topic to similar concepts.

Sentence B is the 4th sentence because it begins with 'critical thinking' and provides more information on it.

Sentence A is the 5th sentence as it is the continuation because it begins with 'also'.

Finally, with the help of the last sentence given, we know sentence C to be the 6th sentence.

So, the correct order of sentences is 1DEBAC7.

Hence, the correct option is (D).

46. The error is in part (2) of the sentence.

According to the 'Proximity rule' of Subject-verb agreement, when a compound subject contains both a singular and a plural noun or pronoun joined by "or" or "nor," the verb should agree with the part of the subject that is closest to the verb. This is also called the rule of proximity.

Also, according to the same rule, **Two singular nouns joined by 'with', 'as well as', 'in addition to', 'together' and 'besides' will have a singular verb as the number of verb is always decided on the basis of the primary subject in a sentence.**

In the above question sentence, 'Shooting' is considered to the primary subject that is singular in number. 'Horse riding' is an addition to the 'Primary subject' i.e. 'Shooting'.

Thus, the error is in part 2 of the sentence as the plural verb form 'are' is incorrect. It should be the singular verb form 'is.'

- For example, Ram, as well as Shyam, was absent during the concert.

Correct sentence: "Shooting as well as horse riding is taught to cadets at the National Defence Academy every morning."

Hence, the correct option is (B).

47. The error is in part (2) of the sentence.

Words joined to a singular subject by 'with', 'as well as', etc., will accommodate the singular verb.

'The President' is singular and is joined by 'along with'. Therefore, the verb should be singular.

Thus, the error is in part (2) of the sentence as the plural verb form 'are' is incorrect. It should be 'is.'

- For example: The newly elected Prime Minister along with his Ministers is keen to reform the economy.

The correct sentence is: "The President, along with several international guests, is to be present during the swearing-in ceremony of the new government."

Hence, the correct option is (B).

48. There is no error in the given question. It is structured correctly.

The correct adjective 'environmental' has been used here which qualifies the noun 'quality'.

The correct sentence is: India has a long way to go to reach environmental quality similar to that enjoyed in developed economies.

Hence, the correct option is (E).

49. The error lies in (1) as the word 'further' means 'more' and it makes no sense here.

The correct word here is the preposition 'beyond' which means that stories take us far away from reality.

The correct sentence is: Stories are all about going **beyond reality** and it is no wonder that they let you understand big concepts with only a little bit of reading practice.

Hence, the correct option is (A).

50. The error lies in (2) as the word 'who' is incorrect here. It is used to introduce a clause giving further information about a person or people previously mentioned. The correct word here is 'which' which goes with the word 'character'.

The correct sentence: Who wouldn't love to chat about **which** character is their favorite, or predict what will happen in a suspense story they are reading?

Hence, the correct option is (B).

51. The passage is about 'Indian economy before 1991'.

Let us refer to this line from the passage, "Prior to 1991, India's economy and financial system were heavily regulated and ___(1)___ by the public sector".

From the above sentence, we get to know that the public sector regulated and controlled India's economy and financial system.

In option (B), 'Dominated' means have power and influence over.

So, 'Dominated' is the correct word for blank (1).

Hence, the correct option is (B).

52. The passage is about 'Indian economy before 1991'.

Let us refer to this line from the passage, "A complicated regulatory regime required firms to obtain licenses for most economic activities, and many industries were ___(2)___ for the public sector".

From the above sentence, we get to know as the public sector had an influence over India's economy and financial system.

The firms required licenses for thier economy activities as most of the industries were specially for the public sector.

In option (D), 'Reserved' means something kept specially for a particular person.

So, 'Reserved' is the correct word for blank (2).

Hence, the correct option is (D).

53. The passage is about 'Indian economy before 1991'.

Let us refer to this line from the passage, "Primarily focused on financing government ___(3)___ and serving government priority sectors such as agriculture".

From the above sentence, we get to know that banks were nationalized and deposits of the public sector increased from 5 to 80 percent.

So, now the primary focus was to financing the government's expenditure and prioritizing sectors like agriculture.

In option (A), 'Deficits' means an excess of expenditure or liabilities over income or assets in a given period.

So, 'Deficits' is the correct word for blank (3).

Hence, the correct option is (A).

54. The passage is about 'Indian economy before 1991'.

Let us refer to this line from the passage, "India's public banks lacked proper lending ___(4)___ and exhibited a high number of non-performing loans".

From the above sentence, we get to know that India's public banks carelessly gave away money, and now they have a high number of non-performing loans(Borrower not paying the installments or loan).

In option (A), 'Incentives' means a payment or concession to stimulate greater output or investment.

So, 'Incentives' is the correct word for blank (4).

Hence, the correct option is (A).

55. The passage is about 'Indian economy before 1991'.

Let us refer to this line from the passage, "Following a balance of payments crisis in 1991, however, a number of structural ___(5)___ were implemented".

From the above sentence, we get to know due to a high number of non-performing loans, in 1991, a number of structural changes brought.

In option (E), 'Reforms' means make changes in (something, especially an institution or practise) in order to improve it.

So, 'Reforms' is the correct word for blank (5).

Hence, the correct option is (E).

56. Informative is the correct tone of the passage.

The whole passage is about mosquitoes, diseases they could carry, genes, etc. and it gives you a sense that the author is giving details with facts and figure so we can easily conclude that the tone of the passage is 'Informative'.

Hence, the correct option is (A).

57. Malarial fever is caused by a virus transmitted to humans primarily by the bite of Aedes aegypti mosquitoes.- is the correct option

After going through the passage we can conclude that the above statement is false.

Hence, the correct option is (A).

58. Transcription means an act, process, of copying something.

Copy means a thing made to be similar or identical to another.

Thus, the word 'copy' is the synonym of the word 'transcription'.

Hence, the correct option is (B).

59. Sustained means maintained at length without interruption or weakening.

Sporadic means occurring occasionally, singly, or in irregular or random instances.

Thus, 'sporadic' is the correct antonym of the given word 'sustained'.

Hence, the correct option is (B).

60. Here we need a word that means to establish the identity of, thus 'identify' is the most suitable word.

Identify means establish or indicate who or what (someone or something) is.

Hence, the correct option is (C).

61. Follow the BODMAS rule according to the table given below:

B	Brackets in order ( ), { }, [ ]	ब्रेकट ( ), {}, [ ] क्रम
O	Of	का
D	Division (÷)	विभाजन (÷)
M	Multiplication (×)	गुणा (×)
A	Addition (+)	जोड़ (+)
S	Subtraction (-)	घटाव (-)

Given,

$$(4698 - 3625 - 857) = ?^3 - 42 - \sqrt{7225}$$

$$\Rightarrow 4698 - 4482 = ?^3 - 42 - 85$$

$$\Rightarrow 216 = ?^3 - 127$$

$$\Rightarrow ?^3 = 216 + 127$$

$$\Rightarrow ?^3 = 343$$

$$\Rightarrow ? = 7$$

Hence, the correct option is (C).

62. Follow the BODMAS rule according to the table given below:

B	Brackets in order ( ), { }, [ ]	ब्रेकट ( ), {}, [ ] क्रम
O	Of	का
D	Division (÷)	विभाजन (÷)
M	Multiplication (×)	गुणा (×)
A	Addition (+)	जोड़ (+)
S	Subtraction (-)	घटाव (-)

Given,

$$\left(\frac{?}{37}\right) = \left(\frac{15}{?}\right) \times \left(\frac{1}{2145}\right) \times \left(\frac{1}{9.25}\right) \times 676 \times 143$$

$$\Rightarrow ?^2 = \left(37 \times 15 \times 676 \times 143 \times \frac{1}{2145} \times \frac{1}{9.25}\right)$$

$$\Rightarrow ?^2 = \left(37 \times 15 \times 676 \times \frac{143}{2145} \times \frac{1}{9.25}\right)$$

$$\Rightarrow ?^2 = \left(37 \times 15 \times 676 \times \frac{1}{15} \times \frac{1}{9.25}\right)$$

$$\Rightarrow ?^2 = \left(37 \times 676 \times \frac{1}{9.25}\right)$$

$$\Rightarrow ?^2 = 4 \times 676$$

$$\Rightarrow ? = \sqrt{4 \times 676}$$

$$\Rightarrow ? = \sqrt{4} \times \sqrt{676}$$

$$\Rightarrow ? = 2 \times 26$$

$$\Rightarrow ? = 52$$

Hence, the correct option is (E).

63. Follow the BODMAS rule according to the table given below:

B	Brackets in order ( ), { }, [ ]	ब्रेकट ( ), {}, [ ] क्रम
O	Of	का
D	Division (÷)	विभाजन (÷)
M	Multiplication (×)	गुणा (×)
A	Addition (+)	जोड़ (+)
S	Subtraction (-)	घटाव (-)

Given,

$$\sqrt{441} \times (985.35 - 969.35) = ?^{\frac{1}{2}} + 305$$

$$\Rightarrow 21 \times 16 = ?^{\frac{1}{2}} + 305$$

$$\Rightarrow 336 = ?^{\frac{1}{2}} + 305$$

$$\Rightarrow 336 - 305 = ?^{\frac{1}{2}}$$

$$\Rightarrow ?^{\frac{1}{2}} = 31$$

$$\Rightarrow ? = 31^2$$

$$\Rightarrow ? = 961$$

Hence, the correct option is (D).

64. Follow the BODMAS rule according to the table given below:

B	Brackets in order ( ), { }, [ ]	ब्रेकट ( ), {}, [ ] क्रम
O	Of	का
D	Division (÷)	विभाजन (÷)
M	Multiplication (×)	गुणा (×)
A	Addition (+)	जोड़ (+)
S	Subtraction (-)	घटाव (-)

Given,

$$\left[\frac{3}{2} + \frac{1}{2}\left\{\frac{3}{4} - \frac{1}{2}\left(\frac{7}{8} - \frac{3}{4}\right)\right\}\right] = ?$$

$$\Rightarrow ? = \left[\frac{3}{2} + \frac{1}{2}\left\{\frac{3}{4} - \frac{1}{2}\left(\frac{7-6}{8}\right)\right\}\right]$$

$$\Rightarrow ? = \left[\frac{3}{2} + \frac{1}{2}\left\{\frac{3}{4} - \frac{1}{2}\left(\frac{1}{8}\right)\right\}\right]$$

$$\Rightarrow ? = \left[\frac{3}{2} + \frac{1}{2}\left\{\frac{3}{4} - \frac{1}{16}\right\}\right]$$

$$\Rightarrow ? = \left[\frac{3}{2} + \frac{1}{2}\left\{\frac{12-1}{16}\right\}\right]$$

$$\Rightarrow ? = \left[\frac{3}{2} + \frac{1}{2}\left\{\frac{11}{16}\right\}\right]$$

$$\Rightarrow ? = \frac{3}{2} + \frac{11}{32}$$

$$\Rightarrow ? = \frac{48+11}{32}$$

$$\Rightarrow ? = \frac{59}{32}$$

Hence, the correct option is (B).

65. Follow the BODMAS rule according to the table given below:

B	Brackets in order ( ), { }, [ ]	ब्रेकट ( ), {}, [ ] क्रम
O	Of	का
D	Division (÷)	विभाजन (÷)
M	Multiplication (×)	गुणा (×)
A	Addition (+)	जोड़ (+)
S	Subtraction (-)	घटाव (-)

Given,

$$\left(4 + 3\sqrt{2}\right)^2 - \left(3 + 2\sqrt{2}\right)^2$$

We know that,

$$(a+b)^2 = a^2 + b^2 + 2ab$$

Now, apply above relation in given equation, we get,

$$\Rightarrow ? = \left[(4)^2 + (3\sqrt{2})^2 + 2\times4\times3\sqrt{2}\right] - \left[(3)^2 + (2\sqrt{2})^2 + 2\times3\times2\sqrt{2}\right]$$

$$\Rightarrow ? = \left(16 + 9 \times 2 + 8 \times 3\sqrt{2}\right) - \left(9 + 4 \times 2 + 6 \times 2\sqrt{2}\right)$$

$$\Rightarrow ? = \left(16 + 18 + 24\sqrt{2}\right) - \left(9 + 8 + 12\sqrt{2}\right)$$

$$\Rightarrow ? = \left(34 + 24\sqrt{2}\right) - \left(17 + 12\sqrt{2}\right)$$

$$\Rightarrow ? = 34 + 24\sqrt{2} - 17 - 12\sqrt{2}$$

$$\Rightarrow ? = 34 - 17 + 24\sqrt{2} - 12\sqrt{2}$$

$$\Rightarrow ? = 17 + 12\sqrt{2}$$

Hence, the correct option is (E).

66. Given:

A invests= Rs. 500

B invests= Rs. M

After 8 months, A added Rs. 200 to his investment, and B removes Rs.100 from his investment.

Difference between the profit shares of B and A after a year = Rs. 720.

Total profit = Rs. 3440.

Calculations:

Total investment of A = 500 × 8 + 700 × 4 = Rs. 6800

Total investment of B = M × 8 + (M – 100) × 4 = Rs. (12M – 400)

Ratio of their profit shares = 6800 : (12M – 400)=1700 : (3M – 100)

According to the question,

$$\frac{(3M-100-1700)}{(1700+3M-100)} \times 3440 = 720$$

$$\Rightarrow M = 900$$

Required ratio = 500 : 900 = 5 : 9

∴ The ratio between the initial investment of A and B is 5 : 9.

Hence, the correct option is (D).

67. Let Principal = P, Rate = R% per annum, Time = N years

$$\text{Simple Interest} = \frac{(P\times N\times R)}{100}$$

Given,

$$\Rightarrow 1395 = P\left(1 + \frac{10}{100}\right)^3 - P - \frac{(P\times10\times3)}{100}$$

$$\Rightarrow 1395 = 0.331P - 0.3P$$

$$\Rightarrow P = 45000$$

The principal amount is Rs. 45000.

Given,

Simple Interest

$$= \frac{(45000 \times 4 \times 20)}{100}$$

$$= 36000$$

Hence, the correct option is (A).

68. Let Principal = P, Rate = R% per annum, Time = N years

Simple Interest $= \dfrac{(P \times N \times R)}{100}$

Given,

P = 35000, N = 4, R = 10

$\Rightarrow$ Simple interest $= \dfrac{(35000 \times 4 \times 10)}{100}$ = Rs. 14000

$\Rightarrow$ Total amount = 35000 + 14000 = Rs. 49000

Given,

$$P = 35000 \times \frac{6}{7} = \text{Rs. } 30000$$

$\Rightarrow$ Simple Interest $= \dfrac{(30000 \times 4 \times 10)}{100}$ = Rs. 12000

$\Rightarrow$ Total amount = 30000 + 12000 + 5000 = Rs. 47000

$\Rightarrow$ Total loss Raj has = 14000 - 12000 = Rs. 2000

Hence, the correct option is (D).

69. Given,

The percentage distribution of the JIO users in Bihar = 22%

The total number of JIO users in Bihar = 22% of 60000000

$$= 60000000 \times \frac{22}{100}$$

= 13200000

The total number of airtel users in Bihar = 13200000 – 2500000

= 10700000

Hence, the correct option is (A).

70. Given,

The percentage distribution of the JIO users in Delhi = 28%

The percentage distribution of the Idea users in Delhi = 15%

The total number of JIO users in Delhi = 28% of 6 crores

$$= \frac{28 \times 6}{100} \text{ crores}$$

= 1.68 crores

The total number of Idea users in Delhi = 15% of 2.5 crores

$$= \frac{15 \times 2.5}{100} \text{ crores}$$

= 0.375 crores

The required percentage $= \dfrac{(1.68 - 0.375) \times 100}{0.375}$

= 348

Hence, the correct option is (C).

71. Given,

The percentage distribution of the JIO users in Delhi = 28%

The percentage distribution of the JIO users in Kerala = 16%

The percentage distribution of the JIO users in UP = 18%

The percentage distribution of the JIO users in Bihar = 22%

The sum of the JIO users in Delhi and Kerala together = (28 + 16)% of 6 crores

= 44% of 6 crores

The sum of the JIO users in UP and Bihar together = (18 + 22)% of 6 crores

= 40% of 6 crores

The required difference = (44 – 40)% of 6 crores

= 4% of 6 crores

$$= \frac{4}{100} \times 6 \text{ crores}$$

= 0.24 crores

= 2400000

Hence, the correct option is (A).

72. Given,

The percentage distribution of the JIO users in Karnataka = 16%

The percentage distribution of the JIO users in Bihar = 22%

The number of JIO users in Karnataka = 16% of 6 crores

The number of JIO users in Bihar = 22% of 6 crores

The required percentage $= \dfrac{(22 - 16) \times 100}{22}$

$$= \frac{600}{22}$$

= Approximately 27.27%

Hence, the correct option is (C).

73. Let the total number of JIO users in Bihar $= 11x$

The total number of Airtel users in Kerala $= 5x$

Given,

The percentage distribution of the JIO users in Bihar = 22%

The percentage distribution of the JIO users in Delhi = 28%

Total number of users of the JIO users in five different states = 6 crores

Then,

$11x = 22\%$ of 6 crores

$\Rightarrow 11x = 1.32$ crores

$\Rightarrow x = 0.12$ crores

Therefore, the total number of Airtel users in Kerala = 5x

$= 5 \times 0.12 = 0.6$ crores

The total number of JIO users in Delhi = 28% of 6 crores

$= \dfrac{28 \times 6}{100}$ crores

= 1.68 crores

The required $\% = \dfrac{(1.68 - 0.6) \times 100}{1.68}$

= 64.29%

Hence, the correct option is (D).

74. Given: A train moving $\dfrac{3}{4}$ of it's original speed after an accident.

Formula used:

$$\text{Speed} = \dfrac{Distance}{time}$$

Calculations:

Let the speed of train be 'x' and time taken to reach the destination is 't'.

Distance = Speed × time = xt

After accident, speed = $\dfrac{3}{4x}$

After accident, time = $\left(t + \dfrac{1}{4}\right)$hr

As distance is same,

$xt = \dfrac{3}{4x} \times \left(t + \dfrac{1}{4}\right)$

$\Rightarrow \dfrac{xt}{4} = \dfrac{3}{16x}$

$\Rightarrow t = \dfrac{3}{4}$ hours

$\Rightarrow t = \dfrac{3}{4} \times 60 = 45$ min.

∴ The usual time taken by train to reach the destination is 45 min.

Hence, the correct option is (C).

75. Given:

Total number of subjects = 5

The incorrect ratio = 13:10

Increase in marks = 27

Total marks increase = 5 × 27

= 135

Let the original number be ab and xy.

Their reverse order is ba and yx.

As the rest of the numbers remain the same the increase is only in the two numbers

So,

ba + yx – ab – xy = 135

$\Rightarrow$ 10b + a + 10y + x – (10a + b + 10x + y) = 135

$\Rightarrow$ 9 (b – a) + 9 (y – x) = 135

$\Rightarrow$ (b – a) + (y – x) = 15

The sum of the difference of the digits of the two numbers is 15.

Multiplying both 13 and 10 by a number like 5, 6, 7, 8, etc we will get:

13 × 7 = 91

10 × 7 = 70

91, 70 as the only combination where the sum of the difference of digits is 15 (9 – 1 + 7 – 0)

The original numbers are 19 and 07 and their sum = 19 + 7

= 26

Hence, the correct option is (D).

76. Let the man's usual speed be x km/hr and the distance to be covered = y km.

We know that,

$$Time = \dfrac{Distance}{Speed}$$

So,

His usual time is $\left(\dfrac{y}{x}\right)$ hours.

When his speed is $\dfrac{5}{3}$ his usual speed the time taken is $\left(\dfrac{3y}{5x}\right)$ hours

∵ Time is inversely proportional to speed when distance is constant.

Now, $\left(\dfrac{y}{x}\right) + \dfrac{20}{60} = \left(\dfrac{3y}{5x}\right)$

$\Rightarrow \left(\dfrac{y}{x} - \dfrac{3y}{5x}\right) = \dfrac{20}{60}$

$\Rightarrow \dfrac{(5y - 3y)}{5x} = \dfrac{1}{3}$

$\Rightarrow \dfrac{2y}{5x} = \dfrac{1}{3}$

$\Rightarrow \dfrac{y}{x} = \dfrac{5}{6}$

So, $\dfrac{5}{6}$ hour change in minutes = $\left(\dfrac{5}{6}\right) \times 60$

His usual time is 50 minutes.

Hence, the correct option is (B).

77. From equation I) we get,

$$3x^2 + 19x + 20 = 0$$

$$\Rightarrow 3x^2 + 15x + 4x + 20 = 0$$

$$\Rightarrow 3x(x + 5) + 4(x + 5) + 20 = 0$$

$$\Rightarrow (x + 5)(3x + 4) = 0$$

$$\therefore x = -5, -\frac{4}{3}$$

From equation II) we get,

$$6y^2 + 19y + 15 = 0$$

$$\Rightarrow 6y^2 + 10y + 9y + 15 = 0$$

$$\Rightarrow 2y(3y + 5) + 3(3y + 5) = 0$$

$$\Rightarrow (2y + 3)(3y + 5) = 0$$

$$\therefore y = -\frac{3}{2}, -\frac{5}{3}$$

∴ The relationship between x and y cannot be established.

Hence, the correct option is (E).

78. From equation I) we get,

$x^2 = 256$

$x = + 16, - 16$

From equation II) we get,

$y^2 + 18y + 17$

$\Rightarrow y^2 + 17y + y + 17$

$\Rightarrow y (y + 17) + 1(y + 17)$

$\Rightarrow (y + 17) (y + 1)$

$\therefore y = -17, - 1$

∴ x = y or the relationship between x and y cannot be established.

Hence, the correct option is (E).

79. From equation I) we get,

$x^2 - 15x + 56$

$\Rightarrow x^2 - 7x - 8x + 56$

$\Rightarrow x (x - 7) - 8(x - 7)$

$\Rightarrow (x - 7)(x - 8)$

$x = 7, 8$

From equation II) we get,

$y^2 + 17y + 72$

$\Rightarrow y^2 + 8y + 9Y + 72$

$\Rightarrow y (y + 8) + 9(y + 8)$

$\Rightarrow (y + 8) (y + 9)$

$\therefore y = -8, -9$

Comparison between x and y:

Value of x	Value of y	Relation
7	-8	x > y
7	-9	x > y
8	-8	x > y
8	-9	x > y

∴ x > y

Hence, the correct option is (A).

80. Lets speed of boat in still water and speed of current be x and y respectively:

Upstream speed of boat = (x-y)

Downstream speed of boat = (x+y)

According to the question,

Equating, Time taken by downstream speed = Time taken by upstream speed

$$\frac{D}{(x+y)} = \frac{\frac{D}{2}}{(x-y)}$$

$$\Rightarrow 2x - 2y = x + y$$

$$\Rightarrow x = 3y$$

First part $= 240 \times \dfrac{12}{40}$

$= 72 \; km$

Second part $= 240 \times \dfrac{13}{40}$

$= 78 \; km$

Third part $= 240 \times \dfrac{15}{40}$

$= 90 \; km$

Now, putting the value,

$$\frac{72}{x+y} + \frac{78}{x+y} + \frac{90}{x+y} = 19.15$$

$$\Rightarrow \frac{72}{3y+y} + \frac{78}{3y\times\frac{3}{4}+y} + \frac{90}{\frac{3y}{2}+y} = 19.5$$

$$\Rightarrow \frac{4680+6240+9360}{260y} = 19.5$$

$$\Rightarrow y = \frac{20280}{260\times19.5}$$

$$\Rightarrow y = 4 \; km/hr$$

Now putting the value of x

Boat usual speed $x = 3y$

$= 3 \times 4$

$= 12 \ km/hr$

Hence, the correct option is (A).

81. Given series:

2, 8, 28, 102, 432, ?

The pattern is:

2 × 1 + 6 = 8

8 × 2 + 12 = 28

28 × 3 + 18 = 102

102 × 4 + 24 = 432

432 × 5 + 30 = 2190

So, the missing number is 2190.

Hence, the correct option is (C).

82. Given series:

6, 16, 44, 126, 370, ?

The pattern is:

6 × 3 − 2 = 16

16 × 3 − 4 = 44

44 × 3 − 6 = 126

126 × 3 − 8 = 370

370 × 3 − 10 =1100

So, the missing number is 1100.

Hence, the correct option is (A)

83. Given series:

51, 77, 175, 250, 279, ?

The pattern is:

$$51 + (5^2 + 1^2) = 77$$

$$77 + (7^2 + 7^2) = 175$$

$$175 + (1^2 + 7^2 + 5^2) = 250$$

$$250 + (2^2 + 5^2 + 0^2) = 279$$

$$279 + (2^2 + 7^2 + 9^2) = 413$$

So, the missing number is 413.

Hence, the correct option is (B).

84. Given series:

2, 2, 5, 15.5, ?, 267.125

The pattern is:

2 × 0.5 + 1 = 2

2 × 1.5 + 2 = 5

5 × 2.5 + 3 = 15.5

15.5 × 3.5 + 4 = 58.25

58.25 × 4.5 + 5 = 267.125

So, the missing number is 58.25.

Hence, the correct option is (A).

85. Given series:

219, 223, 232, 248, ?

The pattern is:

$$219 + (1^2 + 1 + 2) = 223$$

$$223 + (2^2 + 2 + 3) = 232$$

$$232 + (3^2 + 3 + 4) = 248$$

$$248 + (4^2 + 4 + 5) = 273$$

So, the missing number is 273.

Hence, the correct option is (D).

86. Given,

Number of people = 30

A handshake needs 2 people. So total ways of two people shaking hands with each other = $^{30}C_2$

We know that,

$$^nC_r = \frac{n!}{r!(n-r)!}$$

where n = 30 and r = 2

Therefore,

$$^{30}C_2 = \frac{30!}{2!(30-2)!}$$

$$= \frac{30×29×28!}{2×1×28!}$$

$$= \frac{30×29}{2}$$

$$= 435$$

Hence, the correct option is (B).

87. Let breath be x cm and length be y cm

⇒ Perimeter = 2(length + breadth)

⇒ 2(x + y) = 44

⇒ x + y = 22

⇒ x = 22 − y   ----(1)

Now,

⇒ Area = length × breadth

⇒ xy = 120

⇒ y(22 − y) = 120 (∵ from equation 1)

⇒ 22y − y² = 120

$\Rightarrow y^2 - 22y + 120 = 0$

$\Rightarrow y = 12, 10$

Now, for y = 12

$\Rightarrow x = 22 - 12 = 10$

As, length > breadth

∴ Length of rectangle is 12 cm

Hence, the correct option is (D).

88. Given:

Pipe P can fill the tank = 8 hours

Pipe Q can fill the tank = 10 hours

We know that,

$$\text{Efficiency} = \frac{\text{Total capacity}}{\text{Time}}$$

Total capacity = LCM = 40

Pipe	Time	Total capacity	Efficiency
P	8 hours	40	$\frac{40}{8} = 5$
Q	10 hours	40	$\frac{40}{10} = 4$

First hours P comes fill tank = 5

Second Q comes fill the tank = 4

Tank fill in 2 hours = 5 + 4 = 9

Tank fill in 8 hours = 9 × 4 = 36

Remaining = 40 – 36 = 4

Now, P comes and fill the remaining part of the tank $= \frac{4}{5} = 0.8$ hours

Total time = 8 + 0.8 = 8.8 hours

∴ Total time taken by pipes to fill the tank alternately is 8.8 hours.

Hence, the correct option is (A).

89. Given,

Number between 107 to 1006 $= 900$

Number of possible outcomes $= n(S) = 900$

Numbers from 107 to 1006 divisible by 11 and 37 both $= \{407, 814\}$

$= 2$

Numbers on cards not divisible by both 11 and $37 = 900 - 2$

$= 898$

∴ Probability $= \dfrac{n(\text{Favourable Events})}{n(\text{Possible outcomes})}$

$= \dfrac{898}{900}$

$= 0.998$

Hence, the correct option is (A).

90. Given:

The cost price of a set of 2 pants + 4 shirts or 1 pant + 6 shirts is Rs. 5,600. A shopkeeper decided to sell them separately. He sells 10 shirts for Rs. 6,000.

Cost price of a set of 2 pants + 4 shirts = cost price of a set of 1 pant + 6 shirt

1 pant = 2 shirt

$\Rightarrow$ 2 pants + 4 shirt = 4 shirt + 4 shirt = 8 shirt

Cost price of 8 shirt = Rs. 5600

Cost price of one shirt = Rs. 700

Selling price of 10 shirt = Rs. 6000

Selling price of one shirt = Rs. 600

Loss = Rs. (700 - 600) = Rs. 100

∴ Loss occurred per shirt = Rs. 100

Hence, the correct option is (D).

Reasoning Ability

Ques (1-5):Direction: Study the following information carefully and answer the question given below.

Eight boxes are kept one above another to make up a stack. The topmost box is numbered as 8 while the bottommost box is numbered as 1. Each box is filled with different colours: Blue, Yellow, Black, Pink, Green, Red and Purple, But not necessarily in the same order. One of the boxes in the arrangement is empty.

Green colour box is immediately above Red colour box. Red colour box is an even number box below box number 5. Three boxes are kept between Red colour box and Yellow colour box. Two boxes are kept between Pink colour box and Purple colour box. Purple Coloured box is not kept at the top. Blue colour box is immediately below Pink colour box. One of the boxes above box number 5 is empty. Black colour box is an odd number box.

Q.1 Which of the following condition is true?

A. Red - 2nd   **B.** Yellow - 8th

C. Black - 4th   **D.** Purple - 5th

E. None of these

Q.2 How many boxes are there between Yellow colour box and Pink colour box?

A. 6   **B.** 3

C. 5   **D.** 4

E. None of these

Q.3 Which colour box is at the bottom?

A. Black   **B.** Red

C. Blue   **D.** Pink

E. None of these

Q.4 Which colour is filled in box number 5?

A. Purple   **B.** Pink

C. Green   **D.** Blue

E. None of these

Q.5 Which number box is empty?

A. 8   **B.** 7

C. 6   **D.** 5

E. None of these

Ques (6-8):Direction: Study the information given below carefully and answer the question that follow.

Anamika starts at her house lying 5 km towards the east from the three-way junction. Now she moves 10 km towards north and reaches tuition. After her tuition she then moves 10 km towards the west to reaches her friend's house, and after that both finally moves 5 km towards the south to reach the restaurant.

Q.6 In which direction is restaurant with respect to three way junction?

A. South   **B.** North

C. North-east   **D.** North-west

E. South-west

Q.7 In what direction is tuition with respect to friend's house?

A. North   **B.** East

C. South   **D.** North East

E. South East

Q.8 What is the shortest distance between three way junction and friend's house?

A. 13 km   **B.** 12 km   **C.** 15 km   **D.** 10 km

E. $5\sqrt{5}$ km

Ques (9-10):Direction: Read the following information carefully and answer the question that follow:

A, B, C, D, E, F, and H are family members related to each other. A is the father of D who is the brother of F. E is the husband of H. F is the sister of E. B is the son of D and husband of C.

Q.9 Who is the grandson of A?

A. D   **B.** F   **C.** E   **D.** C

E. B

Q.10 How is H related to F?

A. Sister-in-law   **B.** Sister

C. Mother   **D.** Mother-in-law

E. Aunt

Ques (11-13):Direction: Study the following information carefully and answer the given questions.

In a certain code language

'he si fi ka' means 'his health is affected',

'si wi ni he' means 'health is wealth indeed',

'pi si re fe' means 'he is super fit',

'ka li hi wi ' means 'his uncle has wealth'.

Q.11 Which of the following means 'wealth' in that code language?

A. si   **B.** wi   **C.** ni   **D.** he

E. li

Q.12 Code 'fi' is for which word in the given language?

A. wealth   **B.** health   **C.** is   **D.** affected

E. fit

Q.13 What would be the code for 'his wealth is affected indeed'?

A. ka wi si fi ni   **B.** hi wi fi si ni

C. ka he si fi ni   **D.** ka re fe ni wi

E. ka wi si pi re

Ques (14-18):Direction: Read the information carefully and answer the questions given below.

Eight people Amar, Brijesh, Pinky, Deep, Eshwar, Nancy, Gurkamal and Harsh are sitting around a circular table. All are facing towards the center but not necessarily in the same order.

Nancy is third to the right of Pinky and second to the left of Harsh. Deep is not an immediate neighbour of Pinky or Harsh. Eshwar is to the immediate right of Amar, who is second to the right of Gurkamal.

Q.14 Who is second to the left of Pinky?

A.   Amar

B.   Eshwar

C.   Brijesh

D.   Deep

E.   Either Amar or Deep

Q.15 Who is to the immediate right of Pinky?

A. Amar

B. Brijesh

C. Brijesh or Deep

D. Deep

E. Eshwar

Q.16 Which of the following pair of persons has the first person sitting to the right of the second person?

A.   Pinky and Brijesh

B.   Amar and Eshwar

C.   Nancy and Gurkamal

D.   Harsh and Amar

E.   Deep and Brijesh

Q.17 Who sits between Gurkamal and Deep?

A. Harsh

B. Deep

C. Nancy

D. Brijesh

E. None of these

Q.18 Which of the following is the correct position of Brijesh with respect to Harsh?

I. Second to the right

II. Fourth to the right

III. Fourth to the left

IV. Second to the left

A. Only I

B. Only II

C. Only III

D. Both II and III

E. None of these

Ques (19-22):Direction: Study the following information carefully to answer the given question.

M 1 E & D 2 G 9 $ F @ 4 N Z W © 8 C Y A * 6

Q.19 If all the numbers in the above arrangement are dropped, then which of the following will be the tenth from the right end?

A. $

B. D

C. F

D. Z

E. None of these

Q.20 Four of following five are alike in a certain way based on their positions in the above arrangement and so form a group. Which is the one that does not belong to that group?

A. ME2

B. G$4

C. NWC

D. YA6

E. None of these

Q.21 How many letters are there between the fourth element from the left and the eleventh element from the right end of the given arrangement?

A. None

B. One

C. Two

D. Three

E. More than three

Q.22 Which of the following is the fifth to the left of the eleventh element from the right end of the above arrangement?

A. H

B. G

C. %

D. D

E. None of these

Q.23 In a row of children, Deepa is 9th from the left and Vijay is 13th from the right. When these two interchange their positions, Deepa becomes 17th from the left. Tell where will Vijay be from the right?

A. 9th   **B.** 21st   **C.** 20th   **D.** 7th

E. 14th

Q.24 In a row of students, Ramesh is ninth from the left and Suman is sixth from the right. When Ramesh and Suman interchange their places, Ramesh becomes fifteenth from the left. Tell what will be the position of Suman from the right after the interchange?

A. 6th   **B.** 13th   **C.** 15th   **D.** 12th

E. 14th

Q.25 Study the following information and answer the question based on it.

(A) 'Srikanth' is younger than Neelima.

(B) Pratima is taller than Srikant.

(C) Subhash is taller than Neelima but shorter than Hembrum.

(D) 'Nilima' is taller than Pratima.

If all of them are made to stand in a row in the order of their height, then who among them will be exactly in the middle of the row?

A. Shrikant

B. Nilima

C. Pratima

D. Hembram

E. Subhash

Q.26 If in the word 'FAVOURITE' all the consonants are arranged on the left in reversed alphabetical order after that on the right of these consonants all the vowels are arranged in alphabetical order then how many letters are there in alphabetical series between third letter from right end and fourth letter from left end?

A. 2   **B.** 5   **C.** 6   **D.** 8

E. 9

Ques (27-29):Directions: In the question, three statements are given, followed by three conclusions. You have to consider the statements to be true even if they seem to be at variance from commonly known facts. You have to decide which of the given

conclusions, if any, follows from the given statements and select the appropriate option.

Q.27 Statements:

1. Some P are D.

2. All C are A.

3. No P is A.

Conclusions:

I. No C is P.

II. No C is D.

III. Some A are definitely D.

A. Only I follows

B. Only I, II, III follows

C. Only II, III follows

D. Only I, III follows

E. No conclusion follows

Q.28 Statements:

1. All C are X.

2. All X are P.

3. No Q is C.

Conclusions:

I. Some X are not Q.

II. Some Q may be both X and P.

III. Some P are not Q.

A. Only I follows

B. Only I, II, III follows

C. Only II, III follows

D. Only I, III follows

E. No conclusion follows

Q.29 Statements:

1. No F is E.

2. No E is C.

3. No Y is E.

Conclusions:

I. Some F are C.

II. Some Y are F.

III. Some C are Y.

A. Only I, II follows

B. Only I, II, III follows

C. Only II, III follows

D. Only III follows

E. No conclusion follows

Q.30 Direction: In the question below given two statements followed by two conclusions numbered I, and II. you have to take the given statements to be true even if they seem to be at variance with commonly known facts. Read all the conclusions and then decide which of the given conclusions logically follows from the given statements disregarding commonly known facts.

Statements:

All boys are student.

No student is a girl.

Conclusion:

I. No boy is a girl.

II. It is a possibility that all students are boys.

A. Only conclusion I follows

B. Only conclusion II follows

C. Both I and II follows

D. Either I or II follows

E. None follows

English Language

Ques (31-35):Direction: Read the passage given below carefully and then answer the following questions.

Russia _______ (1) its space satellite Arktika-M on Sunday on a mission to monitor the climate and environment in the Arctic amid a push by the Kremlin to expand the country's activities in the region.

The Arctic has _______(2) more than twice as fast as the global average over the last three decades and Moscow is seeking to develop the energy-rich region, investing in the Northern Sea Route for shipping across its long northern flank as the ice melts.

The satellite _______ (3) reached its intended orbit after being launched from Kazakhstan's Baikonur cosmodrome by a Soyuz rocket, Dmitry Rogozin, the head of Russia's Roscosmos space agency, said in a post on Twitter.

Russia plans to send up a second satellite in 2023 and, combined, the two will offer round-the-clock, all-weather _______ (4) of the Arctic Ocean and the surface of the Earth, Roscosmos said.

"There is also an element of data nationalism that is feeding into all this. Countries, especially those that see themselves as _______(5) powers, want to be able to rely on their own satellites and data to inform their activities, whether commercial or military in nature," she said.

Q.31 Which of the following is the most appropriate option for blank 1?

A. crashed **B.** taxied **C.** sprung **D.** flew

E. launched

Q.32 Which of the following is the most appropriate option for blank 2?

A. frozen **B.** grappled

C. stagnated **D.** warmed

E. cooled

Q.33 Which of the following is the most appropriate option for blank 3?

A. randomly **B.** mistakenly

C. successfully **D.** unsuccessfully

E. unfortunately

Q.34 Which of the following is the most appropriate option for blank 4?

A. Morphing **B.** Monitoring

C. Altering **D.** Suffocating

E. Pleasing

Q.35 Which of the following is the most appropriate option for blank 5?

A. space **B.** rocket
C. flying **D.** NASA
E. monitoring

Ques (36-40):Directions: In the following questions, some part of the sentence is underlined. Which of the options given below the sentence should replace the part underlined to make the sentence grammatically correct? If the sentence is correct as it is given then choose option E 'No Correction required' as the answer.

Q.36 In quick time she got acquainted with the new environment.

A. In enough time
B. In small time
C. On time only
D. in no time
E. No correction required

Q.37 It was quite clear that the athlete can be able to improve upon his own record.

A. will be able to
B. should be able to
C. would be able to
D. be able
E. No correction required

Q.38 He is a very lazy person and hate doing any kind of work.

A. hated doing
B. hate does
C. hates do
D. hates doing
E. No correction required

Q.39 She opened the door as she know the person very well and had spent quite a few mornings with him.

A. as she knows
B. as she was knowing
C. as she knew
D. as she knowing
E. No correction required

Q.40 Usha could not thinking of traveling without her car and feared the crowd.

A. could not think
B. cannot thinking
C. cannot think
D. could not thinks
E. No correction required

Ques (41-45):Direction: In the following question, part(s) of the sentence may have an error. Find out which part of the sentence has an error and mark the remaining, i.e., the errorless combination as your answer.

Q.41 Formulation of schemes (A)/ for betterment from the (B)/ youth is one of the prime (C)/ objectives of the mayor. (D)

A. ACD **B.** ABC **C.** BCD **D.** BD
E. No Error

Q.42 Hardly had I (A)/ finished my Tiffin than (B)/ the bell rang signifying (C)/ the end of recess. (D)

A. ABC **B.** ABD **C.** BCD **D.** ACD
E. No Error

Q.43 As soon as (A)/ I saw the bananas that (B)/ I knew the monkey (C)/ was hiding in the room. (D)

A. ABC **B.** ACD **C.** ABD **D.** BCD
E. No Error

Q.44 Neither the choreographer/(1) nor the dancers/(2) are following/(3) the steps properly./(4) No error /(5)

A. 1 **B.** 2 **C.** 3 **D.** 4
E. 5

Q.45 Choose the statement from the given options that is grammatically and contextually correct.

A. The secretary had appointment the same person for the post.
B. Even as though he knew they were safe, he couldn't stop fighting.
C. He has every attribute of a dog except loyalty.
D. The council would have been approve the decision.
E. The domain owner may currently been creating quite a spectacle.

Ques (46-50):Direction: Read the passage given below and then answer the questions given below the passage. Some words may be highlighted for your attention. Read carefully.

The Indian pharma industry is flourishing overseas, touching almost every part of the world. With low cost, speed and high-quality advantage, India is gearing up to become the hub for contract research and manufacturing. Having a competitive edge is, one thing and maintaining it is another. Canada provides tax benefits up to 6 percent for research carried out within the country. It also protects the intellectual property rights of the original developers Others like Korea and China (without a large pool of scientists) make up by facilitating foreign research in every conceivable way. India does not do any of this and faces many hurdles - diseases that it has been inflicted with since independence like Malaria and TB while Indian companies have only focused on reverse engineering blockbuster drugs from MNCs, overseas scientists have displayed little interest in researching sub-continent specific diseases (like malaria and TB) as there are more profits and public interest in lifestyle drugs such as obesity which in turn fund their research. In the interest of Indian research industry, a decision must be taken quickly on the implementation of data protection laws.

India is one of the few countries where data exclusivity provisions are not prevalent. Data protection is a contentious issue, wholly debated by the government and the industry. A pharma company wishing to market a drug is required to submit data to the drug controller to show that the drug is both effective and safe. The first (originator) company that makes the application for marketing approval has to submit its data relating to the clinical trials to the drug controller, who once satisfied that the drug is safe and effective will register it. Another drug company wishing to market the same drug only requires to show a bio equivalence company. Thus, as per the prevailing laws, the regulator in India can rely on an innovator's data to approve the competitor's product. While the system, in general, is responsible for maintaining the necessary secrecy, it is not accountable for the same—the competitor gets an unfair advantage over the innovator even when he is clandestinely abusing an innovator's intellectual property. Consequently, research-based pharma companies are being forced to undertake vital clinical trials abroad. Huge expenditures are incurred overseas, draining precious foreign exchange when this could be done at home at a fraction of the cost.

Q.46 Which of the following statements is NOT true in reference to the passage?

A. Countries like Canada and Korea have an edge over India when it comes to the pharmaceutical industry.

B. The Indian Pharma Industry has a propensity to promote costlier and less required drugs.

C. Drug trials are often carried out overseas in spite of the huge expenditure.

D. The drug controller has the power to accept or reject a new drug based on data submitted.

E. Intellectual property rights are valued highly by the Indian government.

Q.47 According to the passage, what kind of diseases are the overseas scientists not interested in studying?

A. Pediatric diseases like sickle cell disease

B. Skin diseases like melanoma

C. Lung diseases like cystic fibrosis

D. Sub-continent specific diseases like TB and Malaria

E. Renal diseases like kidney failure

Q.48 Which of the following is the most SIMILAR in meaning to the given word?

PREVAILING

A. Fashionable **B.** Regular

C. Current **D.** Limited

E. Uncommon

Q.49 Why does Canada have a competitive edge over India when it comes to pharma industry?

A. Canada has a competitive edge over India when it comes to pharma Industry as it provides a tax benefit for related research carried out within the country.

B. Canada has a competitive edge over India when it comes to pharma Industry because not only does it provide a tax benefit for related research carried out within the country but also because it protects the intellectual property rights of the original developers.

C. Canada has a competitive edge over India when it comes to pharma Industry as it protects the intellectual property rights of the original developers.

D. Canada has a competitive edge over India when it comes to pharma Industry as it facilitates foreign research in every possible manner.

E. Canada has a competitive edge over India when it comes to pharma Industry as there are fewer rules and

regulations regarding over the counter selling of drugs which leads to profit maximisation.

Q.50 Which of the following would be the most appropriate title of the passage?

A. Drawbacks affecting the Indian pharma Industry

B. The advantages of the pharma industry

C. Intellectual Property Rights in India

D. Drug Control in India

E. A study of the international pharma Industry

Ques (51-54):Direction: In the given question, a statement with a blank has been given, followed by three words out of which more than one can complete the sentence grammatically and contextually. Find the word (s) which can fill the blank and choose the option accordingly.

Q.51 The party's _____________ were based on prejudice rather than on any coherent ideology.

I. Basis

II. Policies

III. Founders

A. Only I **B.** Only II

C. Only III **D.** Both I and II

E. Both I and III

Q.52 The book is hard to obtain, because of _____________ demand following the author's appearance on TV.

I. Excess

II. Access

III. Assess

A. Only I **B.** Only II

C. Only III **D.** Both I & II

E. Both I & III

Q.53 The company's spending has also _____________ following the launch of a new Sunday magazine.

I. Risen

II. Made

III. Decreased

A. Only I **B.** Only II

C. Only III **D.** Both I and II

E. Both I and III

Q.54 Lewis was annoyed that Adam did not show _____________ respect and deference to him.

I. Multiple

II. Enough

III. Least

A. Only I **B.** Only II

C. Only III **D.** Both I and II

E. Both I and III

Ques (55-59):Direction: The following sentences form a paragraph. The sentences are numbered as P, Q, R, S nd T. These five parts are not given in proper order. Read the sentences and choose the alternative that arranges them in the correct order

P. The stolen money was in ₹ 500 and ₹ 1,000 denomination notes that were later demonetized

Q. In which ₹5.75 crore cash assigned to the Reserve Bank of India was looted from a moving train couple of years ago

R. The unprecedented train robbery occurred on the Salem-Chennai Express on the night of August 8, 2016,

S. In a major breakthrough, the Crime Branch CID of the Tamil Nadu police has cracked the sensational train heist case

T. After a gang broke into the parcel van containing ₹342 crore of soiled but usable currency and took away ₹5.75 crore

Q.55 Which of the following is the FIRST sentence of the paragraph?
A. S   **B.** R   **C.** Q   **D.** T
E. P

Q.56 Which of the following is the SECOND sentence of the paragraph?
A. R   **B.** S   **C.** Q   **D.** P
E. T

Q.57 Which of the following is the THREE sentence of the paragraph?
A. R   **B.** S   **C.** Q   **D.** T
E. P

Q.58 Which of the following is the FOURTH sentence of the paragraph?
A. S   **B.** T   **C.** Q   **D.** R
E. P

Q.59 Which of the following is the FIFTH sentence of the paragraph?
A. P   **B.** Q   **C.** S   **D.** R
E. T

Q.60 Direction: In the given question, a sentence is given with a part of it missing and represented by a blank. Choose the phrase that can be placed in the given blank to make a meaningful and grammatically correct sentence.

Computing professionals ___________ of almost every aspect of the modern world.
A. are trying to be conspicuous
B. are evident
C. are on the front lines
D. are participating
E. None of these

Numerical Ability

Q.61 The area of the trapezium is 504 cm². If the ratio of value of parallel side of trapezium is in the ratio of 4 : 5 and the height is 16 cm. The multiplication of parallel side is ______ m.
A. 98   **B.** 0.98
C. 0.098   **D.** 980
E. None of the above

Q.62 If selling price is doubled, the profit triples. What is the profit percent?
A. $105\frac{1}{3}\%$ **B.** $66\frac{2}{3}\%$
C. 120%   **D.** 100%
E. None of these

Ques (63-67):Direction: What should come in place of the question mark '?' in the following number series?

Q.63 79, 108, 139, 176, 217, ?
A. 301   **B.** 260   **C.** 264   **D.** 273
E. 274

Q.64 8, 16, 48, 192, 960, ?
A. 5660   **B.** 5460   **C.** 5760   **D.** 5560
E. 5570

Q.65 500, 475, 426, 345, 224, ?
A. 51   **B.** 52   **C.** 53   **D.** 54
E. 55

Q.66 144, 164, 194, 234, 284, ?
A. 400   **B.** 344   **C.** 564   **D.** 564
E. 369

Q.67 11, 13.5, 18.5, ?, 36
A. 23   **B.** 24   **C.** 21   **D.** 26
E. 28

Q.68 A, B and C entered into a partnership with capitals 1 : 5 : 4. After four months A increases its capital by 50% and C increases its capital by 25%. At the end of year total profit earned is Rs. 4950. Find the share of A.
A. 600   **B.** 300   **C.** 900   **D.** 450
E. 200

Q.69 Two candidates A and B appear for a job interview. The probability of getting selected in the job is for A and B are $\left(\frac{1}{5}\right)$ and $\left(\frac{1}{6}\right)$ respectively. What is the probability that both A and B will not be selected in job interview?
A. $\frac{2}{15}$ **B.** $\frac{1}{6}$
C. $\frac{2}{3}$ **D.** $\frac{29}{30}$
E. None of these

Q.70 A tap can fill a tank in 6 hrs . After half the tank is filled, three more similar taps are opened. What is the total time taken to fill the tank completely?
A. 3 hrs 15 min   **B.** 3 hrs 45 min
C. 4 hrs   **D.** 4 hrs 15 min
E. 4 hrs 20 min

Q.71 Simple interest on a certain sum of money for 3 years at 8% per annum is half the compound interest on Rs. 4000 for 2 years at 10% per annum. The sum placed on simple interest is:
A. Rs. 1550   **B.** Rs. 1650   **C.** Rs. 1750   **D.** Rs. 2000
E. Rs. 1500

Ques (72-76):Direction: The following line graph gives the annual percent profit earned by a Company during the period 1995 - 2000.

Q.72 If the expenditures in 1996 and 1999 are equal, then the approximate ratio of the income in 1996 and 1999 respectively is:

A. 1:1   **B.** 2:3   **C.** 13:14   **D.** 9:10

E. 11:12

Q.73 If the income in 1998 was Rs. 264 crores, what was the expenditure in 1998?

A. Rs. 104 crores   **B.** Rs. 145 crores

C. Rs. 160 crores   **D.** Rs. 185 crores

E. Rs. 180 crores

Q.74 In which year is the expenditure minimum?

A. 2000

B. 1997

C. 1996

D. 1998

E. Cannot be determined

Q.75 If the profit in 1999 was Rs. 4 crores, what was the profit in 2000?

A. Rs. 4.2 crores

B. Rs. 6.6 crores

C. Rs. 6.8 crores

D. Rs. 7.6 crores

E. Cannot be determined

Q.76 What is the average profit percent earned for the given years?

A. $50\frac{2}{3}\%$ **B.** $55\frac{5}{6}\%$ **C.** $60\frac{1}{6}\%$ **D.** 335%

E. $52\frac{5}{6}\%$

Q.77 The value of $\dfrac{(0.625\times0.0729\times28.9)}{(0.0017\times0.025\times8.1)}$ is:

A. 3825   **B.** 3.825   **C.** 38.25   **D.** 382.5

E. 0.3825

Q.78 What approximate value will come in place of question mark (?) in the following question?

$$441.01 - 232.99 + 1649.99 = ? + 1225.92$$

A. 602   **B.** 632   **C.** 660   **D.** 691

E. 720

Q.79 Direction: What will come in place of question mark (?) in the following questions?

(764 × ?) ÷ 250 = 382

A. 115   **B.** 145

C. 135   **D.** 125

E. None of these

Q.80 Direction: What will come in place of question mark(?) in the following question?

$$\left(\frac{1}{4}\right) \times (4856 \times 0.5) \times 12 = ?$$

A. 7284   **B.** 7462

C. 7262   **D.** 7414

E. None of these

Q.81 Direction: What will come in place of question mark(?) in the following question?

853 + ? ÷ 17 = 1000

A. 2516   **B.** 2482

C. 2499   **D.** 16147

E. None of these

Q.82 What is the downstream speed of a boat when the speed of the boat in still water is 10 m/s and the speed of the stream is 20% of the speed of the boat?

A. $8m/s$ **B.** $12m/s$ **C.** $4m/s$ **D.** $9m/s$

E. $13m/s$

Ques (83-85):Direction: In the given question, two equations numbered I and II are given. Solve both the equations and mark the appropriate answer.

Q.83 I. $x^2 - 13x + 30 = 0$

II. $y^2 + 5y + 4 = 0$

A. x > y

B. x < y

C. x ≥ y

D. x ≤ y

E. x = y or relationship between x and y cannot be established

Q.84 I. $x^2 + 17x + 72 = 0$

II. $y^2 + 11y + 30 = 0$

A. x > y

B. x < y

C. x ≥ y

D. x ≤ y

E. x = y or relationship between x and y cannot be established

Q.85 I. $2x^2 - 39x + 189 = 0$

II. $y^2 - 16y + 63 = 0$

A. x > y

B. x < y

C. x ≥ y

D. x ≤ y

E. x = y or relationship between x and y cannot be established

Q.86 Train A running with the speed of 36 km/hr crosses a pole in 20 seconds. Another train B whose length is 100 metre more than length of train A is running with the speed of 18 km/hr. Find the time taken by train B to cross a platform of length 500 metre.

A. 200 seconds
B. 150 seconds
C. 160 seconds
D. 140 seconds
E. None of these

Q.87 In a colony, there are 55 members. Every member posts a greeting card to all the members. How many greeting cards were posted by them?

A. 990
B. 890
C. 2970
D. 1980
E. 2780

Q.88 The average of three numbers is 77. The first number is twice the second and the second number is twice the third. The first number is:

A. 33
B. 66
C. 77
D. 132
E. None of These

Q.89 For how many minutes does a bus stop per hour, if including the stoppages the bus travels at a speed of 67.96 kmph and excluding stoppages the speed of the bus is 81.57 kmph.

A. 10.011
B. 10.110
C. 10.119
D. 10.991
E. 10.911

Q.90 A person gets Rs. 644 on a sum of Rs. 4600 in 3.5 years. If the interest rate is decreased by 50%, then find the simple interest received, if the same sum is invested for 4.5 years.

A. Rs. 41.4
B. Rs. 4140
C. Rs. 414
D. Rs. 322
E. Rs. 325

// Smart Answer Sheet //

Correct — Indicates percentage of students who answered questions correctly.

Skipped — Indicates percentage of students who skipped questions.

Q.	Ans.	Correct / Skipped	Q.	Ans.	Correct / Skipped	Q.	Ans.	Correct / Skipped	Q.	Ans.	Correct / Skipped	Q.	Ans.	Correct / Skipped
1	B	63.71 % / 1.12 %	17	C	86.72 % / 0.0 %	33	C	46.2 % / 1.87 %	49	B	54.09 % / 1.15 %	65	E	61.6 % / 1.55 %
2	D	41.64 % / 1.82 %	18	D	65.13 % / 1.41 %	34	B	64.66 % / 1.02 %	50	A	69.36 % / 1.5 %	66	B	78.07 % / 0.0 %
3	A	82.14 % / 0.0 %	19	C	89.96 % / 0.0 %	35	A	42.21 % / 1.45 %	51	B	62.07 % / 1.79 %	67	D	26.33 % / 4.47 %
4	C	77.87 % / 0.0 %	20	D	89.09 % / 0.0 %	36	D	60.01 % / 1.86 %	52	A	62.91 % / 1.91 %	68	A	43.35 % / 1.49 %
5	B	83.17 % / 0.0 %	21	D	78.65 % / 0.0 %	37	C	40.77 % / 1.82 %	53	D	46.19 % / 1.14 %	69	C	85.88 % / 0.0 %
6	E	52.18 % / 1.67 %	22	B	86.46 % / 0.0 %	38	D	57.31 % / 1.64 %	54	C	41.99 % / 1.32 %	70	B	40.16 % / 1.2 %
7	B	55.03 % / 1.58 %	23	B	62.87 % / 1.91 %	39	C	64.8 % / 1.48 %	55	A	67.2 % / 1.37 %	71	C	83.78 % / 0.0 %
8	E	47.26 % / 1.07 %	24	A	22.05 % / 4.56 %	40	A	45.94 % / 1.91 %	56	C	49.5 % / 1.81 %	72	D	65.16 % / 1.9 %
9	E	47.12 % / 1.27 %	25	B	12.97 % / 3.05 %	41	A	47.22 % / 1.12 %	57	A	45.4 % / 1.29 %	73	C	50.27 % / 1.63 %
10	A	56.06 % / 1.82 %	26	A	19.24 % / 4.5 %	42	D	69.37 % / 1.11 %	58	B	56.05 % / 1.98 %	74	E	64.11 % / 1.75 %
11	B	54.7 % / 1.27 %	27	A	47.18 % / 1.92 %	43	B	68.73 % / 1.86 %	59	A	48.02 % / 1.52 %	75	E	67.3 % / 1.97 %
12	D	53.46 % / 1.46 %	28	B	55.24 % / 1.48 %	44	E	68.33 % / 1.84 %	60	C	65.98 % / 1.02 %	76	B	78.46 % / 0.0 %
13	A	63.38 % / 1.18 %	29	E	47.57 % / 1.97 %	45	C	61.5 % / 1.72 %	61	C	46.6 % / 1.18 %	77	A	44.63 % / 1.01 %
14	A	53.31 % / 1.43 %	30	C	49.41 % / 1.13 %	46	E	63.79 % / 1.98 %	62	D	43.23 % / 1.02 %	78	B	82.69 % / 0.0 %
15	B	76.29 % / 0.0 %	31	E	48.36 % / 1.18 %	47	D	45.34 % / 1.83 %	63	B	30.67 % / 4.42 %	79	D	51.69 % / 1.94 %
16	E	64.02 % / 1.31 %	32	D	64.19 % / 1.63 %	48	C	51.25 % / 1.97 %	64	C	13.84 % / 3.24 %	80	A	53.89 % / 1.22 %

Q.	Ans.	Correct		Q.	Ans.	Correct		Q.	Ans.	Correct		Q.	Ans.	Correct		Q.	Ans.	Correct
		Skipped				Skipped				Skipped				Skipped				Skipped
81	C	89.39 %		83	A	46.0 %		85	C	24.28 %		87	C	69.31 %		89	A	50.76 %
		0.0 %				1.75 %				4.05 %				1.15 %				1.66 %
82	B	63.96 %		84	B	66.3 %		86	C	20.1 %		88	D	88.24 %		90	C	44.77 %
		1.42 %				1.55 %				4.31 %				0.0 %				1.26 %

Performance Analysis	
Avg. Score (%)	37.78%
Toppers Score (%)	73.33%
Your Score	

//Hints and Solutions//

Ques (1-5):Boxes: 1 to 8 in descending order

Colours: Blue, Yellow, Black, Pink, Green, Red and Purple

1) Green colour box is above Red colour box.

2) Red colour box is an even number box below box number 5.

3) Three boxes are kept between Red colour box and Yellow colour box.

Box	Case 1	Case 2
8	Yellow	
7		
6		Yellow
5	Green	
4	Red	
3		Green
2		Red
1		

4) Two boxes are kept between Pink colour box and Purple colour box.
5) Blue colour box is immediately below Pink colour box.

Box	Case 1	Case 2
8	Yellow	Pink
7		Blue
6	Purple	Yellow
5	Green	Purple
4	Red	
3	Pink	Green
2	Blue	Red
1		

6) One of the boxes above box number 5 is empty.
7) Black colour box is an odd number box.

Box	Case 1	Case 2
8	Yellow	Pink
7		Blue
6	Purple	Yellow
5	Green	Purple
4	Red	
3	Pink	Green
2	Blue	Red
1	Black	Black

As case 2 does not fulfil the above condition, it is thus eliminated. The final arrangement will be:

Box	Colour
8	Yellow
7	
6	Purple
5	Green
4	Red
3	Pink
2	Blue

1	Black

1. As Yellow colour is filled in 8th number box.

So, the condition Yellow - 8th is true and the other conditions are false.

Hence, the correct option is (B).

2. So, 4 boxes are there between Yellow colour box and Pink colour box.

Hence, the correct option is (D).

3. So, Black colour box is at the bottom.

Hence, the correct option is (A).

4. So, Green colour is filled in box number 5.

Hence, the correct option is (C).

5. So, 7 number box is an empty box.

Hence, the correct option is (B).

Ques (6-8): The figure according to the information given in the question will be as follows:

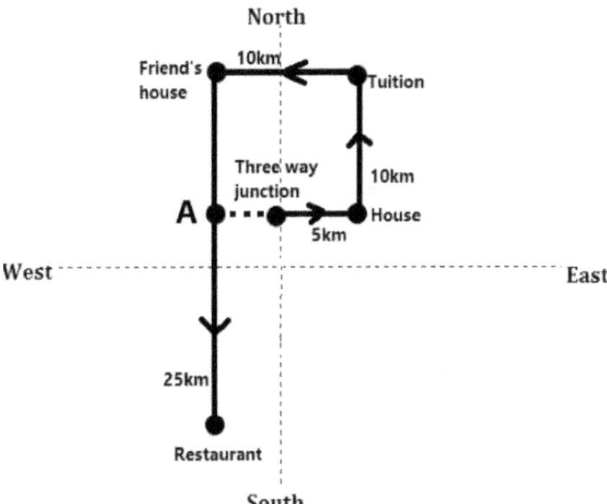

6. So, restaurant is in South-west direction with respect to three way junction.

Hence, the correct option is (E).

7. So, tuition is in East with respect to friend's house.

Hence, the correct option is (B).

8. Let,

friend's house → R

Three way junction→ X

By Pythagoras' theorem,

$$RX^2 = RA^2 + AX^2$$

$$RX^2 = 5^2 + 10^2 = 125$$

So, the shortest distance between a friend's house and a three-way junction is 5√5 km.

Hence, the correct option is (E).

Ques (9-10): From the given information,

Symbol in Diagram	Meaning
○	Female
□	Male
═══	Married Couple
───	Siblings
│	Difference of A Generation

1) A is the father of D who is the brother of F (means D is the brother of F)

2) E is the husband of H.

3) F is the sister of E.

4) B is the son of D and husband of C

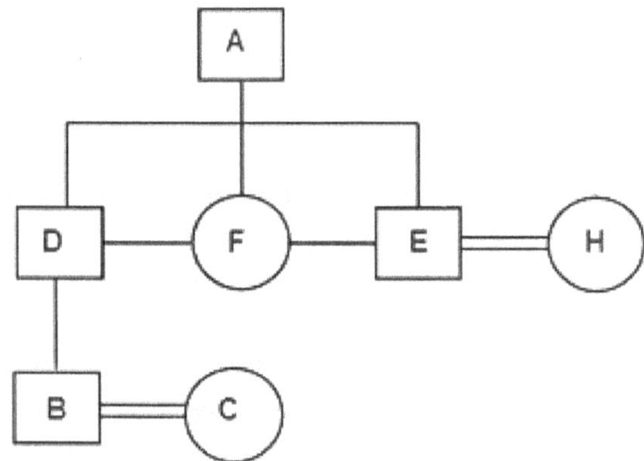

9. So, B is the grandson of A.

Hence, the correct option is (E).

10. So, H is the sister-in-law of F.

Hence, the correct option is (A).

Ques (11-13): In certain coding language,

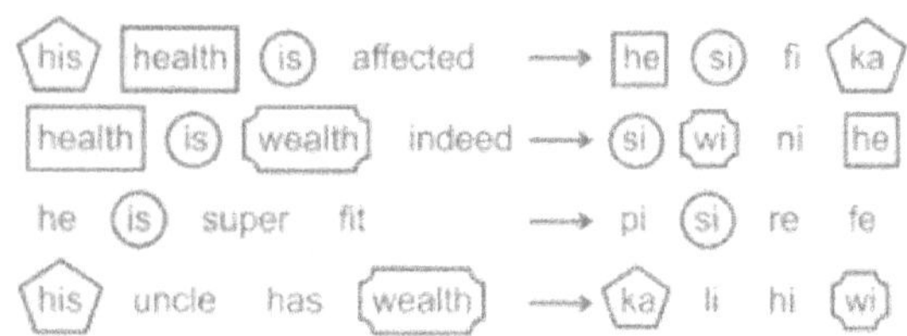

11. Thus, 'wealth' is coded as 'wi'.

Hence, the correct option is (B).

12. Thus, 'fi' is code for 'affected'.

Hence, the correct option is (D).

13. Code for 'his' is 'ka',

Code for 'wealth' is 'wi',

Code for 'is' is 'si',

Code for 'affected' is 'fi',

Code for 'indeed' is 'ni'.

Thus, the possible answer is 'ka wi si fi ni'.

Hence, the correct option is (A).

Ques (14-18): Eight people: Amar, Brijesh, Pinky, Deep, Eshwar, Nancy, Gurkamal and Harsh

1) Nancy is third to the right of Pinky and second to the left of Harsh.

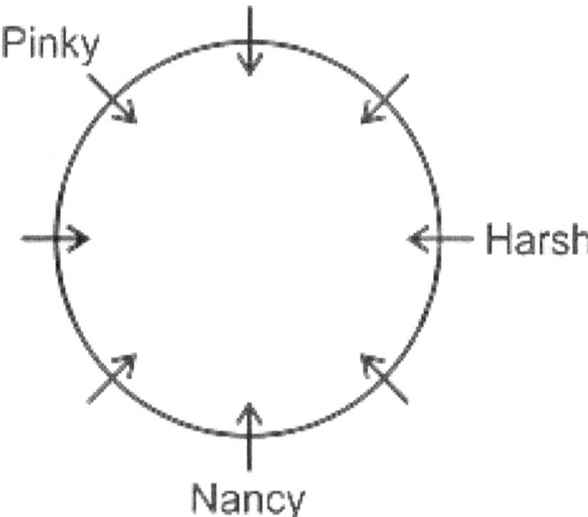

2) Deep is not an immediate neighbour of Pinky or Harsh.

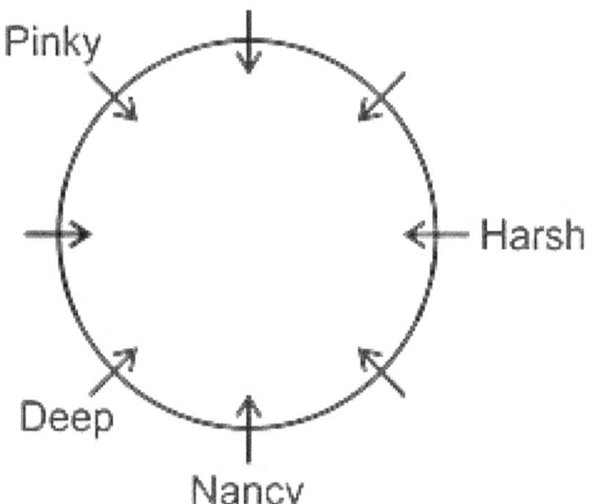

3) Eshwar is to the immediate right of Amar, who is second to the right of Gurkamal.

Here the only position possible for Aman is to the immediate right of Harsh.

Thus, the vacant place is occupied by Brijesh.

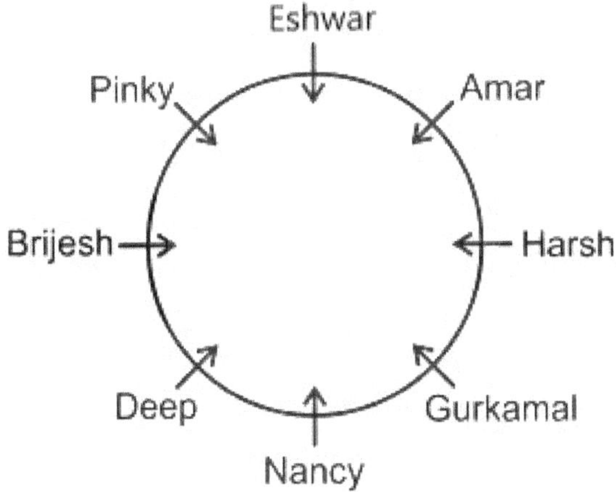

14. Thus, Amar is second to the left of Pinky.

Hence, the correct option is (A).

15. Thus, Brijesh is to the immediate right of Pinky.

Hence, the correct option is (B).

16. Here Deep is sitting to the right of Brijesh. Thus, the correct pair is Deep and Brijesh.

Hence, the correct option is (E).

17. Thus, Nancy sits between Gurkamal and Deep.

Hence, the correct option is (C).

18. Brijesh is sitting in front of Harsh, so Brijesh is both fourth to the right and fourth to the left of Harsh.

Hence, the correct option is (D).

19. Given series:

Left Side M 1 E & D 2 G 9 $ F @ 4 N Z W © 8 C Y A * 6 Right Side

If all the numbers are dropped:

M E & D G $ F @ N Z W © C Y A *

Then, the letter/symbol that is tenth from the right end is 'F'.

Hence, the correct option is (C).

20. Given series:

Left Side M 1 E & D 2 G 9 $ F @ 4 N Z W © 8 C Y A * 6 Right Side.

Here the group is formed in which second element is to the second next of the first element and the third element is third next to the second.

Therefore, YA6 does not belong to the group.

Hence, the correct option is (D).

21. Given series:

Left Side M 1 E & D 2 G 9 $ F @ 4 N Z W © 8 C Y A * 6 Right Side.

1) 4th element from the left end is '&'.

2) 11th element from the right end is '4'.

& **D** 2 **G** 9 $ **F** @ 4

Therefore, there are 3 letters between the fourth element from the left and the eleventh element from the right end D, G and F.

Hence, the correct option is (D).

22. Given series:

M 1 E & D 2 G 9 $ F @ 4 N Z W © 8 C Y A * 6

As, Right + Left = Right

11th from the Right + 5th from the left = 16th from the Right

Clearly, 16th from the Right is G.

Hence, the correct option is (B).

23. Given,

In a row of children, Deepa is 9th from the left and Vijay is 13th from the right. When these two interchange their positions, Deepa becomes 17th from the left.

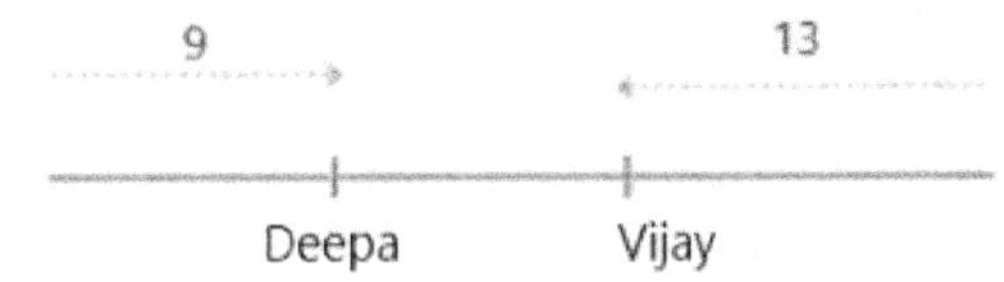

After interchanging,

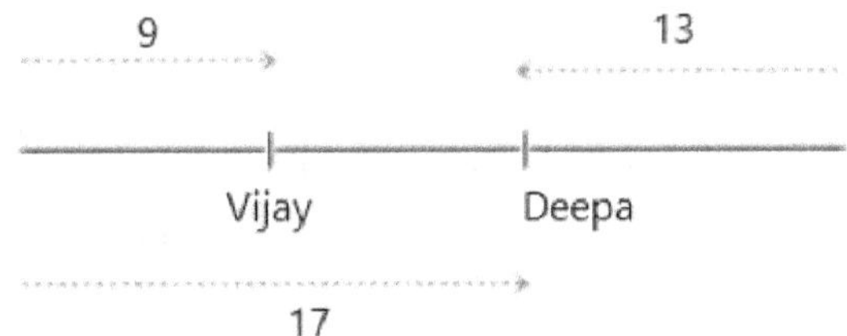

Then,

Present position of Deepa = 17

Former position of Deepa = 9

Difference of present and former position of Deepa = 17 - 9 = 8

Former position of Vijay = 13

Present position of Vijay = difference of present and previous position of Deepa + former position of Vijay

$$= (17 - 9) + 13 = 21\text{st}$$

Hence, the correct option is (B).

24. Given,

In a row of students, Ramesh is ninth from the left and Suman is sixth from the right. When Ramesh and Suman interchange their places, Ramesh becomes fifteenth from the left.

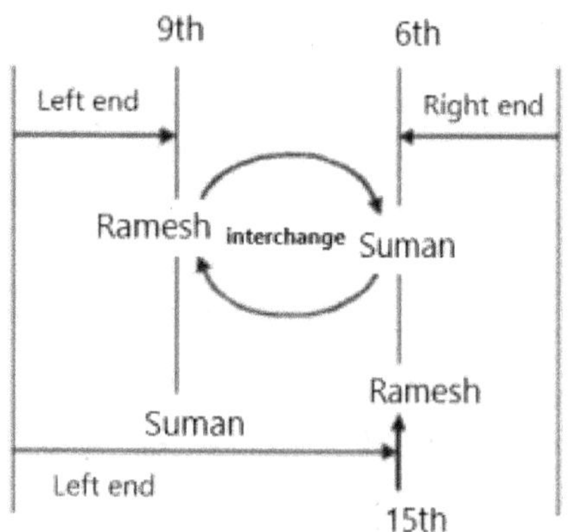

Thus the position of Suman changed from right to $= 6 + 5 +$ Suman

$$= 6 + 5 + 1 = 12$$

Thus Suman will be 12th from the right.

Hence, the correct option is (A).

25. According to the given information, their sequence in the order of height in the queue is as follows-

Shrikant < Neelima = Neelima > Shrikant ...(i)

Pratima > Shrikant ...(ii)

Hembram > Subhash > Neelima...(iii)

Neelima > Pratima ...(iv)

Here ' > ' means 'longer than' and '<' means 'shorter than'.

On arranging their order from equations (i), (ii), (iii) and (iv),

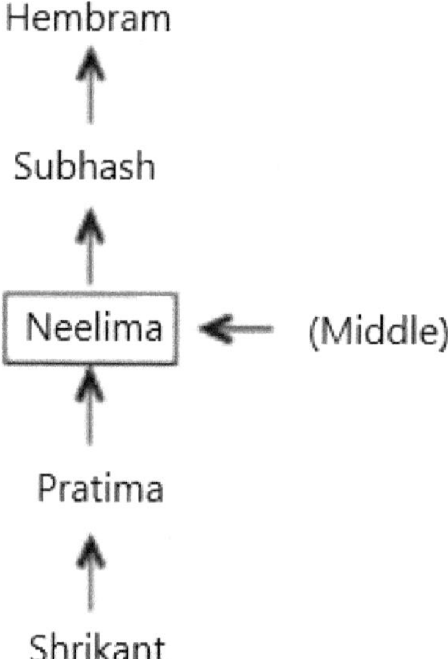

Thus, Neelima will be right in the middle of the row.

Hence, the correct option is (B).

26. The given word:

FAVOURITE

After arranging all the consonants on the left in reversed alphabetical order, we get:

VTRF

Now, arranging all the vowels on the right of these consonants, we get:

VTRFAEIOU

Here, the third letter from the right end is I and the fourth letter from the left end is F.

And, we know that there are two letters between F and I in alphabetical series.

Hence, the correct option is (A).

27.

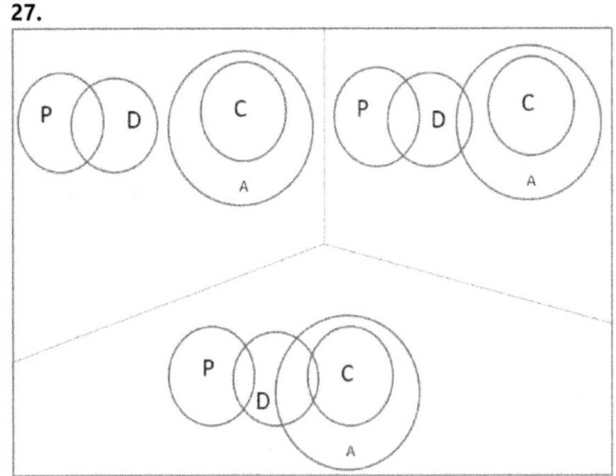

From all the diagrams we can see that all C are A and No P is A so no C is P.

From all the diagrams we can see that Some C maybe D.

From all the diagrams we can see that Some A may/may not D.

So, we can say that only I conclusion follow.

Hence, the correct option is (A).

28.

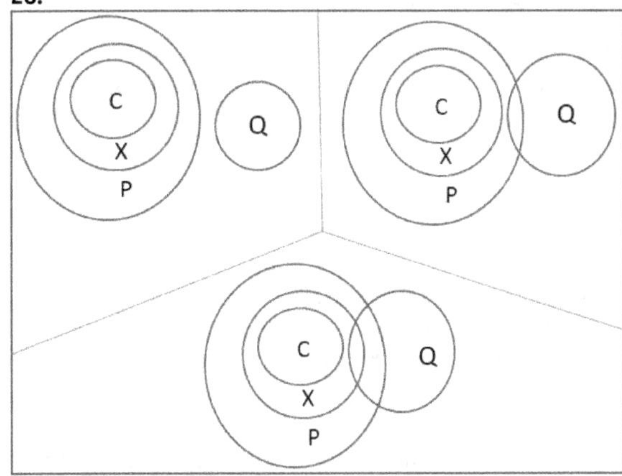

From all the diagrams we can see that all C those are part of X and P can't be Q so conclusions I, III follows.

From all the diagrams we can see that Some Q may be both X and P.

So, we can say that only all I, II, III conclusion follows.

Hence, the correct option is (B).

29.

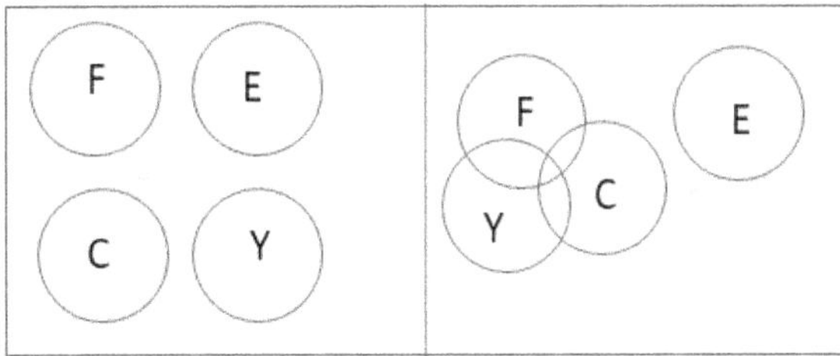

From both the diagrams, we can see that Some F may/may not be C.

From both the diagrams, we can see that Some Y may/may not be F.

From both the diagrams, we can see that Some C may/may not be Y.

So, we can say that no conclusion follows.

Hence, the correct option is (E).

30. The least possible Venn diagram for given statements is as follows:

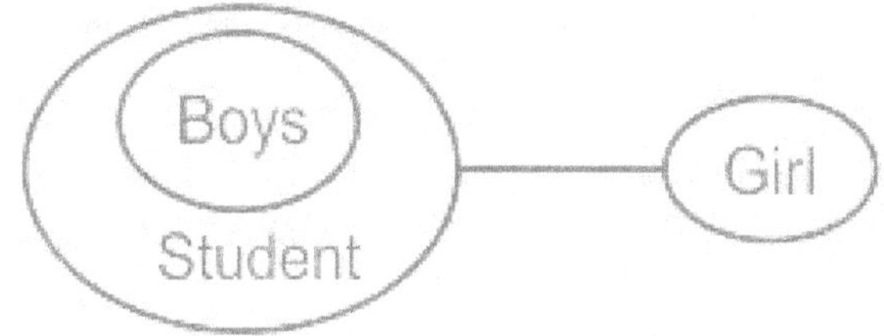

Conclusion:

I. No boy is a girl → True (Because no student is a girl makes no boy is a girl)

II. It is a possibility that all students are boys → True (possibility is possible)

Thus, Both conclusions I and II follow.

Hence, the correct option is (C).

31. The passage talks about the Russian space satellite Arktika-M and what it will do once it reaches the Arctic.

- The sentence with the first blank introduces the topic to the reader and mentions that something happened to Arktika-M and explains its mission.
- When it comes to spaceships and any space-related vehicles, although they seem to be flying in the air, they move in an almost vertical-upward direction and require a very strong and powerful take-off.
- Thus, it makes sense that the space satellite 'launches' into space than 'flies'.

Thus, the correct answer is 'launched' which means 'sent (a missile, satellite, or spacecraft) on its course.'

Hence, the correct option is (E).

32. The passage talks about the Russian space satellite Arktika-M and what it will do once it reaches the Arctic.

- The sentence with the second blank mentions something happening to the Arctic at twice the normal rate.
- The end of the sentence mentions that the ice is melting.
- The Arctic is on the Northern Pole of the Earth, meaning that it has an extremely cold temperature.

- It would not be worrisome if the climate there got colder, but it would be more worrisome if the climate there was getting unusually warmer.

Thus, the correct answer is 'warmed'.

Hence, the correct option is (D).

33. The passage talks about the Russian space satellite Arktika-M and what it will do once it reaches the Arctic.

- The sentence with the third blank talks about the space satellite reaching its intended (expected) location after being launched from Kazakhstan.
- The use of the word 'intended' here is crucial, 'intended' refers to something that was 'planned or meant to be'.
- This means that it was expected of the satellite to reach where it did. The plan made for the launch and destination of the satellite was a success.

Thus, the correct answer is 'successfully'.

Hence, the correct option is (C).

34. The passage talks about the Russian space satellite Arktika-M and what it will do once it reaches the Arctic.

- The sentence with the fourth blank talks about how Russia has a plan to send a second satellite up into space in 2023 and how both the satellites would then do something regarding the climate in the Arctic.
- The very first line of the passage talks about how Russia sent the satellite Arktika - M in order to monitor the climate and environment in the Arctic.
- If the second satellite is also going to be doing the same things as the first one, it would be right to assume that both satellites would do the job of monitoring the climate and environment in the Arctic.

Thus, the correct answer is 'monitoring' which means 'maintaining regular surveillance over'.

Hence, the correct option is (B).

35. The passage talks about the Russian space satellite Arktika-M and what it will do once it reaches the Arctic.

The sentence with the fifth blank mentions that countries that consider themselves as 'something' prefer to rely on data that they themselves have collected.

The only word that makes sense here is 'space'.

- Space powers are those nations that have the capability to conduct and influence activities to, in, through, and from space to achieve their objectives.
- Being a space power also means " having the ability to use space while denying reliable use to any foe".

Thus, the correct answer is 'space'.

Hence, the correct option is (A).

36. The phrase 'In quick time' must be replaced with 'In no time' which means very quickly and is more appropriate under the context.

Hence, the correct option is (D).

37. The underlined part 'can be able to' must be replaced with 'would be able to' to match the tense in the sentence.

Other similar examples:

Ex. He came at 8: 30 pm, freshened up and sat (not sit) by the window with his favourite novel.

Ex. It was obvious that he smoked (not smoke) in nobody's presence.

Ex. He said he would (not will) go to Lucknow on Friday.

Hence, the correct option is (C).

38. The underlined part must be replaced with 'hates doing' as the verb 'hate' has to be in agreement with the the subject 'He' which is singular in number.

Hence, the correct option is (D).

39. In this sentence, the underlined part must be replaced with 'as she knew' as the clause has to be in agreement with the tense which is simple past.

So, the correct sentence is: She opened the door *as she knew* the person very well and had spent quite a few mornings with him.

Hence, the correct option is (C).

40. As In simple modal sentences, modal verbs are followed by the base form of a verb. The underlined part hence must be replaced with 'could not think' to make it a grammatically correct sentence.

Hence, the correct option is (A).

41. The error lies in part (B).

The sentence uses the preposition 'from', which is incorrect, given the context. The betterment will be 'of' the youth and not 'from' it. So, the correct preposition here is 'of'.

So, the errorless combination is ACD.

Correct sentence - Formulation of schemes for betterment of the youth is one of the prime objectives of the mayor.

Hence, the correct option is (A).

42. The error lies in part (B).

The sentence uses the conjunction phrase 'Hardly had...when', which shows an immediate succession of events in a sentence. The sentence uses the conjunction 'than', which is used to compare between two things and is incorrect here. The correct conjunction to be used here is 'when'.

e.g. Hardly had I started my work when the boss came.

So, the errorless combination is ACD.

Correct sentence - Hardly had I finished my Tiffin when the bell rang signifying the end of recess.

Hence, the correct option is (D).

43. The error lies in part (B).

The sentence uses the conjunction phrase 'as soon as', which shows a quick following of two events in a sentence. The part B uses the conjunction and preposition 'that', which is incorrect. There is no need to use another conjunction with the phrase 'as soon as'. This makes the use of another conjunction redundant.

So, the errorless combination is ACD.

Correct sentence - As soon as I saw the bananas I knew the monkey was hiding in the room.

Hence, the correct option is (B).

44. There is no error.

The order and usage of helping verbs are correct.

Hence, the correct option is (E).

45. Option (A) uses the noun 'appointment' after the auxiliary verb 'had'. This is incorrect. It should be the verb form 'Had appointed'.

Correct sentence: The secretary had appointed the same person for the post.

Option (B) incorrectly uses the adverb/conjunction 'as'. Removal of the word makes the sentence meaningful.

Correct sentence: Even though he knew they were safe, he couldn't stop fighting.

Option (D) uses the incorrect form 'would have been approve'.

Correct sentence: The council would have approved the decision.

Option (E) uses the incorrect form 'may currently been creating'.

Correct sentence: The domain owner is currently creating quite a spectacle.

Hence, the correct option is (C).

46. The given passage talks about the disadvantages that the pharma industry in India is facing in spite of rapid development. Option (A) is true as the passage mentions the various benefits that the pharma industry has in countries like Canada and Korea.

Option (B) is true as the passage clearly states that Indian pharma industries "have only focused on reverse engineering blockbuster drugs from MNCs,"

The last line of the passage makes option (C) true.

Option (D) is also true as a pharma company wishing to market a drug is required to submit data to the drug controller to show that the drug is both effective and safe.

But option (E) is not true. The passage clearly states that the protection of relevant data with regards to intellectual property (in this case the data regarding new drugs) is a very debatable issue in India.

Hence, the correct option is (E).

47. The passage states that - '...overseas scientists have displayed little interest in researching sub-continent specific diseases...' making option (D) the correct answer.

Hence, the correct option is (D).

48. 'Prevailing' = be widespread or current in a particular area or at a particular time in the context of the given passage.

Thus options (D) and (E) are opposite in meaning to the given word as they refer to something restricted or unusual. Option (C) is the most similar in meaning to the given word as it means in common or general use.

Hence, the correct option is (E).

49. According to the passage, Canada provides tax benefits up to 6 percent for research carried out within the country in the context of pharma industries. Again, India does not have stringent rules regarding data protection, which often forces research-based pharma companies to undertake vital clinical trials abroad. Huge expenditures are incurred overseas, draining precious foreign exchange when this could be done at home at a fraction of the cost.

Thus option (B) is the correct answer as it mentions both the points that give Canada an edge over India.

Hence, the correct option is (B).

50. The given passage talks about the disadvantages that the pharma industry in India is facing in spite of its rapid development. It focuses mainly on the reasons that are causing problems in the said industry and hampering its full development.

Thus, option (A) is the best-suited title for the given passage.

Hence, the correct option is (A).

51. The blank requires a plural noun as it followed by 'were'. 'Basis' is singular. So, option I is wrong.

Founders refer to the people who established the party. People can't be based on something. So, option III is also wrong.

Hence, the correct option is (B).

52. Excess means an amount of something that is more than necessary, permitted, or desirable.

Access means approach or enter (a place).

Assess means evaluate or estimate the nature, ability, or quality of.

The blank requires an adjective. 'Access' and 'assess' are verbs and 'excess' is an adjective.

Hence, the correct option is (A).

53. Here, 'spending' is used as a gerund. The verb in the blank must be suitable for this gerund. 'Spending' cannot be made. It can, however, rise or decrease.

Hence, the correct option is (D).

54. 'Multiple' is used for countable nouns. 'Respect' is not countable. Option I is wrong.

People don't get annoyed when they are not least respected. So, option II is also wrong.

Hence, the correct option is (C).

55. The passage is about a robbery. And that police has successfully cracked or solved the mystery behind it. So, the First sentence is **S**. It should be followed by sentence **Q**, which is a continuation of the "**the** sensational train heist case." Third sentence is **R**, which presents us more details about the incident, and continues with sentence **T**, which is the fourth sentence. Thus, the Last sentence is P.

Thus, the correct chronological order for the passage is **SQRTP**.

The ordered paragraph will be: In a major breakthrough, the Crime Branch CID of the Tamil Nadu police has cracked the sensational train heist case in which ₹5.75 crore cash assigned to the Reserve Bank of India was looted from a moving train couple of years ago. The unprecedented train robbery occurred on the Salem-Chennai Express on the night of August 8, 2016, after a gang broke into the parcel van containing ₹342 crore of soiled but usable currency, and took away ₹5.75 crore. The stolen money was in ₹ 500 and ₹ 1,000 denomination notes that were later demonetized.

Hence, the correct option is (A).

56. The passage is about a robbery. And that police has successfully cracked or solved the mystery behind it. So, the First sentence is **S**. It should be followed by sentence **Q**, which is a continuation of the "**the** sensational train heist case." Third sentence is **R**, which presents us more details about the incident, and continues with sentence **T**, which is the fourth sentence. Thus, the Last sentence is P.

Thus, the correct chronological order for the passage is **SQRTP**.

The ordered paragraph will be: In a major breakthrough, the Crime Branch CID of the Tamil Nadu police has cracked the sensational train heist case in which ₹5.75 crore cash assigned to the Reserve Bank of India was looted from a moving train couple of years ago. The unprecedented train robbery occurred on the Salem-Chennai Express on the night of August 8, 2016, after a gang broke into the parcel van containing ₹342 crore of soiled but usable currency, and took away ₹5.75 crore. The stolen money was in ₹ 500 and ₹ 1,000 denomination notes that were later demonetized.

Hence, the correct option is (C).

57. The passage is about a robbery. And that police has successfully cracked or solved the mystery behind it. So, the First sentence is **S**. It should be followed by sentence **Q**, which is a continuation of the "**the** sensational train heist case." Third sentence is **R**, which presents us more details about the incident, and continues with sentence **T**, which is the fourth sentence. Thus, the Last sentence is P.

Thus, the correct chronological order for the passage is **SQRTP**.

The ordered paragraph will be: In a major breakthrough, the Crime Branch CID of the Tamil Nadu police has cracked the sensational train heist case in which ₹5.75 crore cash assigned to the Reserve Bank of India was looted from a moving train couple of years ago. The unprecedented train robbery occurred on the Salem-Chennai Express on the night of August 8, 2016, after a gang broke into the parcel van containing ₹342 crore of soiled but usable currency, and took away ₹5.75 crore. The stolen

money was in ₹ 500 and ₹ 1,000 denomination notes that were later demonetized.

Hence, the correct option is (A).

58. The passage is about a robbery. And that police has successfully cracked or solved the mystery behind it. So, the First sentence is **S**. It should be followed by sentence **Q**, which is a continuation of the "**the** sensational train heist case." Third sentence is **R**, which presents us more details about the incident, and continues with sentence **T**, which is the fourth sentence. Thus, the Last sentence is P.

Thus, the correct chronological order for the passage is **SQRTP**.

The ordered paragraph will be: In a major breakthrough, the Crime Branch CID of the Tamil Nadu police has cracked the sensational train heist case in which ₹5.75 crore cash assigned to the Reserve Bank of India was looted from a moving train couple of years ago. The unprecedented train robbery occurred on the Salem-Chennai Express on the night of August 8, 2016, after a gang broke into the parcel van containing ₹342 crore of soiled but usable currency, and took away ₹5.75 crore. The stolen money was in ₹ 500 and ₹ 1,000 denomination notes that were later demonetized.

Hence, the correct option is (B).

59. The passage is about a robbery. And that police has successfully cracked or solved the mystery behind it. So, the First sentence is **S**. It should be followed by sentence **Q**, which is a continuation of the "**the** sensational train heist case." The third sentence is **R**, which presents us with more details about the incident, and continues with sentence **T**, which is the fourth sentence. The Last sentence thus is **P**.

Thus, the correct chronological order for the passage is **SQRTP**.

The ordered paragraph will be: In a major breakthrough, the Crime Branch CID of the Tamil Nadu police has cracked the sensational train heist case in which ₹5.75 crore cash assigned to the Reserve Bank of India was looted from a moving train couple of years ago. The unprecedented train robbery occurred on the Salem-Chennai Express on the night of August 8, 2016, after a gang broke into the parcel van containing ₹342 crore of soiled but usable currency, and took away ₹5.75 crore. The stolen money was in ₹ 500 and ₹ 1,000 denomination notes that were later demonetized.

Hence, the correct option is (A).

60. The given sentence describes the importance of computing professionals throughout the world. Option (C) fits correctly as 'on the front lines' means 'playing a very important part (in something); influential'. Someone who is in the front line has to play a very important part in defending or achieving something.

So, the correct sentence is: Computing professionals *are on the front lines* of almost every aspect of the modern world.

Hence, the correct option is (C).

61. Area of the trapezium = 504 cm²

Height of trapezium = 16 cm

Ratio of parallel side of trapezium = 4 : 5

∵ Area of trapezium = $\left(\dfrac{1}{2}\right)$ × (sum of parallel side) × (height of trapezium)

⇒ 504 = $\left(\dfrac{1}{2}\right)$ × (4x + 5x) × 16

⇒ $\dfrac{(504 \times 2)}{(16 \times 9)}$ = x

⇒ $\dfrac{1008}{144}$ = x

⇒ x = 7

For value of side,

Larger side = 5x = 7 × 5 = 35 cm = 0.35 m

Smaller side = 4x = 4 × 7 = 28 cm = 0.28 m

For require answer,

Desire value = multiplication of parallel side

⇒ Desire value = 0.35 × 0.28

∴ Multiplication of parallel side = 0.098 m

Hence, the correct option is (C).

62. Let cost price $= x$ and Selling price $= y$

Then, profit $= y - x$

If selling price is doubled,

Selling price $= 2y$

Profit $= 2y - x$

$2y - x = 3(y - x)$

⇒ $2y - x = 3y - 3x$

⇒ $y = 2x$

Profit $= (y - x) = (2x - x) = x$

Profit percent $= \dfrac{x \times 100}{x} = 100\%$

Hence, the correct option is (D).

63. The pattern is as follows:

Logic: Addition of Prime numbers

79 + 29 = 108

108 + 31 = 139

139 + 37 = 176

176 + 41 = 217

217 + 43 = 260

∴ The value of ? is 260.

Hence, the correct option is (B).

64. The pattern is as follows:

Logic: Multiplication of Consecutive numbers starting from 2

8 × 2 = 16

16 × 3 = 48

48 × 4 = 192

192 × 5 = 960

960 × 6 = 5760

∴ The value of ? is 5760.

Hence, the correct option is (C).

65. The pattern is as follows,

$500 - (5)^2 = 475$

$475 - (7)^2 = 426$

$426 - (9)^2 = 345$

$345 - (11)^2 = 224$

$224 - (13)^2 = 55$

∴ The value of ? is 55.

Hence, the correct option is (E).

66. The pattern is as follows:

144 + 20 = 164

164 + 30 = 194

194 + 40 = 234

234 + 50 = 284

284 + 60 = 344

∴ The value of ? is 344.

Hence, the correct option is (B).

67. The pattern is as follows:

11 + 2.5 × 1 = 13.5

13.5 + 2.5 × 2 = 18.5

18.5 + 2.5 × 3 = 26

26 + 2.5 × 4 = 36

∴ The value of ? is 26.

Hence, the correct option is (D).

68. Let the capital of A be x.

And the capital of B be 5x and the capital of C is 4x.

It is given that, after four months A increases its capital by 50%.

A's investment for next (12 - 4) = 8 months is (x + 50% of x) $= \dfrac{3x}{2}$

And C Increases its capital after 4 months by 25%.

C's capital for next (12 - 4) = 8 months is (4x + 25% of 4x) = 5x

Ratios of their profit is:

A	:	B	:	C
$x \times 4 + \dfrac{3x}{2} \times 8$	:	$5x \times 12$	:	$4x \times 4 + 5x \times 8$
16x	:	60x	:	56x
4x	:	15x	:	14x
4	:	15	:	14

A's share = $\dfrac{4}{33} \times 4950$ = Rs. 600

∴ Share of A is Rs. 600.

Hence, the correct option is (A).

69. Probability of A for not getting selected in interview = 1 – $\left(\dfrac{1}{5}\right)$ = $\dfrac{4}{5}$

Probability of B for not getting selected in interview = 1 – $\left(\dfrac{1}{6}\right)$ = $\dfrac{5}{6}$

So the required probability = $\dfrac{4}{5} \times \dfrac{5}{6} = \dfrac{2}{3}$

Hence, the correct option is (C).

70. Given,

Time taken by tap to fill the tank = 6 hrs

Time taken by tap to fill half of the the tank = 3 hrs

Part filled by the four taps in 1 hr $= 4 \times \dfrac{1}{6}$

$= \dfrac{2}{3}$

Remaining part $= 1 - \dfrac{1}{2}$

$= \dfrac{1}{2}$

Therefore,

$\dfrac{2}{3} : \dfrac{1}{2} :: 1 : x$

$\Rightarrow x = \dfrac{1}{2} \times 1 \times \dfrac{3}{2}$

$= \dfrac{3}{4}$ hrs

$= \dfrac{3}{4} \times 60$ mins

= 45 mins

∴ The total time taken to fill the tank completely is 3 hrs 45 mins.

Hence, the correct option is (B).

71. Given,

Principal = Rs. 4000, Time period = 2 years, Let the rate = 10%

As we know,

Amount = Principal $\left(1 + \dfrac{Rate}{100}\right)^{n}$

Simple interest = $\dfrac{(P \times R \times T)}{100}$

And compound interest = Amount - Principal = $4000 \left(1 + \dfrac{10}{100}\right)^{2}$ - 4000 = Rs. 840

It is given that simple interest is half the compound interest.

$\Rightarrow 420 = \dfrac{(P \times 8 \times 3)}{100}$

$\Rightarrow$ P = Rs. 1750

∴ The sum placed on simple interest is Rs. 1750.

Hence, the correct option is (C).

72. Let, the expenditure in 1996 = x

Also, let the incomes in 1996 and 1999 be I_1 and I_2 respectively.

Then,

For the year 1996, we have:

$55 = \dfrac{I_1 - x}{x} \times 100$

$\Rightarrow \dfrac{55}{100} = \dfrac{I_1}{x} - 1$

$\Rightarrow I_1 = \dfrac{155x}{100}$ ... (i)

For the year 1999, we have:

$70 = \dfrac{I_2 - x}{x} \times 100$

$\Rightarrow \dfrac{70}{100} = \dfrac{I_2}{x} - 1$

$\Rightarrow I_2 = \dfrac{170x}{100}$ ...... (ii)

From equation (i) and (ii), we get:

$\dfrac{I_1}{I_2} = \dfrac{\left(\dfrac{155x}{100}\right)}{\left(\dfrac{170x}{100}\right)}$

$\Rightarrow \dfrac{I_1}{I_2} = \dfrac{155}{170} \approx \dfrac{0.91}{1} \approx 9 : 10$

Hence, the correct option is (D).

73. Given,

The income in 1998 was Rs. 264 crores

Let the expenditure is 1998 be Rs. x crores.

Then,

$65 = \dfrac{264 - x}{x} \times 100$

$\Rightarrow \dfrac{65}{100} = \dfrac{264}{x} - 1$

$$\Rightarrow x = \frac{264 \times 100}{165}$$

$$= 160$$

$\therefore$ Expenditure in $1998 =$ Rs. 160 crores.

Hence, the correct option is (C).

74. The line-graph gives the comparison of percent profit for different years but the comparison of the expenditures is not possible without more data. Therefore, the year with minimum expenditure cannot be determined.

Hence, the correct option is (E).

75. From the line-graph we obtain information about the percentage profit only. To find the profit in 2000 we must have the data for the income or expenditure in 2000.

Therefore, the profit for 2000 cannot be determined.

Hence, the correct option is (E).

76. Percentage profit earned in different years:

In the year 1995 = 40%

In the year 1996 = 55%

In the year 1997 = 45%

In the year 1998 = 65%

In the year 1999 = 70%

In the year 2000 = 60%

Average profit percent $= \frac{1}{6} \times [40 + 55 + 45 + 65 + 70 + 60]\%$

$$= \frac{335}{6}\%$$

$$= 55\frac{5}{6}\%$$

Hence, the correct option is (B).

77. Given:

$$\frac{(0.625 \times 0.0729 \times 28.9)}{(0.0017 \times 0.025 \times 8.1)}$$

Using BODMAS rule to solve this question,

This is a simple simplification.

$$0.0729 = 8.1 \times 0.009$$

$$0.625 = 0.025 \times 25$$

$$28.9 = 0.0017 \times 17000$$

$$\therefore \frac{(0.625 \times 0.0729 \times 28.9)}{(0.0017 \times 0.025 \times 8.1)}$$

$$= (0.009 \times 25 \times 17000)$$

$$= 3825$$

Therefore, the value of $\frac{(0.625 \times 0.0729 \times 28.9)}{(0.0017 \times 0.025 \times 8.1)}$ is 3825.

Hence, the correct option is (A).

78. Given expression is-

$$441.01 - 232.99 + 1649.99 =? + 1225.92$$

Using BODMAS rule to solve this question,

$$? + 1226 \approx 441 - 233 + 1650$$

$$\Rightarrow ? + 1226 \approx 1858$$

$$\Rightarrow ? = \approx 1858 - 1226$$

$$\Rightarrow ? = \approx 632$$

From above 632 (approx.) in the place of '?'.

Hence, the correct option is (B).

79. Given,

$$\left\{ \frac{(764 \times ?)}{250} \right\} = 382$$

Using BODMAS rule to solve this question,

$$\Rightarrow ? = \left\{ \frac{(382 \times 250)}{764} \right\}$$

$$= 125$$

Therefore, the value of '?' is 125.

Hence, the correct option is (D).

80. Given,

$$\left(\frac{1}{4}\right) \times (4856 \times 0.5) \times 12 =?$$

Using BODMAS rule to solve this question,

$$\Rightarrow \left(\frac{1}{4}\right) \times 2428 \times 12$$

$$? = 7284$$

Hence, the correct option is (A).

81. Given,

$$853 + \left(\frac{?}{17}\right) = 1000$$

Using BODMAS rule to solve this question,

$$\Rightarrow \left(\frac{?}{17}\right) = 1000 - 853$$

$$= 147$$

$$\Rightarrow ? = 17 \times 147$$

$$= 2499$$

Hence, the correct option is (C).

82. Given,

The speed of the boat in still water $= 10m/s$

The speed of the stream $= 20\%$ of the speed of the boat

Let the speed of the boat in still water is u m/s and the speed of the stream is v m/s

Then,

The speed of the boat in still water $= 10m/s$

The speed of the stream $= 20\%$ of $10m/s$

$= 10 \times \dfrac{20}{100}$

$= 2m/s$

Downstream speed = speed of the boat in still water + speed of the stream

Downstream speed $= (10 + 2)$

$= 12m/s$

Hence, the correct option is (B).

83. I. $x^2 - 13x + 30 = 0$

$\Rightarrow x^2 - 3x - 10x + 30 = 0$

$\Rightarrow (x - 3)(x - 10) = 0$

$\Rightarrow x = 3, 10$

II. $y^2 + 5y + 4 = 0$

$\Rightarrow y^2 + y + 4y + 4 = 0$

$\Rightarrow (y + 4)(y + 1) = 0$

$\Rightarrow y = -4, -1$

Value of x	Value of y	Relation
3	−4	x > y
3	−1	x > y
10	−4	x > y
10	−1	x > y

So, x > y

Hence, the correct option is (A).

84. I. $x^2 + 17x + 72 = 0$

$\Rightarrow x^2 + 9x + 8x + 72 = 0$

$\Rightarrow (x + 8)(x + 9) = 0$

$\Rightarrow x = -8, -9$

II. $y^2 + 11y + 30 = 0$

$\Rightarrow y^2 + 5y + 6y + 30 = 0$

$\Rightarrow (y + 5)(y + 6) = 0$

$\Rightarrow y = -5, -6$

Value of x	Value of y	Relation
−8	−5	x < y
−8	−6	x < y
−9	−5	x < y
−9	−6	x < y

So x < y

Hence, the correct option is (B).

85. I. $2x^2 - 39x + 189 = 0$

$\Rightarrow 2x^2 - 18x - 21x + 189 = 0$

$\Rightarrow 2x(x - 9) - 21(x - 9) = 0$

$\Rightarrow (x - 9)(2x - 21) = 0$

$\Rightarrow x = 9, \dfrac{21}{2}$

II. $y^2 - 16y + 63 = 0$

$\Rightarrow y^2 - 7y - 9y + 63 = 0$

$\Rightarrow y(y - 7) - 9(y - 7) = 0$

$\Rightarrow (y - 7)(y - 9) = 0$

$\Rightarrow y = 7, 9$

Value of x	Value of y	Relation
9	7	x > y
9	9	x = y
$\dfrac{21}{2}$	7	x > y
$\dfrac{21}{2}$	9	x > y

$\therefore x \geq y$

Hence, the correct option is (C).

86. Given:

Length of platform $= 500$ m

Time required by train A to cross a pole $= 20$ seconds

Speed of train A $= 36$ km/hr

Speed of train B $= 18$ km/hr

Length of train B $=$ Lenght of Train A $+100$ m

We know that:

$$S = \dfrac{D}{T}$$

(where, S $=$ speed, D $=$ Distance, T $=$ Time taken)

Speed of Train A and train B in m/s

Train A $= 36 \times \left(\dfrac{5}{18}\right)$

$= 10$ m/s

Train B $= 18 \times \left(\dfrac{5}{18}\right)$

$= 5$ m/s

The length of the train A $= 10 \times 20$

$= 200$ m

The length of the train B $= 200 + 100$

$= 300$ m

Time taken by train B to cross-platform

$= \dfrac{(500+300)}{5}$

$= 160$ seconds

∴ The time taken by train B to cross a platform of length 500 metres is 160 seconds.

Hence, the correct option is (C).

87. First player can post greeting cards to the remaining 54 players in 54 ways. Second player can post greeting cards to the 54 players. Similarly, it happens with the rest of the players. The total numbers of greeting cards posted are

$54 + 54 + 54 \,...$

$54(55 \text{ times}) = 54 \times 55 = 2970.$

Hence, the correct option is (A).

88. Let the third no. be $= x$

Then second number $= 2x$

First number $= 4x$

Average of the numbers $= 77$

$\Rightarrow \dfrac{x+2x+4x}{3} = 77$

$\Rightarrow 7x = 77 \times 3$

$\Rightarrow x = 33$

First number $= 4 \times 33 = 132$

∴ 132 is the first number.

Hence, the correct option is (D).

89. From the question it's known that the bus travels at a speed of 67.96 kmph including stoppages and without stoppages 81.57 kmph.

So it's very clear that some time is wasted due to decrease in speed of the bus

Decrease in speed of bus = 81.57 kmph – 67.96 kmph = 13.61 kmph

Every hour 13.61 km is wasted due to stoppages, we know that

Time $= \dfrac{distance}{speed}$

So if it would have travelled this 13.61 km with a speed of 81.57 kmph, it would have saved

$\Rightarrow \dfrac{13.61}{81.57} = 0.1668 \text{hrs} = 10.011$ minutes

∴ The bus stops 10.011 minutes per hour due to these stoppages.

Hence, the correct option is (A).

90. Given:

Principal = Rs. 4600

Interest received in 3.5 years = Rs. 644

Formula used:

$SI = \dfrac{PRT}{100}$

Where P = principal

R = rate

T = time

Calculation:

$SI = \dfrac{PRT}{100}$

For 3.5 years,

$644 = \dfrac{(4600 \times R \times 3.5)}{100}$

$\Rightarrow 644 = 161R$

$\Rightarrow R = 4$

For 4.5 years,

$SI = \dfrac{(4600 \times 0.50R \times 4.5)}{100}$

$\Rightarrow \dfrac{(4600 \times 0.50(4) \times 4.5)}{100}$

$\Rightarrow$ Rs. 414

∴ Simple Interest received for 4.5 years is Rs. 414.

Hence, the correct option is (C).

Q.1 How many such vowels are there in the above arrangement, each of which is immediately followed by a symbol and preceded by a letter?

A. 0   **B.** 1   **C.** 2   **D.** 3
E. 4

Q.2 Which of the following element is 5th to the left of the 9th from the left end of the above arrangement?

A. %   **B.** 6   **C.** F   **D.** #
E. 4

Q.3 How many symbols are between the highest number and the 2nd smallest number?

A. 0   **B.** 1   **C.** 2   **D.** 3
E. 4

Ques (4-5):Direction: Follow the given series to answer the question.

J U & 5 R 3 1 7 @ & M I 6 R 2 F S @ I M $ 9 L 7 1 6 A # 9 B Z $

Q.4 How many such symbols are there in the above arrangement, each of which is immediately preceded by a symbol and immediately followed by a letter?

A. 2   **B.** 1   **C.** 4   **D.** 0
E. 3

Q.5 If all the vowels from the above arrangement are dropped, which of the following element will be the 11th to the right of the element, which is 17th from the right end?

A. M   **B.** R   **C.** J   **D.** @
E. 6

Ques (6-8):Direction: Study the following information carefully and answer the given questions.

In a certain code language, 'bank is open today' is written as 'sd cb vi zn', 'winter is coming' is written as 'ri dm zn', 'today is bank holiday' is written as 'zn vi cb pq', and 'they are coming today' is written as 'dm vi ki rt'.

Q.6 Code 'vi zn sd ri' is for which of the following sentence in the given language?

A. Winter is bank holiday
B. Bank are close today
C. Winter is coming today
D. Today is open winter
E. Open holiday is coming

Q.7 Code 'pq' is for which word in the given language?

A. Are   **B.** Today   **C.** Open   **D.** Bank
E. Holiday

Q.8 What is a code of 'bank'?

A. cb   **B.** sd   **C.** vi   **D.** zn
E. ki

Ques (9-11):Direction: In the following question assuming the given statements to be true, find which of the conclusion among given conclusions is/are definitely true and then give your answers accordingly.

Q.9 Statements:

A > B > C = P, R < B > Q, P ≥ S = T

Conclusions:

I. A > R

II. C = T

III. B > S

A. All follow
B. Only I follow
C. Only II follows
D. Only I and III follow
E. None follow

Q.10 Statement: A > B > C = D = E

Conclusion:

I. A > E

II. D < B

III. A > C

A. Only II is true
B. Only I is true
C. Only II and III are true
D. Only II and I are true
E. All conclusions follow

Q.11 Statement:

N ≥ T > J ≤ R, J ≥ P ≥ M

Conclusions:

I. M < R

II. N = P

III. R = M

A. Only III is true
B. Only either I or III is true
C. Only II is true
D. Only I is true
E. None is true

Q.12 Direction: Study the information given below carefully and answer the question that follow.

A person starts walking in north direction from Bus-stop, after walking 15 m he reached Park, then he takes right turns and walks 7 m to reach at Electronic Shop after that he walks in south direction and walks 10 m to reach Cafe. General store is 5 m east of Cafe. Lighthouse is 22 m north of General store. School is 10 m west of Lighthouse.

What is the direction of Lighthouse with respect to person's initial position?

A. North   **B.** West
C. South-west   **D.** North-East

E. None of these

Q.13 Direction: Study the information given below carefully and answer the question that follow.

A person starts walking in north direction from Bus-stop, after walking 15 m he reached Park, then he takes right turns and walks 7 m to reach at Electronic Shop after that he walks in south direction and walks 10 m to reach Cafe. General store is 5 m east of Cafe. Lighthouse is 22 m north of General store. School is 10 m west of Lighthouse.

What is the shortest distance between Electronic Shop and General store?

A. √125 m   **B.** √124 m   **C.** √135 m   **D.** √175 m
E. √165 m

Q.14 Direction: Study the information given below carefully and answer the question that follow.

A person starts walking in north direction from Bus-stop, after walking 15 m he reached Park, then he takes right turns and walks 7 m to reach at Electronic Shop after that he walks in south direction and walks 10 m to reach Cafe. General store is 5 m east of Cafe. Lighthouse is 22 m north of General store. School is 10 m west of Lighthouse.

What is the direction of Bus-stop with respect to General store?

A. South-east   **B.** North-west
C. South-west   **D.** East
E. None of these

Q.15 If in the word 'CAPITALIZATION' all the letters are arranged in alphabetic order then how many vowels are replaced by a new vowel?

A. Zero   **B.** One
C. Two   **D.** Three
E. More than three

Ques (16-17):Direction: Read the information carefully and answer the questions asked below.

K is the aunt of R, who is the son of M. M is the spouse of N. N is the daughter-in-law of L, who is the father of K.

Q.16 How N is related to R?

A. Daughter   **B.** Mother
C. Son   **D.** Cousin
E. Niece

Q.17 If K is married to J. How J is related to M?

A. Son-in-law   **B.** Father-in-law
C. Brother-in-law   **D.** Sister-in-law
E. None of these

Q.18 Suresh is heavier than Anil but not as heavy as Raju. 'Anil' is heavier than Jayesh. 'Krishna' is heavier than Suresh but lighter than 'Raju'. Who is the lightest among them?

A. Krishna   **B.** Suresh   **C.** Jayesh   **D.** Raju
E. Anil

Q.19 Sahil and Gaurav are standing in a row of persons. Sahil is 12th from the left side and Gaurav is 18th from the right side of the row. If they interchanged their positions Sahil becomes

25th from left. What is the total number of persons standing in the row?

A. 42   **B.** 52   **C.** 45   **D.** 46
E. 56

Q.20 In a School, there are 147 people, the ratio of girls : boys is 1:6. Soumya is a girl who stands 15th from the top of that row and 7 girls are in front of her. How many boys are behind her?

A. 100   **B.** 119   **C.** 110   **D.** 120
E. 125

Ques (21-25):Direction: Read the information carefully and answer the questions given below.

At a reunion party, eight friends named A, B, C, D, E, F, G and H sit together on a round table facing the centre. Interestingly all eight friends are pursuing bachelor's degree in different subjects namely Mathematics, Economics, English, History, Physics, Chemistry, Sociology and Hindi. They are not necessarily seated in the mentioned order. A sits adjacent to D who is studying Economics. B is studying History and does not sit adjacent to C or D. F is sitting fifth to the left of A and is studying Physics. One who is studying Chemistry sits immediate left to F. G sits opposite to A. Neither H nor E is immediate neighbour of G. One who is studying Hindi sits fifth to the left of G, who is learning Sociology. C does not study chemistry. E is studying English and sits next to the one who is studying Hindi.

Q.21 What does the person study who is sitting third to the left of C?

A. Mathematics   **B.** Physics
C. Sociology   **D.** History
E. None of these

Q.22 Who is diagonally opposite to B?

A. D   **B.** A   **C.** H   **D.** F
E. G

Q.23 Who sits between A and E?

A. D   **B.** H   **C.** C   **D.** B
E. F

Q.24 Which subject is A studying?

A. Sociology   **B.** English
C. Chemistry   **D.** History
E. Mathematics

Q.25 Who is studying Chemistry?

A. A   **B.** B
C. F   **D.** H
E. None of these

Ques (26-30):Direction: Answer the question based on the information given below:

Seven kids A, B, C, D, E, F and G were born in different months among January, February, April, May, July, August and November in different years among 1998, 2003, 2006, 2008, 2010, 2014 and 2015 not necessarily in the same order.

Note: If a person is n (=1, 2, 3, 4, so on) years elder than another person, consider only the years. F was born in

2003. C, who was born in July, is five years elder than D. D was born in a month, which consists of only 30 days. A is at most two years elder than the one, who was born in February. B is elder than E, who was not born in 2014. G was not born immediately before the one, who was born in April. The kid, who was born in January, is elder than the one, who was born in April. The kid, who was born in May is not elder than the one, who was born in April. Kid, who was born in 1998, was not born in January.

Q.26 __ is three years elder than __.

A. B, F

B. A, E

C. C, G

D. F, A

E. None of the above

Q.27 Who was born in the month of May?

A. G

B. A

C. F

D. B

E. None of the above

Q.28 The eldest child was born in ___ while the youngest child was born in ___.

A. August, May

B. April, November

C. April, August

D. August, November

E. None of the above

Q.29 Kid, who was born in May, is __ years younger than F.

A. 11

B. 2

C. 9

D. 16

E. None of the above

Q.30 Which among the following statements is/are true?

A. B was born in May

B. F was born in a leap year

C. 2nd eldest kid was born in January

D. G was born in a month, which has only 30 days

E. None of the given statements is true

// Smart Answer Sheet //

Correct — Indicates percentage of students who answered questions correctly.

Skipped — Indicates percentage of students who skipped questions.

Q.	Ans.	Correct / Skipped	Q.	Ans.	Correct / Skipped	Q.	Ans.	Correct / Skipped	Q.	Ans.	Correct / Skipped	Q.	Ans.	Correct / Skipped
1	B	85.32 % / 0.0 %	7	E	78.95 % / 0.0 %	13	A	60.3 % / 1.56 %	19	A	69.51 % / 1.39 %	25	D	77.65 % / 0.0 %
2	B	82.75 % / 0.0 %	8	A	76.06 % / 0.0 %	14	C	66.52 % / 1.1 %	20	B	45.67 % / 1.64 %	26	D	26.31 % / 3.45 %
3	C	88.1 % / 0.0 %	9	D	69.37 % / 1.98 %	15	C	77.98 % / 0.0 %	21	C	17.08 % / 3.0 %	27	A	69.7 % / 1.32 %
4	B	80.14 % / 0.0 %	10	E	55.75 % / 1.95 %	16	B	61.02 % / 1.49 %	22	A	43.54 % / 1.5 %	28	D	52.21 % / 1.89 %
5	E	88.38 % / 0.0 %	11	B	22.04 % / 4.25 %	17	C	68.13 % / 1.85 %	23	C	83.33 % / 0.0 %	29	A	42.86 % / 1.67 %
6	D	88.83 % / 0.0 %	12	D	43.11 % / 1.04 %	18	C	54.09 % / 1.42 %	24	E	41.23 % / 1.41 %	30	C	10.72 % / 3.98 %

Performance Analysis	
Avg. Score (%)	60.0%
Toppers Score (%)	66.67%
Your Score	

//Hints and Solutions//

1. Given Series,

B T % 6 P A & 8 4 @ S O G # 9 C 5 U 2 % F M

Requirement: Letter → Vowel → Symbol

There is only one such a pair.

P A &

Hence, the correct option is (B).

2. Given Series,

B T % 6 P A & 8 4 @ S O G # 9 C 5 U 2 % F M

For calculating the element which is 5th to the left of the 9th from the left end of the above arrangement, we will substract the numbers to get the desired number from the left end.

9 - 5 = 4th from left end.

B T % **6** P A & 8 4 @ S O G # 9 C 5 U 2 % F M

Hence, the correct option is (B).

3. Given Series,

B T % 6 P A & 8 **4** @ S O G # **9** C 5 U 2 % F M

So, there are 2 symbols i.e., @ and # between the highest number and the 2nd smallest number.

Hence, the correct option is (C).

4. Given series is:

J U & 5 R 3 I 7 @ & M I 6 R 2 F S @ I M $ 9 L 7 1 6 A # 9 B Z $

After finding such symbols are there in the above arrangement, each of which is immediately preceded by a symbol and immediately followed by a letter, we get

J U & 5 R 3 I 7 @ & M I 6 R 2 F S @ I M $ 9 L 7 1 6 A # 9 B Z $

So, there is only one such symbol.

Hence, the correct option is (B).

5. Given series is:

J U & 5 R 3 I 7 @ & M I 6 R 2 F S @ I M $ 9 L 7 1 6 A # 9 B Z $

After dropping all the vowels from the above arrangement, we get

J & 5 R 3 7 @ & M 6 R 2 F S @ M $ 9 L 7 1 6 # 9 B Z $

After finding the 11th to the right of the element, which is 17th from the right end.

J & 5 R 3 7 @ & M **6** R 2 F S @ M $ 9 L 7 1 6 # 9 B Z $

Thus, 6 is that element.

Hence, the correct option is (E).

Ques (6-8): First, let's decode the words,

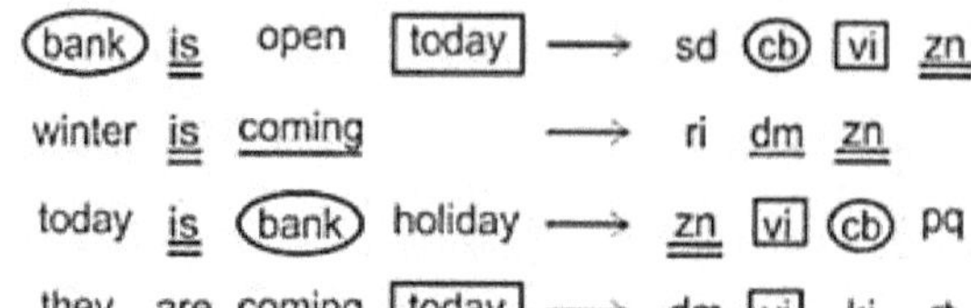

After decoding,

bank → cb

is → zn

open → sd

today → vi

winter → ri

coming → dm

holiday → pq

They → ki or rt

Are → ki or rt

6. So, code 'vi zn sd ri' is for 'today is open winter'

Hence, the correct option is (D).

7. So, "holiday" is the correct answer.

Hence, the correct option is (E).

8. So, "cb" is the correct answer.

Hence, the correct option is (A).

9. Given statements: - A > B > C = P, R < B > Q, P ≥ S = T

On combining: A > B > C = P ≥ S = T, R < B > Q

Conclusions:

A > R → True (because A > B > R, implies A > R)

C = T → False (as C = P ≥ S =T, implies C ≥ T, thus C = T is not definite)

B > S → True (because B > C = P ≥ S, implies B > S)

So, only I and III follow.

Hence, the correct option is (D).

10. Given statement: A > B > C = D = E

Conclusion:

I. A > E → True (As, A > B > C = D = E → Thus, it is clear that A > E)

II. D < B → True (As, D = C and C < B → Thus, it is clear that D < B)

III. A > C → True (As, A > B > C → Thus, it is clear that A > C)

Therefore, all conclusion follows.

Hence, the correct option is (E).

11. Given: N ≥ T > J ≤ R, J ≥ P ≥ M

On Combining: R ≥ J ≥ P ≥ M, N ≥ T > J ≥ P ≥ M

Conclusions:

I. M < R → False (as R ≥ J ≥ P ≥ M, therefore R ≥ M).

II. N = P → False (as N ≥ T > J ≥ P, therefore N > P).

III. R = M → False (as R ≥ J ≥ P ≥ M, therefore R ≥ M)

Conclusion I and III form a complementary pair.

So, either conclusion I or III is true.

Hence, the correct option is (B).

12. We have drawn the figure according to the information given in the question,

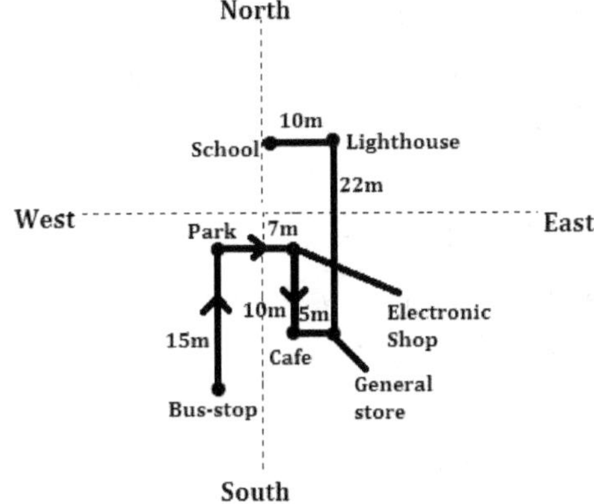

So, Lighthouse is in the North-East direction.

Hence, the correct option is (D).

13. We have drawn the figure according to the information given in the question,

Let us take Electronic Shop as Q, General store as B and cafe as M

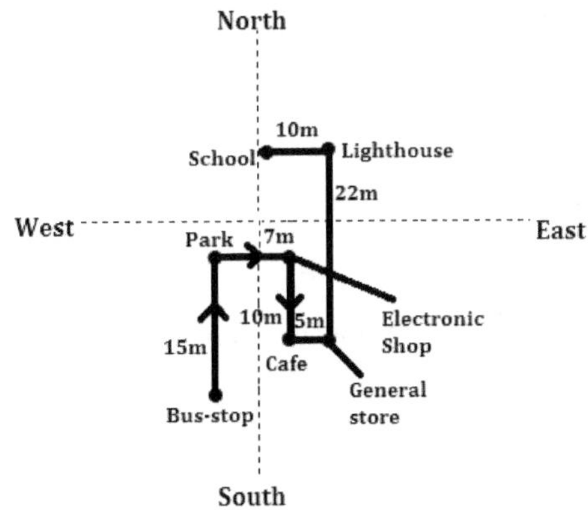

The shortest distance between Electronic Shop and General store

$$= \sqrt{QM^2 + \overline{MB}^2}$$

$$= \sqrt{10^2 + 5^2} = \sqrt{125}$$

So, the shortest distance between Q and B ie., Electronic Shop and General store is √125.

Hence, the correct option is (A).

14. We have drawn the figure according to the information given in the question,

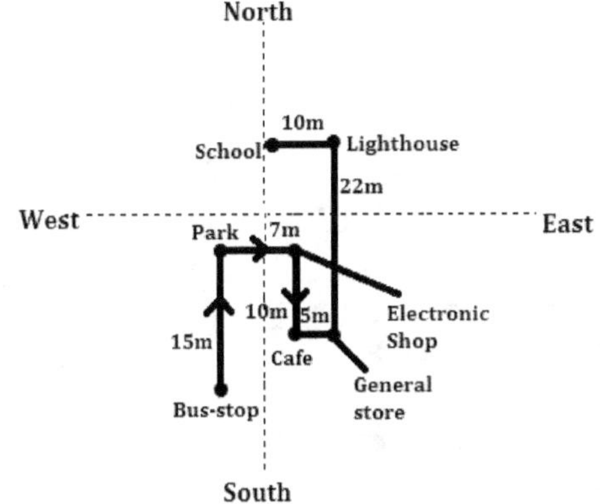

So, the direction of Bus-stop with respect to General store is South west.

Hence, the correct option is (C).

15. The given word:

CAPITALIZATION

After arranging the letters in alphabetic order the word becomes:

AAACIIILNOPTTZ

The final arrangement of new and old words are:

C	A	P	I	T	A	L	I	Z	A	T	I	O	N
A	A	A	C	I	I	I	L	N	O	P	T	T	Z

Here, there are two such vowels which are replaced by a new vowel.

Hence, the correct option is (C).

Ques (16-17): From the given information

Symbol in Diagram	Meaning
◯	Female
▢	Male
═══	Married Couple
───	Siblings
│	Difference of A Generation

1) K is the aunt of R, who is the son of M.

2) M is the spouse of N.

3) N is the daughter-in-law of L, who is the father of K.

16.

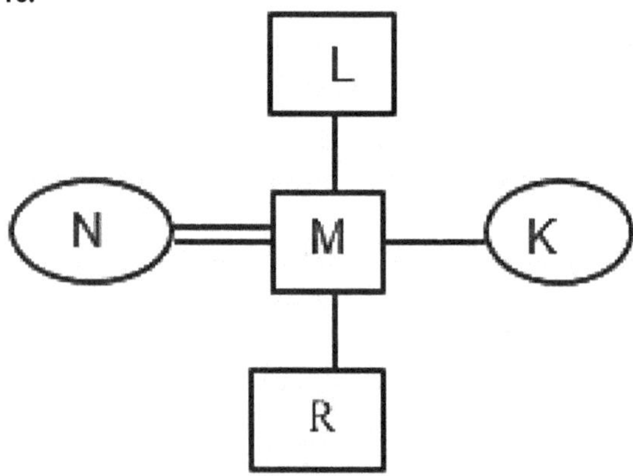

So, N is the mother of R.

Hence, the correct option is (B).

17. If K is married to J,

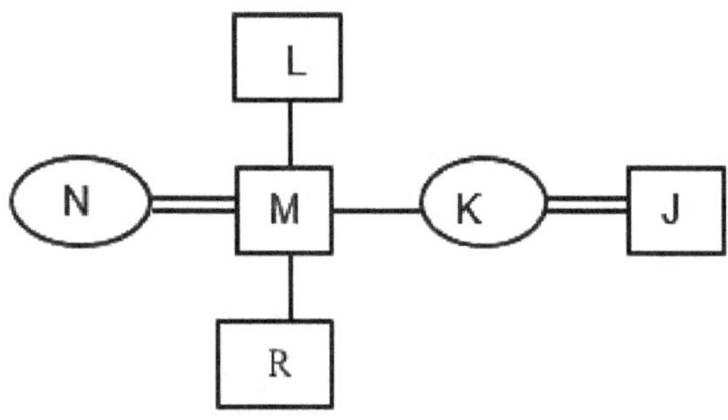

So, J is the brother-in-law of M.

Hence, the correct option is (C).

18. Given,

Suresh is heavier than Anil but not as heavy as Raju. 'Anil' is heavier than Jayesh. 'Krishna' is heavier than Suresh but lighter than 'Raju'.

The sequence is as follows,

Raju $>$ Krishna $>$ Suresh $>$ Anil $>$ Jayesh

Thus the lightest one is 'Jayesh'.

Hence, the correct option is (C).

19. Given,

Sahil and Gaurav are standing in a row of persons. Sahil is 12th from the left side and Gaurav is 18th from the right side of the row.

Position of Sahil from Left = 25 (after interchanging)

Total person = Position from Left + Position from right - 1

Position of Sahil from Right = 18 (position of Sahil from right end is same as Gaurav after interchanging) -1

Total person $= 25 + 18 - 1 = 42$

Thus, there are 42 persons in the row.

Hence, the correct option is (A).

20. Given,

In a School, there are 147 people, the ratio of girls: boys is 1:6. Soumya is a girl who stands 15th from the top of that row and 7 girls are in front of her.

Total number of students $= 147$

Girls : Boys $= 1 : 6$

Let the number of girls be x and the number of boys be $6x$.

Then,

$$x + 6x = 147$$

$$\Rightarrow 7x = 147$$

$$\Rightarrow x = 21$$

Then the number of girls = 21

The number of boys $= 6 \times 21 = 126$

Now Soumya is in 15th position from the top and 7 girls are in front of her.

Now boys are in front of him $= 7$ as total 14 students are in front of him.

So, the number of boys, behind him = $126 - 7 = 119$

Hence, the correct option is (B).

Ques (21-25):Eight friends: A, B, C, D, E, F, G and H

Subjects: Mathematics, Economics, English, History, Physics, Chemistry, Sociology and Hindi

1) A sits adjacent D who is studying Economics.

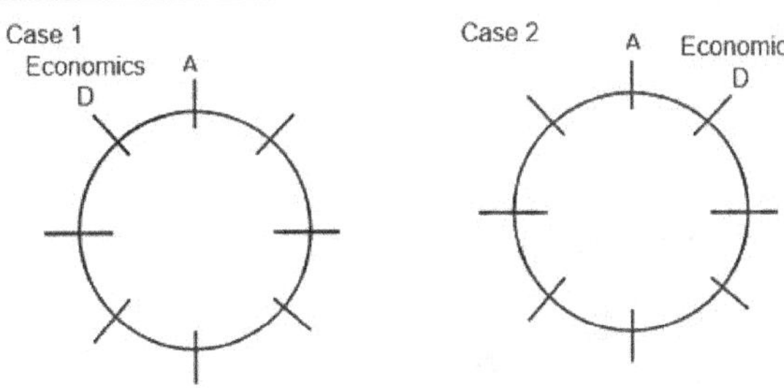

2) F is sitting fifth to the left of A and is studying Physics.

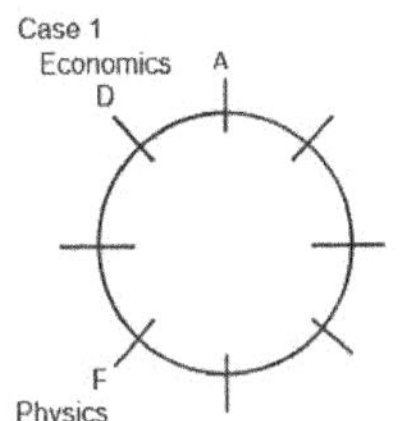

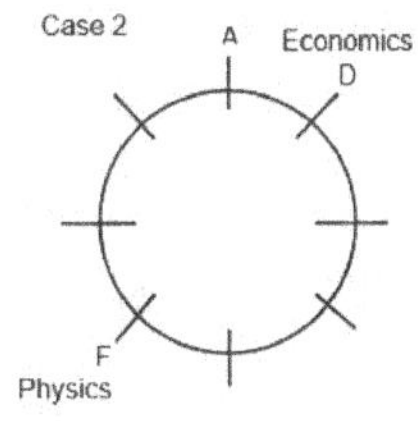

3) One who is studying Chemistry sits left to F.

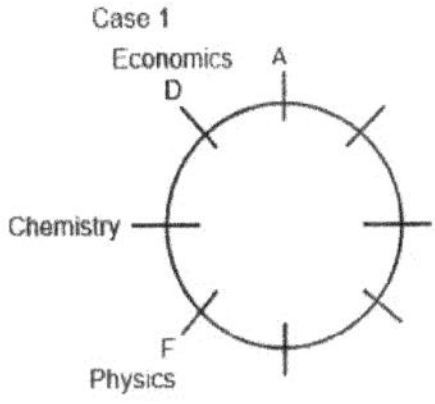

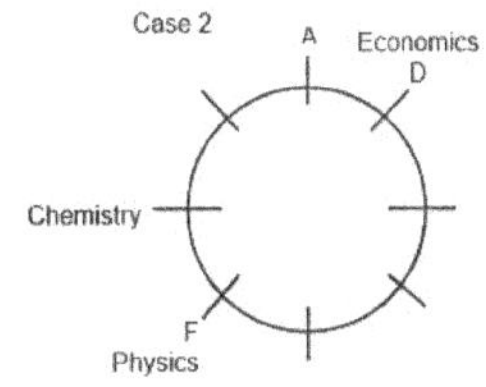

4) G sits opposite to A.

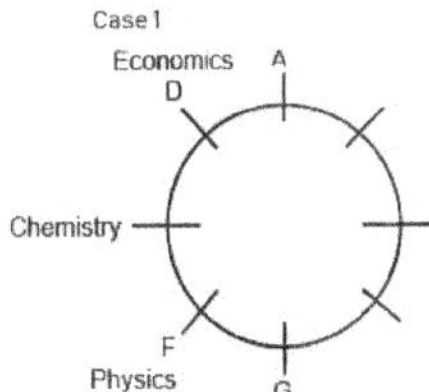

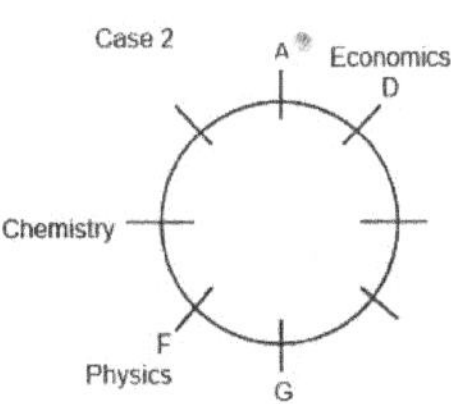

5) One who is studying Hindi sits fifth to the left of G, who is learning Sociology.

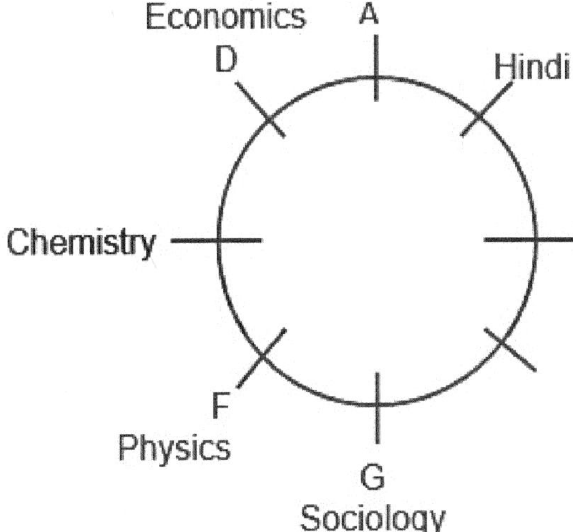

Thus, case 2 has been ruled out.

6) E is studying English and sits next to the one who is studying Hindi.

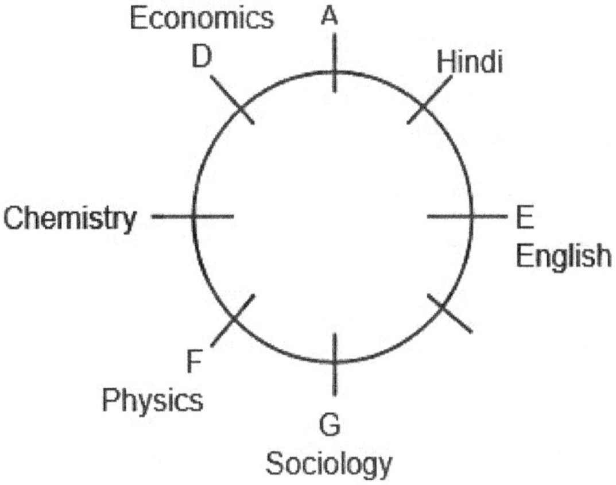

7) B is studying History and does not sit adjacent to C or D. Neither H nor E is immediate neighbour of G.

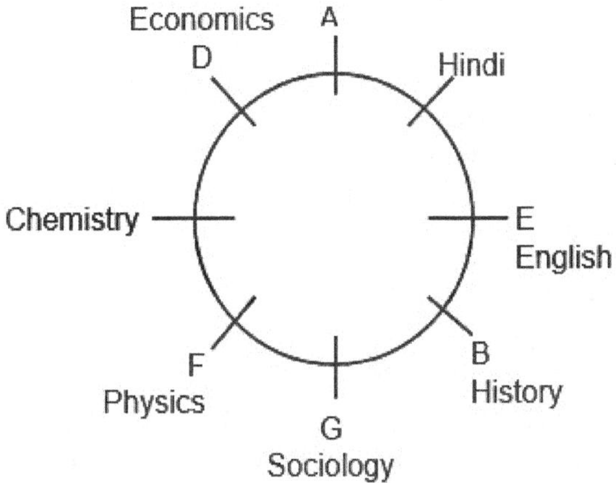

8) C does not study chemistry.

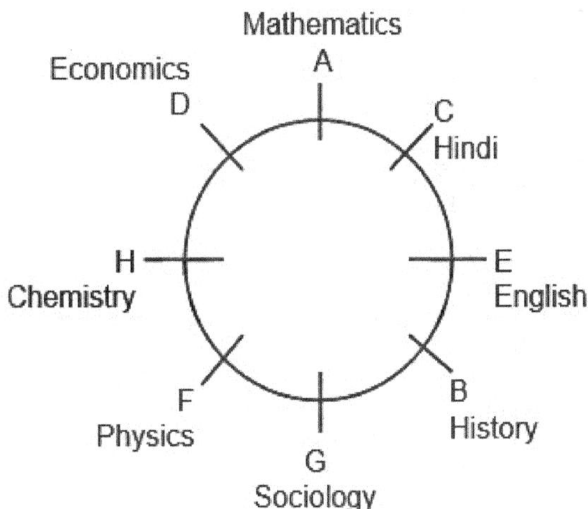

21. Thus, G is sitting third to the left of C and studies Sociology.

Hence, the correct option is (C).

22. Thus, D is sitting diagonally opposite to B.

Hence, the correct option is (A).

23. Thus, C sits between A and E.

Hence, the correct option is (C).

24. Thus, A is studying Mathematics.

Hence, the correct option is (E).

25. Thus, H is studying Chemistry.

Hence, the correct option is (D).

Ques (26-30):1. F was born in 2003. C, who was born in July, is five years elder than D.

		1998
F		2003
		2006
		2008
C	July	2010
		2014
D		2015

2. D was born in a month, which consists of only 30 days.
3. A is at most two years elder than the one, who was born in February.
So, D was born either in April or November. A was born in 2006 and the one, who is born in February, is born in 2008.

		1998
F		2003
A		2006
	February	2008
C	July	2010
		2014
D	April/November	2015

4. B was elder than E, who was not born in 2014.
5. G was not born immediately before the one, who was born in April.
So, B was born in 1998. E was born in 2008. G was born in 2014 and D was born in November.

B		1998
F		2003
A		2006
E	February	2008
C	July	2010
G		2014
D	November	2015

6. The kid, who was born in January, is elder than the one, who was born in April.
7. The kid, who was born in May is not elder than the one, who was born in April.
8. Kid, who was born in 1998, was not born in January.
So, F was born in January. A was born in April. G was born in May. B was born in August.
The final table is given below:

B	August	1998
F	January	2003
A	April	2006
E	February	2008

C	July	2010
G	May	2014
D	November	2015

26. F is three years elder than A.

Hence, the correct option is (D).

27. So, G was born in the month of May.

Hence, the correct option is (A).

28. The eldest child was born in August while the youngest child was born in November.

Hence, the correct option is (D).

29. So, Kid, who was born in May, is 11 years younger than F.

Hence, the correct option is (A).

30. So, the true statement is 2nd eldest kid was born in January

Hence, the correct option is (C).

Ques (1-3):Direction: Study the following information carefully and answer the questions that follow.

Pavan starts walking form point T. He walks for 5 km in north direction from point T to reach point W. Then he turns towards west and walks for 7 km to reach point K. From point K he turns towards South and walks for 10 km to reach point H. From point H he turns towards east and walks for 15 km to reach point F. Then he turns towards south and walks 5 km to reach point G. Finally he turns towards west and walks for 10 km to reach the final point C.

Q.1 Point W is in which direction with respect to point C?

A. North   **B.** South
C. North - East   **D.** North - West
E. West

Q.2 Point G is in which direction with respect to point H?

A. South   **B.** East
C. West   **D.** South - East
E. South - West

Q.3 What is the total distance covered by Pavan?

A. 50 km   **B.** 51 km   **C.** 53 km   **D.** 54 km
E. 52 km

Ques (4-6):Direction: Study the following information carefully and answer the given questions.

In a certain code language,

(i) 'si la mi' means 'flower are red'

(ii) 'si za bi ta' means 'steel industry are shrinking',

(iii) 'la ha pi bi' means 'steel component holds flower',

(iv) 'ma za ha sa' means 'component need better shrinking'

Q.4 Which of the following means 'better' in the code language?

A. ma
B. ha
C. sa
D. Either (A) or (B) or (C)
E. Either (A) or (C)

Q.5 Which of the following means 'industry' in that code language?

A. ta
B. za
C. sa
D. mi
E. Cannot be determined

Q.6 What will be the code for the sentence 'steel component are red'?

A. ha la mi si

B. bi ha si mi
C. la bi mi si
D. ha mi si la
E. Cannot be determined

Ques (7-11):Direction: Study the following information carefully and answer the question given below.

In a store seven boxes of different names are kept. They are: P, Q, R, S, T, U and V. Each box has a number written on it from 1 to 7 but not necessarily in the same order. The boxes are arranged in a stack in ascending order with the lowest number on the top.

Box Q is immediately above the box T. T is place on an odd number. Two boxes are kept between Q and S. Not more than one box is placed between S and P, in which S is placed above P. Two boxes are kept between T and R. The box V is placed immediately below box T but not immediately above the box U.

Q.7 Which of the following condition is true?

A. R - 8th   **B.** U - 1st
C. V - 6th   **D.** P - 3rd
E. None of these

Q.8 How many boxes are there between box Q and R?

A. 2   **B.** 5
C. 4   **D.** 3
E. None of these

Q.9 Which box is at the bottom?

A. P   **B.** S
C. U   **D.** T
E. None of these

Q.10 Box V is which number box?

A. 3rd   **B.** 6th
C. 4th   **D.** 5th
E. None of these

Q.11 Which box is kept between box S and P?

A. V   **B.** R
C. Q   **D.** T
E. None of these

Ques (12-16):Direction: Read the following information carefully and answer the given question:

Ten students are sitting in a straight line. Some of them are facing north while some of them are facing south. They all likes different subjects viz. Hindi, English, Maths, Physics, Biology, History, Geography, Computer, Commerce and Account but necessarily in the same order.

A likes Computer sits third from one of the extreme ends. A faces the same direction as C. Three students sit between A and H, who likes Math. G sits second to the right of H, who is not facing south direction. G sits third to the left of J and both are facing the same direction. The one who likes History is neither an immediate neighbor of the one who likes Math's nor A. B likes History and sits third to the right of F, who likes Commerce. Neither B nor F sits at extreme ends. The one who likes Biology and the one who likes Account are the immediate neighbors of each other. The students sit at extreme ends are facing the opposite direction.

There are as many students sit between C and the one who likes English as between D and one who likes English. C does not like Account. B and F are facing the same direction (Same direction means if B faces north then F also faces north and vice-versa). The one who likes Geography is not an immediate neighbor of E. E and I face the same direction as D, who faces the opposite direction of B. The one who likes Physics sits third to the left of the one who likes Hindi.

Q.12 Four among the following are the same in a certain way and thus form a group. Who among the following does not belong to that group?

A. A   **B.** I   **C.** H   **D.** D
E. E

Q.13 Which among the following statement is not true about J?

A. J likes English
B. J is facing south direction
C. J sits immediate right of B
D. Only one student sits between J and F
E. All statements are true

Q.14 E likes which of the following Subject?

A. Geography   **B.** Physics
C. Hindi   **D.** Account
E. Biology

Q.15 Who among the following student likes Physics?

A. D   **B.** I   **C.** E   **D.** C
E. G

Q.16 How many students are facing in the south direction?

A. Two   **B.** Three   **C.** Four   **D.** Five
E. Six

Q.17 Height of five students A, K, L, M and T are compared. Height of K is more than only two students. Height of M is greater than T and Height of T is greater than K. How many students are smaller than T ?

A. 3   **B.** 4   **C.** 5   **D.** 1
E. 2

Q.18 Among A, B, C, D, and E, A is taller than B but shorter than C. B is taller than only E. If C is not the tallest, then who will be in the middle keeping them in order of height?

A. A   **B.** B   **C.** C   **D.** D
E. E

Q.19 In a class of 60 students in which the number of girls is twice the number of boys, Kamal's rank is 17th from the top. If there are 9 girls ahead of Kamal then how many boys are behind him in the rank?

A. 3   **B.** 7   **C.** 12   **D.** 23
E. 20

Ques (20-22):Direction: In the question below are given three statements followed by two conclusions. You have to take the given statements to be true even if they seem to be at variance with commonly known facts. Read all the conclusions and then decide which of the given conclusions logically follows from the given statements disregarding commonly known facts.

Q.20 Statement:

I. All cars are bikes
II. No bikes are track
III. Only few tracks are laps

Conclusions:

I. Some cars are laps.
II. No cars are track.

A. Only conclusion I follows
B. Only conclusion II follows
C. Either conclusion I or II follows
D. Neither conclusion I nor II follows
E. Both conclusion I and II follows

Q.21 Statement:

I. Some hockey is tennis
II. All football is basketball
III. No football is hockey

Conclusions:

I. Some tennis is not football
II. Some basketball is hockey

A. Only conclusion I follows
B. Only conclusion II follows
C. Either conclusion I or II follows
D. Neither conclusion I or II follows
E. Both conclusion I and II follows

Q.22 Statement:

I. Only a few switches are USB
II. Only a few USB are wires
III. Some switches are not chargers

Conclusion:

I. Some chargers are wires
II. Few USB are chargers

A. Only I follows
B. Only II follows
C. Either I or II follows
D. Neither I nor II follows
E. Both I and II follows

Ques (23-24):Direction: These questions are based on the following information.

There are seven family members – P, Q, R, S, T, U, and V. R is the maternal grandmother of V. Q is the husband of R. S is the brother-in-law of Q. P is the nephew of S. T is the mother of V. U is the son-in-law of Q. There are four males in the family.

Q.23 How is V related to P?

A. Daughter
B. Nephew
C. Niece
D. Son
E. Cannot be determined

Q.24 How is P related to Q?
A. Daughter **B.** Son
C. Nephew **D.** Son-in-law
E. None of these

Ques (25-29):Directions: Study the following arrangement of alphabets and answer the questions given below:

Q W E R T Y U I O P A S D F G H J K L Z X C V B N M

Q.25 Which letter is fifth to the left of the seventh letter to the right of the eighteenth letter from the right end?
A. A **B.** W **C.** X **D.** P
E. G

Q.26 If all the vowels in the series are dropped, which letter would be the tenth to the right of the fifteenth letter from the right end?
A. J **B.** C
C. S **D.** D
E. None of these

Q.27 If the group of the first 5 letters is interchanged with the group of the last 5 letters such that the order of the letters within the group remain the same, then which letter will be the seventh to the left of the ninth letter from the left end?
A. C **B.** W **C.** V **D.** B
E. Y

Q.28 If the alternate letters are dropped starting from the first letter, which letter will be the fifth to the left of the eight-letter from the right end?
A. M **B.** C **C.** P **D.** W
E. Z

Q.29 Which letter is fifth to the right of the letter which is second to the right of the seventeenth letter from the left end?
A. Q **B.** J **C.** L **D.** O
E. B

Q.30 If the letter of the words 'FUTURISTIC' are arranged in alphabetic order from left to right then what would be the third letter of the meaningful English word formed using third, fifth, sixth and eighth letter of the word formed after arranging? (If no word is formed mark 'L' as your answer and if more than one word are formed mark 'M' as your answer)
A. R **B.** I **C.** S **D.** L
E. M

// Smart Answer Sheet //

Correct   Indicates percentage of students who answered questions correctly.

Skipped   Indicates percentage of students who skipped questions.

Q.	Ans.	Correct / Skipped	Q.	Ans.	Correct / Skipped	Q.	Ans.	Correct / Skipped	Q.	Ans.	Correct / Skipped	Q.	Ans.	Correct / Skipped
1	C	60.74 % / 1.64 %	7	B	40.85 % / 1.11 %	13	C	41.01 % / 1.04 %	19	C	61.09 % / 1.48 %	25	A	24.96 % / 4.51 %
2	D	86.94 % / 0.0 %	8	D	69.94 % / 1.85 %	14	C	89.67 % / 0.0 %	20	B	42.03 % / 1.06 %	26	B	47.61 % / 1.77 %
3	E	32.5 % / 3.38 %	9	A	78.47 % / 0.0 %	15	B	48.47 % / 1.3 %	21	A	76.01 % / 0.0 %	27	C	69.8 % / 1.54 %
4	E	51.71 % / 1.39 %	10	C	63.83 % / 1.78 %	16	E	51.19 % / 1.29 %	22	D	43.28 % / 1.18 %	28	D	41.55 % / 1.34 %
5	A	76.16 % / 0.0 %	11	B	66.69 % / 1.25 %	17	A	55.87 % / 1.89 %	23	C	45.25 % / 1.43 %	29	E	44.24 % / 1.08 %
6	B	40.16 % / 1.22 %	12	A	24.69 % / 4.99 %	18	A	54.75 % / 1.44 %	24	B	53.48 % / 1.03 %	30	B	20.61 % / 3.27 %

Performance Analysis

Avg. Score (%)	63.33%
Toppers Score (%)	63.33%
Your Score	

//Hints and Solutions//

Ques (1-3): According to the given information,

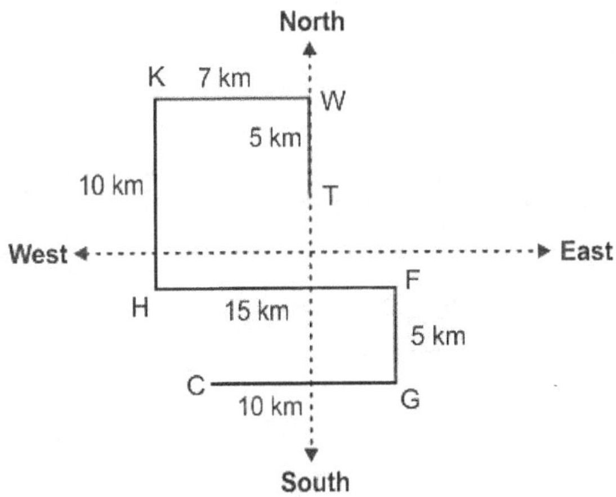

1. Thus, North - East is the correct answer.

Hence, the correct option is (C).

2. Thus, Southeast is the correct answer.

Hence, the correct option is (D).

3. Total distance covered by Pavan = 5 + 7 + 10 + 15 + 5 + 10 = 52

Thus, 52 km is the correct answer.

Hence, the correct option is (E).

Ques (4-6):

si (la) mi ⟶ \flower/ are red

si (za) (bi) ta ⟶ [steel] industry are (shrinking)

(la) [ha] pi (bi) ⟶ [steel] [component] holds \flower/

ma (za) [ha] sa ⟶ [component] need better (shrinking)

4. So, better is coded as either ma or sa.

Hence, the correct option is (E).

5. So, industry is coded as 'ta'.

Hence, the correct option is (A).

6. Code for steel = bi

Code for component = ha

Code for are = si

Code for red = mi

So, "steel component are red" is coded as "bi ha si mi".

Hence, the correct option is (B).

Ques (7-11): Boxes: 1 to 7 in ascending order

Boxes names: P, Q, R, S, T, U and V

1) Box Q is immediately above the box T.

2) T is place on an odd number.

3) Two boxes are kept between Q and S.

Box	Case 1	Case 2	Case 3	Case 4
1			S	
2	Q			
3	T			S
4		Q	Q	
5	S	T	T	
6				Q
7		S		T

4) Not more than one box is placed between S and P, in which S is placed above P.

Box	Case 1	Case 2	Case 3	Case 4	Case 5
1			S		P
2	Q				
3	T		P	S	S
4		Q	Q		
5	S	T	T	P	
6				Q	Q
7	P	S		T	T

As case 2 and 5 does not fulfil the above condition, it is thus eliminated.

5) Two boxes are kept between T and R.

6) The box V is placed immediately below box T but not immediately above the box U.

Box	Case 1	Case 3	Case 4
1	U	S	
2	Q	R	
3	T	P	S
4	V	Q	R
5	S	T	P
6	R	V	Q
7	P	U	T

As case 3 and 4 does not fulfil the above condition, it is thus eliminated.

The final arrangement will be:

Box	Names
1	U
2	Q
3	T
4	V
5	S
6	R
7	P

7. As U is the 1st number box.

So, the condition U - 1st is true and the other conditions are false.

Hence, the correct option is (B).

8. So, 3 boxes are there between box Q and R.

Hence, the correct option is (D).

9. So, box P is at the bottom.

Hence, the correct option is (A).

10. So, box V is 4th number box.

Hence, the correct option is (C).

11. So, Box R is kept between box S and Box P.

Hence, the correct option is (B).

Ques (12-16):(1) A likes Computer sits third from one of the extreme ends.

(2) Three students sit between A and H who like Maths.

(3) G sits second to the right of H, who is not facing south direction.

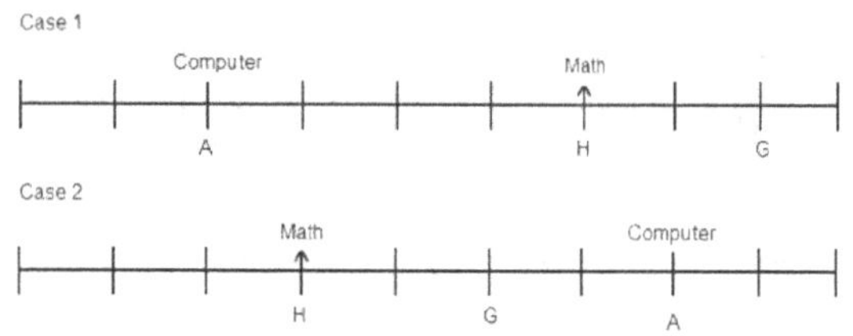

(4) G sits third to the left of J and both are facing the same direction. (This creates one more case in case 2 so here we say case 3)

(5) The one who likes History is neither an immediate neighbor of the one who likes Maths nor A.

(6) B likes History and sits third to the right of F, who likes Commerce. Neither B nor F sits at extreme ends. (Here again, one more case with case 1 because in case 1 F can be either side of B. we name that condition Case 4)

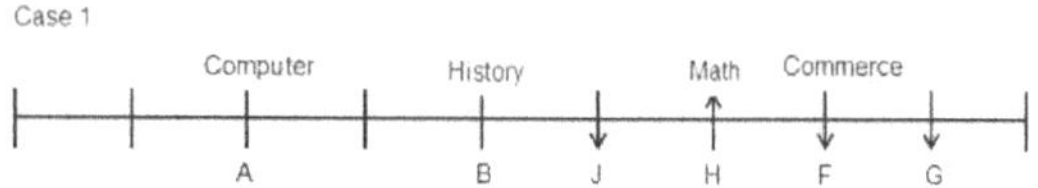

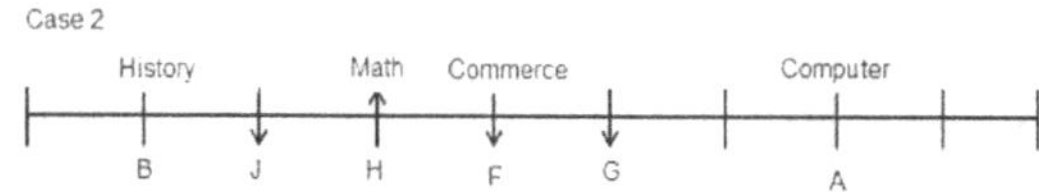

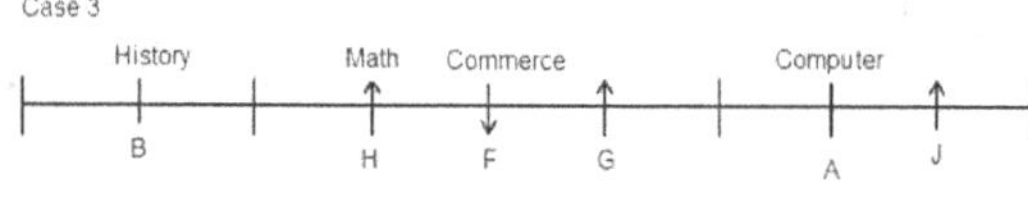

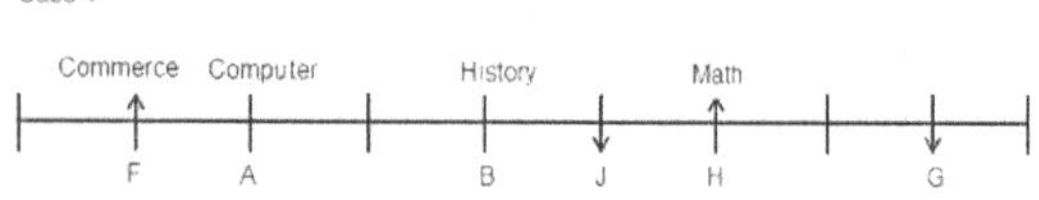

(7) There are as many students sits between C and the one who likes English as between D and one who likes English. (This eliminates case 2 and case 3)

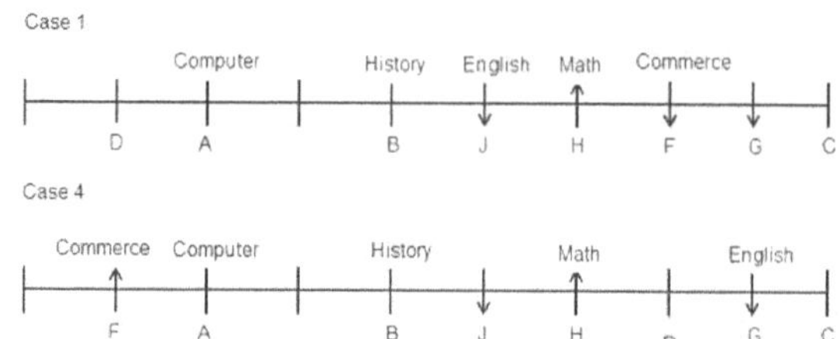

(8) The one who likes Biology and the one who likes Account are the immediate neighbors of each other. (This eliminates case 4)

(9) C does not like Account.

(10) B and F are facing the same direction

(11) E and I face the same direction as D, who faces the opposite direction of B.

(12) The one who likes Physics sits third to the left of the one who likes Hindi.

(13) The one who likes Geography is not an immediate neighbor of E.

(14) The students sit at extreme ends are facing the opposite directions.

(15) A faces the same direction as C.

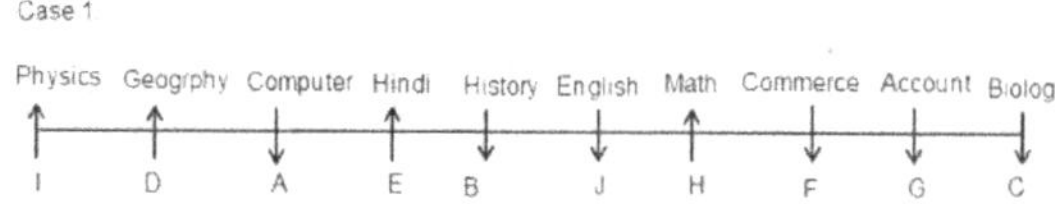

12. All are facing north except A.

So, A does not belong to that group.

Hence, the correct option is (A).

13. So, Clearly, J sits immediate left of B.

Hence, the correct option is (C).

14. So, E likes Hindi.

Hence, the correct option is (C).

15. So, I likes Physics

Hence, the correct option is (B).

16. Clearly, Six students are facing south direction.

Hence, the correct option is (E).

17. Given,

Height of five students A, K, L, M and T are compared. Height of K is more than only two students. Height of M is greater than T and Height of T is greater than K.

Five students -A, K, L, M and T are compared.

1. Height of K is more than only two students.

_ > _ > K > _ > _

2. Height of M is greater than T and Height of T is greater than K.

M > T > K

From condition 1 and 2, we get

M > T > K > _ > _

So, 3 students are smaller than T.

Hence, the correct option is (A).

18. Given,

Of A, B, C, D and E A, B is longer than A, B but shorter than C. B is longer than E only. If C is not the longest.

According to the given information,

D > C > A > B > E

A will be in the middle if they stand in the order of height.

Hence, the correct option is (A).

19. Let the number of boys be x.

Then, the number of girls $= 2x$

According to the question,

$\therefore x + 2x = 60$

$\Rightarrow 3x = 60$

$\Rightarrow x = 20$

Hence, the number of boys $= 20$

And the number of girls $= 40$

Number of students behind Kamal in rank $= (60 - 17) = 43$

Number of girls ahead of Kamal in rank $= 9$

Number of girls behind Kamal in rank $= (40 - 9) = 31$

$\therefore$ Number of boys behind Kamal in rank $= (43 - 31) = 12$

Hence, the correct option is (C).

20. The least possible Venn diagram for the given statements is as follows:

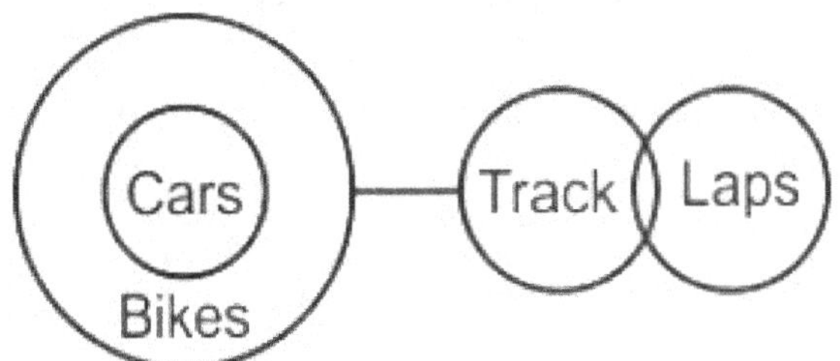

Conclusions:

I. Some cars are laps → False (It is possible, but there is no definite positive or negative relation is given between the elements, therefore it is false)

II. No cars are track → True (Because all cars are bikes and no bikes are track → no cars are track)

So, only conclusion II follows.

Hence, the correct option is (B).

21. The least possible Venn diagram for the given statements is as follows:

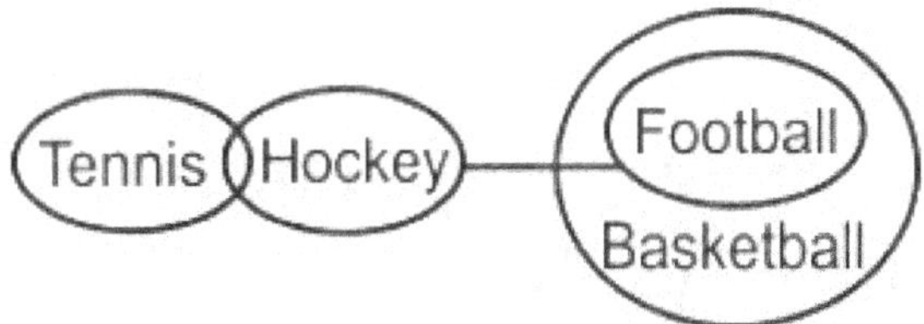

Conclusions:

I. Some tennis is not football → True (Because some tennis are hockey and no hockey is football, which implies that the tennis which is hockey will not be football)

II. Some basketball is hockey → False (It is possible, but there is no definite positive or negative relation is given between the elements, therefore it is false)

So, only conclusion I follows.

Hence, the correct option is (A).

22. The least possible Venn diagram for the given statements is as follows:

Conclusion:

I. Some chargers are wires → False (As there is no definite relation between chargers and wires, We cannot determine some chargers are wires or not)

II. Few USB are chargers → False (As there is no definite relation between chargers and USB, We cannot determine few USB are chargers or not)

So, Neither I nor II follows.

Hence, the correct option is (D).

Ques (23-24): From the given information,

(i) T is the mother of V. R is the grandmother of V.

(ii) Q is the husband of R. S is the brother-in-law of Q.

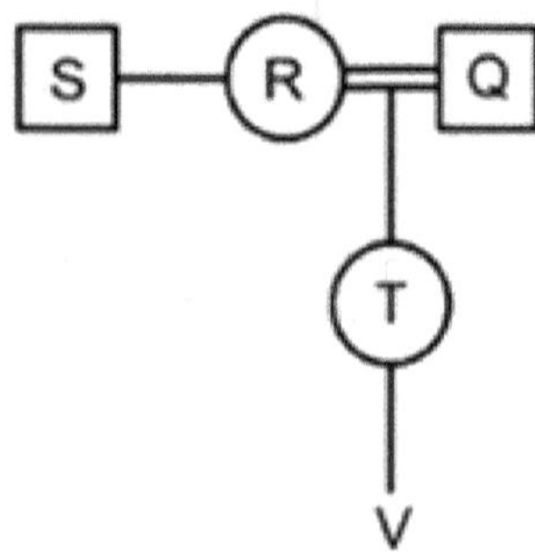

(iii) U is the son-in-law of Q. P is the nephew of S.

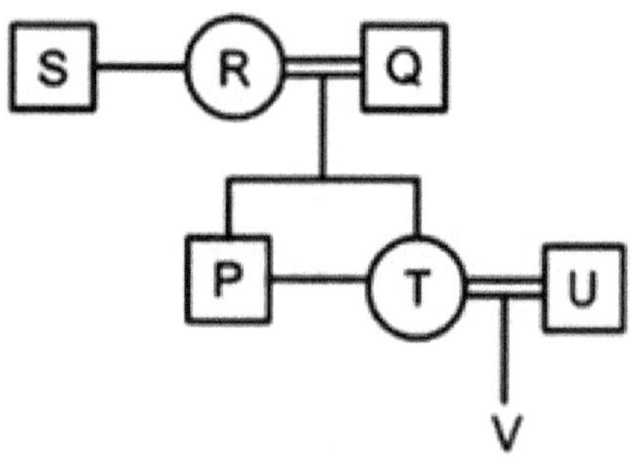

(iv) There are 4 males in the family. It means V is female.

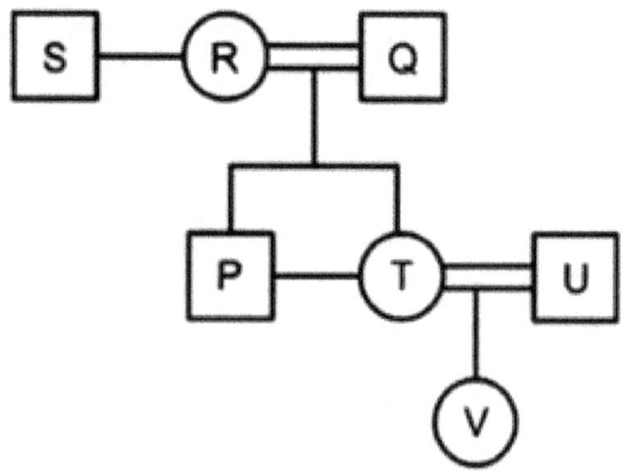

23. So, V is the niece of P.

Hence, the correct option is (C).

24. So, P is the son of Q.

Hence, the correct option is (B).

25. Eighteenth letter from the right end → O

Seventh letter to the right of O → H

Fifth letter to the left of H → A

Hence, the correct option is (A).

26. After removing all the vowels, the series becomes:

Q W R T Y P S D F G H J K L Z X C V B N M

Now, the fifteenth letter from the right end → S

Tenth letter to the right of S → C

Hence, the correct option is (B).

27. After interchanging,

C V B N M Y U I O P A S D F G H J K L Z X Q W E R T

Now, the ninth letter from the left end → O

Seventh letter to the left of O → V

Hence, the correct option is (C).

28. The series formed after dropping alternate letters starting from the first letter:

W R Y I P S F H K Z C B M

Eighth letter from the right → S

Fifth letter to the left of S → W

Hence, the correct option is (D).

29. Q W E R T Y U I O P A S D F G H J K L Z X C V B N M

Seventeenth letter from the left end → J

The second letter to the right of J → L

Fifth to the right of L → B

Hence, the correct option is (E).

30. The given word:

FUTURISTIC

After arranging the letters of the word in alphabetic order from left to right, we get:

CFIIRSTTUU

Now, the third, fifth, sixth and eighth letters of the word 'CFIIRSTTUU' are I, R, S and T.

The meaningful English word that can be formed using I, R, S and T is STIR.

Here, the third letter of the word 'STIR' is 'I'.

Hence, the correct option is (B).

Ques (1-3):Direction: Study the following information carefully and answer the given questions.

In a certain code of language,

'David is going school' is coded as 'da mi ge he',

'David stays there' is coded as 'da ta ri',

'school is there' is coded as 'he mi ri'

'Roshni stays in school' is coded as 'ra ta li he'

Q.1 How will 'David is Roshni' be written in that language?

A. da mi ra   **B.** da mi li

C. da mi ri   **D.** Either (A) or (B)

E. Either (A) or (C)

Q.2 What is the meaning of 'li' in that language?

A. Roshni   **B.** Davide

C. in   **D.** stays

E. Either (A) or (C)

Q.3 What does 'ta' mean in that language?

A. there   **B.** David   **C.** is   **D.** stays

E. school

Ques (4-6):Direction: In the following question assuming the given statements to be True, find which of the conclusion among given conclusions is/are definitely true and then give your answers accordingly.

Q.4 Statements: A > B ≥ C , C < D

Conclusion:

I. A > D

II. A > C

A. Only I is true

B. Only II is true

C. Neither I nor II is true

D. Both I and II are true

E. Either I or II is true

Q.5 Statements:

C ≤ D ≥ F < B > Q, Q < Y ≥ O > P

Conclusions:

I. F > Y

II. B > P

A. Only conclusion I follows

B. Only conclusion II follows

C. Both conclusion I and II follows

D. Either conclusion I or II follows

E. Neither conclusion I nor II follows

Q.6 Statements:

T < H ≤ W, D > S ≥ M, T > D

Conclusions:

I. W > D

II. M < T

III. H > S

A. All follow

B. Only I follow

C. Only II follow

D. Only I and III follow

E. None follow

Ques (7-11):Direction: Study the following information carefully and answer the given question.

Eight persons are sitting in two parallel rows in which four persons are sitting in each row A, B, C and D are sitting in row-1 and all of them are facing south. While in row- 2 P, Q, R and S are sitting and all of them are facing north.

Hence, in the given seating arrangement each member sitting in a row faces another member of the other row. They all like different colours.

B sits second to the right of the one who likes the yellow colour. C sits opposite to the one who likes the Orange colour, who sits second to the left of S. Q sits immediately the left of the one who likes black colour. A sits immediate right of the one who likes gray colour. The one who likes white color sits opposite to B. P sits opposite to the one who likes green color but does not sit at the end. C likes neither Olive color nor Blue colour. The one who likes Blue color faces south.

Q.7 Who sits between A and the one who likes the Blue colour?

A. B

B. C

C. D

D. The one who likes black

E. The one who likes gray

Q.8 Who among the following sits at the extreme ends of the rows?

A. Q and the one who likes white

B. R and the one who likes Olive

C. S and the one who likes Orange color

D. D and the one who likes Blue

E. A and the one who likes Green

Q.9 Who among the following faces the one who likes Olive?

A. The one who likes green color

B. The one who likes Blue color

C. The one who likes gray color

D. The one who likes yellow color

E. D

Q.10 Who among the following likes the Blue colour?

A. B

B. C

C. D

D. A

E. Cannot be determined

Q.11 Who among the following likes white colour?

A. R

B. C

C. D

D. A

E. Cannot be determined

Q.12 If all the letters of the word 'UNIDENTIFIED' are arranged in the alphabetical order then the position of how many letters will be remain unchanged?

A. Zero

B. One

C. Two

D. Three

E. More than three

Ques (13-17):Direction: Study the following information to answer the questions.

Ten persons are sitting in two parallel rows containing five person each in such a way that there is an equal distance between adjacent persons. In row 1 P, Q, R, S, and T are seated and all of them are facing South. In row 2 A, B, C, D, and E are seated and all of them are facing North. Therefore, in the given seating arrangement each member seated in a row faces another member in the other row. S sits third to the right of Q where either of them is sitting on any of the extreme ends of the row. The one who faces Q sits second to the right of E. Two persons are sitting between B and E. Neither A nor C sits at an end of the row. The immediate neighbour of A faces the person who sits immediately to the right of Q. R and T are immediate neighbours of each other. T does not face the immediate neighbour of D.

Q.13 Who among the following is facing P?

A. S   **B.** R   **C.** Q   **D.** P

E. B

Q.14 Which of the following statements is true regarding R?

A. R faces one of the immediate neighbors of D.

B. P is one of the immediate neighbors of R.

C. None of the given statement is true.

D. R sits to the immediate right of Q.

E. All of the given statements are true.

Q.15 Who among the following is facing T?

A. D   **B.** E   **C.** B   **D.** C

E. A

Q.16 What is the position of C with respect to A?

A. Second to the left

B. Immediate left

C. Immediate right

D. Third to the right

E. Second to the right

Q.17 Four of the following five are alike in a certain way and so form a group, find the one which does not belong to the group?

A. S   **B.** P   **C.** D   **D.** B

E. C

Q.18 Kamal is 11th from the front in a row of girls. Leela is 3 places ahead of Sunita, who is 22nd from the lead. How many girls are there between Kamal and Leela in this row?

A. 6

B. 8

C. 7

D. 9

E. Cannot be determined

Q.19 In a row of children, Kailash is fifth from the left and Mona is sixth from the right. When they interchange their positions, then Kailash becomes thirteenth from the left. What will be the position of Mona from the right?

A. Fourth

B. Fourteenth

C. Eighth

D. Fifteenth

E. Cannot be determined

Q.20 Direction: Read the following information carefully and answer the question that follows.

In a row of 35 children, M is 15th from the right and there are 10 children between M and R. What is the position of R from the left end of the row?

A. 15th

B. 5th

C. 30th

D. 20th

E. Cannot be determined

Ques (21-22):Directions: Read the following information carefully to answer the question that follows:

There are six members P, Q, R, S, T and U in the family of three generations. There is no single parent in the family. U is paternal aunt of T. R is mother-in-law of S's husband. Q has only one child. S and Q are not married to each other.

Q.21 How is U related to S?

A. Daughter

B. Sister-in-law

C. Sister

D. Mother

E. Daughter-in-law

Q.22 Who is the father of S?

A. Can't be determined

B. P

C. Q

D. T

E. None of these

Ques (23-25):Direction: Read the following information carefully and answer the question that follows:

Darshana moved 1 km South to reach point P. She turns 60° to her left and goes 7 km to point Q. She takes a 150° turn to her right and goes 12 km to reach point R. Now she turns 120° to her right and goes 9 km to reach S.

Q.23 Starting Pointis in which direction with respect to R?

A. Northeast

B. Northwest

C. Southeast

D. East

E. Southwest

Q.24 Point S is in which direction with respect to point Q?

A. Northwest   **B.** Southeast
C. Northeast   **D.** East
E. Southwest

Q.25 What is the total distance covered by Darshana when she reaches point S?

A. 25 km   **B.** 49 km   **C.** 30 km   **D.** 29 km
E. 20 km

Ques (26-30):Direction: Study the following information carefully to answer the given question:

Y W @ 1 & C N 3 P L B 9 ↑ = D ◊ E 2 £ M V $ 7 # 4 F G 5

Q.26 How many such symbols are there in the above arrangement which are not immediately preceded by a number and also not immediately followed by a letter?

A. Nil   **B.** One
C. Two   **D.** Three
E. None of these

Q.27 C 1 3 W : 7 4 V G in the same way as N @ B = : ?

A. $ 4 2 D   **B.** V F 2 D   **C.** $ F 2 ◊   **D.** $ F £ D
E. $ F 2 D

Q.28 If the numbers immediately preceding the symbols are attached the value double their numerical value, then what will be sum of the value of all such numbers?

A. 22   **B.** 26
C. 36   **D.** 38
E. None of these

Q.29 Four of the following are alike in a certain way based on the above arrangement and hence form a group. Which one does not belong to the group?

A. ◊ V 2 M   **B.** ↑ 2 D E   **C.** L D B =   **D.** V F 7 4
E. & L N P

Q.30 If Y W @ 1 are written in the reverse order, & C N 3 are written in the reverse order and so on, then in the new arrangement which of the following will be exactly in the middle between 9 and $?

A. ↑   **B.** =
C. D   **D.** M
E. None of these

// Smart Answer Sheet //

Correct — Indicates percentage of students who answered questions correctly.

Skipped — Indicates percentage of students who skipped questions.

Q.	Ans.	Correct / Skipped
1	D	80.4 % / 0.0 %
2	E	87.55 % / 0.0 %
3	D	88.17 % / 0.0 %
4	B	77.93 % / 0.0 %
5	E	44.83 % / 1.86 %
6	A	61.82 % / 1.04 %

Q.	Ans.	Correct / Skipped
7	B	28.56 % / 3.46 %
8	D	28.76 % / 3.97 %
9	D	41.23 % / 1.13 %
10	A	43.1 % / 1.77 %
11	A	61.92 % / 1.87 %
12	B	81.4 % / 0.0 %

Q.	Ans.	Correct / Skipped
13	E	65.57 % / 1.68 %
14	A	80.02 % / 0.0 %
15	D	18.52 % / 3.91 %
16	B	42.15 % / 1.31 %
17	E	81.53 % / 0.0 %
18	B	46.03 % / 1.01 %

Q.	Ans.	Correct / Skipped
19	B	64.7 % / 1.46 %
20	E	48.66 % / 1.67 %
21	B	19.98 % / 3.29 %
22	C	42.89 % / 1.52 %
23	A	47.15 % / 1.49 %
24	A	51.18 % / 1.75 %

Q.	Ans.	Correct / Skipped
25	D	63.6 % / 1.36 %
26	C	78.09 % / 0.0 %
27	E	61.11 % / 1.73 %
28	D	67.16 % / 1.74 %
29	C	79.94 % / 0.0 %
30	A	88.21 % / 0.0 %

Performance Analysis

Avg. Score (%)	33.33%
Toppers Score (%)	56.67%
Your Score	

//Hints and Solutions//

Ques (1-3):

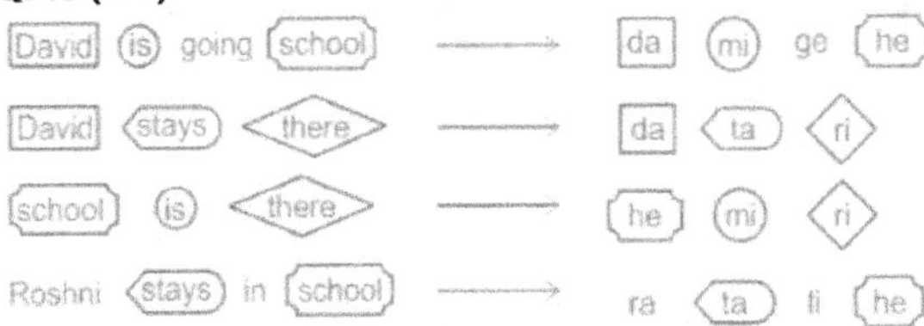

Therefore, in the given code language,

'da' means 'David'

'mi' means 'is'

'he' means 'school'

'ge' means 'going'

'ta' means 'stays'

'ri' means 'there'

1. Either 'da mi ra' or 'da mi li' means 'David is Roshni.'

Hence, the correct option is (D).

2. Therefore, 'li' means either 'Roshni' or 'in' in that language.

Hence, the correct option is (E).

3. Therefore, 'ta' means 'stays' in that code language.

Hence, the correct option is (D).

4. Given statements: A > B ≥ C, C < D

Conclusions:

I. A > D → False (as A > B ≥ C < D)

II. A > C → True (as A > B ≥ C → A > C)

So, only II is true.

Hence, the correct option is (B).

5. Given statements: C ≤ D ≥ F < B > Q, Q < Y ≥ O > P

On combining,

C ≤ D ≥ F < B > Q < Y ≥ O > P

Conclusions:

I. F > Y → False (As per C ≤ D ≥ F < B > Q < Y ≥ O > P → Relationship between F and Y can't be determined)

II. B > P → False (As per C ≤ D ≥ F < B > Q < Y ≥ O > P → Relationship between B and P can't be determined)

So, neither conclusion I nor II follows.

Hence, the correct option is (E).

6. Given statements: T < H ≤ W; D > S ≥ M; T > D

On combining: W ≥ H > T > D > S ≥ M

Conclusions:

I. W > D → True (W ≥ H > T > D → W > D)

II. M < T → True (T > D > S ≥ M → T > M)

III. H > S → True (H > T > D > S → H > S)

Thus, all the conclusions follow.

Hence, the correct option is (A).

Ques (7-11):

According to the given information,

First of all, we will decide the position of the B, person who likes yellow colour, C and the one who likes orange colour. The one who sits second to the left of S. Here the word 'who' is used for the person who likes orange color-

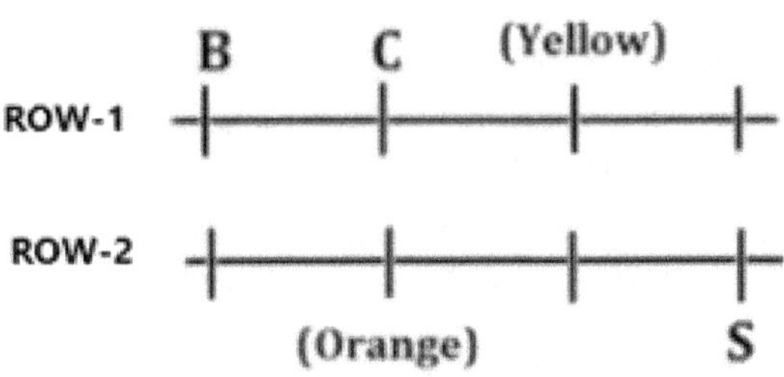

P is opposite to the one who likes Green, and he does not sit at the end also, similarly, C does not like Olive color and he is also not at the end, so on these clues, we can determine the final seating arrangement as follows-

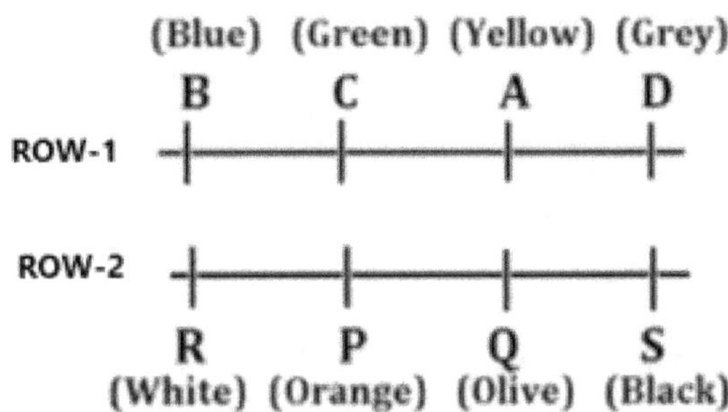

7. As per above seating arrangement C sits between A and the one who likes the Blue colour.

Hence, the correct option is (B).

8. As per the above seating arrangement D and the one who likes Blue sits at extreme ends.

Hence, the correct option is (D).

9. As per above seating arrangement the one who likes the Yellow color faces the one who likes Olive.

Hence, the correct option is (D).

10. According to the above seating arrangement, among the following B likes Blue colour.

Hence, the correct option is (A).

11. R likes white color as per above seating arrangement.

Hence, the correct option is (A).

12. The given word:

UNIDENTIFIED

After arranging the letters in alphabetical order:

DDEEFIIINNTU

The final arrangement of old and new words are:

U	N	I	D	E	N	T	I	F	I	E	D
D	D	E	E	F	I	I	I	N	N	T	U

On comparing both the words we will find that the position of only 1 letter viz. I is unchanged.
Hence, the correct option is (B).

Ques (13-17): Facing South: P, Q, R, S, and T (Row 1)

Facing North: A, B, C, D, and E (Row 2)

(1) S sits third to the right of Q where either of them is sitting on any of the extreme ends of the row.

(Here, there are two possible cases, Case 1: Q sits at the extreme right end of the row, Case 2: S sits at the extreme left end of the row.)

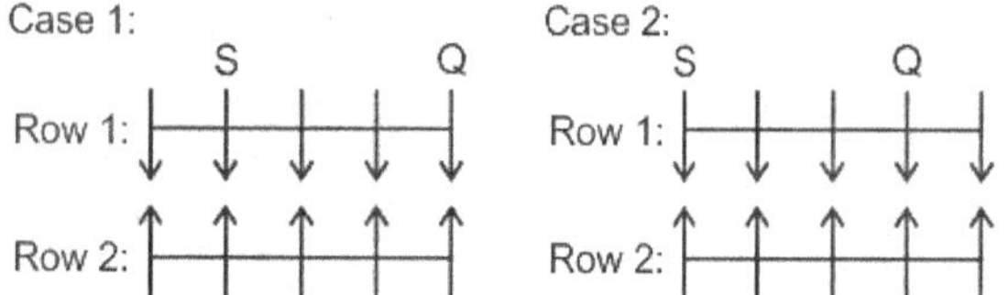

(2) The one who faces Q sits second to the right of E.

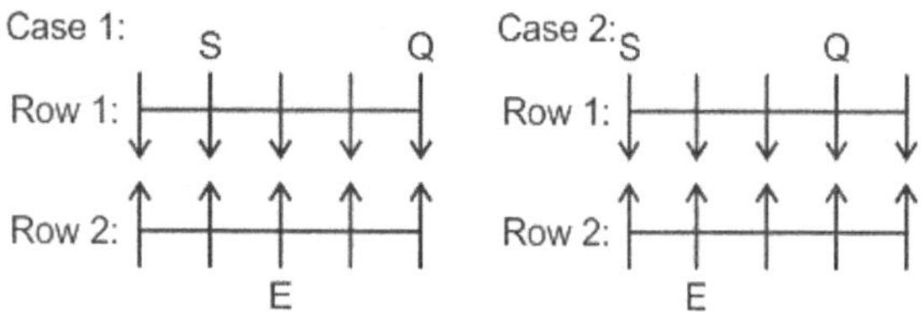

(3) Two persons are sitting between B and E.

(Here we can eliminate Case 1)

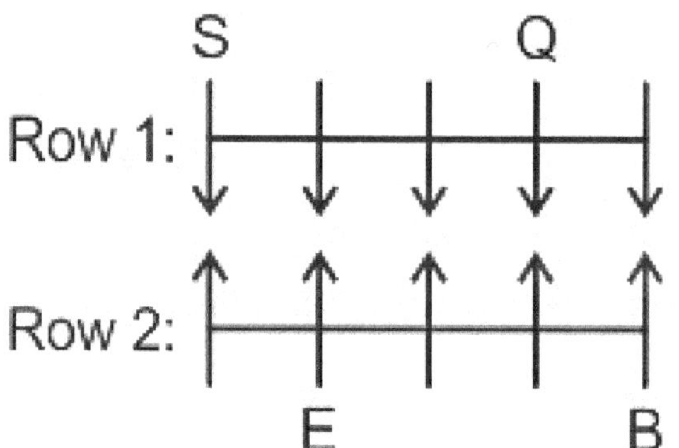

(4) Neither A nor C sits at an extreme end of the row.

(So D sits at the extreme end of row 2)

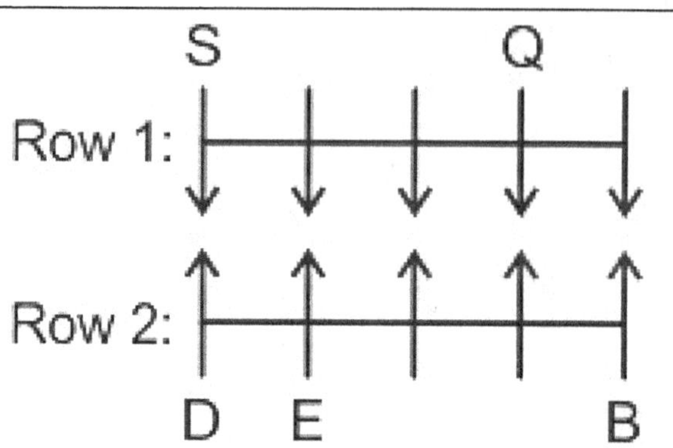

(5) The immediate neighbour of A faces the person who sits immediately to the right of Q.

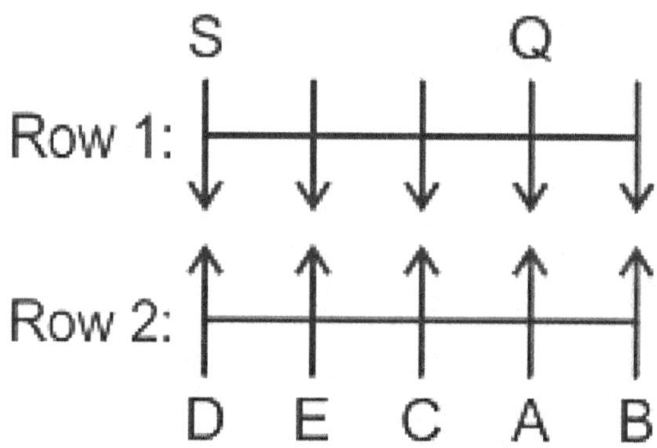

(6) R and T are immediate neighbours of each other.

(7) T does not face the immediate neighbour of D.

The final arrangement will be as follows.

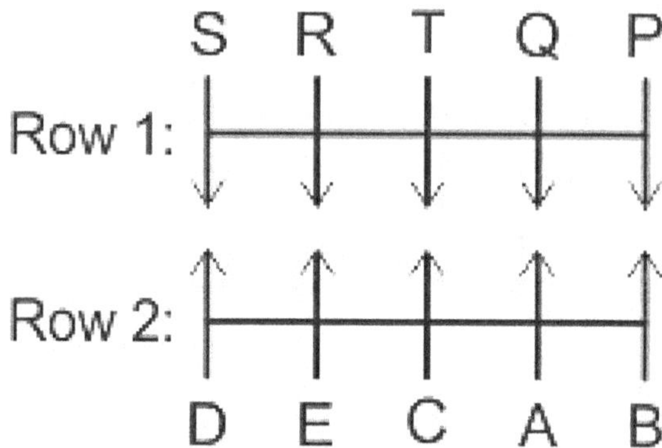

13. Thus, B is facing P.

Hence, the correct option is (E).

14. Thus, R faces one of the immediate neighbours of the D is a true statement.

Hence, the correct option is (A).

15. Thus, C is facing T.

Hence, the correct option is (D).

16. Thus, C sits immediate left of A.

Hence, the correct option is (B).

17. S, P, D, and B are sitting at the extreme ends of the row. C sits in the middle of the row.

Thus, C does not belong to the group.

Hence, the correct option is (E).

18. Kamal is 11th from the front in a row of girls. Leela is 3 places ahead of Sunita, who is 22nd from the lead.

According to the given information,

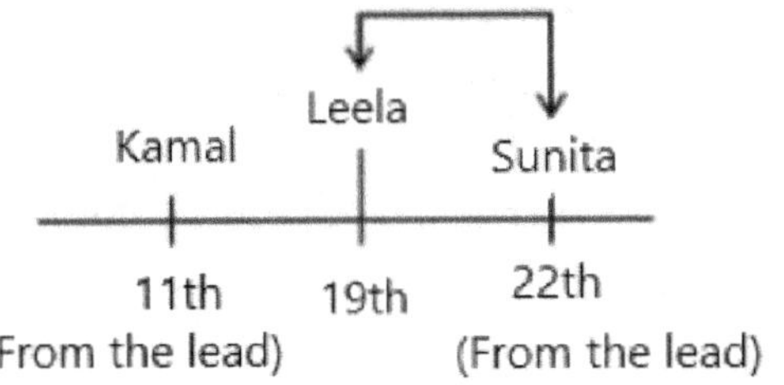

Girls in row between Kamal and Leela = 19 - 11 = 8

Hence, the correct option is (B).

19. Given,

In a row of children, Kailash is fifth from the left and Mona is sixth from the right. When they interchange their positions, then Kailash becomes thirteenth from the left.

According to the given information,

After changing the position,

1 2 3 4 ⑤ 6 7 8 9 10 11 12 ⑬ 14 15 16 17 18
Mona   Kailash

We can say after looking at the diagram, Mona's position will be fourteenth from the right.

Present position of Kailash = 13

Former position of Kailash = 5

Difference of present and former position of Kailash = 13 - 5 = 8

Former position of Mona = 6

Mona's present position = Difference of Kailash's present and former position + Former position of Mona

= 8 + 6 = 14

Hence, the correct option is (B).

20. Given,

In a row of 35 children, M is 15th from the right and there are 10 children between M and R.

According to the given information,

$$
\begin{array}{c}
\text{M} \qquad \text{R} \\
\hline
20 \quad \text{15th} \quad 10 \quad 4 \\
\text{(Left end)} \qquad \text{(Right end)}
\end{array}
$$

Or,

$$
\begin{array}{c}
\text{R} \qquad \text{M} \\
\hline
9 \quad \text{10th} \quad 10 \quad \text{15th} \quad 14 \\
\text{(Left end)} \qquad \text{(Right end)}
\end{array}
$$

Thus, the position of R cannot be determined.

Hence, the correct option is (E).

Ques (21-22): From the given information,

Symbol in Diagram	Meaning
◯	Female
▢	Male
═══	Married Couple
───	Siblings
│	Difference of A Generation

1. U is the paternal aunt of T. R is the mother-in-law of S's husband.

2. Q has only one child.

3. S and Q are not married to each other.

Based on the given data, we can draw the family tree,

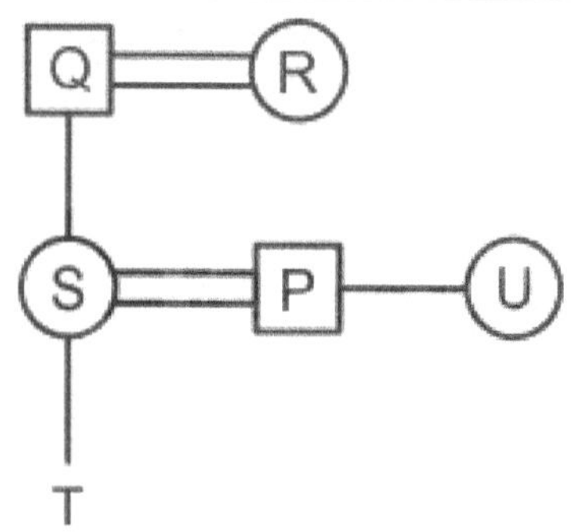

21. So, U is the sister-in-law of S.

Hence, the correct option is (B).

22. So, Q is the father of S.

Hence, the correct option is (C).

Ques (23-25): We have drawn the figure according to the information given in the question,

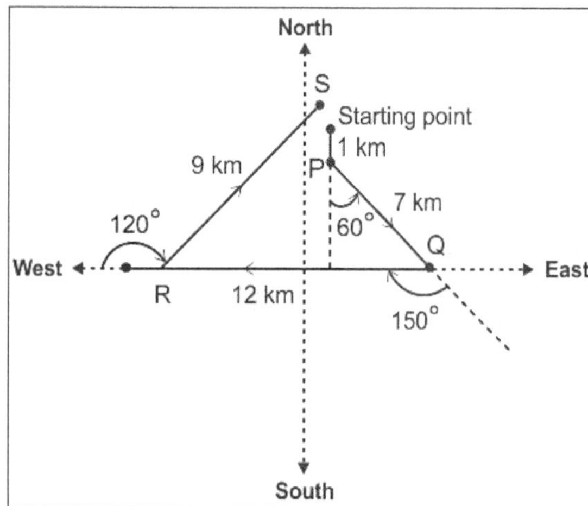

23. So, Starting Point is in Northeast direction with respect to R.

Hence, the correct option is (A).

24. So, Point S is in the Northwest direction with respect to point Q.

Hence, the correct option is (A).

25. Starting point to P + P to Q + Q to R + R to S = 1 + 7 + 12 + 9 = 29 km

So, the total distance covered by Darshana when she reaches point S is 29 km.

Hence, the correct option is (D).

26. Given Statement :

| Y | W | @ | 1 | & | C | N | 3 | P | L | B | 9 | ↑ | = | D | ◊ | E | 2 | £ | M | V | $ | 7 | # | 4 | F | G | 5 |

Condition: Symbols which are not immediately preceded by a number and also not immediately followed by a letter

| Y | W | @ | 1 | & | C | N | 3 | P | L | B | 9 | ↑ | = | D | ◊ | E | 2 | £ | M | V | $ | 7 | # | 4 | F | G | 5 |

So, two is correct.

Hence, the correct option is (C).

27. Given Statement :

| Y | W | @ | 1 | & | C | N | 3 | P | L | B | 9 | ↑ | = | D | ◊ | E | 2 | £ | M | V | $ | 7 | # | 4 |

In each pair, the corresponding elements of both the terms occupy the same position from the beginning and end of the given sequence.

So, $ F 2 D is correct.

Hence, the correct option is (E).

28. Such numbers may be shown in the sequence as follows:

| Y | W | @ | 1 | & | C | N | 3 | P | L | B | 9 | ↑ | = | D | ◊ | E | 2 | £ | M | V | $ | 7 | # | 4 |

Therefore, required sum = 2 * (1 + 9 + 2 + 7) = 2 * 19 = 38

So, 38 is correct.

Hence, the correct option is (D).

29. In all other groups, the first element moves five steps forward to give the second element, the second element moves three steps backward to give the third element; the third element moves two steps forward to give the fourth element.

So, L D B = does not belong to the group.

Hence, the correct option is (C).

30. The new arrangement is :

| 1 | @ | W | Y | 3 | N | C | & | 9 | B | L | P | ◊ | D | = | ↑ | M | £ | 2 | E | # | 7 | $ | V | 5 |

There are 13 elements between 9 & $.

So, the middle one will be 7th element to the right of 9, which is ↑

Hence, the correct option is (A).

Ques (1-4):Direction: In the given question, a part of the sentence is printed in bold. Below the sentence alternatives to the bold part are given at (A), (B), (C) and (D) which may help improve the sentence. Choose the correct alternative. In case the given sentence is correct, your answer is (E), i.e., "No correction required".

Q.1 He nonetheless continued to hold that all violence was wrong, and was not even **tempted by the implausible lenient idea** that, if something is not one's fault, it can only be apparently wrong.
A. Tempted by the implausible lenient ideae
B. Tempted with the implausible lenient idea
C. Tempted by the implausibleness lenient idea
D. Tempted by the implausibly lenient idea
E. No correction required

Q.2 **Dig deep into** the subject, he traces the origins of the plant from which hashish is made.
A. The object being assimilated into
B. The transformation of the object into
C. Delving deep into
D. A series of an investigation into
E. No correction required

Q.3 Indians involved **with agriculture have less access** to basic education and healthcare necessities.
A. In agriculture have the least access to
B. With agriculture have the least access to
C. To agriculture have the lest access to
D. In agriculture has the less access to
E. No correction required

Q.4 **Donald should have consider** all his options before taking such a life-changing decision.
A. Donald should have been considering
B. Donald should considered
C. Donald should have considered
D. Donald should have to consider
E. No correction required

Ques (5-10):Direction: Fill in the blank with the most appropriate word.

Q.5 The referee allowed the teams to play on without blowing the final whistle ______ one of them scored a winning goal.
A. unless   B. still   C. until   D. through
E. yet

Q.6 Either my cousin or **I is held** responsible for the broken tool.
A. myself is held
B. I are held
C. me is held
D. I am held

E. No correction required

Q.7 A painter **always is having** his own vision of life.
A. each time will have
B. every time is having
C. always has
D. every time will have
E. No correction required

Q.8 As there was no time, the remaining items **were deferred into** the next meeting.
A. Are deferred till
B. Were deferred till
C. Were deferred to
D. Had deferred with
E. No correction required

Q.9 They **are not beware of** all the facts
A. Are not aware for
B. Are not aware of
C. Are not to be aware
D. Must not to be aware for
E. No correction required

Q.10 The man who has committed such a serious crime must **get the mostly severe** punishment.
A. Be getting the mostly severely
B. Get the most severe
C. Have got the most severely
D. Have been getting the severe most
E. No correction required

Ques (11-15):Direction: Arrange the following randomly given sentences: (A), (B), (C), (D), (E) and (F), into a meaning order to form a paragraph, then answer the given question.

A. But its tail was cut down by a trap when it tried to escape from the trap.

B. It worried because all other foxes would mock at its lost tail. Hence it planned a trick.

C. Now all other faxes understood the trick of the fox and mocked at it. The ashamed fox ran away into the forest.

D. A greedy fox stealthily entered a garden to eat the grapes.

E. When all foxes ridiculed it and said, "I have cut down the tail myself because it is a great hindrance. Now I am free and happy without my tail. So you too cut down your tails. It will be very convenient to all of you."

F. An old wise fox laughed at the tricky fox and said, "I will also join you after losing my tail when I try to steal the grapes. It looks very nice to be with a tail and I am proud of it."

Q.11 Which of the following should be the SECOND sentence after rearrangement?

[SBI PO, 2021], [IBPS Clerk, 2021]

A. A **B.** C **C.** D **D.** E
E. F

Q.12 Which of the following should be the FIRST sentence after rearrangement?

[SBI PO, 2021], [IBPS Clerk, 2021]

A. A **B.** B **C.** E **D.** F
E. D

Q.13 Which of the following should be the THIRD sentence after rearrangement?

[SBI PO, 2021]

A. D **B.** E **C.** C **D.** B
E. A

Q.14 Which of the following should be the FOURTH sentence after rearrangement?

[IBPS Clerk, 2021]

A. D **B.** C **C.** B **D.** E
E. F

Q.15 Which of the following should be the LAST(SIXTH) sentence after rearrangement?

A. A **B.** C **C.** D **D.** B
E. F

Ques (16-19):Direction: The following questions consist of a single sentence with one blank only. You are given five words as answer choice and from the five choices, you have to pick up one correct answer, which will make the sentence meaningfully complete.

Q.16 The Computer Practical is likely to be taken on November 13th, two days ahead of the ______ date.

A. conventional **B.** suitable
C. convenient **D.** common
E. desired

Q.17 A ______ of scientists now agree that the 'ozone hole' developed over Antarctica is due to the greatly increased use of Chlorofluorocarbons.

A. group **B.** creed **C.** majority **D.** range
E. band

Q.18 His utter ______ and disregard for the rules of the jungle lead him to his demise.

A. vigilance **B.** studious
C. careful **D.** ignorance
E. existence

Q.19 The Louvre pyramid is one of the most ______ landmarks in France.

A. dismal **B.** shallow
C. iconic **D.** crude
E. contempt

Ques (20-24):Direction: Read the following paragraph and choose the correct answer from the choices given below.

It seems quite **clearly unjust** to pay two people different amounts of money for doing the same work. But it is not as easy as it appears at first sight to introduce equal pay for equal work.

First of all, one must be sure that the work is in fact equal. Two people may be working side by side in a factory and doing the same work, but one may be doing it twice as fast as the other; or one may, be making no mistakes, while the other is making a lot. In some kinds of work, one can solve the problem of speed if one pays by the amount of work done and not by the hour: work paid for in this way is called piece-work. But it is not always possible to do this, so it is sometimes useful to pay workers at different rates, which make differences in **skill** into account. This usually means that the younger and therefore less experienced worker gets less than the older and more experienced one, which seems reasonable enough.

What does not appear to be so **reasonable** is when two equally skilled, equally fast workers receive different rates of pay. In some countries, for instance, women are paid less than men for the same work.

The employers' argument in places where this happens is that men usually have a wife and children to support and women usually have not. They say that most women workers are either unmarried and have no one to support, or have husbands who also work and bring home money so that it would be unjust for them to be paid as much as a man who has a wife who does not work because she has several children at home to **look after**.

This, of course, is quite true; but you do find some men workers who are unmarried and have no one to support, and some women workers who are widows and have children to support. Other women workers, though they have no children, may have old or sick parents and young brothers and sisters who cannot yet work.

The fact is that the problem of paying workers according to their family needs cannot be solved **simply** by giving the men more and the women less. The answer is to pay both alike, and to leave it to the state to see that justice is done by **means** of taxation and allowances.

Q.20 What looks unjust?

A. Unequal work unequal payment
B. Women are inferior to men
C. Men are superior to women
D. Equal work unequal payment
E. Equal payment unequal work

Q.21 What is the viable solution to this problem of inequality in payment?

A. Labourers irrespective of sex should be paid according to their skill
B. Young labourers should not be paid more than the old because of their experience
C. A woman with more than three children should not be paid more
D. A male worker having more than one wife should not be paid more
E. None of these

Q.22 How does a male worker define the inequality in payment?

A. Men have the responsibility to look after their wives and children
B. Women don't have such responsibilities
C. Most of the women workers are unmarried
D. Some of the women have husbands to earn
E. None of these

Q.23 What appears to be irrational?

A. Equal pay for equal work
B. Discrimination in payment for the same quantum of work
C. No equality in payment
D. No respect for the skill
E. None of these

Q.24 What is meant by piece-work?

A. Work done in the piece
B. Work completed in a particular hour
C. Quality of work is more important than quantum of work
D. Amount of work done by the hour
E. None of these

Q.25 Direction: In the following sentence, a part of the sentence is bold. Below are given alternatives to the bold part, which may improve the sentence. Choose the correct alternative. In case no improvement is needed, choose the option 'No improvement'.

This will unhinge and overturn all politics, and instead promoting order, leave nothing but anarchy and confusion.

A. And instead to

B. And despite of

C. And instead of

A. Both A and B   **B.** Only C
C. Both B and C   **D.** Only B
E. No improvement

Ques (26-30):Direction: Read the following sentence and determine whether there is any error in it. The error, if any, will be in one part of the sentence. If the sentence is error-free, select 'No error' as your answer.

Q.26 Many a doubt on History/(A) were cleared in the remedial class,/(B) thus proving the maximum/(C) utility of such initiatives. (D)

[IBPS Clerk, 2021]

A. (A)   **B.** (B)   **C.** (C)   **D.** (D)
E. No error

Q.27 The village is facing /(A) the problem of scarcity of water /(B) because much water are wasted /(C) for careless reasons by the villagers. /(D) No Error. /(E)

A. (A)   **B.** (B)   **C.** (C)   **D.** (D)
E. No error

Q.28 After spending (A)/ three years of our (B)/ college life together (C)/ we parted with our friends. (D) No error (E)

A. (A)   **B.** (B)   **C.** (C)   **D.** (D)

E. No error

Q.29 I lived here (A)/ in New York since 1980 (B)/, so I know everything about the city (C)/, its culture, and famous places for tourism. (D) / No Error. /(E)

A. (A)   **B.** (B)   **C.** (C)   **D.** (D)
E. No error

Q.30 Since the education system /(A) in the country has been poorly designed, /(B) there are not many institute /(C) that offer this course. /(D) No error /(E)

A. (A)   **B.** (B)   **C.** (C)   **D.** (D)
E. No error

// Smart Answer Sheet //

Correct — Indicates percentage of students who answered questions correctly.

Skipped — Indicates percentage of students who skipped questions.

Q.	Ans.	Correct / Skipped
1	D	55.58 % / 1.08 %
2	C	65.32 % / 1.73 %
3	A	69.74 % / 1.61 %
4	C	40.99 % / 1.02 %
5	C	24.89 % / 4.28 %
6	D	50.19 % / 1.5 %
7	C	66.07 % / 1.49 %
8	B	65.89 % / 1.36 %
9	B	44.63 % / 1.05 %
10	B	61.68 % / 1.36 %
11	A	53.53 % / 1.04 %
12	E	52.36 % / 1.42 %
13	D	55.97 % / 1.69 %
14	D	44.68 % / 1.57 %
15	B	52.04 % / 1.61 %
16	A	17.81 % / 4.07 %
17	C	59.45 % / 1.71 %
18	D	65.39 % / 1.49 %
19	C	79.25 % / 0.0 %
20	D	18.63 % / 4.51 %
21	A	69.07 % / 1.46 %
22	E	40.28 % / 1.07 %
23	B	66.27 % / 1.77 %
24	E	49.59 % / 1.82 %
25	B	53.26 % / 1.23 %
26	B	59.17 % / 1.76 %
27	C	82.48 % / 0.0 %
28	D	82.04 % / 0.0 %
29	A	78.87 % / 0.0 %
30	C	86.87 % / 0.0 %

Performance Analysis

Avg. Score (%)	53.33%
Toppers Score (%)	60.0%
Your Score	

//Hints and Solutions//

1. It is an error in the adverb. An adverb modifies the meaning of any verb, adjective or other adverb. Here the word 'lenient' is an adjective qualifying for the noun 'idea'. The word 'implausible' is an adjective that cannot be used here to qualify the other adjective.

Hence, an adverb, 'implausibly' should be used here.

Hence, the correct option is (D).

2. After the comma, the subject is 'he,' therefore, in the previous clause, we cannot describe anything other than the author himself. If we describe the "subject", we would commit the modifier error.

Hence, the correct option is (C).

3. You get "involved with" a person (usually in a romantic relationship) and "in" a process. Since "agriculture is a process, the preposition 'in' should be used instead of "with". Also, 'less' should be in the superlative degree as it is preceded by the article 'the'.

Hence, the correct option is (A).

4. The tense in the underlined part is incorrect. The present perfect is formed by using have/ has + past participle form of verbs. Thus, "have considered" should be written.

Hence, the correct option is (C).

5. The referee allowed the teams to play on without blowing the final whistle **until** one of them scored a winning goal.

- A word which expresses the idea of 'up to the point of the even mentioned' i.e scoring the winning goal should be used here.
- Until is a word that acts as a preposition and conjunction.
- Here we find that the referee has allowed the teams to play up to the point where one scores the winning goal.
- Which means up to the point in time or the event mentioned.
- Example: The kidnappers have given us until October 11th to deliver the documents.
- Thus from the given meaning we can conclude that the correct word to be used here is Until.

Hence, the correct option is (C).

6. In 'either...or' type sentences, the verb agrees with the latter subject. So it should be 'I am'. Therefore, the correct phrase is "I am held'.

Hence, the correct option is (D).

7. The statement is a fact. We can see this from the generalized way the sentence has been stated and the use of the article 'a'. Facts that are still valid today are to be stated in the simple present tense. So the correct phrase would be 'always has'.

Hence, the correct option is (C).

8. The sentence uses the past tense as can be seen from the use of the word 'was'.

This means that the other verb in the sentence must also be in the past tense.

The verb 'deferred' can take one of two pronouns after it. Either you 'defer to someone or you 'defer till' sometime, depending on the object of the verb. Here we have been given a time - the 'next meeting'. So we use 'till' after the verb. So the correct phrase is 'were deferred till'.

Hence, the correct option is (B).

9. Here, we can see that the statement is almost correct except usage of "beware" in the sentence. "Beware" means to be careful. The usage of "be careful" is not correct in the context of the sentence. So, instead of beware, we will use "aware" which means careful. The word 'aware' always takes the preposition 'of' after it.

Hence, the correct option is (B).

10. The only problem here is the usage of "mostly severe" punishment which indicates that the part of the punishment should be severe which is not what was meant in the sentence. What the sentence is trying to convey is that this man deserves a punishment more severe than any other. So, instead of 'mostly severe' we should use 'most severe' in the sentence. The sentence uses the present tense. The first verb is in the present perfect tense indicating this was the first action so the second verb must be in the simple present tense indicating a subsequent action. So the correct answer is 'get the most severe'.

Hence, the correct option is (B).

11. The correct sequence is **DABEFC.**

The above mentioned passage is based on a moral story of a greedy fox.

It is mentioned that greed and selfishness does not help any person in life. Since, we need a character to introduce the passage.

So, D is the first sentence. Now, **the sentence has an object 'garden of grapes'.**

So, she must have cut her tail in order to escape from the garden.

Therefore, A is the second sentence, thus DA. Now, since it cut its tail, and that worried about it. So, B is the third sentence i.e. DAB. Now, the trick is being discussed in the passage, so that other foxes do not make fun of its cut tail.

So, E is the next sentence, i.e. DABE. Another character is being introduced in the passage, i.e. a wise old fox.

Therefore, F is the fifth sentence, i.e. DABEF. And, last is C, i.e., DABEFC.

Hence, the correct option is (A).

12. The correct sequence is **DABEFC.**

The above mentioned passage is based on a moral story of a greedy fox. It is mentioned that greed and selfishness does not help any person in life. Since, **we need a character to introduce the passage.**

So, D is the first sentence. Now, the sentence has an object 'garden of grapes'. So, she must have cut her tail in order to escape from the garden. Hence, A is the second sentence, thus DA. Now, since it cut its tail and that worried about it. So, B is the third sentence i.e. DAB. Now, the trick is being discussed in the passage, so that other foxes do not make fun of its cut tail.

Therefore, E is the next sentence, i.e. DABE. Another character is being introduced in the passage, i.e. a wise old fox.

So, F is the fifth sentence, i.e. DABEF. And, last is C, i.e., DABEFC.

Hence, the correct option is (E).

13. The correct sequence is **DABEFC.**

The above mentioned passage is based on a moral story of a greedy fox. It is mentioned that greed and selfishness does not help any person in life. Since, we need a character to introduce the passage. Hence, D is the first sentence. Now, the sentence has an object 'garden of grapes'. So, she must have cut her tail in order to escape from the garden. Hence, A is the second sentence, thus DA. Now, since **it cut its tail, and that worried about it.**

So, B is the third sentence i.e. DAB. Now, the trick is being discussed in the passage, so that other foxes do not make fun of its cut tail. Hence, E is the next sentence, i.e. DABE. Another character is being introduced in the passage, i.e. a wise old fox.

Therefore, F is the fifth sentence, i.e. DABEF. And, last is C, i.e., DABEFC.

Hence, the correct option is (D).

14. The correct sequence is DABEFC.

The above mentioned passage is based on a moral story of a greedy fox. It is mentioned that greed and selfishness does not help any person in life. Since, we need a character to introduce the passage.

So, D is the first sentence. Now, the sentence has an object 'garden of grapes'. So, she must have cut her tail in order to escape from the garden.

Therefore, A is the second sentence, thus DA. Now, since it cut its tail and that worried about it. So, B is the third sentence i.e. DAB. Now, **the trick is being discussed in the passage, so that other foxes do not make fun of its cut tail.**

So, E is the fourth sentence, i.e. DABE. Another character is being introduced in the passage, i.e. a wise old fox.

Therefore, F is the fifth sentence, i.e. DABEF. And, last is C, i.e., DABEFC.

Hence, the correct option is (D).

15. The correct sequence is **DABEFC.**

The above mentioned passage is based on a moral story of a greedy fox. It is mentioned that greed and selfishness does not help any person in life. Since, we need a character to introduce the passage.

So, D is the first sentence. Now, the sentence has an object 'garden of grapes'. So, she must have cut her tail in order to escape from the garden.

Therefore, A is the second sentence, thus DA. Now, since it cut its tail, and that worried about it. So, B is the third sentence i.e. DAB. Now, **the trick is being discussed in the passage, so that other foxes do not make fun of its cut tail.**

So, E is the next sentence, i.e. DABE. Another character is being introduced in the passage, i.e. a wise old fox.

Therefore, F is the fifth sentence, i.e. DABEF. And, last is **C, i.e., DABEFC.**

Hence, the correct option is (B).

16. Out of the options mentioned above, **'conventional'** would be the correct option as it means based on or in accordance with what is generally done or believed.

Conventional suits the meaning of the sentence best as November 13th is considered as a date on which computer practical is generally taken making option (A) as the correct answer.

Hence, the correct option is (A).

17. The most appropriate word here would be **'majority'.** The sentence is talking about a disputed scientific claim, namely, ozone layer depletion. The words 'range', 'creed' and 'band' cannot be used for scientists.

The word 'group' and **'majority'** sound appropriate. Among these, 'majority' is more appropriate since if a majority of scientists say something, its credibility would be strongly established.

Hence, the correct option is (C).

18. The word **ignorance** means lack of knowledge or information.

Reading the above line we find that it is talking about a person's lack of knowledge and disregard for the rules of the jungle which resulted in his death. Thus, **"ignorance"** fits best in the sentence.

Hence, the correct option is (D).

19. The word **"iconic"** means widely recognized and well-established; famous as an icon.

Here the sentence is talking about the Louvre pyramid which is a famous monument in France. Thus, **"iconic"** fits best in the sentence.

Hence, the correct option is (C).

20. Let's look at the 1st line from the 1st paragraph given below:

"It seems quite clearly unjust to pay two people different amounts of money for doing the same work."

Upon the perusal of the given extract, it is obvious that equal work unequal payment looks unjust.

Hence, the correct option is (D).

21. Let's look at the last line from the last paragraph given below:

"The answer is to pay both alike and to leave it to the state to see that justice is done by means of taxation and allowances."

Upon the perusal of the given extract, it is obvious that the viable solution is to pay according to their skill irrespective of sex.

Hence, the correct option is (A).

22. Nowhere in the passage is it mentioned how a male worker defines the inequality in payment.

It cannot be defined that how a male worker defines the inequality in payment.

Thus, "None of these" is the correct answer.

Hence, the correct option is (E).

23. Let's look at the 1st line from the 3rd paragraph given below:

"What does not appear to be so reasonable is when two equally skilled, equally fast workers receive different rates of pay."

Upon the perusal of the given extract, it is obvious that discrimination in payment for the same quantum of work is irrational.

Hence, the correct option is (B).

24. Let's look at the 3rd line from the 2nd paragraph given below:

"In some kinds of work, one can solve the problem of speed if one pays by the amount of work done and not by the hour: work paid for in this way is called piece-work."

This line denotes that- piece work denotes If one paid for the amount of work done instead of the hour, the issue of speed (working of an individual)will be resolved.

So, the mentioned line is not given in any of the options; thus the correct answer is None of these

Hence, the correct option is (E).

25. The sentence uses the form and, instead, which is incorrect and needs improvement.

Given the context, the sentence should contain a preposition like 'of' after instead, which makes the sentence meaningful.

The only alternative that improves the sentence is C.

None of the other alternatives can make the sentence meaningful.

Note that 'despite' does not need a preposition like 'of' to be used along with it.

Hence, the correct option is (B).

26. The error lies in the wrong usage of the verb 'were' in Part (B).

'Were' should be replaced by 'was' because a singular verb always comes after 'many a', 'each', 'either', 'neither', 'everyone'.

Therefore, the singular verb 'was' should be used instead of the plural verb 'were' to make the sentence correct.

So, the correct sentence is:

"Many a doubt on History **was** cleared in the remedial class, thus proving the maximum utility of such initiatives."

Hence, the correct option is (B).

27. The word water is an uncountable noun.

So, the singular verb 'is' should be used in place of the plural verb 'are'.

So, the correct sentence is 'The village is facing the problem of scarcity of water because much water is wasted for careless reasons by the villagers'.

Hence, the correct option is (C).

28. The error is in part (D) of the sentence.

The preposition should be 'from' instead of 'with'.

The tense used in the sentence talks about an action which has already been carried out previously which refers to past continuous tense.

The pronouns used in the sentence is the first person along with the subject, for example, we is used with 'our'.

Hence, the correct option is (D).

29. There is an error in part (A) of the sentence

There is a use of a time adverbial since in this sentence.

Since is used to talk about action from the past which still continues in the present. So, we have to use the present perfect tense in part (A).

Therefore, in part, (A) of the sentence 'have' should be inserted before 'lived'.

The correct sentence is: I have lived here in New York since 1980, so I know everything about the city, its culture and famous places for tourism.

Hence, the correct option is (A).

30. The adjective the 'many' before the noun 'Institute' suggests that there is more than one institute.

So, the noun 'institute' has to be in its plural form that is 'institutes'.

Therefore, the correct sentence is Since the education system in the country has been poorly designed, there are not many institutes that offer this course.

Hence, the correct option is (C).

Ques (1-4):Direction: In the question given below, the sentence is divided into three parts I, II and III. For each part, an alternate statement is given. You have to determine if a part requires correction, and then mark that as your answer.

Q.1 The Indian Space Research Organisation is standing/testimony to the public sector's capacity to deliver outstanding results,/ when provided to autonomy and resources.

I. The Indian Space Research Organisation was standing

II. testimony for the public sector's capacity to deliver outstanding results,

III. when provided with autonomy and resources.

A. I only   **B.** II only   **C.** III only   **D.** I and III
E. II and III

Q.2 The government must consider setting up a dedicating agency/under the Ministry of Labor to deal with developing standards, monitoring/ establishments, and enforcement of standards through the economy.

I. The government must consider setting up a dedicated agency

II. under the Ministry of Labor to dealing with developing standards, monitoring

III. establishments, and enforcement of standards across the economy.

A. I only   **B.** II only   **C.** III only   **D.** II and III
E. I and III

Q.3 Most research suggests / that highly intelligent people tend to be outgoing, well adjusted / and popular contradict to popular belief.

I. Most research suggest that

II. highly intelligent people tends to be outgoing, well adjusted

III. and popular contrary to popular belief.

A. Only I   **B.** Only III
C. Only II   **D.** Both I and II
E. Both II and III

Q.4 In what became known as a "taper tantrum", markets / balking at the Fed's first hint at withdrawing crisis-era / accommodation by foreshadowing an end to QE asset purchases.

I. In what become known as a "taper tantrum", markets

II. balked at the Fed's first hint at withdrawing crisis-era

III. accommodate by foreshadowing an end to QE asset purchases.

A. I only   **B.** II only
C. Both I and II   **D.** Both II and III
E. I, II and III

Ques (5-9):Direction: In the following question, some part of the sentence may have an error. Find out which part of the sentence has an error and select the appropriate option. If a sentence is free from errors, select the option 'E'.

Q.5 So we paid an enormous /(A) amount of money for /(B) the meal, the food was /(C) terribly disappointing. /(D) No error/(E)
A. A   **B.** B   **C.** C   **D.** D
E. E

Q.6 Apart for a few less /(A) experienced individuals, all /(B) of the recent applicants /(C) were taken on. /(D) No error/(E)
A. A   **B.** B   **C.** C   **D.** D
E. E

Q.7 Nepal has recently signed U.S. \$2.4 billion connectivity /(A) and infrastructure deals with China /(B) which includes linking China to /(C) Kathmandu through the Himalayan railways. /(D) No error /(E)
A. A   **B.** B   **C.** C   **D.** D
E. E

Q.8 Politicians have to /(A) believe in himself if /(B) they expect the people /(C) to believe in them. /(D) No error /(E)
A. A   **B.** B   **C.** C   **D.** D
E. E

Q.9 Millions of parents and educators around the country /(A) has deep-rooted and extremely /(B) outdated mental models /(C) of what education should be. /(D) No error /(E)
A. A   **B.** B   **C.** C   **D.** D
E. E

Ques (10-14):Direction: Read the passage and answer the question that follows.

As Spring advances, many flowering plants bloom. In some areas of the Northern hemisphere, Spring begins in February. Furthermore, temperate areas have a dry Spring which brings flowering. Also, in sub-arctic regions, Spring does not begin until May. Spring certainly is the result of warmth. Furthermore, this warmth is due to the changing of Earth's axis relative to the Sun. Unstable weather can also occur in Spring. This happens when warm air invades from lower latitudes, while cold air pushes from the Polar Regions. In Spring, flooding is common in mountainous areas. This is because of the snowmelt acceleration by warm rains. In recent years, a new Spring phenomenon known as season creep has been observed. Most noteworthy, due to season creep, signs of Spring are now **occurring** earlier than expected. This trend is prevalent in many regions of the World. Spring Season certainly brings with itself many health benefits. One important benefit of the Spring Season is the mental boost. The Winter season can cause depression and anxiety in many people. Spring replaces those feelings with fresh and positive energy. People are able to come out of winter hibernation. Most **noteworthy**, the Spring Season is a period of **rejuvenation** and joy. Probably many individuals consume comfortable foods during Winter Season. This certainly results in increased weights for many individuals. Spring is a time for eating diet food. During Spring Season healthy fresh local food is available. Above all, many vitamin-

rich vegetables reach their prime during Spring. Some of these vegetables are asparagus, kale, and peas.

Q.10 What happens when warm air invades from lower latitudes?

A. It causes winter

B. It causes rains

C. It causes a pleasant weather

D. It causes spring

E. None of the above

Q.11 Which region's spring brings flowering?

A. Arid areas

B. Temperate areas

C. Semi-arid areas

D. Tundra

E. None of the above

Q.12 Why flooding is common in the mountainous region during spring?

A. Spring brings heavy rains

B. Its rainy in mountainous regions

C. Winter weather

D. Melting of snow by warm rains

E. None of the above

Q.13 Give the synonyms of the given word "noteworthy".

A. Unexceptional

B. Boring

C. Ordinary

D. Interesting

E. None of the above

Q.14 Give the antonym of the given word "occurring".

A. Happen

B. Transpire

C. Chance

D. Stopping

E. None of the above

Ques (15-19):Direction: Read the passage given below carefully and then answer the following question.

The _______ (1) laden with vaccines had just rolled to a stop at Santiago's airport in late January, and Chile's president, Sebastián Piñera, was beaming. "Today," he said, "is a day of joy, emotion, and hope."

The source of that hope: China – a country that Chile and dozens of other nations are depending on to help rescue them from the COVID-19 _______ (2).

China's vaccine diplomacy campaign has been a surprising success: It has pledged roughly half a billion doses of its vaccine to more than 45 countries, according to a country-by-country tally by The Associated Press. With just four of China's many vaccine makers able to produce at least 2.6 billion _______ (3) this year, a large part of the world's population will end up inoculated not with the fancy Western vaccines boasting headline-grabbing efficacy rates, but with China's humble, traditionally made shots.

Amid a dearth of public data on China's vaccines, fears over their efficacy and safety are still pervasive in the countries depending on them, along with _______ (4) about what China might want in return for deliveries. _______ (5), inoculations with Chinese vaccines have begun in more than 25 countries, and the shots have been delivered to another 11, according to

AP's tally, based on independent reporting in those countries along with government and company announcements.

Q.15 Which of the following is the most appropriate option for blank (1)?

A. helicopter

B. cart

C. ship

D. plane

E. train

Q.16 Which of the following is the most appropriate option for blank (2)?

A. catastrophe

B. pandemic

C. incident

D. accident

E. calamity

Q.17 Which of the following is the most appropriate option for blank (3)?

A. policies

B. antidote

C. doses

D. vial

E. injection

Q.18 Which of the following is the most appropriate option for blank (4)?

A. concerns

B. concern

C. surprise

D. surprises

E. pleasure

Q.19 Which of the following is the most appropriate option for blank (5)?

A. furthermore

B. afterwards

C. unless

D. as a result

E. nonetheless

Q.20 Directions: Fill in the blank(s) with the correct word(s).

Mandarin Chinese is the second most _______ language in the world.

A. heard

B. spoken

C. written

D. translated

E. read

Q.21 Directions: In the following question, one sentence is given in which certain words are in bold and numbered from A to E. Below the sentence are given five options with possible pairs of interchange of those bold words. Choose the pair(s) of words which are needed to be interchanged to make the sentence grammatically correct and meaningful.

The (A)**growth** for connected consumers' devices in 2020 will be (B)**masses** by cellular and Wi-Fi connectivity to consumer electronics for mass markets making (C)**several** 'luxury' products (D)**available** to the (E)**driven** during the year.

A. (D)-(E)

B. (B)-(E)

C. (C)-(D)

D. (A)-(B) and (C)-(E)

E. (A)-(C) and (B)-(D)

Ques (22-25):Direction: In the following question, fill in the blanks in the sentence with the correct option.

Q.22 It is absurd to _______ the majority of mankind as below the intellectual average.

A. depart

B. denounce

C. detach

D. detail

E. divert

Q.23 I would rather ______than beg.

A. accept
B. propose
C. die
D. accuse
E. All of the above

Q.24 The internship is an ________ aspect of our grades.

A. neglected
B. important
C. useful
D. marked
E. massive

Q.25 We were supposed to _______ for dinner, at the nearby bar.

A. visit
B. make
C. meet
D. deliver
E. cook

Q.26 Direction: In each of the sentences below, a portion (a phrase or a group of words) is marked in bold. Choose the best replacement for the part in bold, as per the options are given below, to make the sentence meaningful and grammatically correct.

It was past midnight, Raj told his kids **to hand a sack.**

I. Uprise

II. Doze off

III. Awake

A. Only I
B. Only II
C. Only III
D. Only II and III
E. No improvements

Ques (27-30):Directions: In each question, a part of the sentence is made bold. Below are given alternatives to the bold part at (A), (B), (C) and (D) which may improve the sentence. Choose the correct alternative. In case no replacement is needed, mark (E) as your answer.

Q.27 One should lay out one's doubts and insecurities before entering the examination hall.

A. One should lay outside
B. One should lay aside
C. One should lay inside
D. One should lay behind
E. No correction required

Q.28 The idea of a single bad bank where the NPAs of all PSBs may be **transferred as a white bullet** to clean up PSB balance sheets must be rejected.

A. transferring as a white bullet
B. transferred as a black bullet
C. transferred as a silver bullet
D. transferred as a platinum bullet
E. No correction required

Q.29 The Indian banking system is beleaguered with **non-performing assets.**

A. in non-performing assets
B. for non-performing assets
C. from non-performing assets
D. under non-performing assets
E. No correction required

Q.30 The dog made over the biker but was soon left behind in the empty street.

A. dog made before the biker
B. dog made after the biker
C. dog made out the biker
D. dog made onto the biker
E. No correction required

// Smart Answer Sheet //

Correct Indicates percentage of students who answered questions correctly.

Skipped Indicates percentage of students who skipped questions.

Q.	Ans.	Correct / Skipped
1	C	44.9 % / 1.82 %
2	E	50.29 % / 1.92 %
3	B	42.24 % / 1.4 %
4	B	49.77 % / 1.54 %
5	A	66.73 % / 1.24 %
6	A	40.95 % / 1.42 %
7	C	22.82 % / 4.26 %
8	B	49.26 % / 1.25 %
9	B	40.81 % / 1.81 %
10	D	76.04 % / 0.0 %
11	B	41.96 % / 1.2 %
12	D	89.32 % / 0.0 %
13	D	79.52 % / 0.0 %
14	D	83.81 % / 0.0 %
15	D	42.08 % / 1.5 %
16	B	67.05 % / 1.78 %
17	C	48.26 % / 1.32 %
18	A	67.9 % / 1.57 %
19	E	59.7 % / 1.19 %
20	B	57.28 % / 1.15 %
21	B	63.41 % / 1.61 %
22	B	64.38 % / 1.38 %
23	C	53.32 % / 1.86 %
24	B	58.84 % / 1.17 %
25	C	68.97 % / 1.12 %
26	B	59.75 % / 1.16 %
27	B	45.45 % / 1.69 %
28	C	60.1 % / 1.42 %
29	E	47.12 % / 1.56 %
30	B	42.4 % / 1.94 %

Performance Analysis	
Avg. Score (%)	60.0%
Toppers Score (%)	60.0%
Your Score	

//Hints and Solutions//

1. The error lies in part 3 only.

Parts I and II are grammatically correct parts and hence do not require any corrections.

Part III uses 'to' which is incorrect here. It should be 'with' as there is a sense of assistance.

Hence, the correct option is (C).

2. The error lies in parts I and III.

Part I uses 'dedicating' which is the incorrect adjective here. It should be 'dedicated' as the action has been completed.

Part II is a grammatically correct part and hence does not require any correction.

Part III uses 'through' which is incorrect here. It should be 'across' as there is a sense of the entire nation.

Hence, the correct option is (E).

3. The error lies in the III part of the sentence.

The verb 'contradict' which means 'deny the truth of (a statement) by asserting the opposite' should be replaced by **the adjective 'contrary'** which means 'opposite in nature, direction, or meaning.'

Correct sentence:

Most research suggests that highly intelligent people tend to be outgoing, well adjusted and popular contrary to popular belief.

Hence, the correct option is (B).

4. The error lies in part II.

The sentence uses the present progressive tense verb 'balking', which does not make the sentence meaningful; as it is the main verb.

The correct verb should be the simple past tense 'balked'.

Parts I and III are grammatically correct and hence do not require any corrections.

Hence, the correct option is (B).

5. In part A of the sentence, the usage of 'So' is incorrect instead, use 'Although'

Where the idea of one clause is in some way opposing the idea of the other, we have to use 'Although/though/but' as a conjunction because these conjunctions show the contrast.

Correct sentence: Although we paid an enormous amount of money for the meal, the food was terribly disappointing.

Hence, the correct option is (A).

6. In part A of the sentence, the usage of 'Apart' is incorrect instead use 'Except'.

'Apart' is an adverb that means 'separated by a specified distance.' and 'Except' is a conjunction that means 'not including, other than'.

To show 'exceptions', we use the prepositions 'Apart from, but for, except for'.

Correct sentence: Except for a few less experienced individuals, all of the recent applicants were taken on.

Hence, the correct option is (A).

7. In part C of the sentence, the usage of 'includes' is incorrect instead, use 'include'.

According to the rule of subject-verb agreement, whenever we use a relative pronoun the verb next to it will be according to the antecedent of the relative pronoun. In the given sentence, the antecedent is 'deals' which is a plural noun hence the verb 'includes' should be in a plural form which is 'include', and 'with china' is a prepositional phrase that doesn't have any effect on the verb.

Correct sentence: Nepal has recently signed U.S. \$2.4 billion connectivity and infrastructure deals with China which include linking China to Kathmandu through the Himalayan railways.

Hence, the correct option is (C).

8. In part B of the sentence, the usage of 'himself' is incorrect instead, use 'themselves'

According to the rule of grammar, whenever we have a plural subject and we want to denote it with a pronoun then always use a reflexive pronoun in a plural form.

Correct sentence: Politicians have to believe in themselves if they expect the people to believe in them.

Hence, the correct option is (B).

9. In part B of the sentence, the usage of 'has deep-rooted' is incorrect instead use 'have deep-rooted'.

In the given sentence, 'Millions of' is a quantifier which is used for the nouns 'parents and educators' and this is the subject of the sentence which is in a plural form and according to the subject-verb agreement rule whenever we have a plural subject use a plural verb.

Correct sentence: Millions of parents and educators around the country have deep-rooted and extremely outdated mental models of what education should be.

Hence, the correct option is (B).

10. According to the passage, "Unstable weather can also occur at Spring. This happens when warm air invades from lower latitudes, while cold air pushes from the Polar Regions".

From the given lines we get to know that when warm air comes in contact with lower latitudes, this results in unstable weather which can also cause spring.

Hence, the correct option is (D).

11. According to the passage, "Furthermore, temperate areas have a dry Spring which brings flowering".

From the given line we get to know that temperate areas are which are neither hot nor cold so, in this region, spring bears flowers.

Hence, the correct option is (B).

12. According to the passage, "In Spring, flooding is common in mountainous areas. This is because of the snowmelt acceleration by warm rains".

From the given line we get to know that mountainous regions are covered with snow. So when spring comes, all this snow melts and it leads to flooding.

Hence, the correct option is (D).

13. The given word 'noteworthy' means worth paying attention to, interesting or significant.

The word 'Interesting' means arousing curiosity or interest, holding or catching attention.

So, 'Interesting' is the correct synonym for the given word.

Hence, the correct option is (D).

14. The given word 'occurring' means happen, take place.

The word 'Stopping' means (of an event, action, or process) to come to an end, cease to happen.

So, 'Stopping' is the correct antonym for the given word.

Hence, the correct option is (D).

15. The passage talks about how China has surprisingly been able to deliver vaccines to so many countries and how different countries are reacting to it.

The sentence with the first blank talks about a 'vehicle' filled with vaccines from China that arrived at the Santiago airport in late January.

The sentence mentions the 'airport' in 'Santiago', this is a city in Chile and thus any cargo coming from China would have to come into the city through some mode of international transportation.

If it were a 'helicopter', the 'helipad' would have been a better option as compared to 'airport'.

Hence, the correct option is (D).

16. The passage talks about how China has surprisingly been able to deliver vaccines to so many countries and how different countries are reacting to it.

The sentence with the second blank talks about how there are dozens of countries - including Chile - which are dependent on China for the vaccine against COVID-19.

The word in blank would be a noun that would categorize COVID as something.

Although COVID is a catastrophe and calamity in the general sense of the term, these titles are generic when it comes to 'pandemic' which is a specific term for a disease that is spread globally.

Hence, the correct option is (B).

17. The passage talks about how China has surprisingly been able to deliver vaccines to so many countries and how different countries are reacting to it.

The sentence with the third blank talks about how China's vaccine-giving ability has been surprising for everyone as it has only 4 companies that are producing the vaccine and China alone has been able to produce 2.6 billion 'units' of the vaccine.

The word in the blank has to be a plural noun.

'Antidote' is a response to someone being poisoned and it is administered after one already has the poison inside one, while 'vaccine' is precautionary and preventative. So, it's incorrect.

Thus, the correct answer is 'doses' which means 'quantities of a medicine or drug taken or recommended to be taken at a particular time'.

Hence, the correct option is (C).

18. The passage talks about how China has surprisingly been able to deliver vaccines to so many countries and how different countries are reacting to it.

The sentence with the fourth blank talks about how there is a lack of information about the vaccines from China and there are also certain doubts about its efficiency and ability to do what it is supposed to.

Along with this, there is also the worry about what China might expect in return for these vaccines that it has pledged to provide for now.

The blank is preceded by the term 'along with' which means 'in the company of' or 'at the same time'.

This means that the word in the blank would have a similar connotation to 'fears'.

The previous phrase mentions 'fears about the power and the safety of the vaccines'. Since this noun 'fears' is in the plural, it may be safe to assume that the noun in the blank would also be in its plural form.

Hence, the correct option is (A).

19. The passage talks about how China has surprisingly been able to deliver vaccines to so many countries and how different countries are reacting to it.

The sentence with the fifth blank talks about how the vaccination against COVID has begun in 25 countries and the vaccine has been delivered to 11 countries, courtesy of China.

The previous sentence talks about how there are fears and concerns in certain countries about the efficiency and safety of the vaccines from China and what the Chinese government might want in return for them.

These fears would deter someone from not using the vaccines, but the sentence with the blank mentions how 25 countries have already started vaccinations and vaccines have been delivered to 11 more countries.

This implies that the 2 sentences present logically contradictory information. Thus, the first word of the second sentence should represent this contradiction.

'Nonetheless' means 'in spite of' or 'despite' i.e. despite there being doubts about the intention of China and the safety of its vaccines, 25 countries used the vaccines.

Hence, the correct option is (E).

20. Complete sentence: Mandarin Chinese is the second most spoken language in the world.

Let's look at the meaning of the given words:

- Heard: To perceive with the ear the sound made by someone or something.

- Spoken: To put across meaning or opinions by mode of speech.

- Written: Past participle of write; mark letters on a paper with a pen or pencil.

- Translated: To express the sense of words or text in another language.

- Read: To look at words and symbols and to understand what they mean.

Thus from the given meanings, we find that the most appropriate meaning of the given sentence is Spoken.

Hence, the correct option is (B).

21. We can look into the sentence the following way:

The (A)______ for connected consumers' devices in 2020 will be (B)______ by cellular and Wi-Fi connectivity to consumer electronics for mass markets making (C)______ 'luxury' products (D)______ to the (E)______ during the year.

It is clear that (A) and (C) has grammatically and meaningfully correct words. Also (D) justifies its bold word.

But from the point of view of grammar, (B) should be a verb and (E) should be a plural noun.

Driven is a verb meaning "(of a device) powered or operated (another device)."

Masses means "the ordinary people."

So, (B) and (E) should be interchanged.

Correct sentence: The (A)**growth** for connected consumers' devices in 2020 will be (B)**driven** by cellular and Wi-Fi connectivity to consumer electronics for mass markets making (C)**several** 'luxury' products (D)**available** to (E)**masses** during the year.

Hence, the correct option is (B).

22. It is absurd to denounce the majority of mankind as below the intellectual average.

The context of the sentence suggests that the blank should contain a word that means 'describe' or 'consider as lower than something or someone'. It can also mean 'insult', as the sentence refers to the mankind as 'below average'.

Let's look at the meanings of the words:

- Denounce- publicly declare to be wrong.

- Depart- leave, especially in order to start a journey.

- Detach- disengage (something or part of something) and remove it.

- Detail- give full information about.

- Divert- distract (someone) from something.

Hence, the correct option is (B).

23. I would rather "die" than beg.

Let us look at the meanings of the words given in options.

- 'Accept' means 'to receive with consent'.

- 'Propose' means 'to suggest something'.

- 'Die' means to 'perish'.

- 'Accuse' means 'to charge someone with a crime'.

Given the context, which expresses a dramatic tone, the correct word to use in this sentence should be 'die'. It talks about a drastic step one is ready to take but still not beg. Such a drastic situation would be death and nothing else from the given options.

Hence, the correct option is (C).

24. The internship is an "important" aspect of our grades.

Let us examine the meanings of the given alternatives:

- Neglected means to fail to care for something properly.

- Important means to be of great significance or value.

- Useful means to be able to be used for a practical purpose or in several ways.

- Marked means to be clearly noticeable.

- Massive means to be exceptionally large.

- In the above sentence, the speaker is talking about the significance of an internship on their grades, thus 'important' is the most apt filler.

Hence, the correct option is (B).

25. We were supposed to "meet" for dinner, at the nearby bar.

Let us examine the meanings of the given alternatives:

- Meet means to arrange or happen to come into the presence or company of someone.

- Visit means to go to see and spend time with someone.

- Make means to form something by putting parts together or combining substances.

- Deliver means to bring and hand over goods to the proper recipient or address.

- Cook means to prepare food, by combining, heating and mixing the ingredients.

- In the above context, the subject is going to have dinner with an acquaintance.

Hence, the correct option is (C).

26. to hand a sack is a wrong phrase, the correct phrase being **to hit the sack** which means **to go to bed** so the correct word replacing it would be **doze off.**

Up rise means **to wake up** and the same goes for **awake.**

Hence, the correct option is (B).

27. The original sentence is erroneous.

Reason: Usage of the phrasal verb 'lay out' which means 'One should lay aside' is inappropriate in this sentence.

'Lay aside' which means 'put away' would be suitable in the context.

E.g.: They agreed to lay aside their differences for the good of their families.

So 'lay aside' should be used in place of 'lay out' to make the sentence grammatically and contextually correct.

Among the given choices, only option B replaces the given bold part most appropriately.

The sentence after replacement becomes:

One should lay aside one's doubts and insecurities before entering the examination hall.

Hence, the correct option is (B).

28. The original sentence is erroneous.

Reason: The term 'white bullet' does not make any sense. The correct expression is silver bullet'.

Silver bullet (Noun):

Meaning: A simple and seemingly magical solution to a complicated problem.

E.g.: There is no silver bullet that can prevent flooding entirely.

So 'silver bullet' should be used in place of 'white bullet' to make the sentence grammatically correct.

Among the given choices, only option C replaces the given bold part most appropriately.

The sentence after replacement becomes:

The idea of a single bad bank where the NPAs of all PSBs may be transferred as a silver bullet to clean up PSB balance sheets must be rejected.

Hence, the correct option is (C).

29. The original sentence is absolutely correct and hence the bold part needs no replacement.

Hence, the correct option is (E).

30. The original sentence is erroneous.

Reason: Usage of the phrasal verb 'make over' which means 'to officially make someone else the owner of something ' is inappropriate in this sentence.

'Make after' which means 'to begin chasing someone or something' would be suitable in this context.

E.g.: I made after the bus, but there was no way I could catch it.

So 'made after' should be used in place of 'made over' to make the sentence grammatically and contextually correct.

Among the given choices, only option B replaces the given bold part most appropriately.

The sentence after replacement becomes:

The dog made after the biker but was soon left behind in the empty street.

Hence, the correct option is (B).

Ques (1-4):Direction: A part of the sentence is underlined. Five alternatives are given to the underlined part which will improve the meaning of the sentence. Choose the correct alternative. In case no improvement is needed, click the option corresponding to "No improvement."

Q.1 Converting to more sustainable energy sources is one way to reduce the <u>reliant on</u> oil products.

A. reliant at   **B.** reliance on

C. reliant of   **D.** reliance from

E. No improvement

Q.2 <u>Despite of the</u> rise of electric car manufacturers, it's clear that economics is the main driver of carbon emissions from transportation.

A. Instead of the   **B.** Within the

C. While the   **D.** Despite the

E. No improvement

Q.3 Non-bank financing facilitates competition <u>between financing providers</u> and supports economic activity.

A. among financing providers

B. between financing provider

C. among financing provider

D. into financing providers

E. No improvement

Q.4 The country has made improvements over the past decades to <u>both availability</u> and quality of municipal drinking water systems.

A. both available   **B.** both the availability

C. both a availability   **D.** both an availability

E. No improvement

Ques (5-9):Direction: Read the passage and answer the questions that follow.

India has two national languages for central administrative purposes: Hindi and English. Hindi is the official, and the main link language of India. English is an associate official language. The Indian Constitution also officially approves twenty-two regional languages for official purposes.

Dozens of distinctly different regional languages are spoken in India, which share many characteristics such as grammatical structure and vocabulary. Apart from these languages, Hindi is used for communication in India. The homeland of Hindi is mainly in the north of India, but it is spoken and widely understood in all **urban** centers of India. In the southern states of India, where people speak many different languages that are not much related to Hindi, there is more resistance to Hindi, which has allowed English to remain a lingua franca to a greater degree.

Since the early 1600s, the English language has had a toehold on the Indian subcontinent, when the East India Company established settlements in Chennai, Kolkata, and Mumbai,

formerly Madras, Calcutta, and Bombay respectively. The historical background of India is never far away from the everyday usage of English. India has had a longer exposure to English than any other country which uses it as a second language, its distinctive words, idioms, grammar and rhetoric spreading gradually to affect all places, habits and culture.

In India, English serves two purposes. First, it provides a linguistic tool for the administrative cohesiveness of the country, causing people who speak different languages to become united. Secondly, it serves as a language of wider communication by including a large variety of different people covering a vast area. It overlaps with local languages in certain spheres of influence and in public domains.

Generally, English is used among Indians as a 'link' language and it is the first language for many well-educated Indians. It is also the second language for many who speak more than one language in India.

One can see a Hindi-speaking teacher giving their students instructions during an educational tour about where to meet and when their bus would leave, but all in English. India is, without a doubt, committed to English as a national language. The impact of English is not only continuing but increasing.

Q.5 Which word means the same as 'the refusal to accept or comply with something'?

A. Cohesiveness   **B.** Distinctive

C. Influence   **D.** Domains

E. Resistance

Q.6 Which of these is opposite in meaning to 'urban'?

A. Town   **B.** Rural

C. Household   **D.** City

E. Suburb

Q.7 The conclusion of the passage is:

A. Speaking English is unavoidable

B. The impact of English can decrease

C. The impact of English will increase

D. People should continue speaking English

E. None of these

Q.8 Hindi speaking teachers:

A. Always speak English

B. Use English to give instructions

C. Never speak English

D. Don't understand English

E. None of these

Q.9 How does English serve as a language of wider communication?

A. By giving importance to regional languages

B. By many adopting it as a first language

C. By serving administrative purposes

D. Both (B) and (C)

E. None of these

Q.10 Directions: In the sentence, certain words are in bold and numbered from (A) to (E), which are the possible pairs to be interchanged. Choose the pair(s) of words that need to be interchanged to make the sentence grammatically correct and meaningful.

The duty of the **(A) preach** parent is plain: to save the child by any possible means, to **(B) skeptical** the uselessness of the **(C) sacrifice** in season and out of season, and to **(D) endure** patiently whatever penalty the law may **(E) indict** for evasion.

A. (A)-(C)

B. (B)-(D)

C. (A)-(B)

D. (A)-(E)

E. None of these

Q.11 Direction: Choose an appropriate word from the options to suitably fill the blank in the sentence below so that the sentence makes sense, both grammatically and contextually.

Coconut water is the _______ and most hygienic water found on the earth.

A. pure

B. purer

C. purest

D. as pure as

E. None of the above

Ques (12-16):Direction: Below, a set of eight statements is given, out of which the first sentence, given in bold, is fixed. The rest are jumbled in any random order. Out of the remaining seven statements, one does not belong to the passage. Rearrange the remaining sentences in the correct order and then answer the questions.

A. Until the early 2000s, Bollywood remained the main source of entertainment for the Himalayan monarchy of Bhutan.

B. As the industry continues to boom, a new parallel cinema movement, made mostly for an international audience, is emerging.

C. Arun Bhattarai's The Next Guardian, a bittersweet documentary set in a remote monastery, also features a character going through a sexual identity crisis.

D. Passionate, self-taught film-makers, armed with themes ranging from magical realism to social justice and sexual identity, have begun to appear in major international film festivals in recent years.

E. The advent of the internet brought along a tidal wave of new content and a nascent parallel voice has also begun taking shape.

F. It was a love triangle about two college boys falling for the same girl, that birthed the commercial Bhutanese film industry.

G. Two decades later, commercial Bhutanese films continue to ride on Bollywood influences, with staple themes of mawkish drama, syrupy duets and acrobatic action sequences featuring prominently.

H. It was in 1999 when the late Tshering Wangyel released the first Dzongkha-language movie called Rewaa (Hope).

Q.12 Which of the following sentences is SECOND in the correct order?

A. B

B. G

C. E

D. H

E. F

Q.13 Which of the following sentences is FOURTH in the correct order?

A. E

B. C

C. G

D. B

E. H

Q.14 Which of the following sentences does not belong in the given passage?

A. E

B. F

C. G

D. H

E. C

Q.15 Which of the following sentences is FIFTH in the correct order?

A. C

B. E

C. B

D. F

E. H

Q.16 Which of the following sentences is SIXTH in the correct order?

A. E

B. D

C. C

D. B

E. G

Ques (17-21):Directions: Read the following sentence and determine whether there is an error in it. The error, if any, will be in one part of the sentence. If the sentence is error-free, select 'No Error' as your answer.

Q.17 The farmers, including the (A) village's Sarpanch were late (B) in paying their due to the zamindar, (C) caused the zamindar to confiscate their lands. (D)

A. (A)

B. (B)

C. (C)

D. (D)

E. No error

Q.18 Mark would (A) always remembered (B) his dog, Molly (C) with fondness. (D)

A. (A)

B. (B)

C. (C)

D. (D)

E. No error

Q.19 His parents were very (A) hopeful that he would (B) one day achieve one's ambitions (C) and make them proud. (D)

A. (A)

B. (B)

C. (C)

D. (D)

E. No error

Q.20 "The driver will (A) be waiting for (B) you at the airport (C) to pick you up." (D)

A. (A)

B. (B)

C. (C)

D. (D)

E. No error

Q.21 Michael insisted paying (A) for the meal, (B) but Halley wanted (C) to split the bill. (D)

A. (A)

B. (B)

C. (C)

D. (D)

E. No error

Ques (22-25):Direction: Fill in the blanks with the appropriate word.

Q.22 I had some chances of winning _______ I started a little slow.

A. either

B. but

C. neither

D. or

E. in

Q.23 APJ Abdul Kalam _______ in Tamil Nadu.
A. born
B. is born
C. had born
D. has given birth
E. was born

Q.24 The play was ___ good to be true.
A. by
B. to
C. too
D. as
E. None of the above

Q.25 I missed the bus _______ I was late.
A. yet
B. although
C. though
D. however
E. because

Ques (26-30):Directions: For the blank in the passage, there are five choices provided. Select the word that makes the most sense when placed in the blank.

An objection is often raised against realistic biography because it reveals so much that is important and even sacred about a man's life. The real objection to it will rather be found in the fact that it reveals about a man the precise points which are unimportant. It reveals and asserts and insists on exactly those things in a man's life of which the man himself is wholly unconscious; his exact class in society, the circumstances of his ancestry, the place of his present location. These are things which do not, properly speaking, ever arise before the human ___(1)___. They do not occur to a man's mind; it may be said, with almost equal truth, that they do not occur in a man's life. A man no more thinks about himself as the inhabitant of the third house in a row of Brixton villas than he thinks about himself as a strange animal with two legs. What a man's name was, what his income was, whom he married, where he lived, these are not sanctities; they are ___(2)___.

A very strong case of this is the case of the Brontës. The Brontë is in the position of the mad lady in a country village; her ___(3)___ form an endless source of innocent conversation to that exceedingly mild and bucolic circle, the literary world. The truly glorious gossips of literature, like Mr. Augustine Birrell and Mr. Andrew Lang, never tire of collecting all the glimpses and ___(4)___ and sermons and side-lights and sticks and straws which will go to make a Brontë museum. They are the most personally discussed of all Victorian authors, and the limelight of biography has left few darkened corners in the dark old Yorkshire house. And yet the whole of this biographical investigation, though natural and picturesque, is not wholly suitable to the Brontës. For the Brontë, genius was above all things deputed to ___(5)___ the supreme unimportance of externals. Up to that point, the truth had always been conceived as existing more or less in the novel of manners.

Q.26 What will come at a place of __(1)__?
A. experience
B. remark
C. fathom
D. occurance
E. vision

Q.27 What will come at a place of ___(2)___?
A. sanctimonious
B. heresies
C. irrelevancies
D. ordinary

E. inimical

Q.28 What will come at a place of ___(3)___?
A. eccentricities
B. outgoing
C. events
D. peeves
E. friends

Q.29 What will come at a place of ___(4)___?
A. sightings
B. lives
C. amusements
D. anecdotes
E. passions

Q.30 What will come at a place of ___(5)___?
A. remark
B. implement
C. assert
D. define
E. play

// Smart Answer Sheet //

Correct Indicates percentage of students who answered questions correctly.

Skipped Indicates percentage of students who skipped questions.

Q.	Ans.	Correct / Skipped
1	B	65.31 % / 1.94 %
2	D	77.72 % / 0.0 %
3	A	41.25 % / 1.95 %
4	B	78.33 % / 0.0 %
5	E	53.26 % / 1.57 %
6	B	58.86 % / 1.15 %
7	C	46.83 % / 1.04 %
8	B	56.29 % / 1.71 %
9	D	43.53 % / 1.33 %
10	C	65.43 % / 1.83 %
11	C	87.16 % / 0.0 %
12	D	48.82 % / 1.85 %
13	C	55.28 % / 1.49 %
14	E	51.92 % / 1.18 %
15	B	49.85 % / 1.49 %
16	D	54.08 % / 1.74 %
17	D	84.59 % / 0.0 %
18	B	87.25 % / 0.0 %
19	C	81.1 % / 0.0 %
20	E	85.26 % / 0.0 %
21	A	76.74 % / 0.0 %
22	B	43.75 % / 1.6 %
23	E	77.44 % / 0.0 %
24	C	76.54 % / 0.0 %
25	E	89.89 % / 0.0 %
26	E	14.07 % / 3.95 %
27	C	51.29 % / 1.16 %
28	A	45.93 % / 1.17 %
29	D	64.84 % / 1.52 %
30	C	63.6 % / 1.32 %

Performance Analysis	
Avg. Score (%)	43.33%
Toppers Score (%)	63.33%
Your Score	

//Hints and Solutions//

1. In the given sentence, the adjective 'reliant' is used and it is incorrect. The word 'reliant' means 'dependent on someone'.

The dependence on something is mentioned in the sentence. Thus, the noun 'reliance' should be used here instead of the adjective 'reliant'.

Correct sentence: Converting to more sustainable energy sources is one way to reduce the reliance on oil products.

Hence, the correct option is (B).

2. The preposition 'of' is used and it is incorrect.

The meaning of the preposition 'despite' is 'in spite of; without being affected by, 'Of' is not used after the word 'despite'.

Correct sentence: Despite the rise of electric car manufacturers, it's clear that economics is the main driver of carbon emissions from transportation.

Hence, the correct option is (D).

3. The preposition 'between' is used and it is incorrect.

- We can use between for any number of elements, as long as all the elements are separate and distinct.
- Among is used when talking about people or things that are not distinct and are viewed as a group.

In the given sentence, 'financing providers' are viewed as a group. Thus, 'among' should be used here instead of 'between'.

Correct sentence: Non-bank financing facilitates competition among financing providers and supports economic activity.

Hence, the correct option is (A).

4. The word 'availability' is a noun and it is a specific quality of something. Therefore, the definite article 'the' should be used before the word 'availability'.

Correct sentence: The country has made improvements over the past decades to both the availability and quality of municipal drinking water systems.

Hence, the correct option is (B).

5.

- Resistance means the refusal to accept or comply with something.
- Cohesiveness means the quality of forming a united whole.
- Distinctive means characteristic of one person or thing, and so serving to distinguish it from others.
- Influence means the capacity to have an effect on the character, development, or behaviour of someone or something, or the effect itself.
- Domains means specified spheres of activity or knowledge.

Clearly, 'resistance' is correct.

Hence, the correct option is (E).

6. Urban means in, relating to, or characteristic of a town or city.

Let's look at the meaning of the given words-

- Rural means in, relating to, or characteristic of the countryside rather than the town.
- Town means a built-up area with a name, defined boundaries, and local government, that is larger than a village and generally smaller than a city.
- Household means a house and its occupants regarded as a unit.
- City means a large town.
- Suburb means an outlying district of a city, especially a residential one.

Clearly, 'rural' is correct.

Hence, the correct option is (B).

7. It is mentioned that "India is, without a doubt, committed to English as a national language. The impact of English is not only continuing but increasing."

Hence, the correct option is (C).

8. It is mentioned that "One can see a Hindi-speaking teacher giving their students instructions during an educational tour about where to meet and when their bus would leave, but all in English."

Hence, the correct option is (B).

9. Upon reading the passage, we can find that options (B) and (C) together will be the answer.

Hence, the correct option is (D).

10. Meanings of the words given in bold are:

- Skeptical means not easily convinced; having doubts or reservations.
- Preach means earnestly advocate (a belief or course of action).
- Sacrifice means an act of giving up something valued for the sake of something else regarded as more important or worthy.
- Endure means suffer (something painful or difficult) patiently.
- Indict means formally accuse of or charge with a crime.

It is clear that (C) and (D) are correct. Also, (E) justifies the bold word.

At (A), we require an adjective that describes the parent. Preach is a verb whereas skeptical is an adjective. Hence, we need to interchange (A) and (B) to make the sentence correct.

Corrected sentence: The duty of the **(A) skeptical** parent is plain: to save the child by any possible means, to **(B) preach** the uselessness of the **(C) sacrifice** in season and out of season, and to **(D) endure** patiently whatever penalty the law may **(E) indict** for evasion.

Hence, the correct option is (C).

11. Coconut water is the **purest** and most hygienic water found on the earth.

The attribute 'the' denotes that a superlative adjective follows it.

A superlative adjective expresses the extreme or highest degree of a quality. We use a superlative adjective to describe the extreme quality of one thing in a group of things.

Hence, the correct option is (C).

12. The first sentence of a paragraph gives an introduction, which is then elaborated in the following sentences.

A is given as the first, introductory sentence. So, logically, the next sentence must give more information about the Bhutanese cinema circa 2000.

This is only shown by H, which talks about the first commercially successful Bhutanese film. **So, H is the second sentence.**

Sentence F gives more information about the film in H. **So, F is the third sentence.**

The next sentences talk about the current state of commercial cinema. **So, G must be fourth.**

E talks about the emergence of current parallel cinema. **So, E must be fifth.**

It is followed logically by B, which talks about its audience. **So, B is the sixth sentence.**

The remaining sentence, **D, is then, the seventh.**

The correct order is : **AHFGEBD**

Hence, the correct option is (D).

13. The first sentence of a paragraph gives an introduction, which is then elaborated in the following sentences.

A is given as the first, introductory sentence. So, logically, the next sentence must give more information about the Bhutanese cinema circa 2000.

This is only shown by H, which talks about the first commercially successful Bhutanese film. **So, H is the second sentence.**

Sentence F gives more information about the film in H. **So, F is the third sentence.**

The next sentences talk about the current state of commercial cinema. **So, G must be fourth.**

E talks about the emergence of current parallel cinema. **So, E must be fifth.**

It is followed logically by B, which talks about its audience. **So, B is the sixth sentence.**

The remaining sentence, **D, is then, the seventh.**

The correct order is : **AHFGEBD**

Hence, the correct option is (C).

14. The context of most sentences is the emergence of Bhutanese cinema.

Only C talks about Anil Bhattarai's documentary. **So, C is out of context.**

The first sentence of a paragraph gives an introduction, which is then elaborated in the following sentences.

A is given as the first, introductory sentence. So, logically, the next sentence must give more information about the Bhutanese cinema circa 2000.

This is only shown by H, which talks about the first commercially successful Bhutanese film. **So, H is the second sentence.**

Sentence F gives more information about the film in H. **So, F is the third sentence.**

The next sentences talk about the current state of commercial cinema. **So, G must be fourth.**

E talks about the emergence of current parallel cinema. **So, E must be fifth.**

It is followed logically by B, which talks about its audience. **So, B is the sixth sentence.**

The remaining sentence, **D, is then, the seventh.**

The correct order is : **AHFGEBD**

Hence, the correct option is (E).

15. The first sentence of a paragraph gives an introduction, which is then elaborated in the following sentences.

A is given as the first, introductory sentence. So, logically, the next sentence must give more information about the Bhutanese cinema circa 2000.

This is only shown by H, which talks about the first commercially successful Bhutanese film. **So, H is the second sentence.**

Sentence F gives more information about the film in H. **So, F is the third sentence.**

The next sentences talk about the current state of commercial cinema. **So, G must be fourth.**

E talks about the emergence of current parallel cinema. **So, E must be fifth.**

It is followed logically by B, which talks about its audience. **So, B is the sixth sentence.**

The remaining sentence, **D, is then, the seventh.**

The correct order is : **AHFGEBD**

Hence, the correct option is (B).

16. The first sentence of a paragraph gives an introduction, which is then elaborated in the following sentences.

A is given as the first, introductory sentence. So, logically, the next sentence must give more information about the Bhutanese cinema circa 2000.

This is only shown by H, which talks about the first commercially successful Bhutanese film. **So, H is the second sentence.**

Sentence F gives more information about the film in H. **So, F is the third sentence.**

The next sentences talk about the current state of commercial cinema. **So, G must be fourth.**

E talks about the emergence of current parallel cinema. **So, E must be fifth.**

It is followed logically by B, which talks about its audience. **So, B is the sixth sentence.**

The remaining sentence, **D, is then, the seventh.**

The correct order is : **AHFGEBD**

Hence, the correct option is (D).

17.

- The sentence is in the past continuous tense.

- This can be seen from the usage of 2 separate verbs - including and paying - in their continuous form and the usage of the verb 'are' in the past form i.e. 'were'.

- This means that all the verbs in the sentence need to be in the continuous tense.

Thus, 'caused' needs to be replaced with 'causing' in order to make the sentence grammatically correct.

Hence, the correct option is (D).

18. The given sentence in the past tense, this can be seen by the use of the modal verb 'would'.

Even if the verb 'would' were to be replaced by the verb 'will', 'remembered' would still be incorrect as 'will' is in the present tense.

A modal verb has to be followed by the base form of the verb.

Thus, 'remembered' needs to be replaced with 'remember'.

Hence, the correct option is (B).

19.

- The sentence is in the past tense as can be seen by the use of the verb 'were' and 'would' in the past tense.

- The sentence already tells us that the subject of the sentence is 'he/his' and this is the pronoun that is used to refers to him in the rest of the sentence.

- If the sentence already uses one specific pronoun it should be maintained throughout the sentence unless the subject of the sentence changes.

Thus, 'one's' needs to be replaced with 'his' in order to make the sentence grammatically correct.

Hence, the correct option is (C).

20.

- The sentence is in the continuous tense as can be seen by the use of 'ing' form of the verb 'wait'.

- The use of the construction 'will + be' before the continuous form of the verb indicates that the action is yet to occur, but will occur in the future.

- This means that every verb in the sentence should comply with this format of the future continuous tense.

The given sentence has no errors and is grammatically correct.

Hence, the correct option is (E).

21.

- The sentence is in the past tense as can be seen by the use of the verb 'insisted' and 'wanted' in the past tense.

- The verb 'insist' means to 'demand something forcefully or not taking no for an answer'.

- This means that there usually is an idea or a point which one is being 'forceful' about.

- The verb 'insisted' needs to be followed by the preposition 'on' in order to show what point someone is being forced about.

Thus, 'insisted' needs to be followed by the preposition 'on' in order to make the sentence contextually correct.

Hence, the correct option is (A).

22. I had some chances of winning **but** I started a little slow.

- The sentence suggests that the blank should contain conjunction joining the two sentences.

- The context suggests that the word should suggest a condition rather than an antithesis.

- So the blank should contain 'until', 'once', 'but', 'if', etc.

Hence, the correct option is (B).

23. APJ Abdul Kalam **was born** in Tamil Nadu.

- The given sentence is the past tense because 'birth' is something that has already occurred.

- 'Was born' is correct as the sentence is in the passive form.

Hence, the correct option is (E).

24. The play was **too** good to be true.

'too' is the correct answer because it is used for expressing degree. The phrase 'too good to be true' is used to convey that something is so good that it cannot be true i.e., unbelievably good.

Hence, the correct option is (C).

25. I missed the bus **because** I was late.

- The correct conjunction to be used in the blank is 'because' as it means 'for the reason that, since'.

- Here, the speaker was late, and that is why he/she missed the bus.

Hence, the correct option is (E).

26. From the context, we can infer that the missing word is a noun. So, we can eliminate verbs in options (B) and (C). From the paragraph, we can infer that the word means sight or vision. Only something that does not appear in our vision can be considered to be unconscious. So, option (E).

Hence, the correct option is (E).

27. Given the parallel structure of the sentence, the missing word should be a noun. So, we can eliminate options (D) and (E). In the

paragraph, the author is trying to say that these details should not really matter while describing a person. So, the word "irrelevancies" is the most appropriate word for the blank.

Hence, the correct option is (C).

28. From the paragraph, we can infer that the Brontes are heavily gossiped about. So, we can eliminate options (B) and (E) as they do not suit the content of the paragraph. It is given in the paragraph that the gossips collect all sorts of trivia about the Brontes. So, the appropriate word for the blank would be eccentricities.

Hence, the correct option is (A).

29. The missing word is part of the list - glimpses, sermons, sidelights. The author says that all these would be personal details that could go into a museum on the Brontes. We can eliminate option (A) as it would be a repeat of the word glimpses. Lives and amusements do not fit in the list. Between anecdotes and passions, observers are more likely to note anecdotes and preserve them while writing biographies of people.

Hence, the correct option is (D).

30. The author says that Charlotte Bronte, through her work, showed that the exterior was irrelevant. Hence, through her work, she made the assertion about the unimportance of externals. So, the missing word should be asserted.

Hence, the correct option is (C).

Q.1 Amit spends 75 % of his income and saves the rest. If his expenditure is increased by 10 % and savings is increased by 20% then find the percentage increase in his income.

A. 10%   **B.** 11%   **C.** 11.5%   **D.** 12.5%

E. 9.5%

Q.2 A man bought a car at Rs. 700000 and if he gives car on rent then his probability to earn profit is $\frac{2}{5}$ then find selling price if he may earn profit of Rs. 50000?

A. 825000   **B.** 750000   **C.** 748000   **D.** 720000

E. 752000

Q.3 A bag contains 20 yellow balls, 10 green balls, 5 white balls, 8 black balls, and 1 red ball. How many minimum balls one should pick out so that to make sure the he gets at least 2 balls of same color.

A. 7 balls   **B.** 4 balls   **C.** 8 balls   **D.** 6 balls

E. 9 balls

Q.4 X can do a work in 9 days and Y in 18 days. How many days they work together to complete the two-third work?

A. 4   **B.** 6   **C.** 8   **D.** 9

E. 10

Q.5 Direction: In the given question, two equations numbered I and II are given. Solve both the equations and give the appropriate answer.

I. $x^2 - 15x + 54 = 0$

II. $y^2 - 13y + 36 = 0$

A. x > y

B. x < y

C. x ≥ y

D. x ≤ y

E. Relation can't be established or x = y

Q.6 Direction: In the given question, two equations numbered I and II are given. Solve both the equations and mark the appropriate answer.

$x^2 - 13x + 40 = 0$

$y^2 - 11y + 24 = 0$

A. x > y

B. x < y

C. x ≥ y

D. x ≤ y

E. Relation can't be established or x = y

Q.7 Direction: In the given question, two equations numbered I and II are given. You have to solve both the equations and mark the appropriate answer.

I. $x^2 - 7x + 10 = 0$

II. $y^2 - 11y + 24 = 0$

A. If x > y

B. If x ≥ y

C. If x < y

D. If x ≤ y

E. If x = y or the relationship cannot be established

Q.8 A cylindrical bucket of diameter 48 cm is filled with water to some height. If a solid spherical ball of diameter 24 cm is completely immersed, then an increase in the height of water level in the bucket will be:

A. 1 cm   **B.** 2 cm   **C.** 3 cm   **D.** 4 cm

E. 5 cm

Q.9 Direction: What should come in place of the question mark '?' in the following number series?

80, 60, 50, ?, 42.5

A. 42   **B.** 43   **C.** 44   **D.** 45

E. 49

Ques (10-13):Directions: What will come in the place of the question mark (?) in the following series?

Q.10 23, 46, ?, 86, 83, 166

A. 45   **B.** 89   **C.** 83   **D.** 49

E. 43

Q.11 99, 98, 96, 95, 91, 90, 82, ?

A. 80   **B.** 73   **C.** 74   **D.** 81

E. 66

Q.12 4913, 6859, 12167, 24389, ?

A. 42875   **B.** 35937   **C.** 29791   **D.** 27991

E. 29537

Q.13 15, 17, ?, 29, 45

A. 25   **B.** 19   **C.** 23   **D.** 21

E. 22

Ques (14-18):Direction: Read the following bar graph carefully and answer the following questions.

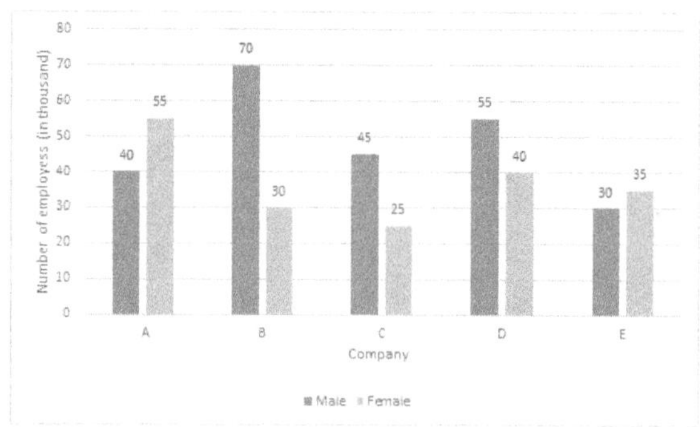

Q.14 Find the difference between the number of male employees and female employees of five companies.

A. 50000   **B.** 61000   **C.** 51000   **D.** 59000

E. 55000

Q.15 Find the male employees of company D are approximately what percent of total male employees of five companies?

A. 29%   B. 28%   C. 30%   D. 23%
E. 26%

Q.16 Find the average number of employees in the five companies.

A. 88000   B. 85000   C. 81000   D. 80000
E. 87000

Q.17 Find the number of female employees of a company E is approximately what percent less than the total employees of the same company?

A. 46%   B. 49%   C. 41%   D. 40%
E. 42%

Q.18 Find the ratio between the number of total employees of company B and C.

A. 1 : 5   B. 7 : 3   C. 5 : 4   D. 10 : 7
E. 3 : 7

Q.19 The average of four consecutive even numbers A, B, C, and D respectively (in increasing order) is 21. What is the product of A and C?

A. 400   B. 350
C. 396   D. 344
E. None of these

Q.20 Three taps A, B and C can fill a tank in 12,15 and 20 hours respectively. If A is open all the time and B and C are open for one hour each alternately, the tank will be full in:

A. 6 hours   B. $6\frac{2}{3}$ hours
C. 7 hours   D. $7\frac{1}{2}$ hours
E. $7\frac{3}{2}$ hours

Q.21 The difference between simple interest and compound interest on a certain sum of money for 2 years at 8% per annum is Rs 120. Find the sum.

[SBI Apprentice, 2019]

A. Rs. 19,750   B. Rs. 17,570
C. Rs. 21,570   D. Rs. 18,750
E. Rs. 20,050

Q.22 Asha has given Rs. 7500 to a labour compounded quarterly for 6 months at the rate 8% per annum. Find the compound interest.

A. Rs. 200   B. Rs. 303   C. Rs. 403   D. Rs. 400
E. Rs. 500

Q.23 A man rows to a place $48\ km$ distant and come back in 14 hours. He finds that he can row $4\ km$ with the stream in the same time as $3\ km$ against the stream. The rate of the stream is:

A. $1\ km/hr$ B. $1.5\ km/hr$
C. $2\ km/hr$ D. $22.5\ km/hr$
E. None of these

Q.24 What value should come in place of question mark (?) in the following question?

$$\sqrt{225} + (1500 \text{ of } 55\%) - \{(45)^2 \div 81 \times 4\} + 20 - 16 = ?$$

A. 744   B. 748   C. 746   D. 752
E. 742

Q.25 What will come in the place of the question mark '?' in the following question?

$$\frac{[(272-32)\times(124+176)]}{(17\times15-15)} = ?$$

A. 240   B. 320   C. 400   D. 380
E. 300

Q.26 What will come in the place of the question mark '?' in the following question?

$$5.8 \times 2.5 + 0.6 \times 6.75 + 139.25 = ?$$

A. 139.80   B. 157.80   C. 156.70   D. 170.70
E. 176.60

Q.27 What will come in the place of the question mark '?' in the following question?

$$(8375 \div 67)^{\frac{1}{3}} + (7.84 \times 25)^{\frac{1}{2}} = (?)^{\frac{1}{2}}$$

A. 456   B. 361   C. 324   D. 338
E. 432

Q.28 What value should come in the place of question mark (?) in the following question?

$$?^{\frac{1}{3}} + 47\% \text{ of } 200 = 60\% \text{ of } 112 + 30\% \text{ of } 136$$

A. 4096   B. 1331   C. 3375   D. 2744
E. 729

Q.29 A, B and C entered into a partnership with investment in the ratio 5 : 4 : 6. After one year A doubled his investment and C withdrew half of his investment amount. At the end of two years, they earned a profit of Rs. 96000, find the sum of the shares of B and C in the profit.

A. Rs. 58500   B. Rs. 56000
C. Rs. 54000   D. Rs. 51000
E. Rs. 53000

Q.30 From 6 programmers and 4 typists, an office wants to recruit 5 people. What is the number of ways this can be done so as to recruit at least one typist?

[UPSC NDA, 2019]

A. 209   B. 210   C. 246   D. 242
E. 250

// Smart Answer Sheet //

| Correct | Indicates percentage of students who answered questions correctly. |

| Skipped | Indicates percentage of students who skipped questions. |

Q.	Ans.	Correct / Skipped
1	D	61.19 % / 1.01 %
2	A	52.52 % / 1.14 %
3	D	79.96 % / 0.0 %
4	A	83.99 % / 0.0 %
5	E	64.94 % / 1.39 %
6	E	58.19 % / 1.96 %

Q.	Ans.	Correct / Skipped
7	E	54.41 % / 1.25 %
8	D	84.31 % / 0.0 %
9	D	23.97 % / 3.52 %
10	E	54.47 % / 1.45 %
11	D	59.59 % / 1.6 %
12	C	62.63 % / 1.67 %

Q.	Ans.	Correct / Skipped
13	D	79.59 % / 0.0 %
14	E	77.39 % / 0.0 %
15	D	58.32 % / 1.01 %
16	B	50.86 % / 1.25 %
17	A	40.65 % / 1.63 %
18	D	43.23 % / 1.15 %

Q.	Ans.	Correct / Skipped
19	C	42.47 % / 1.45 %
20	C	67.66 % / 1.24 %
21	D	28.27 % / 4.47 %
22	B	12.06 % / 3.94 %
23	A	63.68 % / 1.92 %
24	A	82.73 % / 0.0 %

Q.	Ans.	Correct / Skipped
25	E	81.64 % / 0.0 %
26	B	52.71 % / 1.27 %
27	B	44.56 % / 1.64 %
28	D	25.18 % / 4.15 %
29	D	44.78 % / 1.57 %
30	C	68.91 % / 1.75 %

Performance Analysis

Avg. Score (%)	56.67%
Toppers Score (%)	70.0%
Your Score	

//Hints and Solutions//

1. Given:

Amit's expenditure = 75% of salary

Increase in expenditure = 10%

Increase in savings = 20%

Let Amit's salary be 100

Expenditure = 75

Savings = 25

Increased expenditure = 110% of 75 = 82.5

Increased savings = 120% of 25 = 30

Increased income = 82.5 + 30 = 112.5

% Increase in income = $\dfrac{112.5-100}{100} \times 100$ = 12.5%

Hence, the correct option is (D).

2. Let selling price = SP

CP = Rs. 700000

Profit may be earned = $\dfrac{1}{probability}$ × real profit

Real profit = 50000 × $\dfrac{5}{2}$ = Rs. 125000

SP = CP + Real profit = 700000 + 125000 = Rs. 825000

∴ Selling price = Rs. 825000

Hence, the correct option is (A).

3. Suppose he picks 5 balls of all different colours then when he picks up the sixth one, it must match any on of the previously drawn ball colour. thus he must pick 6 balls.

Hence, the correct option is (D).

4. X complete work in 9 days.

X's 1-day work $= \dfrac{1}{9}$

Y complete work in $= 18$ days

Y's 1-day work $= \dfrac{1}{18}$

Both working together for 1 hour $= \dfrac{1}{9} + \dfrac{1}{9}$

Both working together for 1 hour $= \dfrac{(2+1)}{18}$

Time to complete the work together $= \dfrac{18}{3} = 6$ days

∴ Time to complete $\left(\dfrac{2}{3}\right)$ of total work together $=$

$6 \times \left(\dfrac{2}{3}\right) = 4$ days

Hence, the correct option is (A).

5. I. $x^2 - 15x + 54 = 0$

$\Rightarrow x^2 - 6x - 9x + 54 = 0$

$\Rightarrow x(x - 6) - 9(x - 6) = 0$

$\Rightarrow (x - 6)(x - 9) = 0$

$\Rightarrow x = 6$ or 9

II. $y^2 - 13y + 36 = 0$

$\Rightarrow y^2 - 9y - 4y + 36 = 0$

$\Rightarrow y(y - 9) - 4(y - 9) = 0$

$\Rightarrow (y - 9)(y - 4) = 0$

$\Rightarrow Y = 9$ or 4

x	sign	y
6	<	9
6	>	4
9	=	9
9	>	4

∴ Relation can't be established or x = y

Hence, the correct option is (E).

6. I. $x^2 - 13x + 40 = 0$

$\Rightarrow x^2 - 8x - 5x + 40 = 0$

$\Rightarrow x(x - 8) - 5(x - 8) = 0$

$\Rightarrow (x - 8)(x - 5) = 0$

$\Rightarrow x = 5$ or 8

II. $y^2 - 11y + 24 = 0$

$\Rightarrow y^2 - 3y - 8y + 24 = 0$

$\Rightarrow y(y - 3) - 8 (y - 3) = 0$

$\Rightarrow (y - 3)(y - 8) = 0$

$\Rightarrow y = 3$ or 8

x	sign	y
5	>	3
5	<	8
8	>	3
8	=	8

∴ Relation can't be established or x = y

Hence, the correct option is (E).

7. I. $x^2 - 7x + 10 = 0$

$\Rightarrow x^2 - 5x - 2x + 10 = 0$

$\Rightarrow x(x - 5) - 2(x - 5) = 0$

$\Rightarrow (x - 5) (x - 2) = 0$

$\Rightarrow x = 5$ or x = 2

II. $y^2 - 11y + 24 = 0$

$\Rightarrow y^2 - 8y - 3y + 24 = 0$

$\Rightarrow y(y - 8) - 3(y - 8) = 0$

$\Rightarrow (y - 8)(y - 3) = 0$

$\Rightarrow y = 8$ or $y = 3$

Value of x	Sign	Value of y
5	<	8
2	<	8
5	>	3
2	<	3

∴ The relationship cannot be established between x and y.

Hence, the correct option is (E).

8. Radius of cylinder $= \dfrac{d}{2} = \dfrac{48}{2} = 24$ cm

Let level of water will be increased by h cm

Radius of Sphere $= \dfrac{24}{2} = 12$ cm

Volume of cylinder of increased water level is equal to volume of sphere immersed in water,

$$\pi \times r^2 \times h = \left(\dfrac{4}{3}\right) \times \pi \times r^3$$

$$\Rightarrow \pi \times 24^2 \times h = \left(\dfrac{4}{3}\right) \times \pi \times 12^3$$

$$\Rightarrow h = \dfrac{2304}{576}$$

$$\therefore h = 4 \text{ cm}$$

Hence, the correct option is (D).

9. The pattern is as follows:

$80 - 20 = 60$

$60 - 20 \times 0.5 = 50$

$50 - 20 \times 0.25 = 45$

$45 - 20 \times 0.125 = 42.5$

∴ The value of ? is 45.

Hence, the correct option is (D).

10. The given series follows the below pattern.

Multiplication by two and subtraction by three.

$46 = 23 \times 2$

$43 = 46 - 3$

$86 = 43 \times 2$

$83 = 86 - 3$

$166 = 83 \times 2$

So, the required number is 43.

Hence, the correct option is (E).

11. The given series follow this pattern is,

$99 - 1^1 = 98$

$98 - 2^1 = 96$

$96 - 1^2 = 95$

$95 - 2^2 = 91$

$91 - 1^3 = 90$

$90 - 2^3 = 82$

So, the number that follows is $82 - 1^4 = 81$

Hence, the correct option is (D).

12. Each of the numbers given in the series is perfect cube of prime numbers.

$4913 = 17^3$

$6859 = 19^3$

$12167 = 23^3$

$24389 = 29^3$

So, $31^3 = 29791$

Hence, the correct option is (C).

13. The difference between consecutive numbers of the series is getting multiplied by 2.

$17 - 15 = 2$

$21 - 17 = 4$

$29 - 21 = 8$

$45 - 29 = 16$

So, the correct answer to replace the question marks is 21.

Hence, the correct option is (D).

14. Total number of female employees of companies = 55000 + 30000 + 25000 + 40000 + 35000 = 185000

Total number of male employees of companies = 40000 + 70000 + 45000 + 55000 + 30000 = 240000

Required difference = 240000 - 185000 = 55000

Hence, the correct option is (E).

15. Total number of male employees of companies = 40000 + 70000 + 45000 + 55000 + 30000 = 240000

Male employees of a company D = 55000

Required percentage $= \dfrac{55000}{240000} \times 100$

$= 22.91\% \approx 23\%$

∴ The required percentage is 23%.

Hence, the correct option is (D).

16. Total number of female employees of companies = 55000 + 30000 + 25000 + 40000 + 35000 = 185000

Total number of male employees of companies = 40000 + 70000 + 45000 + 55000 + 30000 = 240000

Total employees in five companies = 185000 + 240000 = 425000

Required average $= \dfrac{425000}{5} = 85000$

∴ The required average is 85000.

Hence, the correct option is (B).

17. Total employees in a company E = 30000 + 35000 = 65000

Total female employees of a company E = 35000

Required percentage $= \left(\dfrac{65000-35000}{65000}\right) \times 100$

$= \left(\dfrac{30000}{65000}\right) \times 100$

$= \dfrac{30}{65} \times 100$

$= 46.15\% \approx 46\%$

Hence, the correct option is (A).

18. Total number of employees of a company B = 70000 + 30000 = 100000

Total number of employees of a company C = 45000 + 25000 = 70000

Required ratio = 100000 : 70000 = 10 : 7

∴ The ratio between the number of total employees of company B and C is 10 : 7.

Hence, the correct option is (D).

19. Average of n quantities $= \dfrac{(sum\ of\ n\ quantities)}{n}$

Let's assume that the four consecutive even numbers A, B, C and D are (a − 2), a, (a + 2) and (a + 4) respectively.

∴ $\dfrac{(a-2+a+a+2+a+4)}{4} = 21$

$\Rightarrow 4a + 4 = 21 \times 4$

$\Rightarrow a + 1 = 21$

$\Rightarrow a = 20$

∴ The numbers A, B, C, and D are 18, 20, 22 and 24 respectively.

∴ Product of A and C = 18 × 22 = 396.

Hence, the correct option is (C).

20. Given,

Time taken by tap A to fill the tank = 12 hours

Part filled by tap A in 1 hour = $\dfrac{1}{12}$

Time taken by tap B to fill the tank = 15 hours

Part filled by tap A in 1 hour = $\dfrac{1}{15}$

Time taken by tap C to fill the tank = 20 hours

Part filled by tap C in 1 hour = $\dfrac{1}{20}$

(A + B) 's 1 hour work $= \dfrac{1}{12} + \dfrac{1}{15}$

$= \dfrac{9}{60}$

$= \dfrac{3}{20}$

(A + C) 's 1 hour work $= \dfrac{1}{12} + \dfrac{1}{20}$

$= \dfrac{8}{60}$

$= \dfrac{2}{15}$

Part filled in 2 hours $= \dfrac{3}{20} + \dfrac{2}{15}$

$= \dfrac{17}{60}$

Part filled in 6 hours $= 3 \times \dfrac{17}{60}$

$= \dfrac{17}{20}$

Remaining part $= 1 - \dfrac{17}{20}$

$= \dfrac{3}{20}$

Since the remaining part is $\dfrac{3}{20}$ and this part can be filled by tap A and B in 1 hour.

So, total time taken = 6 + 1

= 7 hours

∴ The total time taken for the tank is 7 hours.

Hence, the correct option is (C).

21. Given:

Difference between simple interest and compound interest on a certain sum of money = Rs. 120

Time $= 2$ years

Rate of interest $= 8\%$

We know that:

Simple interest $= \dfrac{(P \times r \times t)}{100}$ $\quad [\because P = $ principle, $t = $ time, $r = $ rate of interest $]$

Compound Interest $= \left[P\left(1 + \dfrac{r}{100}\right)^t - P\right]$ $\quad [\because P = $ principle amount, $t = $ time, $r = $ rate of interest, $n = $ number of times interest applied per time periods]

Let, the sum i.e., Principal amount $= $ Rs $100x$

∴ Simple interest earned = Rs. $\dfrac{(100x \times 2 \times 8)}{100} = $ Rs. $16x$

$\therefore$ Compound interest earned $=$ Rs. $\left[100x \times \left(1+\frac{8}{100}\right)^2 - 100x\right]$

$=$ Rs. $\left(\frac{2916x}{25} - 100x\right)$

According to the question,

$\left(\frac{2916x}{25} - 100x\right) - 16x = 120$

$\Rightarrow \frac{(2916x - 2900x)}{25} = 120$

$\Rightarrow 16x = 3000$

$\Rightarrow x = \frac{3000}{16}$

$\Rightarrow x = \frac{375}{2}$

$\Rightarrow$ Total Sum $=$ Rs. $\left(\frac{100 \times 375}{2}\right) =$ Rs. 18,750

$\therefore$ Total sum is Rs. 18,750.

Hence, the correct option is (D).

22. Given:

Amount given by Asha to labour = Rs. 7500

Time $= 6$ months

Rate of interest $= 8\%$

$A = P\left(1+\frac{R}{400}\right)^{4n}$ (when interest calculated quarterly)

$A = P\left(1+\frac{R}{400}\right)^{4n}$

$= 7500\left(1+\frac{8}{400}\right)^{4\left(\frac{1}{2}\right)}$

$= 7500\left(1+\frac{1}{50}\right)^2$

$= 7500\left(\frac{51}{50}\right)^2$

$= 7500\left(\frac{2601}{2500}\right)$

$= 7803$

$CI = A - P$

$= 7803 - 7500$

$= 303 Rs.$

$\therefore$ CI for given sum is Rs. 303.

Hence, the correct option is (B).

23. Given,

Distance man can row against the stream $= 3km$

Distance man can row along the stream $= 4km$

Total distance rowed by a man $= 48km$

Total time taken to row that distance $= 14$ hours

Suppose he move $4km$ downstream in x hours Then, Speed downstream $= \frac{4}{x}km/hr$ Speed upstream $= \frac{3}{x}km/hr$

According to question,

$\frac{48}{\left(\frac{4}{x}\right)} + \frac{48}{\left(\frac{3}{x}\right)} = 14$

or

$x = \frac{1}{2}$

So, Speed in downstream $= 8km/hr$

Speed in upstream $= 6km/hr$

$\therefore$ Rate of the stream $= \frac{1}{2}(8-6)km/hr$

$= 1\ km/hr$

Hence, the correct option is (A).

24. Follow BODMAS rule to solve this question, as per the order given below.

Step - 1: Parts of an equation enclosed in 'Brackets' must be solved second, and following BODMAS rule in the bracket

Step - 2: Any mathematical 'Of' or 'Exponent' must be solved next.

Step - 3: Next, the parts of the equation that contain 'Division' and 'Multiplication' are calculated.

Step - 4: Last but not the least, the parts of the equation that contain 'Addition' and 'Subtraction' should be calculated.

Using the BODMAS rule:

$\sqrt{225} + (1500 \text{ of } 55\%) - \{(45)^2 \div 81 \times 4\} + 20 - 16 = ?$

$= 15 + 825 - 25 \times 4 + 20 - 16$

$= 15 + 825 - 100 + 20 - 16$

$= 840 - 100 + 20 - 16$

$= 740 + 4$

$= 744$

$\therefore$ Answer is 744

Hence, the correct option is (A).

25. Follow BODMAS rule to solve this question, as per the order given below.

Step - 1: Parts of an equation enclosed in 'Brackets' must be solved second, and following BODMAS rule in the bracket

Step - 2: Any mathematical 'Of' or 'Exponent' must be solved next.

Step - 3: Next, the parts of the equation that contain 'Division' and 'Multiplication' are calculated.

Step - 4: Last but not the least, the parts of the equation that contain 'Addition' and 'Subtraction' should be calculated.

Using the BODMAS rule:

$$\frac{[(272-32)\times(124+176)]}{(17\times15-15)} = ?$$

$$\Rightarrow \frac{(240\times300)}{(255-15)} = ?$$

$$\Rightarrow \frac{(240\times300)}{240} = ?$$

$$\Rightarrow 300 = ?$$

∴ The value of $?$ is 300.

Hence, the correct option is (E).

26. Follow BODMAS rule to solve this question, as per the order given below.

Step - 1: Parts of an equation enclosed in 'Brackets' must be solved second, and following BODMAS rule in the bracket

Step - 2: Any mathematical 'Of' or 'Exponent' must be solved next.

Step - 3: Next, the parts of the equation that contain 'Division' and 'Multiplication' are calculated.

Step - 4: Last but not the least, the parts of the equation that contain 'Addition' and 'Subtraction' should be calculated.

Using the BODMAS rule:

$$5.8 \times 2.5 + 0.6 \times 6.75 + 139.25 = ?$$

$$= 14.5 + 4.05 + 139.25$$

$$= 157.80$$

Hence, the correct option is (B).

27. Follow BODMAS rule to solve this question, as per the order given below.

Step - 1: Parts of an equation enclosed in 'Brackets' must be solved second, and following BODMAS rule in the bracket

Step - 2: Any mathematical 'Of' or 'Exponent' must be solved next.

Step - 3: Next, the parts of the equation that contain 'Division' and 'Multiplication' are calculated.

Step - 4: Last but not the least, the parts of the equation that contain 'Addition' and 'Subtraction' should be calculated.

Using the BODMAS rule:

$$(8375 \div 67)^{\frac{1}{3}} + (7.84 \times 25)^{\frac{1}{2}} = (?)^{\frac{1}{2}}$$

$$\Rightarrow (125)^{\frac{1}{3}} + (7.84 \times 25)^{\frac{1}{2}} = (?)^{\frac{1}{2}}$$

$$\Rightarrow (125)^{\frac{1}{3}} + (196)^{\frac{1}{2}} = (?)^{\frac{1}{2}}$$

$$\Rightarrow 5 + 14 = (?)^{\frac{1}{2}}$$

$$\Rightarrow (?)^{\frac{1}{2}} = 19$$

Squaring both sides,

$$? = 19^2$$

$$? = 361$$

∴ 361 will come in place of '?'

Hence, the correct option is (B).

28. Follow BODMAS rule to solve this question, as per the order given below.

Step - 1: Parts of an equation enclosed in 'Brackets' must be solved second, and following BODMAS rule in the bracket

Step - 2: Any mathematical 'Of' or 'Exponent' must be solved next.

Step - 3: Next, the parts of the equation that contain 'Division' and 'Multiplication' are calculated.

Step - 4: Last but not the least, the parts of the equation that contain 'Addition' and 'Subtraction' should be calculated.

Using the BODMAS rule:

$$?^{\frac{1}{3}} + (47 \times 2) = \left(\frac{6}{10}\right) \times 112 + \left(\frac{3}{10}\right) \times 136$$

$$\Rightarrow ?^{\frac{1}{3}} + 94 = 67.2 + 40.8$$

$$\Rightarrow ?^{\frac{1}{3}} = 108 - 94$$

$$\Rightarrow ?^{\frac{1}{3}} = 14$$

$$\Rightarrow ? = 2744$$

$$\therefore ? = 2744$$

Hence, the correct option is (D).

29. Let the investment of A, B and C are Rs. $5x$, Rs. $4x$ and Rs. $6x$.

Ratio of shares of A, B and C in the profit

$$= (5x + 5x \times 2):(4x + 4x):\left(6x + \frac{6x}{2}\right)$$

$$= 15x:8x:9x = 15:8:9$$

Sum of the shares of B and C in the profit $= \dfrac{8+9}{15+8+9} \times$

$96000 \,] = \dfrac{17}{32} \times 96000 =$ Rs. 51000

Hence, the correct option is (D).

30. Concept:

The notation C(n, r) is the number of combinations/groups of n different things taking r at a time and is given by:

$$C(n,r) = \dfrac{n!}{r!(n-r)!}$$

Calculation:

Given: 6 programmers and 4 typists, an office wants to recruit 5 people.

Here, n = 10 and r = 5.

Case 1: Group of 5 with 1 typist

1 typist can be chosen from 4 in C(4, 1) = 4 ways

4 programmers can be chosen from 6 in C(6, 4) = 15 ways

⇒ No. of ways to form a group of 5 with 1 typist = 4 × 15 = 60.

Case 2: Group of 5 with 2 typists

2 typist can be chosen from 4 in C(4, 2) = 6 ways

3 programmers can be chosen from 6 in C(6, 3) = 20 ways

⇒ No. of ways to form a group of 5 with 2 typist = 6 × 20 = 120.

Case 3: Group of 5 with 3 typists

3 typist can be chosen from 4 in C(4, 3) = 4 ways

2 programmers can be chosen from 6 in C(6, 2) = 15 ways

⇒ No. of ways to form a group of 5 with 2 typist = 4 × 15 = 60.

Case 4: Group of 5 with 4 typists

4 typist can be chosen from 4 in C(4, 4) = 1 way

1 programmers can be chosen from 6 in C(6, 1) = 6 ways

⇒ No. of ways to form a group of 5 with 2 typist = 1 × 6 = 6.

Total number of ways in forming a group of 5 with at least one typist is = 60 + 120 + 60 + 6 = 246.

Hence, the correct option is (C).

Ques (1-5):Direction: In the following number series, only one number is wrong. Find out the wrong number.

Q.1 3, 5, 13, 53, 177, 891
A. 3 **B.** 5 **C.** 891 **D.** 177
E. 53

Q.2 72, 73, 59, 78, 62, 87, 51
A. 73 **B.** 59 **C.** 78 **D.** 62
E. 51

Q.3 11, 35, 65, 119, 191, 281
A. 191 **B.** 65 **C.** 35 **D.** 119
E. 120

Q.4 20, 10, 40, 5, 85, 2.5
A. 10 **B.** 40 **C.** 85 **D.** 2.5
E. 20

Q.5 7, 29, 61, 128, 211, 349
A. 7 **B.** 61 **C.** 29 **D.** 349
E. 128

Q.6 The average weight of a group of 75 girls was calculated as 48 kg. It was later discovered that the weight of one of the girls was read as 44 kg, whereas her actual weight was 26 kg. What is the actual average weight of the group of 75 girls? (Rounded off to two digits after decimal)?
A. 46.73 kg **B.** 48.76 kg
C. 45.76 kg **D.** 45.85 kg
E. None of these

Q.7 One-third of 12 oranges got rotten. If 4 oranges are taken out randomly, what is the probability that all orange are rotten?
A. $\frac{14}{995}$ **B.** $\frac{1}{495}$
C. $\frac{16}{495}$ **D.** $\frac{8}{495}$
E. None of these

Q.8 Three pipes A, B, and C can fill a tank in 6 hours. After working at it together for 2 hours, C is closed and A and B can fill the remaining part in 7 hours. The number of hours taken by C alone to fill the tank is:
A. 10 hours **B.** 12 hours **C.** 14 hours **D.** 15 hours
E. 16 hours

Q.9 If sum triples in 4 years under simple interest. What is the time that it would take to become 5 time itself at the same rate of interest?
A. 8 years **B.** 9 years
C. 7 years **D.** 5 years
E. None of these

Q.10 Monika invested an amount of Rs. 5800 for 2 years. At what rate of compound interest will she get an interest of Rs. 594.5 at the end of two years?

A. 50% **B.** 20%
C. 15% **D.** 10%
E. None of these

Q.11 A hemispherical cup of inner radius 3 cm is filled with water. The water is poured into another hemispherical cup of inner radius 6 cm. what percentage of the cup will remain empty?
A. 25.6% **B.** 65.8% **C.** 45.2% **D.** 50.4%
E. 87.5%

Q.12 A man spends 40% of his monthly salary on food, 20% on entertainment, 10% on house rent and 15% on travel. If he saves Rs. 3,000 in the month, then his monthly salary is:
A. Rs. 40,000 **B.** Rs. 30,000
C. Rs. 20,000 **D.** Rs. 10,000
E. Rs. 50,000

Q.13 A man can row at a speed of $4\frac{1}{2}\ km/hr$ in still water. If he takes 2 times as long to row a distance upstream as to row the same distance downstream, then the speed of stream (in km/hr) is:
A. 1 **B.** 1.5 **C.** 2 **D.** 2.5
E. 3

Ques (14-18):Direction: The following line graph gives the ratio of the amounts of imports by a company to the amount of exports from that company over the period from 1995 to 2001.

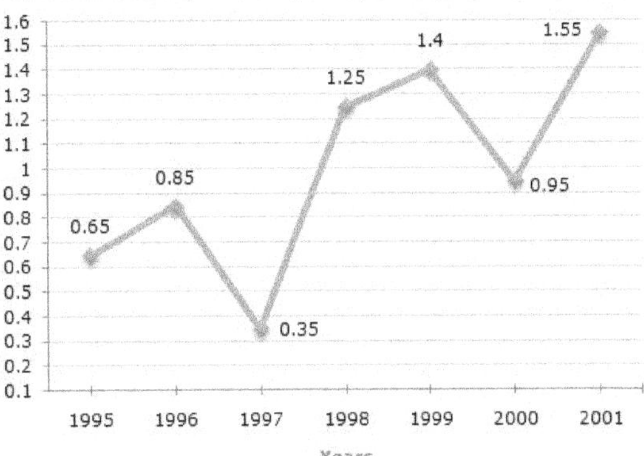

Q.14 If the imports in 1998 was Rs. 250 crores and the total exports in the years 1998 and 1999 together was Rs. 500 crores, then the imports in 1999 was?
A. Rs. 250 crores **B.** Rs. 300 crores
C. Rs. 357 crores **D.** Rs. 420 crores
E. Rs. 405 crores

Q.15 The imports were minimum proportionate to the exports of the company in the year______.
A. 1995 **B.** 1996 **C.** 1997 **D.** 2000

E. 2001

Q.16 What was the percentage increase in imports from 1997 to 1998?

A. 72　　　　　　　　　**B.** 56
C. 28　　　　　　　　　**D.** 25
E. Data inadequate

Q.17 If the imports of the company in 1996 was Rs. 272 crores, the exports from the company in 1996 was:

A. Rs. 370 crores　　　　**B.** Rs. 320 crores
C. Rs. 280 crores　　　　**D.** Rs. 275 crores
E. Rs. 305 crores

Q.18 In how many of the given years were the exports more than the imports?

A. 1　　　　**B.** 2　　　　**C.** 3　　　　**D.** 4
E. 5

Ques (19-21):Directions: In the given question, two equations numbered I and II are given. Solve both the equations and mark the appropriate answer.

Q.19 I. $x^2 + x - 156 = 0$

II. $y^2 + y - 182 = 0$

A.　 x > y
B.　 x < y
C.　 x ≥ y
D.　 x ≤ y
E.　 x = y or the relationship between x and y cannot be established

Q.20 I. $x^2 - 18x + 77 = 0$

II. $y^2 + 3y - 70 = 0$

A.　 x > y
B.　 x ≥ y
C.　 y > x
D.　 y ≥ x
E.　 x = y, Relation doesn't exist

Q.21 I. $3x^2 - 2\sqrt{21}x + 7 = 0$

II. $3y^2 + \sqrt{3}y - 2 = 0$

A.　 x > y
B.　 x < y
C.　 x ≥ y
D.　 x ≤ y
E.　 x = y or relationship between x and y cannot be established

Q.22 In how many ways can arrange the letters of the words ALLAHABAD?

A. 5560　　　**B.** 4560　　　**C.** 7560　　　**D.** 6540
E. 7450

Ques (23-27):Direction: What approximate value should come in the place of question mark (?) in the following question?

Q.23 $\sqrt[3]{\left(\dfrac{1331}{124999}\right)} + \sqrt[3]{\left(\dfrac{26.87}{7.78}\right)} - (2 \times ?^2) = 1$

A. $\frac{3}{5}$　　　**B.** $\frac{2}{5}$　　　**C.** $\frac{1}{5}$　　　**D.** $\frac{4}{5}$
E. 1

Q.24 $6.03 \times 36.06 + \dfrac{131.99}{10.99} + 2^1 = ?$

A. 180　　　**B.** 250　　　**C.** 130　　　**D.** 230
E. 420

Q.25 $\dfrac{[(36.01)^2 - (24.99)^2]}{?} = (8.99)^2 - (4.01)^2$

A. 20　　　**B.** 1　　　**C.** 5　　　**D.** 10
E. 15

Q.26 $311.99 \times 8.88 \times 1.99 \times 9.99 = ? \times 8$

A. 7200　　　**B.** 7000　　　**C.** 7700　　　**D.** 7020
E. 7070

Q.27 $139.95 \times 70.09 - 48.99^2 = ? - 1$

A. 7200　　　**B.** 7300　　　**C.** 7400　　　**D.** 7500
E. 7600

Q.28 A shopkeeper sells 12 pens at a price for which he bought 14 pens. If he has to pay a tax of 10% on the profit obtained, what is his net profit on the overall transaction?

A.　 15.33%
B.　 16%
C.　 16.67%
D.　 15%
E.　 Cannot be determined

Q.29 Ratul invested 20% more than Rakesh and Rakesh invested 50% more than Rudra. If the total amount of their investment is Rs. 3,225, how much amount did Ratul invest?

[SBI Apprentice, 2019]

A.　Rs. 1,450　　　　**B.**　Rs. 1,500
C.　Rs. 1,050　　　　**D.**　Rs. 1,350
E.　Rs. 1,400

Q.30 Sahil do a certain piece of work in 5 days. Karan takes 7 days to complete the same work. Himani takes as long as Sahil and Karan takes working together. Find the time taken by Karan and Himani to complete the work.

A.　$2\frac{1}{17}$ days　　　　**B.**　$2\frac{2}{3}$ days
C.　$4\frac{1}{3}$ days　　　　**D.**　$5\frac{1}{7}$ days
E.　$5\frac{1}{17}$ days

// Smart Answer Sheet //

Correct   Indicates percentage of students who answered questions correctly.

Skipped   Indicates percentage of students who skipped questions.

Q.	Ans.	Correct / Skipped
1	E	80.87 % / 0.0 %
2	B	84.7 % / 0.0 %
3	C	76.24 % / 0.0 %
4	C	31.28 % / 3.62 %
5	E	60.8 % / 1.43 %
6	E	61.0 % / 1.87 %

Q.	Ans.	Correct / Skipped
7	B	81.54 % / 0.0 %
8	C	52.82 % / 1.58 %
9	A	45.14 % / 1.21 %
10	E	87.14 % / 0.0 %
11	E	15.71 % / 4.52 %
12	C	89.93 % / 0.0 %

Q.	Ans.	Correct / Skipped
13	B	61.81 % / 1.78 %
14	D	64.71 % / 1.84 %
15	C	64.33 % / 1.83 %
16	E	65.34 % / 1.02 %
17	B	43.22 % / 1.92 %
18	D	46.27 % / 1.32 %

Q.	Ans.	Correct / Skipped
19	E	62.5 % / 1.4 %
20	B	51.78 % / 1.16 %
21	A	46.47 % / 1.25 %
22	C	69.78 % / 1.48 %
23	A	66.23 % / 1.23 %
24	D	85.9 % / 0.0 %

Q.	Ans.	Correct / Skipped
25	D	49.34 % / 1.27 %
26	D	84.76 % / 0.0 %
27	C	62.82 % / 1.98 %
28	D	60.46 % / 1.42 %
29	D	64.6 % / 1.09 %
30	A	45.08 % / 1.5 %

Performance Analysis	
Avg. Score (%)	53.33%
Toppers Score (%)	63.33%
Your Score	

//Hints and Solutions//

1. The series follows the following pattern:

$3 \times 1 + 2 = 5$

$5 \times 2 + 3 = 13$

$13 \times 3 + 4 = 43 \neq 53$

$43 \times 4 + 5 = 177$

$177 \times 5 + 6 = 891$

Since 43 will come in place of 53.

∴ Wrong number is 53.

Hence, the correct option is (E).

2. The series follows the following pattern:

$72 + 1^2 = 73$

$73 - 2^2 = 69 \neq 59$

$69 + 3^2 = 78$

$78 - 4^2 = 62$

$62 + 5^2 = 87$

$87 - 6^2 = 51$

Since 69 will come in place of 59.

∴ Wrong number is 59.

Hence, the correct option is (B).

3. The series follows the following pattern:

$11 + 18 = 29 \quad (\because 18 = 18 \times 1)$

$29 + 36 = 65 \quad (\because 36 = 18 \times 2)$

$65 + 54 = 119 \quad (\because 54 = 18 \times 3)$

$119 + 72 = 191 \quad (\because 72 = 18 \times 4)$

$191 + 90 = 281 \quad (\because 90 = 18 \times 5)$

Since 29 will come in place of 35.

∴ Wrong number is 35.

Hence, the correct option is (C).

4. The series follows the following pattern:

$20 \div 2^1 = 10$

$10 \times 2^2 = 40$

$40 \div 2^3 = 5$

$5 \times 2^4 = 80$

$80 \div 2^5 = 2.5$

Since 80 will come in place of 85.

∴ Wrong number is 85.

Hence, the correct option is (C).

5. The series follows the following pattern:

$2^3 - 1 = 7$

$3^3 + 2 = 29$

$4^3 - 3 = 61$

$5^3 + 4 = 129 \neq 128$

$6^3 - 5 = 211$

$7^3 + 6 = 349$

Since 128 will come in place of 129.

∴ Wrong number is 129.

Hence, the correct option is (E).

6. The average weight of a group of 75 girls was calculated as 48 kg.

The total weight of a group of 75 girls was = 48 × 75 kg=3600 kg

It was later discovered that the weight of one of the girls was read at 44 kg, whereas her actual weight was 26 kg

The rest of the 74 girls actual weight was = (3600 – 44) kg = 3556 kg

But the actual weight of the girl is 26 kg.

Putting the actual weight of the girl the total weight of 75 girls = 3556 + 26 kg

= 3582 Kg

Now the average weight of the 75 girls = $\dfrac{3582}{75}$ kg

= 47.76 kg

So the answer is 47.76 kg

Hence, the correct option is (E).

7. Total rotten oranges = $\dfrac{12}{3}$ = 4

4 oranges can be selected from 12 oranges in $^{12}C_4$ ways, and four rotten oranges can be selected as a set in $^4C_4$ ways

Probability = $\dfrac{No.\ of\ favourable\ outcomes}{Total\ no.\ of\ outcomes}$

The probability that all oranges are rotten = $\dfrac{^4C_4}{^{12}C_4}$ = $\dfrac{1}{\left(\dfrac{12\times11\times10\times9}{4\times3\times2\times1}\right)} = \dfrac{1}{495}$

Hence, the correct option is (B).

8. Given,

Total time taken by pipe A, B and C to fill the tank = 6 hours

Part filled by A, B and C in 1 hour = $\dfrac{1}{6}$

Part filled by A, B and C in 2 hour = $\dfrac{2}{6}$

$$= \frac{1}{3}$$

Remaining part $= 1 - \frac{1}{3}$

$$= \frac{2}{3}$$

(A + B)'s 7 hours' work $= \frac{2}{3}$

(A + B)'s 1 hours' work $= \frac{2}{21}$

C's 1 hour's work = (A + B + C) 's 1 hour's work - (A + B)'s 1 hour's work

$$\frac{1}{C} = \frac{1}{(A+B+C)} - \frac{1}{(A+B)}$$

$$= \frac{1}{6} - \frac{2}{21}$$

$$= \frac{1}{14}$$

∴ C alone can fill the tank in 14 hours.

Hence, the correct option is (C).

9. Let the amount be P and the rate of interest R.

According to the question, a sum of money becomes three times of itself in 4 years.

So after 4 years the amount will become $3P$.

Therefore, 4 simple interest for years $= 3P - P = 2P$

we know that,

Simple Interest $= \frac{(\text{Principal} \times \text{Rate} \times \text{Time})}{100}$ ...(1)

$$2P = \frac{(P \times R \times T)}{100}$$

$$\Rightarrow \frac{200}{4} = R$$

$$\Rightarrow R = 50\%$$

Let the time taken by the sum to be 5 times T. So the amount after T years $5P - P = 4P$

Substituting the above value of simple interest in equation (1),

$$4P = \frac{(P \times R \times T)}{100}$$

$$\Rightarrow \frac{400}{50} = T$$

$$\Rightarrow T = 8 \text{ years}$$

It will take 8 years to become 5 time itself at the same rate of interest.

Hence, the correct option is (A).

10. Given,

Principal $=$ Rs. 5800

Time $= 2$ years

Compound Interest $=$ Rs. 594.5

We know that, formula:

Compound Interest:

$$\Rightarrow \mathbf{CI} = \left[P \left\{ \left(1 + \frac{r}{100}\right)^t - 1 \right\} \right]$$

Where, $Cl =$ compound interest,

$P =$ principal,

$r =$ rate of interest,

$t =$ time period.

Now, according to the question,

$$594.5 = 5800 \left[\left(1 + \frac{r}{100}\right)^2 - 1 \right]$$

$$\Rightarrow \frac{594.5}{5800} = \left(1 + \frac{r}{100}\right)^2 - 1$$

$$\Rightarrow 0.1025 + 1 = \left(1 + \frac{r}{100}\right)^2$$

$$\Rightarrow 1.1025 = \frac{(100+r)^2}{10000}$$

$$\Rightarrow 1.1025 \times 10000 = (100 + r)^2$$

$$\Rightarrow 11025 = (100 + r)^2$$

$$\Rightarrow 105 = 100 + r$$

$$\Rightarrow r = 5\%$$

The rate of compound interest Monika will get for Rs. 594.5 at the end of two years is 5%.

Hence, the correct option is (E).

11. Volume of Hemisphere $= \left(\frac{2}{3}\right) \times \pi \times r^3$, where r is the radius of hemisphere.

In case of 1st hemisphere,

Inner radius = 3 cm

∴ Volume of water in it $= \left(\frac{2}{3}\right) \times \pi \times 3^3 = 18\pi$ sq. cm.

In 2nd hemisphere,

Inner radius = 6 cm

∴ Volume of water it can contain $= \left(\frac{2}{3}\right) \times \pi \times 6^3 = 144\pi$ sq. cm.

∴ Empty volume = 144π - 18π = 126π sq. cm.

∴ Percentage empty $= \left(\frac{126\pi}{144\pi}\right) \times 100 = 87.5\%$

Hence, the correct option is (E).

12. Monthly salary of man = 100%

Total monthly expenditures = 40% + 20% + 10% + 15% = 85%

Monthly saving = 100% – 85% = 15%

$$\Rightarrow 15 = \left(\frac{3,000}{Monthly\ income} \right) \times 100$$

$$\Rightarrow Monthly\ income\ = \frac{3,00,000}{15} = Rs.\ 20,000$$

∴ Monthly salary of man is Rs. 20,000.

Hence, the correct option is (C).

13. Given,

Speed at which man can row in still water = $4\frac{1}{2}\ km/hr$

let speed of stream $= y\ km/h$

Speed in downstream $= \dfrac{9}{2} + y$

Speed in upstream $= \dfrac{9}{2} - y$

Accroding to question,

$$2 \times \left(\frac{9}{2} - y\right) = \left(\frac{9}{2} + y\right)$$

$$\Rightarrow 9 - 2y = \frac{9}{2} + y$$

$$\Rightarrow 3y = \frac{9}{2}$$

$$\Rightarrow y = 1.5 km/hr$$

Hence, the correct option is (B).

14. Given,

The ratio of imports to exports for the years 1998 and 1999 are 1.25 and 1.40 respectively.

Let the exports in the year $1998 = $ Rs. x crores.

Then, the exports in the year $1999 = $ Rs. $(500 - x)$ crores.

$$\therefore 1.25 = \frac{250}{x}$$

$$\Rightarrow x = \frac{250}{1.25}$$

$$= 200 \quad \text{[Using ratio for 1998]}$$

Thus, the exports in the year 1999

$$= Rs.\ (500 - 200)\ \text{crores}$$

$$= Rs.\ 300\ \text{crores.}$$

Let the imports in the year $1999 = $ Rs. y crores.

Then, $1.40 = \dfrac{y}{300}$

$$\Rightarrow y = (300 \times 1.40)$$

$$= 420$$

∴ Imports in the year $1999 = $ Rs. 420 crores.

Hence, the correct option is (D).

15. The imports are minimum proportionate to the exports implies that the ratio of the value of imports to exports has the minimum value.

Now, this ratio has a minimum value 0.35 in 1997, i.e., the imports are minimum proportionate to the exports in 1997.

Hence, the correct option is (C).

16. The graph gives only the ratio of imports to exports for different years. To find the percentage increase in imports from 1997 to 1998, we require more details such as the value of imports or exports during these years.

So, the data is inadequate to answer this question.

Hence, the correct option is (E).

17. Given:

Imports of the company in 1996 = Rs. 272 crores

Ratio of imports to exports in the year 1996 = 0.85

Let the exports in 1996 = Rs. x crores.

Then,

$$\frac{272}{x} = 0.85$$

$$\Rightarrow x = \frac{272}{0.85}$$
$$\Rightarrow x = 320$$
∴ Exports in $1996 = $ Rs. 320 crores.

Hence, the correct option is (B).

18. The exports are more than the imports imply that the ratio of value of imports to exports is less than 1. Now, this ratio is less than 1 in the years 1995, 1996, 1997 and 2000. Thus, there are four such years.

Hence, the correct option is (D).

19. Equation I.

x² + x – 156 = 0

⇒ x² + 13x – 12x – 156 = 0

⇒ x(x + 13) – 12(x + 13) = 0

⇒ (x + 13) (x – 12) = 0

⇒ x + 13 = 0 or x – 12 = 0

⇒ x = -13 or x = 12

Equation II.

y² + y – 182 = 0

⇒ y² + 14y – 13y – 182 = 0

$\Rightarrow y(y + 14) - 13(y + 14) = 0$

$\Rightarrow (y + 14)(y - 13) = 0$

$\Rightarrow y + 14 = 0$ or $y - 13 = 0$

$\Rightarrow y = -14$ or $y = 13$

Value of x	Value of y	Relation
-13	-14	x > y
-13	13	x < y
12	-14	x > y
12	13	x < y

$\therefore$ x > y and x < y the relationship between x and y cannot be established.

Hence, the correct option is (E).

20. According to the given equations:

I. $x^2 - 18x + 77 = 0$

$\Rightarrow x^2 - 11x - 7x + 77 = 0$

$\Rightarrow x(x - 11) - 7(x - 11) = 0$

$\Rightarrow (x - 11)(x - 7) = 0$

$\Rightarrow x = 7, 11$

II. $y^2 + 3y - 70 = 0$

$\Rightarrow y^2 + 10y - 7y - 70 = 0$

$\Rightarrow y(y + 10) - 7(y + 10) = 0$

$\Rightarrow (y + 10)(y - 7) = 0$

$\Rightarrow y = -10, 7$

x	y	Relation
7	-10	x > y
7	7	x = y
11	-10	x > y
11	7	x > y

$\therefore x \geq y$

Hence, the correct option is (B).

21. I. $3x^2 - 2\sqrt{21}x + 7 = 0$

$\Rightarrow 3x^2 - \sqrt{21}x - \sqrt{21}x + 7 = 0$

$\Rightarrow (\sqrt{3}x - \sqrt{7})(\sqrt{3}x - \sqrt{7}) = 0$

$\Rightarrow x = \dfrac{\sqrt{7}}{\sqrt{3}}, \dfrac{\sqrt{7}}{\sqrt{3}}$

II. $3y^2 + \sqrt{3}y - 2 = 0$

$\Rightarrow 3y^2 - \sqrt{3}y + 2\sqrt{3}y - 2 = 0$

$\Rightarrow (\sqrt{3}y - 1)(\sqrt{3}y + 2) = 0$

$\Rightarrow y = \dfrac{1}{\sqrt{3}}, \dfrac{-2}{\sqrt{3}}$

Value of x	Value of y	Relation

$\dfrac{\sqrt{7}}{\sqrt{3}}$	$\dfrac{1}{\sqrt{3}}$	x > y
$\dfrac{\sqrt{7}}{\sqrt{3}}$	$\dfrac{-2}{\sqrt{3}}$	x > y
$\dfrac{\sqrt{7}}{\sqrt{3}}$	$\dfrac{1}{\sqrt{3}}$	x > y
$\dfrac{\sqrt{7}}{\sqrt{3}}$	$\dfrac{-2}{\sqrt{3}}$	x > y

$\therefore$ x > y

Hence, the correct option is (A).

22. Given,

The word is ALLAHABAD.

In the word, repeated letters are A and L.

The number of times A repeated $= 4$

The number of times L repeated $= 2$

The number of ways to arrange letters $= \dfrac{9!}{(4! \times 2!)}$

$= \dfrac{9 \times 8 \times 7 \times 6 \times 5}{2 \times 1}$

$= 7560$

$\therefore$ The number of ways to arrange the letters of the words ALLAHABAD is 7560.

Hence, the correct option is (C).

23. Given,

$$\sqrt[3]{\left(\dfrac{1331}{124999}\right)} + \sqrt[3]{\left(\dfrac{26.87}{7.78}\right)} - (2 \times ?^2) = 1$$

Approximating the value to the nearest integer, we get

$$\sqrt[3]{\left(\dfrac{1331}{125000}\right)} + \sqrt[3]{\left(\dfrac{27}{8}\right)} - (2 \times ?^2) = 1$$

$\Rightarrow \dfrac{11}{50} + \dfrac{3}{2} - (2 \times ?^2) = 1$

$\Rightarrow \dfrac{86}{50} - 1 = (2 \times ?^2)$

$\Rightarrow \dfrac{36}{50} = 2 \times ?^2$

$\Rightarrow \dfrac{36}{50 \times 2} = ?^2$

$\Rightarrow \dfrac{36}{100} = ?^2$

$\Rightarrow \left(\dfrac{6}{10}\right)^2 = ?^2$

$\Rightarrow \dfrac{6}{10} = ?$

$\Rightarrow ? = \dfrac{3}{5}$

$\therefore$ The value of ? is $\dfrac{3}{5}$.

Hence, the correct option is (A).

24. Given,

$$6.03 \times 36.06 + \dfrac{131.99}{10.99} + 2^1 = ?$$

Approximating the value to the nearest integer, we get

$$6 \times 36 + \dfrac{132}{11} + 2^1 = ?$$

$$\Rightarrow 6 \times 36 + 12 + 2 = ?$$

$$\Rightarrow 216 + 14 = ?$$

$$\Rightarrow ? = 230$$

$\therefore$ The value of ? is 230.

Hence, the correct option is (D).

25. Given,

$$\dfrac{[(36.01)^2 - (24.99)^2]}{?} = (8.99)^2 - (4.01)^2$$

Approximating the value to the nearest integer, we get

$$\dfrac{[(36)^2 - (25)^2]}{?} = (9)^2 - (4)^2$$

$$\Rightarrow \dfrac{[(36+25) \times (36-25)]}{?} = (9+4) \times (9-4)$$

$$\Rightarrow \dfrac{[(61) \times (11)]}{?} = (13) \times (5)$$

$$\Rightarrow \dfrac{671}{?} = 65$$

$$\Rightarrow \dfrac{671}{65} = ?$$

$$\Rightarrow 10.32 = ?$$

$$\Rightarrow ? \approx 10$$

$\therefore$ The value of ? is 10.

Hence, the correct option is (D).

26. Given,

$$311.99 \times 8.88 \times 1.99 \times 9.99 = ? \times 8$$

Approximating the value to the nearest integer, we get

$$312 \times 9 \times 2 \times 10 = ? \times 8$$

$$\Rightarrow 312 \times 180 = ? \times 8$$

$$\Rightarrow 56160 = ? \times 8$$

$$\Rightarrow \dfrac{56160}{8} = ?$$

$$\Rightarrow ? = 7020$$

$\therefore$ The value of ? is 7020.

Hence, the correct option is (D).

27. Given,

$$139.95 \times 70.09 - 48.99^2 = ? - 1$$

Approximating the value to the nearest integer, we get

$$140 \times 70 - 49^2 = ? - 1$$

$$\Rightarrow 20 \times 490 - 49^2 = ? - 1$$

$$\Rightarrow 49 \times (200 - 49) = ? - 1$$

$$\Rightarrow 49 \times (151) = ? - 1$$

$$\Rightarrow 7399 + 1 = ?$$

$$\Rightarrow ? = 7400$$

$\therefore$ The value of ? is 7400.

Hence, the correct option is (C).

28. According to the questio,

Selling price of 12 pens = Cost price of 14 pens

12 × SP = 14 × CP

$$\Rightarrow SP = \left(\dfrac{7}{6}\right) \times CP$$

Profit = $\dfrac{(SP - CP)}{CP} \times 100\% = 16.67\%$

So, if the cost price is 100, the profit is 16.67

Tax = 10% = $\left(\dfrac{10}{100}\right) \times 16.67 = 1.67$

So, net profit = 16.67 - 1.67 = 15

So, the shopkeeper is making a net profit of 15 when the cost price is 100.

$\Rightarrow$ Net profit percentage = 15%

Hence, the correct option is (D).

29. Given:

Ratul invested 20% more than Rakesh

Rakesh invested 50% more than Rudra

Total investment amount = Rs. 3225

Let, Rudra invested Rs. 100x.

Amount invested by Rakesh = 150x

Amount invested by Ratul = 150x + (150x × 20%) = 150x + 30x = 180x

Ratio of their investment = 100x : 150x : 180x = 10 : 15 : 18

Investment amount of Ratul = Rs. 3,225 × $\dfrac{18}{43}$ = Rs. 1,350

$\therefore$ Investment of Ratul is Rs. 1,350.

Hence, the correct option is (D).

30. Given:

Sahil completes the work in 5 days.

Karan completes the work in 7 days.

Himani takes time to complete work as time taken by Sahil and Karan together.

Work done by Sahil in 1 day $= \dfrac{1}{5}$

Work done by Karan in 1 day $= \dfrac{1}{7}$

Time taken by Himani to complete that work $= \dfrac{1}{\left[\left(\frac{1}{5}\right)+\left(\frac{1}{7}\right)\right]} = \dfrac{35}{12}$ days

$\Rightarrow$ Time taken by Karan and Himani to complete that work $=$

$\dfrac{1}{\left[\left(\frac{1}{7}\right)+\left(\frac{12}{35}\right)\right]} = \dfrac{35}{17}$ days

$= 2\dfrac{1}{17}$ days

Hence, the correct option is (A).

Q.1 P is twice efficient than Q, Q is is thrice efficient than R and R does the whole work in 54 days then in how many days P and Q together complete work?

A. 9 days   **B.** 5 days   **C.** 8 days   **D.** 6 days
E. 7 days

Q.2 A dishonest shopkeeper uses a false weight of 800 gm instead of 1000 gm at the time of selling goods. Also, he marks up his goods by 40% above the cost price and gives 10% discount to the customer. In this whole process, find his overall profit percentage.

A. 57.5%   **B.** 52%
C. 48.5%   **D.** 62.5%
E. None of these

Q.3 The volumes of two cones are in the ratio of 11 : 10 and the radius of cones are in the ratio of 3 : 2. what is the ratio of their vertical heights.

A. 22 : 45   **B.** 50 : 21
C. 22 : 37   **D.** 45 : 22
E. None of these

Q.4 An amount of Rs. 400 becomes Rs. 424 in 3 years at a certain rate of simple interest, If the rate of interest increases by 8%, then find what amount will Rs. 400 becomes in 2 years?

A. Rs. 450   **B.** Rs. 425
C. Rs. 480   **D.** Data inadequate
E. None of these

Q.5 A invested in the sum of Rs. 6000 at a rate of interest 20% simple interest and another amount at the rate of interest 15% simple interest. The total interest earned at end of the year on the difference between sums became 50% per annum. Find the largest amount of sum.

A. Rs. 15000   **B.** Rs. 10000
C. Rs. 12000   **D.** Rs. 6000
E. Rs. 8000

Q.6 A invests Rs.400, B invests Rs.600 into a partnership. After 5 months, B adds Rs.100 and C joined them with Rs.800. After 10 months, A adds Rs.300 to his investment. Their total profit is Rs. 2079 after 1 year. Find the difference between the profit shares of C and A.

A. Rs. 30   **B.** Rs. 22   **C.** Rs. 18   **D.** Rs. 40
E. Rs. 36

Q.7 The average of 12 numbers is 35. The average of the first nine numbers is 40. The average of the last two numbers is 25. Find the tenth number.

A. 20   **B.** 10   **C.** 12   **D.** 15
E. 8

Q.8 A tank is 7 m long and 4 m wide. At what speed should water run through a pipe 5 cm broad and 4 cm deep so that in 6 hrs and 18 mins water level in the tank rises by 4.5 m?

A. 10 km/hrs   **B.** 12 km/hrs
C. 8 km/hrs   **D.** 9 km/hrs
E. None of these

Q.9 What should come in place of question mark (?) in the following questions?

$784 ÷ 14 + 1728 ÷ 12 + ? = 70 \% \text{ of } 1600$

A. 820   **B.** 720
C. 1000   **D.** 920
E. None of these

Q.10 What should come in place of question mark (?) in the following questions?

$[3^3 × 2^4] ÷ 16 × 49 – 594 = ?^3$

A. 7   **B.** 11
C. 8   **D.** 9
E. None of these

Q.11 What should come in place of question mark (?) in the following questions?

$7272 ÷ 24 × 3 + ?^2 = 30 \% \text{ of } 6000 + 9$

A. 20   **B.** 27
C. 24   **D.** 30
E. None of these

Q.12 What should come in place of question mark (?) in the following questions?

$$\frac{38}{3} × \sqrt{324} – 35\% \; of \; 1500 = 64 – ?^2$$

A. 29   **B.** 15
C. 21   **D.** 19
E. None of these

Q.13 What should come in place of question mark (?) in the following questions?

$$\sqrt{2809} × \sqrt{1764} + ?^2 = 1369 + 961 – 23$$

A. 19   **B.** 13
C. 11   **D.** 9
E. None of these

Ques (14-16):Direction: In the given question, two equations numbered I and II are given. Solve both the equations and mark the appropriate answer.

Q.14 I. $4x^2 + 3x – 27 = 0$
II. $3y^2 – 20y + 32 = 0$

A. x > y
B. x < y
C. x ≥ y
D. x ≤ y
E. x = y or the relationship between x and y cannot be established

Q.15 I. $4x^2 + 19x + 21 = 0$
II. $3y^2 – 19y – 14 = 0$

A. x > y
B. x < y
C. x ≥ y
D. x ≤ y
E. x = y or the relationship between x and y cannot be established

Q.16 I. $4x^2 - 9x - 9 = 0$
II. $15y^2 - 29y + 12 = 0$
A. x > y
B. x < y
C. x ≥ y
D. x ≤ y
E. x = y or the relationship between x and y cannot be established

Ques (17-21):Direction: Read the below data carefully and answer the following questions.

The pie chart shows the income of seven companies in the financial year 2020 - 2021 in percentage

The table shows the profit percentage of seven companies in the financial year 2020 - 2021

Income of 7 companies in percentage

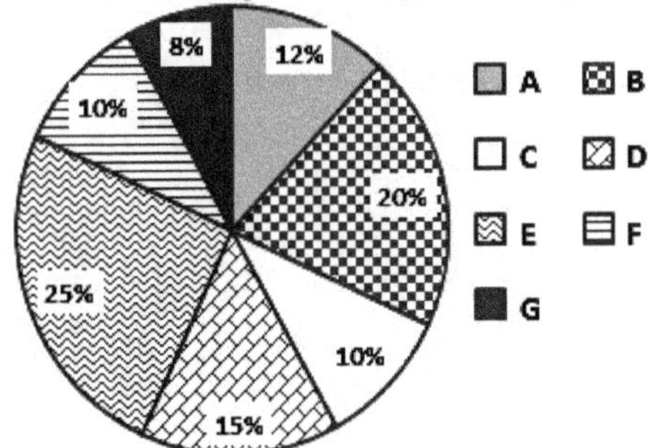

Name of the company	Profit%
A	12%
B	25%
C	15%
D	20%
E	10%
F	10%
G	25%

Q.17 If the income of the company E and company F is Rs. 350 crore, what is the profit of the company C? (Approx value up to two decimal)
A. Rs. 13.04 crore
B. Rs. 14 crore
C. Rs. 15 crore
D. Rs. 13 crore
E. None of these

Q.18 Which of the following company has recorded the maximum profit in this financial year if the combined income of these companies is Rs. 3600 crore? (Approx value up to two decimal)
A. A
B. B
C. C
D. D
E. None of these

Q.19 What is the ratio between the expenditure of company D and company G?
A. 64 : 125
B. 60 : 127
C. 125 : 64
D. 50 : 170
E. None of these

Q.20 If in the given financial year, income of the company D is 450 crore, then find the expenditure of the company B.
A. Rs. 250 crore
B. Rs. 480 crore
C. Rs. 265 crore
D. Rs. 280 crore
E. None of these

Q.21 If the expenditure of company A is Rs. 750 crore, then find the total income of all the company.
A. Rs. 6000 crore
B. Rs. 5000 crore
C. Rs. 7000 crore
D. Rs. 7500 crore
E. None of these

Ques (22-26):Direction: In the following number series, only one number is wrong. Find out the wrong number.

Q.22 10, 9, 16, 32, 176, 875
A. 10
B. 9
C. 16
D. 32
E. 875

Q.23 8, 8, 12, 22, 60, 180, 630
A. 12
B. 22
C. 60
D. 180
E. 630

Q.24 72.9, 71.5, 68.7, 64, 58.9, 51.9
A. 71.5
B. 68.7
C. 64
D. 58.9
E. 51.9

Q.25 112, 87, 67, 50, 42
A. 112
B. 87
C. 67
D. 50
E. 42

Q.26 5, 4, 7, 20, 79, 386, 2363
A. 4
B. 7
C. 20
D. 386
E. 79

Q.27 A committee of 6 HODs is to be formed in a university out of 4 people from engineering department, 5 from management department and 3 from medical department. In how many ways the committee can be formed if two head of department from each department are to be included?
A. 152
B. 180
C. 165
D. 178
E. None of these

Q.28 A boat covers $24\ km$ upstream and $36\ km$ downstream in 6 hours, while it covers $36\ km$ upstream and $24\ km$ downstream in $6\frac{1}{2}$ hours. The speed of the current is?
A. $1\ km/hr$
B. $2\ km/hr$
C. $1.5\ km/hr$
D. $2.5\ km/hr$
E. $3.5\ km/hr$

Q.29 A dice is rolled once. Find the probability of getting a prime even number on a dice:

A. $\frac{1}{3}$ B. $\frac{1}{2}$ C. $\frac{1}{5}$ D. $\frac{1}{6}$

E. $\frac{2}{5}$

Q.30 The population of a town is 20000. It increases by 15% in the first year and decreases by 10% in the second year. What is the population of the town at the end of the second year?

A. 21500   B. 20700   C. 23300   D. 25600

E. 22600

// Smart Answer Sheet //

Correct — Indicates percentage of students who answered questions correctly.

Skipped — Indicates percentage of students who skipped questions.

Q.	Ans.	Correct / Skipped
1	D	48.89 % / 1.4 %
2	A	89.36 % / 0.0 %
3	A	56.04 % / 1.7 %
4	C	20.03 % / 3.8 %
5	C	43.48 % / 1.49 %
6	B	63.89 % / 1.13 %
7	B	89.21 % / 0.0 %
8	A	16.55 % / 4.33 %
9	D	52.37 % / 1.02 %
10	D	14.86 % / 4.99 %
11	D	31.35 % / 3.79 %
12	D	20.93 % / 4.8 %
13	D	45.17 % / 1.21 %
14	B	14.43 % / 4.97 %
15	B	58.3 % / 1.36 %
16	E	45.53 % / 1.97 %
17	A	64.89 % / 1.54 %
18	B	45.88 % / 1.31 %
19	C	29.76 % / 4.36 %
20	B	68.29 % / 1.42 %
21	C	32.34 % / 4.58 %
22	D	45.79 % / 1.88 %
23	B	67.09 % / 1.72 %
24	C	81.24 % / 0.0 %
25	D	84.48 % / 0.0 %
26	D	82.78 % / 0.0 %
27	B	54.26 % / 1.81 %
28	B	25.81 % / 3.86 %
29	D	65.65 % / 1.92 %
30	B	49.87 % / 1.0 %

Performance Analysis

Avg. Score (%)	30.0%
Toppers Score (%)	60.0%
Your Score	

//Hints and Solutions//

1. Given:

P = 2Q

Q = 3R

R can complete a work in 54 days

Concept used:

If A does a work in n days then 1-day work of A is $\dfrac{1}{n}$

Calculation:

According to question,

Let, P's one day work = 6 unit

⇒ Q's one day work = 3 unit

⇒ R's one day work = 1 unit

C can complete work in 54 days

⇒ Total work = 1 × 54 = 54 unit

⇒ (P + Q) can complete work in = $\dfrac{54}{(6+3)}$

⇒ $\dfrac{54}{9}$

⇒ 6 days

∴ P and Q together can complete work in 6 days.

Hence, the correct option is (D).

2. Let CP of 1000 gm = Rs. 100

MP = Rs. 140

SP of 800 gm = Rs. 126

CP of 800 gm = Rs. 80

Profit = SP - CP

= Rs. (126 - 80) = Rs. 46

∴ Overall profit% $= \dfrac{Profit}{CP} \times 100$

$= \dfrac{46}{80} \times 100 = 57.5\%$

Hence, the correct option is (A).

3. Given that:

The ratio between the volume of two cones = 11 : 10

The ratio between the radius of two cones = 3 : 2

We know that,

Volume of cone $= \dfrac{1}{3}\pi r^2 h$

According to the question,

$$\dfrac{V_1}{V_2} = \left(\dfrac{r_1}{r_2}\right)^2 \times \left(\dfrac{h_1}{h_2}\right)$$

$$\Rightarrow \dfrac{h_1}{h_2} = \dfrac{11}{10} \times \left(\dfrac{2}{3}\right)^2$$

$$\dfrac{h_1}{h_2} = \dfrac{22}{45}$$

∴ ratio between vertical heights of cone is $22 : 45$.

Hence, the correct option is (A).

4. Given:

Principle = Rs. 400

Amount = Rs. 424

As we know,

$$R = \dfrac{(S.I. \times 100)}{(P \times T)}$$

S.I = A – P

Where,

R = Rate of Interest

S.I. = Simple Interest

P = Principle

T = Time

A = Amount

S.I. = Amount – Principle

⇒ 424 – 400 = Rs. 24

$$R = \dfrac{(24 \times 100)}{(400 \times 3)} = 2\%$$

It is given in the question that new rate is 8% more than previous rate of interest.

New rate = 2% + 8% = 10%

$$\text{New S.I.} = \dfrac{(400 \times 10 \times 2)}{100} = \text{Rs. 80}$$

New Amount = 400 + 80 = Rs. 480

∴ The new amount is Rs. 480.

Hence, the correct option is (C).

5. Given,

Let other amount invested be Rs. M.

$$\text{Simple Interest} = \dfrac{\text{Principal} \times \text{Rate} \times \text{Time}}{100}$$

$$\text{Simple Interest} = \dfrac{(6000 \times 20 \times 1)}{100} = 1200$$

$$\text{Simple Interest on other amount} = \dfrac{(M \times 15 \times 1)}{100} = \dfrac{3M}{20}$$

$$\text{Total interest} = 1200 + \dfrac{3M}{20}$$

Then,

$$\text{Simple Interest} = (M - 6000) \times 50 \times \frac{1}{100}$$

$$\Rightarrow 1200 + \frac{3M}{20} = \frac{(M-6000)}{2}$$

$$\Rightarrow 2400 + \frac{3M}{10} = M - 6000$$

$$\Rightarrow 24000 + 60000 = 7M$$

$$\Rightarrow M = 12000$$

Largest sum is Rs. 12000.

Hence, the correct option is (C).

6. Given:

Total profit = Rs. 2079

We know that,

Profit ratio = Investment × Time period

Total investment of A = 400 × 10 + 700 × 2 = Rs. 5400

Total investment of B = 600 × 5 + 700 × 7 = Rs. 7900

Total investment of C = 800 × 7 = Rs. 5600

Ratio between their profit shares = 5400 : 7900 : 5600

= 54 : 79 : 56

$\therefore$ Required difference = $\dfrac{56}{189} \times 2079 - \dfrac{54}{189} \times 2079$

= Rs. 22

Hence, the correct option is (B).

7. Given:

Average of 12 numbers = 35

Average of first nine numbers = 40

Average of last two numbers = 25

Formula: Average = $\dfrac{sum\ of\ all\ item}{number\ of\ item}$

Sum of 12 numbers = (35 × 12) = 420

$\Rightarrow$ Sum of 9 numbers = (40 × 9) = 360

$\Rightarrow$ Sum of last two numbers = (25 × 2) = 50

$\therefore$ Value of 10th number = 420 – 360 – 50 = 10

Hence, the correct option is (B).

8. Given,

Length of tank (L) = 7 m

= 700 cm

Breadth of tank (B) = 4 m

= 400 cm

Length of pipe (l) = 5 cm

Breadth of pipe (b) = 4 cm

Since, length, breadth, and height of the tank are given. So we can consider the tank as a cuboidal shape.

Let rate of the flow of water be x cm/min.

Therefore,

Volume of water that flowed in the in 1 min = L × B × H

= 5 × 4 × x

= 20 x cm³

Volume of water that flowed in the tank in 6 hours 18 mins.

$$= (6 \times 60 + 18)$$

$$= 378 \text{ mins}$$

Volume of water that flowed in 378 min = 20 x × 378 cm³

According to the question,

Volume of water of that flowed in 378 min = Toatl volume of the tank

L × B × H = l × b × h

$$20x \times 378 = 700 \times 400 \times 450$$

$$\Rightarrow x = \left(\frac{700 \times 400 \times 450}{20 \times 378}\right)$$

$$\Rightarrow x = \left(\frac{700 \times 400 \times 450 \times 60}{100000 \times 20 \times 378}\right) \text{ km/hours}$$

$$\Rightarrow x = 10 \text{ km/hours}$$

Hence, the correct option is (A).

9. Given:

784 ÷ 14 + 1728 ÷ 12 + ? = 70% of 1600

$\Rightarrow$ 784 ÷ 14 + 1728 ÷ 12 + ? = 1600 $\times \dfrac{70}{100}$

$\Rightarrow$ 784 ÷ 14 + 1728 ÷ 12 + ? = 16 × 70

$\Rightarrow$ 56 + 144 + ? = 16 × 70

$\Rightarrow$ 56 + 144 + ? = 1120

$\Rightarrow$ 200 + ? = 1120

$\Rightarrow$? = 1120 – 200

$\Rightarrow$? = 920

Hence, the correct option is (D).

10. Given:

[3³ × 2⁴] ÷ 16 × 49 – 594 = ?³

$\Rightarrow$ [27 × 16] ÷ 16 × 49 – 594 = ?³

$\Rightarrow$ [432] ÷ 16 × 49 – 594 = ?³

$\Rightarrow$ 432 ÷ 16 × 49 – 594 = ?³

$\Rightarrow$ 27 × 49 – 594 = ?³

$\Rightarrow 1323 - 594 = ?^3$

$\Rightarrow ?^3 = 729$

$\Rightarrow ? = 9$

Hence, the correct option is (D).

11. Given:

$7272 \div 24 \times 3 + ?^2 = 30\%$ of $6000 + 9$

$\Rightarrow 7272 \div 24 \times 3 + ?^2 = 6000 \times \dfrac{30}{100} + 9$

$\Rightarrow 7272 \div 24 \times 3 + ?^2 = 600 \times 30 + 9$

$\Rightarrow 303 \times 3 + ?^2 = 600 \times 30 + 9$

$\Rightarrow 909 + ?^2 = 1800 + 9$

$\Rightarrow 909 + ?^2 = 1809$

$\Rightarrow ?^2 = 1809 - 909$

$\Rightarrow ?^2 = 900$

$\Rightarrow ? = 30$

Hence, the correct option is (D).

12. Given:

$\dfrac{38}{3} \times \sqrt{324} - 35\% \; of \; 1500 = 64 - ?^2$

$\Rightarrow \dfrac{38}{3} \times \sqrt{324} - 1500 \times \dfrac{35}{100} = 64 - ?^2$

$\Rightarrow \dfrac{38}{3} \times 18 - 15 \times 35 = 64 - ?^2$

$\Rightarrow 38 \times 6 - 15 \times 35 = 64 - ?^2$

$\Rightarrow 228 - 525 = 64 - ?^2$

$\Rightarrow -297 = 64 - ?^2$

$\Rightarrow -297 - 64 = -?^2$

$\Rightarrow -361 = -?^2$

$\Rightarrow ?^2 = 361$

$\Rightarrow ? = 19$

Hence, the correct option is (D).

13. Given:

$\sqrt{2809} \times \sqrt{1764} + ?^2 = 1369 + 961 - 23$

$\Rightarrow 53 \times 42 + ?^2 = 1369 + 961 - 23$

$\Rightarrow 2226 + ?^2 = 1369 + 961 - 23$

$\Rightarrow 2226 + ?^2 = 2330 - 23$

$\Rightarrow ?^2 = 2330 - 23 - 2226$

$\Rightarrow ?^2 = 2330 - 2249$

$\Rightarrow ?^2 = 81$

$\Rightarrow ? = 9$

Hence, the correct option is (D).

14. I. $4x^2 + 3x - 27 = 0$

$\Rightarrow 4x^2 + 12x - 9x - 27 = 0$

$\Rightarrow 4x(x + 3) - 9(x + 3) = 0$

$\Rightarrow (4x - 9)(x + 3) = 0$

$\Rightarrow x = \dfrac{9}{4}$ or -3

II. $3y^2 - 20y + 32 = 0$

$\Rightarrow 3y^2 - 12y - 8y + 32 = 0$

$\Rightarrow 3y(y - 4) - 8(y - 4) = 0$

$\Rightarrow (3y - 8)(y - 4) = 0$

$\Rightarrow y = \dfrac{8}{3}$ or 4

Comparison between x and y (via Tabulation):

Value of x	Value of y	Result
$\dfrac{9}{4}$	$\dfrac{8}{3}$	x < y
-3	$\dfrac{8}{3}$	x < y
$\dfrac{9}{4}$	4	x < y
-3	4	x < y

$\therefore$ x < y

Hence, the correct option is (B).

15. I. $4x^2 + 19x + 21 = 0$

$\Rightarrow 4x^2 + 12x + 7x + 21 = 0$

$\Rightarrow 4x(x + 3) + 7(x + 3) = 0$

$\Rightarrow (4x + 7)(x + 3) = 0$

$\Rightarrow x = \dfrac{-7}{4}$ or -3

II. $3y^2 - 19y - 14 = 0$

$\Rightarrow 3y^2 - 21y + 2y - 14 = 0$

$\Rightarrow 3y(y - 7) + 2(y - 7) = 0$

$\Rightarrow (3y + 2)(y - 7) = 0$

$\Rightarrow y = \dfrac{-2}{3}, 7$

Comparison between x and y (via Tabulation):

Value of x	Value of y	Result
$\dfrac{-7}{4}$	$\dfrac{-2}{3}$	x < y
-3	$\dfrac{-2}{3}$	x < y
$\dfrac{-7}{4}$	7	x < y
-3	7	x < y

$\therefore$ x < y

Hence, the correct option is (B).

16. I. $4x^2 - 9x - 9 = 0$

$\Rightarrow 4x^2 - 12x + 3x - 9 = 0$

$\Rightarrow 4x(x - 3) + 3(x - 3) = 0$

$\Rightarrow (4x + 3)(x - 3) = 0$

$\Rightarrow x = \dfrac{-3}{4}$ or 3

II. $15y^2 - 29y + 12 = 0$

$\Rightarrow 15y^2 - 20y - 9y + 12 = 0$

$\Rightarrow 5y(3y - 4) - 3(3y - 4) = 0$

$\Rightarrow (5y - 3)(3y - 4) = 0$

$\Rightarrow y = \dfrac{3}{5}$ or 4/3

Comparison between x and y (via Tabulation):

Value of x	Value of y	Result
$\dfrac{-3}{4}$	$\dfrac{3}{5}$	x < y
3	$\dfrac{3}{5}$	x > y
$\dfrac{-3}{4}$	$\dfrac{4}{3}$	x < y
3	$\dfrac{4}{3}$	x > y

∴ Relation between x and y can't be established

Hence, the correct option is (E).

17. Given:

The income % of company E $= 25\%$

The income % of company F $= 10\%$

The income % of company C $= 10\%$

The profit % of company C $= 15\%$

The income of the company E and company F is Rs. 350 crore

We know that,

Profit $\% = \left\{\dfrac{(\text{Income - Expenditure})}{\text{Expenditure}}\right\} \times 100\%$

As per the question, we can say,

$(25 + 10)\% = 350$

$\Rightarrow 35\% = 350$

$\Rightarrow 10\% = 100$

So, the income of company C is Rs. 100 crore

Let, the expenditure of company C be x

Now, according to the formula, we can say,

$15 = \left\{\dfrac{(100 - x)}{x}\right\} \times 100$

$\Rightarrow 3x = 2000 - 20x$

$\Rightarrow 23x = 2000$

$\Rightarrow x = \left(\dfrac{2000}{23}\right)$

So, the expenditure of company C is Rs. $\left(\dfrac{2000}{23}\right)$ crore

Profit = Income - Expenditure

So, the profit will be $= \left\{100 - \left(\dfrac{2000}{23}\right)\right\} = \left(\dfrac{300}{23}\right) = 13.04$

∴ The profit of company C will be Rs. 13.04 crore.

Hence, the correct option is (A).

18. Given:

The total income of all companies is Rs. 3600 crore.

Name of the company	Profit%	Income%
A	12%	12%
B	25%	20%
C	15%	10%
D	20%	15%
E	10%	25%
F	10%	10%
G	25%	8%

We Know that,

Profit $\% = \left\{\dfrac{(\text{Income - Expenditure})}{\text{Expenditure}}\right\} \times 100\% \ ... \ (1)$

Let, the expenditure of company A be x.

The income of company A $= \left\{3600 \times \left(\dfrac{12}{100}\right)\right\} = 432$

From the given chart, The profit percentage of company A is 12%. Therefore, from equation (1), we get,

$12 = \left\{\dfrac{(432 - x)}{x}\right\} \times 100$

$\Rightarrow x = 385.71$

Profit $= (432 - 385.71) = 46.29$

Let, the expenditure of company B be y.

The income of company B $= \left\{3600 \times \left(\dfrac{20}{100}\right)\right\} = 720$

From the given chart, The profit percentage of company B is 25%. Therefore, from equation (1), we get,

$25 = \left\{\dfrac{(720 - y)}{y}\right\} \times 100$

$\Rightarrow y = 576$

Profit $= (720 - 576) = 144$

Let, the expenditure of company C be z.

The income of company C $= \left\{3600 \times \left(\dfrac{10}{100}\right)\right\} = 360$

From the given chart, The profit percentage of company C is 15%. Therefore, from equation (1), we get,

$$15 = \left\{ \frac{(360-z)}{z} \right\} \times 100$$

$$\Rightarrow z = 313.04$$

Profit $= (360 - 313.04) = 46.96$

Let, the expenditure of company D be p.

The income of company D $= \left\{ 3600 \times \left(\frac{15}{100} \right) \right\} = 540$

From the given chart, The profit percentage of company D is 20%. Therefore, from equation (1), we get,

$$20 = \left\{ \frac{(540-p)}{p} \right\} \times 100$$

$$\Rightarrow p = 450$$

Profit $= (540 - 450) = 90$

Let, the expenditure of company E be q.

The income of company E $= \left\{ 3600 \times \left(\frac{25}{100} \right) \right\} = 900$

From the given chart, The profit percentage of company E is 10%. Therefore, from equation (1), we get,

$$10 = \left\{ \frac{(900-q)}{q} \right\} \times 100$$

$$\Rightarrow q = 818.18$$

Profit $= (900 - 818.18) = 81.82$

Let, the expenditure of company F be r.

The income of company F $= \left\{ 3600 \times \left(\frac{10}{100} \right) \right\} = 360$

From the given chart, The profit percentage of company F is 10%. Therefore, from equation (1), we get,

$$10 = \left\{ \frac{(360-r)}{r} \right\} \times 100$$

$$\Rightarrow r = 327.27$$

Profit $= (360 - 327.27) = 32.73$

Let, the expenditure of company G be k.

The income of company G $= \left\{ 3600 \times \left(\frac{8}{100} \right) \right\} = 288$

From the given chart, The profit percentage of company G is 25%. Therefore, from equation (1), we get,

$$25 = \left\{ \frac{(288-k)}{k} \right\} \times 100$$

$$\Rightarrow k = 230.4$$

Profit $= (288 - 230.4) = 57.6$

$\therefore$ Company B gains the maximum profit.

Hence, the correct option is (B).

19. Given:

Income $\%$ of company D $= 15\%$

Profit $\%$ of company D $= 20\%$

Income $\%$ of company G $= 8\%$

Profit $\%$ of company G $= 25\%$

Let, the total income of all the company is 100%.

So, the income of company D $= 15$

The income of company G $= 8$

Now according to the question we can say,

$$120\% = 15$$

$$\Rightarrow 100\% = \left\{ \left(\frac{15}{120} \right) \times 100 \right\}$$

So, the expenditure of company D $= \left\{ \left(\frac{15}{120} \right) \times 100 \right\}$

Again according to the question we can say,

$$125\% = 8$$

$$\Rightarrow 100\% = \left\{ \left(\frac{8}{125} \right) \times 100 \right\}$$

So, the expenditure of company G $= \left\{ \left(\frac{8}{125} \right) \times 100 \right\}$

So, the required ratio $= \left\{ \left(\frac{15}{120} \right) \times 100 \right\} : \left\{ \left(\frac{8}{125} \right) \times 100 \right\}$

$$\Rightarrow 125 : 64$$

$\therefore$ The ratio between the expenditure of company D and company G is $125 : 64$.

Hence, the correct option is (C).

20. Given:

The income of company D is Rs. 450 crore.

Income $\%$ of company D $= 15\%$

Income $\%$ of company B $= 20\%$

Profit $\%$ of company B $= 25\%$

We know that:

Profit $\% = \left\{ \frac{(\text{Income - Expenditure})}{\text{Expenditure}} \right\} \times 100\% \ ...(1)$

According to the question we can say,

$$15\% = 450$$

Then,

$$20\% = \left\{\left(\frac{450}{15}\right) \times 20\right\} = 600$$

600 rupees is the income of company B.

Let, the expenditure of company B be x

From the given chart, The profit percentage of company B is 25%. Therefore, from equation (1), we get,

$$25 = \left\{\frac{(600-x)}{x}\right\} \times 100$$

$$\Rightarrow x = 2400 - 4x$$

$$\Rightarrow 5x = 2400$$

$$\Rightarrow x = 480$$

$\therefore$ The expenditure of company B in the financial year $2020 - 2021$ is Rs. 480 crore.

Hence, the correct option is (B).

21. Given:

The expenditure of company A is Rs. 750 crore

Income $\%$ of company A $= 12\%$

Profit $\%$ of company A $= 12\%$

We know that:

$$\text{Profit } \% = \left\{\frac{(\text{Income - Expenditure})}{\text{Expenditure}}\right\} \times 100\%$$

Let, the income of company A be x

According to the formula we can say,

$$12 = \left\{\frac{(x-750)}{750}\right\} \times 100$$

$$\Rightarrow 360 = 4x - 3000$$

$$\Rightarrow 4x = 3360$$

$$\Rightarrow x = 840$$

So, the income of company A is Rs. 840 crore

According to the question we can say,

$$12\% = 840$$

$$\Rightarrow 100\% = \left\{\left(\frac{840}{12}\right) \times 100\right\} = 7000$$

The total income of all company $= $ Rs. 7000 crore

$\therefore$ The total income of all company in the financial year $2020 - 2021$ is Rs. 7000 crore.

Hence, the correct option is (C).

22. The series follows the following pattern:

10 × 1 - 1 = 9

9 × 2 - 2 = 16

16 × 3 - 3 = 45 ≠ 32

45 × 4 - 4 = 176

176 × 5 - 5 = 875

Since 45 will come in place of 32.

$\therefore$ Wrong number is 32.

Hence, the correct option is (D).

23. The series follows the following pattern:

8 × 1 = 8

8 × 1.5 = 12

12 × 2 = 24 ≠ 22

24 × 2.5 = 60

60 × 3 = 180

180 × 3.5 = 630

Since 24 will come in place of 22.

$\therefore$ Wrong number is 22.

Hence, the correct option is (B).

24. The series follows the following pattern:

72.9 - 71.5 = 1.4

71.5 - 68.7 = 2.8

68.7 - 64.5 = 4.2 ≠ (68.7 - 64 = 4.7)

64.5 - 58.9 = 5.6

58.9 - 51.9 = 7.0

Since 64.5 will come in place of 64.

$\therefore$ Wrong number is 64.

Hence, the correct option is (C).

25. The series follows the following pattern:

112 - 87 = 25

87 - 67 = 20

67 - 52 = 15 ≠ (67 - 50 = 17)

52 - 42 = 10

Since 52 will come in place of 50.

$\therefore$ Wrong number is 50.

Hence, the correct option is (D).

26. The series follows the following pattern:

5 × 1 − 1 = 4

4 × 2 − 1 = 7

7 × 3 − 1 = 20

20 × 4 − 1 = 79

79 × 5 – 1 = 394

394 × 6 – 1 = 2363

Since 394 will come in place of 386.

∴ Wrong number is 386.

Hence, the correct option is (D).

27. Given,

A committee of 6 HODs is to be formed in a university.

From engineering department $= 4$ people

From management department $= 5$ people

From medical department $= 6$ people

Number of ways of selecting 2 people out of 4 from Engineering $= {}^4C_2$

Number of ways of selecting 2 people out of 5 from Management $= {}^5C_2$

Number of ways of selecting 2 people out of 3 from Medical $= {}^3C_2$

Required number of ways to form the committee where 2 persons are included from each department $=$ ${}^4C_2 \times {}^5C_2 \times {}^3C_2$

$$= \left[\frac{4!}{2!(4-2)!}\right] \times \left[\frac{5!}{2!(5-2)!}\right] \times \left[\frac{3!}{2!(3-2)!}\right]$$

$$= 6 \times 10 \times 3$$

$$= 180$$

Therefore, the number of ways to form the committee is 180.

Hence, the correct option is (B).

28. Given,

Time taken by boat to cover 24 km downstream and 36 km upstream = 6 hours

Time taken by boat to cover 36 km downstream and 24 km upstream = $6\frac{1}{2}$ hours

let speed of boat in still water = $x\ km/h$

Speed of stream current = y km/h

According to question,

$$\frac{24}{x-y} + \frac{36}{x+y} = 6h \quad \text{(i)}$$

$$\frac{36}{x-y} + \frac{24}{x+y} = \frac{13}{2}h \quad \text{(ii)}$$

In these type of questions, make factor of 24 and 36 and choose the common values which satisfy the above equations.

$$24 = 2,3,4,6,8,12$$

$$36 = 3,4,9,12$$

Choose the common factor i.e. Put this value in equation (i)

$$\frac{24}{x-y} + \frac{36}{12} = 6$$

$$\frac{24}{x-y} + 3 = 6$$

$$x - y = 8$$

$$\therefore x + y = 12$$

$$\therefore x = 10, \quad y = 2$$

Speed of the current, $y = 2\ km/h$

Hence, the correct option is (B).

29. Given:

A dice is rolled once

$$\text{Probability} = \frac{(Number\ of\ favorable\ outcomes)}{(Total\ number\ of\ outcomes)}$$

Total number of outcomes = 1, 2, 3, 4, 5 and 6.

The only prime and even number is 2.

$$\therefore \text{Required Probability} = \frac{1}{6}$$

Hence, the correct option is (D).

30. Given:

Population of town = 20000

Increase % = 15%

Decrease % = 10%

Formula:

If the present population of a village is P and there is an increment or decrement of R1% and R2% in the first and second year respectively, then

Population of town after 2 years = P × $\left[1 \pm \frac{R_1}{100}\right] \times \left[1 \pm \frac{R_2}{100}\right]$

Where, '+' sign for increases and '-' sign for decreases

Calculation:

Here, R1 = +15%, R2 = -10%

According to the question,

Population after 2 years = 2000 × $\left[1 + \frac{15}{100}\right] \times \left[1 - \frac{10}{100}\right]$

$$= 20000 \times \frac{23}{20} \times \frac{9}{10}$$

$$= 20700$$

∴ The population of town after 2 years is 20700.

Hence, the correct option is (B).

// Notes //

// Notes //